THE ARMENIAN MASSACRES 1894–1896

This publication was made possible by a generous grant from

The Dolores Zohrab Liebmann Fund

THE ARMENIAN MASSACRES 1894–1896

British Media Testimony

Edited and with an introduction by
ARMAN J. KIRAKOSSIAN

Foreword by LORD SHANNON

THE ARMENIAN RESEARCH CENTER
University of Michigan–Dearborn
2008

Manufactured in the United States of America
12 11 10 09 08 5 4 3 2 1

Cataloging-in-Publication Data
The Armenian massacres, 1894–1896 : British media testimony / edited and with an intro. by Arman J. Kirakossian ; foreword by Lord Shannon.
614 p. : map ; 23 cm.
Includes bibliographical references and index.
ISBN: 1-934548-01-4
ISBN13: 978-1-934548-01-1
1. Armenian massacres, 1894–1896—Foreign public opinion, British.
2. Turkey—History—19th century—Sources.
3. Armenians—Turkey—History—Sources.
4. Armenia—History—1801–1900—Sources. I. Kirakosi͡an, A. Dzh.
(Arman Dzhonovich).
DS194.A685 2008
956.6'20155—dc22

The paper used in this publication meets the minimum requirements of the American National Standard for Information Sciences—Permanence of Paper for Printed Materials, ANSI Z39.48-1984

Book design based on a design by Betty Pilon.

"We have in the face of the world bound ourselves to secure good government for Armenia and for Asiatic Turkey."

—William Gladstone, 1896

CONTENTS

FOREWORD

I am delighted to be able to read the articles on Armenia and the Armenian question that appeared in the British periodicals more than a century ago. As the first chairman of the British-Armenian Parliamentary Group, I was well aware of the long-standing British commitment to the Armenian people. I first met the editor of this volume, Ambassador Arman Kirakossian, when he was deputy foreign minister on a working visit to London in 1992 for his opening of the Armenian Embassy—the first Armenian diplomatic mission in a European country, evincing the strong nature of British-Armenian relations.

It is a pleasure to see this testimony of the care and concern that the British people have for oppressed minorities and human rights in foreign lands, in this instance during the Armenian massacres in 1894–1896 in the Ottoman Empire. Although the Armenian-populated regions in the Ottoman Empire were far removed from Britain, the British people showed how deeply they cared about the injustices and persecution that were being meted out upon Armenians in all walks of life. They cared enough to set up humanitarian societies, lobby their government, and make the Armenian question an issue in successive parliamentary campaigns as the articles amply show. In this I see a portent of the deeply held humanitarian instincts and sense of justice of the British people, which forced their government to take action again in the course of the twentieth century.

How saddening it is to know now that ultimately the dreams of the Armenians living in the Ottoman Empire to live on their ancestral lands without fear of oppression and persecution were doomed to fail and that the genocide carried out by the Ottoman Empire under the pretense of the First World War erased the presence of the Armenian people from their historic homeland. It was not just an Armenian tragedy; it was a tragedy for humankind and a criminal precedent for the future. It is therefore gratifying to know that a new Armenia was reborn in 1991, also that this Armenia determines to build a democratic, prosperous, and stable society at peace with its neighbors. With all our hearts, we wish it well. It deserves it!

RICHARD BENTINCK BOYLE, THE EARL OF SHANNON*
United Kingdom
September 1, 2004
London, U.K.

*Richard Bentinck Boyle, the Ninth Earl of Shannon, is a renowned British politician and business leader. Lord Shannon served in the House of Lords from 1963 to 1999, sitting as the Baron Carleton, and was a member of its European Communities Committee. He was a captain in the Irish Guards (1942–1953) and has served as director or chairman of several leading public and private institutions and associations in the area of science and technology.

PREFACE

This book, presenting the coverage of the Armenian massacres of 1894–1896 in the British periodicals, follows the publication of its first volume, *The Armenian Massacres 1894–1896: U.S. Media Testimony*, by Wayne State University Press in 2004. I conceived the original idea for the book and collected the materials when I was researching the British policies and public opinion on the Armenian question, as a necessary part of my work *British Diplomacy and the Armenian Question, from the 1830s to 1914* (Princeton and London: Gomidas Institute Books, 2003).

The original spellings and uses of names and places have been preserved throughout the book. I recognize that this may be confusing to some readers. I nevertheless believe that the benefits of having unedited and uncensored text, published in the same form and format in which it originally appeared, far outweigh the expediency of converting all names and terms to modern usage. The articles are presented in chronological order.

I wish to express my sincere gratitude and appreciation to the Dolores Zohrab Liebmann Fund, Edmond Y. Azadian, Alice Nigoghosian, Ambassador Armen Sarkissian, and Richard Bentinck Boyle, the Earl of Shannon. I also thank my wife, Susanna, and son, Aram, as well as Lilit Toutkhalian and Haik Gugarats, for their help in putting this book together, and I owe a debt of gratitude to my family and friends, whose love, respect, and dedication to this project helped bring it to a successful conclusion.

Arman J. Kirakossian
Yerevan, Armenia
February 5, 2005
Washington, D.C.

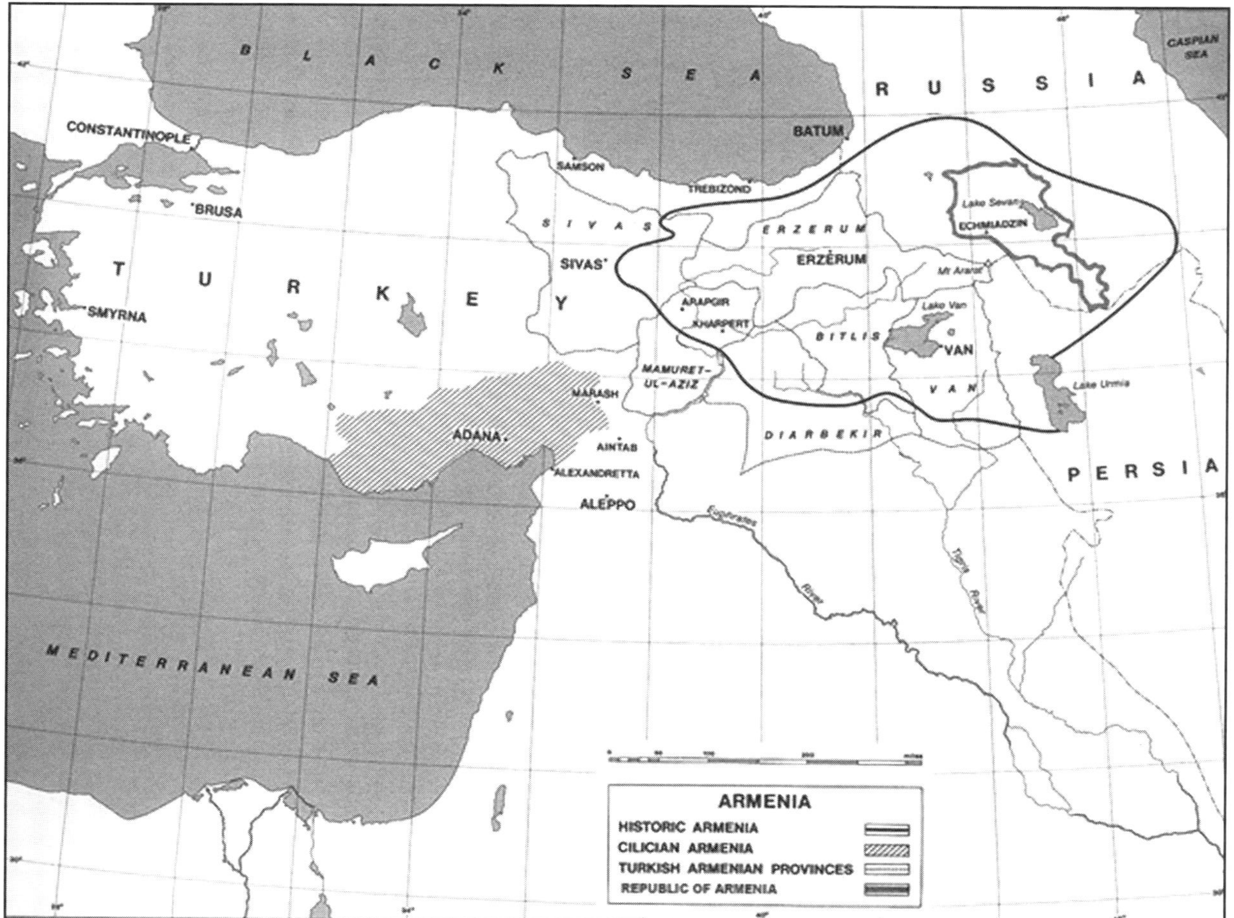

From Robert Mirak, *Torn between Two Lands: Armenians in America 1890 to World War I* (Cambridge: Harvard University Press, 1983). Courtesy of Robert Mirak.

INTRODUCTION[1]

Policy of Great Britain toward the Ottoman Empire, 1830s–70s

At the turn of the eighteenth century, Great Britain had become one of the world's leading colonial, industrial, and trading nations. Britain sought to solidify and guard its commercial advantage, and it already possessed an advanced economy that none of its Continental rivals could compete with. These developments led to increased tension in its relations with other European powers. Pursuing active balance-of-power politics, Great Britain viewed with distrust other powers' colonial expansion plans. Britain would prevent any European nation from accruing too much power and would ally with or challenge any player in this system to maintain the overall balance.[2]

The relative importance of the Near East and the Balkans in European diplomacy gradually started to increase in the 1830s, parallel to increasing tensions among the European powers regarding their attempt to exercise political and economic domination over various parts of the Ottoman Empire. The Ottoman Empire was at the crossroads of major strategic and trade routes, the control of which was, potentially, the key to overall domination by any power. These geopolitical developments turned the Ottoman Empire into one of the key elements in the European balance-of-power system.

The Russian successes in the 1826–28 Russo-Persian and especially the 1828–29 Russo-Turkish wars rekindled the old British mistrust of Russian intentions. The increase in Russia's relative power in the south and its territorial expansion there were viewed as potentially dangerous to the British domination of India.[3] But a key turning point was the Egyptian-Ottoman disagreement of 1831–33 and the Russian-Ottoman treaty of Unkiar-Skelessi, which was viewed as a major victory for Russian diplomacy, since it was achieved implicitly, as a result of the Russian mediation of the Ottoman-Egyptian dispute, rather than on the battlefield. The treaty provided for permanent mutual consultations to ensure "serenity and security" of the contracting parties, as well as for assistance against third-party interference. A secret clause in the treaty would require the Ottoman authorities to close the Straits of the Bosphorus and the Dardanelles to all foreign navy ships should the Russian government request it to do so.

The new British policy toward the Ottoman Empire was crafted during what became known as the Palmerston era. During his long tenure as foreign secretary and then prime minister, Lord Henry John Palmerston[4] was a defining figure in the formulation of British foreign policy. The Near Eastern direction pursued the following objectives: to deny Russia the right to intervene in and assert its protectorate over the Ottoman Empire; to strengthen the British political and economic presence in the Ottoman Empire; and to secure implementation of military, administrative, and legal reforms in the country and equal rights for the Christian subjects of the sultan. The Ottoman government (Sublime Porte) of the day accepted the alliance with the leading world power, believing that reforms were a first step for the survival of the empire.

The British-Turkish commercial treaty of August 1838 was a turning point for British diplomacy, as well as for the Ottoman reforms. The treaty provided for free trade and customs-free maritime navigation through Turkish territorial waters and the Black Sea Straits, as well as an end to monopoly and the forced procurement system. Great Britain was the first European nation that won the right to export agricultural products and natural resources to the Ottoman Empire.

By the middle of the nineteenth century, an important development became apparent in the multiethnic Ottoman Empire: non-Turkish peoples began to play a leading role in the economic activities of the empire. The suppressed minorities showed signs of developing and exercising entrepreneurial skills but were impeded by the ruling Turkish political and feudal elite, which served to deter the overall development of the country. Growing social and political disparity and revolutionary ideas that penetrated the Ottoman Empire in 1789, 1830, and 1848 laid the foundation for a national liberation ideology and movement among the non-Turkish peoples of the empire. From an ethnic perspective, the Ottoman Empire was a composite of more than sixty nationalities of different cultural and religious affiliations and of dissimilar levels of social, economic, political, and cultural development. Against this backdrop, the growing economic strength of the Christian minorities and the reawakening and growing realization of their national identities increased pressure from the European powers on the Porte.

Recognizing the imminence of problems in the internal life of the empire, some representatives of the Ottoman elite advocated a new approach to the status of the Christian minorities as early as the turn of the eighteenth century. Reforms were proposed to revive and modernize the economy, strengthen the central government, and prevent the national liberation movements and any possible interventions by the European powers on behalf, and under the pretext, of the defense of their co-religionists. The national movements among the Slavic peoples in the Balkans and the liberation of Greece in the 1820s were milestones in the development of new approaches to the territorial integrity and governance of the empire, and Sultan Mahmud II was the first ruler to attempt such reforms in the 1820s and 1830s. The first period (1830–50s) of Tanzimat—as this reform movement is known—saw an emergence of new ideas on the treatment of the Christian subjects of the empire. The author of the reforms, Reshid Pasha, called for guarantees for life, property, and dignity for all the subjects of the empire, without exclusions, as explicitly defined in the Royal Decree of Gülhane in 1856.[5]

The British government, which had already supported the cohesiveness, independence, and integrity of the Ottoman Empire, was supportive of the Ottoman officials' reform efforts, especially in the nationalities question. The British Foreign Office concurred that only serious reforms could check the growing strength of the national liberation movements, particularly in the Balkans, and the Christian minorities' struggle to overthrow the sultan's control, usually with the help of Russia. These objectives were foremost on the minds of the British envoys stationed in Constantinople—John Ponsonby and, later, Stratford Canning (Lord Redcliffe). Always raising the specter of Russian-sponsored activities aimed against the Ottoman Empire's territorial integrity, Canning called on the Sublime Porte to implement reforms to alleviate the tension and put down revolts in the Danubian Principalities, Bulgaria, Lebanon, and other regions.

The "Eastern question" increased in intensity in the years leading to the Crimean War of 1853–56 and became the focus of the European powers' policies in the Near East. In the language of diplomacy, the "Eastern question" refers to the relations between the Ottoman Empire and the European powers and Russia, the liberation movements of the oppressed minorities in the empire and their exploitation by other powers, as well as the powers' race to obtain commercial and political concessions from the empire. The first use of the term occurred at the 1822 Verona Conference, during the discussions on the Greek national liberation movement and the situation in the Balkans. By the 1850s, the Eastern question gained in complexity and nuances parallel to the increased tensions in the Near East among the leading European powers of the day. Despite the inevitable conflict of interests among Britain, France, and Austria, these powers shared two main objectives: to secure the political and economic strengthening of the Ottoman Empire by means of reforms and to prevent the liberation movements of the Christian minorities. The two main objectives of the European powers should be seen in the context of their efforts to contain the Russian influence in the Near East, and they led to increased polarization in Russian-Turkish relations.

In early 1853, Russia and Great Britain entered into active political discussions on the future of the Ottoman Empire and the condition of its Christian subjects. But the British government rejected the Russian proposals for dismemberment of the Ottoman Empire. At the same time, the British government warned Russia against any excessive demand or show of military or naval force to coerce the sultan's government.[6]

While the Crimean War between Russia and Turkey was under way, British diplomacy worked industriously to produce a program of reforms for the Christians, and the Porte published the sultan's Gülhane-Hatte-Humayun decree granting equality to the Christian population and promulgating financial, fiscal, legal, and police reforms in the empire.[7] Since the decree had been published before the Paris Conference in 1856, Great Britain pushed for a clause prohibiting powers from individually interfering in the internal affairs of the Ottoman Empire.

One of the results of the Crimean War was the strengthening

of British positions in the Ottoman Empire and the significant weakening of Russia. The Ottoman Empire was nominally one of the victors and became a part of the Concert of Europe but failed to overcome enormous political and economic problems at home. The empire's dependence on the Western powers increased, just as the government's oppression of the Christian minorities increased, parallel to the rise of national liberation movements.

In the 1850s and 1860s, Britain continued to press the Porte to carry out reforms, improve the condition of non-Turkish peoples, and achieve real equality between Christian and Muslim subjects. In the British view, the alternative was the gradual dismemberment and eventual collapse of the empire, resulting in the emergence of several independent states bound to fall within Russia's sphere of influence. British diplomacy encouraged reformist Ottoman activists such as Ali Pasha and Fuad Pasha, who developed the ideology of Ottomanism that would give equal treatment to all subjects of the sultan, independent of their religious and ethnic affiliation.[8] The position of the Foreign Office was reflected in the joint memorandum presented to the grand vizier by the diplomatic representatives of six powers in Constantinople in October 1859. The memorandum stated that the implementation of the reforms should continue independent of the differences in religion and race. The aim of the reforms should be the establishment of a system of government under which all of the sultan's subjects would share in the benefits of the country's development.[9]

The Liberal Cabinet of William Gladstone[10] (1868–1874) set domination of Egypt and the Suez Canal as priorities for the British government, which ran contrary to the British principle of preserving the territorial integrity of the Ottoman Empire. Consequently, the British government displayed almost no interest in the internal problems of the Porte, including the reform process, ignoring consular reports of growing mismanagement, oppression, and abuses of the local authorities, which were increasingly directed against the Armenians and other Christian peoples.

In 1869, Ali Pasha and Fuad Pasha finally succeeded in securing passage of a "fusion" (or melting pot, in modern terminology) law, based on the principle of Ottoman citizenship. According to the law, all inhabitants of the empire, irrespective of their national or religious denomination, were declared subjects of the empire. Superficially, the law was beneficial to non-Muslims, since it was the first time in history that Muslims and Christians received equal status before the law. At the same time, the law would deprive the national minorities of their national identity, since the declared objective was the principle of assimilation or fusion. But the deaths of Fuad Pasha in 1869 and Ali Pasha in 1871 stopped the reform process in its tracks, giving way to traditional conservative policies.

The implemented administrative reforms had not resulted in greater economic efficiency and better government, largely because of the vestiges of the old feudal-style economic relations and the continuing ethnic unrest and persecutions. The European powers further increased their control over the empire's finances, eliminating competitors in the market. The country's weak industrial base stagnated under the double pressure of the authorities' mismanagement and the foreign competition. The British government was perhaps the most successful among the powers vying for control in the Ottoman Empire, not only by its economic power but also as a result of its extensive diplomatic activities. In the 1870s, the Turkish-British trade volume was 12 million to 13 million pounds annually. Most products were transported through the Suez Canal by British ships, and Britain increased its purchases of cotton from the Mesopotamia region from 12,000 pounds to 199,000 pounds during the decade.[11]

The Conservative Party of Benjamin Disraeli (Lord Beaconsfield)[12] led the British government in 1874–80. This period stands out for the active efforts of the government in expansion of British positions abroad, with the government waging colonial wars in India, Afghanistan, and South Africa, suppressing revolts in Ireland and other places. The British government solidified its control over Cyprus, the Suez Canal, and Egypt. Without prior consent or consultation with the Parliament, the Disraeli Cabinet purchased 40 percent of the Suez Canal shares from Ismail Pasha, the previous ruler of Egypt, which set the stage for the British domination of Egypt.

Against the backdrop of the acute economic crisis in the Ottoman Empire and internal instability, the constitutional reform movement gained more supporters. The Porte was now trying to stir up pro-sultan, nationalist, anti-Christian emotions to distract attention from its ongoing political, social, and economic difficulties and as a substitute for the constitutional reform ideas that had gained a foothold in the military, in the administration, and among the intellectuals. The heavy-handed tactics of the sultan's government and the political, economic, and ethnic persecutions during the June 1875 anti-Turkish uprising in Bosnia and Herzegovina sparked an international crisis, usually referred in diplomatic history as the Balkan crisis of 1875–1878. The danger of formation of pro-Russian statelets in the Balkans became a serious issue in international relations. An object of intense diplomatic discussion and competition among the powers, this could have led to a general war. Nineteen years had passed since the Paris Conference, and it became clear that none of the sultan's promises to implement reforms in the Balkans had been completed. The situation in Bulgaria, Bosnia and Herzegovina, Romania, Serbia, and Montenegro actually had deteriorated in the previous two decades.

In December 1876, Disraeli invited all the signatories of the Treaty of Paris to attend a conference in Constantinople to discuss the Eastern question. Representatives of Great Britain, Russia, France, Italy, Germany, Austria-Hungary, and Romania assembled in Constantinople. The British government was represented by then-Secretary of State for India Lord Robert Salisbury,[13] who was instructed to impede any attempts to impose the terms of settlement on Turkey. The diplomatic representatives finally agreed on a common proposal, which would preserve the autonomy of Serbia, grant minor territorial gains to Montenegro, unite Bosnia and Herzegovina into one province, and divide Bulgaria into eastern and western regions, each with a guaranteed right to self-government and freedom of religion. Reforms addressing the situation of the Christian population in those regions were to be carried out under the supervision of the Europeans. Meanwhile, a new constitution for the Ottoman Empire was promulgated in December 1876 by the new sultan, Abdul Hamid II, and the representative of the Sublime Porte rejected the European proposal. The European powers continued to negotiate with the Porte, trying to persuade it to accept the peace program. Salisbury's efforts toward that goal were also outstanding, although the British were well aware of the sultan's contemptuous attitude toward the settlement. The Ottoman government, however, did not make a single concession, and on

January 20, 1877, the European countries declared the conference closed and recalled their ambassadors. Faced with external threats, Sultan Abdul Hamid resorted to extraordinary measures by establishing an authoritarian regime. In February, the head of the constitutional movement, Midhat Pasha, and his supporters were arrested and subsequently exiled.

In early March, Russia presented to the European governments a peace proposal on the Eastern question. Germany, France, Austria-Hungary, and Italy immediately accepted the Russian proposals. The Russian government suggested signing a memorandum in London containing the proposals developed earlier in Constantinople, to be presented to the Porte. The memorandum stated that the participants of the Constantinople conference, aiming for a peaceful resolution of the Eastern question, expressed their general interest in the condition of the Christian population of the Ottoman Empire and appealed to the Porte to implement the necessary reforms. The diplomatic representatives of the powers were to establish control over the reforms. If the powers' appeals were rebuffed and the condition of the Christians deteriorated further, the draft would reserve to the powers the right to provide for the welfare of the Christians and general peace by all necessary means.[14] Convinced that Abdul Hamid would reject the powers' proposal since it would undermine his authority in the eyes of his Muslim subjects, the British government signed the memorandum on March 31.[15]

At about the same time, Abdul Hamid declared at the opening session of the Ottoman Parliament that he would work to improve the welfare of the empire, continue the Tanzimat reforms, and do his utmost to defend the dignity and independence of the empire.[16] On April 9, the Porte expressed dissatisfaction over foreign interference in Turkish internal affairs and rejected the European demands. Russian-Turkish diplomatic contacts were broken off immediately after the Turkish rejection of the London memorandum, and on April 24, Russian Emperor Alexander II signed a decree declaring war on the Ottoman Empire.

Great Britain and the Armenian Question, 1870s–1890s

On the eve of the Russo-Turkish war, Armenia was divided between the Ottoman Empire and Russia. These western and eastern parts of historical Armenia, populated with Armenians, are conditionally called western Armenia and eastern Armenia. More than 3 million Armenians were living in western Armenia, particularly in the provinces of Van, Erzurum, Bitlis, Diarbekir, Kharput, and Sivas, and in other parts of the Ottoman Empire, who were undergoing national and religious persecution. The 1860s and 1870s witnessed a rise in the Armenian liberation movement. The Ottoman government did everything it could to hinder the national consolidation of Armenians. Measures were taken to put an end to the semi-independent existence of some Armenian regions and to arouse fanaticism in the Muslim population.

In the middle of the 1870s, the British Foreign Office increasingly directed its attention to the situation in western Armenia, where the Turkish authorities and the Kurdish feudal elite subjected the Armenian population to systematic oppression, to the degree that robbery, arson, and murder became daily occurrences. According to the British diplomatic sources, as a result of the internal displacement during the 1877–78 Russian-Turkish war, the massacres and atrocities committed by the Kurdish irregulars, and the government-sponsored resettlement of the Circassians, Turks, and Lezgins in eastern Asia Minor, the Armenian population of the six easternmost provinces of the Ottoman Empire was reduced to 35 percent of the total population there in 1878.[17]

The fall of Kars and the occupation of parts of western Armenia by Russia during the war were a cause of grave concern to the British government. In his confidential message to the Foreign Office, Ambassador Henry Layard suggested that the capture of parts of Armenia by the advancing Russian forces would affect British interests. The Russian occupation of Armenia would severely undermine British authority in the East, Layard suggested and, therefore, was to be prevented at all costs and with the help of other European powers.[18] The view of the British ambassador proved to be decisive in formulating the British position on the Armenian question. This position did not at all consider the interests of the Armenians and other minorities in the empire. British diplomacy worked hard to press Russia to withdraw troops from western Armenia in exchange for promises of reforms in those areas under a general supervision of the European powers. This would have tragic consequences for the Armenian population in the years to come.

After the signing of the ceasefire agreement at Adrianople on January 31, 1878, the British diplomatic machine sought to reverse the Russian military advances, protect the Ottoman interests—in exchange for concessions in the Middle East—and secure territorial gains for Great Britain. The British government calculated that both Russia and Turkey were exhausted and that the time had come for Britain to dictate its terms. The Russian-Turkish negotiations were marked by diplomatic pressure from Britain and Austria-Hungary, while a British fleet was deployed in the Straits. The British government was opposed to the bilateral format of the negotiations on the grounds that any agreement between Russia and Turkey had to be approved by other European powers, as required by the Treaty of Paris of 1856 and the London Agreement of 1871.

Under the terms of the San Stefano Peace Treaty, signed on March 3 between Russia and Turkey, the Porte recognized the independence of Romania, Serbia, and Montenegro and the autonomy of Bulgaria and Bosnia and Herzegovina and was forced to cede to Russia Bessarabia, Kars, Ardahan, Bayazid, Batum, Olti, Ardanush, Ardvin, Alashkert, Kaghisman, and Khumar. Article 16 of the San Stefano Treaty read as follows: "As the evacuation by the Russian troops of the territory which they occupy in Armenia, and which is to be restored to Turkey, might give rise to conflicts and complications detrimental to the maintenance of good relations between the two countries, the Sublime Porte engages to carry into effect, without further delay, the improvements and reforms demanded by local requirements in the provinces inhabited by Armenians, and to guarantee their security from Kurds and Circassians."[19] This was the first instance of Armenia and the Armenians appearing in an international document in modern history. Nevertheless, it was obvious that the Russian government was not keen on securing autonomy for Armenia, as happened in the case of the Slav peoples in the Balkans. Russia was satisfied with its status as a protector of the Armenians and promises of reforms there under Russian monitoring. By acknowledging the possibility of reprisals against the Armenian population, the Russian government turned the Ottoman government's promise of reforms in Armenia into a subject of international law.

The British Cabinet discussed the San Stefano Treaty during a special session on March 27. The prime minister proposed to ask the House of Commons to call up reserves, declare Britain's readiness to use force, as well as to occupy Cyprus and Alexandretta with the British troops in India to neutralize the Russian military presence in Armenia. The government position was expressed in a circular sent by Foreign Secretary Salisbury to the British ambassadors abroad and forwarded to other nations as well. The circular condemned the treaty for violating the principles of the Treaty of Paris of 1856 and the London Agreement of 1871 and demanded that it be renegotiated in a European congress. Noting that establishment of a Greater Bulgaria would turn it into a Russian stronghold in the East, Salisbury wrote that occupation of Armenia would make the population of the region dependent on Russia while the European trade routes from Trabzon to Persia could be closed by Russia at will by means of trade barriers.[20]

By raising anti-Russian feelings in the Parliament and threatening war with Russia, the British government prepared the ground for obtaining territorial concessions for Britain. Cyprus was singled out as appropriate compensation, since it could be turned into a springboard for further penetration in the Middle East. In mid-April, Disraeli and Salisbury decided to enter into separate negotiations with the Russians in advance of the Berlin Congress, in order to reach a common ground. The British government made the following points: (1) the territory of an independent Bulgaria should not extend south of the Balkan mountain chain, (2) if Russia were to keep its Asiatic conquest, Britain must receive equivalent compensation to safeguard its interests in Asia.[21] In his letter to Queen Victoria, Salisbury wrote that Britain would be content with the Russian conquest of Kars if Russia recognized the northern borders of the Ottoman Empire in the Balkans. However, if Russia also gained Batum, the British government had to receive an island or a post in the vicinity of Asia Minor to neutralize the Russian presence in Armenia.[22]

Finding itself in an unfavorable international position and under pressure from Great Britain and Austria-Hungary, the Russian government signed a secret Russian-British protocol on amendment of the terms of the San Stefano Treaty. The protocol played down the Russian military gains and turned the terms of the peace treaty into a subject of international mediation. The Russian government had to agree not to create a Greater Bulgaria and to withdraw from some districts in western Armenia. In effect, the powers gathered later in Berlin to endorse the terms of the Russian-English protocol.

Following confidential negotiations, on June 4, the British and Ottoman governments signed the Cyprus Convention, or a "Defense Alliance between England and Turkey." According to Article 1 of the agreement, the British government would come to the aid of the sultan "if Russia were to occupy Batum, Ardahan, Kars or any of the Sultan's possessions in Asiatic Turkey that were kept under the Sultan's domination according to the final peace treaty." In return, Turkey would undertake such reforms as agreed upon between the two governments in order to provide better governance and security for the Christians and other subjects of the empire. Also, the sultan had to agree to the British administration of Cyprus.[23]

Thus, the British government concluded agreements with both Russia and Turkey. Confident that Russia was not going to resume hostilities, Britain nevertheless managed to take advantage of the Ottoman Empire's situation to take control of Cyprus that would guarantee its domination in the eastern Mediterranean while remaining its staunch ally and guarantor of its Asiatic domains. There were no references to western Armenia in the document, and the reforms were guaranteed to the Christians and other subjects of the empire in general. British diplomacy supplanted the self-determination demands of the oppressed peoples with the general overhaul of the Ottoman Empire, which would delay their liberation.

When it became known that the terms of the San Stefano Treaty would be subject to renegotiating at the Berlin Congress, the Armenian community leaders appealed to the powers, sending a delegation to the European capitals. The Armenian delegation was headed by Mkrtich Archbishop Khrimian, who was to present a proposal on establishment of an administrative autonomy in the Armenian-populated regions, under the control of the powers. In early June, following the visit of the Armenian delegation and as a result of the Armenian community's activities, the Armenian question was for the first time discussed in the House of Commons.

MPs Henry Carnarvon (Baron Porchester of Highclere) and Anthony Shaftesbury (Lord Ashley) presented the desperate condition of the Armenians in the Ottoman Empire, noting that the San Stefano Treaty had not guaranteed equal rights for all the Christian minorities, and demanded that the Cabinet make an effort at the Berlin Congress to defend the interests of the Armenians and promote the reforms in western Armenia. In response to the inquiries from the lords, Salisbury said it was impossible to implement special reforms for the Armenians since they were dispersed and lived next to Muslims who would react negatively to such reforms. The foreign secretary stated that the Armenian question was more difficult to address than the issue of Balkan Slavs and that the solution was a general reform of the Ottoman Empire.[24]

The Congress of Berlin opened on June 13, with representatives of Britain, Austria-Hungary, Germany, Russia, France, and Italy, under the chairmanship of German Chancellor Otto von Bismarck. Delegations from Serbia, Romania, Greece, Montenegro, Persia, and the Armenian National Assembly of Constantinople were also present but were not allowed to join the congress and had to content themselves with bilateral talks.[25] On July 4, during the twelfth plenary session, Article 16 of the San Stefano Treaty was discussed by the congress. Agreeing with the language of the article on granting "reforms and improvements to the Armenians," Salisbury demanded that the terms providing for the presence of Russian troops to enforce the aforementioned reforms be dropped, threatening, otherwise, to introduce a new, amended article.[26] The final draft of the article addressing the Armenian question was presented on behalf of the Ottoman and British delegations by Salisbury on July 8, during the fifteenth plenary session.[27] It ran as follows: "The Sublime Porte undertakes to carry out, without further delay, the amelioration and reforms demanded by local requirements in the provinces inhabited by the Armenians, and to guarantee their security against the Circassians and Kurds. It will periodically make known the steps taken to this effect to the Powers, who will superintend their application."[28]

Thus, British diplomacy succeeded in replacing Article 16 of the San Stefano Treaty with Article 61 of the Berlin Treaty and removing the Russian monopoly over Armenian affairs. In the period between the San Stefano Treaty and the Congress of Berlin,

British diplomacy managed to weaken the Russian military gains of the 1877–78 Russo-Turkish war, maintain its influence in the Ottoman Empire, and even secure acquisition of Cyprus, the important isle in the eastern Mediterranean. While under the provisions of Article 16 of the San Stefano Treaty, the withdrawal of the Russian troops was an incentive to carry out the reforms in western Armenia, it was not clear how the powers would "superintend the application of the reforms" under the terms of Article 61. The San Stefano Treaty referred to Armenia as a place name, while the Treaty of Berlin mentions "provinces inhabited by the Armenians." The issue was not merely semantic, since British diplomacy avoided using the geographical place name *Armenia* to preclude even the possibility of establishing autonomy there in the future. The Armenian question became an issue of international relations at San Stefano and Berlin, yet it also continued to be viewed as an internal issue of the Ottoman Empire.

Having benefited from agreement with the British government and taken advantage of the indifference of the powers toward the fate of the Christians residing in mainland Asia Minor, including the Armenians, and abusing the unclear and ineffective language of Article 61 of the Berlin Treaty, Sultan Abdul Hamid set out to redraw the empire's administrative units and intensified the anti-Armenian campaign to reduce the number of the Armenian population so that "provinces inhabited by the Armenians" would cease to exist.

Enforcement of Article 61 of the Berlin Treaty that required the sultan's government to implement reforms for the Armenian-populated provinces became a priority for the Disraeli Cabinet. British consuls were posted to several cities in western Armenia, and their reports on the conditions of the Armenians and the activities of the local administration became a constant source of pressure for the British government in its dealings with the Sublime Porte, as well as an important tool for extracting more concessions from the sultan.

By the spring of 1880, it became evident that Disraeli's and Salisbury's policies of "peaceful penetration" into the region stretching from the Aegean Sea to India had been largely ineffective. Russia checked the Conservative government's designs on Afghanistan and in the Ottoman Empire. The British government's proposals to introduce troops in eastern Rumelia or conclude a secret treaty against the Slav states had been rejected by the sultan, and the British appeals and threats of a naval intervention failed to persuade the sultan to carry out the provisions of Article 61 of the Berlin Treaty. Internal political blunders, the tax increases, and a poor harvest in 1879 contributed to the decline in fortunes of the Conservative Party. In March, Prime Minister Disraeli was forced to call new elections.

The Liberal Party won the general elections in April 1880, and William Gladstone assumed the office of prime minister. Disraeli died in the same month, and the leadership of the Conservative Party passed to Salisbury. During the election campaign, Gladstone made the Conservative government's colonial policy a major target of criticism and promised the electorate that he would pursue peaceful policies based on principles of the "Concert of Europe," joint and coordinated actions by six major European powers to promote peace. Disraeli's position on the Armenian question had been subjected to criticism from this perspective as well. Gladstone made a major foreign policy speech in Edinburgh on November 25, 1879. He noted that England had acquired Cyprus, assumed control of Egypt together with France, and soon would push the frontiers of its colonies in South Africa to the southern borders of the Portuguese domains there. England also had assumed the responsibility to improve the administration of the Turkish provinces in Asia Minor and the rest of Asiatic Turkey, including Arabia, Gladstone said. He noted that England had also pledged to defend the Turkish frontier in Armenia against a Russian attack, a responsibility that would require troops to cross hundreds of miles of mountainous terrain or cross thousands of miles by sea. Gladstone concluded by pledging to reduce the "confusion" of the British obligations.[29] As far as the Armenian question was concerned, this meant joint and coordinated actions by the European powers to force the sultan's government to carry out its obligations under Article 61 of the Berlin Treaty.

The Gladstone Cabinet's new foreign policy was reflected in a circular sent by Foreign Secretary George Granville to the British ambassadors in the European powers on May 4, 1880. The new head of the Foreign Office noted that it was in the interests of Europe to end the delays in implementing several provisions of the

Berlin Treaty and that the coordinated efforts of all the powers were the best means to achieve that objective. The British government proposed that all powers submit, through their envoys in Constantinople, collective notes to the Turkish government to force it to carry out its obligations on the issues of Greece, Montenegro, and Armenia. The document concluded that the Porte had not carried out its obligations on the Armenian question per Article 61 and had not made efforts to secure the supervision of the powers over the reforms. According to Granville, in the view of the continuing appalling state of the Armenian community, the provisions of the article could not remain a dead letter but needed to be enforced by a coordinated effort of the powers.[30] This was the first serious indication that the new government disavowed the Disraeli policy of a unilateral defense of the Ottoman Empire and drew closer to the positions of Russia and the other European powers.

The European ambassadors presented identical notes to the Porte on June 18, 1880. In the note to Turkish Foreign Minister Abeddin Pasha, British Ambassador George Goschen informed him that delays in the implementation of certain articles of the Berlin Treaty by Turkey had become a subject of consultations among the powers. The powers agreed that European interests required an end to delays in execution of the conditions spelled out in the treaty on July 13, 1878. In addition to the issues related to the demarcation of Turkish-Greek and Turkish-Montenegrin borders, the note raised the issue of reforms in the Armenian-populated regions, as provided for in Article 61, since the sultan's government had not done anything in this area. It was mentioned that Article 61 had been rendered dead while the situation in the Armenian-populated areas continued to be unbearable. The powers concluded that only joint and coordinated efforts by them could force the Porte to carry out the reforms, the note claimed. The British government, therefore, demanded that the Porte promptly carry out the reforms and inform the powers in minute detail of the measures it intended to take toward that goal.[31]

Not satisfied with the official reply from the Porte, the British government continued consultations with the other powers seeking joint action to pressure the sultan. Having received the approval of their governments, the ambassadors of Great Britain, Germany, Russia, Italy, France, and Austria-Hungary presented a collective note to the Porte on September 7, 1880. The document stated that the assurances given in the Turkish answer of July 5 did not abide by the spirit and letter of Article 61 of the Berlin Treaty; that the commissions sent to the regions to investigate local conditions produced no tangible results; that the consular officers' reports had indicated no reforms in the judiciary or progress in the establishment of a gendarmerie or improvement in the police. "The language which the Sublime Porte uses in speaking of the crimes alleged to have been committed in the provinces inhabited by the Armenians shows that it refuses to recognize the degree of anarchy which exists in those provinces," the document charged. The powers warned of the gravity of a situation that could lead to wholesale destruction of the Christian population in many districts and noted that no serious proposal had been made for stopping the excesses of the Kurdish and Circassian bandits, who could not be restrained by ordinary laws. The powers urged strong and "exceptionally rigorous" measures to put an end to the harassment that was a continuing source of danger to the property, honor, and life of the Armenians.[32] The note admitted the need for reforms in all parts of the empire but specified the need for immediate action in the Armenian-populated provinces, as provided for in Article 61. While the Porte argued that the reforms should be made for both the Kurdish and the Armenian communities, the collective note suggested that distinctions had to be made between the two ethnic groups, in view of the settled nature of one group and the semi-nomadic state of the other. The powers concluded that the Ottoman proposals did not address the existing situation, did not satisfy the needs of that region's inhabitants, and were not based on the two most important principles of equality and decentralization. The powers urged the organization of census by an independent commission, carrying out prompt reforms to secure the life and property of the Armenians, taking immediate measures against the incursions of the Kurds, implementing the proposed system of finance, and giving to governors-general greater security of office and a more extended responsibility. The powers also urged that the reforms be carried out under their supervision.[33]

The British government's new position on greater coordination between the powers on the Armenian question, it would appear, should have yielded positive results and forced the sultan's government to implement the reforms in the face of European solidarity. In fact, the Porte submitted a reply to the envoys on October 3 giving vague promises without specific proposals or guarantees and showed irritation in the language of the note. The disagreements among the powers on the one hand and the lack of practical control mechanisms on the other placed Britain in an ambiguous position.

In 1881, the British government made a fresh initiative on the Armenian question. On January 12, Granville sent a circular to the British ambassadors asking them to draw the attention of the powers to the Armenian question and proposing to submit another collective note protesting the treatment of the Armenian population and nonexecution of the provisions of the Berlin Treaty in this regard.[34] The French and German governments rejected the proposal on the pretext that it was not appropriate to raise the Armenian question while the Greek-Turkish boundary issue remained unresolved.[35] Conversely, the Italian and Russian governments instructed their envoys in the Ottoman Empire to work jointly with other ambassadors and issue a statement on the implementation of reforms for the Armenian population.[36] On February 14, Granville instructed the British ambassador in Russia to inform the Russian government of Britain's intention to accommodate the position of Germany and France and postpone the joint statement.[37]

On September 9, 1881, the new meeting of the powers' envoys convened in Constantinople under the auspices of the British ambassador. Ambassador Frederick Dufferin opened the conference and noted that the previous collective note, dated September 7, 1880, had not been answered by the Porte, which had not taken any steps toward carrying out its obligations under the Treaty of Berlin. He proposed to send another collective note to the Porte, reiterating the demands set forth in the earlier *demarche*. The British envoy suggested demanding that the sultan immediately end the anarchy prevalent in the eastern provinces of the empire and take steps toward securing the life and property of the Christian subjects. Dufferin proposed that an appointment of an able administrator with full powers in those regions could guarantee the reforms. On September 15, he presented the proposal agreed upon with his colleagues to Sultan Abdul Hamid. The sultan expressed his concern over the conditions in the eastern provinces, admitted the unfortunate "dearth of capable administrators" in Turkey, and promised to carry out the proposals. He thought the idea of appointing a high commissioner to the eastern provinces was an "excellent" one and assured the ambassador that he would make an appointment within a month.[38]

The British government took over Egypt completely in June–September 1882, under the pretext of protecting British lives and investments in the wake of the Egyptian national movement. While formally still a part of the Ottoman Empire, Egypt became a de facto British colony. Consequently, the British government focused its attention on the Egyptian problem and, in an effort to avoid additional points of conflict with the Porte, altogether refrained from any action on the Armenian question.

In the winter months of 1891, the sultan began to organize mounted militia, drafted almost exclusively from the Kurdish tribes and dubbed Hamidiye. Some thirty regiments were set up, with 33,000 members. The formation of the Kurdish militia by the sultan's government meant to stem the Armenian national liberation movement, dramatically alter the balance of power and, wherever possible, the ethnic composition in the provinces where the reforms had been scheduled to take place, and serve as a bulwark against the Russian army in case of renewal of hostilities in the East.

Gladstone's final tenure in office (1892–1894) coincided with the period during which the ground was prepared by the sultan's authorities for the massacres of the Armenian population. Among the measures used were inciting Muslim fundamentalism, spreading anti-Armenian propaganda, permitting robberies and murders of Armenians, forced conversion of Armenians to Islam, stricter censorship, settling Muslim refugees from the Balkans in the Armenian-populated provinces, and unleashing the Kurdish tribes. The government prohibited circulation of Armenian newspapers in the inner provinces of the empire. In 1892, the Porte officially banned the operation of all schools it had not authorized. Another decision limited civil service appointment only to those empire subjects who had graduated from state-sponsored (i.e., Muslim-run) schools. The teaching of Armenia's history and geography was forbidden throughout the empire, books on these subjects were confiscated and burned, and authors and teachers were commonly tried as criminals. After declaring a war on the Christian schools, the sultan's government proceeded to "destroy and exterminate" non-Muslim literature. Banned were such English classics as Shakespeare, Byron, Milton, and Scott.[39] Thus, it became clear that instead of tackling the deep political, socioeconomic, and ethnic issues accounting for the difficult state of the Armenian population, the sultan's government had decided to foment religious hatred and incite Muslim fundamentalism against the Armenian Christians.

Gladstone continued the same policy toward the Ottoman Empire, neglecting the radical changes taking place in the empire and the increasingly intense anti-Armenian actions of the sultan's government. In 1894, Gladstone, now eighty-five, resigned from the office of prime minister and stepped down as the leader of the Liberal Party, passing on his portfolio to Archibald Rosebery. The Foreign Office papers show unequivocally that during Gladstone's last two years in office, his government had not come forward with any substantial initiative to press the Porte for implementation of reforms and improvement in the conditions of the Armenian population.

Great Britain and the Armenian Massacres, 1894–1896

In March 1894, Lord Rosebery assumed the leadership of the shattered Liberal Party and, therefore, also the prime minister's position. His foreign secretary, John Kimberley,[40] did not have a predetermined policy on the Ottoman Empire, while the British ambassador in Constantinople, Philip Currie, was appointed shortly before the change of government and was still navigating the vagaries of Constantinople politics. So, Rosebery merely continued his predecessor's policy on the Armenian question, which was to resort to joint action with the European powers if a crisis broke out again in the Ottoman Empire.[41]

In August and September 1894, the Ottoman authorities organized a massacre of the Armenian population in Sasun, Bitlis province. The pretext for the massacre was created by the local authorities, who had assessed an additional tax on the Armenian population. The Armenian community refused to pay, because of the damages caused by the continual attacks by the Kurdish irregulars. The Ottoman authorities labeled the action insurgency, and regular Turkish troops, gendarmerie, and Kurdish irregulars under the command of Governor Hussein Tahsin Pasha besieged Sasun. The people of Sasun repulsed the attack. Receiving reports of an uprising, the sultan flew into a rage and ordered the brutal suppression of the Armenians.[42]

The sultan's government had successfully blocked the information about the Sasun uprising and subsequent military operations from reaching the outside world and sealed off the entire region completely. Nevertheless, Vice Consul C. M. Hallward, referring to unofficial sources, reported from Van in early October that a massacre had taken place in Sasun the previous month.[43] Kimberley instructed Currie to request that Hallward be sent to Sasun to investigate,[44] but the authorities dismissed the British report as unreliable and refused to authorize his trip on the grounds that the presence of a British official in the rebellious region would be viewed as endorsement and rekindle the uprising that had been suppressed.[45]

On November 2, Currie presented a memorandum to the sultan on the massacre in Sasun, based on reports from the British vice consul. The ambassador was convinced that his report would be disputed or denied by the Porte but decided to insist on an investigation. The ambassador was convinced that the reports of an Armenian uprising had been untrue and urged an independent investigation of the results.[46]

The sultan rejected Hallward's report as not credible and charged the British officials with supporting the actions of nihilists, socialists, and anarchists aimed against his government. The sultan drew parallels with the Bulgarian situation wherein, he noted, the Bulgarians circulated similar stories of massacres, asked for support from the British government, and achieved autonomous status for Bulgaria. The sultan noted that it was not possible to establish Armenian autonomy, since the Armenian population was not concentrated and was not in the majority in any locale. He claimed that the Armenian hopes for autonomy were unrealistic and that the reports of persecution and oppression generating European sympathy were futile. He again complained of the British press publishing the massacre stories, although he did admit that the government had been forced to take tough measures against the "insurgents" who took arms and resisted the government. Abdul Hamid referred to the British government's suppression of the native insurgencies in India and Egypt as examples of similar actions. In the conclusion of his answer, however, the sultan informed Currie that the interior minister had been ordered to conduct an investigation and, should the British reports prove to be true, promised to hold the governor of Bitlis, Hussein Tahsin Pasha, responsible for the incident.[47]

Rosebery tried to prevent the news of the Sasun massacre from spreading in the country and refrained from publicizing the troubling consular reports about the destitute conditions prevalent in Armenia. The news of the massacre, however, reached the British press in early November and generated a wave of public sympathy for the Armenian cause. British public opinion charged its national government with greater responsibility for the conditions of the Armenians, because while it was only one of the signatories of the Treaty of Berlin, the British government was the power most vocal in demanding reforms from the Porte. Also, the Ottoman government undertook a bilateral obligation, under the terms of the Anglo-Turkish Convention, to carry out reforms in the Armenian-populated provinces in exchange for protection from Russian territorial encroachment. Thus, the resurrection of the Armenian question in the press presented a challenge to Rosebery, although he was convinced naively that the crisis would go away on its own.[48]

The British government publicly expressed its preference for acting in concert with the European powers on the Armenian question. Rosebery expressed his personal opposition to unilateral British actions on this issue, stating that joint intervention by the powers would be the only reliable and safe method of achieving their goal, while any independent action would be futile and dangerous.[49]

On November 21, 1894, the sultan announced that a commission had been formed to investigate "cruel actions of the Armenian bandits" and denied the fact of massacre. The Ottoman ambassadors in European nations received a circular telegram with the official version of events, according to which regular troops had been sent to Sasun to stop the crimes committed by the Armenian insurgents and restore law and order. The telegram noted the unfriendly attitude of the European press and claimed that its reports of the Sasun events did not correspond to reality.[50]

On November 27, the British Cabinet decided to take an active stance on the Armenian question and request the cooperation of the French and Russian governments in an investigation of the events.[51] Kimberley instructed the British Embassy to present a *demarche* to the Porte requesting the participation of the European powers in the investigation. The *demarche* stated that under the circumstances, Article 61 allowed the powers the liberty to intervene on the Armenian question.[52] On December 5, Currie met with French ambassador Paul Cambon and Russian chargé M. Jadowsky and proposed that the British, French, and Russian consuls in Erzurum in parallel to the Turkish commission conduct an independent inquiry into the Sasun events. The French and Russian envoys gave their preliminary approval and promised to inform their respective governments of the proposal.[53]

In mid-January 1895, the Turkish commission accompanied by the British, Russian, and French representatives (vice consuls in Erzurum) departed for Mush from Erzurum three days before.[54] While the local authorities had tried to obstruct the meetings between the members of the commission and the local Armenians, the Armenian residents of Sasun succeeded in presenting a petition to the commission describing the massacre. The investigation then ground to a halt after the local authorities arrested a number of Armenian activists in Bitlis and Mush. The European representatives appealed to the Porte, and Governor Hussein Tahsin Pasha was dismissed and replaced by Ömer Bey. The representatives of the powers noted that the Turkish commissioners preferred to read government documents and hear the testimony of government officials, rather than of local residents.[55] On February 8, British representative H. S. Shipley reported to Currie that the commission had conducted twelve hearings to date but heard testimony from only one Armenian witness. According to the vice consul, the Turkish commissioners had been instructed to prove that the Armenian population had been in open rebellion, that Armenians, not Kurds, were the aggressors, and that the Armenians had committed barbaric acts against the Muslims. The European representatives had visited Armenian homes and institutions and interviewed numerous Armenians, which had irritated the sultan's government.[56]

The reports by the British Embassy and consular officers

noted that the harassment of the Armenian population by the sultan's government continued in earnest even while the Sasun commission was functioning. Many Armenians were searched, detained, and held without due process for alleged "revolutionary activities." On March 16, Kimberley informed Currie of intense interest in the Parliament and among the members of the public toward the events in Turkey. Kimberley referred to the reports of the arrest of some eighty Armenian activists in Constantinople for collecting donations for the victims of the Sasun massacre. The press continued to report on the abominable conditions of inmates in Turkish jails and the persecution of Armenians. Kimberley noted that real-life evidence showed that the living conditions of the Christian population had not improved, contrary to the assurances given by the sultan and his government as well as the obligations under the Treaty of Berlin. The ambassador was instructed to draw on this argument to demand that the Porte release the arrested Armenians and allow the foreign consuls to be present at the trials of the Christian subjects. The ambassador was instructed to hold consultations with the powers on the subject of reforms.[57]

After the Russian and French governments endorsed the British proposal and simultaneously expressed their opposition to any coercive measures to enforce it, on May 11, the project was presented to the Porte. The May memorandum contained the following main points: (1) the number of provinces must be reduced; (2) the governors must be selected and appointed with semiofficial approval of the powers; (3) a general amnesty must be proclaimed, releasing Armenian prisoners from custody and allowing exiled and displaced Armenians to return; (4) the judicial and penal systems must be reformed; (5) a high commissioner must be appointed to oversee the reforms process, with the approval of the powers; (6) a permanent commission of control must be established, made up of three Christian and three Muslim government officials; (7) the Armenian victims in Sasun, Talvorik, and other regions where massacres had been carried out must be compensated; (8) the right to change religion must be respected; (9) Armenians' land titles must be respected; (10) the conditions of the Armenian population in other parts of Asia Minor must be improved; (11) the status of local administration officials and members of the police, gendarmerie, and Kurdish and Hamidiye paramilitary forces must be reviewed;

and (12) fiscal administration must be reformed. Under French and Russian pressure, the British government removed important points from its reforms proposal, such as merging six provinces into one which would have established an Armenian administrative unit headed by a Christian governor of the powers' choosing.[58]

Abdul Hamid issued his reply on June 3. The sultan had rejected all of the guarantees for implementation of the reforms, including the appointment of a high commissioner, a commission of supervision, and the vetting of gubernatorial appointments by the powers. The sultan further rejected the proposed reforms of the judiciary, gendarmerie, and police and the demand to allow the displaced population to return to their original domiciles, to declare amnesty, compensate the victims, reform the penal system, and improve the condition of the Armenian population in other provinces.[59]

The moment arrived for a European response to the arrogant position of the sultan. The response never materialized. The British government proved to be indecisive as far as a unilateral action was concerned. The Mediterranean Fleet was deployed near Beirut, at a distance of 200 to 300 kilometers (124 to 186 miles) from Armenia. On June 19, the British Cabinet discussed the possibility of a naval deployment but made no decision. Three days later, the Liberal government resigned for domestic political reasons, and the following day, the queen asked Lord Salisbury to form the new Cabinet on behalf of his Conservative Party.[60]

The British public greeted the return of Salisbury to power with great hopes, and the overall consensus was that the Conservative government would be able to bring the Near Eastern crisis to an end and to stop the anti-Armenian policies of the sultan. Even Lord Rosebery, now the leader of the opposition, noted in August that Salisbury would have the support of not only his party but also the British people.[61] Nevertheless, members of the Liberal Party pointed out the inconsistency of Salisbury's perceived platform and his position during the Congress of Berlin, where British diplomacy succeeded in nullifying some of the provisions of the San Stefano Treaty. As a result, an area with a Christian population was returned to the sultan's rule.

Returning to power, Salisbury also assumed the Foreign

Office portfolio. He granted the British ambassador in Constantinople, Philip Currie, a personal friend of his, the rank of undersecretary of state for foreign affairs, a privilege testifying to the importance of the Near East and the Armenian question for British foreign policy. On the surface, Salisbury seemed to have distanced himself from the traditional Conservative platform on the Eastern question by supporting the historical Russian mission of controlling the Black Sea Straits. In reality, Salisbury had concluded that the collapse of the Ottoman Empire was inevitable, but he would not contribute to hastening that end. On the one hand, the interests of Great Britain required preservation of the territorial integrity of the Ottoman Empire and defending the sultan's government from Russian encroachment, but on the other, any British action would have been rendered useless and ineffective unless supported by Russia and the European powers. Thus, Salisbury worked to secure British-Russian rapport on the Armenian question, while simultaneously preparing the ground for the complete occupation of Egypt and restoring British influence on the Porte, which had been supplanted by closer ties between Russia and Turkey. This was the essence of the delicate maneuvering of British diplomacy on the Armenian question. By proclaiming its intentions to cooperate closely with Germany and Russia on the Eastern issues, the British government was attempting to bring Sultan Abdul Hamid's government back into its sphere of influence.

On July 16, 1895, the commission investigating the Sasun events concluded its work after hearing testimony from nearly two hundred witnesses without making public its final recommendations. On July 20, the European representatives presented their findings to their embassies, with the conclusion that a full-scale massacre of the Armenian population had taken place in Sasun with the participation of regular Turkish troops. The European representatives' report did not confirm the reports of a serious insurgency by the Armenians preceding the events.[62]

In the annual Queen's Speech on August 15, which opened the session of the Parliament, all references to the Armenian question contained tough language. The queen noted that the British government anxiously awaited the response of the Porte to the proposals presented by the British, French, and Russian ambassadors in Constantinople. In his own remarks, Salisbury accused the Porte of openly carrying out anti-Armenian policies and threatened serious consequences if the Porte did not accept the ambassadors' memorandum on the Armenian reforms. He also expressed disappointment with the reluctance of the French and Russian governments to resort to force to press the issue on the Porte. Later that month, in a speech in Dover, Salisbury referred to Turkey as a "center of destruction, a malignant tumor spreading disease to the healthy part of Europe bordering the Turkish dominions," and predicted an imminent collapse of the Ottoman Empire.

Throughout July to September 1895, the British consular officers in eastern Asia Minor continued to submit reports on the critical conditions of the local Armenian population, clashes between Muslims and Christians, Kurdish attacks, and incitement of the Muslim mob against Armenians by local Turkish officials.[63]

Despite the support and sympathy for the Armenian population expressed publicly by Salisbury, Gladstone, and other prominent public figures, as well as overwhelmingly by the public, nothing influenced the implementation of reforms. Moreover, the Armenian political parties, buoyed by the pronouncements of British politicians and the media, rushed to condemn the sultan's anti-Armenian policies. Despite the fact that the recently established Armenian parties carried no real political weight and did not yet enjoy much popular support among the Armenian population, the sultan's government skillfully used the political activities of these groups as a pretext to launch large-scale massacres of the Armenian population.[64]

On September 28, while the British, French, and Russian embassies were holding consultations on the course of the proposed reforms program and finding common ground in negotiations with the sultan, the three ambassadors received identical letters from the Hunchak Armenian Revolutionary Committee. The Hunchaks notified the foreign envoys of their intention to spearhead a peaceful demonstration in Constantinople to demand that reforms be carried out in the Armenian-populated provinces. The organizers expressed hope that the Porte would not deploy the police and troops against the peaceful demonstration and disavowed any responsibility for regretful incidents should the authorities use force to disperse the rally.[65]

On September 30, some two thousand Armenians marched to

the sultan's residence, Bab Ali, demanding an immediate implementation of reform measures. The demonstrators prepared a petition on administrative, economic, and judicial reforms, based largely on the May memorandum. According to Currie's October 1 report to the Foreign Office, the demonstrators were stopped by the gendarmerie and ordered to disperse. The demonstrators defied the ban, and a gunfight ensued during which gendarmerie chief Server Bey, fifteen gendarmes, and sixty Armenian demonstrators were shot and killed. The gendarmerie and police dispersed the demonstration and arrested more than five hundred participants, treating them with the utmost brutality. Then the Muslim mob, armed with clubs, began to attack Armenians randomly on the streets, assaulting and killing without regard to the police, who did not intervene. More than one thousand Armenian residents, including women and children, took refuge in the patriarchal residence. Despite official assurances that law and order had been restored, the killings continued unabated, Currie reported.[66] The firing of gunshots at the gendarmerie chief was used by the Turkish government as a pretext for a massacre that claimed the lives of more than six thousand Armenians.[67]

On the morning of October 2, the ambassadors of six powers met at the Austrian Chancery to draft a joint statement on the Constantinople incident. The ambassadors demanded that the Porte use only government troops to restore law and order, decried the inciting of the mob against the Armenians, and protested the police brutality toward the jailed Armenians.[68] The Turkish foreign minister ignored the *demarche* and told the ambassadors that the government had already taken all measures to restore law and order and provide public safety. He dismissed the claims of massacres as hearsay and accused the Armenian patriarch of provoking the antigovernment demonstrations.[69]

On October 4, Lord Salisbury received a letter from Queen Victoria, who expressed her indignation over the Armenian massacres and suggested occupying the Turkish Straits as the only measure to prevent further massacres of the Armenian population in the Ottoman Empire.[70]

A decision was made at another meeting of the ambassadors on October 5 to present a joint memorandum to the Porte, while the British Cabinet authorized deployment of six warships to Lemnos island.[71] In the memorandum, dated October 6, the European diplomatic missions cited the evidence of the massacres and noted the continuing deterioration of public safety in the capital. The memorandum warned that the disturbances could spread to other parts of the empire if uncontained. The embassies called on the Porte to take measures to check fanaticism in the Muslim and Christian communities and provide security to the Christian subjects and foreign nationals and offered their assistance in the reestablishment of public order, collecting evidence, and conducting an inquiry.[72]

On October 10, Currie had met with the French and Russian ambassadors to discuss the upcoming program of reforms and the protection of the lives and property of the Armenians. The ambassadors' report proposed that the reforms program was to be formalized in the form of an agreement or treaty with the powers and issued as an imperial decree. This program included provisions for (1) a Christian assistant to the chairman of the Governmental Commission of Supervision Shakir Pasha, whose name should be unofficially submitted to the powers for their approval; (2) the participation of Christians in the administration and the posts of governors and deputy governors to be open to Christians; (3) the dragomans having the right of addressing to the Commission of Control any complaint, communication, or information; (4) the Commission of Control fixing the number of Christian functionaries in proportion to each province; (5) Christian assistants being attached to the Muslim governors and vice governors; (6) the ambassadors reserving the right to remonstrate against the appointment of incapable, dishonest, or fanatical governors; (7) the number of rural guards being fixed by the governor on the recommendation of the district police chief and in conformity with local requirements; (8) a note to be addressed by the ambassadors to the Porte respecting prisons, arbitrary arrests, amnesty, reinstatement of emigrants, regulations for the Hamidiye cavalry, and insisting upon their complete and immediate execution; and (9) a stipulation that the principles of the reform scheme would be applied to all regions of Asia Minor where the Christians formed a palpable part of the population.[73]

The three ambassadors met with Minister of Foreign Affairs

Said Pasha and presented him with additional proposals for the reforms program. The Turkish foreign minister assured the ambassadors that the program would be discussed at the Council of Ministers and would be released in the form of an imperial decree. Similar assurances had been received from the newly appointed grand vizier, Kiamil Pasha.[74]

On October 17, the sultan signed a decision promulgating the reforms program negotiated by the three ambassadors and the Turkish foreign minister.[75]

In the beginning of November, Salisbury gave the traditional Guild Hall banquet speech and noted that Abdul Hamid's reforms program could alleviate the grievances of the Armenian population of the Ottoman Empire if the sultan's government carried out the reforms in a genuine and serious way. The prime minister said that the powers were unanimous in their desire to uphold the integrity of the Ottoman Empire to allow a reformed Turkey to rise on its foundations. If it did not happen, the powers would be forced to take matters into their own hands and establish new political entities out of pieces of the empire.[76]

On November 11, Russian Ambassador Alexander Nelidov proposed at the meeting of the European ambassadors that the powers should dispatch gunboats or lightly armed vessels to the vicinity of Constantinople.[77] He said that the presence of the European gunboats would positively affect the positions of the powers vis-à-vis the sultan, stop the spreading of the crisis, and prevent recourse to measures involving political complications. The powers' representatives had expressed a generally positive attitude toward the Russian proposal.

While the powers were staging a largely useless naval demonstration of force, the sultan announced that the British government would be unable to support the Armenians in their quest. Abdul Hamid noted that all attempts to establish an Armenian autonomy, whether by means of a European conference or by a show of force, should be stopped. He complained that the Armenians had boasted about the powers' naval maneuvers as if the actions of the European nations had been intended to help them.[78] Abdul Hamid was convinced that the joint expedition would not take place because of constant disagreements between Britain and Russia.[79]

The sultan's government was bent on obstructing the European naval demonstration in the Straits. On November 19, the sultan requested that the foreign envoys change the decision on the warships, pointing to the efforts to stop disturbances and restore peace. The embassies, in turn, requested that the Porte not obstruct the passage of the fleet and issue a decree authorizing the naval deployment, which would promote peace in the country and prevent recourse to more stringent measures.[80]

In the meantime, the British Embassy continued to receive reports from the provinces on large-scale massacres in the provinces. As the year 1895 drew to a close, British policies on the Eastern question faced a crisis. Traditionally, British demands for reforms in the Ottoman provinces populated by Christian subjects had been made primarily as a means of asserting Britain's influence and advancing its interests. The establishment of a protectorate and the implementation of reforms were the main elements of the political objectives of the Cyprus Convention. These objectives became irreconcilable by 1895, and this period brought to the surface the contradictions in the British position on the Eastern question. The tragedy of the Armenian massacres had completely destroyed British hopes to control and direct the reform measures. Sultan Abdul Hamid's delaying tactics, temporary suspension of the Armenian massacres, and the increasing difficulty of maintaining a common position with the European powers effectively neutralized British diplomacy, preventing it from achieving any positive or practical results. Even the sultan's acquiescence to the naval deployment in the Dardanelles did not bring about an effective change in the reforms issue and did not prevent the spread of disturbances. Salisbury blamed his predecessors, Rosebery and Kimberley, for their inability to recognize the real position of the French and Russian governments on the issue of reforms.[81]

Salisbury even made up his mind to prevent the deployment of the Russian Black Sea Fleet near Constantinople. Salisbury had no doubts about the inability of the sultan's government to maintain the status quo in the Ottoman Empire and the despotic nature of the government and readily admitted that the anti-Russian policy of the Crimean War was a mistake on the part of Britain. At the same time, he hoped that the traditional reputation and authority of the British Navy would prevent the loss of Constantinople to a third power. The prime minister proposed that the Cabinet empower Currie to authorize deployment of the entire Mediterranean Fleet to the Straits to terrorize the sultan and restore British influence. The Cabinet did not concur, while the Admiralty argued that the Franco-Russian alliance had unfavorably altered the naval balance in the Mediterranean.[82]

Salisbury was facing an uphill battle in November and December 1895, as he was trying to explain and justify the British policy to a public greatly agitated by the continuing reports of massacres. The Foreign Office received an enormous number of letters, appeals, and protests from public, humanitarian, and religious groups. Motivated anew by the reports of the massacres, Gladstone began a fresh public campaign against the sultan, whom he had labeled the "Great Assassin."[83] Lack of support for the government's policies from an anxious public and the apparent failure of British-French-Russian efforts to cooperate on the issue of reforms forced Salisbury to rethink his position on the Armenian question. At the same time, he was concerned with the possibility of active cooperation among the five European powers that supported the territorial integrity of the Ottoman Empire—cooperation that he feared would be aimed against British interests. The only specific proposal he made to the powers was to depose Sultan Abdul Hamid. In mid-December, Salisbury refused to meet a delegation of the Armenian Society led by the duke of Westminster and pressured the duke and Gladstone to postpone a rally in support of the Armenian cause. The government's indecisiveness and actions led to its international isolation and loss of public support at home.

Eventually, the sultan granted an authorization for the passage of the warships to Constantinople but only because of the Russian government's intervention.[84] During December 12–16, 1895, a procession of British, French, Russian, Italian, and Austro-Hungarian warships passed through the Straits one by one.[85]

On December 10, Currie proposed to his fellow ambassadors that joint action be taken to address the continuing reports of massacres and robberies throughout Asia Minor. He proposed establishing an international commission to visit the affected provinces, conduct an inquiry into the disturbances, address the issues of compensation, and bring the perpetrators to justice. The Austro-Hungarian and Italian ambassadors endorsed the idea, but Russian

Ambassador Nelidov balked at the proposal, saying he had been instructed to cooperate with other powers only as far as protection of foreign subjects was concerned. He proposed instead that the embassies should forward the reports to the Porte demanding an explanation and that they should ask their respective governments to review Currie's idea if it was officially endorsed by the British Cabinet.

Currie recommended that the Cabinet approve the proposal, despite the disagreements among the powers. The ambassador noted that the situation in the eastern provinces continued to be horrifying, and the provinces where the reforms were to take place had been especially devastated. The Armenians had been subjected to massacres in all the major cities; nearly all of the Armenian settlements had been affected. Almost three hundred thousand Christians were in a state of extreme poverty and misery.[86] The Kurdish attacks continued unabated, the perpetrators of massacres remained at large, many innocent Armenians remained in custody, the called-up reserves were not paid and had resorted to robbing and looting the population, disturbances had broken out in Crete, and more were expected in Macedonia. The financial situation of the sultan's government was hopeless, Currie noted, and would find itself unable to meet its needs as early as spring. He suggested using the Ottoman government's default as an occasion to exact measures establishing public order and preventing further attacks on peace.[87]

In one Armenian populated district, however, the pattern was not the same. The remote and inaccessible town of Zeitoun had been annually shredded by that voracious locust, the Ottoman tax collector, and was thus well prepared for self-defense. In July 1895, the Porte hoped to quiet the agitation by granting the town an amnesty for its seditious activity. But when reports started to reach Zeitoun of the massacres of fellow Armenians, the Zeitountsis started a rebellion. The army had surrounded the Zeitoun rebels and was gearing up for a massacre, having already claimed alleged Armenian atrocities as a justification.The European embassies received letters from the Armenian Apostolic and Armenian Catholic patriarchs, transmitting the request of the Zeitoun rebels to use the good offices of the foreign consuls for talks with the authorities. On December 23, Currie initiated a discussion with other ambassadors, who decided to request their governments to authorize the consuls in Aleppo to travel to Zeitoun.[88] Before the powers could take any action, the Turkish military advanced on Zeitoun, destroyed the citadel, and captured the city; the remaining rebels escaped. The British consul in Aleppo reported that the Turkish military granted unarmed Armenians free passage to Marash, but Kurdish and Circassian gangs terrorized the area.[89] The Porte announced that the military had captured the citadel and surrounded the city but the military commander had been ordered to advance slowly to allow the Armenians to surrender.[90] According to the next consular report, almost five thousand rebels retreated to the nearby strategic hills dominating the region.[91]

On December 28, the powers' envoys decided to offer the Porte the use of the foreign consuls for mediation and, if the offer was accepted, to press for an immediate ceasefire.[92] The offer was made jointly through the embassy dragomans.[93] Several days later, the Turkish foreign minister informed Currie that the Porte agreed to the proposal of negotiation by the consuls in Aleppo and issued appropriate orders to the authorities in the region.[94] On January 6, 1896, the Zeitoun rebels accepted the mediation offer from the consuls, the British consul in Aleppo reported.[95] The mediation effort in Zeitoun ended on January 30, with the signing of an agreement between the rebel leaders and the government delegates. The agreement provided for the Armenian rebels and the Muslims inhabiting the valleys to surrender their weapons.[96] The agreement represented a major victory for the Zeitoun rebels and humiliated the sultan's government, which was forced to sign a treaty with its own subjects and to recognize their demands and rights. The British consul played a crucial role in the signing of the treaty. He had dispensed monetary grants to the people of Zeitoun and stayed there for a few months after the agreement was signed. In April 1896, the sultan's government appointed a Muslim as mayor of Zeitoun but retracted its decision under pressure from the British Embassy and appointed a Greek Christian instead.[97]

The massacres of Armenians that took place in the Ottoman Empire from September 1895 to January 1896[98] were planned in advance. Government agents had been sent to all the provinces with instructions to whip up the fanaticism of the Muslim mob. Government agents would meet with the Muslims gathering to pray at mosques and tell them that the sultan believed all Armenians to be scheming to assault Islam and would call on the faithful to defend Islam and the sultan from the seditious Armenians. The agents played to the greed of the mob by saying that the rules of the holy jihad allowed the property of the rebels to be taken by the faithful; any resistance from the Christians was punishable by death.[99] Single shots would be fired or trumpets would be sounded as a signal to launch the pogroms.[100] Before sacking the urban areas, the Kurdish tribes would attack and commit atrocities in the nearby Armenian villages. The mob, made up of Kurdish, Circassian, or Laz tribal elements, would then enter the city and, joined by the Turkish mob, police, and troops, would massacre and loot the Armenian population.[101] The local authorities issued orders to target males only.[102] Only Armenians were singled out for killing; the Greek and Jewish communities were rarely affected. The massacres of the Armenian population were well organized; regular troops and gendarmerie forces took part in killing and looting. The action would end as suddenly as it started; another signal would be sounded to call it off.[103] The local authorities in many locales would force the Armenian notables to sign a document acknowledging their role in beginning or provoking the disturbances.[104]

Relative calm prevailed in the Ottoman Empire in the spring and summer of 1896. British diplomacy markedly decreased its activities related to the Armenian question. The embassy no longer sent protest *demarches* to the Porte, while British political and public figures no longer addressed Armenian issues with the same frequency and fervor. However, the core problems in the Ottoman Empire had not been solved, and the Porte had no intention to carry out the reforms in the Armenian-populated provinces that it had announced the previous year.

The Armenian efforts to improve their living conditions, their just demands to end constant harassment and persecution by the Turkish authorities and nomadic Kurdish tribes, and the British policy of forcing the sultan's government to carry out reforms in Armenia—a policy directed in part as response to public opinion in Europe and Britain—eventually culminated in an organized and determined effort by the sultan's government to execute massacres of the Armenian subjects of the Ottoman Empire. The sultan's government had successfully created and put into practice an extermination machine targeting the Armenian population in the provinces where they made up a significant percentage of the population. The objective of the extermination campaign was to neutralize the European demands for reforms in the Armenian-populated provinces.

On August 26, 1896, a group of thirty-one Armenian revolutionary activists, primarily from the Armenian Revolutionary Federation (the Dashnak Party), armed with pistols and grenades, took over the Ottoman Bank. The Dashnak activists threatened to blow up the building if the sultan did not take active measures to carry out the announced reforms in the Armenian-populated provinces and prevent further massacres of the Armenian population. The foreign ambassadors in Constantinople received official notices from the party presenting the demands of the revolutionaries.[105] The Turkish authorities had been warned in advance of the plot to seize the bank, but the sultan had chosen not to prevent the attack so as to incite the anti-Armenian mood among the Muslim mob in the capital and score a point with European public opinion.[106] Interestingly enough, the massacre of the Armenian population of Constantinople had begun shortly before the publication of an imperial decree on negotiations with the European powers on the fate of Crete; the Greek population of Crete had demanded to be reunited with Greece. The public announcement of reforms to ameliorate the living conditions of a Christian minority in the Ottoman Empire had been aimed at the European powers. Yet the sultan's government carefully manipulated such announcements to incite the Muslim population and to derail the very reforms it had proclaimed.

The group that had seized the bank sent a deputy director to negotiate with the palace. The negotiators persuaded the Armenian group to leave the bank voluntarily and be transferred to an English ship taking them to safety in exile.[107] Finally, the rebels departed Constantinople in the yacht of the bank's director. Although the main cause of the disturbances had been resolved, the situation did not stabilize. While the bank was still held by the Armenian group, the sultan's government transferred armed groups of Kurds, Albanians, and Lazes to the capital to assist the Muslim mob in carrying out reprisals against the Armenians. The would-be perpetrators of the massacres had been issued sticks with sharpened brass caps, knives, and pistols.[108]

The eyewitness testimonies largely agree on the number of

victims of the Constantinople massacre. The Russian military attaché testified that more than 5,500 Armenians had been killed in two days,[109] while other sources referred to 8,750 victims,[110] or more than 10,000,[111] or even 13,600 deaths.[112]

The six powers made representations to the Porte in vain attempts to stop the massacres; notes of protest were sent on August 27 and 31 and September 15.[113] The European diplomatic missions helped thousands of Armenians flee the massacres. Some 12,000 Armenians moved to Bulgaria, almost 1,000 to Alexandria, another 1,200 to Athens, and several hundred to Marseilles.[114]

The Constantinople massacre was but another in the series of Armenian massacres in the Ottoman Empire organized by the government of Sultan Abdul Hamid. Just as in the previous year, the massacres of the Armenian population in Constantinople in 1896 launched a series of similarly planned and executed pogroms throughout the Ottoman Empire on a bigger scale and in a more brutal fashion. Belgian writer Emil Antoine estimated that 186,655 Armenians perished in Asia Minor in the autumn of 1896.[115] Malcolm MacColl estimated that the 1896 massacres took a toll of 200,000 lives.[116] Almost 12,000 homes and kiosks had been burned, 47,000 homes were robbed, some 40,000 Armenians had been forcibly converted to Islam, and another 400,000 Armenians lost their homes and jobs as a result of pogroms.[117] The total number of Armenian casualties in 1894–1896 reached 300,000.

The Porte remained unpunished while European diplomacy remained indifferent to the suffering and oppression of an entire nation. The mutually exclusive interests of and mistrust among the powers were the main factors preserving the corrupt Ottoman Empire. Abdul Hamid took advantage of these disagreements to get rid of the undesirable Christian elements that he believed threatened the stability and integrity of his empire.

On October 20, 1896, Salisbury sent a circular note to the heads of governments in Europe, urging common and joint initiative on the Armenian question to avoid a clash of competing interests in the Ottoman Empire. He proposed convening a European conference to find a comprehensive settlement to the Eastern question.[118] Salisbury was convinced that the Austro-Hungarian and French governments would endorse the idea of the conference, since they were concerned about the possibility of the Russian occupation of the Straits. Italy was expected to follow the British lead, but Salisbury was unsure about the German position, hoping, however, that Germany would agree with the proposal on account of its alliance with Austria-Hungary. The matter hinged on the support of Russia. Russian Foreign Minister Nikolai Shishkin told the British ambassador that Russia would agree to convene a conference in Constantinople on the condition that use of force against the sultan was ruled out.[119]

Addressing the annual Guild Hall banquet in London on October 29, Salisbury said that Britain had enough resources to penalize the sultan or cause him trouble, if the British people demanded so. At the same time, he said that a punitive expedition would not save the Christian and Muslim population of Turkey from the brutal regime; such an effort would require the consent of as many nations as possible. He said that the combined resources at the disposal of the Concert of Europe were far greater than any other nation's. Therefore, it was dangerous for Britain to act unilaterally, as the other powers could either refrain from joining or oppose the British action by force, leading to a general war. He said that the conflicts of interest and disagreements among the European powers were far too complicated to gamble on the issue of Armenia. He concluded that the amelioration of the state of affairs in the Muslim and Christian communities in Turkey could be achieved through the sultan only.

The conference of the ambassadors representing the European powers began on December 22. The mutual distrust and antagonism among the powers increased after the Russian ambassador insisted on discussing the question of Macedonia first. Currie was concerned that addressing Macedonia would increase Russia's leverage and insisted on discussing the general state of affairs in the Ottoman Empire. He was supported by Austro-Hungarian Ambassador Heinrich von Calice, who noted that any settlement in Macedonia would cause disturbances in the neighboring regions of Austria-Hungary, rekindle the Slavic peoples' national liberation movements, and inevitably lead to the collapse of the Ottoman Empire. When Currie mentioned the need for reforms in the European part of Turkey, Calice noted that reforms would only strengthen Russian influence in the region.[120] The British government also concluded that deployment of the British Fleet in the Dardanelles would inevitably lead to reciprocal Russian action in the Bosphorus, seriously undermining Austro-Hungarian interests.[121]

On January 6, 1897, Currie reported that he had not presented any initiatives out of fear that the envoys would then split into two opposing camps. He said he had preferred to hold bilateral and private discussions.[122] His consultations with the Russian and Austro-Hungarian envoys led to an approval of joint action to prevent further disturbances in Constantinople. The envoys agreed to deploy Austro-Hungarian and Russian warships in the Straits in the event that fresh disturbances and massacres broke out in the capital. The Austro-Hungarian and Russian gunboats were to be deployed in front of the sultan's palace and fire one shot each in its direction—the Austro-Hungarians first, the Russians second.[123]

On January 19, Currie reported that the ambassadors had approved plans to form two international commissions to work on reform programs for the European and Asiatic parts of the Ottoman Empire.[124] On February 2, they prepared a reform program that would provide for seven measures only: (1) establishment of a Supreme Council; (2) formation of a Control Commission to oversee the reforms process; (3) control by the powers over the Turkish treasury; (4) reform of the judicial system; (5) reform of the police system; (6) establishment of municipalities; and (7) guarantees for the freedom of the press.[125] The reforms program was soon forgotten when the Turkish-Greek War broke out in 1897 and the European powers sided with Turkey in its suppression of the rebels in Crete. The ambassadors concluded that "in this time of crisis, it would not be expedient to press for reforms."[126]

The conference of the European ambassadors in Constantinople showed that the powers were unwilling to risk deterioration in their relations with the Porte. By presenting demands diminishing the sovereign rights of the sultan and threatening to reopen the Armenian question, the powers had intended to obtain fresh concessions from the Porte. Meanwhile, Abdul Hamid had organized the massacre of the Armenians, which had become an object of wrangling between the powers and the Porte. When the Turks defeated Greece, the Muslim soul was buoyed, the sultan's authority rose, and it became impossible for the powers to press for implementation of reforms in the Armenian-populated provinces.

Thus, the last serious attempt of British diplomacy to secure reforms in the Ottoman Empire failed. This episode marked the end of the traditional British policies in the Near East. British diplomacy also had been unsuccessful in preventing a rapprochement between Russia and Turkey. Starting in 1897, Salisbury began to prepare ground for radical changes in British policy on the Eastern question. As he wrote to Currie in October 1897, the British policy would be to strengthen its presence in the Nile region and to avoid any and all obligations in Constantinople.[127]

Faced with the complex dynamics of international politics in the early twentieth century, the British government did not raise the Armenian question, fearing that another wave of disorders would result in dismemberment of the Ottoman Empire and instability in the Near East that would be detrimental to British interests. British decision makers still hoped that the Turkish authorities would try to improve conditions in the Armenian provinces by carrying out reforms.

Coming to power in 1908, the regime known as the Young Turks inherited the anti-Armenian policies of the sultan's government, although this movement emerged in reaction to the absolutist rule of Abdul Hamid. The backbone of the movement was formed by young military officers who were especially disturbed by the continuing decline of the Ottoman Empire. Abdul Hamid's reinstatement of constitutional and parliamentary rule ushered in a brief period of legalized political activity by a panoply of reformist Turkish parties as well as Armenian political organizations. The most ideologically committed party in the entire movement, the Committee of Union and Progress, espoused a form of Turkish nationalism that was xenophobic and exclusionary in its thinking. Its policies threatened to undo the tattered fabric of a multiethnic and multireligious society.[128] However, the Young Turks' government was not going to effect any reforms in the country's eastern provinces; it stirred up hostility between the nations and backed and encouraged lawlessness of local authorities, the settlement of the refugees migrated from Balkans, destructive raids by Kurdish detachments on Armenian populated areas, and the robbery and massacre of Armenians. In April 1909, Young Turks carried out the massacre of Armenians in Adana province, slaughtering more than 30,000 Armenians.

In 1912–14, when a new blow was dealt to the Turkish dictatorship as a result of the national liberation struggle of the Balkan peoples, the Armenian question again became the subject of negotiations between the powers and Turkey. A complicated struggle began on carrying out reforms in western Armenia, which continued until the eve of World War I. In 1913, the Russian government presented to the European governments a project of reforms, which was discussed at the meeting of ambassadors in Constantinople. The project, which was worked out by the Russian embassy on the basis of the May program of 1895 and the proposal made by Armenian Patriarchate in Constantinople, envisioned a province uniting six Armenian provinces (Erzurum, Van, Bitlis, Diarbekir, Kharput, Sivas). The governor of that province was to be a Christian subject or a European appointed for a five-year term by the powers' consent. He would exercise the province's executive power and would have a right to appoint and dismiss all the administrative officials. It was proposed to dismiss Kurdish detachments and return the lands captured from Armenians or their equivalent, as well as to prohibit settlement of the Muslims migrated from the Balkans in the Armenian provinces. The powers were to supervise the implementation of the reforms. Great Britain and France mainly agreed with the Russian project; however, Germany and the other powers of the Triple Alliance decisively resisted the main terms of the Russian project, offering to assume the Turkish program as a basis for discussions that preserved the former way of ruling vilayets and most likely was avoiding foreign supervision. In a diplomatic struggle, Russia succeeded in forcing Turkey to sign an agreement on January 26, 1914, by which western Armenia was divided into two parts (Erzurum, Trabzon, Sivas and Van, Bitlis, Kharput, Diarbekir) governed by two foreign general inspectors appointed by the consent of the powers.[129]

Though the agreement was insufficient and didn't give the Armenians the wide range of rights for self-governing envisioned by the Russian program, it created favorable conditions for the future of western Armenia. It was received enthusiastically in Britain, inasmuch as it provided for real reforms in internal administration and did not accord special privileges to either Russia or Germany;

in other words, British interests were not seriously affected. This program of Armenian reforms shared the fate of its predecessors, although it came closest to fruition. World War I put an end to the Russian-Turkish agreement. Britain was unable to secure Turkish neutrality and declared war on Turkey in November.

Thus, from 1830 to 1914, British diplomacy successfully carried out the British government's policy of preventing the Russian takeover of the Straits, Constantinople, and western Armenia but proved unable to force the Ottoman authorities to carry out reforms in Armenia or provide guarantees for the Armenian population in Turkey. As a result of genocide, deportation, and mass-scale massacres of the Armenian population of the Ottoman Empire perpetrated by the Young Turk regime during World War I, western Armenia finally lost its indigenous population.

British Public Opinion and the Armenian Massacres

The influence of public opinion, domestic interest groups, and the political process on the formation of the country's foreign policy and international relations in Britain rose steadily throughout the nineteenth century, parallel to the enfranchisement of the middle class and the liberalization of domestic politics. British public opinion was affected by the press reports of atrocities and disorders in the Ottoman Empire during the Eastern crisis of 1895–1897, and the British government had to take domestic politics into account. Both Conservatives and Liberals engaged in criticism of the sultan and his government. Many prominent members of the British elite also sympathized with the Armenian population in the Ottoman Empire and demanded more forceful actions from their government.

The existence of Armenian societies and *émigré* groups in Britain was a major factor in the development of pro-Armenian opinion in the country. The progressive Armenian groups advocated liberation and the establishment of self-government in western Armenia, preferably under the auspices of Britain. Two Armenian periodicals were published in London, including *Hayastan* (in English and French) and *Hunchak* (in Armenian), the organ of the Social-Democratic Hunchak Party. Many Armenian groups and committees were based in London, including the Armenian Patriotic Union founded in 1888 by Karapet Hagopian. Another prominent group, the Armenian United Association of London, was founded in 1898 and published an English-language magazine, *Ararat: A Searchlight on Armenia*.[130]

Prominent British public figures, politicians, and clergymen were members of Anglo-Armenian societies in the 1890s. Many of these groups lobbied the government to take action on the Armenian question and engaged in charity work to assist the Armenian population in Turkey. One of the groups, the Anglo-Armenian Association, was founded by James Bryce in 1893 and was headed by MP Francis Stevenson and MP Edward Atkin, who later served as chancellor of the exchequer.

Another pro-Armenian group, the Grosvenor House Association, was established with Salisbury's blessing and was headed by the Duke of Westminster (Earl of Grosvenor). One of the more prominent members of this group was Rev. Malcolm MacColl, the canon of Ripon, a notable clergyman and publicist who authored several books on the Armenian question.

The two pro-Armenian groups were affiliated with, respectively, the Liberal and Conservative parties and engaged in partisan politics. Nevertheless, their grassroots activities did much to educate the British public on the Armenian question and bring to light evidence of atrocities and massacres organized in the Armenian-populated regions of Turkey.

Several groups and charities raised funds to alleviate the suffering of the Armenian population in Turkey; the funds were sent to the British and American missionary associations operating in Turkey.

The Armenian Mission of Religious Society of Friends, founded in Constantinople in 1881, was the first British group that carried out charity, medical, and educational activities in the Armenian-populated regions. The mission was established as a medical charity. In 1888, the mission established a Sunday school, a vocational school, and a day school. The number of students in the day school reached one hundred fifty, while four hundred students attended the Sunday school; new buildings had been built for the schools.[131]

The British missionaries were among the few private British

citizens stationed in Turkey and provided assistance and educational opportunities to the Armenian-populated provinces. Many Armenians converted to Protestantism and Catholicism to avoid persecution, although the local governments continued to harass the Protestant Armenians as much as they did the members of the Armenian Apostolic Church.

Another group, called Friends of Armenia, was formed in London in 1897. Lady Cavendish was the president, and Ms. Cantlow was the executive secretary. The society published a monthly, *Friends of Armenia*, with the self-declared objective of the revival of Armenia. In 1899 alone, Friends of Armenia raised 509 pounds from its members in Manchester, Edinburgh, Paisley, and Liverpool. Overall, the society raised nearly 60,000 pounds in ten years to assist the victims of the Armenian massacres.[132]

In March 1897, Friends of Armenia sent Cambridge University professor of paleontology Rendel Harris and his wife, Helen Harris, on a fact-finding trip to Asia Minor. Upon their return to Britain, the Harrises published their correspondence with friends in Britain and missionaries in Asia Minor.[133]

The Women's Relief Fund was another British group assisting the Armenian victims of massacres. The group brought together prominent British women and was headed by Madeleine Cole. The Women's Relief Fund sent money to Van, Diarbekir, Zeitoun, and Urmia; it raised and disbursed more than 16,000 pounds.[134]

The International Association of the Friends of Armenia was founded in 1896 and incorporated the Armenian Information Bureau. Its objectives were to disseminate information and literature on Armenia and educate the British public on the subject, as well as to facilitate interaction among various groups engaged in Armenian relief efforts. The bishop of Rochester was the president of the association, and Lady Henry Somerset was the honorary secretary.[135]

British Media Testimony

Britain's proactive policy on the Armenian question and the views of the British public and political and civic organizations on the massacres of the Armenian population in the Ottoman Empire in 1894–1896 were widely reflected in the contemporary British press and other media accounts. This volume, which contains more than fifty articles published in major British periodicals in the 1890s, including *The Contemporary Review*, *The Nineteenth Century*, *The Fortnightly Review*, *Blackwood's Magazine*, and *The Spectator*, presents a snapshot of British public opinion during the height of the Armenian crisis of the 1890s, as well as rather detailed, and therefore extremely important, factual evidence of anti-Armenian policies carried out by the sultan's government in the Ottoman Empire and the response of the great powers—including Britain—to the massacres.

This volume deliberately omits day-to-day reports from British newspapers covering those events, which by themselves represent a rich factual source. The idea is to include analytical reviews and opinions by leading British public figures; travelers; scientists; political, religious, and civic activists; journalists; and members of Parliament that were published in periodicals of differing political and social affiliations.

The articles cover a wide spectrum of issues that can be broadly divided into several categories:

1. History, culture, and traditions of the Armenian people and the geography, demographics, and nature of western Armenia and other parts of the Ottoman Empire (Ramsay, Dillon, Lynch, Harris).

2. History and contemporary situation of the Ottoman Empire; foreign and internal policy of the Sultan Abdul Hamid and the Ottoman government; issues concerning interaction between Christianity and Islam (Davey, Ghulam-us-Saqlain, Ahmad, Harris, MacColl, Geffcken, Ramsay, Du Cane).

3. Difficult conditions of life among the Armenians in western Armenia; details of massacres of the Armenian population in several cities and provinces of the Ottoman Empire (Stevenson, Dillon, Lynch, MacColl, Gladstone, Geffcken, Rogers, the Earl of Meath, Anthony-Salmoné, Malcolm, Burns, Nazarbek, Ramsay, Lanin, Rogers, Anthony-Salmoné, the Earl of Meath).

4. The policies on the Armenian question carried out by the Liberal and Conservative Cabinets of Great Britain; diplomatic efforts to promote and enforce reforms in western Armenia (Stevenson, Blunt, Dillon, Lynch, MacColl, Russell, Rogers, Ahmad, Gladstone, Burns, Blunt).

5. The policies of Russia, the United States, France, Germany, and other major powers on the Armenian question (Lynch, Dillon, Blunt, Russell, Lanin, Geffcken).

Of particular interest are the materials published in the London-based weekly periodical *The Spectator*. Between 1890 and 1897, it published almost thirty editorials and news reports that allow us to trace the development of the anti-Armenian activities of the Ottoman government and to perceive the main directions of successive British governments on the Armenian question.

Reprinted more than a century after their original publication, the articles are characteristic of the public attitudes in late-nineteenth-century Britain. The positions and perceptions of that period are absolutely different from the principles and values applied to international affairs nowadays. So is British foreign policy, and, for that matter, so is Britain. At the time, Great Britain was the leading world power, whose policies strongly and resolutely influenced the course of international affairs and could play a critical role in the fate of smaller nations, in this instance the population of western Armenia. So the British public, including most authors of the reprinted articles, were highly critical of the British government's policies toward the Ottoman Empire, calling for a more active and decisive involvement, including in the form of military intervention, to defend the Christian Armenian population. The policies of the other European powers were also a subject of criticism and scrutiny because of their perceived complacency.

The sympathetic attitude in Great Britain toward the Armenians was a result of religious feelings that ran deep among a large segment of British society, namely a perceived need to defend Christianity against Muslim encroachment and the widespread negative image of Islam. An important factor influencing public opinion was the perception of Sultan Abdul Hamid II as the ultimate anti-Christian, pan-Islamic ruler. These factors have to be considered when reading the articles, as they explain the negative and even insulting remarks in some of them about Muslims or Turks. Notwithstanding the language that is now justifiably deemed insensitive and offensive, these articles present a vivid picture of the charitable efforts and the humanity of the British public.

At the same time, this edition includes several articles that do not reflect the general positions and trends prevalent in British society. For example, Walter Harris, in "An Unbiased View of the Armenian Question," attempted to show a dispassionate picture of the tragic events of 1894–1896, effectively whitewashing the Ottoman government's anti-Armenian policies. The authors of "The Mussalmans of India and the Armenian Question" and "A Moslem View of Abdul Hamid and the Powers," respectively, Ghulam-us-Saqlain and Rafiüddin Ahmad, presented a criticism of what they viewed as Christian-centric policies of Great Britain in the Near East on the grounds that it totally ignored the interests and opinions of the multimillion Muslim population of the British Empire.

These articles present different approaches and positions on the Armenian question and should help readers understand and study the historical realities of the late nineteenth century in a comprehensive, objective, and impartial manner.

The Spectator,[1] Vol. 65 (August 9, 1890): 172–73

A Vanishing Treaty

Mr. Bryce's[2] question to Sir J. Fergusson[3] on the recent disturbances among the Armenian population in Asia Minor and elsewhere, and his speech on Thursday night, show more appreciation of the dangers and difficulties which lie behind these half-smothered tales of violence than is yet entertained by the Government, if we may judge from the language used by the Under-Secretary of State for Foreign Affairs.

Perhaps it was the direct suggestion, made in the last part of his question, that the Sultan's Government should be informed "that we regard the Anglo-Turkish Convention of 1878 as having lapsed, owing to the neglect of Turkey in introducing the reforms undertaken in that instrument," that inspired Sir J. Fergusson with those conventionalities of official ignorance in which he abounded. But Mr. Gladstone amended his colleague's error by proposing that notice should be given to the Porte that such might be consequences of continued neglect of treaty obligations, and pressed for some acknowledgment of the gravity of the situation. Sir J. Fergusson, however, could add nothing to his rather hopeless admission that "her Majesty's Government make representations only when they think that they will be attended with good effect," from which we must draw the disagreeable inference that representations made on behalf of a population for whose well-being England and Turkey entered into reciprocal obligations of a very binding character are less than welcome to one of the contracting parties. Sir J. Fergusson is "unable to say whether this would be a favourable opportunity for pressing on the Porte the views of her Majesty's Government with respect to remedial measures of a conciliatory character." As the Foreign Office have the best means of knowing the *mollia tempora fandi* of the Porte, we may conclude, in other words, that the

Sultan's Government has turned sulky, and means to let the Armenian difficulty settle itself. But to "smoke the pipe of tranquillity on the carpet of patience" is now no remedy for the race troubles of the Ottoman Empire, where so many outside interests are involved; and Sir J. Fergusson's verbal admission must be read in connection with another which he makes by implication. Mr. Bryce justified his question and suggestion by urging the risk that an insurrection, or an occupation by some other Power, might be provoked by further attempts at repression and denials of justice: and against this Sir J. Fergusson had nothing to say. Unfortunately, both these results are just what may be expected to happen,—a partial insurrection first, with a Russian occupation to follow. This will please neither the admirers of the Turks nor the sympathisers with the Armenians, for an insurrection will be the signal for bloody reprisals by the Kurds, while the ultimate loss of the province to Turkey is certain. But the attitude of Sir J. Fergusson—"Very sorry, but we really can do nothing for you"—is exactly calculated to drive to some rash outbreak a population exasperated by oppression and violence condoned.

That the tales of outrage are true which reach us from the distant vilayets of Moosh, Bitlis, and Alashgird, there is every reason to believe. These provinces are inhabited by the poorest and least-educated Armenians, incapable of conducting an "agitation" themselves, and too dull, perhaps too honest, to be the ready tools of others. But numbers migrate yearly to Constantinople, where they are employed as "Hammals," or porters; there are said to be thirty thousand so employed in the capital. After two or three years they return, with their savings, and their places are taken by fresh arrivals, who bring news, accurate if late, of the state of things they left at home. Moosh has long been a "centre and culminating point of Turkish misrule and oppression," to quote the words of a recent report. The town is about forty miles from Lake Van, with about four thousand Armenian, and twelve thousand Kurd and Turkish inhabitants. In the plain of Moosh, the Turks have arranged an ingenious *modus vivendi* between Kurds and Armenians. In the winter, the Kurds are invited to leave the mountains, and are billeted on the Armenian villagers at free quarters. But love of violence and revenge is too strong in the Kurd to make such an arrangement satisfactory, even to him. Djazzo (query Djezzar—the Butcher?), brother to Moussa Bey, who is still retained in honourable confinement at Constantinople, and other chiefs of his clan, are burning and murdering in the vilayet of Moosh; and in the plain of Alashgird, which is nearer Russian Armenia and Ararat, the inhabitants are asking leave to migrate *en masse* to Russian territory. Such, at least, is the story which comes from Erivan. If England cannot protect them, the Armenians will naturally seek help from Russia; and Russia is prepared to give her aid in the most effective manner. The difficulty in organising a race like the Armenians is great. They are scattered and divided alike by residence and education. The region known by the geographical name of Armenia is mainly inhabited by Turks, Kurds, and Persians. Its population is about two millions, of whom six hundred thousand may be Armenians. These are chiefly of the lowest and poorest class, living in small villages scattered around Ararat and Lake Van. The intelligent and cultivated Armenians live, not in Armenia, but in Constantinople, Smyrna, Rodosto, Adrianople, and other great towns of Turkey. According to the best estimates, the total Armenian population in the Ottoman Empire is about two millions and a half. Another half-million are in Russian Armenia. But small colonies exist in most of the great towns of Asia, giving a false impression of their numbers. To organise a community so scattered, and with such remote traditions of separate national life, is no light task. Even the language has been in many parts forgotten, and Turkish has been adopted. It is rare to find an Armenian anywhere who uses his own language in counting beyond fifty. But the nucleus of a national feeling remains in the common love for the national Church; and the Russian friends of Armenia use this with admirable skill. Just as they secured a separate Church for Bulgaria, thereby detaching the ecclesiastical rule of the then Turkish province from the Greek Patriarch, and more recently gained for their *protégés* the Syrians of Antioch and Jerusalem, the majority in the synods which elect to those Patriarchates, so in the case of the Armenian Church the greatest efforts have been made to secure a friend of Russia in the Patriarch of Constantinople. Spiritually, the Catholicus of Etchmiazin is head of the Armenian Church; but the real authority lies with the Constantinople Patriarch. Narses, next but one before the present holder of the office, was a zealous supporter of Russia. The present Patriarch, however, has always maintained that English aid would in the end promote the best interests of Armenia. The recent riot at the Church of Koom Kapo in Constantinople, was no doubt concerted with a view to putting pressure on the Patriarch, or to destroying the confidence of his countrymen in his fidelity to their case.

Probably, in spite of difficulties, Russia will succeed, unless the English Government can guarantee reasonable freedom to the Armenians; and it is difficult not to sympathise with Russian efforts. What is here called "Russian intrigue" differs from the intrigue of other Governments chiefly because it is clever and successful. It is scarcely forty years since the first book in the Bulgarian language was printed. Yet Russia created a national sentiment and a flourishing State out of materials less promising than those she finds in Armenia, and at a distance from her frontier. If England is unable to secure the Armenians in the enjoyment of the ordinary conditions of liberty and safety, she must be prepared to see the absorption of the country by Russia, when such a move suits the purposes of the Czar's Government.

The Fortnightly Review,[1] Vol. 54 (August 1890): 258–73

Armenia and the Armenian People

E. B. Lanin

It would be difficult to point out a more delightful, soul-inspiring, mysteriously fascinating country on the surface of the globe than Armenia, the land of the Terrestrial Paradise, the resting place of Noah's Ark, the native home of that fear-dispelling wine which has drowned more human lives and wrecked more human hopes than the billows of the tempest-tossed ocean. The most eloquent description in words, the most ideal representation on canvas, would be powerless to produce the ineffable impressions which the traveller experiences when he gazes awestruck on its snow-capped mountains, on whose spotless heights once dwelt the dread deities of forgotten peoples, and which now seem to overhang the world; when he watches its rapid rivers madly tearing along through narrow fissures in the hard unyielding stone; when he views its gigantic rocks, hurled mayhap by the angry Titans in their wars with the gods, whose sides time has covered with a mantle of vegetation; when he contemplates its yellow corn-fields, and threads his way through its sweet-smelling groves and masses of mingling shade. Armenia is a country of strong contrasts, of opposite extremes, of heat and cold, light and shade, drought and moisture, and contains more dark mysteries awaiting the solution of the future naturalist, geographer, philologist, and historian than Central Africa, Central America, and Hindostan taken together. The ethnologist is still in doubt to what branch of the great Indo-European family the Armenian people belongs; the philologist has not yet classified their language; the antiquarian knows next to nothing of their early history. There are rivers in Armenia whose course, like that of the Bitlis, has still to be explored; cities occupying the sites of dried-up lakes; petrifying lakes, the sluggish surge of whose deep-blue waters is the only sound now heard on the spot where populous cities flourished when the human race was young; towns which for part of the year are river-girt islands; woods whose soul-dissolving odour is unknown outside the neighbourhood of old Eden; caves scooped out of massive rocks, which lead through endless windings to mysterious halls and unexplored recesses where "dead men hang their mute thoughts" on the walls around—men whose names were household words before Babylon became Semitic, and when the simple law of Accad was still administered within its walls; adamantine rocks covered with quaint inscriptions and strange devices which the prying eye of an irreverent world has not yet been able to read—like awful spells destined hereafter to save the human race from a second deluge or a universal conflagration; slabs of stone on which are carved, in arrow-headed characters, the childish boasts, the patriotic hopes, and the pious sentiments of Darius the King; cities paved over with the wreck of days departed; stupendous columns and "wild images of more than man," whose history and purpose are no longer remembered, and grey mouldering walls

> "On which dull Time
> Feeds like a slow fire upon a hoary brand."

The centre of this interesting country is Van, with its lake of bitter salt water and solitary species of fish, 4,700 feet above the sea-level, the scenery round which is said to have sent the great Semiramis into ecstasies, which she forthwith embodied in architectural fancies which our grandchildren may yet succeed in interpreting. And in sober truth nothing could be more impressive. To the traveller approaching from the north, and suddenly catching a glimpse of the western shore, it seems a corner snatched from Paradise. To the east the lake is protected by snow-capped mountains, at whose feet lies nestling the island of Akhtamar, like the refreshing shadow of a passing cloud; and on the north, by the ragged Subhan Dagh, on whose crest Noah and his companions are said to have rested after their six weeks' sojourn in the stuffy ark. The citadel of Van, on the dizzy summit of an immense rock rising bolt upright in the centre of a natural amphitheatre, deserves to rank as one of the wonders of the world. The roads leading to Aderbeidjan, Kurdistan, and Western Armenia pass through the venerable town of Van, formerly called Semiramas-city, the vineyards and orchards of which would have gladdened the heart of Hafiz himself. Armenia possesses as many famous cities as Greece or Italy; but they are now mostly dead cities, whose names are unfamiliar to the European. There is Bayazed, the streets of which are paved with fragments of sculpture shaped and fashioned when Moses was a boy and Pharaoh heir-apparent to the throne of Egypt; Ani, the city of colossal ruins, in which the treasures of the kings of kings were preserved; Armavir, to the north of the Araxes, formerly the residence of Armenian monarchs, where the holy plane-trees grew, the rustle of whose palmate leaves was the language chosen by the gods of old to make known their behests to men of goodwill; Vagharshabad, said to have been built by King Erovand I., six hundred years before our era, and now shrunk up to the dimensions of the large but solitary monastery of Etchmiadzin, in which the Catholicos, or Patriarch of all Armenia, resides; Erzeroum, in the valley once occupied by a lake; Kemak, whose walls exhibit the only specimen of a strange style of architecture never seen elsewhere; Egin, in a deep valley of the Euphrates, screened by mountains that rise four thousand feet above the level of the sea, whose slopes are covered with smiling gardens gracefully laid out on terraces one above the other, the houses being buried, as it were, in hursts and groves that subdue into soft twilight the glare of the mid-day sun. Egin may not be precisely the Paradise of the Bible; but it is the Eden of modern Armenians, who toil and moil from youth to middle age, happy if they can lay by a sufficiency to enable them to retire thither, to enjoy the foretaste of the dreamy pleasures and luxurious repose that they hope for in a better world. Then there is the quaint, melancholy city of Takht-i-Soliman, whose venerable ruins are reflected in the clear, cold, petrifactive waters of the tiny lake in their centre, like blades of sapless grass left standing by the scythe of Time. A feeling of intense depression and eeriness steals over one at night, when the ill-boding cry of the spectral screech-owl breaks in upon the deathlike stillness that reigns in the reputed birth-place of Zoroaster, the city in which was jealously guarded for ages the holy fire descended from heaven, at which were periodically lighted all the fires and flames that blazed and burned throughout the world of Magi.

Whithersoever we turn our steps, to the north, south, east, or west, the ground we tread is holy. It is history—stratified. Here it was that the confluent streams of old-world humanity met and mingled, seethed and foamed, leaving a fertilising deposit on the shores of the surrounding countries that proved of inestimable service to the growth of civilisation.

Like most of the principalities and kingdoms that compose what may be termed New Europe, Armenians have a glorious history, and, unlike them, were an ancient people before the Slav or the Englishman, the German or the Scandinavian, was dreamt of. They raised the standard of rebellion against Darius Hystaspes, and he himself informs us with scrupulous minuteness in his longest arrow-headed inscription what endless trouble it cost him to drive them back to their allegiance, first sending an Armenian general to stamp out the insurrection, and after he had won three battles to little purpose, giving the command to a Persian, who had to fight two more before he succeeded in making a lasting impression. Among the bravest of the troops of the ill-starred Xerxes in Greece were Armenian warriors, and in the first century B.C., we find an Armenian king of kings, Tigranes, ruling with a rod of iron over Syria, Phoenicia, Cilicia, Galatia, &c., transplanting whole colonies of Greeks from Cappadocia to Mesopotamia, and Arabs from their native places to the banks of the Euphrates, executing insubordinate vassal kings and warring with the Romans and the Parthians. Numberless have been the rotations of Fortune's wheel since then, bringing alternately change for the better and change for the worse, till to-day we see Armenia, like Poland, parcelled out between three neighbouring powers, Russia, Turkey, and Persia, and her children sitting down by the waters of Modern Babylon and weeping when they remember the faded glories of Van and Ani.

At no period of their history have they lost the wild spirit of independence which characterized them in antiquity. In the fourth century of our era, for instance, they seemed politically to have sunk to the very bottom of a sea of misfortunes and miseries. They were then Persian subjects, and were as much the property of the king of kings as the slave is a chattel of his master. Yet when it was a question of compelling them to change their lately adopted Christianity for the worship of Ormuzd, the Gospel of Christ for the Zend Avesta, they rose up one and all, men, women, and children, and shook the throne of Yezdigerd to its foundations. In like manner a few years ago, when the Russian Government ordered them to consent to change the constitution of that ancient Church of theirs, they steadfastly refused, and men who under different circumstances would almost barter their human dignity for "a ribbon to stick in their coats," resisted the imperial commands like heroes, preferring the apparently inevitable alternative of the mines of Siberia. These and scores of equally well-attested instances of heroic patriotism form a sufficient answer to those who imagine that because there are Armenian merchants in Bombay and in Paris, Hong Kong and Constantinople, whose politics seem absorbed in the *auri sacra fames*, it must be even so with the bulk of the Armenian people.

It is the future of this country, the destinies of these its oldest inhabitants, that are meant by the term Armenian question; and with this difficult problem Europe will be called upon to deal at the conclusion of the coming war, whichever side is victor. As certain eminent statesmen of this country, who may possibly find themselves at that conjuncture at the head of our Government, seem to harbour the idea that Russia alone is fitted by her geographical position, her benevolent proclivities, and her civilising mission to take in hand the settlement of the Armenian difficulty, it may be well to point out plainly some of the chief issues involved. The claims of the present writer to a hearing upon this question are nothing very special or exclusive; his close and prolonged intercourse with Russian and Turkish Armenians; the assiduity with which for many years past he has studied their language and literature, the history of their past and the dreams of their future; and lastly, several interesting conversations upon the various aspects of this question which he has lately had with the most trusted leaders of the Armenian people in the East, furnish him, it may be hoped, with the necessary qualifications for touching upon a problem that bristles with difficulties.

The prevailing idea among many of those politicians and journalists who are contributing by questions in Parliament and letters and articles in the press to keep the Armenian question alive is that, as the dissolution of Turkey is very close at hand, it is greatly to be desired that Armenia should anticipate the beneficial effects of this event on her prospects by entering at once, or as soon as possible, into the enjoyment of those solid benefits which a strong Christian Government, a vast undeveloped empire, and human laws confer; for, whatever the shortcomings of Russian rule may be, they are perfections in comparison with the evils of Turkish misgovernment. Now fifteen years ago much might have been urged in favour of this proposition to hand over Armenia to Russia. Very little can be said for it now; indeed, if we are justified in reading the near future by the strong light of the recent past, there can be little doubt that this way of dealing with the problem would render the last state of the Armenian people considerably worse than the first.

Armenians are perfectly justified in making use of everything that will burn as fuel to generate the steam necessary for the agitation which is to obtain for them national independence. "If the child does not cry," says the Armenian proverb, "the mother gives it no breast." Hence the atrocities of Moussa Bey, the persecution of the Nestorians, Turkish partiality to Armenian Catholics, and a hundred and one other grievances common to most peoples whether independent or not, are very properly turned to account in this really excellent cause. At the same time candid Armenians will admit that of the two evils, Russian Government or Turkish misrule, the latter is the less intolerable. Turkish policy is *laissez faire* applied impartially to all subjects with that sublime disregard of consequences which marks the confirmed fatalist. In substance the Sultan says to his Armenian subjects: "We tolerate you and your ways, however repugnant to our maxims of religion and morality. In our eyes you are strange animals, cross-grained and pig-headed, who do things that ought never to be done. But if we connive at your worship, which is hateful to us and impious in the sight of God, we cannot well display any squeamishness if when you go trading about the country, putting out your money to usury, fleecing your fellow subjects, and making other people's losses your gains, certain sections of your orthodox fellow-subjects adopt a more primitive but franker way of enriching themselves at your expense." This liberty or licence once given to Giaours, it could not well be expected that such good Mahometans as the Kurds would be contented with less; and if tastes and education of the latter lead them to prefer one form of plunder to what Turks consider another—pillage and occasional massacres to trade and occasional extortion—this is a detail that seems mainly to concern the parties themselves. But is the state of things in this respect radically different in Russia? Is life and property a whit more secure in that portion of Armenia which enjoys the benefits in Russian rule than in the Turkish district of Van? Almost every organ of the Russian press that appeared during the past twelve months contains a categorical reply in the negative. They are continually full of reports of unpunished outrages and crimes, which, to put it mildly, are quite as blood-curdling as those which so unutterably horrify the English Liberal press when committed in the dominions of the Turk. Here is a sample of what one reads in the Russian newspapers—it is taken from the semi-official *Novoye Vremya*:—

> "The band of highwaymen who lately robbed the mail between Derbend and Kooba, and has permanently established itself in Daghestan, continues its daring deeds with impunity. Thus, a few days ago, they had a skirmish in the Samoorski district, *with the inhabitants* of the village Mirki, *in which four of the inhabitants were killed and several wounded.* After this the gang of brigands marched on towards the district of Kooba."[2]

The notorious highwayman, Kareem, who sent scores of peaceful Armenians to their last account, wounding, robbing, and dishonouring others, pursued his career of blood and crime with perfect impunity. The Russian soldiers and police, though they hunted him for years, might as well have tried to catch their own shadows. Last August he calmly gave himself up to the Persian authorities, who treated him as a hero; and the diplomatic efforts of Russia to obtain his extradition or his trial were as bootless as the endeavours of the Armenians to bring about the punishment of Moussa Bey.

In the newspapers of the 9th October, 1889, we read:—

> "Near Kooba a skirmish took place between a band of highwaymen and the Russian troops sent in pursuit, in which one private and a guide were killed and two dangerously wounded. The gang of highwaymen escaped with impunity. This conclusion," the *Novoye Vremya* remarks, in a leading article on the question, "has become quite as common as in letters the concluding phrase, 'I remain, dear sir, your obedient servant.' "[3]

But besides abounding in the very worst evils that characterise Turkish misrule in Armenia, Russia has a large number of other grave drawbacks peculiar to herself. Thus you are hopelessly trammelled in all that you undertake, and your movements are impeded by a vast network of rules, regulations, laws, and ukases that a Mezzofanti could not remember nor an angel obey, unless gifted with the power of doing two or more incompatible things at the same moment and in the same place. You can scarcely sneeze in the privacy of your own home without formally breaking, if not some special law against sneezing at improper times, then at least the general one that everything not expressly permitted is *ipso facto* prohibited. Hence the saying among all Armenians who inhabit Russia: "Bribery illumines dark ways." Now this state of things, it need hardly be said, is not precisely what the Armenian has set his heart upon; indeed, so strong is his antipathy to be straitened and stretched and disjointed in order to be fitted for the Procrustean bed of Russian "citizenship" that he almost prefers the slight risk of being suddenly waked up some night to have his throat cut by the Kurd. This intricate labyrinth of ceremonies and formalities through which only a golden Ariadne's thread enables you to find your way is extremely galling to the commercial mind. The extent to which trade and commerce are paralysed by this pernicious pedantry, the enormous power for evil wielded by the pettiest Russian tschinovniks, are not fully realised by Europeans who have only seen Russia as tourists. Here is a scene related by an eye-witness and published by most of the Russian newspapers, which I translate word for word from one of them:—

> "A stoker, attired in a pair of new breeches was stopped by the Russian custom-house authorities in Batoum. As he had no luggage of any kind, however, he was allowed to pass on. But he had scarcely gone a few steps when two soldiers, sent after him, seized him and brought him back to the *tschinovnik*. 'What's that?' asks the official, pointing to the trousers. 'Breeches, your honour.' 'I know they are breeches, but where did you get them?' 'Bought them, your honour.' 'Pay duty on them, then.' 'But they are for myself, your honour. I have no others. The old pair were worn to rags, and I sold them for twopence and bought these.' 'That is all the same, you have got to pay.' 'But, your honour, I have no money. It's all spent.' 'It doesn't matter a rap. Pay, or I'll have the breeches taken from you.' And they were taken from him literally and truly; stripped off in the public street. Two smart lads held the stoker's arms, a third deftly removed his nether garments, and the servant of God was sent adrift in his linen."[4]

This took place four years ago, not in Turkey nor in Dahomey, but in Russia. Perhaps it was an exceptional case, the work of some eccentric official whom swift punishment brought to his senses? It was the deliberate act of all the officials of the custom-house, and perfectly in keeping with their usual practice and traditions. Why, one may ask, does not the Armenian Society in this country dwell on these things? It requires but little reflection, however, to see that such a course of action would be simply suicidal. They are compelled to act in accordance with their own shrewd saying: "My heart is not a table-cloth that it should be spread out before every man." Such cases might be multiplied *ad infinitum*; I must content myself, however, with giving one other equally characteristic and more disgraceful that occurred in the same year, and in the same place, the victim being the wife of a well-known landowner, Madam Dzaparidze. The *New Review* of August, 1885, relates, with the dry conciseness of an annalist, that this lady had a dress of Chinese silk on her when she entered the Batoum Custom-House, on her way to the railway station. She had no luggage whatever. The custom-house officials, however, required her to pay duty for the dress she wore. She refused. Her husband who accompanied her was indignant, and qualified the demand as unjustifiable extortion. In answer to these protests the official said simply: "All right, I confiscate the dress." And Madam Dzaparidze, who at once became hysterical, *was forthwith undressed and was obliged to traverse the city from one end to the other*— in returning to her hotel—*in her linen*. The passers-by were indignant.

"Now treatment of this kind," said an Armenian friend of mine the other day, "and the entire system of trammels and restrictions it implies, paralyses enterprise, kills trade, and renders the name of Russians hateful to all men of peaceful pursuits, Armenians and others." Nor is this all. The profound conviction prevails among Armenians of Turkish as well as of the Russian provinces, that the annexation of Turkish Armenia by Russia would be followed in a comparatively short space of time by the utter blotting out of those distinctive marks of national individuality which the people have jealously preserved from the action of time, the violence of fire and sword, and the subtle poison of corruption. This impression, which cannot with truth be termed unfounded, contributes in no small measure to foster that political hatred of Russia which Poles, Finns, Jews, Germans, and Georgians possess in common with Armenians. With the last-named people, however, it is not a race hatred. No one could be more obstinately blind to the beams in his neighbour's eye than the smiling, self-satisfied Armenian, who, like the constable who arrested a gentleman engaged in dancing a mazurka at a public ball, takes people pretty much as he finds them. "If the bread is good and wholesome," says an Armenian proverb, "I don't care a rap whether it is a Jew or Turk who has baked it." The feeling that animates the masses and such leaders in the country as are in touch with them, is the same spirit of political hate that endowed their hero Vartan and his men with almost superhuman strength to smite the armies of Persia fifteen hundred years ago. They feel that in the Russian Empire, vast as it is, there is no place for a united Armenian people, who are bound to disappear as the Poles are disappearing in German Posen, and the Georgian and Ossetinians in the Caucasus.

We may be told of Caucasians, as we have lately been told of all Asiatics, by a magnanimous Conservative tourist who, after a dash through a country, of the languages of which he pretends to no knowledge, assures us that Russia's rule is "loyally accepted by, and acceptable to, the bulk of her Asiatic subjects." This, no doubt, is magnanimous in a Conservative. But magnanimity properly comes after justice, and an accurate knowledge of facts would seem essential to them both. The generosity of a Chandos who, with princely munificence, gives away the thousands that belong to his creditors, is a spectacle calculated to excite contemptuous pity rather than respectful admiration. The present writer is neither Russophobe nor Russophile in politics; and in every-day life he loves the Russian people with all the cordiality compatible with intimate knowledge. It is his acquaintance with the facts that prevents him from accepting conclusions founded upon personal appreciation eked out with considerable insight and delivered with an air of conviction. Russia has two ways of dealing with her Asiatic subjects. When the population is considerable, united, homogeneous, she subordinates her appetite to her assimilating powers, leaves them pretty much to themselves, and even guarantees them certain privileges. They are then in the position of the captive reserved for slaughter in ancient Mexico, who used to be well fed, sumptuously dressed, married to four young girls, and generally made much of till the feast of Tezcatlipoca came around, when his heart was torn out by the priests, his head stuck on a spike, and his body eaten as sacred food. This is the method applied to the Baltic provinces, Little Russia, Poland, and Finland. The feast of Tezcatlipoca has already arrived for the first three people; it will soon come round to the fourth.

When the populations are weak, disunited, scattered, they are at once assimilated; and should this prove impossible, life is made so uncomfortable for them that they flee from before the Russian advance as North American Indians vanish before the white man. Ask the brave Circassian whether Russian rule is acceptable to him and his race, and he will tell you what few Englishmen seem to be aware of, that his people have disappeared from before the Russians as a flock of sheep from before a pack of hungry wolves. Thousands of Circassians emigrated from Batoum when that district was ceded to Russia; tens of thousands have been steadily emigrating ever since, and now a memorial column might be appropriately erected in the centre of the picturesque country once inhabited by the vanished Circassian race. Nor is this all. Half the Mahometan population of the Government of Kars have joined the exodus. One shipowner alone in Novorossisk—and this statement is borne out by the official reports of several foreign consuls to their Governments—shipped sixty-two thousand Mahometan inhabitants of the Kuban district and Daghestan from Novorossisk to Turkey in the course of last year alone! These things require no commentary; they afford no scope for the display of magnamity.[5]

But it may be urged with apparent reason that the vast difference in aptitudes and character between Circassians and Armenians would of itself guarantee a correspondingly wide difference in the treatment of the latter people, who possess a common language enshrined in a national literature to unite and consolidate them, a glorious history to inspirit, and a Church to console and nerve them. To this there is a categorical answer, the cogency of which can only be lessened by the disproval of the facts on which it is based, namely, that all these elements of union, strength, and national individuality are being systematically rooted out by the Russian Government. The Church of Armenia, which withstood the persecutions of Sassanian kings, the blandishments of Byzantine emperors, the fiery onslaught of fanatic Mussulmans, and the more dangerous intrigues of its own schismatic members, is now gradually succumbing to a judicious combination of all forms of persecution and cajolery employed by Russia. From the days of St. Gregory, the scion of a royal house and first Patriarch of Armenia, the Church has been governed as an absolute monarchy by his successors, called "Catholicos," until a comparatively recent period, when the "natural protector of Oriental Christians" forcibly introduced government by a Synod—the right of veto being invested in the Catholicos—as the thin end of the wedge, which has been hammered and driven in considerably since then. The next important move was made a few years ago, on the death of the late Catholicos, Mgr. Kevork, who hated the Russian Government with the thoroughness and cordiality of which only a Christian ecclesiastic is capable. Theretofore it was customary for the delegates of the Turkish Armenians, who possessed a voice in the election of the Catholicos, to select, for economy's sake, one or two of their number, to whom they delegated their voting powers. These would then set out for Etchmiadzin, in Russia, where the election takes place. On the death of Mgr. Kevork, however, the Government suddenly refused to sanction the practice of voting by proxy, and the electors were informed that unless they undertook, one and all, the costly journey to Russia, they must forfeit their votes. Against this the whole Armenian Church protested, and the Government straightway threatened the existence of their schools. The privilege—which in Turkey and China would be the indefeasible right—of having parochial schools attached to Armenian parish churches was suddenly made conditional upon the priests and inspectors accepting the new additions made to their ancient ecclesiastic constitution. They replied that according to the canons of their Church no modifications could be lawfully introduced or accepted unless first sanctioned by the Catholicos, and as there was no Catholicos they felt unable to take the matter into consideration. On this, the police entered the schools, drove out the weeping children, and closed the premises. Still the Synod stood firm. Then Prince Doudukoff-Korsakoff pointed out to the members of that body that according to Article 329 of the Penal Code, the penalty for their contumacy was hard labour in the mines of Siberia, inasmuch as the objectionable clauses had been promulgated in a Ukase of the Most High (*i.e.*, Tsar). The Synod was deaf to these threats. The Emperor, directly appealed to by his representative, telegraphed reiterating his commands, but the Synod repeated its *non possumus*.

The elections at last took place, two candidates were chosen according to custom, the right being vested in the Russian Government, as the natural protector of all Oriental Christians, to approve either of them. It had never before exercised that right to prefer the favourite candidate of the Synod to an unpopular one put forward merely in obedience to *force majeure*. On this occasion, determined to avail itself of this right of selection, the Government took steps to have one of the candidates a Russophile. The ecclesiastical electors, over whose heads the penalties decreed by Art. 329 were hanging, were informed that their crime would be left unpunished if they voted for Archbishop Magar [Macarius]. Hoping or believing that the candidate of the majority would be approved by the Russian authorities, the ecclesiastical electors purchased pardon on these seemingly easy terms. They, and they only, to the number of fourteen, voted for Magar, while both they and the lay electors chose Archbishop Muradjian, who was thus unanimously elected with thirty-one votes.[6] The Government at once selected the unpopular Magar and materially contributed to originate a schism in the Church of a people, the majority of whom live in Turkey. Several bishops and priests refused at first to recognise the new Catholicos, others struck his name out of prayers during divine service, and even now many venerable ecclesiastics are only restrained from protesting and transferring their allegiance to another by considerations of prudence and patriotism. Impotence to resist only intensifies the feeling of hatred with which most Armenians regard the Russian Government for its systematic endeavours to sweep away the national Church, this last repository of traditions, hopes, and aspirations of a brave people. That the closing of the schools was not merely a transient form of punishment for disobedience, but one of the means deliberately employed to crush out the national spirit, is evident from the galling conditions attached to their reopening after the Government had scored a success in the election of the present Catholicos. The schools were declared to have permanently forfeited several of their "privileges," their programme was considerably narrowed, they were forbidden to have more than two classes, so that the utmost they can now do is to teach a child to read a little, and in the girls' school not even so much, as they can possess but one solitary class.

Those details are dry. Ecclesiastical questions no longer occupy the prominent place in the social and political life of Western peoples that was accorded to them in the Middle Ages. Still in the East, where religion and politics are inextricably interwoven, the study of the one necessitates a thorough knowledge of the other; and it is only from such seemingly uninteresting details as the above that correct views of one important aspect of the Armenian question can be formed. What may probably seem more interesting to most readers is the Russian method of dealing with the agricultural population of Armenia. Tens of thousands of Armenian peasants, whose industry, patient toil, and capital had made the District of Kars the granary of an immense area of Southern Russia, became subjects of the Tsar, when at the close of the late war all that country was added to Russia. The welcome extended to them by "the only Christian power qualified to deal with the Armenian Question" was not of a nature to inspire the rest of their countrymen in Turkey with a lively desire of sharing it. They were driven from their homesteads, their land was parcelled out and distributed among Russians rent free with remission of the taxes for ten years, and they were forbidden ever again to set foot in the district, unless they came to live in the cities. The peasants sent deputation after deputation to the authorities entreating permission to return, offering to pay any rent, any taxes, their only wish being to be allowed to live and work and die in the homes where they were born, on the land sanctified by the dust of their parents and relatives. They might as well have been entreating their old god Ormuzd to give them the elixir of life. The foreign settlers, totally unacquainted with the conditions of the new climate and soil, failed so completely in their slipshod attempts to till the land that a famine resulted in that part of Russia which was dependent for its corn supply upon the District of Kars. The evicted tenants retired to Erivân, where there was great dearth of arable land and a superabundance of tillers of the soil.[7] Their arrival augmented the general misery, and during the famine that ensued women ate their own children. It would be idle to expect that the recital of these recent events, which are surely horrors as genuine as those coupled with the name of Moussa Bey, should excite compassion or indignation in England, which must be evoked or appeased by the talisman of a party cry. Nor is it intended that they should. They do seem, however, to be not wholly devoid of force as arguments against the position maintained by certain organs of the English press and by the illustrious leader of the Liberal party that the settlement of the Armenian Question should, in the interests of Christianity, morality, humanity itself, be entrusted to the Russian Government. I lately had a conversation with an Armenian from the city of Artvin on the Tschorokh, a little to the south of Batoum, a man well stricken in years, who trembled with rage when I asked him what he thought of the plan to extend to the Turkish Armenians the benefits of Russian rule. "We helped the Russian during the late war," he said, with the accents with which the Ancient Mariner may be supposed to have related how he killed the albatross; "our knowledge of the country, of the mountain-passes, of the enemy's position, made us invaluable allies. We wanted to better our position and we acted like a horse that called in the man to help him and rued it ever afterwards. Great God! we tear the hair off our heads in rage and despair when we think of the flood-gates of misery we then threw open. In the coming war there is not a man—nor a woman either, for the matter of that—who will not strain every nerve to assist the Turks. If legislative independence could be bought at the price of military services, we would put a splendid army in the field warranted to wipe off old scores with Russia."

The fondness of Armenians for their national literature must appear, to those foreigners who have any knowledge of it, like the intense love a mother manifests for her deformed child at whom strangers glance and shudder. Ancient Armenian Literature is a collection of dry dusty annals enshrining deeds of daring, glorious achievements that would have made Dryasdust himself a second Homer had he undertaken to describe them; and yet in Armenia they are mere matter-of-fact annals, the poetry of which it needed all the asceticism of Oriental Christianity to suppress. The literature of modern times is more diversified but less original. It is still in the translation-period; the classic works of other literatures being rendered accessible to Armenian readers who live outside the pale of civilisation in Aberbeidjan and at the foot of Mount Ararat. Noble efforts, however, are being made by all classes to contribute to its development. Russian Armenians, for instance, support two daily newspapers, one weekly and three monthly reviews; and translations from French and English works are being continually published. The [censor], however—that blight of literature and clog of all intellectual progress—is also at work, and to considerable purpose. The difficulties with which the Armenian press has to contend in Russia are enormous: whole pages are cut out of the reviews, long paragraphs suppressed in the daily newspapers, all of which have to be examined and approved in writing by these literary policemen before they can be published. Armenian publications printed elsewhere are carefully revised and expurgated before being put in the hands of their readers in Russia. The Shah of Persia, whose partiality for his Armenian subjects is as well known as their exemplary loyalty to their sovereign, lately paid a visit to the Catholicos of the Armenians at Etchmiadzin, but the Russian authorities strictly forbade the Armenian papers to give a detailed account of the visit or to allude to it otherwise than in the measured words used by the official journal in its few casual remarks on this event.

Another instance—and the last that I shall bring forward—of the earnest determination of the Russian authorities to cut down every growth of national life is as incredible in appearance as it is imprudent in fact. In the hope of enlarging the intellectual horizon of the common people, and arousing in them an enlightened interest in questions of history, literature, science, a series of cheap little primers were issued in Armenian, containing each the story of the life of some hero, or an account of some memorable event in the world's history, in simple words perfectly free from all objectionable tendencies; so free indeed that the [censor], so chary of its imprimatur to Armenian publications, approved the little pamphlets, which were printed. Very soon, however, the Government declared that, although each little book was in itself quite harmless, yet the fact that the series contained the lives of such persons as Joan of Arc, William Tell, &c., related in a way that charmed the minds of the people, coupled with the circumstance that these primers were bought up in a very short time, was a sufficiently clear indication of a state of feeling which the Government could not tolerate. And the further issue of these little books, *some of which were literal translations of sketches written and published by Russian pedagogues for Russian children*, was forthwith prohibited.[8]

There are many systems of political ethics which have no

words of blame for persecution like the above. Against these doctrines, when honestly and consistently proposed, I have nothing to object. But surely ordinary respect for simple truthfulness should suffice to prevent those who advocate Russia's interference in Armenian affairs from mixing up with the only intelligible grounds upon which this opinion can be upheld considerations of religion or humanity. It is bad enough for a man to be stripped of his possessions, put in irons, and persecuted to death, without being still further exasperated by the assurance that all this is done in his own interest, at a heavy sacrifice to the doer, and in the name of mercy and charity.

It is not surprising that in this age of resuscitated peoples, when the dry bones of withered nations live again like those to which Ezekiel once prophesied, one of the oldest branches of the Indo-European family should look forward with hope and wistful yearnings to the re-establishment of its former power and prestige. The opportunity for effecting this change is far more favourable than it ever was for the liberation of Bulgaria, Servia, Greece, or Roumania, and the benefits to Europe would prove at least equally great. A vitality equalled only by that of the Jews, political aptitudes as marked as those of the Hungarians, a combination of European love of progress and Asiatic tact and diplomacy, silence all doubts as to the qualifications of Armenians to play the important part that would of necessity devolve upon one of the principal heirs to the Turks' dominions. "The Armenian," says a native proverb, "has understanding in his head, the Georgian in his eye." The logical outcome of the present agitation should—and possibly will—be the establishment of a small principality, the center of which should be Seitun in Cilicia, or the Vilayet of Van, which would stand in the same relation to Turkey as Bulgaria. Tiflis, Kars, and the rest of the Russian provinces would constitute Armenia *irredenta*, which would always display a natural tendency to unite with the independent principality.

At present this is but a *pium desiderium*, and it would be ridiculous to imagine that considerations of abstract humanity, or motives of ideal philanthropy, or a sentiment of compassion aroused by the recital of the most blood-curdling atrocities, will ever induce this country to embark in a Quixotic attempt to realise it. And it is well that this should be known to all the friends and enemies of the children of Haik. But in this age of materialism self-interest is stronger than chivalric impulses; and the few statesmen who still believe that England has interests in the east of Europe, who having tasted of the fruit of experience have been driven from the fool's paradise of fancied security, in which most of our politicians seem to live and dream, will admit that no better or more effectual plan could well be conceived to promote those interests than the re-establishment of Armenian independence.

Russia, we are being constantly reminded by enthusiastic Liberals, must one day absorb Turkey, Persia, all Central Asia, Corea—in a word, the whole of the eastern world. Those who really know what Russian as at present constituted and governed is, would infinitely prefer a repetition of the incursions of the Goths and Vandals and Huns, the Mongols, or any of the other Plagues of God who darkened the face of civilisation since history began to be written. But no sane man can believe that the realisation of Russia's programme is as irresistible as the decrees of Fate, until strenuous, well-advised efforts have been made to prevent it, and have been made in vain. And no more efficacious scheme could be devised than the establishment of a new power to divide with her the spoils of Turkey, and if needs be of Persia. It is no small recommendation in its favour that its execution is compatible with the strictest neutrality and the most scrupulous attention to the requirements of international comity. Thus the fulfilment of the engagements contained in Article 61 of the Treaty of Berlin would not cost a single soldier nor a single pound. The coming war, if precipitated before Russia succeeds in distancing her competitors, who now seem to be drawing dangerously near the limits of military strength, will in all human probability prove exceptionally disastrous to the Empire of the Tsar, in which case it would be appropriately wound up by a new Congress of Berlin, at which, among other changes of the map of Europe, Germany might take the Baltic Provinces, Austria Russian Poland, and the principality or kingdom of Van annex Tiflis, Batoum, and Armenia *irredenta*.

The Spectator, Vol. 65 (September 13, 1890): 329–30

The True Danger in Armenia

There will be trouble, and that very speedily, in the Foreign Office about Armenia, and probably trouble also in the Unionist Party. The situation there, as we understand it, is of this kind. The Armenians are sinking into despair. All the promises made them at Berlin, in which they half-trusted, as suffering nations will, though they knew their chances were small, have been broken; the Koords, who harass them worse than the reivers ever harassed our Border Counties, remain unpunished; the acquittal of Moussa Bey showed them that even an appearance of redress was not to be expected from Constantinople; and the appeal made to Europe has resulted in nothing except those promises of "reforms" which the Porte is ready to issue in reams, but which remain, and are intended to remain, mere words. The whole nation is therefore hopeless, and has recently become, moreover, panic-stricken. It believes that the Koords have been assured of impunity, and that the Mussulmans of Armenia itself, more especially in the towns, have been secretly armed in order to meet the eventuality of a rising. The Armenians know what this means, and of all peoples understand thoroughly what Turks are, good-humoured because indifferent rulers while they are unresisted, but when defied or alarmed, revealing the old temper of the steppe, a temper horribly cruel, and capable of using extermination as a weapon. The scene at Batuk, which seemed to Western Europeans so horrible, was merely a scene of steppe warfare, and would not have impressed Tartars as at all unusual. The Armenians therefore, made apprehensive by centuries of oppression, seeing around them repeated cases of unpunished violence and rapine, and conscious no doubt of their own hatred to their immediate masters, live from day to day in expectation of an outbreak, in which their position would be that of citizens in a town just taken by a savage soldiery. Human nature cannot endure a protracted misery of that kind, even if it is partly based on exaggerated reports, and the Armenians turn for help to the only men who will help them, to their own countrymen in Russia, who often hold highly influential positions; to the Russians themselves, always moved by Christian despair when it arises from Mussulman enmity; and possibly to the Imperial family, which, from feeling as well as traditional policy, is always friendly to the Armenian race. They beg of all these for rescue, in accents not less persuasive because of the necessary secrecy. We have no doubt, if the truth were known, that many Armenians have said or written treasonable things across the frontier, and that while the stories of Russian aid and sympathy are grossly exaggerated, Russian Armenians, and religious Russians also, have promised or sent arms and "incitements"—which means, we take it, advice to resist by force—into Armenia. Many leading Armenians, too, believe that, though insurrection is hopeless without arsenals, insurrection, and the consequent explosion of Tartar fury, would bring the Russians to their aid, and that it would be better to run that awful risk than await in patience the Mussulman outbreak, which any accidental incident may provoke. In such a situation, anything may produce a massacre, and if it comes, we may rely on it Russia will not be quiet. Not only will she, as the Russophobes say, "seize her opportunity," as we should do under the same circumstances, but she cannot help herself. The Russian Government is very strong; but it must respect the religious feelings of its people; must show itself fearless to its Army; must keep up the tradition, the perfectly true tradition, that as against Turks or Tartars, it is and will remain Protector of the Faith. It has, moreover, nothing to fear. The German Emperor, even if he has not given the Czar a free hand in Armenia, is not going to waste his trained Pomeranians' lives in order to protect Koords in spoiling Armenians at will; and there is no one else with the power to interfere, not even we ourselves, for we should be too deeply divided, and France would instantly declare herself the "friend of humanity and the ancient people of Armenia." She would do it if only to strengthen her claim to a Russian alliance, and to indulge the grudge against England which has tormented her like an envy ever since M. de Freycinet threw away her chance of a dual dominion on the Nile. The Russian force in the Caucasus and Russian Armenia would be quite strong enough for the work, which might be a defensive campaign; the invaders would be among friends who would bring them information and supplies, and who know Constantinople through and through; the war would be a rapid one, and at its close Armenia would be a State dependent on St. Petersburg. It is all very well to call that prospect a dream; but it is a simple calculation, based upon facts admitted on every hand—for those who deny that ground exists for the Armenian panic do not question the existence of the panic itself—and justified by the unbroken experience of a hundred years. When Turkey drives a Christian province to revolt, Turkey, beaten, or victorious, loses that province.

The remedy, and the only possible remedy, is for Turkey to anticipate Russia, and convert Armenia from a Turkish province into a Turkish dependency. The Sultan's promises of reforms are mere illusions. He may wish to fulfill some of them—for no Sovereign ever quite loses the sense of responsibility for his subjects, except under the influence of bigotry, and it is not probable that Abdul Hamid, jealous as he is of his position in the Mussulman world, and proud as he is of the Khalifate, is secretly a Mussulman fanatic—but he cannot fulfill them. It is the steady policy of his Court not to break with the Koords, and to tolerate their excesses in order to use their valour in suppressing any Christian or Russophile uprising in the wilder and most eastern districts of the Empire. It is also its policy to keep alive a certain fanaticism among Mahommedans who might otherwise be lost in a Christian population, and to cultivate the pride of ascendency by a steady, though often hidden, protection in the Courts. This policy in a country like Armenia is perfectly intelligible, and only more wicked than our own policy in Ireland three hundred years ago because Asiatics, once broken loose, will do things of which scarcely any European race is capable. The Sultan, thus hampered, cannot act energetically, and round him stand persons of much more gloomy tempers, who hold that the old Turkish policy is the right one, that force is the only remedy for disaffection, and that Christians who rise against Mussulmans in a country clearly belonging to the Faith ought to be and must be terrorised till they despair. Orders of protection are, therefore, not executed, and they never will be except under a European pressure which of itself destroys the Sultan's authority without completely sheltering the Christians, and will be there, and powerless, years after the European pressure has been withdrawn. The only cure is to turn Armenia into a Principality; or, if that is too great an immediate concession, into a Governor-Generalship, with a Governor appointed for life and directed to raise a strong Armenian corps for local service and protection. It hardly matters what his faith is, though he had much better be an Armenian; for if he is an able man, he will govern decently for his own sake, and if he is not, the Armenians, who are very shrewd and capable, will either guide him or, in extremity, buy him. They, if once armed, will soon provide a force sufficient to keep in check the Koords, who, after all, are uncivilised warriors, and in India would be reduced to order in three years by a few regiments of cavalry; and the province, once quieted, could afford to pay a heavy tribute to the Sultan's private fisc. Turkey under this plan would not be weakened but strengthened, for Armenia would be interposed between her and Russia, just as Bulgaria is, and would speedily have as many people. They would be loyal, too, if they were at ease; for they have not the abstract hostility to the Porte felt by the Christians of the Balkan and the Orthodox Church, and they dread, for religious reasons, being absorbed in a community at once so aggressive and so irresistible as the Russian Slav. They are almost as separate as Jews; they are proud of the antiquity of their race and Church; and they have a confidence, justified in every country they enter, in their own efficiency in the ordinary business of life. They are potentially good soldiers, too, as they show in the Russian regiments, and could both organise and fill a *corps d'armée*, which, in the event of a Russian invasion, would be a solid help towards the defence of Turkey. Constantinople, in fact, would lose nothing except places for a few Pashas; while if the State were a Russian dependency—and that is the only alternative credible to practical politicians—St. Petersburg would have advanced three hundred miles nearer to the Mediterranean. It is this scheme which should be pressed on the Sultan both by England and the Armenians themselves, who, at all events, ought to be able to conciliate his Majesty with money, and not unreal reforms or favours for an ecclesiastical authority which may be entitled to respect within its own functions, but cannot disarm a single

Koord. It is of no use whatever asking for a good police, or impartial tribunals, or fair taxation, or security for property from the Turk. He may not be indisposed to grant all those good things, and he will always talk civilly about them; but the Empire is too far gone to risk changes. It has nothing solid left in it except the Army, and the only way to escape the effects of the ruinous condition of the old edifice is to step outside. If the Armenians are not permitted to do this, and helped to do this, there is no alternative except to permit Russia to carry out a design which, however tainted with ambition, will be nevertheless a work of mercy towards an ancient Christian people. Most certainly it will not be the duty of Great Britain to arrest that work.

The Spectator, Vol . 67 (July 18, 1891): 85–87

The Armenian Debate

It is unfortunate that Lord Salisbury is not able to defend his own foreign policy, at least on Turkish affairs, in the House of Commons. Sir James Fergusson's speech in the debate on the Armenian Question on Friday week will be read by the Porte as an encouragement to persevere in its maladministration of Armenia. Lord Salisbury's attitude has been very different. In his speech at Glasgow, for instance, the other day, he paid a graceful tribute to the leader of the Opposition for his generous support of the foreign policy of the Government. Mr. Gladstone, in relation to foreign policy at all events, has never shown any sympathy with the dictum of Lord Randolph Churchill, that "the business of an Opposition is to oppose." He has invariably supported in Opposition any Ministerial policy of which he really approved; and he has been a generous critic of Lord Salisbury's foreign policy because Lord Salisbury's conduct of foreign affairs has commanded his approval. The truth is, that in foreign politics Lord Salisbury has always been a Liberal,—or, to put it more accurately, he has always sympathized with the traditional foreign policy of England down to the Crimean War, rather than with a turbulent and cynical Jingoism which Lord Palmerston introduced and Lord Beaconsfield developed to the verge of caricature. When Mr. Gladstone in 1858 proposed the union of Moldavia and Wallachia he was supported in a brilliant speech by Lord Salisbury, then a youthful Member of the House of Commons, and was opposed by Mr. Disraeli and Lord Palmerston in speeches which commanded the confidence of the large majority of Parliament at the time, but of which events soon afterwards demonstrated the folly. Lord Salisbury has been imbued with the craven fear and jealousy of Russia which latter-day Toryism has inherited from Palmerston. We all remember his scornful recommendation to our Russophobists, in one of the acute phases of the controversy on the Eastern Question in 1877, to put themselves through a course of study in large maps; and if he had been allowed a free hand at the Conference of Constantinople, there is hardly a doubt that he would, in concert with Russia, have persuaded the Conference to extort from the Porte by moral pressure most of the concessions which Russia alone extorted afterwards by war. His subsequent approval of the reunion of divided Bulgaria, in violation of the Treaty of Berlin, is a pretty plain indication of his opinion of the blunder which Lord Beaconsfield regarded as the crowning glory of the "peace with honour." Lord Salisbury's stern denunciation at Glasgow of misrule in Morocco is a further proof of the entire difference of tone and feeling which separates his foreign policy from that of Lord Beaconsfield.

It is, therefore, in no censorious or unfriendly spirit that we press on Lord Salisbury the urgent need of speedy and energetic action in the affairs of Armenia. Mr. Clifford Lloyd's record in Ireland, and afterwards in the Mauritius, shows that he was an uncompromising advocate of firm and resolute government, and did not allow himself to be unduly influenced by humanitarian considerations, or sentimental sympathy with nationalist aspirations on the part of native races. Yet Mr. Clifford Lloyd's experience as British Consul at Erzeroum confirms the reports which have reached this country from other sources of the anarchy and reign of terror which prevail among the Christians of Armenia. That intrepid traveller, Mrs. Bishop, has lately returned from a tour through Armenia, and she describes the condition of the Armenians as simply intolerable. As Christians they are taxed much more heavily than the Mussulman, yet they are absolutely without any vestige of protection for life, property, religion, or the honour of their women. Forbidden to bear arms, they are at the mercy of the Kurds, who carry off their cattle, their crops, and their women, without let or hindrance, for any resistance is immediately resented by wounds and death. An appeal to the law is out of the question, for there is no law for the Christian subjects of the Porte. Their evidence is not admissible against a Mussulman, and no Mussulman will give evidence on behalf of a Christian against a "true believer." The Turkish Government has lately armed the Kurds with modern weapons, and enrolled a considerable number of them as commissioned officers of the Sultan. The ostensible reason for this is the Sultan's desire to make the Kurds amenable to discipline. The reason given by the Kurdish officers themselves, and believed by the Armenians, is the Sultan's desire that the Kurds should "diminish the population" of native Christians. That is a favourite device, from Pharaoh downwards, on the part of Oriental despots to keep down an energetic subject race. Chefket Pasha exhibited in Constantinople the official orders which he had received from the Grand Vizier to commit the massacre of Batak; and it is recorded in official despatches from our Consuls in Bulgaria that the Turkish officials openly boasted that they had orders from head-quarters "to diminish the population." The Porte is afraid of the Armenians, afraid of their intelligence, their courage, their indomitable national aspirations, and their contiguity to the Russian frontier, beyond which there are a million of Armenians living under Russian rule, and supplying Russia with some of her ablest generals and civil administrators. It really looks as if the Porte had determined to terrorise the whole of the Armenians now under Turkish rule to depart into Russian territory.

But what can the British Government do? England, let it be remembered, is under a triple bond of duty and honour to use its best endeavours to coerce the Porte to reform its infamous misrule of Armenia. By the Treaty of San Stefano Armenia was placed under the protectorate of Russia. If that protectorate had remained, there can be no question that the fear of Russian annexation would have compelled the Porte to make the conditions of life at least tolerable for the Armenians. England was the power that insisted on withdrawal of the Russian protectorate, substituting for it the 61st Clause of the Treaty of Berlin, which provides for substantial reforms in the Turkish administration of Armenia under the supervision of the Great Powers. England is thus immeasurably more responsible than her co-signatories for the due execution of that clause. But, in addition to the Treaty of Berlin, England made a convention with Turkey, stipulating for reforms in return for English co-operation with the Turkish Government in defence of Armenia and Asia against Russian aggression. We all remember the glowing description which Lord Beaconsfield's Under-Secretary for the Colonies gave of the blessings to the Christian races of Asiatic Turkey which were to follow in the train of the Cyprus Convention. The wretched inhabitants would gladly dispense with the "steam-plough" and other accessories of modern civilisation which Lord Harrowby promised them, if they could only obtain security for the ordinary conditions of tolerable existence. But do we possess any means of enforcing the fulfillment of her treaty obligations on Turkey? War is, of course, out of the question, nor is it necessary. Sir James Fergusson said not very long ago that the Cyprus Convention had lapsed through the Porte's disregard of its part of the contract. In the debate of Friday week he corrected his first and more correct impression, and then said that the Cyprus Convention "is in abeyance." Very well. Let the Government declare openly that during the abeyance of Turkey's duty the defense of Turkish territory will be left by England to Turkey alone. Indeed, that would be nothing more than common fairness to the Porte in any case. For it is certain that under no circumstances would public opinion in this country suffer any Government to wage war on behalf of Turkey against Russia. It is cruel to the Turks to let them live in their fool's paradise of belief that England will ever again lift up sword for the integrity of the Ottoman Empire. We know, on the authority of Midhat Pasha himself, that the Porte would never have dared to go to war with Russia if it had not believed in the cooperation of England. But there need not be a public declaration on the subject. Let Lord Salisbury tell the Porte in unmistakable language that, unless the Porte begins at once to put the 61st Clause of the Treaty of Berlin in force, England will not hinder Russia by deed, or even by word, from annexing Armenia. That argument would have effect; no other argument will. The obligations incurred by the Sultan in the 61st Clause of the Treaty of Berlin involve a violation of the Sacred Law of the Koran, and no Sultan would dare to enforce them except under coercion. But the same law, which forbids obedience without coercion, commands it if there should be any probability of damage to the cause of Islam from non-compliance. Ordinary remonstrances in diplomatic language are worse than useless. "Lord Derby," said a Turkish official of high rank in 1877, after one of Lord Derby's feeble remonstrances, "is but a drum—skin and wind." We can conceive nothing better calculated to encourage the Turks in their misdoings than the tremulous anxiety of Sir James Fergusson to prevent any word being said in his presence which may perchance ruffle the tender susceptibilities of the Turks. He will not even allow the Armenians to be spoken of as a nation lest it should give umbrage to the Sultan. Remonstrances delivered in that tone are not likely to have much effect. Had Russia or Germany been bound as England is to protect the Armenians, we may be sure that the 61st Clause of the Berlin Treaty would long ago have been enforced. Fear is the only motive-power which ever influences the Turkish Government. Russia has massed an army of one hundred thousand men on the frontiers of Armenia, and a hint from England to the Sultan that the Russian legions might cross the frontier without remonstrance from England would have an instantaneous effect. We trust that Lord Salisbury will adopt a more virile tone on this subject than the apologetic and deferential speeches of his Under-Secretary.

The Contemporary Review,[1] Vol. 65 (June 1894): 847–65

The Armenian Question

I.—In Russia

H. F. B. Lynch[2]

The reality and the importance of the Armenian question are facts of which a careful study of the subject in the country itself has convinced me. The Power whose true interests will most directly be promoted by a practical solution of this question is the Ottoman Empire. The Russian frontier is already within fifty miles of the Turkish fortress of Erzerum, which immediately commands the roads to the interior of Asia Minor and to the capital. The further advance of Russia will not only establish her as mistress of this position, but will extend her border beyond the spine of the Ararat system to the shores of the Lake of Van, where she will be situated at the head of the passes which lead towards Mosul and Bagdad. It needs no long memory to recall the causes which were avowed by Russia as a justification for her past aggression upon Turkish territory; nor is any large measure of foresight necessary to enable us to realise that an aggravated political situation in the provinces which adjoin her Asiatic frontier may invite her intervention again. Those who are acquainted with the true state of these provinces will find it difficult to deny that there exists such a situation, or to affirm that it is occasioned by adventitious fermentation, and not by the action of deep-seated conditions in the life of the body itself. There is a party not only in Turkey, but also in this country, who desire to remain blind to these issues; and it is not the least dangerous symptom of this tendency that those who encourage it find a sure avenue to favour at Constantinople which the more candid among Turkish officials must forego. There are friends of Turkey in England who must deplore this tendency and the policy which it is calculated to promote. They know that the development under the rule of the Sultan, a rule which is usually mild, of the stronger and more hopeful races, who can best preserve their individual existence while remaining his subjects, can alone save this empire from decay. On the other hand, they are aware that the pursuit of a different policy will inevitably issue in the sequel of a further extension of Russian dominion in Asia, which they do not consider desirable whether on general or on patriotic grounds.

England cannot afford to remain indifferent to a question which involves such contingencies as these. For what is the plain significance of an occupation by Russia of Armenia? It means no less than her complete supremacy in the nearer East, by which I mean the countries which extend between India and the Mediterranean. Throughout history the geographical position of the country has invested it with a special importance in the politics of this part of Asia. It was not to gain an Eastern conquest that the statesmen of the Roman Empire extended Roman influence to Armenia; and it was not to settle within her upland plains that the Seldjuks, and the Mongols, and the hordes of Tatars and Turks swept westwards across them from the steppes beyond the Caspian Sea. The strategical value of the country consists in its character as a land of passage and in the command which its possession ensures of the roads to the south, to the west, and to the east. The Romans, who held Asia Minor and the fertile lowlands through which the Euphrates and Tigris flow, could ill afford, in spite of the comparative weakness of their Eastern rivals, to see others paramount there. In our times the arguments which have operated through history have become more momentous than before. In the first place, the principal and almost the only avenue which is followed by the commerce of Europe with northern Persia leads from Trebizond to the Persian border through the plains just south of the Russian frontier, which afford a natural passage from west to east. The value of this trade already amounts to about a million sterling a year, of which Great Britain controls more than one-half. The immediate effect of any addition to Russian territory in this region would be the extinction of this trade route, and it is for this reason that I mention it first. In the second place, the construction by Russia of the Georgian military road through the Caucasus has opened a new and direct passage between the north and the south, and, while the comparatively easy undertaking of an extension of the Tiflis railway to Kars is among the more pressing projects which are announced and abandoned every year, the connection of Tiflis itself with the Russian railway system is scarcely likely, even in present circumstances, to be much longer delayed. The Caucasus, shorn of its terrors, no longer opposes an impassable barrier to the advance of the peoples of the north, and the fourth arm has been added to the ancient signpost which points from Armenia to the conquest of the adjacent lands. Policy must also counsel Russia to advance through this region to the south. Persia is more defenceless, and it would be easy to march from the valley of the Araxes or from the fringe of Khorassan to waters of the Persian Gulf; but such a course would at once excite war with England, while the flank of Russia on the side of Turkey is now open to damaging attack. The mere distance of Armenia from India, and the unfamiliarity of most Englishmen with anything that concerns it, are advantages which Russian statesmen are too wise to overlook; while, once in possession of the country, they are not only more secure on the west, but they command all the passes to the plains of the Tigris which extend without the intervention of any natural obstacle from Diarbekr to Syria on the one side and to the Persian arm of the Indian Ocean on the other. The following extract from a despatch by Sir Henry Layard, when ambassador in Constantinople at the time of the Russo-Turkish war, resumes the contemporary importance of the country in relation to the position of England in the East:

> "Should Russia desire to annex at this time any of the European provinces of Turkey, European interests would probably be called into play, and she would be prevented from carrying out her intentions. . . . But as regards the acquisition by her of territory in Asia Minor, the case is different. The interests of England would then be alone concerned. It would probably signify little to the rest of Europe whether Russia retained Armenia or not. But England has to consider the effect of the annexation to Russia of this important province upon the British possessions in India. Russia would then command the whole of Asia Minor and the great valley of the Euphrates and Tigris, which would inevitably fall into her hands in course of time. Persia, moreover, would be placed entirely at her mercy."

Here he mentions a suspicion that secret overtures had been made to Persia by Russia that the former should cede Ghilan and Mazanderan, receiving in exchange the province of Bagdad with its Shiah shrines.

> "The possession of the entire coast of the Caspian Sea and the direct road through a rich and well-inhabited country to Herat and Afghanistan, and ultimately to India, is a matter of vast political importance to Russia. . . . The possession by Persia of the province of Bagdad would be, as far as England is concerned, its possession by Russia. It must not be forgotten that the possession of Armenia by Russia, as regards any designs she may have upon India, supposing her to entertain them, would be very different from that of any part of Turkestan or Central Asia. In Armenia and the north of Persia she would have a hardy and abundant population, affording her excellent materials for a large army ready at any time to advance upon our Indian frontier, and resting upon a convenient and sure base of operations in direct communication, by the Caspian Sea and by Batoum, with the heart of the Russian Empire."[3]

The arguments which have been urged for and against the supposition that Russia has designs upon India have, I confess, in judging her future and our own, seemed to me to be of secondary importance. Nations, like individuals, need not consciously make plans; they go on and they fulfil. What is the issue? To the west of our Indian Empire a long succession of countries and peoples extends to the Mediterranean and to the threshold of Europe. The historical prosperity of this part of Asia, and the wealth of its natural resources, contrast with the squalor of its present condition and the state of desolation to which it has declined. From the west the tide is recoiling upon it, and again the pulse of life throbs. But the infirmity of all its better elements renders it incapable of resistance to any organised force from whatever quarter it may come. The plain policy of England—a policy which she has recognised, but failed to enforce—is, while abstaining from any direct intervention both in Turkey and in Persia, to work for the strengthening of whatever elements of stability either empire may be found to contain. If she shrinks from this task the preponderance of Russia is only a matter of time. To succeed in our efforts towards renovation and construction we must convince both Turkey and Persia of the sincerity of our intentions and of the strength of our will, and, above all, we must concentrate ourselves upon particular problems, and not be disheartened and disgusted if we fail to solve all at once.

Such a problem is this Armenian question. It has been very imperfectly understood. Those who have even a superficial acquaintance with it would probably be unable to narrow the issues further than to explain that it was a question of Turkish misgovernment in Asia Minor and the outcome of a general system of oppression and persecution of the Christians by their Mohammedan rulers, the Turks. To such it is replied by the adherents of the Turkish policy that the Government of the Sultan is actuated by motives of the broadest tolerance, and that, although undoubtedly it is susceptible of improvement, still the evils of which the Armenians complain are shared by the Mohammedan population as well as by the Christians of different race who inhabit the same provinces in which the agitation exists without joining in or otherwise abetting it. There is the usual grain of truth in both these statements which is just sufficient to make either mislead us. Yet the same vagueness of issue which is displayed by such lay views as these has unfortunately attended the whole treatment of the question at the hands of those who might have done much to resolve it. What has been its history? The Armenians first, I believe, brought their cause officially before Europe at the Congress of Berlin in 1878. They came forward with a proposal for the constitution of an autonomous province; but they do not seem to have possessed any clear conception of the practical difficulties which would have to be encountered by any such administrative scheme.[4] A clause was inserted in the Berlin Treaty, which, if it means anything, must be taken as a hint to the Armenians to go home and prove their case.[5] Immediately after the Berlin Treaty England, acting under the Cyprus Convention, despatched a number of able consular officers over the whole of Asia Minor with instructions to report upon the general condition of the country and upon the measures of reform, extending over the whole field of Turkish administration, which it would be necessary to recommend. In the case of the Armenians in particular our ambassador obtained the signature of his colleagues to his representations and acted under the Treaty of Berlin. It must be confessed that he was very indifferently served by the Armenians themselves, for whom he was working; they supplied him with misleading statistics and seem never to have inspired him with any real confidence as to the soundness of their cause.[6] As a consequence, no definite plan was placed before the Porte, and, what is more important, no definite policy seems ever to have been brought to the mind of our ambassador or of his colleagues representing the signatory Powers. The activity of England in Asia Minor, and the reports of misgovernment in every direction which she showered upon the Porte, seem not only to have alarmed Turkey but the European Powers as well; and it only required a word from Prince Bismarck to dismiss the whole question of Armenian reforms.[7]

Since that time our diplomacy at Constantinople has been occupied by endeavours to obtain redress in particular cases of wrong suffered by individual Armenians, but it has not been assisted in any material manner by our co-signatories of the Treaty of Berlin. The settlement of the Armenian provinces has not progressed, while our interests in other matters have undoubtedly suffered owing to the irritation in Turkish Government circles which our intervention in such cases excites. During my recent journey in Armenia, which covered a very wide field, and included both the Russian and the Turkish territory, certain specific issues were present to my mind which I shall endeavour to express in the following manner: What is Armenia? In other words, what is the area of the region to which we give this name, and which we assume to possess a special historical and contemporary individuality? As a necessary preliminary to the study of the subject in Turkey, what capacity and character have the Armenians who live in that portion of the country which is subject to the rule of Russia displayed, and, as an important but subsidiary issue, what measure of success may the rule of Russia in Armenia be said to have attained? In the Turkish territory and in *the provinces inhabited by the Armenians* is there any area which can be held to require separate treatment from the other provinces of Asiatic Turkey, and, if so, what are the limits of such area and what is the composition of the population who inhabit within it? To the first two of these questions I propose in this and the following paper to address myself, and to begin with a brief but necessary excursion into the field of geographical research.

The limits of the Armenian plateau, according as we look to the north and south, or to the west and east, present the contrast of well-defined geographical features in the first case, with vague and arbitrary divisions in the second. Mountain terraces, whose general direction is from west to east, rise with successive steps and slow gradation both to its northern and its southern edge, and although the southern chain, from the magnitude of its scale and scope, has rightly earned the independent designation of the Taurus range, it may well be questioned whether the proper correspondence of ideas to words would justify the name of Little Caucasus, which is sometimes applied to the north-eastern buttress of the plateau, where it sinks to the flat and dreary steppes which border the middle and lower course of the Kur. The northern zone of terraces follows on the west the shores of the Black Sea; the saturated air of that warm seaboard clothes it with luxuriant woods in which the massive forest trees, the oak, the beech, the elm, alternate with the graceful varieties of the fir. Stretching up north towards the chain of the Caucasus, it again assumes its easterly direction along the rich valley of the Rion, joins hands with the Caucasus itself in the picturesque belt of mountain scenery which the railway from Tiflis to Batum crosses by the pass of Suram, leaves the soft climate which fed its forests, and extends with a bleak succession of parallel ridges along the trough of the Kur river towards the Caspian Sea. I had seen on a former journey, which took me from the Caspian to Tiflis, the eastern portion of this northern buttress range where it rose on the left hand from the steppe which the Caucasus bordered on the right. On the present occasion I came from the banks of Rion, struck westward across its level plain, scaled the walls of the range by a winding road which leads through a forest landscape of the greatest beauty, and reached the rim of the great plateau at an altitude of over 7000 feet. This clearness of geographical feature on the north is answered by no less marked characteristics when you descend from the plateau on the south. Terrace upon terrace of ridge and trough leads down to the vast plains of Mesopotamia, and form that long line of bold escarpments which some years ago I remember to have followed from the neighbourhood of Diarbekr to the Persian Gulf. On the west and east the limits of the plateau are much more difficult to define, and any division can at best be arbitrary in the continuous stretch of lofty upland which extends from the Mediterranean to the Indian plains. It is of greater usefulness to determine the nature of any special features which in that long series the Armenian plateau may present and which may invest it with a distinctive character and an individuality of its own. Its elevation above the contiguous levels, its projection northwards between the Caspian and the Black Sea, the vast scale of the great operations which Nature has worked upon it, and the mighty rivers which rising within it feature the surrounding lands—these are its claims to individual existence, whether we judge it from the standpoint of our senses or measure it in a sober estimate of the geography of the nearer East. The deep trough of the Araxes, which in the latitude of Erivan lie as low as 2500 feet, while the Lake of Van on the south is no less than over 5000 feet, and the Lake of Sevanga on the north is over 6000 feet high, presents a convenient point at which to consider the plateau on the east. North of the river the Karabagh system, which, commencing east of Lake Sevanga, contains within itself the features both of table-land and terrace and sinks to the flat steppes of the Caspian from uplands which are 6500 feet high, is but the imposing eastern buttress of the plateau on the side of the Caspian Sea. On the southern bank any limits are artificial; it is the same country and the same landscape as you pass from Lake Van to Lake Urumiah, from Armenia to Azerbaijan. The western boundary may be placed at the great southern bend of the western Euphrates: there a most interesting mountain system, whose connection with the main structure of the country has not been sufficiently established, divides the two branches of the Euphrates, and under the name of the Deyrsim still calls for exploration and research.

If from the parched plains of the upper Tigris, from the coast of the Black Sea, or from the trough of the middle Kur, we have crossed the zone of parapet and terrace and emerged on the plateau edge, the landscape for many long days of travel will, in spite of the varieties of local action, develop a consistent and continuous plan. The surface of the great table-land has been denuded by melted snows and raised by the upheaval of volcanic forces into long and irregular convexities of mountain and hummock and hill. But its true character is never lost among these complex features, however large and majestic their scale. The main watersheds do not decline from mountains but from the almost imperceptible gradations of the surface of the plateau itself. The valleys of the rivers are often bordered by gigantic cliffs whose steep sides rise to level summits, from trough to table-land. Even the long volcanic spine which divides the Russian from the Turkish provinces and culminates in the mass of Ararat does little more than start the scanty stream of the upper Murad and drive the impetuous Araxes northwards from its natural course. It is from vast tracts of comparatively level country that the waters gather and diverge. In the case of the Russian territory, which I crossed from Akhalzik to Erivan, the streams which feed the Kur on the west and the Araxes on the south decline from far-stretching upland plains at an altitude of about 7000 feet. In Turkey the most lofty portion of the plateau lies in the country south of Erzerum, and as I followed the winter road from Mush to this city by the plain of Khinis, across levels which varied in altitude from 4500 to 5000 feet, the sharp rim of this higher region followed my course for nearly fifty miles, till I mounted to the deep snow which already lay upon it at a height of over 7000 feet.

The great altitude of the higher portions of the plateau is an obstacle to the full and free development of human life upon them even in these southern latitudes; yet it would be a mistake to suppose that the climate of the country as a whole is unduly severe and inclement. The plain of Erzerum is situated at an elevation of just over 6000 feet; yet the thermometer during the month of December maintained an average of 27° Fahrenheit at ten o'clock in the forenoon. Snow fell on the hills which form the northern border of the plain of Mush for the first time last autumn on the 29th of November, and in March the hot sun already commenced to fill the torrents and free the land from its winter covering. When I arrived in Van at the commencement of November the trees had not yet lost their golden leaves and spread the full glory of an Indian summer over the dirty avenues of the garden town. If you cross the Russian territory from north-west to south-east, you are at a height which varies from 3000 to 4000 feet in the plain of Akhalzik, and you rise to 5500 feet in the plain of Akhalkalaki; the scarcely perceptible decline to the watershed of the Araxes commences at 7000 feet, and leads to the plain of Alexandropol, which has a mean elevation of about 5000 feet. The valley of the Araxes itself is as low as 2500 feet in the neighbourhood of Erivan, and not quite as high as 4000 feet where I crossed it again as far as Kagizman. The plain of Alashkert, where first I entered the Turkish provinces, is about 5500 feet above the sea; the rich land about Lake Van a little more than 5000 feet; the plain of Mush does not exceed 4400 feet. The average height of the great plains within Turkish territory may be placed at

5500 feet. Cereals flourish here at this altitude, and, while the cotton plant thrives in the valley of the Araxes, the vine and the tobacco plant enrich and embellish the neighbourhood of Mush. The salubrity of the mountain atmosphere, the fertility of the volcanic soil, the extent of the area which can be cultivated and the profusion of water which may take the place of rain, are natural gifts which any land might envy and which less in this land than in others have been devoted to the service of man. Where the air is keen in summer while at midwinter the sun is warm it would seem that nothing is wanting to foster a strenuous race. Yet nowhere in this half of Asia is the standard of life lower, and in scarcely any old country is the imprint of man less marked. The burrows of the Armenian and the Kurd are scarcely discernible in the landscape, and the only roads which give access to the interior are the main avenues of military communication which lead towards the Russian frontier from the north.

Such are the geographical conditions upon which, perhaps, in a general survey it is most useful to dwell. When we come to deal with questions of population it is important to note the distinction, to which I have already alluded, between the plateau itself and the land of terrace which on its northern as well as on its southern side leads up like a ladder to its edge. The breadth of these zones of mountainous country—which according to the point of view from which we regard them may be considered either as the buttresses of the plateau or as the steps which lead down from it to the sea on the north and to the low alluvial plains of the Tigris on the south—does not admit of such exact definition as the metaphors which I have used might suggest, and varies at different points of the belt according to those general or local causes which have operated at the particular place. Where I crossed the belt upon entering the country, its depth in a direct line from the village of Bagdad, on the first slopes of the systems which meet the Rion plain to the pass of Zikar at the plateau rim, does not exceed 15 miles. The more westerly portion of this same northern zone, across which I rode on my homeward journey, which took me from Erzerum to Trebizond, has, on that line, from the pass of Vavuk to the sea, a depth of about 40 miles. On the south of the mountain range which immediately borders the southern shores of Lake Van and stretches right across the country on the left bank of the eastern Euphrates, or Murad

Tchai, may be regarded as the northern limit of the southern zone. The importance of a clear conception of these features is apparent when we consider that they coincide in a general manner with the local distribution of races, and that, while on the one hand the steep mountains and inaccessible valleys both of the northern and of the southern zone have at all times been inhabited by pirates and nomad shepherds—Lazis and Adjars on the north, Kurds and Kizzilbashes on the south—the great plains, on the other hand, which expand upon the plateau have afforded a spacious settling ground for the agricultural peoples and are the original habitation of the Armenians and the adopted home of their Mussulman conquerors—the Tatars and the Turks. The Greek colonies, which established themselves on the sea-board and maintained themselves as an important political factor down to a period as late as that of the Greek kingdom of Trebizond, have not contributed any large element to the present population of the plateau, although their numbers are still considerable upon the coast. On the plateau within the whole area with which I am dealing the numbers of the Greek population may be placed at 52,000 souls.

To a greater degree than has any other race among the peoples who inhabit it the Armenians have impressed their individuality upon the face of this lofty and extensive table-land. In the immense expanse of the landscape, in which blue lakes lie lapped in treeless plains whose ochre-hued surface swells from hummock and hill to the long descending mountain outlines which sweep from the summit of some snow-crowned cone, the note which is uttered by man is lost. Yet there is scarcely a remote valley or lonely island which does not attract a band of pilgrims to worship in the beautiful monasteries which date from the time of the kings of Armenia, and keep alive the story of the past. I regret that it is without the scope of this paper to develop this side of the general subject; I am more concerned in this place to delimit in a more particular manner the area of the Armenian country and to endeavour to present some tangible conception of it by means of a brief analysis dealing with the numbers of the different races and the distinctive character which belongs to each. For the sake of clearness, no less than of convenience, I shall in the first place address myself to that portion of the country which lies within the empire of the Czar.[8]

The solid block of territory over which Russia now rules on

the plateau is neither a new acquisition nor the fruit of a single conquest. At the commencement of the present century she gained a foothold upon it by the voluntary accession of the Georgian kingdom and its constitution into a Russian province in 1802. This event, the outcome of the folly of the Mussulman powers who had driven the Christians to despair, was followed by new acquisitions: from Persia, Karabagh in 1813 and the important Khanate of Erivan in 1828; from Turkey, the district of Akhalzik in 1829 and the fortress and province of Kars in 1878. Appearing as a deliverer to the Christian peoples, and profiting by their aid, she has succeeded in advancing her border beyond the Araxes and to the threshold of Erzerum, and in establishing herself behind a well-rounded frontier which comprises the venerated mountain of Armenia and the seat of the supreme spiritual government to which the Armenians bow.

The admirable volume of statistics of Transcaucasia which we owe to the labours of M. de Seidlitz and the Transcaucasian statistical committee, and which was published by order of the civil government during the past year, presents us with the most detailed information concerning the Russian provinces, the numbers of the different races and of the votaries of the different religious sects, and as to how the inhabitants may be classed and labelled as noble or clergy, as tradesmen or as tillers of the soil. I do not propose to forestall by quoting from its serried columns of figures the pleasure which the perusal of this work is sure to bring to every well-regulated mind, but its aid will be useful, and indeed indispensable, in determining the elements of population within the area with which I deal, and in fixing upon a surer foundation the more general conceptions and conclusions which the experience of travel suggests. While the country on the north of the plateau, the plain of the Rion on the north-west and the wide trough of the Kur on the north, is inhabited by various branches of the Georgian family and by the settlers of Turco-Tatar race; while the Caucasus itself, the northern boundary of the whole geographical system, contains within its countless recesses a Homeric catalogue of nations whose names it is difficult to pronounce and whose languages are as mysterious as their names, the distribution of the people upon the plateau itself is a subject which may be presented with comparative ease, and which is free from the perplexing entanglement in which the study of the neighbouring peoples is involved. In order to adapt as nearly as possible the governmental areas upon which the statistics are based to the geographical area with which I deal, I have been obliged in the case of the Government of Tiflis to separate those administrative districts which belong to the plateau from those which lie outside; but both in the case of Erevan government and also in the case of Kars the limits of the governmental areas coincide in a fairly satisfactory manner with the limits of the plateau on the west and of that portion of it lying on the east with which I have gained a personal acquaintance during the journey which I have brought to a close. The boundary of the area comprised by these administrative districts, the statistics of which I propose to resume, includes the whole frontier of the Russian territory on the south from a point in the neighbourhood of Ordubad on the Araxes in the east to the vicinity of Ardanutch on the west, follows thence the edge of the plateau northwards to a point a little west and north of the town of Akhalzik, stretches eastwards along the belt of terrace to about the longitude of the western shore of Lake Sevanga, descends abruptly southwards to the lake itself and, following its northern shore in a south-easterly direction, declines to the point from which it started just east of Ordubad. The superficial measurement of this area amounts in round numbers to 22,000 square miles, which is about three times the area of Wales. The extensive Government of Elizabetpol, which, in addition to other territories quite outside the plateau, includes the whole system of Karabagh, I omit from the present inquiry, partly because I have never been in Karabagh, but chiefly because the Karabagh system may more justly be included in the land of terrace which I propose to exclude, as far as may be convenient, from the scope of the whole subject which I treat. In presenting the figures of the population of these Russian provinces upon the plateau within the area which I have already described I have only to remark that in the case of the Government of Kars I have made use of later official statistics than those which are furnished by the volume to which I have referred. The figures stand thus:

Armenians	519,238	Georgians	31,102
Tatars	306,310	Russians	28,844
Kurds	68,864	Karapapachs	27,247
Greeks	47,763	Others	19,357
Turks	46,985	Total	1,095,710

About 8 per cent must be added to these figures if it is assumed that the number of females is at least equal to that of the males. Of a total population in Transcaucasia of 4,700,000 souls, the Armenians number one-fifth; their total number is given as 939,131. The census on which these figures are based is that of 1886, and later calculations place their present number at 965,000. It is safe to assume that there are now at least five millions of people in the Transcaucasian provinces of Russia, and that of these the Armenians number one million souls. The importance of the Armenian element must be measured, not by its numerical strength, but by the solidarity of the Armenian people as compared with the peoples among whom they live. In the Russian provinces they are little divided by religious differences; the Roman Catholics are a mere handful among the solid ranks of the Gregorians, and the Gregorian Church is not only the symbol of national existence, but the stronghold of national hopes. Two other races in Transcaucasia exceed the Armenians in number: the Tatars with 1,139,000, and the different divisions of the Georgian family, who number over a million souls. But the bitter religious antipathies of Sunni and Shiah divide the Tatars, and the Georgians are in a period of transition from their old feudal system to a new and more settled social order, while the union of their Church with the Orthodox Church of Russia has deprived them of the natural rallying-point for that community of sentiment which is based on a consciousness of race pride. The distribution of the Armenians in Transcaucasia outside the area which I am treating is as follows: In the Government of Elizabetpol, which includes Karabagh, they number 258,000; but only in the governmental divisions of Shusha and Zangezur, that is to say in the tract of country between the Araxes on the east, and the south-eastern shore of Lake Sevanga on the west, do they constitute the numerically preponderating race, while in the other divisions, and in the whole government, they are largely outnumbered by the Tatars, who are nearly twice as numerous as they. The Government of Tiflis contains nearly 212,000 Armenians, of whom I have included 99,000 in my estimate for the plateau itself: the remainder are distributed over the other divisions of the government, and in the town of Tiflis, where they attain the imposing number of 55,000 in a total population of 145,000. In the Government of Baku, out of a total Armenian population of 55,000, there are over 24,000 in the town of Baku itself, where they are engaged in commerce and in the oilworks; they are also numerous in the town and district of Shemakha, which lies to the west of Baku. In the Government of Kutais they are only 16,000, and most of these reside in the towns. These figures, when added to the number which I have given for the Armenians on the plateau, will produce a result in excess of the total, which I have taken from the statistics of 1886, for the Armenians in Transcaucasia: I have to say, in explanation, that these statistics only show a total population for the town of Tiflis of 78,000, while the larger figure which I give both for the total population of Tiflis, and for the Armenian element in it, is the result of the latest official estimate which I know.

An analysis of the figures which I have given for the plateau will show that the stronghold of the Armenians, the locality in which they are most numerous, is the rich country through which the Arpa Tchai flows on its way to join the middle course of the Araxes. There is situated the fortress and modern town of Alexandropol, which is inhabited almost exclusively by Armenians, and there, a little further south, are the remains of the ancient city of Ani, whose deserted site still testifies to the taste and splendour of their kings. The upland plains about Akhalkalaki on the north are dotted with Armenian villages, while the valley of the Araxes on the south, from Kagizman to Erivan, and especially in the district of Etchmiadzin, contains a considerable Armenian population. The town and district of Novo-Bayazed, on the western shore of Lake Sevanga, is for the greater part Armenian. On the other hand, the eastern portion of the Araxes valley, commencing from the town of Ordubad, is held in large numbers by the Tatars, who run the Armenians close in the extensive and important area which is covered by the Government of Erivan. It must be remembered, in reference to the Armenian population of the Russian provinces, that their numbers have been considerably augmented by emigration from Turkey. It is computed that not less than 10,000 families from the district of Erzerum followed the Russian army out of Turkey in 1829, and I am informed that, during the past year, 3500 passports have been registered for emigrants from Turkey by the Russian Consulate in Erzerum.

Next to the Armenians, the most numerous element in the

population of the plateau are the Tatars, who extend from the Persian frontier up the valley of the Araxes, and cover with their settlements the eastern portion of the plateau and the whole of Karabagh. According to M. Vambéry, the Tatars of Transcaucasia represent a section of those warriors of Turkish race who, from the time of the appearance of the Seldjuks down to the end of the last century, were driven by political conditions to this country from the northern provinces of Persia—that is from Azerbaijan, and from the eastern shores of the Caspian Sea. Within the area with which I deal they belong almost entirely to the Shiah sect, and, besides sharing the religion of Persia, contain an admixture of Persian blood. It is not so long ago that these districts formed a Persian Khanate, and were administered by Persian Serdars; and the wealthy families who flourished during that period are still the owners of extensive gardens, and live on the proceeds of their skill in all those methods of working mud which are practised in the East; they are plasterers, wall-makers, skilled men in the construction of works of irrigation; while most of the little tradesmen, the hucksters and fruitsellers, are Tatars, and many of the gardeners and drivers of carts. In the country they have passed from the nomadic stage, and are prosperous settlers upon the land. In the town of Erivan, where their numbers equal those of the Armenians, many of the largest gardens are owned by Tatar families, and many of the most prosperous houses of business are in Tatar hands. The degree of religious tolerance which they had achieved in that town was a matter of extreme astonishment to me when I remembered how often I had resented in vain the bigotry of the Persian Shiahs who are unable to enforce reciprocity in their country and to repay us for the pleasure and the profit which they may derive in inspecting the great religious buildings of Europe by suppressing and impounding the vicious fanatics who drive us from the doors of their mosques. It is a pleasure to offer a well-deserved tribute to that sense of respect for themselves and for their religion in which the Shiahs of Erivan give so striking a proof by admitting the stranger, whatever his creed, into the innermost courts of their spacious and beautiful mosque; and it is not imprudent to hope and to expect that the narrow path which they are still treading may widen as the years increase. On the other hand, it is not without disappointment that we may note the small progress they have hitherto made in availing themselves of the opportunities of education which the Russian Government have placed within their reach. In the High School of Erivan, among 260 scholars, only eighteen are Tatars, and it appears that only those among them show signs of serious application whose means are incommensurate with their appetite for vacuous repose. When the amiable headmaster of this well-managed school called upon his Armenian pupils to stand up, it seemed to me that the entire school rose in a body to their legs; but when the same command was addressed to the Tatars one little boy at the extreme end of the class confronted his seated schoolmates as the representative of the Tatar race.

The remaining peoples native to the country, at whom it is necessary before proceeding further to take a passing glance, are the Kurds, the Greeks, the Turks, the Georgians, and the Karapapachs. The Kurds within the Russian territory have not yet abandoned their nomadic habits; they are found as far north as the country about Batum, but their principal pasture-grounds are on the Turkish frontier and in Karabagh. The Kurds in the neighbourhood of Ararat take two main directions for their summer wanderings; one body proceeds towards the north, through the districts of Etchmiadzin and Alexandropol, and stations itself upon the highlands about Akhalzik and Akhalkalaki; the other takes an easterly course and enters the Government of Elizabetpol. The total number of Kurds in Transcaucasia is given as 100,000, of whom the larger part inhabit within the area with which we are concerned; the rest are found in greatest number in Karabagh. The Greeks have several villages, principally in the Government of Kars; those which I saw were prosperous, and the gay dresses and trinkets of the women betokened a somewhat higher stage of comfort than that which is usual in the country as a whole. These Greeks speak Turkish and are learning Russian; their versatile genius enables them to change nationality as we take a change of air. They are excellent miners and road engineers; the fine *chaussée* which has just been completed up the valley of the Toparavan river to Akhalkalaki was constructed by the skilled labour of Greek workmen. The small number of Georgians who are included in our area are found, as would be expected, in the valley of the Kur. In many places the race has received such a large admixture of Turkish blood that the inhabitants, although classed as Georgians, would call themselves

Turks, and are in religion Mussulman. In such villages I found much discontent with the existing order, and the evident outward signs of breaking up and decay. The Turks are found almost exclusively in the Government of the Kars, which is also the seat of a hybrid tribe called Karapapachs, or "Black Caps," from the black lambskin caps which they wear.

Not the least interesting element in the population of these Russian provinces is the Russian settlers themselves, the extreme fixed outpost of the northern empire and its tangible embodiment as a permanent force. The geographical situation of Russia, the habits which her rigorous climate imposes upon her people, would seem to point to this lofty plateau as a natural settling ground for her surplus population, where, without regretting the bracing keenness of their native air, they might realise that dream of northern peoples, the sun of a southern sky. The insignificant number of these colonists, while it seems to dispose of the theory that a colonial outlet is at present required by the economical condition of Russia, is the more remarkable when we examine the causes which have brought them from their home. They are those whom the national church of Russia has driven from her presence and her sight as an element of danger and contagion which requires to be removed and isolated. They bear the hated character of sectaries; Molokans and Duchoborians are the names under which the two sects who inhabit the plateau are known. I had occasion to pass through two zones of country in which these people live. The Duchoborians I met on the way from Akhalkalaki to Alexandropol, where their villages are situated on the high land from which the waters of the Kur diverge on the one slope, and those of the Arpa Tchai on the other; the Molokans between Kars and Kagizman, in that province which Russia has acquired the most recently and where the presence of colonists who belong to the ruling race may be supposed to constitute the strongest barrier against any attempt to wrest it from her rule. Whether the religious opinions which these people hold would dispose them, under all circumstances, to offer an active opposition to any change in merely secular allegiance, is a question which can be suggested rather than answered; it is more useful to inquire what influence they exercise, or are likely to exercise, upon the people and in the country of their adopted home. When we consider the social condition of the country, no circumstance is more striking than the complete separation of one race from another and the entire absence of a natural fusion of the different elements upon a common plane. Cases exist where, whether from a sense of advantage or by compulsion, the people of a particular district will have adopted the religion of their rulers and have come, by inter-marriage and closer intercourse, to be absorbed by the dominant race. We find an example in those villages in the Kur valley whose inhabitants, not much to their present advantage, adopted the Mohammedan religion when the Mohammedan power was supreme. But the differences which make for separation are only aggravated by such instances as these: prejudices become animosities, and the tendency to fusion, should it exist, is retarded rather than advanced. Had the Russian colonists come out to the country in search of a better provision than they were able to obtain at home, and, mixing freely with the people, taken wives from among them, the barriers which now separate them from their neighbours would have fallen in the course of time. But they came in the shape of whole villages of peasants, with their women and their children and their household goods: their communities are self-sufficient, and the law of Russia rivets isolation upon them by obliging the sectary, should he marry an Armenian wife, to bring up the children in the orthodox faith of Russia, which neither of the parents professes. The fact, too, that their villages are grouped together provides them with a larger area for social intercourse without obliging them to leave their own ranks. It is a bit of Russia let down in Armenia; the curious stare and pass on. The higher material standard of their life—their neat stone houses, their spacious carts, their ploughs and field implements—does not seem to have inspired the neighbouring Armenians to improve their agricultural methods and to emerge from their unhealthy burrows into the light and comfort of glass windows and solid walls of stone. At the same time, the Russian peasant does not stand so high in the scale of nature as to be able, even were his numbers larger, to master the other elements and mould them to his will. Unlike his neighbours, whom many centuries of oppression have accustomed to live on that extreme margin where life is just possible and no more, he is a man of method and order, who is well acquainted with the higher qualities of forethought, and care, and thrift. But his mood is passive and his ideals are low. I had heard that he was given to superstition and to the use of symbols which suggested Pagan rites. What I found was an extreme form of Protestantism engrafted on a child's nature, which finds it difficult to discriminate between the emotions of worship and love. In the village of Gorelovka, on the high land south-east of Akhalkalaki, there died, about seven years ago, a woman, who had made herself remarkable as the leader, both spiritual and in temporal matters, of the Russian sectaries who lived around. Her name was Lukeria Vasilievna Kalmakoff: she was obeyed and honoured like a queen. Her good actions, her devotion to their welfare, and the high example which she set, inspired simple people with an affection which partook in some measure of the nature of a religious cult. They built for her a little pavilion, where in summer she would live and teach, and planted it round with rose bushes and flowers, which she had brought them to cultivate and admire. The skill which they possess in carving wood they lavish upon this pleasant place; and it seems that the imputation which attributes to them the use of religious symbols was suggested by the figures of doves and by those ornaments of fancy with which they embellished their work. After her death both her house and the pavilion were preserved in the neatest order as though she inhabited them still; the flowers still bloom within the deep embrasures of windows in the simple room in which she was wont to receive the congregation and to lead their services of prayer. But the exaggeration of sentiment, however amiable, brings with it its own revenge: the reign of peace was to issue in discord, and discord in severe return to reason when the Russian official appeared upon the scene. Scarcely a year had elapsed from the time of her death when a pretentious successor arose, a boy who I believe claimed relationship with her and who assumed to be worthy to wear the mantle which had hitherto descended on none. The arrest of this youth by the Russian Government, and his expulsion to Siberia from the scene of strife, have served to allay the more dangerous passions of adversaries and partisans but the dissentions which he caused have not yet subsided, at present the dark side of a simple story, which seems to repeat in miniature the history of a larger world.

The Contemporary Review, Vol. 66 (July 1894): 91–107

The Armenian Question

II.—In Russia

H. F. B. Lynch

The close of the preceding paper was occupied by an analysis of the elements of the population inhabiting the plateau under the rule of Russia: it remains to measure the political system, under which the subject peoples live, both with reference to their dispositions towards it, and to the results material and moral which it may be considered to have achieved. It is also necessary, in order to obtain some clearer and more definite conception of the political condition of the Armenians in Russia, to proceed to an examination of the contemporary position of the Armenian Church, an institution which is at once a spiritual organisation, and the centre and stronghold of Armenian hopes, and which constitutes a factor of the highest importance in the consideration of the Armenian question as a whole.

The administration by Russia of Armenia has been brought to deal with races whose more recent political history consists in their passage from one domination to another; and the presence of discontent in certain quarters may be regarded as the inevitable outcome of the change. The Mussulman adherents of the Turkish dominion share with their neighbours of Turkish origin the humiliation of a fallen state, and their Turkish sympathies and connections, while they excite the suspicions of the Russian Government, dispose them to yield to the lightest pressure, and to cross the border into Turkish soil. The Armenians, who have supported Russia both in her Persian and in her Turkish wars, whose lands were swept by the tide of battle, and who can recall the memory of conflicts which extended even to the walls of their sanctuary, the cloister of Etchmiadzin, are inclined to temper their sentiments of gratitude with the consciousness of the services which they rendered, and which many among them may be disposed to consider have scarcely been adequately repaid. North of the plateau the Georgian races, whose kingdom harassed by Mohammedan peoples was driven to seek assistance outside, have not yet forgotten the disappointment of the hope which many among them had cherished that Russian intervention might assume the form of a protectorate rather than of a complete absorption of the Georgian element into the Russian State. But such regrets and disillusionments are but the familiar sequel to the constitution of empire upon a new soil, and human nature, under such circumstances, is more prone to count the loss than to recognise the gain. Nearly twenty years have now passed since Russia completed her subjugation of the Caucasus, whose peoples, untamed for so long a period, menaced the base of her advance; order and peace have been given to the country, and life and property are safe. Georgian children are no longer sold into slavery, and a middle class is forming amongst that people whose traditional relation to one another was that of noble and serf. An experience traveller, who visited the Armenian provinces in 1868, and passed through the more fertile regions of the country between Kars and Kagizman, has left on record a striking picture of the misery of those times. He was crossing the district of Shuragel, the ancient Shirac of the Armenians, and he speaks of deserted towns and villages, of Armenian peasants who clung to their ruined homes with a pertinacity of affection which neither poverty nor oppression could subdue, of the dispossession of the Christians by the Turkish Beys, and of the exactions and forays of the Kurds, which had curtailed agriculture and stifled industry, and had reduced both to the extreme limit on which human life is able to subsist. If, at the present time, the Armenian peasant gathers for himself the crops which he has grown, and the restless Kurd consults his safety by a sober respect for the law, it is to Russia that the people owe this deliverance from the license and anarchy of former years.

Had the Russian Government confined its energies to the amiable and disinterested task of establishing and maintaining public order as the guardian of a distracted country and the knight-errant who clears the land of thieves, it would have received the ungrudging gratitude of the Armenians, until, in the maturity of time, they had learnt to walk unaided and to cope alone with those lawless elements which might still resist the yoke of law. When that happy state had been accomplished it might only be natural to suppose that the progressive tendencies of the Armenian would lead him to take counsel with his neighbours and friends, to thank his protectors for past benefits, and to submit that the continuance of foreign tutelage was neither necessary nor desirable in the interests of the further advancement of a country to whose welfare they had contributed so much. To the Russians such a possible outcome of all their strenuous efforts was scarcely calculated to present so rosy an appearance as their ingenuous wards might have expected or hoped, and, if the advantages which the Russian empire offered were not sufficiently apparent by themselves, it was necessary to reform and to educate a perversity which sooner or later would yield. The Russians are not a commercial people, and would be content to see the Armenians conduct the commerce of their native country and develop its vast resources could they only collect the means; but only on one condition could they approve and encourage such activity: that their subjects should become Russians, and that the province should be joined to the Russian empire not only by the slender thread of annexation, but by the abiding tie of a common patriotism founded on a community of sentiment with themselves. But just at this point the real difficulties of empire arise. Races who stand on a low scale in nature have become absorbed into the Russian system by the exertion of little further energy than was required to ingrain in them that wholesome respect for their northern conqueror which the first sharp conflict had inspired; and the broad, expansive Russian character has been able to assimilate them to itself. It is different when, whatever the degree of degradation to which foreign oppression may have reduced them, a people is conscious of elements of vitality which impel them to higher ideals and standards than those which guide the powerful protectors under whom they have commenced to breathe. An empire which is confronted with such a situation has few alternatives among which to choose: if it cannot attract the subject people towards it, if it cannot accomplish that task of self-change which is more difficult than any which the exercise of empire may present, it will sooner or later be driven to adopt the more forcible expedients of coercion and repression and to lower the plane of civilised life by arresting the race for progress in which it was unfitted to compete.

Such a political situation can best be gauged and appreciated if we approach it from several different points of view. The nature of the Russian system, the attitude of the Armenians towards it, the true significance of such struggles in the larger issues of the outside world—such are various aspects of the general subject which it may be well in the interest of clearness to select. The kindness and hospitality of the Russian people, the amiable disposition which, in spite of official exigencies, makes them wish the traveller well, the real desire which a large and increasing number among them cherish for social progress at home, are features in the Russian character which the shortest acquaintance will recognise with respect, and which make for the true advance of Russia as a civilised nation among her peers. But the moment that the elements of progress in Russia have asserted their right to rule, the Russian system, as we know it, will die and disappear, and the laws which govern its existence will be subject to new conditions which may make for closer national concentration rather than for expansion abroad. Such reflections, although not new, are pertinent in this place. The element of finality, always relative, may justly appear in the eyes of many Armenians to be wanting to the political system and to the Government under which they live; and the abhorrence which that system inspires tempts them to convert the thought into a wish. The ultimate outcome of any revolution in the affairs of Russia is too uncertain, and the present evils of her Government are too substantial and apparent to induce them willingly to cast in their lot with the Russian people, and to abandon their hope of fulfilling their destiny in their own manner and by themselves.

A people whose commercial activity has brought them into contact with the most progressive races of Europe, and whose natural instinct renders them eager to assimilate Western thought can scarcely be blamed if they chafe under a system which assumes to establish the opinions they shall hold and to select the books which they shall read, and which subjects every action of their daily life to an inquisitorial control. Such methods are only the manifestations of a settled and uniform plan. The Armenian must sink his individuality and resign his initiative into other hands. He must imbue himself with the ideas which his rulers have prepared for him, and which may be opposed to the tendencies and the capacities with which he has been endowed. In such a prospect he recognises nothing to admire and much to fear. He sees the more capable races either driven from the Russian Empire or made the object of a constant jealousy and antipathy rather than of increasing respect. He feels the grip of an organisation which is founded on European methods, and commands all the resources which those methods provide, but he distrusts the hands which wield these weapons, and he is indifferent to the objects to which they are turned. Even the material results of such a system leave him little hope beyond what he has attained. The resources of the country still lie dormant, and the Government seems to lack the means or else the will to turn them to account. He sees the rich forests of the terrace land, which might yield a considerable revenue in return for an outlay which would be comparatively small, left unexploited and neglected, while shiploads of wood are entering the ports to supply the requirements of the oil industry. That industry itself he sees promoted by foreign capital in Russian guise, while the jealousy of all foreign capital has closed the door to its beneficent action in the provinces of his home. Not a mile of railway traverses the plateau, and there is scarcely a road upon it except such as are rendered necessary by the exigencies of the military arm. A few examples of the economical condition of these provinces may emphasise and explain such statements of a general kind. The two principal towns on the plateau are Alexandropol and Erivan: yet the road which joins them makes the colossal circuit by the northern shore of Lake Sevanga where it meets the main avenue of traffic between Tiflis and Erivan. From a point further west on this roundabout line of communication a road has been cut with the laudable object of shortening the distance between the two points; but the same contempt for the smaller and more irksome duties of life, to which we become accustomed in purely Eastern countries, has allowed it to fall into ruin by neglect, and we are met by the sight, so familiar to the traveller in the East, of yawning culverts and broken bridges and parallel tracks which have diverged and avoided the perilous surface of the metalled way. In Erivan itself, the chief town of a district where capital might be turned to the greatest advantage both to the people and to itself, it is impossible or difficult to find a foreign newspaper, while the industrial skill of the advanced races of Europe is not represented by a single foreign enterprise or, so far as I know, by a single foreign man of business or industrial employee. Persons who know the country well have told me that from the point of view of irrigation, so important a requirement in a land which suffers from want of rain, it has gone back since the times of the Persians, who are experts in such arts. As a consequence of this economical stagnation the spectacle is often presented in a country which enjoys security and repose of miserable villages, pinched by the scantiest resources and in appearance scarcely more prosperous than those on Turkish soil. I cannot help thinking that many of these evils are due to excessive centralisation in the Russian capital. When the Governor of the Trans-Caucasian provinces was a Grand Duke residing at Tiflis he was able to gratify his personal interest in their welfare by the exercise of a large measure of independent initiative and control; at the present day the smallest projects are referred to St. Petersburg, and are made subservient to the general economic policy which governs the empire as a whole. But such an explanation serves only to display and emphasise the character of the Russian system itself; how small are the prospects which it offers in return for the leaden yoke which it brings.

But the time has not yet come when Russia might consider it opportune to apply more drastic methods, and to impose upon the newest of her adopted children the full measure of a disciplinary *régime*. The larger part of the plateau still belongs to another master, whose lessons are not so attractive as to turn his pupils from the hope of change. It would be the worst policy to alienate by the example of severity sympathies which in former wars have stood her in such good stead. Meanwhile the Armenians have shown no signs of natural inclination to adopt Russian ways of thought. On the contrary, they have made use of the greater material prosperity of their country to draw more closely together and to apply themselves, now that they can better afford it, to the study of their national history and literature and of the purer language of former days. On the practical side they may well be satisfied with what they have already achieved. In every trade and in every profession, in business and in Government services, the Armenian sees himself without a rival and in full possession of the field. He equips the postal service by which you travel, and if you are so fortunate as to find an inn the landlord will be an Armenian. If the local governor attaches to your service the head of the local police it will be a stalwart Armenian in Russian uniform, who will either find you a lodging or a shady garden in which to erect your tents. If you remark on the way some well-built edifice which aspires to architectural design it will be the work of an Armenian builder from Alexandropol. In that town itself, where the Armenians are most numerous, the love of building, which was so marked a characteristic of their forefathers, has blossomed again among kinder circumstances: a spacious cathedral and several large churches stand among new stone houses fronted with ambitious façades. In Erivan each richer merchant has lodged himself in an agreeable villa, whose Italian architecture will rise from the shade of poplars and willows and fruit trees laden with fruit. The excellent wine which is found in Erivan is made according to the newest methods by an Armenian who has studied for two years in Germany the most modern appliances of the industry in Europe. The monetary transactions of the country are in the hands of Armenian bankers. The skilled workmen, jewellers, watchmakers, carpenters, are Armenians. Even the ill-miened officer of mounted frontier police, whose long association with the wilder elements, Kurds and robbers of small and large degree, has lent him the appearance of a chief of brigades, will bear, not much to its honour, an Armenian name. The large majority of the people do not speak Russian, or speak it very imperfectly. Indeed, were it not that the governors and chief police officials of large districts were Russian, and that Cossacks and Russian regular soldiers may here and there be seen, the traveller would not suspect that he was in a Russian province, and would go the way he listed with the most serene composure until he was rudely awakened by some abrupt collision with the Russian system and brought to his proper mind. As it is, the Armenian has edged out the Russian, and if peace were allowed its conquests unhindered he would ultimately rule in the land.

Such a situation is suggestive; and it ought not to surprise us if the Armenian has exercised his oriental imagination upon it in a manner less prudent than may be calculated to appeal to the slower veined races of the West. The idea of a modern Armenian kingdom has set the spark to that national enthusiasm which the perusal of his historical records has fed. The example of Eastern Europe has seemed to justify his speculations. When I come to deal with the

Turkish provinces, I shall endeavour to analyse the premisses on which such speculations must rest; but I do not believe that any such details have influenced his somewhat more general conceptions, and they are not pertinent here. I shall only remark that if we could leap all political obstacles and be given the run of the plateau as a whole, we should find as a basis for our political calculations, that the Armenians number about one-half of the total population with which we should have to deal. The vision of an independent Armenian State, could it ever, indeed, be realised, will not appeal to all minds alike. Many will see a real danger to human progress in the creation of these small States. The national sentiment they would place among those realised ideals upon which, as our civilisation widens, it is necessary to build anew. The magnitude of the conflict, should any of the greater nations enter the arena of war, acts as a wholesome preventive to ambitions which the small State is prone to indulge on the least pretence. The gratification of such ambitions causes bad administration and ends in bankruptcy, while few of the advantages which are offered by a great European empire can the people of a little country enjoy. Such considerations have great weight, and it would probably be well if, whenever it were practicable, our political actions were founded upon them; yet they scarcely apply to the present case. The Armenian, who is a convert to such views, might justly ask in what quarter he should look. The Turkish Empire will not even protect him, and thwarts his activity wherever it may; while, if he turns his eyes to Russia, he sees no prospects of material advantage which would enable him to rise above the economic stage to which he has already attained, and fails to find there, under present circumstances, any hope of moral or intellectual gain. Confronted with such an outlook, he seeks refuge within himself; and, if he consults his more sober perceptions, he will labour in silence and without ostentation to supply the requirements which his race still needs; to raise the peasant from his present degradation, to purify the Church, to promote the interest of his richer neighbours in work for the common good. These are the more legitimate ambitions which, however tedious, are certain of success, and which will establish, whatever be the revolution of politics, his right to influence the history of his country as the only stable element of progress in the East.

If, before concluding these reflections, we turn to the broader issues upon which such questions bear, and, having examined the comparative failure of Russia in Armenia, consider its significance to the larger world, we may find that the very strength of the Russian system as a powerful factor in international life derives from the same character which has denied her victory here. Had Russia through a natural process of attraction been able to draw towards her the higher races who stood on her path she would have been a greater nation, but perhaps a less formidable force. Round her she groups the less cultivated peoples, the nomads of Asia, the wanderers of the steppe, and arms them with the might of a European organisation which the intellect of Europe, impressed into her service, perfects as a weapon for her use. The dangers which such results threaten can only imperil the improvident and those whose nervous powers are unstrung; but the world has not yet advanced sufficiently to render those dangers unreal. The indolence of mind which shrinks from facing difficulties and leaves them to solve themselves is not the least element of weakness in her neighbours by which she profits and through which she grows; but the victory will now as always be given to those who unite with a higher civilisation a spirit of enterprise still healthy and powers still unimpaired.

I shall now pass without further preface to the second division of my subject, the bearing of which, on the general question, I have endeavoured at the commencement of this paper to define—namely, to a brief examination of the national Church of Armenians, its relations to the Russian authority, and its place in the national life.

The supreme ruler of the Armenian Church—the Catholikos Megerditch Khrimian—has for many years been in the forefront of the Armenian movement, and has more than any man inspired the Armenians with a sense of their own dignity and of the worthiness of their past. A people whose spirit has been crushed and whose manhood has been degraded gather new life from such a teacher and learn to become men. If some of his newest proselytes have displayed a zeal for self-assertion at which many have been inclined to smile, they may at least console themselves with the reflection that they are superior to those of their nation who, where possible, have denied their origin and pandered to a misplaced shame. The teacher in mien and person justifies his own lessons, and the race may well be proud of the example which in him is offered of itself.

At the interesting ceremony of his consecration, which took place at Etchmiadzin in October last, it seemed as if at the foot of Ararat the ancient spirit were still alive, and that the oil which descended upon that venerable head from the beak of a golden dove anointed a law-giver to his people who announced the divine word. The stately figure, the handsome and engaging face, fine brown eyes, and bold but regular features, above a full beard grown grey, are typical of the great personal beauty which distinguishes some Armenians, but which is often spoiled by a certain coarseness that grows with the advance of age. The refinement of a high purpose is written in every line of this interesting face, and few men unite to a nobler appearance a greater personal charm. Through a long life he has exercised a magnetic influence upon his countrymen, and, while he is loved and esteemed by all, he is the object of an almost superstitious veneration on the part of the humble and the poor. When I visited his native province, and, as it happened, was winding up the slopes of Mount Varakh to the ancient monastery where he lived so long, teaching in the school which he had founded, and often taking this very path from the cloister to preach in the little church of Hanguesner, on the outskirts of the gardens of Van, I was shown a spot where several years ago an assassin had lain in wait for him, deputed by his enemies to kill him as he rode unaccompanied towards the town. The story is told that when the man saw him and raised his rifle to his shoulder a sudden fear seized upon him, his arm shook like a wand, and he fell on his knees before his victim whose look he had been unable to bear. The simple surroundings among which his life has been passed recall a setting of a Bible story and place us in another age. As I alighted before the house which he once occupied in Van, and which he has now devoted to a school for girls, a man with the appearance and the clothes of a peasant offered to hold the reins of my horse; this was the nephew of the Catholikos and the brother of the refined and charming man who has accompanied his uncle to Etchmiadzin. At the time when within the walls of that famous monastery the ceremonies in connection with his accession to the patriarchal office were being celebrated, and the courts were occupied by the staff of the Emperor's representative, generals and Russian officials of high degree, I remember one evening to have been called into his bedroom where he had retired after the fatigues of the day. I entered a bare apartment: beside the wooden Eastern couch a single rug was suspended upon the whitewashed wall. The simplicity, which in our complex Western life, although often affected, seems unreal and untrue, sits naturally upon a personality which has grown upon this soil. As a writer he has expressed, through the vehicle of a prose which is full of poetry and emotion, conceptions of Scripture and thoughts upon the troubles of his times which might have sprung from the warm imagination of the early Christians in the East. The strong reality which he has given the old Armenian history is shown by an act which those who are wanting in sympathy with such a character might almost regard as childish. In his cloister of Varakh are buried the remains of Senacherim, king of the Van country, who abdicated his kingdom at the will of the Greek Emperor, and retired to the town of Sivas, in Asia Manor, which he received in exchange. Over his tomb a wooden altar had been built and decorated in a manner befitting royal rank; but such honours, paid to so unworthy a monarch, shocked the keen sense of the patriot in him; he stripped the frame of its ornaments, and the structure stands bare to this day. His activity has not been confined to the less contentious sides of life; it was he who pleaded the Armenian cause at the Congress of Berlin. He has often suffered for the fire of his sermons, and he was the easiest and most graceful speaker during the festivities which followed his elevation to the patriarchal throne. But perhaps the most striking quality in a character which presents much to admire and love is the ever-willing kindness and open-armed sympathy with which he shares the troubles of his fellow-men. As the throng pressed round him, the holder of their highest office, and endeavoured to kiss his hand or gain a glimpse of his face, the mind travelled back to that solemn scene in which the old Greek king received his stricken and distracted people: "Oh! my poor children, known to me, not unknown is the subject of your prayer; well I know that you are sore afflicted all; yet, though you suffer, there is not one among you who suffers even as I. For the grief you bear comes to each one alone—himself for himself he suffers—and to none other else; but my soul mourns for the State and for myself and you."[1]

The Church over which he has been called to rule is at once remarkable for its great antiquity and for the steadfastness with which through times of great trial its adherents have clung to it. It is not part of my present purpose to enter into an historical disquisition concerning the Armenian Church; but it is important to the student of modern politics to obtain some clear conception of its dogma and religious standpoint as compared with the Greek Church, the Church of Russia, on the one hand and that of Rome on the other. Both these churches have endeavoured with much persistence to effect a union of the Armenian Church with themselves; but, while the Church of Russia, still nourishes the hope that the whole body will come over to her, and, following the example of the neighbouring Church of Georgia, will seek within her bosom both spiritual and political repose, the Church of Rome has been obliged to content herself with the less splendid ambition of making individual proselytes chiefly upon Turkish soil. Without hazarding myself or the reader for too long a time on the tight-rope of religious dogma, the following account, which I received at Etchmiadzin of the distinctions and differences which separate the Armenian communion from those of Greece and of Rome, may serve to present a notion which will be more imperfect than untrue. While the Armenian Church was represented at the Council of Nice and accepts both its dogma and its canons, it, on the other hand, expressly rejects Chalcedon in which Council it took no part. It therefore differs both with the Greek and with the Roman Church on the subject of the natures of Christ. It holds that in Christ there is one person, one nature, one will, and one energy, and its liturgy expresses this dogma in a striking manner in the Trisagion, which runs: "Oh! God, holy God, mighty God, everlasting God, who wast crucified for us." The Armenians have therefore been branded as monophysites; but they reject the heresy of Eutyches with as much warmth as the Chalcedonists themselves. Except on this point their disagreements with the Greek Church are few: for instance, they mix no water in the wine and eat the bread without salt. It is rather in the part which religion takes in the daily life of the people that an important difference exists: you will not find in Armenian rooms those religious pictures, set in encrusted metal, which the Russians, children of the Byzantine Church, place in conspicuous positions and honour with daily reverence as emblems of their tutelary saints. On the other hand, as regards Rome, the dogmatic breach is deeper: the Armenian Church, in common with that of Greece, rejects the *Filioque*. Nor do the Armenians admit any cult of the Virgin Mary, although from the number of the churches in their country which are dedicated to the Mother of God it might be supposed that they also participated in this particular homage of the Church of Rome. The infallibility of the head of that Church they, in common with others, deny.

The relations of the Armenian Church to the Russian Government are regulated in a long document which received the signature of the Emperor Nicholas on March 23, 1836, and which, while reciting the internal constitution of the Church and the rules which govern the conduct of its own affairs, defines at the same time its privileges and its duties in connection with the Russian State. By this document Russia accords freedom of worship to the Armenian Church, and recognises her as the equal of the other religious bodies which subsist under the Emperor's rule. The clergy are exempt from all civil burdens; but of course they are subject to the civil law in purely civil affairs. The spiritual supremacy of the Catholikos of Etchmiadzin is recognised; but Russia emphasises and develops the constitutional position of the Synod in the government of the Church, and then very wisely frames regulations which aim at making the Synod subservient to herself. This Synod consists of four archbishops or bishops and four archimandrites all residing at Etchmiadzin; the Catholikos, if present at the sitting, presides. The Emperor fills up any vacancy in the body, two names being submitted to him by the Catholikos from which to make his choice. The Synod is to meet at least twice in each week; it addresses itself to the multifarious business which pertains to the general government of the Church. In matters which are purely spiritual, such as the proper doctrine of the Church on a particular point or its ritual, the Catholikos takes counsel with the Synod, but need not necessarily accept its advice; and such matters cannot be settled by the Synod during a vacancy in the patriarchal chair. But in all the other business of Church government which comes before the Synod the Catholikos has only the casting-vote, which his position as president confers. It is true he might act by Bull, and it is also true that according to the traditions of the Armenian Church the members of the Synod would be expected to obey him as the inferior obeys the superior priest. But such action, were it contrary to the resolutions of the Synod, would create a situation of great tension, and would in any case be a departure from the usual custom by which the supreme Patriarch acts through his Synod in the general government of his Church. The Synod must conduct its affairs according to the Russian laws which govern colleges, and it is under the supervision of the Minister of the Interior. The Russian Government also appoints a *Procureur* or Controller who speaks both Armenian and Russian and whose business it is to reside at Etchmiadzin and to supervise all the decrees of the Synod and pronounce upon their legality and their consonance with the powers which that body holds. These decrees are headed "By the order of the Emperor of Russia," the Emperor being the titular head of the Synod. The members of the Chancellery, who conduct the clerical work of the Synod, must be chosen with the approval of the Russian Controller, and at present they work under him. Nor is the Catholikos in a position of complete freedom even when he acts with his Synod. He cannot punish a member of Synod or even a diocesan bishop without notifying his intention to the Emperor and receiving his consent. If he happens to have any matter pending with any foreign State he must communicate with the Emperor through the governor of the province of Erivan. If he wishes to leave Etchmiadzin for more than four months he must obtain the permission of the Emperor through the Minister of Interior; nor can he sanction the absence of a bishop abroad for more than the same period without having previously consulted the Imperial will. Every bishop of a diocese is appointed by the Emperor, to whom the Catholikos presents the names of candidates. But perhaps the most serious, because the most insidious, weapon against the independence of the Armenian Church is the provision which enacts that a year shall elapse between the death of a Catholikos and the election of his successor. This clause was accepted with singular want of foresight in a time when travelling was even slower than it is now, and when it was difficult to collect the delegates, who elect the two candidates among whom the Emperor chooses, before a considerable time. In practice it is difficult for a Catholikos to take up his position immediately after his election even if the Emperor confirms with the greatest promptitude the candidate who has most votes, and, as a consequence, a long *interregnum* ensues during which it is possible for the Government to play off one party against another, and to obtain those concessions which might be resisted during the occupancy of the chair.

The method of electing the supreme Patriarch is set forth in the same document. On the decease of a Catholikos the Synod sends invitations to all Armenian dioceses in Russia and elsewhere, calling upon them to name each two deputies, one clerical and one lay, who shall repair to Etchmiadzin within a year. There, in the Church of the Illuminator, they first elect four candidates, and then proceed to choose two names from among this number, which are submitted to the Emperor through the Governor of the Caucasus. There are only six dioceses in Russia, and the number is not specified of those in foreign parts. As a general rule, there are fifty-two dioceses in Turkey and two in Persia—namely, those of New Julfa and Tabriz. The Armenian communities in the other parts of the world have not as yet sent delegates. In addition to these deputies from the dioceses the members of the Synod and seven of the oldest archimandrites in the community of Etchmiadzin are *ex-officio* members of the elective assembly. In that assembly, therefore, the balance of power lies with the clericals. The Emperor, having signified the choice which he has made and in which he is influenced by the number of votes which either candidate has received, confirms the new Patriarch in his office and receives his oath of allegiance through a representative whom he sends to the patriarchal seat. The Patriarch is then consecrated according to the customs of the Armenian Church.

I have dwelt upon these matters at the risk, perhaps, of becoming tedious, because the Armenian Church occupies a position of a special and peculiar nature in the life of the Armenian people, and is a factor of the first importance in the politics of the country at the present time. In the first place it is the only stable institution which the Armenian people possess. In the next place it provides them, speaking generally, with whatever leaders they have. If we allow our historical sense to correct and temper our democratic tendencies we must recognise the salutary influence which a ruling class must exercise upon the life of a nation by reason of its permanent traditions, by the habits of mind which it inherits rather than acquires, and by the appearance at once glamorous and solid which it presents to the outside world. No people, perhaps, have stood in greater need of such a class of natural leaders than the Armenians. How much of the harassing friction, how many of the silly annoyances to which their daily life is subjected might have been mitigated or even avoided had they been able to follow men who, while intimately bound up with their interests, could speak with the authority of a recognised position and act with the experience and discretion which long exercise of that authority had ingrained! Nothing is at first sight more surprising than the complete want of tact with which so intelligent a people have conducted their relations with the powerful States under whose protection—or oppression—they live. It may be too general a statement, but it is nevertheless materially true, that those who have assumed to speak for them are either cringeing time-servers who inspire contempt, or windy fanatics who excite resentment in their rulers and promote an ill-founded alarm. Nor are the conditions favourable for the rise to eminence of an individual behind whom might be ranged the solid ranks of the strong and prosperous middle class. The Church alone, at once an asylum and a stronghold from which to move, is capable, if provided with the proper material, of guiding and controlling the people and of leading along the surest channels a movement which must necessarily be peaceful and which must look to moral progress for success. But however patriotic the Armenian clergy as a body may be, and however keenly they may share the national hopes and fears, it can scarcely be denied that they compare most unfavourably with the better among their lay brethren in capacity, in education, and in the grade to which they belong. In the country they are ignorant peasants chosen by the villagers from among their own ranks; in the towns they are not the most promising scholars whom the schools send out into the world. On no better task could the present Catholikos bestow an assiduous activity than on the reform of this dangerous state of things. To no more essential object could the richer Armenians both in Russia and Turkey contribute some necessary support. The career must be made a little more attractive than present circumstances permit it to be. If ever in every larger village there should reside an enlightened teacher who is able to raise the life of his congregation and to minister to their new needs, not only would the social welfare of the whole people be promoted, but an organisation which is of the greatest contemporary value to the Armenians and on which the fabric of their nationality is based would be saved from the extinction which must ultimately overtake it should it continue as it is today.

Intimately bound up with the Church and deriving their organisation and permanent revenue from it, the Armenian schools present an exception to the general school system of the Russian Empire, but amply justify their separate existence by the good work which they do. Although the advantages which they offer are as yet very imperfectly extended to the country districts, still, where they exist, their lay teachers are usually the best educated among the Armenians, while many have received their instruction in Europe, principally in Germany, and are men of far higher attainments than the standard of teaching, which is limited by Government, requires. It will not surprise us, when we consider the uniformity at which continental educational methods aim and the intimate connection between public instruction and the State which the Russian Empire requires, that the career of these schools has been chequered and that their prospects of continued existence are not bright. These schools are recognised in the long document which I have already cited in connection with the Armenian Church, and they, therefore, stand upon a constitutional foundation in the Russian State. But the nature of the education which they offer is there defined to be religious and moral, although it is added, presumably with reference to the seminaries, that it is most important for the clerical calling to know the language, the history, and the geography of Russia. Whatever the intention of the framers of this document may have been, it is certain that for a long period after its promulgation, and until the Government took measures to limit their scope, the schools which are attached to many of the Armenian churches provided a high standard of elementary education which was by no means confined to religious instruction or to the preparation of candidates for the Church. The degree of instruction which a school offers in Russia is defined and understood by the number of classes it has. Each class represents a standard and not a convenient numerical division of pupils, and of these classes the lowest is the first. Schools of five classes were often attached to the Armenian churches, and the scholars who desired to pursue their studies still further passed to the so called religious seminaries which each diocese is permitted to maintain. In this manner it was possible for an Armenian youth to receive all but the highest university education in his native language and in schools of his own Church. In 1884, during a vacancy of the patriarchal chair, a Ukase was promulgated which aimed a serious blow at these schools. Every Church school which has more than two classes is placed on the same basis as a private school, that is to say, the whole of the instruction which it gives is required to be conducted in Russian language. In the case of a school of two classes only the lessons may be given in the Armenian language, but it is obligatory to teach the Russian language and, where general geography and history are included, the history and geography of Russia must be taught in Russian. The *curriculum* of a school must be submitted to, and approved by, the Russian educational authorities, who are also invested with the right to apply to the Armenian spiritual government for the dismissal of a teacher of whom they do not approve, and, failing redress in this quarter, they can place the matter before the Governor of the Caucasus, who can order as he thinks fit. The seminaries, one of which is attached to each diocese and which provide a higher education, are exempted from the provisions of this decree, but their object is defined to be the preparation of clergymen to meet the requirements of the Armenian Church.

The bitter feelings which this decree aroused among the Armenians have not yet subsided, and the policy it foreshadows is plain. Yet the Armenians are not altogether without blame in the matter, and their whole treatment of this question has been deplorably wanting in skill. The Synod did not accept the decree, but represented that its consideration should be allowed to stand over until the new ruler had been chosen, and had taken possession of the vacant chair. The Government replied by closing the schools. Nor were they again opened until, in 1886, the new Catholikos Makar consented to agree to its provisions with some small concession as to the meaning which should be attached to the limit of two classes which had been imposed. It could scarcely be expected that the Government would for long sit quiet while Armenian children were being brought up in ignorance of the Russian language and of the institutions of the Russian people, yet no adequate but voluntary measures had been taken to supply them with this necessary need. At the present day an order is on record, which, although neglected on a former occasion, has been renewed, that every teacher in an Armenian school shall be furnished with a certificate from the Russian pedagogic seminary, and shall have passed in the Russian language the necessary examination which entitles him to receive this award. This order will come into force during the present year, but how many of the teachers will have complied with its provisions, or be within measurable distance of complying with them is a matter upon which I prefer not to speculate, but to guard in silence the impression which I received. Meanwhile, the Russian school system is extending itself in the country, and you may visit schools in which the teachers, although Armenians, have been students in the Russian pedagogic seminary at Erivan. In these schools the instruction is given in Russian and is governed by the general regulations which are in force in Russian elementary schools. The Armenian Church schools are limited to two classes, and the higher schools which formerly existed have not been re-opened under the new conditions which have been established by the decree.

If, from this plain statement of fact, I may be permitted to proceed to a suggestion, it will be that the Armenians should to a far greater extent make use of their educational organisation to supply the undoubted requirements of their Church. It is not enough that the members of their monastic order should have received a seminarial education; no clergyman should be ordained who has not attained the same or a similar grade. The academy at Etchmiadzin is admirably equipped to provide the centre for such instruction, and there are seminaries at Erivan and Tiflis. I shall not examine too curiously how many of the scholars of these institutions proceed to holy orders of their Church; yet that Church is the real and tenable stronghold of Armenian nationality, and might be made a more efficient minister to social and national needs.

The Contemporary Review, Vol. 66 (September 1894): 435–56

The Armenian Question

III. (Conclusion.)—In Turkey

H. F. B. Lynch

In the course of the two preceding papers I have endeavoured to present a description which, although general, may perhaps be sufficient of the Armenian country as a whole. I have also touched upon the importance of the Armenian Question in its relation to the larger politics of the nearer East. But the greater part of the space at my disposal has been devoted to a study of the conditions political and social which prevail upon that portion of the plateau which lies within Russian territory and which at once illustrate and determine the measure of progress achieved by the Armenians under Russian rule. Such a discussion, although it may appear academical, is, in my opinion, not only indispensable to any adequate presentation of the whole subject, but is also of the highest practical importance in its bearing upon the Armenian problem in Turkey. In these Russian provinces the Armenian element, strengthened by continuous emigration from Turkey, composes the principal part of the population, and the Armenians have been able at least to give earnest of whatever capacities they possess. I was so much impressed with the results of their activity and with the variety of interest which their country presents that, when once the ascent of Ararat had been accomplished, I resolved to prolong my journey across the frontier and to devote the autumn and winter to a tour in the provinces of Van and Erzerum.

The line of the Russian frontier, as it marches with the borders of Turkey and of Persia, corresponds with a remarkable geographical feature in the configuration of the plateau. The middle course of the Araxes waters a vast plain which, on the northern skirts of the Ararat system in the neighbourhood of Erivan, lies far beneath the normal level of the table-land, and, varying in breadth as the long volcanic ranges approach or recede from the river, extends to the Caspian Sea. This great depression of the surface is the leading feature of the country on the east of Kagizman, West of that town the ranges close together and present the appearance of a surging ocean still lashed by the violence of the storm; the impetuous torrent of the Upper Araxes, coming from the neighbourhood of Khinis, breaks from one to another trough as it threads these serried ridges and reverses the direction of its former course. This confused and troubled mountain scenery has probably been caused by the action of denudation, operating upon the higher levels of the plateau on a scale which is magnificent and immense, and contrasts with the solemn restfulness of the landscape through which the river, exhausted by canalisation, flows eastwards slowly to the sea. Between the long and almost horizontal outline of Alagöz on the north, and the serrated summits of the Ararat system on the south, this noble plain of the Araxes widens as it opens to the east, and attains perhaps its greatest dimensions just west of Erivan. At that point the massive fabric of Ararat, advancing from its satellite system alone, attains the great elevation of nearly 17,000 feet above the sea; and the whole structure of the mountain from the base to the dome of snow may be seen across a space, which is comparatively level, at a distance of nearly 50 miles. From Kagizman to the Caspian this depression which marks the Araxes valley appears to bisect the plateau into two distinct halves, and this valley is separated from the country on the south, at first by the rugged chain of Ararat, and then by the mountains of Azerbaijan. Thus the territory of Russia is divided from that of Turkey and of Persia by no artificial line; while the majestic slopes of Ararat itself are the meeting-place of three empires which come from the Mediterranean, the Baltic, and the Persian Gulf.

Several passes lead from the valley of the Middle Araxes across the wild range which I have called the Ararat system, and which is known in the country under the name of Aghri Dagh. That by which I travelled attains a height of over 8000 feet, and descends into Turkish territory at the plain of Alashkert. The Sultan still holds the greater portion of the plateau, and some of its richest districts are subject to his rule. If Russia is supreme in the valley of the Middle Araxes, the fertile country about Lake Van belongs to Turkey; the plains of Mush and Bulanik and, further west, the populous plain of Kharput are all within the Turkish border, and compose an area of grain-growing country which is capable of supporting a population far more numerous than that which it at present maintains. On the north of these plains, of which those of Mush and Kharput are the least elevated, although the plain of Mush is situated at an altitude of over 4000 feet above the sea, the level of the country rises, the plateau gathers into a compact and solid mass which divides the two branches of the Euphrates, and constitutes the roof of the three watersheds of the Black Sea, the Caspian and the Persian Gulf. On the section between Mush and Erzerum the true character of the great table-land is displayed in a wholeness and simplicity of feature, which it is difficult to mistake. You are here at the heart of the whole geographical system, at the culminating point from which the waters gather to start on their long and strenuous journey to different and distant seas. It is over a wide expanse of level land, clothed for the greater portion of the year with a continuous canopy of snow, that the prospect ranges to distant chains of mountains whose summits are scarcely higher than the ground upon which you stand. The surface of the upland has been broken by volcanic action which has reared the crater of the Bingöl Dagh, or mountain of a thousand springs; yet that mountain is but a minor incident in a large and comprehensive plan which I shall endeavour on a future occasion to analyse according to the conception of it which I have formed, but which only bears on my present purpose in its leading and ultimate results. On the west and east as well as on the north and south of this section of the plateau between Mush and Erzerum, the processes of denudation must have operated on a scale which the existing natural conditions make it difficult to conceive. Not only have these processes contributed to form that confused mountain scenery which on the west and east of this central section distinguishes the head waters of the Araxes and the valley of the Western Euphrates below Erzerum, but they have also resulted in a natural phenomenon which no traveller can have omitted to remark. It often occurs that the banks of the rivers are bordered by plains which are perfectly flat, and which present an appearance exactly similar to the dry bed of a lake. The usual direction of these plains is that of the drainage, namely, east and west, and the chains of mountain which enclose them are in reality but the rim of higher levels, the banks of these gigantic cuttings in the surface of the table-land. The most noticeable example of this phenomenon is presented by the valley of the Western Euphrates just north of Erzerum, but the feature is characteristic of the whole plateau and distinguishes it from the land of terrace, where chain succeeds chain in rapid succession in obedience to lateral forces, and to the law of shrinkage and fold. I should not insist on these natural features if they had not contributed in so marked a manner to determine the character of the different peoples with whom we are here concerned. Whatever opinion we may hold of the value of political geography—and indeed there can scarcely exist another study which is so often and so wilfully misused—the large scale on which Nature has worked in Asia, and the great differences both of climate and of natural conditions which distinguish the lofty highlands from the buttress ranges which support them, and from the low alluvial plains, have combined with ethnological causes to produce a large correspondence of distinct geographical areas with natural and important political divisions in the distribution of the human race. It is therefore useful for our present purpose to define in a convenient manner the limits of the plateau within Turkish territory on the north and on the south. On the north, and on the section between Erzerum and the coast, the plain between Baiburt and the Vavuk Pass, which appears to belong to the same characteristic formation as that which has just been described, and on which the remains of ancient Armenian churches still testify to the historical extension of Armenia to this point, may be regarded as the meeting-place of the plateau with the ranges of the northern terrace land. On the south the serrated mountain system, which, like the gloomy wall of a Norwegian fiord, overhangs the southern shore of Lake Van, and which is continued along the plain of Mush and westwards to the neighbourhood of Kharput, has already been mentioned in these papers as the northern limit of the southern terrace zone.

In estimating the population of these Turkish provinces I have found it convenient to follow the method which was adopted in the case of the Russian territory, and to select those existing governmental divisions which correspond in a general manner to the area of the plateau. The area of these governmental divisions composes the political area with which we shall deal. For this purpose I have taken the following Governments, or divisions of Governments: the whole of the Government of Erzerum, that portion of the Government of Van which constitutes the Sandjak or governmental division of Van, the whole Government of Bitlis with the exception of the Sandjak of Sert, which belongs to the terrace land. On the west I have included that small portion of the Government of Diarbekr which is formed by the Caza or governmental sub-division of Palu, and the whole of the Government of Kharput, which includes Deyrsim with the exception of the Sandjak of Malatia. The superficial measurement of the area obtained in this manner amounts to about 42,000 square miles, which compares with the figure of 22,000 given in the first paper as the area of the Russian portion of the plateau within the boundary there defined. Although the Turkish territory, thus delimited, overlaps on the south with the terrace land and includes the heads of the great passes which lead down from the plateau to the Arab plains, yet I think it will be found that we are avoiding a serious error which even some of our ablest consular officials appear to me to have made. When Mr. Goschen was actively pursuing his inquiries and endeavouring, in connection with the Armenian Question, to discover *sure ground upon which to build*, the statistics which were supplied to him not only represented the population of the plateau but also included in one and the same estimate extensive districts which lie outside it and which present conditions so entirely dissimilar as to render such a co-ordination misleading, at least for those purposes of practical construction which were present to his mind. A single instance of such error will illustrate what I mean. The Government of Van includes the Sandjak of Hakkiari, a wild and seldom visited region which belongs to the terrace land. It is inhabited by Kurds, who for the greater part are in the pastoral and nomadic stage, and by Nestorian Christians, whose ancestors fled from persecution to these mountains and who are scarcely more civilised than the Kurds. So difficult of access is this rugged country, and so remote from the seat of Government are the principal centers which it contains, that it would be a work of no small difficulty to administer it efficiently from Van. As a consequence it enjoys a practical immunity from authority, a boon much appreciated by the Kurds. I have purposely omitted this division of the Government of Van from the area and from the statistics with which we are concerned; yet it has been included by others in their estimate of the population of the Armenian provinces, although the number of Armenians who may have filtered into it must be infinitesimally small. The problems which are presented to a governor on the plateau by reason of the difference in religion and in habits of the peoples over whom he is called to rule are quite sufficient to absorb his attention without the addition to his jurisdiction of districts which, if Russia were mistress of the country, would be constituted into a military government and subjected to military law.

In the case of these Turkish provinces I have found it a task of the greatest difficulty to arrive at a statistical estimate of the population upon which it might be possible to rely. The results which I am about to present are the outcome of a long and laborous investigation pursued in the country itself, in which I was sometimes aided, but more often bewildered, by the lists which I had in my possession, and which have either already been published, or were furnished to me by private friends. In the absence of a census conducted on scientific principles any figures can only be approximately correct. Two possible sources of information exist which, in the first instance, it is natural to consult. The first are the official lists which are published in the almanacs of each Government, and which profess to give the numbers both of Mohammedans and of Christians inhabiting each Caza or administrative sub-division. The second are the books of the diocesan authorities who, under the 14th and 96th Articles of the so-called Armenian constitution, are enjoined to maintain complete records of all births and deaths among Armenians in the diocese, and to provide copies to the Central Bureau of the Patriarchate in Constantinople. But the diocesan authorities are chary of recording information which conflicts with the number of Armenians who are placed for purposes of taxation upon the Government lists, and these lists themselves are founded upon a system whose essential tendency it is to underrate the number of the population, Mohammedan and Christian alike. Owing to the seclusion of women in the East no serious attempt is made to count the female population; while in the case of males, the figures in the official statistics derive from the military census, which is at best a very imperfect record, and which each man strives his utmost to evade. All Mohammedan males are liable to be enrolled in the army, while the Christians are obliged to pay an annual tax which exempts them from military service, and which is incident at birth. In the case of the sedentary population it is probable that the Christians evade this census to a greater extent than their Mohammedan neighbours: for the budget of a Christian family is immediately menaced by the birth of a male child. On the other hand, there are extensive districts on the southern portion of the plateau in which the Kurdish tribes inhabiting them are in a state approaching independence, and have never been counted at all. The officials lists must for these reasons be used with much discrimination and care. In one Government they will be compiled with some measure of completeness; in another they will be defective as regards the Armenians; in yet another as regards the Kurds. In addition to this source of information there are the estimates which have been made in particular districts by private people engaged in business, and who know their own district well. The figures which emanate from the Armenian Patriarchate, and which have found their way into the Blue Books, have evidently been designed to subserve political purpose, and may be dismissed under a sense of disappointment and disgust. Before presenting in summary form the results at which I have arrived, two points suggest themselves to me as calling for remark. In the first place I am satisfied that the total population of the country is in excess of the figure which I give. That figure only shows a percentage of population to the square mile of about 30; in the Russian provinces, which can scarcely be called populous by comparison, although they probably contain less waste land, the percentage is about 47. Secondly, while the greatest care has been taken to get the totals of the different peoples at least correct in the proportion which they bear to one another, it is probable in the case of the Armenians and of the Kurds that even for this purpose the figures are a little too low. I have preferred to content myself with reproducing the statistical materials which, however imperfect, I consider the best, and only to mention in this connection the general impression which I have received. The population of the plateau within Turkish territory for the area already delimited may be conveniently divided in the following manner:[1]

Mussulmans	Turks (Sunni Mohammedan)	442,946
	Kurds (Sunni Mohammedan and Kizzilbash)	410,812
Christians	Armenians (Gregorians; some Roman Catholics and Protestants)	387,746
	Greeks	4,604
	Others	6,733
	Total	1,252,841

It may also be useful to add these figures to those which I have given for the Russian provinces. The population of the whole plateau within the political limits which I have traced will then be represented by the following figures:

Armenians	906,984	Russians	28,844
Turks	489,931	Others	84,439
Kurds	479,67	Total	2,348,551
Tatars	306,310		
Greeks	52,367		

Among the inhabitants of these Turkish provinces who are classed as Mussulmans there exist considerable differences both of race and of religion; but for our present purpose it is most useful to distinguish them according as they are Turkish or Kurd. Under the former name I have counted the Mussulman population of the northern portion of the Government of Erzerum. Or, to use more specific language, of the entire Government of Erzerum, with the exception of the Sandjak of Bayazed and the Cazas of Khinis, Keghi, and Terdjan. I have also included as Turkish one-half of the Mussulman inhabitants of the Caza of Passin. In the Governments of Van and of Bitlis the only portion of the population which I have thought it safe to number as Turkish are the Mussulmans in the towns of Van, Bitlis, and Mush: as citizens in governmental centres they are attached, if not by a common origin, at least by a common character and common sympathies, to the interests of the ruling race. In the case of the Government of Kharput and of the governmental division of Palu I have been unable to verify by general acquaintance the estimates which I have adopted as the best: these estimates make the Turkish about as strong as the Kurdish element in the Sandjak of Kharput, and a little less numerous in the Caza of

Palu. That part of the Mussulman population of the Sandjak of Deyrsim who are counted as adherents of Government may most usefully be classed as Turkish and have been included in the roll of Turks. In the several Governments the remainder of the Mussulman inhabitants compose the total which has been given for the Kurds.

To express these results in general language, we may say that the seat of the Turkish population is the country on the north of Erzerum, while the Kurds inhabit the more southerly districts which extend to the southern terrace land. But what is the meaning of the name Turkish, which has been used to distinguish the one from the other element? We must certainly guard ourselves from the danger of attributing to a convenient political designation an ethnological sense. We are justified in declaring that the Mussulman inhabitants of the northern districts of the Government of Erzerum are not of Kurdish origin; on the other hand, the ground is less tenable if we suppose that they belong to the Turkish race. How large an admixture of Turkish blood may flow within their veins is a question which it is impossible to determine: it was rather the fertile country on the west of the Euphrates that presented the most attractive settling ground to the invading hordes of Turks. I am given to believe that a considerable number derive from the widely spread Georgian family; but that family has here mixed with other race elements of which the Turkish is one. In what pertains to national solidarity, in the possession of common interests and common sentiments, these Mussulman inhabitants of the northern districts may justly be classed as Turks. But even this statement is subject to exception and can not be universally applied. Just as in the northern zone of terrace there still exist whole districts of which the inhabitants have adopted the Mohammedan religion, but retain their essential affinity to the Greek race to which they belong, so on the plateau itself among the ranks of the Mussulmans may be found considerable aggregates of people who, although of Armenian origin, profess the dominant creed. In the northern province an important instance of this change in religion rather than in nationality is found in the district of Tortum between Erzerum and the town of Olti; the Mussulman inhabitants of the district are said to be the descendants of the ancient Armenian families who are known to have inhabited it within historical times.

While the Turkish inhabitants are engaged in agriculture and in those pursuits of urban life which attach to the service of Government or of individuals, or to the less ambitious among the requirements of industry and commerce, the Kurdish population, on the other hand, present a variety of social development which includes both the sedentary and the nomadic state, the organisation of the commune and the tribe. A people who were known to a remote antiquity and whose character is already sufficiently familiar in Europe, the Kurds who inhabit the plateau are not only distinguished from one another according to the plane of social life to which they have attained, but are divided by essential differences of language and of creed. From the neighbourhood of the town of Sivas in Asia Manor to beyond Malatia on the south, and between the two branches of the Euphrates to the vicinity of Mush, the Kurds, although classed in the official lists as Mussulmans, neither practise the orthodox religion nor speak the same dialect as their neighbours of the kindred race. Branded throughout the nearer East under the opprobrious name of Kizzilbash they harbour a sullen hatred of the Turkish Government, whose attempts to convert them to orthodoxy they resent; while towards the Christians they are drawn by the impulse of a common antagonism to the existing order, and by the respect in which they hold the Christian religion, in the person of whose Founder they recognise an incarnation of God. Their religion, so far as we know it, bears the impress of the Aryan mind, which seeks for a human embodiment of the Deity; they invest with divine attributes Moses and Jesus, Mohammed and Ali. Their language, although a branch of the Kurdish, contains an admixture both of Persian and Armenian words, and is said to differ so greatly from the prevailing dialect of the Kurdish tongue that those who are familiar with the one are unable to understand the other. While they practise the rite of circumcision and have adopted certain of the observances of Islam, the contempt in which their religion is held by Mussulman neighbours of the Sunni sect disposes them against the dominant creed in which they recognise the most dangerous enemy of their own peculiar faith. In brief, they constitute a separate element in the Kurdish population of the plateau, and the numerical value of this element may be placed at a third of the total figure which I have given for the Turkish Kurds. Their geographical position between and about the two branches of the Euphrates invests them with some contemporary importance from a military point of view; and they hold the wild and mountainous country on the south of the headquarters of the Turkish Army Corps at the town of Erzingan. In this district, which is known under the name of the Deyrsim, they have long resisted and continue to resist the imposition of the Turkish yoke. They are here in the tribal and pastoral state, but they have been obliged, by the rigour of the climate, to build houses, and they cultivate small strips of land. In the country on the west and east of the Deyrsim the Kizzilbashes are peaceful and industrious peasants, of whom most travellers have spoken with respect.

If we draw on the map an imaginary line from Mush through Erzerum towards the sea, the Mussulman population of the Turkish provinces are distributed in the following manner over the area of the plateau. On the north of Erzerum, and on either side of this line, the Turkish population extend from the Russian border on the east, along the banks of the Western Euphrates on the west, to its junction with the eastern branch. The country south of Erzerum and on the west of this line is the seat of the Kizzilbash Kurds, while on the east are situated the Kurds who profess the orthodox religion, and speak the prevailing dialect of Kurdistan. The territorial extension of the Kurdish people varies as the forces of order are strengthened or decline, but their original home and natural habitation are the mountains of the terrace land. From the Euphrates on the west to the Persian Gulf upon the south the zone of buttress ranges which support the plateau of Armenia and Persia, and which we know at first under the name of Taurus and then under that of Zagros, is inhabited by tribes of Aryan origin, who are distinguished by considerable variations in dialect and in religion, but who present the common characteristic of an inveterate aversion to settled life and to the imposition of the yoke of law. Their manner of living is directly determined by their geographical position. As spring develops into summer and the yellow drought creeps higher and higher up the slopes of the mountain sides, they ascend from one to another step, from a lower to a higher chain, and arrive, perhaps at the approach of autumn, on the fringe of the table-land. When at length the season is verging upon winter the migration southwards begins. A continuous throng of sheep and goats and horses and weather-worn people of either sex and every age flows slowly down the blighted country, filing by tortuous tracks between the boulders or pausing, about the noonday hour, by the bed of a shaded stream. At the foot of the range, on the verge of the vast alluvial plains through which the Tigris winds, is placed their winter encampment: their tents are sufficient shelter against the climate of the low country, which even through the colder months is temperate and mild. These yearly migrations of the Kurdish tribes are not conducted without great suffering on the part of the settled population; their granaries are plundered by the shepherd army, and the land which they might have cultivated is occupied by the nomads during winter as pasture for their flocks. But this is a problem which belong to the land of terrace, and which applies in a less essential manner to the population of the plateau. On the plateau, these Kurds are an alien element; the great distance of their pastures from the plains of the Tigris makes it difficult for them, if not impossible, to pursue their usual migration; the rigorous winter obliges them to discard their tents and inhabit villages, and to take the first step towards a more settled order where further development may justly appear to them incompatible with their tribal organisation and their independent life.

We may place at the kernel of the Armenian Question in Turkey the difficulties which arise from the presence of this Kurdish population upon the plateau. It is true that a considerable number among them have become industrious cultivators and subsist on the fruits of their own toil. According as the period which separates them from their former life is long or short, or the name of their more lawless kinsmen is despised or respected, these peasants will answer the traveller who inquires to what people they belong either by replying that they are Osmanli or by owning to their being Kurds. In the first case they rank themselves with the settled Turkish population; in the second they acknowledge the bond which attaches them to the free life of the tribe. But the weight of this agricultural element lies in the scale of peace; it is otherwise with those Kurds who retain to the full their tribal organisation and who pasture their flocks on the lofty highlands which extend to the plain of Erzerum. It is possible that from a remote period the nomads of the terrace land may have advanced the limit of their summer journey beyond the plain of Mush to return at the approach of winter to the neighbourhood of Diarbekr. How far their migration should be extended would be determined by the distance which separated them from their winter quarters and by the degree of resistance which the settled peoples might be able to offer to their unwelcome approach. The fall of the feudal system in Turkey and the decline of the power of the Turkish Beys may no doubt have contributed in a sensible manner to open a breach to the Kurds; but it appears that a powerful colony of this people were brought to their present seats through a definite act of public policy on the part of the Turkish Power. After the defeat of the Persians in the plain of Chalderan in 1514 it became necessary to arrive at a permanent settlement of the Kurdish provinces; and it formed part of the plan pursued by Edrisi, the distinguished Minister of Selim the First, and himself a Kurd of Bitlis, to remove a portion of this turbulent people from the country of their home and to settle them along the new frontier of Turkey in the districts bordering upon Persia and Georgia which had been acquired from the Shah. It is said that they were granted a perpetual immunity from taxation on the condition that they would act as a permanent militia upon the border which had been given them to guard. Neither the evidence of subsequent history nor the contemporary political situation upon the plateau can be taken to have established the wisdom of a policy which appears to have overrated the capacity of the Kurds whether for benefit or for harm. On the one hand, by adding to the area inhabited by them, the Turkish Government seems rather to have increased the difficulties which have always beset their efforts to hold this people in check; and, on the other, their experience of the value of this militia can scarcely be so pleasant a memory as their persistent continuance in a worn-out ideal might lead us to expect. During the two campaigns against Russia of 1829 and 1854 the Kurdish chiefs played off one Power against another, and are even said to have assisted the invading armies by affording a passage through their country and by providing them with supplies. In the campaign of 1877 they were the most dangerous element in the Turkish Army, and are described by an eye-witness of the several actions in Asia as a grotesque corps of irregular cavalry breaking into groups when resisted and altogether unfitted for the serious operations of war. Their atrocious cruelty towards the wounded and their mutilation of the dead [were] visited upon the heads of their afflicted protectors in a general execration of the Turkish name. Yet even the bitterness of this disappointment and the scarcely doubtful lesson of several minor wars, which within the course of the present century they have been obliged to conduct against the Kurds, seem not to have convinced the Turkish Government of the folly of endeavouring to humour a people who will only then be of assistance to them when they have lost for ever the power of resistance, and ranged themselves on the side of law. The reigning Sultan in his dealings with them has inclined to the old policy; he has sought at once to civilise them and to render them more efficient from a military point of view. In the wild and seldom visited country between the plain of Alashkert and the Lake of Van I was able to gain a practical acquaintance with the methods which are being pursued. In the village of Patnotz, the principal seat of the notorious tribe of Haideranli, a solid stone structure, which has been designed to serve the several purposes of a mosque, a school, and a residence for the chief, stands out from the usual cluster of mud hovels, a palace among ant-hills. In every larger Kurdish village I found a petty officer of the Turkish army bewailing the sad fate which had brought him to this exile and his own impotence to control the slippery people and constrain them to attend his drills. A new name, that of Hamidieh, has been given to this irregular cavalry, and they have been liberally supplied with uniforms from the Turkish magazines. The headquarters of the corps are at Melazgerd on the Eastern Euphrates or Murad Su, and over thirty regiments have already been registered upon the area of the plateau. Each regiment has a nominal strength of about 600 men. But they have never yet maneuvered together, and when in 1892 a detachment from each regiment paraded at Erzerum, I am informed that the whole number did not amount to 2000, and the sorry spectacle was presented to the general of a motley company of aged men and half-grown youths mounted on horses which wanted muscle and had perhaps never tasted corn. It is pleasant to acknowledge the good intentions of the Sultan in endeavouring to educate the Kurds and to organise them in a more efficient manner for the purposes of serious war: the ideal which has no doubt been present to the mind of his military advisers is the example of the Russian corps of Cossacks. But the mild measures at present in favour will never attain this result; it is not under such a policy that the Kurds will be subjected to the regular discipline of a camp. Either the young men must be taken from their native province and trained in the armies of the empire at a distance from their homes, or the entire people must be made to bend to the yoke of an equal civil law, whose provisions they at present evade and whose ministers they successfully defy.

While the Turkish Government have little reason to be satisfied with the results of their experiments with the Kurds, the effects which derive from their presence on the plateau are disastrous in the extreme. Yet it is not the Mussulmans so much as the Armenians who are afflicted by this scourge. Let us pursue a little further our original analysis. Transplanted from their natural camping grounds, and obliged through the long months of an arctic winter to provide themselves and their animals with shelter and with food, this pastoral people were quartered on the Armenian villages, but were required by Government to pay an annual tax in return for the accommodation which during winter they received.[2] But an arrangement which was based on the just principle of insuring to the Armenian a fair remuneration for the lodging which he furnished, and the fodder which he supplied, was put into practice by the local authorities in a characteristic manner: the proceeds of the tax were committed to their own coffers and their proper destination was ignored. In 1842, after the promulgation of the celebrated chapter of reforms which is know under the name of the Hatti-Sherif of Gulkhane, a beginning was made towards the abolition of the system; the Kurds in the neighbourhood of Mush were allotted certain villages which had been vacated by the Armenian emigrants, and the Armenians of the district were relieved of the heavy burden which they had previously been obliged to bear. At the present day, the pastoral Kurds of the plateau have all their own villages, and the old system, except in isolated instances, may be said to have disappeared. Yet even now they justify their raids upon the Armenians on the ingenious plea of the ancient right of quarter which they consider they are entitled to enforce. Policy also dictates a course which their tender conscience has approved. The Armenians are at once the most immediate and the least redoubtable among their neighbours. The courageous Kurd equips himself for the foray with a rifle of modern Russian pattern and belts bristling with cartridges; his victims, by a cruel and cynical provision, have been deprived by Government of all arms. If the Kurd is caught red-handed and is arraigned before the civil authority he will scornfully defy the civil jurisdiction and claim to be tried by his military superiors as a trooper in the Hamidieh Corps. When the civil branch has been successfully thwarted, the military authorities are cajoled, while the injured party is rewarded by the visitation of a fresh injury, which he endures without complaint. I can understand that in the land of terrace the Kurdish problem presents some difficulty: it must always be a task of some magnitude to control a people whose migrations extend over so wide an area and whose country hides within its recesses such inaccessible retreats. On the plateau, the case is quite elementary; the pastoral Kurd belongs to a village, and that village is situated in the neighbourhood of the pastures from which he is driven by the winter snows. It is not a matter of great difficulty to follow up the robbers to their homes. It is well within the capacity of the existing authorities to enforce against them the necessary measures of police. But the tribal chiefs are well aware of the consequences which would flow from such a change in Turkish policy towards them, and they exert all the means at their disposal to avert it. Upon the plateau, they enjoy a parasitical prosperity. Once prevented from levying their grain supplies upon the Armenians, and restricted to the legitimate operations of barter with the peasantry or reciprocal trade, their tribes would gradually melt away, and, while a large number would join the ranks of the agricultural population, a remnant only would remain to continue the shepherd calling and the tribal life.

The Armenians are distributed in the following manner over the political area of the Turkish provinces. Compared with the number of the Mussulman inhabitants they are in greater strength in the Government of Van than in any other Government: taking that Government as a whole, but of course excluding the Hakkiari, they exceed by about one-third the total of the Mussulman population. In the town of Van the proportion of Armenians to Mussulman is about two to one. In the Government of Bitlis they are in a majority in the neighbourhood of Mush, and in the fertile district of Bulanik, north-west of the Lake of Van. On the other hand, they are outnumbered by the Mussulmans in the populous Sandjak of Kharput, and in the Caza or governmental sub-division of Palu. In the Government of Erzerum there is scarcely a district in which they are not less numerous than their Mussulman neighbours. Yet when estimating the relative strength of the Armenian element, we deceive ourselves if we dwell with complacent insistence on the fact of its numerical inferiority. Several factors essential to such an analysis deserve and require attention. In the first place, the most fertile portion of the country is held by the Armenians; the beautiful region about Lake Van, the vast plains of Bulanik, of Mush, and of Kharput are the principal seats of the Armenian peasantry, a peasantry as sturdy as the Mussulman settlers, and far more industrious and progressive than they. Another advantage possessed by the Armenians is their favourable geographical situation in relation to the Turks and the Kurds: the Armenian population compose a mass of varying compactness, which extends from the east to the west of the plateau, and may be said, in a general manner, to divide as with a wedge the two branches of the Mussulman inhabitants. Or the Armenian may be compared to the middle bedfellow of three. Again, the solidarity of the Armenian element, both from a political and a social point of view, is a fact which must not be ignored. Nowhere in a more conspicuous manner than upon the plateau has the Gregorian Church resisted the advances of Rome. According to the statistics supplied by the Roman Catholic patriarch to Mr. Goschen, the number of the Roman Catholics within the limits of our political boundary can not amount to 20,000 souls. Of these the great majority inhabit the northern districts of the Government of Erzerum, while in the country of Van and Mush, which is essentially Armenian, there are scarcely any adherents of Rome. It is true that the Protestant community is growing: if we include the mission of Mardin outside the plateau they are over 16,000 strong. But the ultimate object which is present to the Protestant missionaries is not to subvert the national Church or to attach it to their own denomination, but rather to raise the standard of the national religion and to improve the social condition of the people among whom they have come to live. Finally, we must not overlook the high place which the Armenians already occupy in the economical order of the country, and the fact that the Armenian population is capable of very rapid expansion under kinder circumstances. I have already spoken of the Armenian peasantry: yet while agriculture suffers from the disappearance of the Armenian from the soil, the place which he now occupies in the less rudimentary grades of civilised life can never be supplied. The worn and crippled machine of industry functions through him alone. His advancement means the progress of the country; his removal is the cause of its decay. Yet the stream of emigration continues, and is gathering fresh volume every year. The general exodus of the Armenian population, which ensued upon the retirement into Russian territory of General Paskiewitch in 1839, has been followed by a gradual process of depletion, which varies in intensity according as harvests are good or disastrous and the Kurds are encouraged or restrained. During my stay in the country the Armenian peasantry of considerable districts were exerting themselves to pay off their debts, and to obtain permission to leave. Many were flying to the Russian frontier to seek an asylum from the Kurds. A change in policy is alone needed to transform a country which is rapidly becoming a desert into a prosperous and progressive province. Behind the Armenian population of the plateau stand their kinsmen who inhabit the less distracted districts of Asia Minor. At the first approach of a better era many of these would seek with eagerness the ancient home of their race. Many of the emigrants into Russia would return to their old seats. The tide now setting to America, whence the Armenians, like the Irish, transmit large sums of money to their less prosperous relations at home, would slacken if it did not cease. A country which even in its wildest regions still retains the traditions of Armenian civilisation, and is adorned with the remains of Armenian architecture, would resume the old order in a spirit essentially new.[3]

Hitherto our study of the Armenian Question has been confined to a definite political area corresponding in a general manner with the area of the Armenian plateau. It remains to connect the analysis which has here been presented with the wider subject to which it belongs, and to resume with a view to a practical solution the results at which we have arrived. A treatment in outline of this portion of the inquiry is all that the space at my disposal will permit.

1. I have already alluded to the vagueness of idea which underlies the language of the clause in the Berlin Treaty, under which the Porte engages to introduce reforms in the *provinces inhabited by the Armenians.* The literal application of that clause would extend over so wide an area, and would be encountered by such a variety of local conditions that any attempt to enforce it in the letter is doomed, under present circumstances, to a barrenness of result. The total number of the Armenians in Turkey was given by the delegates at the Berlin Congress as amounting to 3,000,000 souls.

This figure is certainly too high. An Armenian clerical writer, who appears not to err on the side of exaggeration,[4] has placed the total of Armenians in Turkey belonging to the Gregorian faith, that is, of the great bulk of the Armenian population, at 1,263,900 souls. It is reasonable to suppose that the Armenian subjects of the Sultan number upwards of one and a half millions, of whom some half million may be taken to inhabit the political area with which we have been dealing, after considerable but somewhat arbitrary additions have been made to supply the shortcomings of the statistical lists. The remainder are distributed over the provinces of Asia Minor, or collected in Constantinople and the large towns. It is true that the recent recrudescence of the Armenian Question has occurred on ground outside the plateau; the towns of Asia Minor in the neighbourhood of the port of Samsun have been the scene of several dangerous collisions between Armenians and the Turkish authorities. But I have not been able to learn that the condition of those districts presents any cause for permanent disaffection, and I do not believe that this recent revolutionary movement was either spontaneous in its nature or indigenous in its growth. The extreme severity with which the outbreaks upon the plateau during 1890 and in former years have been quelled has cowed the spirit of the Armenians in the country of their home; and however great and real are the wrongs which they there endure they have learnt to bear them in silence, and without attempting to obtain redress. The movement, suppressed in the place of its origin, has broken out on new ground. The revolutionary party, disappointed of support in Van, and Mush, and Erzerum, have transferred their efforts to the peaceful towns of Asia Minor, where they work on virgin soil. They appeal to the patriotic instincts of the Armenians, to their sympathies with their more afflicted kinsmen, to the sense of their own inequality with the Mussulmans, and to the hopes which the example of Eastern Europe has fed. But it is not the condition of the Armenians in Asia Minor which invests the Armenian cause with reality, and provides it with a reasonable aim. It is rather the aggravated political situation in the country with which we have been concerned, and the definite political problems which that situation presents, that constitute at once the justification of the cause, and its solid foundation on fact. The Armenian Question in Turkey, considered as a practical issue in the politics of the present day, is a question of the proper government of the provinces inhabited by the Armenians and the tribal Kurds. Thus we are brought back to the field of the foregoing analysis, and to the subjects to which it has been addressed.

2. It is true that in another and much more general sense the Armenian Question is only part of a larger issue arising out of the inequality which exists in Turkey between the Christians and the Mussulmans. Just as within some stagnant pool the folded life of Nature is revived by the returning tide, so our Western civilisation, recoiling upon Asia, arouses the hopes which have slept for centuries in the breasts of the Christians of the East. It is not that they are denied religious freedom, as some of their partisans are bold enough to assert. The tolerance of the Sultan is active throughout his empire. The traveller who has marvelled in the streets of the capital at the liberty, almost amounting to license, which is allowed to the votaries of the several creeds, fermenting human material controlled by an invisible force, will only be confirmed in his original impression by the wider experience of a provincial tour. In the country the sound of Christian bells falls upon the silence of the landscape as he ascends to the lonely cloister nestling in a lap of the hills. In the towns the observance of Sunday effects a change in city life which is almost as marked as in the West: trades are suspended, shops are closed, chimes ring from the churches. It is political equality which is denied to the Christians, and it is most often their efforts to snap the yoke of their subservience that embitter their relations with the dominant race. The edicts which have pronounced in favour of equality are in abeyance. Were these edicts enforced the empire of the Sultan would enter upon a fresh lease of life. His Armenian subjects, in common with other Christians, would find in the empire a wider field for their activity than could be furnished by an autonomous Armenian State. The sentiment of a larger nationality would arise as advantages and apprehensions were shared by all in an equal measure and without distinction of creed.

3. These are the hopes or prospects of the future which individuals, according to their temper or experience, will be inclined to cherish or reject. The practical necessities of the present situation are far from raising an issue at once so momentous and so large. Apart from the Kurdish questions, grave vices beset the conduct of

government in Armenia. Judged even by the standard of Turkish administration in other parts of the empire, the methods pursued by the provincial governors can only be described in the blackest terms. In spite of the numerical inferiority of the Armenians, and of the fact that they are without arms, a reign of terror has been established in the country which poisons the lives of the unfortunate people and drives them to treachery or despair. An elaborate system of espionage follows their footsteps, even into the privacy of their homes. Their national literature, the works of their classical authors, have been confiscated and placed under a ban. Our own great writers who have found their way into these distant regions, Shakespeare and Milton, are proscribed. Their printing presses, the legitimate pride of their cloisters, have been seized. The most innocent poem, the most trivial song, is sufficient evidence to support a charge against their young men, which brings them to the prison cell. I am inclined to believe that a large number of the so-called rebellions are instigated or even invented by the governors themselves in order to establish a reputation for zeal. Were it not for the suffering which is caused, the ridiculous aspect of such actions would be likely to impress us most. They would appear to resemble the clumsy gyrations of the blind Cyclops afflicted with panic by a pigmy hand. Yet the blame and the ridicule which attach to such a policy can not with justice be visited upon the heads of the governors alone. It is a policy which receives the approval of the Porte. In the capital itself the sittings of the Armenian National Assemblies, which are guaranteed by the Constitution of 1863, and which were designed to control both their religious and their secular affairs, have been suspended. The Patriarch of Constantinople, who directs the affairs of the national Church in Turkey, but whose powers are limited and defined by that constitution, is reduced to impotence by the action of the opposing forces of the Government on the one side and the people on the other. In adopting these methods the Turkish Government are digging the grave of their empire in Asia. On the one hand they are engaged in maintaining a situation which, when once the opportunity offers, will call for solution at the hands of Russia. On the other, they are recklessly discarding those very advantages, the habitual mildness of their secular rule and the tolerance of their religious policy, which, in face of a dogmatic and censorious rival, are at once the safeguard of their dominion and its strongest justification as a contemporary fact.

4. It is necessary to notice two schemes for the government of the Armenian provinces which have been put forward, the one by Nubar Pasha,[5] himself an Armenian by birth, the other by the Armenian delegates to the Congress of Berlin. It would be presumptuous in me to criticise the various provisions, dealing with the local government of the country, which men so familiar with the local conditions have framed. It is probable that whatever be the form of government a great part of their recommendations will be adopted in time. But I believe that both these plans, regarded as a whole, are open to two serious objections, the one fundamental, the other arising out of an important omission in the adequate presentation of their case. In the first place, both authorities postulate a preponderance over others of the Armenian element which subsequent investigation has not confirmed, and they recommend the appointment of an Armenian Governor-General whose tenure of office shall be guaranteed. Secondly, although the Armenian delegates accompanied their proposal with a map upon which they delimited the geographical area to which they should apply, still neither Nubar Pasha, who speaks in general terms of an Armenian province, nor even the delegates themselves have presented us with any definite conception of the principle upon which delimitation should proceed. It has been my object during the course of this paper to throw light upon both these points. If ever an Armenian province should be created the limits which have been drawn in these pages will, I think, be found to correspond in a general manner with the practical necessities of the case. The area which we have been considering, while it answers most nearly to the geographical extension of the Armenian plateau in Turkey, comprises a country in which the relative strength of the Armenian element is greater than it is within the larger limits which it has been usual to assign. Yet the proportion which the number of the Armenians within that area bears to that of the other races is very different from the proportion which the Armenian projects assume. Having regard to the constitution of the population of the province, and to the prejudices and animosities which exist, I cannot help thinking that his Christian religion and his Armenian nationality would be a serious disadvantage to a governor in the inauguration of a new *regime*. I may add that, while I was in the country, I gathered from several influential Armenians that this opinion was shared by them. It is possible to name several

Mohammedan officials, high in the Turkish service, who have proved themselves capable governors, and who would be well fitted to administer the new province should it ever become a fact. There is little doubt that the country could be governed more efficiently from a single centre than under the present system of several different governments, of which each is independent of the other. That centre should be chosen in the country south of Erzerum, and north of the Lake of Van. The position of the town or village of Akhlath on the north-western shore of that lake has already in this connection attracted the attention of the Turkish authorities: in the year 1848 the plan which was framed by Osman Pasha of providing that place with the requirements of a capital came near to being carried into effect. A governor acting from Akhlath would conduct at the greatest advantage the administration of the plateau; while the different conditions which obtain in the southern land of terrace, the home of the nomads, the proper Kurdistan, could best be dealt with by military officials provided with a suitable force. However, when once peace had been established on the plateau the Armenians who inhabit these inaccessible districts would emigrate into the protected sphere. But, even if it be impossible to convince the Porte of the advantages of such an administrative reform, it is at least reasonable, having regard to the pledges which have been given by Turkey to Europe in general, and to the moral responsibility which lies upon Great Britain in particular in respect of the Armenians, that we should seriously exert ourselves with the Turkish Government to secure the appointment of suitable officials to the governorships of Erzerum, Bitlis, and Van, and that we should require of them, at least within the area of the plateau, to secure to the Armenians complete immunity from the depredations of the Kurds. On the other hand, the Armenians who inhabit the wilder districts of the neighbouring regions might reasonably be expected to draw more closely to the centres of government. Should such and similar measures, conceived in a kindred spirit, be taken by the Porte, neither they nor we are likely to be disturbed by the exigencies of an Armenian Question; the Armenians, as loyal subjects of the Sultan, would find in the wide extent of his empire a more appropriate field for their enterprise than within the narrower limits of the country of their original home. In the contrary case it is probable that a solution for the present difficulties will ultimately be found in the constitution of a separate province under definite guarantees.

The Spectator, Vol. 73 (December 15, 1894): 839–40

The Armenian Claim on Europe

We do not quite understand the sort of hesitation expressed by some of our contemporaries as to the right of the British Government, or any other Government in Europe, to interfere for the protection of the Armenians. That right rests not only upon positive treaty recognised and quoted by the oppressing Power, but upon a claim much broader and, to our minds, more definite even than that. Europe now arrogates to herself a distant right to interfere in the affairs of Asia, and to distribute Africa as she pleases upon the ground of her own superior civilisation. She dictates internal reforms to the Ottomans, and compels them to surrender provinces now to the Greeks (Thessaly), and then to insurgent Slavs (Bulgaria), again to Austrians (Bosnia), and yet again to Great Britain (Cyprus), because such reforms and such cessions are for the general benefit of mankind. It is not by conquest but by a European mandate that we are now administering the Valley of the Nile. Europe compels the Japanese to abandon their isolation, to open their ports, and to enter against their will into the general comity of mankind. She coerces the Chinese into trade they do not seek or wish, divides the islands of the Eastern Archipelago, and gives her sanction to annexations like those of Russia, Great Britain, and France as if she were, as regards the distribution of power, the rightful mistress of the world. As regards Africa, she acts with even more imperial authority; and at this moment over half the surface of that Continent those who decide the fate of her peoples can plead no title, not even conquest, except the fiat of civilisation as represented by the greater Powers who sometimes, without even signing treaties, have assented to huge redistributions of African territory and population. It is vain to deny that in these great operations Europe has sought her own advantage as well as that of mankind; or that if one consideration is disregarded, they constitute in the aggregate a huge dacoity. This consideration is the protection of the peoples affected by our acts, their immunity from gross oppression, the securing to them of the right to live, and progress, free from any violence which Europe has not explicitly allowed. We ought to secure more than that; but not to secure that, is to forfeit all moral claim to the position we have acquired. If, for example, Europe permits the savages of the Soudan to lay waste Egypt, or the Ottomans to massacre the Armenians, or Russia to slaughter out the Tatars, or the Japanese to make China suffer more misery than is probably for her own good in waking her from her torpor, she gives up, as it seems to us, the moral basis of her general right to rule. That Europe has not yet formulated her authority, or arranged for its legal exercise through a defined agency, has little or nothing to do with the matter. It is certain that her consent, tacit or expressed, is essential to every great change made in the two subordinate Continents; it is certain that this consent is given, or withheld, in part on considerations of European advantage; and it is certain, therefore, that an obligation is created to give, in return, the largest possible measure of protection against miseries arising from external violence. We cannot imagine where the answer to this proposition is, or can be, and regard the statement that we have no right of interference to protect the oppressed, as directly contrary to the visible fact that, whenever it suits our policy or our commercial interests, we do unhesitatingly interfere. The claim to put Egypt straight for the benefit of Europe, involves to our minds the obligation to put Armenia straight for the benefit of Armenians.

We are perfectly aware that the principle thus broadly stated, must be applied under strict limitations both from common sense and from general good policy. Europe is as yet unfederated, even for action in Asia and Africa; and is not bound on behalf of anybody to break her own sword in her hand, or terminate her power of future beneficial action. If she cannot, for example, put an end to a great oppression without a great European war, her obligation ceases, just as the obligation of a civil Court would cease if its officers were resisted by superior military force, or if it could act only by provoking a civil war. Nor, we conceive, is Europe bound to interfere if its interference would produce a convulsion involving greater misery than the misery it was intended to relieve. That would be the case, for example, or might be the case, if we demanded resolutely that throughout the Mussulman world the status of slavery should abruptly cease. The statesmen of Europe must consider the consequences of their decrees just as carefully as Judges consider the effects of their orders in a suit, and with as much precaution to prevent injustice to third parties flowing from them. But when, without such evil consequences, the protection to the oppressed can be given, then we hold we are bound by an obligation which is not based on contracts, though it is greatly strengthened by them, to afford the protection even though it requires an exercise of force. There was just such a case created by the atrocities in Bulgaria; there is just such a case created by the atrocities in Armenia. All the Powers should insist on punishment for the past and security for the future; and if any of them shrink back from the enterprise, the remainder who are willing to act should unhesitatingly go forward. There is no danger of European war from their action; there is no risk of a convulsion producing misery greater than that we relieve, and the obligation therefore on the two Powers which acknowledge it, will, when once the alleged facts are established as true, be immediate and complete.

But we shall be told that the Russian Government, even if it professes disinterestedness and willingness to keep step with ourselves, is in reality only anxious now, as always, to acquire another and fertile province. Well, we meet that difficulty honestly and face to face. We are more willing that Russia should acquire a certain accession of strength than that the domination of the Turks over Christian populations should continue. That domination is of necessity so evil, that in suffering it to continue when we have the opportunity of bringing it to a close, we surrender our moral right ever to interfere in the Ottoman Empire for our own advantage. We have, if we desert the Armenians, no rightful business in Egypt. As a matter of fact, however, we do not when demanding that Armenia shall be made a Principality increase the chance that Armenians will fall under Russian domination. The moment the Principality is organised, national feeling will wake up, the Armenians will resist absorption as the little States of the Balkan have resisted it, and the Ottomans, for their own sake, will be compelled to aid in that resistance. The Principality, well armed, and with an Ottoman Army as its ally, will be indefinitely more likely to remain independent than Armenia is now, when Russia could with a word summon its Christians inhabitants to aid her arms by insurrection. We all know what happened in Bulgaria. That Principality was enfranchised by an effort of Russia sanctioned and controlled by Europe, and is now the strongest bulwark of the Ottoman Empire, the spear-head, as it were, of the Ottoman Army of defence. Nothing can be conceived better for Europe than the situation as it exists; and five millions of Christians who were subject to unendurable tyranny, a tyranny which not only justified insurrection but made submission shameful, are now as contented and progressive a population as any in Eastern Europe. That there is a risk to be run we fully admit, just as there is a risk caused by the attitude of Russia towards Bulgaria; but the risk is less and not greater than that involved in the present condition of affairs, which is rapidly tending to this result. Some day, and that soon, the Russian people will be unable to bear any longer the cry of men whom they regard as co-religionists, they will signify that feeling to the Czar, and Armenia will be snatched from Turkey by Russia with the consent of her people, but avowedly as ceded territory. No Power in the world, except Great Britain, would be even inclined to interfere, and no Government of Great Britain could or would for so evil a cause enter on a great war. Parliament would not vote it, and at least half the population would regard themselves as morally disgraced by supporting it. If the two Powers act together and guarantee a moderate tribute, Armenia can be enfranchised without a war; and if Russia, dreading the rise of an independent Armenia, refuses to act, our duty will be to apply the physical pressure which liberated Thessaly without a single shot being fired. The desire of all Arabs to be free of the Sultan is as strong now as it was when Mr. Gladstone, who, when strongly moved, in foreign politics has a depth of insight, used that lever to secure the Sultan's submission. The Admiralty knows the road to Besica Bay, and what would follow the second appearance of a squadron there.

The Fortnightly Review, Vol. 62 (February 1895): 197–210

Turkey and Armenia

Richard Davey

Anyone who takes the trouble to read books of travel in Turkey, published not earlier than twenty years ago, must acknowledge that a wonderful progress has been made in the country in the present reign. Abdul Ahmed had done more for education than all the Sultans, his predecessors, put together. It would take pages to enumerate the educational establishments he has founded or favoured. He is, I should think, the only sovereign in Europe who entertains at a picnic annually all the school-children of both sexes in his capital, and of every denomination. He has endowed the Ottoman University with many scholarships, and founded schools of law and medicine. Breaking with all the traditions of Muhammedanism, he has given a free hand to His Excellency Hamdi Bey to organize in the deserted kiosks in the Old Seraglio a splendid museum of sculpture and antiquities, and has attached to it a capital school of fine art and design. Needless to say the education imparted in these schools is not perhaps all that might be desired. This cannot be expected. Everything is too new. Teachers of what we should consider third order, even, are sadly needed. But it is a step in the right direction, and its ultimate results may indeed be surprising, for the population of Turkey—Mohammedan and Christian—is remarkably intelligent. It is curious, however, that the Sultan, who has opened out excellent roads in the provinces, should neglect those in the immediate vicinity of his capital. This is probably due to that morbid nervousness which prevents his leaving the confines of Yildiz, and realising for himself the filthy condition of the ill-paved dog-infested streets of Constantinople.

Unfortunately, Abdul Ahmed, by concentrating the reins of government in his own hands, has established in his dominions two terrible curses; a system of espionage which renders life unendurable for anyone in the least connected with political life; and a censorship, the silliness of which baffles belief. The spy system is sapping the foundations of the Empire, demoralising even otherwise honourable men. It is one of the indirect causes of the troubles in Armenia and other parts of the Empire; when a man is paid to spy upon his neighbours, you may be certain that when he has nothing to report, he invents, and thus many an Armenian has been dragged to jail simply because some official spy was beginning to feel that there was no work for his idle hands to do. The childish obstacles thrown in the way of honourable correspondents, who earnestly wish to be just, and to give accurate news to the papers they represent, I firmly believe to be one of the reasons for the exaggerated reports which are appearing about Armenian atrocities.

It is impossible to withhold sympathy and respect for a Sultan of such blameless private life as Abdul Ahmed, who works incessantly at what he believes to be the welfare of his people. To accuse him, as I have seen lately, even in respectable English papers, of being a sort of Tackleton who delights in tormenting his Armenian subjects as that worthy did in scrunching crickets, is not only unjust but in preposterously bad taste. In the first place, the Sultan is so free from the spirit of cruelty which disgraced some of his ancestors, that it is difficult to get him to sign even the death-warrant of a murderer. He invariably commutes the sentence to imprisonment. He has much to contend with. The old Oriental spirit has not yet passed away, and so far the reforms have only influenced the capital and the larger cities, and these only superficially. Fanaticism is still rampant, and Yildiz, like the Seraglio of the "good old times," contains all the *dramatis personae* of the tales of Sheherazaide, the eunuchs, mollahs, pashas, beys, astrologers, slaves, sultanas, kadines, dancing-women, Circassian and Georgian odalisques, whose main object in existence is their own self-advancement. Above this ant-hill of picturesque folk the interesting figure of the Sultan stands out in striking relief. He seems to be watching the West, watching for the return of that civilisation which ages ago started from the land of the rising sun on her troublesome pilgrimage, which has ended at the golden gates of San Francisco. She is returning, and very fast too, for she comes three times a week by the Orient Express; she sleeps at the Grand Hotel de Pera; she takes a luxurious steamer for Jaffa; thence by train to Jerusalem, stopping at the *buffet* Jericho, *dix minutes d'arrêt*, for luncheon. When she is comfortably installed in Zion's brand new hotel, she purchases a twopenny tramcar fare to the Holy Sepulchre. Decidedly she is not picturesque! She is, however, essentially utilitarian. There is no driving her back. The Sheik-ul-Islam himself and all his mollahs could not do it. By-and-by she will send the pilgrims to Mecca by train *de luxe*; or who knows, perhaps by balloon.

However, be this as it may, education has firmly established itself in Turkey. What the result on Muhammedanism will be, time alone will show. It stands to reason, however, that in course of time Islam, if it is to endure, will be obliged to accommodate itself to a great intellectual change. "God made the world," the Muhammedan still repeats, "why do you want to know how He made it?" If we wish to be happy, we have only to do nothing wicked, obey the Koran, and wait patiently until Allah calls us to our reward." This fatalistic doctrine was possible in other times. There is unrest to-day in the hearts of the peoples of the whole world; they are gathering together in one common bond whose object is implacable war against falsehood and cruelty. Science and reason are synonymous, and unless both are thoroughly and reverently understood by education, education becomes worse than useless. If Islam can throw off her lethargy and her fatalism, and frankly accept what the Christian religions have obliged to accept, humanitarian progress, well and good. Under these circumstances alone can we say of her, that her mission is not ended. I had several conversations with learned Sheiks, who spoke to me in this sense. They apparently believe that the Koran can be adapted to altered circumstances, and evidently saw the necessity of great reforms in their religion, as not only possible, but imperative. Inshallah! With better educated and progressive men at the helm, Turkey might yet rise to greatness. But the tone of that education must be very different from that of the Galata Seraï, which from its position in the heart of Pera, a truly cosmopolitan city, is not calculated to create a high sense of honour and manly dignity in the hearts of its scholars. What I say of this particular school—in the Turkish sense the most important in Turkey—I say of all French and other foreign Lycées. The instruction may be excellent, but the tone is simply disastrous.

After all, Turkey is a country in an acute state of transition from an old to a new civilisation. We must not expect too much from her. We must be patient and firm, but also reasonable. To treat the Sultan, the chief of a great religion, a mighty emperor and an old friend, as if he were a naughty little boy who wantonly breaks his toys, is bad manners. It will do no good, and possibly much harm. It certainly will not solve the Armenian question.

I am pretty certain that if ten Englishmen, who apparently interest themselves so clamorously in the Armenian Question, were cornered and cross-questioned even as to where Armenia is, at least eight of them would answer hesitatingly, "Oh! Armenia—a province in the north of Turkey—to be sure—like Bulgaria, you know—principally inhabited by Armenians, whom the Turks persecute because they are Christians." Our old friend Mrs. Gamp used to talk a great deal about a certain Mrs. Harris, but it turned out in the long run that there was no "sich a person." So with Armenia—there is no such place—at present. There was once, but for many a century it has been merely a geographical expression. In 1242 the whole of Armenia was overrun by the Mongols, and this was undoubtedly the greatest disaster that ever befell the Armenians, for such an enormous number of them were slaughtered that they subsequently never recovered their numerical strength. Sultan Selim I., in 1513, conquered the western half of the kingdom, and the Egyptians subjugated a great portion of the eastern half. A little later the Tartars overran and plundered the plateau of the Taurus, and the Khurds and the Persians, by their incessant acts of brigandage, made life unbearable to the peaceful Armenian farmers. By this time almost every vestige of ancient civilisation had been swept away, and possibly there is no other country in the world of such undoubted antiquity in which the past imprint of man has left fewer marks. There are, I believe, some very fine and little-known ruins of ancient fortresses and palaces—the villa of Semiramis at Van, for instance, and some exceedingly interesting old monasteries—but otherwise there is very little of interest beyond the splendid scenery to attract the traveller. Mr. H. F. B. Lynch, in his recent admirable series of papers on the Armenian Question, describes the burrows of the Armenian and the Khurd as scarcely discernible in the landscape. The extent of territory included in Turkish Armenia combined could easily accommodate and provide for a population of twenty millions of people. At the present moment the population of both divisions of the plateau of the Taurus does not exceed three millions. On the Turkish side of Mount Ararat the population, according to the best calculation, is about 1,500,000 souls, among whom there are, perhaps, 500,000 Armenians, 500,000 Turks, 450,000 Khurds, 5,000 Greeks, others 7,000. On the Russian side the population is about 1,100,000, of whom *circa* 520,000 are Armenians. The total Armenian population of the world is about 3,000,000, of whom about 2,500,000 are in Turkey, and the rest in other parts of Europe, Egypt, and America. I take these figures rather roughly from three separate sources, from Quinet's *Empire Ottoman*, published in 1891; from statistics supplied me by the Jesuit missionaries, and those given by Mr. Taylor, our late Consul at Erzeroum, and by Mr. Lynch. But it is almost impossible to obtain an exact census of the population of this part of the world. The Muhammedans, for instance, will not consent to give the number of their women; and the Christians, in order to evade the military tax on male children, are extremely reticent; and as to the Khurdish tribes, as they dwell in inaccessible places, they have never been properly counted at all. In their case it is mere guesswork.

The Jesuit missionaries, who make a point of collecting all sorts of information in the countries in which they labour, as a rule count the number of houses; thus, ten houses to the Muhammedans, five to the Armenians, six to the Greeks, and so forth. However, what is essential to my purpose is to show that the kingdom of Armenia has had its confines so frequently changed that it can now only be considered as "a geographical expression," and that the Armenian population is so numerically inferior to that of the other nationalities among which they live that it is absurd to compare their condition with that of the Bulgarians, who were as three to four to the Turks. I will not enter into particulars as to the geography of this interesting part of the world. It has been so admirably and so recently done by Mr. Lynch. It is quite true, that of all the peoples who inhabit this region, the Armenians are the most remarkable. Descendants, according to their own belief, of Haig, the great-grandson of Japhet, they are much more probably the issue of a cross between the Persians and the various Turanian populations. They have, however, strongly marked Semitic features and peculiarities and are remarkably shrewd in business; so adroit, indeed, are they in their financial transactions, that it is popularly said throughout the East that "no Jew can flourish within ten miles of an Armenian." When all the tribes among whom they live were lost in the intellectual sloth of barbarism, the Armenians had a noble literature. Almost all the Armenians in Asia speak Turkish, the pure Haican language being, however, taught in the schools. It is a rather curious fact that there are several daily papers published in Turkish expressly with Haican characters for the benefit of such Armenians who cannot speak their national language. A great movement in favour of popular education occurred among them as early as 1830. Assisted by wealthy Armenian emigrants and exiles, they have established schools for boys and girls at Zeitoum, Hadjin, Marasch, Aleppo, Angora, Cæsaria, Van, Mouch, Bitlis, Erzeroum, &c. This movement is all the more remarkable when we consider the painful circumstances of their condition, surrounded by hordes of armed barbarians, Khurds, Circassians, Lazes, Kazaz, Kizilbaches (devil worshippers), who have rendered their lives for ages, especially in the rural districts, almost unendurable, and have made their history that of one prolonged martyrdom. It is a mistake, however, to imagine, as some people seem to do, judging from the daily papers, that the Armenians have only been exposed to these terrors during the last twenty-five years. A few examples taken at random will easily prove the contrary.

In the year 404 John Chrysostom, after having denounced in burning words, and to her face too, the evil life led by the Empress Eudoxia in Constantinople, was exiled to Cucusus, a small town situated in one of the vilayets of the Taurus, at a point where the high road, leading from Cappadocia into Persia, is crossed by another passing through the Syrian provinces of Upper Armenia. It was a military station of some little importance, established to ensure the safety of the few travellers who went that way. The saint tells us himself that the town was a wretched little place, from the walls of which you could see, dotting the valley below, the rare huts of the peasantry. Here he dwelt with one, Dioscorus, but he was not long installed in his new quarters when a heavy fall of snow covered with its mantle the town and its neighbourhood. It was so extremely cold, St. John says, that it was impossible for him, in the enfeebled state in which he then was, to leave his chamber. Some of his friends came one day to him with the appalling news that the Isaurians—read Khurds—had descended from their lairs in the mountains into the plain below. In a few days they ascended to the town, which they began to pillage. The soldiers in the garrison were powerless to defend the place, and the brigands plundered the houses of the wealthy, burnt farms, carried off the women and cattle, and massacred all who ventured to oppose them. John Chrysostom, with many others of the unfortunate inhabitants, fled into the woods, and, after many adventures, eventually reached the city of Arabissus. The Isaurians, when they had devastated Cucusus, followed the refugees and continued their depredations. "Like ferocious beasts," says the great orator, "they fell upon the unhappy inhabitants of Armenia and devoured them. Trouble and disorder are everywhere. Hundreds of men, women, and children have been massacred; others have been frozen to death. The towns and villages are desolated; everywhere you see blood; everywhere you hear the groans of the dying, the shouts of the victors, and the sobs and the tears of the vanquished." In reading the passages in the letters of St. John Chrysostom referring to this matter, one would almost imagine oneself reading a sensational account in one of our evening papers headed "Fresh outrages in Armenia."

When I was in Genoa some years ago I translated some documents connected with a very ancient, so-called likeness of the Saviour, preserved in the Armenian church of St. Bartholomew in that city. From them I learnt that somewhere in the first quarter of the fourteenth century four Basilian monks arrived from the neighbourhood of Van, and implored the Archbishop of Genoa, Porchetto Spinola, to whom they were recommended by a Latin priest in Constantinople, to grant them permission to found a monastery of their order in his diocese. They were kindly received by the Archbishop, on whom their narrative of the dreadful massacres in their native country, from which they had escaped, produced a profound impression. The "savages and the Saracens" had, they assured him, desolated their villages, burnt and pillaged their monasteries, and massacred so many people that the stench of the their unburied bodies had produced a dreadful plague. Passing over several centuries, we come to the eighteenth, when the unsafe condition of the Christian population in Asia Minor began to attract the attention of Europe. The archives of the Franciscan and Jesuit missionaries contain hundreds of minute accounts of fearful visitations of the Khurds, and other barbarous tribes, in the plateaux of the Taurus and elsewhere in Armenia. In 1825 a massacre took place which was the subject of diplomatic representations to Sultan Mahmud II. I have before me, whilst I am writing, a report presented by the Armenian Patriarch of Constantinople to the Sultan. . . . It gives a long and concise list of the yearly massacres and vexations to which the Armenians in the Taurus regions and in Asia Minor had been subjected during the years extending from 1860 to 1877. Armenian massacres are, therefore, literally as old as the nation itself. The most wonderful feature about them is, that the Armenians have not long ago followed the example of the man in the Gospel, and taken up their beds and walked. But unlike the Turks, who can make their homes anywhere, the Armenians have an exaggerated affection for the roof that shelters them.

About 1850 an emigration commenced, especially from Constantinople, of a better class of Armenians than had hitherto appeared in any considerable numbers in the rest of Europe and America. Wealthy Armenian merchants now began to establish branch houses connected with their business in Boston, Philadelphia, London, and Paris, and sent thither their sons to superintend them. The plan has evidently succeeded, for I am assured at the present moment that there are not less than 6,000 Armenians in the city of Boston alone, and, what is more, that they are all well-to-do people. That love of self-improvement, which has distinguished the Armenians under even the most adverse circumstances, and has raised them above their neighbours, is one of their marked features wherever they go. They study at our schools and universities with admirable results; but although one or two generations may be born among us, like their first cousins the Jews, they never thoroughly assimilate themselves with us. They remain a people apart. Their love of their desolated and unpeopled fatherland, even though they have never visited it, is intense; and they dream that the day may come when they shall be gathered together amid the corn and the cotton fields, the vines and the splendid forests of that glorious country where Semiramis was wont to pass the summer months.

Imbued, both in America, England, and France, with liberal, not to say revolutionary, ideas, they are easily deceived by certain adventurers of their own race, professional patriots I will call them, who find that their patriotism pays them well. I have had personal acquaintance with more than one of these gentlemen, and I confess that, although I cannot lift my hat to their integrity, I must make them a profound bow for their uncommon shrewdness and plausibility. Their industry is incessant. They form associations and, by their singular persuasiveness, manage to obtain permission—sometimes enthusiastically granted—to place certain conspicuous names upon their committee lists. Their well-organised meetings are not unfrequently presided over by cabinet ministers and other distinguished persons, who should really know better than to have anything whatever to do with such proceedings. Every man of heart must admire, nay reverence, the nobility of the Armenian character, and its steadfast adherence to its old institutions and its ancient religion, through sorrows and trials which would have driven other peoples to despair, and applaud their pluck in keeping their wrongs before the public. But surely it is not for us to endorse falsehoods and exaggerations without taking the trouble to verify them. A few examples will serve my purpose better than a long dissertation. One of these associations established in London publishes a little newspaper yclept *The Anglo-Armenian Gazette*. I cull a few gems from its columns to show the method with which these "patriots" work. In the February number for 1894 I find this: "Some thirty years ago an Armenian published a pamphlet to prove the descent of Queen Victoria from the ancient kings of Armenia. Since which time the Armenians have been wondering why Her Majesty does not annex Armenia to her dominions." This would be merely silly if it were not extremely mischievous. There exists at the Sublime Porte a sort of official Romeike, presided over by an Armenian clerk, whose duty it is to cut out of the foreign newspapers everything he can find that is disagreeable to the Sultan. These he translates into Turkish, and they are sent up every evening to Yildiz for His Majesty's perusal—*en parenthèse*, His Majesty must have had a good deal of unpleasant reading during the last few months! Now, when he reads such a paragraph as the above, and finds that it emanates from an association presided over by some of Her Majesty's Cabinet Ministers and Members of Parliament, he, whose mind is eastern and not western, puts his own construction upon it, and comes to the conclusion that it is an indirect but, nevertheless, semi-official suggestion as to the propriety of our annexing a part of his dominions. In another number I find the following question asked: "Is it not a beautiful sight to see the Armenians of Constantinople going about the streets in rags and tatters rather than, by renouncing their ancient religion, accepting the golden epaulets and decorations of a Pasha?" This is an insinuation that no Armenian can accept office under the Turkish Government unless he turns Muhammedan. There happen to be, at the present moment, no less than eleven Armenian, four or five German, and three English Pashas, not one of whom has ever been requested to change his religion. As to the "rags and tatters," the Armenian population of Constantinople, which is exceedingly active and industrious, is very fairly well off—some few very rich. At least a quarter of the officials in the Government employ are Armenians, for the Turks cannot do without the assistance of their superior intelligence. Moreover, a good third of the commercial and banking interests of Turkey are in the hands of Armenians. On the other hand, undoubtedly the Anglo-Armenian and American-Armenian Associations—by flooding Turkey with revolutionary pamphlets, principally sent over the Persian frontier from Tabriz, where there is a headquarter of Armenian revolutionary propaganda, by notoriously exaggerating the proportions of the unfortunate events which take place in Armenia, and by creating secret societies whose avowed object is the overthrow of the Sultan—have made the very name of Armenia odious to him. Aided by busybodies and notoriety-hunters in England and America, they have greatly impeded the action of the ambassadors, and done more harm to the cause of their compatriots than they can ever undo. The truth must prevail, and the truth about Armenia is terrible enough, without the aid of hysterical sensationalism.

If anyone wishes to form an idea of how Armenian atrocities are manufactured and exaggerated, let him read the Blue-books on "affairs at Aleppo," 1879. The London papers, inspired by the "patriots," announced, with a great flourish of trumpets, that 500 Armenians had been tortured and massacred in the neighbourhood of that city; and there was, so to speak, a great Armenian horrors' boom all over the western world and America too. Well, after all this sensationalism, the number of slain was eventually reduced by our own and the American consul to eight.

Within the past six weeks the London papers have been gloating over the "atrocities" committed upon Armenians at, and in, Sasoun. The number of the killed was at first 2,000, then 3,000, and finally, thanks to a telegram from Boston, from "one who had received a letter from Sasoun"—how the letter had time to reach America, and how it had been allowed to get out of Turkey, were details never explained!—it was declared that the "massacred Armenians exceeded 10,000." In all these despatches, and in the articles commencing upon them, Sasoun is almost invariably described as a "town" or "village." As a matter of fact Sasoun is neither the one nor the other, but a wild district in the Upper Valley of the Tchaï-Batam, a branch of the Tigris, and separated from the basin of the Euphrates by high mountains. It is remoter from Erzeroum, but about equal distance from Diabekir, Mousch, and Bitlis. Nothing can be imagined more terrifically grand than the scenery of this desolate country. The gorges and ravines which cross it are as dreadfully gloomy as the one described by Shelley's *Beatrice*. A score of cataracts and waterfalls tumble headlong from the black precipices, and gathering together their waters rush desperately towards the Tigris and Euphrates, at the foot of the various dangerous defiles and passes. As a contrast to the stern grandeur of this awe-inspiring scenery are certain smiling valleys and platforms which the Armenians cultivate with all their well-known industry. This autumn the Khurds happened to select the Sasoun, or Sasounkh as it is called, as the scene of their dreaded exploits. They fell upon the Armenian farmers with a view of stealing their cattle and carrying off their women and provisions. The Armenians resisted, and a fight took place, in which at first the farmers seemed to have had a well-earned advantage. Matters grew so serious that a zealous Armenian rode off for help to Bitlis, the Governor of which place lost his head and called to his aid the regular troops reinforced by two regiments of the Hamadyeh, and by the cavalry from Erzeroum, under the command of Zekhi Pasha. The Armenians, frightened out of their lives at this display of force, entrenched themselves in the Khandosch Dagh. Pursued by the Hamadyeh, they were killed in great numbers in their mountain retreats, but the number of slain did not reach 2,000, let alone 10,000, which would certainly exceed the entire population of the district. Most probably it did not pass 1,000. Further than this we really know nothing positive. The papers have condemned the action of both the Governor of Bitlis and of Zekhi Pasha. But is it fair to do so until we are in a position to judge accurately? The capital error made in this unhappy affair was the bringing upon the scene of the Hamadyeh. When we read of Turkish "regular troops" we are perhaps apt to imagine our own dear Tommy Atkins in a fez; but a Turkish "regular" is very much of a savage in a sort of German uniform, and when his martial ardour is inflamed in active service, his unamiable traits appear only too conspicuously, and he is apt to commit every sort of atrocity. As to the Hamadyeh,[1] one of the greatest mistakes ever made was this of incorporating the Khurds into a sort of well-armed irregular troop. The Sultan doubtless had in his mind the success of the Russian Emperor with his Cossack regiments, when he gave permission for these barbarians to be supplied with uniforms and arms. The only distinction they obtained in the war of 1877 was for their blood-curdling atrocities on the poor wretches who fell into their hands, and their diabolical mutilation of the dead. Their headquarters are at Melaigerd, on the Eastern Euphrates, and there are about thirty regiments of them registered in the area of the plateau, each regiment consisting of from 500 to 600 men. They will not, and possibly cannot, accept discipline, and their natural savageness is rendered ten times more dreadful when they are provided with modern arms and ammunition and taught how to use them.

The Powers ought to insist upon their being immediately disarmed and disbanded. As to their religion, concerning which we have heard so much, they are not Muhammedans except in name—only savages. The Khurds and their allies the Hamadyeh do not scruple to attack Muhammedans when they have no better prey to hand, and only last year they tied the brother of a Greek I became acquainted with in Pera to a tree, whilst they pillaged his farm. I have a copy now before me of his letter to his brother M. X———, describing that unpleasant scene. He would have lost his life but for some friendly Turks. Civilisation in Turkey is, I repeat, superficial, and confined to certain classes in the large towns. The few examples I have given will prove, I hope, sufficiently and satisfactorily that the Armenian atrocities are purposely exaggerated, though for what good purpose I fail to perceive. There is a great deal of excitement in England just now about the matter, but hitherto I have read scarcely a sensible suggestion—unless from Mr. Lynch and Mr. Edward Dicey—as to a possible solution of the question. I do not think it is the policy of the Czar to provoke a conflict with the Turks, and, if victorious, annex the plateau of Taurus, which is the high road to India, and therefore of vast importance to us. If he thinks so, then this agitation in England is pernicious alike to our own interests and to the Armenians—to our own, because we shall be told we provoked the hostile movement on the part of the Russians against Turkey, as we did in the case of Bulgaria; to the Armenians, for I do not see that this unfortunate people will gain much by passing from the rule of the Sultan to that of the Czar. As to ourselves, what can we do in the matter? Only give the best advice we can to the Sultan, who is far more likely to accept it if we are civil, than if we are so abominably rude as to declare in our public meetings that even the Ambassador of "such a tyrant" is unfit to kiss the "pure tender hand of our spotless Queen." We have not the remotest idea of going to war for the sake of the fine eyes of the Armenians. If we had we could not, and even if we did, where on earth should we get sufficient troops from, to occupy so vast a tract of country once we had upset the entire machinery of its present administration? The solution of the question is one, I believe, which time and the advance of civilisation alone can effect. Civilisation must eventually absorb, not only Turkey, but the whole of the East. It will certainly not be solved by untruth, intrigue, self-glorification, mutual admiration and exaggeration. These impede the action of our very able Ambassador, and irritate the Sultan who, be assured, desires the pacification of his dominions quite as ardently as do Canon McColl, M. Thoumayan, and Mr. Stevenson. As to the much talked of commission, I believe it will do very little or no good. It will not be able to go further into the interior than Erzeroum, for the journey beyond there at this season of the year is equivalent to an Arctic expedition. The witnesses will be so timid of the eventual consequences to themselves of their revelations, that they will say nothing of any importance or else invent. What is really wanted is a European Congress on the subject, to which the Sultan should be invited, not as a refractory naughty boy, but as a great Sovereign who has at heart the welfare of his people. The troubles of Armenia might then be thoroughly investigated, and some practicable remedy found for their alleviation. I shall be told that this was done at the Berlin Congress. A close examination of the documents published concerning that Meeting will, I think, clearly prove that the Congress had altogether too much to do to enter fully into the Armenian question. It was treated very lightly indeed, and the famous Article 61 was passed without mature reflection.

In conclusion I would call attention to another amusing feature of the procedure of the patriots, their endeavour to make their English friends believe that the Armenian religion is a branch, if not a twin sister, of the Church of England as by law established. Hence it is generally spoken of as "holy" and "venerable" and "national"—epithets which would certainly not be bestowed upon its real twin sister, the scarlet lady of the Vatican. A distinguished gentleman the other day in presenting a chalice from the Armenians to another and much more distinguished gentleman informed him "that the Armenian church was the oldest national church in the world, having been founded by Gregory the Illuminator at the beginning of the fourth century, before Constantine was converted to Christianity." The truth is otherwise. The Armenian church did not become national or independent until the Synod of Dovin in 596. Christianity was introduced into Armenia according to universal tradition of the Eastern Churches, by the Apostles Bartholomew and Thaddeus. I have elsewhere mentioned the existence of a curious icon in Genoa, which represents, it is stated, the face of Jesus Christ. The legend concerning it, which is still preserved and is written in very ancient Armenian, relates that Abgarus, King of Edessa, having heard of the miracles and wonders wrought by Our Lord, wished to possess himself of His portrait. He therefore sent to Jerusalem an artist named Ananias, who tried in vain to sketch the Divine lineaments. Christ, seeing his fear and sorrow, lest he should have to return with his mission unfulfilled, took the canvas and pressed it upon His face, which remained imprinted upon it. The icon, which is very beautifully painted in the Byzantine style, is surrounded by a series of medallions representing, amongst other things, the conversion of a number of Armenians to the Christian faith by the saints Bartholomew and Thaddeus. I give the legend for what it is worth. It, however, affords a proof, if one were needed, of the extreme antiquity of the origin of Christianity in this part of the world. Gregory the Illuminator, towards the end of the third century and the beginning of the fourth, gave form to the liturgy and ritual of the Armenian Church, but he neither added nor abstracted to or from those dogmas, which she held in common with the Greek and Latin Churches with which she was in communion. Gregory, who was Bishop of Cæsarea, established the chief seat of ecclesiastical administration at Etchmijadzen, where it has remained ever since, but there was a hierarchy long before his time; and as a proof that he did not attempt to render the Armenian Church independent, he was canonised at a very early period by the Latin Church, and still has his place in its hagiology among the doctors of the Church. St. John Chrysostom was in intimate communication with the Armenian bishops, who received him in his exile with proud reverence, which he would certainly not have allowed had they, at this period, been monophysites. It was, therefore, not till the year 560, that is, nearly three hundred years after the death of Gregory the Illuminator, that the Armenian Church became national in the full meaning of that term. Then it adopted the monophysite doctrine, that in Christ there was but one nature, a heresy which has never been accepted by any of the Western Protestant Churches, by whom the Armenian Gregorian or National Church must logically be considered heretical. It is possibly owing to this doctrine that the Armenians use pure wine, without the addition of any water, in the Mass. Beyond this doctrine and the non-recognition of the Papal supremacy, the Armenian Church and the Latin differ so slightly, that when an Armenian Gregorian or schismatic passes over to Rome, he finds in the united branch of this Church no change whatever in liturgy or ritual. I defy any casual observer to tell the difference which exists between the two Churches in matter of ceremonial and general arrangement. In both he will see the same three altars, raised on a marble platform about four feet high, the centre one, a mass of artificial flowers and lights towering up to the ceiling, being the high altar. It is screened at the moment of the Consecration of the Host by a gorgeous curtain drawn around a circular pole of brass, exactly like the curtain of a "tester" bedstead. The priests wear the same beautiful flowing robes, perform exactly the same ceremonies to the accompaniment of a delightfully picturesque orchestra, consisting of a band of acolytes who, seated in a circle in front of the altar, beat upon tambourines, cymbals, and little drums, whilst they chant in the usual nasal tones of the East the various hymns and psalms appropriate to the service.

The use of images, or pictures, is less exaggerated than in the Latin and Greek Churches, but they are venerated nevertheless, and the relics of the saints on certain festivals are presented to the faithful to kiss. The Virgin Mother and other saints are invoked, and they have their shrines and sacred pools and wells, precisely as in the Greek and Roman Churches. In short, as I have already said, the difference between the two religions is very slight. Mgr. Azarian, the Catholic Patriarch of Constantinople, assured me that when an Armenian congregation joins the Roman, no change whatever is made in their ritual; the priests are not reconsecrated and they are allowed to retain their wives. I may here add that Mass is said in the old Armenian languages in both Churches. It was not until 1827 that the Roman Catholic Armenian Church was thoroughly organized. There is, however, a complete and unbroken list of the Armenian patriarchs who never subscribed to the monophysite doctrine from the time of the Council of Dovin to the present; and the last of these is Mgr. Azarian, the actual Romano-Armenian Patriarch of Constantinople. This Church has a well-organized hierarchy, and numbers some 110,000 members, principally, however, in the large towns, for which reason they are rarely comprised in the troubles which afflict the rural districts. In the annals of the Dominican Friars at Galata, I found a number of entries for the payment of sermons preached by them in the Gregorian churches in the last century. This seems to me a proof that the monophysite heresy, although the original cause of the schism with the Greek and Latin Churches, has never been well defined by the Gregorians.

There are only two original orders in either the Latin or Gregorian Church—the Hermit of St. Anthony of Egypt and the Basilians. The Mechitarists of Venice are Latin Basilians. The priests are allowed to marry once, in both Churches, and the bishops are only selected from the regular clergy. The Gregorians have the same orders as the Roman Catholics, and like them reckon the Subdiaconate among the greater orders. In the seventeenth century, I feel persuaded, the Gregorian Church in Asia Minor felt the influence of the Catholic revival in the East under the Jesuits. The decoration of the high altar is exactly like the Roman, being surcharged with artificial flowers and lights. Then, too, unlike the Greeks, they allow of a certain amount of progress in art, and do not scruple to use images manifestly imported from Italy, and mostly by inferior seventeenth century artists. At about this period, too, the tall Roman mitre was introduced, and this essentially post-Reformation in its design. Blue vestments are used on feasts of the Virgin in both the Gregorian and the United Church.

Of the very numerous works written on the Armenian Church, the best will be found to be Le Quien's *Oriens Christianus*; *Le Patriarcat Armenien*, of L. D. Vernier; the Père de Damas' *Arménie*; and the very elaborate, most erudite and curious *Storia del Armenia*, published by the Friars of the Mechitarist Monastery, at Venice, in 1782.

The Contemporary Review, Vol. 67 (February 1895): 201–9

Armenia

Francis Seymour Stevenson[1]

By the sixty-first article of the Berlin Treaty the condition of the Armenians in the provinces of Asiatic Turkey was raised to the dignity, and was invested with the importance, of an international question. Each successive year which has witnessed the postponement of the stipulated reforms has augmented the gravity of the situation, and has helped to render more difficult the peaceful solution of the problem. In spite of the express provisions of the "Charter of the Orient," the security of the Armenians has not been guaranteed against the Kurds and the Circassians, the Porte has entirely failed to fulfil its obligations, and no adequate or earnest attempt has been made by the signatory Powers to act up to the responsibilities which they incurred, and to enforce and supervise the execution of the promised improvements. The accumulated evidence of sixteen years exemplifies the hopelessness of the present position of affairs, so long as existing conditions are maintained, and points to the necessity for definite, serious, and immediate action. The Sasun incidents have brought matters to a head, although they constitute merely one connecting link in a long chain of acts of oppression and outrage. Unless steps are taken at once to compel the Porte to carry out the provisions of clause sixty-one in their spirit and intention, and in such a manner as to secure, not merely a temporary abatement of outrages, but the introduction of permanent reforms, there is grave reason for fearing that what has now become an international question may soon develop into an international crisis.

Before proceeding to examine the available remedies, and the manner in which they are capable of being applied, it may be well to consider some of the fallacies which are frequently urged at the present juncture with the object of lulling the public mind into a state of indifference, or even of acquiescence in the condition of affairs which prevails in the Armenian provinces. It is stated, for example, (1) that the Sasun occurrences constitute an isolated event of so exceptional a character as not to justify the interferences which it is sought to deduce from it; (2) that, pending the report of the Commission recently appointed, the whole of the Armenian agitation should be brought to a standstill; (3) that the object of the movement is hostile to Mohammedanism, and is calculated to exasperate the adherents of that religion; and (4) that the question does not concern the government and inhabitants of that country to a greater extent than that to which it concerns the government and inhabitants of other European countries. The error of those statements is due in part to a misapprehension or distortion of facts, and in part to an imperfect process of reasoning. The Sasun incidents, in the first instance, differ not so much in kind as in degree from similar occurrences of which other districts of Armenia have been the scene, and it would be impossible, therefore, to describe them as isolated and exceptional phenomena. The papers relating to the misdeeds of [Moussa] Bey contain the record of atrocities no less revolting, though on a smaller scale, and other consular reports published previous to 1891 contain numerous references to acts of cruelty to which Armenians have been subjected, and to the general insecurity of their lives and properties owing to the habitual ravages of the Kurds and the prevailing misgovernment. Without referring to the earlier reports of 1879, 1880, and 1881, it is sufficient, perhaps, to quote the following sentence from a despatch addressed to the Foreign Office by the late Mr. Clifford Lloyd, consul at Erzeroum, which appears in the Blue-book, Turkey, No. 1 (1890–91):

> "Putting aside isolated instances of depredation, there has been pillage on the most extensive scale, with much slaughter, by Kurds in various parts of Armenia during the past few months, as will be observed from my despatches dated the 21st of August and the 1st of October, 1890. This year the record is an exceptionally large one, but the position of the defenceless Armenian peasantry with reference to the Kurds, who are all armed, varies only in degree, and, looked at from any point of view, is one calling for immediate relief."

Matters have retrogressed since the date of that report from bad to worse. The organisation of the Hamidie, or Kurdish irregular cavalry under Turkish officers, has placed a new weapon of offence in the hands of the oppressors, and, far from producing the results which might, perhaps, have been anticipated from their subjection to military discipline, has rendered them more powerful for evil and more and more difficult to restrain. Outrages without number have been committed in the vilayets of Erzeroum, Van, Bitlis and Diarbekir. The whole country is under a reign of terror, to which the judicial administration affords no redress and no mitigation. "In all crimes of violence," writes Mr. Clifford Lloyd in the despatch already cited, "of which the Christians have been the victims during the past year in the province of Erzeroum, no one has been punished, nor, with very few exceptions, has any effort been even made to bring the offenders to justice." Everybody is acquainted with the history of the sham trial at Angora, in which the incidents at Marsovan culminated; and Professor Thoumaian has related some of the tortures of which he was the eye-witness, as well as the treatment to which he himself was subjected. The number of Armenian prisoners confined in Turkish gaols or exiled to Arabia, Tripoli in Barbary, and elsewhere, was estimated not long ago, on the highest authority, at the figure of 2000; and, although a certain number have since then been released—at any rate on paper—a further increase has taken place in the number of those who have been incarcerated, so that the total is understood to stand higher now than it did some few months back. Whilst the ravages of the Kurds are conducted with impunity, and the rapacity of the Turkish officials remains unchecked, their victims are also subjected to the terrors of a law unjustly applied, and to indignities inflicted by those who should act as their protectors. Well might Mr. Clifford Lloyd quote from the Identical Note presented by the Powers in 1880 the reference, which is as appliable now as it was then, to the "gravity of a state of things, which, if permitted to continue, would in all probability lead to the destruction of the Christian population of vast districts."

The second argument which is sometimes put forward at the present time is that, pending the verdict of the Commission appointed to inquire into the Sasun incidents, an open mind should be preserved with regard to the Armenian question as a whole, and the agitation should be suspended. But the Sasun outrages, as has been pointed out, do not stand alone, and merely represent the latest, most conspicuous, and most startling development of the situation. Even, therefore, if they are to be regarded as being temporarily *sub judice*, it does not follow that silence ought to be kept with regard to the events of the past sixteen years and to the convincing proof, which their testimony supplies, of the necessity for thorough reforms under European supervision. A good deal of misapprehension, however, exists with respect to the constitution of the Commission of Inquiry. It is not an international but a Turkish Commission, and, to judge by past experience, Turkish Commissions are instruments by which truth is suppressed and issues are obscured. It is satisfactory that representatives of Great Britain, France and Russia will have the opportunity of examining the *procès-verbaux*, besides being present at the sittings of the Commission and credit is due to the British Foreign Office for having taken the initiative in securing this concession; but it must be remembered that the powers of the international representatives will be strictly limited, and that they will not be able to guarantee the security of the witnesses. They will be little more than spectators. The winter months, involving as they do necessary delays, are favourable to the kind of work which followed the perpetration of the Bulgarian massacres, and which was intended to render difficult, and almost impracticable, the collection of trustworthy testimony; in spite of which efforts, however, it became possible for Mr. Baring, acting independently of any Turkish Commission, to draw up and present a report in which he confirmed, apart from certain details, but in all essential features, the accounts which had been published. In view of the difficulties which surround the path of the international representatives who are to watch the Turkish Commission of Inquiry into the "acts of brigandage" in the Sasun district, it may be well to recall the weighty words with which the remarkably well-informed Constantinople correspondent of the *Speaker* prefaced the letter which appeared in that journal on the 12th of January:

> "I fear there can be no doubt about the essential facts. We have already the official reports of the consuls of Van, Erzeroum, Sivas, and Diarbekir, which have not yet been published, but which, we know, confirm the most horrible statements made in the newspapers.

> We have the reports of the Armenian refugees who were eye-witnesses. We have the reports sent to the Armenian Patriarchate here, and the reports of the Catholic and Protestant missionaries in the vicinity of Sasun. Beyond this, and most horrible of all, we have the testimony of the Turkish soldiers who took part in the massacres. These soldiers . . . have talked with the greatest freedom in public places, and to all who would listen, boasting of their deeds. We have full reports from all these places of the statements made by hundreds of these soldiers, and they agree in all essential points."

In the face of such an accumulation of testimony, can it be properly asserted that silence should be maintained even with regard to the Sasun incidents? Is it not more in accordance with right reason to maintain that the real object which the Sasun inquiry may be assumed to have in view, is not the question whether outrages have been committed—a question to which there can be only one possible answer—but the questions, what has been the extent of the outrages, and upon whose shoulders does the responsibility rest? That Turkish officials should deny the elementary facts of the case is not surprising, but those denials cannot be expected to impose either upon the Powers or upon European nations as a whole. Perhaps some traveller, accompanied by half a dozen Zaptiehs, and obtaining all his information through interpreters appointed by Turkish authorities at Constantinople, may be led astray; but he cannot lead others astray. Silence, I repeat, may reasonably be expected to be observed with regard to the responsibility for these particular outrages, though not with respect to the outrages themselves. But there is no reason why the constitution of a Turkish Commission to inquire into these occurrences should necessitate the cessation of an agitation which takes as its basis the existing condition of affairs in the whole of the Armenian provinces, and which aims at the removal of the causes which have brought that state of things into existence.

A third objection to which it is necessary to refer is the argument which is based upon the supposition that Mahommedanism, as such, is an object against which an attack is directed. That is not so. Christians have, no doubt, been the principal sufferers from the existing misgovernment. Their bishops, pastors, and teachers have been repeatedly arrested on false pretexts, and have been kept in confinement or exile without trial or after mock trials. The cases of the Archbishops of Marash and Zeitoun, of the Bishop of Moush, of the Bishop of Hadjin, of Messrs. Thoumaian and Kayayan, and numerous others, may be cited in support of that contention. Christian evidence is not held valid in the courts as against Mussulman testimony, as is shown again and again in the published consular reports. But Mahommedans, though they have not been massacred or outraged, have also grievous grounds of complaint against the present methods of administration, and letters from various parts of Asia Minor show that their feeling of dissatisfaction with Turkish officialism is rising rapidly. Turkish officialism is the object of attack and not Mahommedanism, and the reforms for which the demand is urged would be of advantage to all sections of the community, irrespective of creed, and would not confer upon the Christians any privilege which the Mohammedans would not equally share. Nothing in the agitation against the methods of Turkish administration in Asia Minor can reflect upon our Mohammedan fellow-subjects in India; and those who bear in mind the times when caliphs occupied the seats of power at Bagdad and at Cordova, when the former was the centre of civilisation in the East and the latter the mainspring of culture in the West, will be the last to assert that Mohammedan rule is incompatible with material or intellectual advance. They will, however, also remember that the Arabic influence which reigned at Bagdad and at Cordova has now disappeared, and with it the higher force which it implied. The Ottoman Turks, as they now exist, depend for the continuance of their rule partly upon the arts of cajolery, mainly upon the exercise of brute force. To compare them with the Haroun-al-Raschids or the Abdabrahmans of the past is to confuse distinct races, and to prevent the teaching of history. At any rate, Mohammedanism is not strengthened by those who attempt to identify its interests with those of Turkish officialism; and it may, perhaps, be considered a question to which the future—possibly a not very distant future—may supply an answer, whether, if the Arabs were to set up a caliph at Mecca he would not occupy a position in which, by virtue of the *religio loci* and owing to other causes, he would command the respect of Mohammedans in other parts of the world to a greater extent than can be the case with a caliph whose seat is on the Bosphorus.

The fourth fallacy against which we must guard ourselves is the assumption that we have no more concern in the Armenian question than have the other signatory Powers which are parties to the Berlin Treaty. That supposition ignores the existence of the Cyprus Convention, and does not take into account the moral liability incurred by this country when, by its influence, it procured the substitution of Article 61 of the Berlin Treaty for Article 16 of the Treaty of San Stefano, and thereby removed the material guarantee which the clause in the earlier Treaty provided for the execution of the required reforms. No doubt the most desirable course, in theory, is that which would involve the joint action of all the signatory Powers; but it is obvious that certain of the Powers have a more direct interest in the Armenian question than others, and it is therefore unnecessary that all should co-operate directly in the task of demanding and enforcing the fulfillment by the Porte of its neglected obligations. It is sufficient that the Powers which are chiefly concerned, such as England and Russia, should act cordially together in the interest of justice and humanity; and those who remember how France and England were able, in the case of the Lebanon, to bring about the introduction of a system of government which has worked satisfactorily, and which has conferred upon the inhabitants of that region the security they required for their lives, their creed, and their property, will welcome the adhesion that France has given to the efforts which have been made by the other two nations in connection with the Sasun inquiry, and which will, it is to be earnestly hoped, be followed by a determined and successful attempt to bring about real, permanent and definite reforms.

The precise nature of those reforms is a matter on which certain differences of opinion may be reasonably anticipated, though there can be no doubt as to the general lines on which they should be carried out, or as to the imperative necessity for their introduction. The Anglo-Armenian Association, which was founded in 1890 for the purpose of appealing to public opinion with the object of securing the executive and judicial reforms stipulated by the sixty-first article of the Berlin Treaty, has placed its policy repeatedly upon record. In the first place, it is necessary that there should be a Governor-General for the Armenian provinces, appointed by the Sultan with the assent of the Powers, and with conditions as to tenure of office of such a character as to free him from the deleterious influences which can now be brought to bear. In the next place, this authority should be supported by a mixed *gendarmerie*, with a certain percentage of European commanders. Thirdly, in order that the Kurds may remain under proper control, they should be made universally liable to military service, and kept under military discipline, with Europeans among their principal officers. Fourthly, the courts of the law should be reorganised somewhat on the basis suggested by Nubar Pasha's well-known scheme. It must be borne in mind that promises have been repeatedly made by the Porte to inaugurate reforms, as, for instance, in reply to the Identical Note and the Collective Note of 1880, but that these promises have never been carried out. The essential condition on which should depend the acquiescence of the Powers in any arrangement that might be proposed, is that the execution of the reforms should be carried out without delay under European supervision. Nothing short of some form of European control will afford a guarantee that they are carried out in their spirit and intention.

It will be sufficient to offer a few words of explanation with respect to the four heads of reform to which reference has been made. The effect of setting up a Governor-General for the Armenian provinces would not necessarily mean the destruction of the system of vilayets, but would mean that the valis would henceforth be responsible to the Governor-General, whose residence would probably be at Erzeroum, and whose hands would be strengthened for good by his immunity from interested interference, and by the presence of European supervisors. In addition to the vilayets of Erzeroum, Van, Bitlis, and Diarbekir, it would be desirable to include in the above arrangement those of Mamuret-el-Aziz and Sivas; for it must be remembered that, as it is not proposed to give to Christians any special privileges which their Mussulman neighbours will not enjoy, it is not a serious question whether Christians or Mohammedans are in a majority or a minority in a particular province. With regard to the Armenians scattered over other parts of Asia Minor, it would undoubtedly be necessary to extend to them the benefit of administrative and judicial reforms; buy they would not be affected by the appointment of a Governor-General under the conditions specified, and they are not at present exposed to Kurdish inroads, so that their case stands on a somewhat different footing. It will be observed that a large number of places containing a considerable Armenian population are situated outside the sphere of authority of the proposed Governor-General. Some readjustment of the boundaries of provinces might, perhaps, be found necessary. It might be well, for instance, to include the mountainous region of the vilayet of Aleppo in which Marash and Zeitoun are to be found, whilst, on the other hand, certain portions of the vilayet of Sivas might without serious objection be omitted. Districts, such as those which contain Cesarea, Yozgat, Angora, and other cities in the more western portion of Asia Minor, as well as portions of Cilicia of which the vilayet of Adana is the present representative, ought unquestionably to be brought under a scheme of administrative and judicial reform, though it would not be necessary to apply to them the special organisation to be adopted in the vilayets previously mentioned. It is probable, however, that a considerable migration of Armenians will take place from other districts of Asia Minor into the region with which their name is specially associated, if once they are satisfied that they will obtain in it the conditions of security which they demand and to which they are entitled.

The establishment of a mixed *gendarmerie* officered, to a certain extent, by Europeans, and the introduction of a European element into the ranks of those who are in command of Kurdish troops, are reforms which have been frequently proposed and approved. Experienced men of the type of British officers in India, or of Russian officers in Turkestan would, no doubt, be most desirable; but it might be found necessary, on political grounds, to make the selection from officers belonging to other nationalities. With respect to the administration of justice, there is clearly room for the introduction of mixed tribunals, with Europeans as presidents in the case of higher courts and courts of appeal. It is a matter of deep regret that the capacity which the Armenians have exhibited in many parts of the world for the discharge of the duties of government, and which is exemplified at the present time in the person of the Prime Minister of Egypt, should find no scope for usefulness in the land with which they have been connected during a span of national existence extending over so many centuries, and it is earnestly to be hoped that in any modification of the existing *régime* their talents may be utilised for the benefit of their fellow-countrymen. It is also to be hoped that the exclusion of Armenians from all branches of the army, with the exception of the medical staff, may no longer be allowed to remain in force.

Reforms of the type which has been described are the logical and inevitable outcome of a due regard for treaty obligations and international responsibilities. That they have not hitherto been carried out has been due to the narrow obstinacy of the Porte and the negligence of the contracting Powers. The patience of Europe shows signs, at length, of becoming exhausted, and the time appears to be opportune, in view of the better understanding between the country and Russia, for the Powers principally concerned to apply such pressure as will compel compliance with the elementary laws of humanity and justice. The necessity arises, not out of the perpetration of this or that outrage, but out of the prolongation and aggravation of a state of things which can no longer be endured, and which is incompatible with the conditions on which the Turkish Empire has been suffered to remain in existence. The claims of the Armenians on our attention are clear, paramount, and instant. The problem cannot be solved by an intermittent fever of activity, but by pressure steadily and resolutely applied. To delay its solution can only result in a menace of the utmost gravity to the peace of the civilised world.

The Spectator, Vol. 74 (May 11, 1895): 642–43

The Armenian Meeting

We wonder who it is that had the choice of speakers at the Armenian Meeting in St. James's Hall, and on what principle the selection was made. If we look at the majority of the speeches, they were just and reasonable. If there was sound, there was also sense. But these good qualities were neutralised by an extraordinary outburst from Lady Henry Somerset. Of the rhetoric of the speech we have nothing to say. We presume that Lady Henry Somerset's oratory has its admirers, and if so, we can only congratulate them on the rich banquet provided for them on Tuesday. But the good sense and judgement shown in asking Lady Henry Somerset to speak does call for some remark. In a serious meeting assembled for a serious purpose, it is only fitting that some regard should be paid to the effect which a speech is likely to have. Lady Henry Somerset's leading object was to show that one main cause of the persecution of the Armenians is their monogamy; "that their home had one central figure rather than a group of women despoiled of their choicest heritage,—the lifelong fidelity of one man to whom their own had been faithfully pledged." And she further described herself as standing on the platform as the representative of the "holy indignation and burning love" which a hundred thousand women who wear the White Riband feel on behalf of "their sisters yonder in the clutch of the harem-despot of Constantinople." So far as these words were anything more than words, they were directly calculated to defeat the object for which the meeting was called. In themselves, indeed, they had nothing whatever to do with that object. That a man has four wives, or forty, or four hundred, is no reason why he should outrage and murder the wives of other people. But this want of connection will not be noticed. What will be noticed—at least we fear so—is that Lady Henry Somerset, one of those chosen speakers at the great English meeting, identified cruelty with polygamy. If some astute friend of the Porte had wished to give it the means of representing the Armenian agitation as really directed against the principles of the Mahommedan religion, this is precisely the sort of speech he would have wished to be made. The purport need only be communicated to the Turkish people to create in them a temper of ardent resistance to any proposed action on the part of England. Such action, they will say, is not prompted so much by pity for the Armenians as by hatred for us. England wishes to restrain our lawful liberty in the matter of marriage. She cannot even observe the decent civility which is due to a foreign Sovereign. He becomes, in the language of Lady Henry Somerset, "the harem-despot of Constantinople," and, if she has her desire, he will promptly be given notice to quit. It is much better for us, these same Turks will say, to meet threats by threats, and to prove to a West which seeks to impose Christian morality on a Mahommedan population, that it can only do so at the sword's point. We do not blame Lady Henry Somerset. Misplaced, and therefore mischievous, rhetoric is so natural to her that she could not restrain it even if she would. But we do blame those who invited her to speak, and thereby evoked those "loud and prolonged cheers," every one of which made the action of the English Government more difficult and less likely to be supported by other Powers.

Lady Henry Somerset had not a monopoly of unwisdom at St. James's Hall, for there were other speeches which raised questions which, in the interest of the Armenian people, had better have been let alone. But the fault of these other speeches was chiefly that they said things which it is not well to say any sooner than can be helped, though it may be necessary to say them some day. What is really important at this moment is to make the English Government understand that it will be warmly supported in bringing all necessary pressure to bear upon the Sultan, in order to make any repetition of these Armenian horrors impossible. No language can be strong which helps on this end. But some of the speeches on Tuesday seemed expressly directed against this end. The speakers were more anxious to end the Turkish Government than to mend it. What they look forward to with most satisfaction, is the ruin which is to overtake the Turks when they refuse to listen to our remonstrances. Now if the English Government is supposed to be simply seeking a good excuse for washing its hands of the Eastern question, two things are likely to follow. The first is, that the Sultan will be encouraged to resist any pressure that England may use to secure the Armenians against further cruelties. He will argue that he has nothing to do but to go on as he has been doing to ensure a larger measure of liberty, at all events, so far as England is concerned. We do not deny that the recent action of the Ottoman Government has given us ample justification for withdrawing the protection we have hitherto given it. We do not deny that, if it should prove that we have absolutely no means of obtaining from the Ottoman Government the guarantees which we are bound to exact, it would be our duty to withdraw that protection. But we are not at all sure that if the Sultan believed that this would be the worst thing that could happen to him if he refused these guarantees, he might not be tempted to refuse them. The Turk is seldom unwilling to trust to the chapter of accidents, and the prospect of being left to make his own terms with Russia, might seem less terrible than the necessity of satisfying England as well as Russia. The second consequence of any threat on the part of England to retire from the position she has hitherto maintained on the Eastern question, would be an immediate lessening of the interest of Russia in the present aspect of that question. Russia naturally wishes a free hand in South Eastern Europe. The purport of some of the speeches on Tuesday was to suggest to the English Government to tell Russia that, unless adequate securities against a repetition of the recent massacres can be obtained from the Sultan, we shall give her that free hand. But if Russia does not heartily co-operate with England it is very doubtful whether England will succeed in extorting these securities. Consequently, to proclaim beforehand what steps we shall take if we fail in obtaining them, is to make it appear the direct interest of Russia to withhold her co-operation. By that means she will drive England into withdrawing her protection from the Turks, which is the very thing that would most advance Russian policy.

The outcome of all this is that the true policy of England in the matter—the policy that ought to be most strenuously urged upon the English Cabinet—is to exert all the force it can command at Constantinople, and to exert it in the first instance in the most intimate combination with Russia and France. Nothing will do so much to ensure the co-operation of these two Powers as the belief that if we cannot obtain it we shall try what we can achieve by acting alone. We may be sure that Russia will not care to leave the protection of Christians under Turkish rule to a Protestant Power. It would be contrary to all her traditions and to the most deeply-rooted sentiment of her people. We may be equally sure that France will not care to see England playing a great part in the Mediterranean while she herself repeats the blunder which deprived her of her share in the administration of Egypt. Provided therefore that England continues to urge the adoption by Russia and France of the demands which she proposes to press upon the Porte, and at the same time leaves them in no doubt that though she would prefer concerted action, she will not shrink from individual action, she stands a very good chance of bringing round Russia and France to her view of the question. Nothing, on the other hand, could be more inimical to the ultimate adoption of her policy than language which encouraged Russia and France in the opinion that if they interpose sufficient delays, England will retire in disgust, and leave Turkey to her fate.

In formulating an Ultimatum to the Sultan, more will depend upon the nature of the guarantee than upon the precise terms guaranteed. It would be easy for the Turkish Government to frame an Armenian Constitution which should embody the more important provisions of every Constitution in Europe or America, and in the end be as worthless as a dishonoured bill. The one essential condition is that the Governor of Armenia should in effect be appointed by the Powers, and be irremovable, except with their consent. There would be no need to make the real independence of the Sultan which this high functionary would really enjoy, unnecessarily visible. On the contrary, it would be expedient to spare the susceptibilities of the Sultan in every possible way. Provided that he was willing to appoint the person recommended to him by the Powers, their share in the transaction might be kept completely in the background. It is necessary to deprive the Sultan of all real power in Armenia, but assuming that this condition is satisfied, his nominal power might be left undisturbed. Whether the Governor be a Christian or a Mussulman is, to our thinking, a secondary point. It would be far better, for example, to have a Mussulman removable only by the Powers than a Christian removable by the Sultan. The character of the Governor's rule will in the end be determined by the character of the authority to which he is responsible. Other things being equal, it would no doubt be better that he should be a Christian. It would give the Armenians a greater sense of security, and be, to some extent, a compensation for their past sufferings. But the qualification, "other things being equal," should be strictly insisted on; the Sultan should not have any concessions made him in such matters as appointment and revocation in consideration of his undertaking to nominate a Christian. The best security for good government the Armenians can possibly desire, is the knowledge on the part of the Governor that his tenure of office depends on his ruling so as to merit the confidence of the Powers, while it will be wholly unaffected by the favour or displeasure of the Sultan.

The Spectator, Vol. 74 (May 18, 1895): 674–75

The Armenian Reforms

It is difficult to speak at all positively upon the value of the scheme of reform which has been submitted to the Sultan by the Ambassadors of the three Powers, so long as we are ignorant of its exact nature. In matters of this kind, distinctions which at first sight may seem little more than verbal may turn out to have very serious consequences. It is quite on the cards, therefore, that the criticism we propose to offer on the telegrams which profess to state the general drift of the scheme, may in the end prove wide of the mark. It will naturally be asked why, with this possibility in front of us, we should offer any criticisms at all. The proposed reforms will, by and by, be printed as a Parliamentary paper—white or blue, as the case may be—and we have only to wait for their appearance in this shape to give our remarks the accuracy which, as it is, they necessarily want. Our justification for what may seem undue haste is to be found in the fact that by the time this certainty, in itself so desirable, has been attained, criticism will be of no use. The reforms will probably not be made public until they have been accepted by the Sultan, and have acquired the force, if not taken from the form, of a definite Treaty. Then criticism will be purely academical. The demands of the Powers will have been made and granted, and journalists, like the public in general, will have nothing to do except to see how far the acceptance of them meets the case. Those who, like ourselves, have formed a clear conception of what is necessary, if the Armenians are to be delivered from their present wretched condition, will naturally be unwilling to exercise a patience which may defeat its own object. They will prefer to speak while the negotiations are only beginning, in the hope that what they say may have an influence, however small, upon the policy of their own Government. The delays incident to all negotiations with the Porte may in this respect be beneficial. So many counter-proposals are like to be made that the Powers will have time to modify in various ways the demands originally put forward. Concessions in one direction may be balanced by greater urgency in another.

The first remark suggested by the proposed reforms, as they appear in the telegrams of the last three days, is that they are very much too detailed. They seem, at all events, to amount to a series of instructions to the Sultan how he is to govern his Christian subjects. Stress, we are told, is laid on the appointment of fit and competent Governors, upon whose appointment the Powers shall have a right of veto. Then, in order that these fit and competent Governors shall have the assistance of an equally fit and competent staff, one-third of the officials in the Armenian provinces shall be Christians, and the gendarmerie, who will carry out their orders, shall be recruited both from Mahommedans and Christians. Assize Courts are to be established, and prisons are to be inspected, though no particulars are yet given as to the composition either of the Courts or of the inspecting authority. The collection of the taxes is to be intrusted not to the gendarmes, but to the tax-gathers appointed by the Communal Councils. This regulation might, it is obvious, lead to much irregularity in the receipts; but this is guarded against by a provision that the inhabitants of the commune shall be liable for the total amount. It is difficult to foresee the precise extent of this liability, or the nature of the machinery by which it would be enforced, though any scheme which abolishes the farming of the taxes must be an improvement on the present system. The heads of the communes will have the right to retain out of the taxes a sum sufficient for the needs of the local administration. In itself, of course, this is a most excellent and reasonable arrangement. But it is also one which is likely to lead to a good deal of friction between the communes and the central authority; and we cannot but doubt whether the position of a head of a commune who proposed to keep back more than the Government thought necessary would be altogether enjoyable. When so much new machinery is being created in the provinces, it is only natural that some addition should be made to the machinery at headquarters. Accordingly, a Commission composed of Christians as well as Mahommedans is to sit at Constantinople and watch over the administration of the Armenian vilayets. All these reforms will, of course, take time to carry out, and so long as it lasts, the process is to be under the supervision of a High Commissioner, of whom nothing is as yet to be learnt beyond the fact that he is not to be a European, and that his appointment is to be subject to the approval of the three Powers. Finally, the Kurds are to be disarmed when their arms are not in use, and are thus to be reduced, at intervals, to the level of the Armenians.

The more we look at these proposals, supposing them to be accurately described in the telegrams, and supposing also that they contain nothing of importance which is not there described, the more unsatisfactory they seem to us to be. The one wheel in the whole machine upon which the three Powers can make their influence effectively felt, is the High Commissioner; but though the appointment of this great personage is to be subject to the approval of the three Powers, we hear nothing as to his removal. He is to remain in office until the reforms are accomplished. But how if his supervision prove languid or partial? The Sultan is not likely to dismiss him for these faults, and apparently the Powers will have no right to do so. They can, of course, remonstrate with the Porte on the inertness of the High Commissioner, just as, if there were no High Commissioner, they might remonstrate with the Porte on the inertness of the Governors or of the officials of the gendarmerie. But the Porte by this time is pretty well used to remonstrances, and Europe generally is pretty well used to nothing coming of remonstrances. If this weapon is all we have to look to for the execution of these reforms, how are we better off than we have been under the Treaty of Berlin? All the rights conferred by that instrument were not enough to prevent the recent massacres. Why should the rights conferred by this new instrument, if the method of enforcing them is identical, be enough to prevent—we will not say similar massacres, for these probably the Porte will for some time to come be careful to prevent in its own interest—but that constant steady oppression which, if it does not kill, makes life all but unendurable? It may be said, perhaps, that the consent of the Powers to the appointment of the High Commissioner will be sufficient security against any such failure on his part. But it will be very much safer not to say this until we know who the High Commissioner is. It is true, of course, that if Lord Dufferin or Lord Cromer were going to Constantinople in this capacity, we should be quite at ease upon this point; and no doubt there are Frenchmen and Russians whose names, to those who know them, would convey an equal sense of confidence. But Englishmen, Frenchmen and Russians have at least this in common, that they are Europeans, and on this ground, therefore, they are alike ineligible. We do not deny that there may be an Asiatic—which we suppose is what is meant by not a European—who would be willing and able to ensure the proper fulfilment of the Sultan's engagements. But we cannot feel certain that the Powers would know enough of the Asiatic candidates for the post to veto all but the right men; and supposing a man to be appointed, of whom the best that can be said is that nothing is known against him, the fact that he cannot be dismissed by the Powers takes away the only real guarantee for the proper exercise of his functions. An official must have an exceptionally high sense of duty, if his reading of it is not affected by what he knows to be desired and expected of him by his own Government.

The same objections apply with much greater force to the provision that the Powers shall have a veto on the nomination of the Provincial Governors. Of the High Commissioner it is probable that the Ambassadors will have some knowledge, or that, if they have not, they will be able to get information about him. But the further down we go in the official scale the more difficult it becomes to get this information. A veto on the appointment of one man, whose place is at Constantinople, has some value, though, as we think, an inadequate value. A veto on the appointment of many men, whose places will be in the various provinces of the Turkish Empire, will have no value whatever. If Russia and France wished to influence the administration of the law in England there might be some sense in giving them a veto on the appointment of the Lord Chancellor. But what sense would there be in giving them a veto on the appointment of County Court Judges? We would far rather have the details of the scheme left to the discretion of the High Commissioner, provided that he were made a permanent officer, and were removable by the Powers as well as appointed by their consent. This in some shape we believe to be the one essential condition of any lasting reform in Armenia. Any arrangement which stops short of this will not give the Christians of Turkey the indispensable minimum of protection, no matter what it may give them in other ways. As to the occasional disarming of the Kurds, we will only remark that it would be very much more effectual to give the Armenians the right of carrying arms.

The Spectator, Vol. 74 (May 25, 1895): 709–10

Our Duty in Armenia

We do not see any particular advantage in holding more meetings about the Armenian question. The English people are quite convinced that the Turkish government of all Christians, in Macedonia scarcely less than in Armenia, is atrociously bad, so bad as to deserve the terrible sentence in which Mr. Gladstone described the government of Ferdinand of Naples. It was, he said, "the negation of God erected into a system." They know that the Pashas let loose on these unhappy provinces commit oppressions so ghastly that they could only be described in a Blue-book; that there is no redress for the wronged, or punishment for the wrongdoers; and that if the people, driven mad, attempt resistance, the soldiers receive instructions which almost, or in isolated instances quite, point to an intention to exterminate the rebellious. The sufferings of Germans in the Thirty Years' War, which were horrible, are the sufferings of Armenian and Greeks in time of peace, aggravated by the fact that the marauding soldiers have the foul passions of Asiatics. The entire Press, with scarcely an exception, has agreed as to the facts, and so far as we can perceive, the general mind believes that any extent of interference with Turkey has been amply justified. We have as much right to interfere with Constantinople as with Coomassie; that is the nearly universal opinion. It is not as to the facts that opinion is weak, but as to the line of action that the facts justify, and this is the fault of the House of Commons. Occupied with internal affairs, none of them of pressing importance, the Members have abstained from pressing the Government to act, and the weak Government in the absence of such pressure, has shrunk from incurring any responsibility. It has been afraid of the vague dangers involved in stirring the Eastern question, it has been afraid of making an opening for Russian aggression, and it has been afraid of the traditional Tory feeling that the Turk must always, under all circumstances, be protected. It has therefore allowed itself to be content with a compromise, suggested by Russia though supported by France, which appears to all who desire a thorough reform in Turkey to involve the maximum of interference with the Sultan's Government and the minimum of safety for the unhappy Christians. There is to be a High Commissioner to watch future oppression, but he is not to be a Viceroy, and will therefore be only a dignified reporter; he is not to appoint all officials and command all gendarmes, and will therefore not be genuinely responsible; and he is not to be a European, and will therefore not even try to govern for the great European ends of equal justice, personal safety, and industrial advance. Such an appointment, considered as a remedy for outrageous oppression, much of which is interwoven with the Turkish system of keeping Christians down, is an unstatesmanlike subterfuge, which might have been suggested by the most cunning of Pashas. They will still be practical rulers, and they will still of necessity be intrusted with the power of "arrest,"—that is, of inflicting tortures such as Dante never imagined,—on any one who resists their will.

It seems to us that the time has arrived when the House of Commons itself should remonstrate against this fiasco, and should inform the Government, in unmistakable terms, that, rather than suffer the atrocious misgovernment of Armenia to go on, the people of Great Britain are willing to encounter a certain amount of risk. That risk, for it is necessary to speak plainly, can only be of one kind. The Russian Government cannot permit the British Government to take up the position of Foremost Protector of the Christians of the East, and cannot therefore either resist her action or threaten her with war. The one thing the Czar could do, if England were in advance of him in coercing the Seraglio, is to insist on full protection for Armenians, and occupy Armenia with his troops as a material guarantee that his full demand should be conceded. It is at least possible that Nicholas II. might take that resolve, and at least possible also that the withdrawal of those troops might be matter of infinite negotiation, or might be delayed for ever. France will not resist; the movement would be of no importance for Germany; and Great Britain will not fight a great war in order to replace enfranchised Christians under a loathsome slavery. We admit fully that this risk exists; and we say deliberately that rather than the present condition of Armenia should continue, the risk ought to be incurred. The Russian system of government is not a good one; but it is as much better than that of Turkish Pashas as Italian Government is better than government by Dahomey. The Russian government at least requires provocation before it orders slaughter; and its soldiers, when resistance ceases, abstain from outrage and murder. It does not, either, grudge prosperity of its subjects, and as regards Armenians, at all events, it does not hold a difference of creed to be an excuse for rejecting evidence of wrong. That Russia would be strengthened by the acquisition of such a province we greatly doubt; but if she were, our duty ought to be done, even though that evil consequence must necessarily follow. We have no more right to sell the Armenians, to whose protection we are pledged, for a political advantage, than we should have to sell them for money.

In reality we do not believe that the risk to be run is at all serious, and conceive that had Mr. Gladstone been in power and aware of the frightful facts known to the Foreign Office, his policy would have been substantially this. He would have warned the Sultan that the patience of Great Britain was at an end, and that a European Viceroy, responsible to the Powers, must be appointed by July 1st, or the British Government would seek a material guarantee in the shape of a great Turkish Custom-house. And the Mediterranean Fleet would at the same time have appeared off Smyrna ready for immediate action. The Sultan did not face that menace before, and he could not face it now, for he knows it would affect the security of his Mahommedan possessions. He understand that his Christian subjects will ultimately be liberated, and care nothing how they suffer, but he hopes to retain the Mussulman Khalifate, and to that one condition is essential. He must reign over both Osmanlis and Arabs, the latter of whom loathe the former with a hatred which springs not only from difference of race, but from centuries of baffled hope. If the Arabs can revolt they will, and with any loss of prestige within tracts of which the Desert people know the history, the Turkish Khalifate, the greatest misfortune which ever befell Islam, would come at once to an end. Neither the Sultan nor his advisers would run that risk even for the luxury of absolutism in Armenia; the "impossible" would at once be done, as it was in the case of Thessaly, the Viceroy would at one be conceded, and the Palace would console itself with the thought that at least the tribute from Armenia would be regularly paid. The Sultan, in fact, would act too rapidly and too decidedly for the Czar to set a corps d'armée in motion, or provide for the eventualities of a possible second Turkish war. This, we say, is our belief; but our counsel that the Fleet should be sent to Smyrna is independent of that calculation. Nations have disagreeable or dangerous duties to perform sometimes, like individuals; and the rescue of Armenia has fallen to the lot of the British people. No one denies our right of interference, whether it be based on specific treaty, as it is, or on the ordinary right claimed by the civilised Powers of arresting any acts which constitute those who commit them enemies of the human race; and possessing the right, we are, in a case so terrible, to blame for not employing it. We are, to put the matter plainly, skulking from a task which, nevertheless, we acknowledge has fallen to our lot. We need not say we acknowledge fully the need of judgment and caution in all foreign affairs; but there is need of boldness too, and this has in the Armenian matter hitherto been lacking. We have temporised and delayed with full information in our hands; and even now we shall probably be told that we must wait for the Report of the Commission, which, when the object was to put off the nations with a feeble compromise, has not been waited for.

There is one more risk connected with interference in Armenia which is so unreal that we are reluctant to allude to it, but which we mention because "practical men" are fond of throwing it in our teeth. It is said that if we coerce the Sultan into doing justice, we shall alienate the sympathies of our Indian Mahommedan subjects, who look to the Sultan as their Khalif. The objection is demonstrably unfounded. The Mussulmans of India care no more about the Khalif than French soldiers when fighting Catholics care about the Pope. In 1855 we spent fifty millions and wasted at least 50,000 lives in defending the Sultan. That defence was successful, and in 1857, two years afterwards, the Mussulman soldiery were springing at our throats, and both Hindoos and Mussulmans strove to supersede us by a Mussulman dynasty. There was no gratitude to service to the Sultan, and there will be no anger at disservice done him. It is not as if the Khalif were going to be dethroned, though even in that case, so long as Mecca was safe and accessible, the Indian Mussulmans would not care a jot. The dangerous section of the Indian Mussulmans are under Wahabee influence, and the Wahabees are all Arabs.

The Nineteenth Century,[1] Vol. 38 (June 1895): 926–39

The Mussalmans of India and the Armenian Question

Ghulam-us-Saqlain

Now that the question of the alleged Armenian atrocities is under the consideration of a Commission composed of the representatives of various European Powers that have shown an interest in that question, it may appear injudicious to write anything for or against either the Government which is held to be responsible for the alleged barbarities, or those persons who are responsible for the agitation which has led to the appointment of this Commission. Public opinion ought to remain silent and neutral regarding the main questions at issue; it should wait for the judgment which the Commissioners, after due investigation, would pronounce. When the public opinion of Europe, acting upon the Governments of their respective countries, has succeeded in effecting the appointment of a Commission composed of members who are expected to be impartial and independent, it is natural that the agitated feelings and popular outbursts should stop for a moment, and give way to a feeling of expectancy.

But it is not on the appointment of the Commission, or the truth or falsehood of the current reports regarding Armenian cruelties, that I propose to write. Indeed, Armenia and the Commission are of secondary importance as regards my present subject. I hope the Commission will publish a correct and impartial report of the doings of the Sultan's officials and the Armenian agitators, so that a fair man, a man of ordinary common sense, may be able to distribute his sympathies on either side, without feeling the pricking of his conscience which must be experienced when he bases his sympathy or his hatred on a one-sided, incomplete, and distorted view of any matter. At the same time, I must say that such commissions, whether they are appointed for the investigation of any political, or diplomatic, or legislative question, have as yet proved of little practical utility; and that if a history of hundreds and thousands of Government commissions were written, they would be found conspicuous only by their negative results. However, it is but just to hear the judgment of competent judges before sentence is pronounced; and all men who are either interested in the Eastern Question, or whose sympathetic natures are shocked by the tales of unheard-of barbarities committed by a fiendish soldiery on an inoffensive people, must speak only after they have heard the evidence on both sides.

But the interest which the English Government has in the Eastern question generally, and in this particular instance of the "Armenian atrocities," is much greater than, and of quite a different nature from, the interest which it would have as one of the European Powers merely, or even as one of the signatory Powers of the treaties of Berlin and Paris. The interest which Great Britain has in all questions relating to the welfare and vitality of Turkey is not merely a platonic interest. England is certainly a Christian Power; and as such it has, and should have, natural sympathies and antipathies; but then she is something more. She is, in one sense, the greatest Muslim Power in the world. This is a phrase which has been often repeated, but few realize the true significance of this single fact.

Any person who has carefully studied the numerous elements of which the vast Empire of Britain is composed will be struck with the enormous number of the Muhammadans who owe allegiance to the British sovereign. Excluding those scattered numbers of the Mussalmans that are found in almost every English colony or possession in Africa, Asia, and in Australia, the Muhammadan population of the Indian Empire, according to the latest census, is *more than fifty-seven millions.* So that Her Majesty is the ruler of a far greater number of Mussalmans than the Sultan of Turkey, or the Shah of Persia, or both of these together, rule.

This aspect of the question should never be lost sight of. In her dealings with other Powers, England has accordingly duties and responsibilities which no other Power has in the same degree. Here is a unique instance of an Empire which comprehends almost all religions and races on the face of the earth, and which is so situated that by the very force of circumstances it cannot, and should not, adopt any policy other than that of the large-hearted and noble-minded Emperor Akbar, whose vast dominions it has inherited by a series of unforeseen and fortuitous circumstances.

Now, if we except the Christian, or rather the European, element, which is naturally the governing and dominant element, the Muhammadans are, as a people, the most important portion of those innumerable masses of human beings in India that own our Queen Victoria as their rightful sovereign. Not only an account of their numbers, but also by reason of their being the most loyal subjects of Her Majesty, they form an important part of the British Empire.

There is one thing more. The Indian Muhammadans are the only ones who are being largely influenced by the pressure of the civilisation of the West. They are the only followers of the Prophet who are intellectually free, and who can study any sciences and arts they like; who can expound new philosophical theories, evolve new religious speculations, or entertain new ideas of social life; and who can, in short, enter into the race for progress and civilisation without any hindrance. If Egypt be partially excluded, the Mussalmans of no other country but India possess the right of free speech, and have a free press. All these things combine to make them more or less united, and to produce amongst them a sense of nationality and a public spirit which is in most respects new to the East.

It is true that Muhammadans of India, when compared even with other important portions of the community, are in a miserable plight, and are far from being a wealthy or prosperous people. But such is the case all over the world, the difference being only this, that in the case of the Indian Mussalmans there has been, for the last quarter of a century, a new movement and a real awakening on their part. The eloquent writings and speeches of the Honourable Sir Syed Ahmed Khan Bahadur and of Nanah Mohsin-ul-Mulk Mahdi Ali, and the incomparable poems of the great national poet Hali, have raised in many of the Mussalmans quite a new spirit. Some of them are making earnest efforts to reform their abuses, and to do away with all those prejudices that are a bar to their progress, and to infuse new and high ideas in them, and to impart high English education to the Muhammadan youths. This movement for the progress and regeneration of the Indian Mussalmans has only just begun, and it will be premature to say that it has, to any great extent, succeeded; yet some effects of the movement are already observable. The Mussalmans have established, for diffusing high education amongst them, a Muhammadan Anglo-Oriental college at Aligarh, in which more than three hundred Mussalman youths from all parts of the country permanently reside, and which may in time become the nucleus of a great Islamic university. They hold a Muhammadan Educational Conference in different parts of India, to devise means for the general spread of Western education amongst themselves; they edit several hundred vernacular papers; they write articles and publish pamphlets—in short, not a few are earnestly trying to ameliorate the condition of their co-religionists, an attempt in which they have often the cordial support of the Government officials in the country. The results of these endeavours can be easily ascertained in the number of the Mussalmans who have recently raised themselves in the Indian world of letters and politics. Mr. Syed Mahmud, lately of the Allahabad High Court, whose genius as a lawyer and jurist has made his name famous throughout the legal world, and Mr. Justice Amir Ali, the learned author of the *Spirit of Islam*, are distinguished examples of the product of English education. Such men can hold their own in the society of great English writers and lawyers.

Now this education, imparted in the colleges and schools of India, is gradually producing Mussalmans who are sufficiently versed in the English language, and who study the writings of English authors and the speeches of English statements almost as eagerly as Englishmen themselves. These men read and admire the writings of Thackeray and Carlyle; write articles on Tennyson and Macaulay; peruse the works of Mr. Herbert Spencer and Darwin, and the treatises of Mr. Morley and Mr. Frederic Harrison. Some of them follow the debates of Parliament and read the speeches of Mr. Gladstone, Lord Salisbury, Lord Rosebery, and Sir William Harcourt. They can thus understand the course of English policy and the drift of European diplomacy, and they appreciate ordinary English literature as much as any Englishman who reads his morning papers and studies his monthly magazines. Such men, even if they might not understand the doings of Europeans and correctly appreciate the policy of various English statements, *think* that they know the tendency of the European politics of the day. They eagerly read and discuss whatever is said in any quarter of the "civilised world" about the Muhammadans; for the press makes them acquainted with all such matters. They praise and condemn, admire and abhor, and every Mussalman in British India who can read and understand the vernacular of the country (*i.e.* Urdu) has the benefit of the opinions expressed even in the remotest corner of the world, and forms his conclusions regarding the question.

Now such an important portion of Her Majesty's subjects must never be omitted from the consideration of English statesmen. England, if she is fully conscious of her duty, as by far the greatest Moslem Power in the world, governing in all nearly 60,000,000 Muhammadans, is bound by the very nature of the circumstances in which she is placed to widen her political horizon, to regard every political question that comes out not merely in the provincial spirit, to which some of her politicians are apt to tend. There are some questions which affect not only the feelings of the inhabitants of England, Scotland, and Ireland, but also the feelings and sentiments of innumerable masses of human beings whose sentiments, mistaken though they may be, and whose feelings, though they might not be fully understood by European statesmen, are not for that reason to be neglected and despised.

Now, of the political feelings of the Mussalmans of India, perhaps the most firmly seated is an attachment to the Mussalman Powers that still exist in the world.

Of the Mussalman kingdoms, Turkey is the most important, both on account of its vastness and power, and also because of the position she occupies as the guardian of Mecca and Medina, the former being the centre of Islam, the latter being the adopted home of the Prophet, where he is buried. These two places are the resort of hundreds of thousands of pilgrims from all parts of Asia and Africa; and even those who cannot visit them entertain a profound reverence for these holy places of Islam. The less cultured of the Indian Mussalmans have also a dim idea that His Majesty the Sultan of Turkey is somehow or other their Caliph, or religious head. This is an opinion which is hardly supported by competent authorities and traditions; but the mass of the people, not merely in India and Asia, but everywhere in the world, are despotic in their nature, and will brook no contradiction or rational correction of their notions and prejudices. From one point of view they are right. The greatest Moslem Empire, which rules those parts of Asia and Africa where the former caliphates were situated, cannot fail to strike the imagination of an ordinary Moslem. He naturally thinks of that Power as something more than an ordinary secular Mussalman Power, which may have a natural claim on his sympathy, but not on his reverence. The great proportion of the Mussalmans of India are moreover of the Sunni or orthodox sect, to which the Sultan belongs. The Sunnis constitute the bulk of the Mussalman population, the rival sect of the Shias (adherents of Ali) being chiefly confined to the upper classes and the older families. The Shias, like the enlightened Sunnis, have no religious reverence for the kingdom, yet they cannot forget that it is a Moslem Power, and that its fall will lower the prestige of Islam throughout the world.

I do not think that the Mussalmans of India regard themselves bound to the Turkish Empire so much that they would rise in rebellion against the English Government if, in their opinion, it took an unfair advantage of the weakness of Turkey, and brought about its downfall. Such a supposition would be pronounced absurd on the very face of it by every person who has ever lived and moved amongst the Indian Mussalmans. They are loyal to England through conviction and interest. They are perfectly assured that their present position, though by no means prosperous, is very satisfactory. They are *safe* under the rule of Britain. Their religious freedom is secured. They have a possibility of future progress and development such as no Moslem country allows to its inhabitants. Their staunch loyalty to England cannot be doubted, and, with the exception of a few old-fashioned Englishmen, who might be still haunted by the phantom of a supposed Wahabi insurrection, it has been universally acknowledged by the English officials in the country that the Muhammadans of India are the most loyal of Her Majesty's subjects.

But suppose that a crusade is proclaimed against the remaining Moslem kingdoms of the world, that Christian fanatics in various parts of Christendom preach against Islam and the Mussalmans, and stir up bad blood in the followers of both religions by abusing the Prophet and insulting the religion of the Muhammadans, and by hounding on the Christians to attack and annihilate the Mussalmans—then it is not difficult to conceive that the loyalty of the Muhammadans will not remain unshaken. Let us assume that their religion is false and inhuman, which is a very irrational assumption; still, that is no reason why they should not feel insulted and injured by such treatment. We may even take another and more probable case of English statesmen giving way before the torrent of invective and calumny which has been for centuries past directed by the enthusiastic, the philanthropic, the ignorant, and the bigoted against the "unspeakable Turk," and, joining with the *Christian* policy of annihilating Turkey, pursue with regard to the Mussalmans the policy of Russia; this will again produce ill-feeling and anger in the Mussalman population.

I trust, indeed, that time may be very far from us. The leaders of both English parties, at present, pursue the same foreign policy. Lord Rosebery's foreign policy is believed to be even more imperialistic than the policy of his great rival, Lord Salisbury; and an imperialistic policy is nothing if it does not carefully take into account the wishes and feelings of the various nations that people the vast dominions of which the Prime Minister of England is for the time being the executive head. On the other hand, there is a provincial policy which would limit the horizon of English statesmanship, and would make the foreign policy of the Empire subservient to the sentimental desires of a few noisy clubs and societies. A statesman of this school would be indifferent to that public opinion of his fellow-subjects that exists outside the limits of his own ken. He would be carried away, not by deep and broad principles, as he may think, but by a very narrow-minded and short-sighted policy. Such a statesman might be a model ruler for a small State, unconcerned with the rest of the world, having no interest in common with other peoples, but such an one is evidently not fitted to rule the Empire of Britain.

I have made it sufficiently clear that the elements of Christian prejudice and bigotry should be wholly eliminated from the foreign relations of Britain; for while the natural prejudices and sentiments of the Christian population are neutralised by the equally strong prejudices of the Mussalman population of the Empire, the question remains, as it ought ever to remain, in the domain of secular politics. It is not as Christians *versus* Mussalmans that the responsible rulers of this vast Empire should view this question, nor do I think that they have generally viewed it in this light; but a campaign of reckless abuse, led by prominent English politicians, and even by members of the Cabinet, would make it not impossible that those statesmen might try such a course. It is not impossible that racial and religious prejudices might at last triumph over reason.

No single person can be pointed out as the originator of the prejudices held by many Englishmen against the Turks. The history of such prejudices against the Muhammadans in general, and against the Turks in particular, would be very interesting. It dates back to the commencement of the Crusades; and the feeling strengthened and became intense in the Middle Ages, when narrow-mindedness was looked upon as the greatest imaginable virtue, and bigotry was synonymous with piety and religion. This "Age of Chivalry" and darkness, as Burke eloquently expresses, and Carlyle, with emphatic scorn, confirms, "is gone," but it has still left in the minds of not a few persons, otherwise enlightened and cultured, an inheritance of prejudice and bigotry. It is due to the laws of "heredity" that the European mind cannot completely purge itself of those erroneous notions which the former generations had accumulated. To many Englishmen the word Turk or "Mahometan" has very disagreeable associations. It means a tyrannical, loathsome creature, unscrupulous in his conduct, callous as to human suffering, dull and inactive, and a confirmed polygamist. He is supposed to have, to use Mr. Gladstone's witty phrase, "a double dose of original sin." We need not believe in an "angelic theory" (to quote Mr. Balfour's equally brilliant retort) to affirm that the Turks are, as a rule, made like other men, that they have their virtues and vices, their excellences and their faults. No nation has a right to attribute to itself all moral excellence, and to assign to some other nation, particularly disliked, everything that is disagreeable or distasteful. But the Turks have long suffered from such unreasonable prejudices. They have a different religion, a different nationality, and their name has become in Europe a byword for all unnatural and inhuman vices. This is to many persons a sufficient reason why they should always pronounce their infallible judgment against them, and expel them from all the civilised parts of the world.

Such a state of mind may be very natural, and even excusable, in the case of the ignorant and the unthinking masses. But when persons of undoubted ability and information, who advocate the equal and liberal treatment of all mankind, irrespective of class, colour, and religion, and who profess to regard man as a noble being, and as such an object of their natural sympathy, forget all those professions of justice and fair dealing, and declaim against a whole race, representing them as worse than brutes, then indeed we are surprised, and cannot but condemn. They draw, as Burke said, an indictment against an entire nation. Granted that there are many shortcomings, and even perverse principles, in the Turkish system of government, two questions naturally arise. Do these things exist nowhere but in Turkey, and have no other government and no other people in the world, or even what is called the civilised world, any such faults? And do the gentlemen who constantly declaim against the Turkish Empire sincerely desire that it should reform its system of government and make a real internal progress, unchecked and unhindered?

For if there are faults in the system of government, and honest efforts are being made by the Sultan and his Court to improve the machinery of the Government, to develop the resources of the Empire, and to advance the education and the civilisation of the people as far as may be possible, no rational man will condemn them simply because the rate of the progress is not as rapid as in his opinion it ought to be, and because they move slowly and do not adopt all that their critics want them to adopt. If such critics of the Turkish Empire were really desirous of its moving with the spirit of the times and adopting the most improved forms of government and administration, no one could blame them. They would be the true friends of that country, though they might be somewhat impatient critics. It might be said in their favour that they really desire the welfare of the people under the Turkish rule, though they do not clearly appreciate the enormous and harassing difficulties which the Sultan and his advisers have to overcome before they introduce effective reforms into the country. But, in fact, those who condemn Turkey, condemn it root and branch: they think that from the beginning to the end it has been a curse to mankind, and that the Turks never do and never will do any good—a contention which implies that the critics are all-wise, and that their judgment is free from errors and their actions are above criticism. With such immaculate beings it is impossible to argue.

Of the two questions mentioned above, I wish to briefly discuss the latter question first—Whether the critics of the Turks earnestly desire the amelioration of the condition of those various races that own the sway of the Sultan? If they do, they certainly do not adopt the best method to effect their ends. I do not deny that these gentlemen are honest in their intentions and sincere in their professions of benevolence and philanthropy; though the benevolence is somewhat partial and the philanthropy somewhat mixed with something other than love. Yet they either fail to recognize or knowingly shut their eyes to the fact that, on the whole, Turkey has been steadily trying to reform its old abuses and to change itself according to the requirements of the age. This change towards improvement is observable in every department. Leaving aside its older history, and coming to the very recent times after the last Russo-Turkish war, one fact will be evident to every careful and honest student of the course of Turkish politics and Turkish history. The present reigning monarch, Sultan Abdul Hamid Khan, is as conscientious and hard-working a prince, and is as much desirous of the welfare and progress of his subjects, as any of his contemporaries can be. In the performance of his duty he does not spare himself. He constantly strives to improve every department of his Government. If the force of circumstances, or the prejudices and notions developed by the laws of what is called "heredity" in the philosophy of Mr. Herbert Spencer, has not allowed the Empire to advance to an ideal State, or has not allowed it to advance as much as might satisfy its ardent critics, we can only condemn the laws of nature, and not any particular set of men. If once it is conceded that personally the Sultan and his Ministers are honestly working for the good of the Empire as a whole, then it becomes the duty of every one interested in the fate of the Christian or the Moslem subjects of Turkey to assist and encourage that Government in its good resolves. Violent invectives against the Turkish nation, and reckless abuse of their religion, and stormy agitation in the country, are the worst possible means to strengthen the hands of Turkish authorities or to make them desirous of working in the right direction.

But that is the only encouragement the Sultan and his Ministers ever get. Not a single peaceful period is given to them for working out internal reforms and making progress. A periodical cry is raised against them that they have been weighed and found wanting. They are told that the respite allowed to them has expired, but they have not mended their ways. They are made the victims of rhetorical attacks and of abuse not very scrupulous. Such treatment makes the Turk doubly angry. It grievously wounds his pride, and he is naturally disgusted and mortified. He looks back fondly to the old system of government, when no one dared raise his voice against the constituted authorities, and when the rights granted to the subjects and the alien races were the free gifts of the sovereign, and not demanded with such violence. He beshrews the day in which he was forced by Sultan Mahmud to partially adopt the Western methods; for every concession is followed by another agitation. Every act of his is misrepresented and distorted into some hideous crime; and a mountain is made of a molehill, and invectives and abuse are the only rewards which he gets for his toleration. Such behaviour makes him angry. It wounds his pride, and he determines once more to return to the former methods of government, and to oppose inch by inch every attempt that is made to drag him against his will to the new schemes. So the good that is done is greatly neutralised by the evil effected by these military campaigns and the campaigns of abuse directed against it by Christian Europe.

But our adverse critics give neither the Sultan nor his advisers any credit for good intentions. As I have said, they seem to think the Turkish race to be an incarnation of the evil principle of Nature, from which no good can be expected, and to whose destruction they should direct their energies. They have made in their mind a picture of the Turk and his government, and they persist in regarding this abnormal creature, which has only a subjective existence, as having an objective reality. Unless they bring an impartial and unprejudiced mind to the consideration of the evidence that might be produced in favour of Turkey, no facts will convince them; for their subjective picture will effectually bar the entrance of the notion of the real Turk into their minds. This only can be respectfully recommended to their consideration: whether a race of human beings can be so abnormally wicked and unspeakably cruel as they represent and suppose the Turk to be. If they think there is some exaggeration in that, it would be better if they considered the question apart from racial and religious prejudices. Let them judge the Turk as they would judge any Christian people similarly placed. If they cannot do so, they have no right to insist that their fancies should be taken as real and patent facts.

The other question is this: Are the abuses complained of in Turkey such as exist in no other part of the world, and is the Turkish system more decidedly corrupt and cruel than the system of any other Christian Government in the world? If this fact should be conclusively settled against Turkey, then indeed there would be strong reason for condemning a Government which suffers such barbarities to be perpetrated, and allows such laws to exist in its dominion as are entirely foreign to the civilised sense of the world, and wholly given up by every other State. But no statesman, even no ordinary politician, who knows enough of the general character of the different Governments, not to say of the world, but of Europe only, will venture to make any such sweeping assertion. No one, however strongly prejudiced he may be against Turkey, can deny that the severe and oppressive despotic system of Russia, according to which system half the European continent is governed, is in no way less lenient, less barbarous, or more humane than the corresponding Turkish system. The world cannot easily forget the late heartless expulsion of hundreds of thousands of Jews. Men were driven from their homes, where they had lived for centuries, their property was confiscated, and they were driven out in absolute poverty, and pushed forcibly on into other reluctant countries. It is impossible to calculate the amount of human suffering brought about by this expulsion; yet the collective humanity of civilised Europe was hardly powerful enough to save one Jew from being expelled from his native place. The press did not raise its mighty voice, the indignant protest of hundreds and thousands of enlightened friends of the human race did not make the Russian officials anxious. The press either uttered some cold phrases of reprobation, or even justified the action of the Russian authorities by specious reasoning.

The Mussalmans of India, informed by the vernacular papers of all these contemporary events, take notice of these facts, and generally look upon all such professions of philanthropy and human sympathy as hypocritical pretensions. No doubt they are wrong in their sweeping condemnation, which is owing to their not being fully acquainted with the political ideas and principles current in Europe, and with the methods in which the Europeans express their opinions. But though they may be erroneous, they are excusable. Any man of common understanding, not gifted with an extraordinarily subtle and discriminating conscience, would fail to find any reason why laws and practices in a Christian country should be passed over in silence, while similar laws and practices, which entail even lesser evils, when found in a neighbouring Moslem kingdom, should be denounced from all public places, from the senate, the pulpit, and the platform. In such cases there must be either a strong religious antipathy, or racial hatred, or both; and if so, the humanitarian gentlemen come down almost to the level of vulgar agitators and the bigots who excite the religious animosities of the masses.

I do not mean to say that the Turkish system is even comparatively perfect. There are, indeed, grave errors of principle, as well as of detail, in the administration. The most important and perhaps the greatest grievance is the absolute suppression of the liberty of the press. The fact that no paper or book can be published or brought into the country without passing through the severe ordeal of being inspected and "corrected" by a very watchful and ruthless licenser is shocking to the minds of men who have been bought up in the midst of a free press and free discussion. This practice is the greatest curse to the people. It stagnates the minds of men, and retards every kind of intellectual progress. For the sake of human nature itself such a benumbing influence should be cautiously and gradually taken away by the Sultan from his subjects; and a reform in this direction would make the name of Sultan Abdul Hamid doubly illustrious in the history of this century. No doubt a Government placed in such a delicate and difficult position cannot safely act according to abstract propositions. It has to look carefully upon the results of the practical applications of such philosophical principles. But even if we take into account all the evils of a moderately free press and free institutions in such an empire as Turkey, the advantages of such institutions far outweigh any incidental evils that might accrue.

But Mussalmans of India naturally suppose that the English public have no right to denounce Turkey for its suppressions of the liberty of the press before they exert themselves to give a free press to the Christians of Russia, by inducing their Christian ally to grant that right to its subjects. When we consider that it was only few years back (1878) that an Act was passed by the Governor-General of India in Council to take away the liberty of the native press, an Act which was repealed by the truly sympathetic Viceroy, Lord Ripon; and when we see that even now not a few Englishmen of India, who are known as the Anglo-Indians, loudly desire to suppress the liberty of the native newspapers, we ought to be a little more lenient in condemning the Oriental Government of Turkey. The Mussalmans of India also think that the alleged cruelties in Armenia do not exceed what is said and written about the cruelties suffered by the Siberian prisoners; but while the former are still hypothetical, the latter are certain and patent facts; yet all the eloquence of a great English party and a great press is exhausted depicting the unnameable Turkish horrors, while only a faint and cold sympathy is given to their suffering co-religionists and fellow-men in another part of the world.

Such considerations produce anger and contempt in the minds of the Mussalmans, who repose even less confidence in the partial philanthropy of interested politicians than the diplomats have in the political treaties. It was a few days ago that I heard some leading Muhammadans saying in perfect good faith, without thinking themselves cynical in expressing such sentiments, that treaties between unequal powers are only so much waste paper! The stronger always consider them worthless, in so far as they are in favour of the weaker powers, while any terms in favour of the stronger power are most sternly enforced by that power. The general treatment of the weak Asiatic and African Governments by the powerful military kingdoms of Europe is regarded in no better light than this! International morality may be realised between equals, or perhaps (but this I say with great reserve) between the Europeans; but as to an equitable dealing between the Europeans and the poor weak people of Asia, the belief does not exist in the Oriental mind. I think that they exaggerate the examples of selfishness which they find in the Europeans, and that they forget that the Europeans are also men, and so have natural faults; but the truth is that such instances of European partiality and prejudice come into strong relief, owing to the professions of a sublime morality, and the claim of their having a high idea of justice, which are unfortunately seldom realised. The

Mussalmans of India, like other Orientals, are not, as a rule, favourably impressed by the political and the diplomatic methods of the European statesmen and diplomats. They have come to look upon the public avowal of humane sentiments and noble principles as the diplomatic screening of very questionable purposes.

Such an unfavourable idea of the Europeans formed on the part of their Asiatic fellow-beings, however partial and erroneous that idea may be, is much to be regretted. I have tried here to prove that, if such ideas are held by a large number of the Indian Mussalmans, they are not wholly to be blamed; and that Englishmen also contribute to the formation of such prejudices.

It is impossible to write on the questions of England and Turkey, and on the sentiments of the Indian Mussalmans, without mentioning the name of Mr. Gladstone. I have not the least wish to say one word against this illustrious and veteran statesman. Personally speaking I have the highest admiration for this great Liberal leader of the century. Indeed I may sincerely say that amongst the Mussalmans I am perhaps his greatest admirer. His pure and lofty character, his genius and eloquence, and the services that he has done to the Liberal party of England, will make his name retain an honourable place in the history of the nineteenth century. I think the greatest achievement of his life is this: he has introduced a high moral tone in all political and diplomatic questions of the day. He has established noble principles, where formerly expediency alone prevailed. Even regarding the Turkish Empire his attitude is far from being entirely indefensible. Whatever he did and wrote and spoke against Turkey was quite natural in a gentleman of warm sympathies, of great susceptibilities, who is easily carried away by his emotions, and who is moreover a sincere believer in all the ecclesiastical dogmas of modern Christianity—dogmas which teach him that the Muhammadans, being non-Christians, are infidels, who have as such no right to desecrate the sacred soil of Europe. With all these qualities, anybody having only defective and one-sided information, and no opportunities of calmly deliberating over the remote result of his actions, might be expected to do exactly what Mr. Gladstone did with regard to Turkey. Mr. Gladstone fondly believes tales of horrors that are told to him by scheming persons. He has a natural prejudice, almost antipathy, to the very name of the "Turk." His mind is some important respects resembles that of some pious, learned, but narrow-minded priest of the middle ages; and his unreasoning prejudice against the Turk is indeed mediaeval, and worthy of those dark ages of blind belief and Quixotic chivalry.

A person of such character, however graphic and sublime it may be, should not have such great political influence on the minds of millions of his fellow-beings—he should not be at the head of such a vast Empire as that of England of to-day—if he cannot control his emotions and his ecclesiastical prejudices. He is a sublime moral leader of men, but a statesman of Mr. Gladstone's position should be more calm, more deliberate, and should weigh his words more carefully before he speaks. He should take great care that his writings and speeches do not wound the feelings of millions of his fellow-subjects. The late Prime Minister of England has seldom thought of the very existence of the Indian Mussalmans, but the Indian Mussalmans often think of him. They hear every word that he utters about the Turks. I do not know, though I can imagine, what the Turkish Mussalmans think of Mr. Gladstone; but amongst the Indian Mussalmans he is far from being popular. To his true admirers, like myself, this is very painful. But Mr. Gladstone never thinks on both sides of the Turkish question. Carried away by his ardent imagination and his rushing eloquence, he delivers speeches and writes pamphlets, which, however noble they may be from a Christian (or rather a dogmatic) and anti-Turkish point of view, are neither statesmanlike in spirit nor sound as to facts.

But it is not of Mr. Gladstone as an individual, but of Mr. Gladstone as a leader of a great political party, that the actions in this respect ought not to be approved. If the British and the Irish people, either Conservative or Radical, calmly think over the great responsibilities which they have, as the rulers of the greatest Empire now existing in the world, and if they clearly appreciate their duty as the rulers of the greatest Moslem community in the world, they will not be carried away by racial or ecclesiastical prejudices. They will calmly and impartially judge before they condemn or agitate against any Moslem power or kingdom with which sixty millions of their fellow-subjects have strong sympathies. They will not readily take part in any outcry against Turkey, or any Mussalman State, simply because the latter is not a Christian or a European State.

"*Noblesse oblige*," says the proverb, and it may be said, with equal truth, that vast empires and large dominions have also their peculiar obligations.

The Nineteenth Century, Vol. 38 (July 1895): 156–64

A Moslem View of Abdul Hamid and the Powers

Rafiüddin Ahmad

The long-looked-for answer of the Sultan to the notes of the Three Powers regarding reforms in Armenia has at last been received. It is understood to be unfavourable. What does England propose to do next? Is she going to war with Turkey? Before the responsible Ministers of the Crown take decisive action in this most difficult matter, it is necessary that they should hear not only the voice of the "Predominant Partner," but also the feeble echoes of such minor partners in the firm of the Empire as the Mohammedan subjects of the Queen-Empress. England is the greatest Mohammedan Power upon earth, and the Queen's Moslem subjects are the mainstay of the British rule in the East. The Moslems, therefore, not unnaturally expect that the Cabinet which governs the fate and guides the policy of the whole Empire should listen to their views, at least whenever questions affecting Moslem kingdoms in the East are under its consideration. Moreover, the advice of the Mohammedan would, for obvious reasons, be received with more attention and effect by the Moslem monarchs than that of the most trustworthy Christian. Unfortunately, it is not always easy for Moslems to have their voice heard in England on important occasions. I gladly take the opportunity which the kindness of the Editor of this Review has placed at my disposal of placing a Moslem view of the question before the British public.

I have been closely studying the origin and development of what is wrongly termed the Armenian question. I have read the British Christian opinion, and my recent visit to Constantinople in connection with the Meccan Pilgrim question has enabled me to learn Turkish Moslem opinion regarding the Armenian problem. As there is no free press in Turkey, and the Turks are naturally suspicious of all Europeans, it is always difficult, if not impossible, for this country to know Turkish public opinion on any question. I think it important that the readers of this Review should know what intelligent Turks have to say in this matter. I happened to be in Constantinople when the demonstration was held at St. James's Hall. It was immediately after the meeting that the Ambassadors presented a cut-and-dried system of reforms to the Porte.

When the full report of the meeting reached the capital of Turkey the indignation of the Moslems knew no bounds. The speech of the Duke of Argyll was undeniably sensible and statesmanlike, but the speeches that followed his were ignorant, spiteful, and fanatical. The enthusiasm of the speakers robbed them of their judgment. The speakers themselves displayed too openly the signs of religious fanaticism and racial rancour which they had assembled there to denounce. One of the speakers, a very influential clergyman, "let the cat out of the bag." What bewilders the mature judgments of statesmen in Europe and makes even the most Radical politicians pause was to him an easy matter. For, speaking of the reopening of the Eastern question, the reverend gentleman is reported to have said, "If the Eastern question meant the abolition of the open scandal of the worship of Mohammed in the first great Christian church erected by the first great Christian emperor, the sooner the question was reopened the better."

This confirmed the belief of the Turks that behind the humanitarian movement in England there was a desire to see Santa Sophia in the possession of some Christian Power. I assure my readers that the so-called friends of Christians in Turkey have ill served the objects of their sympathy. They have raised false hopes in the breasts of the Moslem subjects of the Porte, and instead of extinguishing fanaticism in the East, they have rekindled the smouldering embers of religious and racial hatred, the result of which may be disaster to all alike.

Moreover, the irresponsible verbosity of ecclesiastical agitators and the mischievous scribbling of political dreamers have added enormously to the diplomatic difficulties of the representative of England in Turkey, and each fresh act of indiscretion in this country tends to accentuate the tension between the British Embassy and the Sublime Porte. One of the immediate effects of the meeting at St. James's Hall was the increase of attendance of the faithful at the evening prayers at the Mosque of Santa Sophia.

The Turks are surprised at the action of England. The Commission appointed by the Sultan and supervised by the delegates of the Three Powers has not yet concluded its labours. Only a short time ago Lord Kimberley, and even Mr. Gladstone, publicly declared that nothing practical would be done in regard to Armenia till the publication of the report of the Commission. It was believed to be an injustice to Turkey to condemn her before trial. They condemned her without trial. It is said that the British Foreign Office possessed facts enough to know the truth about the Sassoon affair. That, the Turks argue, it possessed long before the appointment of the Commission.

Why, then, the Turks ask, did the British Government send a delegate to Armenia and put itself as well as the Porte to useless expense and inconvenience? When the Sultan invited England to send a delegate, why did not the Government say that, in its opinion, the appointment of a Commission was superfluous, as it had already obtained the necessary information? Why did not the Government at once prepare a scheme of reform, and present it to the Porte soon after the receipt of consular reports from Asia Minor, instead of losing eight precious months? Probably the authorities will return a satisfactory answer to each of these questions when the time comes; but meanwhile the opinion prevails in Turkey that the Government yielded to the Armenian agitation, the object of which had been to condemn the Commission and prejudge the question.

What the Moslems in Turkey cannot understand is the nature of the English people. England says that France and Russia are signatories to the Treaty of Berlin; yet France and Russia have not allowed the Armenian question to upset their minds. Their newspapers have not made more than passing allusions to recent incidents in Armenia. How is it, then, that England alone of all the Powers has whipped herself to fever-heat? Is she more humane or more conscientious in her duties than the rest of the Christian Powers? Neither the Continental Powers nor the Turks would admit that. The Turks do not understand English customs. They take it that every meeting or every article in the English newspapers reflects the opinion of the responsible authorities.

While the Turks thus interpret popular agitations in this country, the Russians draw altogether different conclusions. When this country was denouncing Russia for her barbarous treatment of the Jews at Guildhall, Madame Novikoff communicated to the *Times* the following remarkable information for the British public:—"Women when their hearts are full, when their nerves are overstrained, indulge in a good cry. Englishmen when their nervous system is upset find their chief consolation in speechifying at public meetings. But idle talk may degenerate into impertinence." And again, regarding the gullibility of the English nation, she wrote:—"If one of the Nihilist murderers, who seem so popular in England, were to write that all Russian husbands kill their wives, and all Russian mothers kill their children, I make no doubt such interesting statements would be published with avidity, and would perhaps necessitate other meetings at Guildhall. The real difficulty is to introduce into the English press a word of truth about Russia."

The Turks assert that their Government was ill-advised in ceding Cyprus to England. By the Convention of Cyprus England undertakes to defend the Asiatic possessions of the Sultan against the aggression of Russia. Russia, as every one knows, desired to establish a protectorate over Armenia in 1878. England would not listen to Russian intervention in the Asiatic provinces of Turkey in any form. Yet England, after a lapse of a decade, is the first to propose to deprive the Sultan of his full and direct sovereignty over Armenia. Undoubtedly, they say, the Porte by the Cyprus Convention undertakes to introduce reforms by force of arms. What England might do at the utmost is to refuse to defend Turkey when she is attacked by Russia, on the ground that Turkey has not observed one of the terms of the contract, and thus rescind it. The Turks, therefore refuse to admit that the Cyprus Convention has given England the right of dictating to the Sultan his policy in Asia Minor, much less any right to deprive him of sovereign power in any of his provinces. The only right of intervention to which she could lay claim is the clause in the Berlin Treaty; but that right is to be exercised by the Powers conjointly.

Some people advise the Government to coerce the Sultan into obedience by *force majeure*. A well-known friend of the Armenians says that, as soon as the Turks observe the British fleet in the Bosphorus, the Sheikh-ul-Islam will issue a *fatwa* advising the Sultan to accept all the terms. The reverend gentleman states that, according to one of the principles of Islam, the Sultan is bound to yield whenever Christian Powers compel him to do so, or whenever he sees no chance of success in war. This principle of Islam exists only in the imagination of Armenian agitators. The example of the Prophet himself, the practice of the distinguished Caliph Omar, and the whole history of Islam contradict it. The Koran has no unchangeable injunction to the Moslem monarchs in political matters.

Quite erroneous and misleading impressions obtain here regarding the duties and functions of the Sheikh-ul-Islam. The Sheikh, in the first place, is not a necessary institution in Islam. However despotic he may have been in former times, in the present reign his power is narrowly limited. He has very little to do with important political matters. The Sultan alone transacts all diplomatic business. The Sheikh holds office at the will of his Majesty. Whenever the ministry is changed, the Sheikh resigns office and a new Sheikh takes his place. To say that the Sheikh decides the question of peace or war in modern times is the grossest absurdity. Of course, as a minister he is consulted along with other ministers; but he has not one bit more influence with his Majesty than any other minister.

I have seen it stated that the real rulers of Turkey are the several Sheikhs that reside in Constantinople. It is said that these Sheikhs bully the Sultan into obedience by threatening to depose him. I have resided too long in Stamboul to believe any such twaddle. No doubt the Sultan maintains some Sheikhs in Constantinople out of his own civil list, and, as is customary with all Eastern princes, he tries to please every learned man, and possibly prevents him from backbiting and mischief by his munificence. But, as every ambassador to Turkey knows, these Sheikhs have very little influence with his Majesty, though every one of them believes that he alone is the favourite of the Caliph.

A glance at the document of the Powers, which advocates doubtless a well-meaning change, will convince every one who has the least acquaintance with Turkey that so elaborate a system as is therein urged is incapable, at any rate for the moment, of being put into execution. The country is too wild and unsettled to admit of so complicated an arrangement, which will appear to be compatible only with the inherited traditions and habits of a highly civilised community. Paper constitutions are notoriously deceptive works of art, and their value is solely proportionate to the fitness of the people on whom they are conferred to assimilate their provisions. As compared with Asiatic Turkey, India is in advance a hundred years; but I doubt very much whether it will be possible to carry out the system even in the most enlightened parts of India. The main objections to the system are very [lucidly] summarized by an M.P. in *England.* These are:—

1. It interferes directly with the sovereign rights of the Sultan and sets up a dual control.

2. It interferes directly with the functions of the Sublime Porte, as it sets up a dual system of administration.

3. It establishes many new officers and sets of officials, whose cost is to be paid out of the slender resources of the poorest provinces and districts of Turkey.

4. It is unjust to the Moslems of Turkey in Asia, inasmuch as it proposes to establish a much larger proportion of Christian officials than is warranted by their numbers, the proportion of Moslems to Christians in Asiatic Turkey being at least five to one.

By a curious coincidence, on the very day when the Sultan sent his answer to the Powers, and at the very moment when all the newspapers of England were discussing the prospects of war, the followers of the Prophet from all parts of the world assembled at Mecca for the Hajj. This assemblage of the faithful in the birthplace of Islam at such a time is an event of great importance. The pilgrims to Mecca represent not only the orthodoxy, but also the aristocracy and intellect, of Islam. Moreover, many of them owe political allegiance to England, France, Russia. The recent tragic incident in Jedda, which necessitated the departure of the venerable Shareef of Mecca to the scene of the tragedy, must have caused great excitement and general confusion among the pilgrims. The attitude of the Christian Powers towards the protector of the Holy Shrines must have come under their discussion. The speeches and writings of European statesmen regarding the Caliph and his country find their way into the mosques and cafés of Islam, much to the annoyance of the Turkish authorities. The pilgrims must have seen with their own eyes the dangers to the prestige of the Caliph and to his authority in the very birthplace of Islam. They will go back to their respective countries filled with regret and indignation, and the tale of woe they will carry to their homes will naturally cause grief and pain to the entire Moslem community. At such a time the eyes of the Moslems are bent upon the Power that will extend a helping hand to the Caliph. Hitherto England has been recognised to be the best friend and Russia the worst enemy of Islam. Lately this traditional belief has been strengthened by the sympathetic answer which Mr. Fowler, the Secretary of State for India, made to me in connection with the grievances of the Indian pilgrims to Mecca and the humane dispatch which he sent to the Viceroy, practically removing all the complaints of the pilgrims which I had brought to his notice. I now hear that Russia is secretly trying to play the part of the friend of Turkey in order to win the affections of the Moslem populace in Asia Minor. Whether this be true or not, it is deplorable to see England grouped with Russia against her old friend and ally. Nothing would be more impolitic than a war with Turkey, and nothing more foolish than an empty demonstration of the fleet in the Bosphorus. The Turks are used to threats from European Powers. England has already committed a great mistake in threatening the late Sultan of Morocco, which act destroyed her influence in that country altogether. If it is to be war, one might ask, not the clergy, but the statesmen of England, For what are you going to war with your old friend and protégé? The probable answer would be, "Because the Sultan does not accept the scheme of reforms presented to him." But the scheme of reforms is not, by the admission of many Englishmen themselves, the most perfect or even the most practical scheme that can be offered. Is it impossible to make any change in, or to make any concession in regard to, the scheme? Is there nothing else but "the pound of flesh" or the acceptance of the scheme? If it is humiliating for England to grant any concession at all, is it not equally so for the Sultan to swallow the bitter pill offered to him by the Powers?

I do not mean to say that there is no misgovernment in Turkey. I have told Turkish statesmen themselves that the only possible reason for the maintenance of their rule in Europe would be a thorough change in the administration of the country. Nor do I think that England is wrong in giving advice to the Turks. I think (and many Turks agree with me) that the best friend of Turkey is England. I differ from English statesmen when they advocate reforms only for the sake of the Christians, while poor Moslem subjects of the Porte are left high and dry. The misgovernment in Turkey is injurious alike to the Christians and to the Turks, and all reforms must benefit the two races equally. If the British Government in India introduced reforms in that country exclusively for the Moslems, would not the Hindoos grow discontented and furious? Englishmen are told that the Turk will do anything through fear and nothing through love. Now, the Turk, whatever else he may not be, is brave. He is not afraid of his life. Turkish history proves that the Turk prefers death to dishonour. But the Turk, along with other warlike and brave people, has his weakness. He is ridiculously self-sacrificing as a friend. If you ask him to do a thing for you as a *friend*, you stand a very good chance of obtaining what you want.

In order to understand clearly the political situation in the East, it is indispensable that my readers should know the real character, position, and influence of the Sultan Abdul Hamid. Apart from his political importance, the ruler of Turkey, as Caliph of Islam and protector of her Holy Shrines, exercises a moral influence over countless millions which is quite unrivalled in this age of skepticism and unbelief. European writers, as a rule, do not do him justice, though some there are who have praised him too much. He has his shortcomings as a statesman; but as Caliph of Islam he is the most popular prince that ever came to the throne. The question naturally arises whether a Moslem Caliph can render any service to England. Although the Turkish Sultans have no direct political influence among the Moslems beyond their own Empire (nor have they ever been desirous of extending their political influence outside their territory), they exercise great moral authority in the Islamic world. This authority was once used in favour of England at a very critical time. Upon that subject I will quote the views of the late Prime Minister of Hyderabad, son of the most distinguished Indian statesman of the century. Sir Salar Jung, in an article in this Review (December 1887), says:—

> "England has in India some fifty millions of Moslem subjects, including in their mass the most warlike of the native races, the races upon whom England must chiefly rely to roll back the tide of Russian aggression; and England is not likely to forget that it was these very races who, in 1857, at the bidding of their Caliph, the Sultan

> Abdul Medjid, gave their united support to the British connection at that supreme moment when their defection might have cost the life of every white man and woman in India. My late father frequently assured me that the whole influence of the Caliphate was used most unremittingly from Constantinople to check the spread of mutiny, to rally round the English standards the Mussulman races of India; and that in this way the debt that Turkey owed to Great Britain for British support in the Crimea was paid in full. And the time may come again when the devotion of the Mussulmans to their Caliph and the shrine of St. Sophie may be not less necessary to Great Britain than in 1857."

European writers describe the Sultan as a very suspicious man. Granting that he is so, show me one man who would not become suspicious under similar circumstances. There are the ambassadors of the six Great Powers, each trying to play the game of his own country, and repeatedly misrepresenting the ideas of his rival. The Sultan believed, and suffered. Christian Europe has done little to abate his difficulties. When he *knows* a person he believes him; but, unfortunately, the person does not always deserve to be trusted. There is another popular error regarding the Sultan's character. It is believed that his Majesty yields only through fear; hence some people always advise the British ambassador to bully the Sultan. No greater mistake could ever be committed by diplomats. I asked a Turkish gentleman who is intimately connected with his Majesty how it was that French and Russian diplomacy succeeded better than British diplomacy, more especially when the English are known to be the best friends of Turkey. He assured me that somehow or other the French and the Russian ambassadors manage to become private friends of his Majesty. The Sultan hates official pressure of whatever kind. The French and the Russians get many things done in the name of their Governments. His Majesty is an extremely kind-hearted man, and when an appeal is made to his friendship or to his generosity he cannot resist it.

On the other hand, he is a very sensitive monarch, and he resents any encroachments upon his dignity as an independent sovereign. I wish Englishmen would take a little more pains than they do to learn Oriental nature. The sooner the policy of bullying Oriental monarchs is abolished, the better it will be for this country.

It is believed by many people that it is useless to appeal to his

Majesty for redress of any grievance. It is said that he turns a deaf ear to all the appeals, and even if he has the will to remedy a complaint, he has not the power to do so. The belief is groundless. I admit that, owing perhaps to too much centralisation, his Majesty has not always time enough to attend to important matters; but when a matter is brought to his notice, he is ready to decide it in an impartial manner. I will relate my personal experience.

I had been trying for some years to bring to the notice of the Turkish authorities the grievances of the Indian pilgrims to Mecca in the Holy Land. I communicated with one or two Turkish officials without much success. Then I went to Constantinople. I saw the Sultan and told him of the complaints. He received me graciously, and listened attentively to what I told him. He assured me that he would do everything in his power to get all the reasonable grievances of the pilgrims removed; that he thought it his duty to listen to complaints from all persons, irrespectively of their nationality and religion. He was as good as his word. I am informed he has sent medical men and a large sum of money to Arabia to carry out the necessary reforms.

I advise Her Majesty's Ministers to adopt a conciliatory mood. There are persons in this country who are trying to put an end to the traditional alliance between England and Turkey. There is a desire in certain quarters to popularise the "Divine Figure of the North." Now, I cannot forget that the greatest rival of England in the East is Russia, and I have a belief in the common sense of Englishmen. The recurrence of danger to British interests in the south-east of Europe (as well as to the north-west of India) is more than possible. The steps of the multiplication table are no less beyond suspicion than is the fact that during a European war, in which Russia is involved, the Divine Figure of the North will become a diabolical figure in the South. In order to cripple her power in Europe, Russia will attack England on the borders of India. She has an enormous army, and can easily afford the diversion. England cannot do better than maintain her traditional alliance with Turkey. When we are establishing buffer States on all our frontiers abroad, are we to permit the disestablishment of the buffer State which lies between England's possessions in the East and the hordes of the myriad Sclavs? Surely England will not suffer her Eastern Empire to be overrun by savagedom, the civilisation of centuries to be wrecked, and the achievements of her Imperial genius to be brought to ruin?

The Armenian Question

Now that the dust and confusion of the General Election have subsided, Lord Salisbury will be able to turn his attention to foreign affairs, and not too soon, for if we mistake not, there is a thorny question not merely in each hemisphere, but in every continent. Lord Rosebery's one strong point was supposed to be foreign affairs, but we venture to say that if the country ever learns what Lord Salisbury learned as to our position when he first went to his Department, they will take a very different view of the matter. Nerveless dexterity and supple ingenuity may do for a time in home politics, but when they are tried against, and in competition with, the ablest of European diplomatists, they mean a series of tergiversations and humiliations. Fortunately, Lord Salisbury is just the man to get the affairs of the nation put into better case. He has a profound knowledge of foreign affairs, he is greatly respected in Europe, and not a little feared, and he has at his back a virtually unanimous people prepared to trust his judgment and enforce it. In only one quarter of the world are we the least anxious as to Lord Salisbury's policy. We doubt whether in the case of Armenia he is prepared to act quite as strongly and with as clear a purpose as he ought, if he is to make England play a part which is worthy of her. That Lord Salisbury is sincerely anxious to help the Christian populations of Armenia, and to put an end to Turkish misrule, we do not doubt for a moment. Our fear is that he may take up an attitude of despair in the matter. His fault is a certain inclination towards pessimism in public affairs, and we feel that there is a danger of his arguing that the attempt to relieve the Armenian Christians may only end in greater miseries for them and for the whole world, by raising the Eastern question in its acutest and most aggravated form, and that, therefore, any scheme for succouring them must be strictly limited and conditioned by the dread of ulterior difficulties.

We believe that this pessimistic way of treating the matter is in reality likely to lead to far greater evils than those it seeks to avoid. The Eastern question is a stinging-nettle that had much better be grasped boldly and firmly. Lord Rosebery made little or no progress in the matter of relieving Armenia, because he would do nothing except in conjunction with the other Powers,—would take, that is, no independent action of his own. We trust that Lord Salisbury will assume a line worthier of the position of England, and will insist upon the Turk taking real measures for the better government of Asia Minor, whether he is able to secure the co-operation of the Powers, or not. The Sultan's policy is trembling in the balance. Hitherto he has hung back from doing what is required of him because he hoped that the result of the Elections would help him. If he finds out that he was mistaken, and that British policy has not changed except to become stronger, he will probably be induced to yield with little or no difficulty. We do not desire to enter here into details of what our policy should be. It may be noted, however, that the one essential thing is that the Powers should be given the right of superintending the carrying-out of reforms, and that the new Governor of, or Commissioner for, Armenia should feel himself responsible not to the Sultan, but to Europe. We care very little whether the Governor is a Christian or a Mahommedan, so long as he feels that his tenure of office depends upon the goodwill of the Embassies and not on that of the Porte. To put it plainly, the Governor of Armenia must, on the one hand, not be dismissed without the leave of the Powers; and on the other, they must have power to enforce his dismissal. If the Governor or Commissioner is removable at will by the Sultan, he will feel that he may at any moment be overthrown by a Palace intrigue. Especially will this be the case if, like Shakir Pasha, the official just nominated, he is a Mahommedan. Some one will whisper at Court that he is a bad Mahommedan, and if this is confirmed locally, the Sultan, who is not only personally somewhat of a fanatic, but who believes that his very existence as a monarch is bound up with an exhibition of strenuous Mohammedanism, will be certain to take alarm, and to compass the downfall of the Governor. But the charge of being a bad Mahommedan is certain to be confirmed locally in the case of an impartial Governor. The man who prevents the Turks from treating the Christians as their natural prey, who really holds the balance fairly and prevents pillage and outrage in the homes of the Christians, or who punishes their perpetrators, will soon come to be regarded as the enemy of the faithful. If the new Governor of Armenia is to be directly dismissible by the Porte, he will be forced to secure his position by allowing a certain amount of oppression and outrage. If, however, he knows not only that he cannot be dismissed by the Sultan, but that he will certainly be got rid of on a protest from the Powers, he may be relied on to keep some sort of hold on the Turkish population of the province. Dependence on the goodwill of the Sultan means, sooner or later, the old tale of murder and rapine. Dependence upon the Powers will mean respect for the public opinion of Europe.

And a strong policy in Armenia not only commends itself as the safest and wisest policy judged by external considerations. It is also the safest and wisest policy at home. If Lord Salisbury fails to take a strong line in Armenia, and if the Turks, as they almost certainly will, argue therefrom that they are to be allowed their own way in the matter of massacres, the effect at home will be most disastrous. Already missionaries and special correspondents are, it is said, convinced that there is very grave danger of another outbreak of massacre in Armenia. All that is wanted to produce another outbreak of fanaticism and outrage is the spread of the belief that England's attitude has changed, and that Turkey is not to be interfered with. Of course Lord Salisbury will mean anything rather than to give such a hint, but the Turks are stupid, and it may well happen that they will treat a lack of strength in dealing with the Sultan as evidence that they are to have their will with the Christian people in Armenia. But another and worse massacre in and around Van, and it is nothing less that is feared, would create an outburst of feeling in England such as characterised the agitation as to the Bulgarian atrocities. We should see Mr. Gladstone back on the platform, and the Gladstonian party trying to put the whole blame on the Ministry. Under such circumstances, Lord Salisbury would have to do one of two things,—either to face a great outbreak of popular feeling which would be as strong among his own supporters as among the Opposition, or else to let the force of opinion carry him into violent diplomatic action, which very likely would be ill-judged and indefensible. Then indeed we should see the Eastern question raised with a vengeance. Is it worth while to risk not only a new massacre, but also so disagreeable a situation, in order to avoid deciding what we mean to do about Russia's claim to go some day to Constantinople?—for that is in a great measure the explanation of the dread felt by English statesmen in regard to raising the Eastern question. That, however, is not the present question. Our object is to point out that if the result of any weakness in dealing with the Armenian question should be a fresh massacre, the Opposition will be given their one chance of injuring the Ministry.

While on the subject of Armenia, and the dealings of the Porte with its Turkish subjects, we must not forget to refer the very able and informing article on Islam in the current number of the *Quarterly*. We are glad to see the position that effectual protection for the Christian population of Turkey cannot be obtained in provinces which are not under the tutelage of Europe.

The Contemporary Review, Vol. 68 (August 1895): 153–89

The Condition of Armenia

E. J. Dillon[1]

A pretty story is told of a little girl, who, fearing to lie in bed in the dark, begged her mother not to take the candle away until sleep should render it needless. "What are you afraid of, darling?" asked the strong-minded parent. "Of darkness," was the reply. "But remember, dear, that God is here in the room with you, and God is light itself. He will stay with you all night to keep you company." The silence that followed this dogmatic announcement seemed to show that the intended effect had been produced, until it was softly broken by the sweet voice of the child: "Then, please mamma, take God away and leave the candle."

The attitude of the Armenian population in Turkey towards the humane peoples of Western Europe who, to fiendish tortures and bloody massacres, hopefully oppose well-timed expressions of righteous indignation and moral sympathy, offers considerable analogy to the frame of mind of that untutored child. "We can dispense with your sympathy and pity if only you guarantee us security for life and property." So reasons the grateful Armenian. The impartial outsider, acquainted with the horrible condition of country and people, would naturally go a step further, and fearlessly affirm that the expression of sympathy at public meetings, followed, as in England, by supine inactivity, is not merely inferior to effective material aid, but is positively disastrous. Formerly the Turks disliked the Armenians, and the blood-bath of Sassoun offers a fair indication of the vehemence of their feeling. At present, after the wanton humiliation inflicted upon them by the European friends of their victims, they loathe the very name of Armenia, and deem no cruelties sufficient to satisfy their outraged self-love. The Vali (Governor-General) of Erzeroum, when the foreign consuls of that city lately brought an unusually crying case of injustice to his notice, told the Dragomans that the Turkish Government and the Armenian people stood to each other in the relation of husband and wife, and that outsiders who felt pity for the wife when her husband maltreated her, would do wisely and well to abstain from interfering. And the remark is quite true, *if the pair are to go on living together;* for the brutal husband can always choose his own time and place to vent his feelings on his helpless mate. And this is what is being actually done in Turkish Armenia. Under the eyes of the Russians, English, and French delegates at Moush, the witnesses who had the courage to speak the truth to the representatives of the Powers were thrown into prison, and not a hand was raised to protect them; and at the present moment, within a stone's throw of the foreign consuls and missionaries, loyal Armenians are being hung up by the heels, the hair of their heads and beards plucked out one by one, their bodies branded with red-hot irons and defiled in beastly ways that can neither be described nor hinted at in England, their wives dishonoured in their presence, and their daughters raped before their eyes. And all that the philanthropic English nation has to offer these its *protégés*, is eloquent indignation and barren sympathy. Would it not have been much more benevolent to hush up the massacres of Sassoun and ignore the Pits of Death than to irritate the Turk to the point of madness and then leave him free to vent his fury upon Christians who are shielded only by our sentimental eloquence?

What reason the Armenians have to feel grateful to this country is a mystery which threatens to prove insoluble, unless indeed we define gratitude to be a lively sense of favours to come. For the net result of our interference with Russia in 1878, if considered from a purely philanthropic point of view, was to perpetuate a system of horrors in the five Armenian provinces, compared with which those of negro slavery in the Southern States were literally light blemishes. We solemnly abolished purgatory and deliberately connived at the inauguration of hell. We undertook to see that the abuses engendered by misgovernment in the Armenian cantons of Turkey should be speedily and definitely swept away; and not merely have we neglected to fulfil this self-imposed duty, with which we refused to entrust Russia, but we have allowed a loose system of misrule gradually to develop into a diabolical policy of utter extermination, without venturing to make our power felt, or daring to recognise our impotence. Even the massacre of Sassoun, which provoked such wild outbursts of indignation among English-speaking peoples, has had no more tangible effect upon our late Liberal Government than that of stirring them up to increase the number of letters, telegrams, and consular reports. It is perfectly true, though not perhaps generally known, that the Liberal Cabinet were in possession of the main facts of that butchery as long ago as last September, left nothing undone to conceal them from the public from that to the day of their resignation; and it is notorious that the Armenians are being hounded down and vivisected with even greater cruelty at present. We are still cheerfully waiting for something to turn up. The responsibility of this wanton waste of time should, we are told by certain well-informed politicians, fall upon the shoulders of Russia, whose "underhand scheming" is rendering the energetic efforts of England abortive. The wily ways of Muscovite diplomacy are too well known to need comment—a vague hint is [deemed] sufficient; the intelligent public can be trusted to draw a pretty accurate picture for itself.

"What do you say hinders you from going to school this morning, George?" asked a mild mother of her wayward boy one fine summer morning. "The mud, mother." "The mud? You are dreaming, child. The streets are perfectly clean; where is the mud?" "It is too deep for detection, mother." The same thing may be predicted of the underhand scheming of the Russian Government.

I speak in the light of facts. I have seen and conversed with the official representatives of that Power, in various parts of Turkey. I have watched their work, observed their methods, and have seen exceptionally trustworthy data for forming an opinion as to the attitude they assume on this question of the Sassoun massacre—the only issue as yet before the Powers—and I have not the slightest hesitation in affirming that, whatever obstacles our Government may have encountered in the work of assisting Armenia, none of them [took] their origin in Muscovite intrigues. Russia acceded to our request to inquire into the Sassoun massacre, and accomplished exactly and conscientiously everything she promised. No efforts were spared by her representatives to clear up the question; no personal prejudice or political interests were allowed to stand in the way of thorough investigation; men who personally dislike the Armenians and admire the Moslems unhesitatingly raised their voices in favour of the latter without wantonly irritating the Turks, with whom they are on more friendly terms than ourselves, they revealed the whole truth, and Russia can now afford to await further developments and complications with the interest of an intelligent observer.

The Armenian problem has, no doubt, a political side, regarding which it is impossible to say what the views of Russia are likely to be, but it is natural to assume that the present Tsar will be guided in his policy solely by considerations of justice and benevolence. One may say, however, without any hesitation that Great Britain ought to treat the Armenian Question on the basis either of pure politics or of pure benevolence. We cannot do both. We ought not openly to offer alms, and secretly endeavour to obtain the market rate of interest on the sum ostensibly given away; build a house for the roofless and stipulate that it shall be used as a protection for ourselves and a barrier against the advance of possible enemies, whom we continue to treat as friends, and whom we invite to help us in the work of construction. Russia's attitude is absolutely correct; it is more, it is highly benevolent; for she has given hospitality to nearly 20,000 Armenian refugees, whereas we, who are morally responsible for the weltering chaos that prevails on her borders, have turned away the sufferers with naught but gaseous sympathy and frothy promises.

And yet the duty of this country is simplicity itself; we should either put a speedy end to the horrors of Turkish Dahomey or publicly proclaim our inability to fulfil our obligations in Armenia, at the same time repudiating our gigantic engagement to maintain the integrity of the Turkish Empire in Asia. For as it was a grievous blunder to raise this Armenian Question last winter without having first made sure that we could work it out to a satisfactory issue, it is little less than a crime to give the Turks the needful time to carry out their nefarious plans by our obstinate refusal to look the facts in the face.

Those who are familiar with the condition of the five provinces and their Christian inhabitants will unhesitatingly acquiesce in this view of the subject; for those who are not, the following brief sketch may prove instructive.

Turkey's real sway in Armenia dates from the year 1847, when Osman Pasha gave the final *coup de grâce* to the secular power of the Koordish Derebeks in the five south-eastern provinces (Van, Bitlis, Moush, Bayazed, and Diarbekir). During that long spell of nearly fifty years, we can clearly distinguish two periods: one of shameful misgovernment (1847–1891), and the other (1892–1894) of frank extermination. Suasion or remonstrance may do much to remedy the abuses that flow from the former system; force alone can achieve anything against the latter. And in this sense Lord Salisbury's recently expressed view of the matter is absolutely correct.

In the year 1891 the Sublime Porte fearing serious dangers from the promised introduction of reforms into Armenia, and from the anticipated hostility in war time of the Christians living in provinces bordering upon Russia, resolved to kill two birds with one stone, and created the so-called Hamidieh cavalry, composed exclusively of Koords. It was an application of the principle, on which rebels and rioters throw open the prison doors and invite convicts to rob and kill the members of the upper classes. The plan as propounded by some of the highest officials of the Empire was that the Armenians were to be driven out of the border lands, such as Alashkerd, their places to be taken by Mohammedans, that their numbers in all the five provinces were to be so considerably reduced that the need of special reforms for them should pass away, and that in case of war the Koords should act as a counterweight to the Cossacks.

This plain policy of extermination has been faithfully carried out and considerably extended from that day to this, and unless speedily arrested, will undoubtedly lead to a final solution of the Armenian problem. But a solution which will disgrace Christianity and laugh civilisation to scorn. The enlisted Koords were left in their native places, exempted from service, supplied with arms, invested with the inviolability of ambassadors, and paid with the regularity characteristic of the Sublime Porte. And they fulfilled their mission with scrupulous exactness: robbing rich Armenians, looting houses, burning corn and hay, raiding villages, lifting cattle, raping young girls of tender age, dishonouring married women, driving away entire populations, and killing all who were manly or mad enough to attempt to resist. Armenians are now among the poorest and most wretched people on the globe.

Perhaps the Turkish authorities did not foresee, nor Turkish justice approve, these results? The authorities not only expected them, but aided and abetted, incited and rewarded those who actually committed them; and whenever an Armenian dared to complain, not only was he not listened to by the officials whom he paid to protect him, but he was thrown into a fetid prison and tortured and outraged in strange and horrible ways for his presumption and insolence.

The massacre of Sassoun itself is now proved to have been the deliberate deed of the representatives of the Sublime Porte, carefully planned and unflinchingly executed in spite of the squeamishness of Koordish brigands and the fitful gleams of human nature that occasionally made themselves felt in the hearts even of Turkish soldiers.

To complain, therefore, of the insecurity of life and property in Armenia, so long as the country is irresponsibly governed by the Sublime Porte, is as reasonable as it would be for a soldier to object to the great danger to life and limb from the enemy's bullets during a sanguinary engagement. The result complained of is precisely the object aimed at, and its completeness the most conclusive proof of the efficiency of the means employed. An eminent foreign statesman who is commonly credited with Turcophile sentiments of uncompromising thoroughness, lately remarked to me in private conversation that Turkish rule in Armenia might be aptly described as organised brigandage, legalised murder, and meritorious immorality. Protests against such a system may be right and proper, but they can hardly be considered profitable. A philanthropist visiting a prison may feel shocked when he discovers one of the convicts with his hands and feet tied with cords; but he will scarcely spend time in complaining if he learns that the prisoner has been condemned to death, and is about to be hanged by the executioner.

The first step in carrying out the Plan of Extermination was the systematic impoverishment of the people. This is natural in a country whose officials are kept waiting eight or ten months for their salaries, and must then content themselves with but a fraction of what is due. "I have not received a para[2] for the past twenty weeks, and I cannot buy even clothes," exclaimed the official who was told off to "shadow" me day and night in Erzeroum. "Do they pay you your salary regularly?" I inquired of the head of the telegraph office at Kutek. "No, Effendi, not regularly," he replied; "I have not had anything now for fully eight months. Oh yes, I have; a month's salary was given to me at Bairam."[3] "How do you manage to live, then?" "Poorly." "But you must have some money to go on with, or else you could not keep body and soul together?" "I have a little, of course, but not enough. Allah is good. You have now given me some money yourself." "Yes, but that is not for you; it is for telegrams, and belongs to the State." "Well, my shadow will have grown considerably less before the State beholds the gleam of it. I keep for myself all the money paid in by the public. I take it as instalments of my salary. It does not amount to very much. But whatever it happens to be, I pocket it." These men are, of course, petty officials, but their case is not essentially different from that of the majority of their betters, and judges, officers, deputy-governor, and valis, &c. &c., are to the full as impecunious and incomparably more greedy.

Tahsin Pasha, the late Governor-General of Bitlis, is a fair specimen of the high Turkish dignitary of the epoch of extermination. An avaricious skinflint, he was as cruel as Ugolino's enemy, Ruggieri, and as cold as Captain Maleger in Spenser's "Faëry Queen." He cultivated a habit of imprisoning scores of wealthy Armenians, without any imputed charge or show of pretext. Liberty was then offered them in return for exorbitant sums representing the greater part of their substance. Refusal to pay was followed by treatment compared with which the torture of the Jews in mediæval England, or the agonies of the eunuchs of the princesses of Oude in modern India were mild and salutary chastisements. Some men were kept standing up all day and night, forbidden to eat, drink, or move. If they lost strength and consciousness cold water or hot irons soon brought them round, and the work of coercion continued. Time and perseverance being on the side of the Turks, the Armenians generally ended by sacrificing everything that made life valuable, for the sake of exemption from maddening pain. It was a case of sacrificing or being sacrificed, and that which seemed the lesser of the two evils was invariably chosen.

In the Vilayet of Bitlis several hundred Armenians who possessed money, cattle or crops, were arbitrarily imprisoned and set free on the payment of large bribes. Some of them, unable to produce the money at once, were kept in the noisome dungeons until they raised the sum demanded, or were released by death. About one hundred Armenian prisoners died in the prison of Bitlis alone. The following petition signed and sent to me—and if I mistake not, also to foreign delegates at Moush—from a well-known man whose name and address I publish, will help to convey some idea of how the Vali of Bitlis governed his province, and prospered the while: "We, who have served the Turkish Government with absolute loyalty, are maltreated and oppressed, more particularly of late years, now by the Government itself now by Koordish brigands. Thus last year (1894) I was suddenly arrested at my own house by Turkish police and gendarmes, who escorted me to the prison of Bitlis, where I was insulted and subjected to the most horrible tortures. Having been kept four months there I was released on condition of paying £450, by way of ransom. No reason, no pretext has been given for this treatment. On my return home, I found my house in disorder, my affairs ruined, my means gone. My first thought was to appeal to the Turkish Government for redress, but I shrank from doing so, lest I should be condemned again. Hearing that you have come to Armenia for the purpose of investigating the condition of the people, I ventured to request you, in God's name, to take notice of the facts of my case. Signed, Boghos Darmanian, of the village of Iknakhodja of the Kaza of Manazkerd."

In 1890, the village elder of Odandjor in Boolanyk, Abdal by name, was a wealthy man, as wealth goes in that part of the world. He possessed 50 buffaloes, 80 oxen, 600 sheep, beside horses, &c. The women of his family wore golden ornaments in their hair and on their breasts, and he paid £50 a year in taxes to the Treasury. That was in 1890. In 1894 he was a poverty-stricken peasant, familiar with misery and apprehensive of death from hunger. His village and those of the entire district had been plundered, and the inhabitants stripped, so to say, naked, the Turkish authorities smiling approval the while. During the year 1894, in the districts of Boolanyk and Moush alone, upwards of ten thousand head of cattle and sheep were driven off by the Koords.

This was the method in vogue all over the country; the details varied according to the condition of things, places, and kinglets, but the means and end never varied. The result is the utter disappearance of wealth and the rapid spread of misery, so intense, so irremediable, so utterly loathsome in its moral and physical effects as to have inspired some of its victims with that wild courage akin to madness which always takes its rise in despair.[4]

Between the Vali or Governor-General and the Zaptieh or tax-gatherer the rungs of the administrative ladder are many, and to each and all of them some portion of the substance of industrious Armenians adheres. No doubt there are far worse things than the loss of one's property, and unemotional Englishmen would rather save their sympathy for those who have endured them. But surely even that is bad enough when the outcome [is] not of crime, accident, or carelessness, but of shameless and defiant injustice, and where the loser has a family of some fifteen to twenty persons. And that the loss of property very often entailed far greater losses will be evident from some of the following facts.

In July 1892, a captain of his Majesty's Hamidieh Cavalry, Idris by name, an ornament of the Hassnanlee tribe, came with his brother to demand a contribution of fodder from the inhabitants of Hamsisheikh. They accosted two of the Armenian notables, Alo and Hatchadoor, and ordered them to provide the hay required. "We do not possess such a quantity in the whole village," they replied. "Produce the hay without more ado, or I'll shoot you dead," exclaimed Idris. "But it does not exist, and we cannot create it." "Then die," said the gallant captain, and shot them dead on the spot. A formal complaint was lodged against Idris, and the Kaimakam, to his credit, arrested him and kept him in prison for four weeks, when the valiant Koord having paid the usual bribe was set at liberty. About thirty similar murders were committed in the same district of Boolanyk during that season, with the same publicity and the same impunity.

At first the Armenians were wont to complain when their relatives or friends were killed, in the hope that in some cases the arm of the law might be raised to punish the murderers and thus produce a deterrent effect upon others who might feel disposed to go and do likewise. But they were very soon weaned of this habit, by methods the nature of which may be gathered from the following incident: In July 1892 a Koord named Ahmed Ogloo Batal rode over to Govandook (District of Khnouss) and drove off four oxen belonging to an Armenian named Mookho. In 1892 the law forbidding Christians to carry arms was not yet strictly observed, and Mookho possessing a revolver, and seeing that the Koord was about to use his, fired. Both weapons went off at once and both men fell dead on the spot. What then happened was this: Nineteen Armenians of the village, none of whom had any knowledge of what had occurred, were arrested and put in jail and told that they would be released on payment of a heavy bribe. Ten paid it and were set free at once. The remainder, refusing, were kept in prison for a long time afterwards. None of the Koords were molested. "Why should Mohammedans be punished for killing Armenians?" asked a Koordish brigand who was also a Hamidieh officer, of me. "It is unheard of." Why indeed? That the relatives of the murdered people should be punished and punished severely for complaining of those who have made them widows or orphans seems meet and proper to the Mohammedan mind—perhaps because it is usual.

In August 1893 the Djibranlee Koords attacked the village of Kaghkik, plundered it, and wounded a merchant named Oannes, who was engaged in business in his shop. Next day Oannes went to the Deputy Governor (Kaimakam) in Khnoussaberd and lodged a complaint, whereupon the Kaimakam put him in prison for "lying." The sufferings inflicted upon him in that hotbed of typhoid fever exceed belief—but that is another story. After eight days his neighbours brought a Koord before the Kaimakam who bore out their evidence that Oannes had been really wounded in the matter described, and that he was not lying. Then, and then only, the authorities *allowed the people* to pay a bribe of ten pounds for the release of the wounded man.

The inhabitants of Krtaboz (a village in Bassen) told me several horrible stories of what they had to endure lately from the Koords who drove off their twenty-three oxen, twenty-eight horses, sixty cows, and twenty sheep. One which illustrates the method of *Turkish* justice will suffice to give the reader an inkling of their nature. "Last May (1894) twelve mounted Hamidiehs attacked our village and seized our priest, Der David. They promised to release him if he paid them six pounds. He borrowed the sum, gave it to his captors and was set free. The troops fired upon the other villagers, who ran away. Next day Guil Beg went to Hassankaleh to complain to the authorities. They abused him, called him a liar and ordered him to be imprisoned. After having spent forty days in the horrible hole called a prison, he was permitted to pay a bribe of seven pounds and go home."

There is no redress whatever for a Christian who has suffered in property, limb, or life at the hands of Mohammedans; not because the law officers are careless or lethargic, but because they are specially retained on the other side. And the proof of this, if any proof were needed, is that the complainants themselves are speedily punished for lodging an information against their persecutors. But whenever a Koord or a Turk is the victim of a "crime," or even an accident, the energy of the Government officials knows no bounds. In the spring of last year, when the snows were thawing and the waters rose high in the rivers and streams, some needy Koords were moving along the bank of the river, hard by Hussnakar. They were wretched beggars, asking alms, and battling with fate. In an attempt to ford the river they were carried away and drowned. Forthwith the villagers were accused of having murdered them, and four Armenian notables were arrested and imprisoned in Hassankaleh of this trumpery charge, the real object of which was not disguised. After the lapse of seven or eight months the villagers were told that on payment of a bribe of £75 the prisoners would be discharged. The money had to be scraped together and paid to the authorities, whereupon the men were released. I saw two of them, Atam and Dono, myself.

The taxes levied upon Armenians are exorbitant; the bribes that invariably accompany them, and are imposed by the Zaptiehs, may swell to any proportions, and assume the most repugnant forms, while the methods employed to collect both constitute by themselves a sufficient justification for the sweeping away of Ottoman rule in Armenia.

To give a fair instance of the different rates of taxation for Christians and Mohammedans in towns it will suffice to point out that in Erzeroum, where there are 8000 Mohammedan houses, the Moslems pay only 395,000 piastres, whereas the Christians, whose houses number but 2000, pay 430,000 piastres.

In the country districts everything without exception is highly taxed by the Government, and the heaviest burden of this legal exaction is light when compared with the extortion practised by its agents, the Zaptiehs. A family, for instance, is supposed to contribute, say, £5, and fulfils its obligation. The Zaptiehs, however, ask for £3 or £4 more for themselves, and are met with a rash refusal. Negotiations, interlarded with violent and abusive language, ensue, and £1 is accepted. But the Zaptiehs' blood is up. In a week they return and demand the same taxes over again. The Armenians wax angry, protest and present their receipt; whereat the Zaptiehs laughingly explain that the document in question is no receipt but a few verses from a Turkish book. The villagers plead poverty and implore mercy. Greed, not compassion, moves the Zaptiehs to compromise the matter for £3 more, but the money is not forthcoming. Then they demand the surrender of the young women and girls of the family to glut their brutal appetites, and refusal is punished with a series of tortures over which decency and humanity throw a veil of silence. Rape, and every kind of brutal outrage conceivable to the diseased mind of Oriental profligates, and incredible to the average European intelligence, varied perhaps with murder or arson, wind up the incident.

I have seen and spoken with victims of these representatives of the Sublime Porte; I have inspected their wounds, questioned their families, interrogated their priests, their persecutors, and their gaolers (some of them being incarcerated for complaining), and I unhesitatingly affirm not merely that these horrors are real facts but that they are frequent occurrences. The following is the translation of an authentic document in my possession, signed and sealed by the inhabitants of Melikan (Kaza of Keghi), addressed as recently as March 26 of the present year of his Beatitude, the learned and saintly Metropolitan Archbishop of Erzeroum, a dignitary who enjoys the respect and esteem of friends and foes:

> "For a long time past the four or five Zaptiehs charged with the collection of the imperial taxes have chosen our village for their headquarters, and compel the inhabitants of the outlying country to come hither to pay their contribution. They eat, drink and feed their horses at our expense, undisguisedly showing that they are resolved to reduce us to beggary.
>
> "Lately seven other Zaptiehs, who had not even the pretext of collecting the taxes, entered our village, beat the inhabitants, insulted the Christian religion, and dishonoured our wives and daughters, after which they seized three men who protested—Boghos,

> Mardig, and Krikor—bound them with a twofold chain and hung them up by the feet from the rafters. They left them in this position until the blood began to blow from their nostrils. These poor men fell ill in consequence. The Zaptiehs, however, declared publicly that they had treated the people thus merely in obedience to the special orders of the chief of the police.
>
> "We therefore appeal to imperial justice to rescue us from this unbearable position. The inhabitants of the village of Melikan, Kaza of Keghi.
>
> "(Signed) Katshere.
>
> "26th March, 1895."

Here is another petition from another village of the same Kaza, likewise addressed to the Metropolitan Archbishop of Erzeroum:

> "A number of Zaptiehs, on pretext of gathering the taxes, rode into our village at five o'clock Turkish (about ten o'clock A.M.) broke open the doors of our dwellings, entered the inner apartments, clutched our wives and children, who were in a state of semi-nudity, and cast them into the road along with the couches on which they lay. Then they beat and maltreated them most cruelly. Finally they selected over thirty of our women, shut them up in a barn, and wrought their criminal will upon them. Before leaving they took all the food and fodder we possessed, as is their invariable custom. We beg to draw your attention to these facts and to implore the imperial clemency. The inhabitants of the village of Arek, Kaza of Keghi.
>
> "(Signed) Mooradian, Ressian, Berghoyan, Melkonian.
>
> "26th March, 1895."

I was present myself in the house of an Armenian peasant, of the village of Kipri Kieu, when a number of mounted Zaptiehs arrived, woke up the inmates, and insolently demanded food for themselves, barley for their horses, and couches for the night. What more they would have called for I am not prepared to say, but I extricated my host from the difficulty by refusing them admittance on the ground that I had hired the house for the night. No wonder that the peasants of the District of Khnouss complain, in the petition which they asked me to lay before "the noble and human people of England," "That the once prosperous and fertile country is now deserted, waste and desolate."

These, then, are the horrors which are connoted by the phrase so flippantly uttered by certain enlightened English people: "These Armenians and Koords are eternally quarrelling and a little bloodshed more or less would not seem seriously to affect the general average." It is true enough in the sense in which it is correct to say that sheep and wolves are perpetually at war with each other, and in this sense only. The Armenians are naturally peaceful in all places: passionately devoted to agriculture in the country, and wholly absorbed by mercantile pursuits in the towns. Lest their inborn aversion to bloodshed, however, should be overcome by the impulse of duty, the instinct of self-defence, or deep-rooted affection for those near and dear to them, they are forbidden to possess arms, and the tortures that are inflicted on the few who disregard this law, would bring a blush to the cheek of a countryman of Confucius.[5] They must rely for protection exclusively upon the Turkish soldiers and the Turkish law.

The nature of the protection afforded by the Imperial troops was sufficiently clearly revealed last August and September on the slopes of Frfrkar and the heights of Andok, in the hamlets of Dalvorik and in the valley of Ghellyegoozan. The villages of Odandjor, Hamzasheikh, Kakarloob Kharagyul, flourishing and prosperous in 1890–1891, did not contain one sheep, one buffalo, one horse in 1894. The stables were all tenantless, the stalls all empty, and the ashes of seventy enormous stacks of corn told the rest of the tale. This was the congenial work of the Koords, whose friends, the Turkish troops, were quartered, to the number of 200 horse soldiers in Yondjalee, half an hour distant from Odandjor, 200 in Kop, and 100 in Shekagoob. The protection which they afforded was given to the Koords, and the reward they received was a share in the spoils.

The protection given by Turkish law is of a like nature, only incomparably more disastrous to those Armenians who venture to have recourse to it. Two or three instances, vouched for by a host of witnesses, verified by foreign consuls and authenticated by official documents, will throw light enough for all practical purposes upon the strange forms assumed by Turkish justice in the provinces of Armenia.

Kevork Vardanian, of the village of Mankassar (Sandjak of Alashkerd) testified, among other things, as follows: "In 1892, a Koord, Andon by name, son of Kerevash (of the tribe of Tshalal) came with his comrades to my house and took five pounds in gold belonging to me which I had saved up to buy seed corn with. I lodged a complaint against him, but the authorities dismissed me with contempt. Andon hearing of my attempt to have him punished, came one night with twelve men, stood on our roof and looking down through the aperture fired. My daughter-in-law, Yezeko, struck by a bullet, fell dead. Her two boys and my child Missak (two years old) likewise lost their lives then and there. Then the Koords entered the apartments and took my furniture, clothing, four oxen and four cows.[6] I hastened to the village of Karakilisse and complained to Rahim Pasha. Having heard my story, he said: 'The Hamidieh Koords are the Sultan's warriors. To do thus is their right. You Armenians are liars.' *And we were imprisoned.* We did not obtain our release until we had paid two pounds in gold.

"The following winter two hundred soldiers entered our village under the leadership of Rahim Pasha himself. He at once told us that it was illegal to complain of the doings of the Koords. Then he quartered himself and his troops upon us and demanded daily eight sheep, ten measures of barley, besides eggs, poultry, and butter. Forty days running our village supplied these articles of food gratis, receiving curses and blows for our pains. Rahim Pasha angry with his host, Pare, for grumbling, had a copper vessel hung over the fire and, when heated, ordered it to be placed on Pare's head. Then he had him stripped naked and little bits of flesh nipped out of his quivering arms with pincers.

"These ruffians had scarcely quitted our village when Aïpé Pasha, with sixty horsemen took their places. Seeing that there were no more sheep to be had in the village, they slaughtered and ate our cows and oxen, and having inflicted much suffering upon us during six days, they too left. To whom could we address our complaints seeing that the legally constituted authorities themselves perpetrated these things? Nothing was left for us but to quit the country, which we did."

Take another case, in which the victim was the wife of a Protestant Armenian missionary, Madame Sookyassian, of the village of Todoveran (District of Bassen). I am personally acquainted with that family, and possess the portraits of all the members of it, including the lady who was afterwards murdered. "On September 12, 1894," deposed Armenag Sookyassian, the son of the missionary's wife, "we were seated at table in my father's house, when a boy came and told us that the Turks and Koords had come to attack us Christians.[7] My brother crossed over to the other side of the street, where our shop was, to fetch a revolver. Sixteen Koordish horsemen meanwhile entered the street, ascended the roofs and opened fire. We barricaded the door, but they broke it in. A bullet struck my mother on the shoulder, but without inflicting a serious wound. She defended herself (being on the roof) by throwing stones. Meanwhile one of the Mohammedans levelled his gun and, taking aim, fired. The bullet struck her on the cheek and passed out under the ear, carrying away the whole side of her face. She dropped, was carried in, and asked for water, which could only be given by raising her upper jaw. Next morning she was dead. We complained, but no one was punished."

One more typical instance and I shall have done with this branch of the subject. The case which I am now about to narrate is taken not merely from the depositions of the parties interested, but from the official records, signed and sealed by Government employés, which I myself have seen. It throws a more powerful light upon Turkish justice, and teaches a more useful lesson to those who still honestly believe in Turkish promises than the most eloquent diatribe.

In the month of June, 1890, the village of Alidjikrek was the scene of a double crime. The Armenian shepherds who were tending the flocks of the villagers rushed in excitedly asking for help. "The Koords of Ibil Ogloo Ibrahim came up with their sheep and drove us out of the village pastures." It was one of the commonplaces of village life in Turkish Armenia. Four young men set out to reason with the Moslems and assert the rights of property; but scarcely had they reached the ground, when the Koords opened fire and killed one of the youths, named Hossep, on the spot. Another fell mortally wounded; his name, Haroothioon. Their comrades fled in horror to the village; the people, dismayed, abandoned their work; the parish priest and several of the principal inhabitants ran to the scene of the murder, others rode off to inform the gendarmes.

The Zaptiehs (gendarmes) accompanied by an official were soon on the spot. They found Hossep dead, and the parish priest, Der Ohannes, administering the last consolations of religion on the dying Haroothioon. They ordered the prayers to cease and menacingly asked, "Where are the Koordish murderers?" "They have fled," was the reply. "Indeed. Probably you, dogs, have killed them, and buried them out of sight. You are all my prisoners." (Turning to the priest.) "You too, come!" And they were all taken to Hassankaleh and thrown into the loathsome dungeon there. After a time they were transferred to the prison of Erzeroum.

The parish priest, Der Ohannes, was a well-to-do man. The process of systematic impoverishment was then only beginning. His brother Garabed, and their ten comrades in misfortune, were likewise men of substance, and it seemed desirable to the officials that their property should change hands. They were left therefore to soak in the fetid vapours of a reeking Eastern prison-house. The time dragged slowly on, day by day, week by week, and month by month, till they seemed to have been completely forgotten. Their families were in an endless agony of fear, their affairs were utterly neglected, their health was wholly undermined. In this pandemonium they passed a year—the most horrible period of their lives.

Then they humbly besought their persecutors to help them to their liberty and to name the price. The terms were agreed to and they were advised to send Koords to hunt up traces of the Koordish murderers whom they were accused of having murdered in turn. "If they be found you will be set free." The cost of this advice and of the ways and means of carrying it out amounted to about £400, which the prisoners were compelled to borrow at 40 per cent interest.

The search was of course successful, Koordish and Turkish assassins, when their victims are Christians, having no need to hide their persons, no motive to hang their heads. What they do is well done. These particular heroes were found enrolled in a battalion of his Majesty's favourite cavalry—the Hamidieh of Alashkerd. They confessed and did not deny; a cloud of witnesses—Turks and Koords of course, Christians being disqualified—testified in court in favour of the twelve Armenian prisoners, who were then set at liberty, with ruined fortunes and broken health. The sentence of the court set forth that the Armenians, charged with the crime of having killed certain Koords who had assassinated two Armenian villagers, had proved their innocence, the Koords in question having been discovered living and well, serving the Commander of the Faithful in the Hamidieh Corps.

The Koordish murderers, about whose precious lives so much fuss was made, were left in peace, and they still continue to serve his Majesty the Sultan with the same zeal and contempt of consequences as before.

A dog will bark if another dog be shot in its presence. These Armenians did not even grumble; they simply called in the representatives of Imperial law and justice, who proceeded to deal with them as with murderers. But Christians in Armenia dare not aspire to be treated with the consideration shown to obedient dogs by good-natured masters.

The stories told of these Koordish Hamidieh officers in general, and of one of them, named Mostigo, in particular, seemed so wildly improbable that I was at great pains to verify them. Learning that this particular Fra Diavolo had been arrested and was carefully guarded as a dangerous criminal in the prison of Erzeroum, where he would probably be hanged, I determined to obtain, if possible, an interview with him and learn the truth from his own lips. My first attempt ended in failure; Mostigo being a desperate murderer, who had once before escaped from jail, was subjected to special restrictions, and if I had carried out my original plan of visiting him in disguise, the probability is I should not have returned alive. After about three weeks' tedious and roundabout negotiations, I succeeded in gaining the gaoler's ear, having first replenished his purse. I next won over the brigand himself, and the upshot of my endeavours was an arrangement that Mostigo was to be allowed to leave the prison secretly, and at night, to spend six hours in my room, and then to be re-conducted to his dungeon.

When the appointed day arrived the gaoler repudiated his part of the contract, on the ground that Mostigo, aware that his life was forfeited, would probably give the prison a wide berth if allowed to leave its precincts. After some further negotiations, however, I agreed to give two hostages for his return, one of them a brother Koord, whose life the brigand's notions of honour would not allow him to sacrifice for the chance of saving his own. At last he came to me one evening, walking over the roofs, lest the police permanently stationed at my door should espy him. I kept him all night, showed him to two of the most respectable Europeans in Erzeroum, and, lest any doubt should be thrown on the story, had myself photographed with him next morning.

The tale unfolded by that Koordish noble constitutes a most admirable commentary upon Turkish régime in Armenia. This is not a place to give it in full. One or two short extracts must suffice.

> *Q*. "Now, Mostigo, I desire to hear from your own lips and to write down some of your wonderful deeds. I want to make them known to the 'hat-wearers.' "[8]
>
> *A*. "Even so. Announce them to the Twelve Powers."[9]

There were evidently no misgivings about moral consequences; no fear of judicial punishment. And yet retribution was at hand; Mostigo was said to be doomed to death. Desirous of clearing up this point, I went on:

> *Q*. "I am sorry to find that you are living in the prison. Have you been long there?"
>
> *A*. "I, too, am sorry. Five months, but it seems an age."
>
> *Q*. "These Armenians are to blame, I suppose?"
>
> *A*. "Yes."
>
> *Q*. "You wiped out too many of them, carried off their women, burned their villages, and made it generally hot for them, I am told?"
>
> *A*. (scornfully). "That has nothing to do with my imprisonment. I shall not be punished for plundering Armenians. We all do that. I seldom killed, except when they resisted. But the Armenians betrayed me and I was caught. That's what I mean. But if I be hanged it will be for attacking and robbing the Turkish post and violating the wife of a Turkish Colonel who is now here in Erzeroum. But not for Armenians! Who are they that I should suffer for them?"

After he had narrated several adventures of his, in the course of which he dishonoured Christian women, killed Armenian villagers, robbed the post and escaped from prison, he went on to say:

> "We did great deeds after that: deeds that would astonish the Twelve Powers to hear told. We attacked villages, killed people who would have killed us, gutted houses, taking money, carpets, sheep and women, and robbed travellers. . . . Daring and great were our deeds, and the mouths of men were full of them."

Having heard the story of many of these "great deeds," in some of which fifty persons met their death, I asked:

Q. "Do the Armenians ever offer you resistance when you take their cattle and their women?"

A. "Not often. They cannot. They have no arms, and they know that even if they could kill a few of us it would do them no good, for other Koords would come and take vengeance; but when we kill them no one's eyes grow large with rage. The Turks hate them, and we do not. We only want money and spoil, and some Koords also want their lands, but the Turks want their lives. A few months ago I attacked the Armenian village of Kara Kipriu and drove off all the sheep in the place. I did not leave one behind. The villagers, in despair, did follow us that time and fire some shots at us, but it was nothing to speak of. We drove the sheep towards Erzeroum to sell them there. But on the way we had a fight near the Armenian village of Sheme. The peasants knew we had lifted the sheep from their own people, and they attacked us. We were only five Koords and they were many—the whole village was up against us. Two of my men—*rayahs*[10] only—were killed. We killed fifteen Armenians. They succeeded in capturing forty of the sheep. The remainder we held and sold in Erzeroum."

Q. "Did you kill many Armenians generally?"

A. "Yes. We did not wish to do so. We only want booty, not lives. Lives are of no use to us. But we had to drive bullets through people at times, to keep them quiet; that is, if they resisted."

Q. "Did you often use your daggers?"

A. "No; generally our rifles. We must live. In autumn we manage to get as much corn as we need for the winter, and money besides. We have cattle, but we take no care of it. *We give it to the Armenians to look after and feed.*"

Q. "But if they refuse?"

A. "Well, we burn their hay, their corn, their houses, and we drive off their sheep, so they do not refuse. We take back our cattle in spring, and the Armenians must return the same number that they have received."

Q. "But if cattle disease should carry them off?"

A. "That is the *Armenians'* affair. They must return us what we gave them, or an equal number. And they know it. We cannot bear the loss. Why should not they? Nearly all our sheep come from them."

After having listened to scores of stories of his expeditions, murders, rapes, &c. &c., I again asked: "Can you tell me some more of your daring deeds, Mostigo, for the ears of the Twelve Powers?" to which I received this characteristic reply:

> "Once the wolf was asked: Tell us something about the sheep you devoured? And he said: I ate thousands of sheep, which of them are you talking about? Even so it is with my deeds. If I spoke and you wrote for two days, much would still remain untold."

This brigand is a Koord, and the name of the Koords is legion. *Ex uno disce omnes.* And yet the Koords have shown themselves to be the most humane of all the persecutors of the Armenians. Needing money, this man robbed; desirous of pleasure, he dishonoured women and girls; defending his booty, he killed men and women, and during it all he felt absolutely certain of impunity, so long as his victims were Armenians. Is there no law then? one is tempted to ask. There is, and a very good law for that corner of the globe were it only administered; for the moment he robbed the Imperial post and dishonoured a Turkish woman, he was found worthy of death.

Laws, reforms and constitutions therefore, were they drawn up by the wisest and most experienced legislators and statesmen of the world, will not be worth the paper they are written on so long as the Turks are allowed to administer them without control. The proof is contained in the life and acts of Turkish officials any time during the past fifty years.

Here, for example, is an honourable record of an energetic administrator, his Excellency Hussein Pasha, Brigadier-General of his Majesty the Sultan, which will bear the closest scrutiny. Commanding a gang of Koordish brigands, which could be increased to about 2000 men, he continually harassed the peaceful inhabitants of the province, plundering, torturing, violating, killing, till his name alone sent a thrill of terror to the hearts of all. The Armenians of Patnotz suffered so much from his depredations that they all quitted their village *en masse* and migrated to Karakilisse, where the Kaimakam resides; whereupon Hussein surrounded the house of the Bishop of Karakilisse with a large force and compelled him to send the people back. Even the Mohammedans felt so shocked at his doings, that the Mussulman priest of Patnotz, Sheikh Nari, complained of him to the Vali (Governor-General) of Erzeroum.

Hussein then sent his men, who murdered Sheikh Nari and frightened his daughter-in-law to death. In one expedition he carried off 2600 sheep, many horses, kine, &c., took £500, burnt nine villages, killed ten men, and cut off the right hands, noses and ears of eleven others. Early in the year 1890 he raped five Christian girls of Patnotz, and in September and October of the same year he levied a contribution of £300 on the people of the same district. *For none of these crimes was he ever tried.* In December 1890 he sent his brother to raise more money, which was done by raiding twenty-one villages of the Aintab District, the net result being £350 and 200 *batmans* of butter (=3000 lbs.). Hatsho, an Armenian of Patnotz, who could not, or would not, contribute a certain sum to his coffer, had his house raided in his absence, and his wife and two children killed. All this time the gallant Hussein occupied the post and "discharged the duties" of a Mudir or Deputy Sub-Governor. One day he drove off 1000 sheep and 7 yoke of buffaloes from Patnotz and Kizilkoh, and sold them in Erzeroum to a merchant, after which he confiscated a fine horse belonging to Manook, an Armenian of Kizilkoh, and sent it as a present to the son of an Erzeroum judge. One night towards the end of February, 1891, Hussein, his nephew Rassoul, and others, entered the house of an Armenian, Kaspar, for the purpose of carrying away Kaspar's handsome daughter-in-law. The inmates, however, shouted for help, whereupon Hussein, raising his revolver, shot the young woman dead. A petition was presented asking that he be punished, but the Vali of Erzeroum declined to receive it, and Hussein was summoned to Constantinople, welcomed with cordiality, decorated by his Majesty, raised to the rank of Pasha, and appointed Brigadier-General. When the troops went to Moush and Sassoun last year, Hussein was one of the heroes, and when "order" was restored there, he returned to Patnotz with several young Sassounian girls whom he abducted, and he now lives happily and respected. No doubt there are missions which might be entrusted to a gentleman like Brigadier-General Hussein Pasha and men of his type. But is the government of a Christian people one of them? And if we assume that the then Vali of Erzeroum and the other administrators of the country were men of a much higher moral standard than he, of what avail were their noble character and admirable intentions, seeing that they allowed him to plunder, ravish, burn and kill unchecked? And is it reasonable to blame Hussein Pasha for deeds, after the perpetration of which, he was honoured and promoted by the guardian of all law and order, the Commander of the Faithful?

Not all of the officials have the same tastes or the same degree of courage as his Excellency Hussein Pasha. There are others—many others no doubt—who, whatever their private proclivities may be, feel moved by their official sense of the fitness of things to cast about for a pretext for acts for which there could be no conceivable justification. And the follies which they commit in pursuit of this shadow would seem incredible were they not notorious. The following case has been inquired into and verified by the foreign representatives in Turkey. In the spring of 1893 Hassib Pasha, the Governor of Moush, feeling the need of some proofs of the disaffection of the Armenians of Avzoot and the neighbouring villages, despatched Police Captain Reshid Effendi thither to search for arms. Reshid set out, made careful inquiries and diligently searched in the houses, on the roofs, under the ground, but in vain. There were no firearms anywhere. He returned and reported that the villagers had strictly observed the law forbidding them to possess weapons of any kind. But Hassib Pasha waxed wroth. "How dare you assert what I know to be untrue?" he asked. "Go back this minute and find the arms. Don't dare return without them!" The Police Captain again rode off to Avzoot and searched every nook and corner with lamps, so to say, turning the houses inside out. But he found nothing. Then he summoned the village Elder and said: "I have been sent to discover the hidden arms here. Tell me where they are." "But there are none." "There must be some." "I assure you you are mistaken." "Well, now listen. I have to find arms here, whether there are any or none, and I cannot return without them. Unless you deliver me some, I shall quarter myself and my men upon your village." This meant certainly plunder and probably rape. The Elder was dismayed. "What are we to do?" he asked. "We have no arms." "Go and get some then, steal them, buy them, but get them." Two or three persons were accordingly sent to the nearest Koordish village, where they purchased three cartloads of old daggers, flintlock guns and rusty swords, which were duly handed over to Reshid. With these he returned to the Governor of Moush exulting. Hassib Pasha, seeing the collection, rejoiced exceedingly and said: "You see now, I was right. I told you there were arms hidden away there. You did not seek for them properly at first. Be more diligent in future."

Verto Popakhian, an inhabitant of the village of Khalil Tshaush (Khnouss), narrated the following, the story of his troubles, which throws a curious sidelight on Turkish justice and Armenian peasant-life generally:

> "A Koord, named Djundee, endeavoured to carry off my niece, Nazo, but we took her to Erzeroum, and gave her in marriage to an Armenian. We often have to give our young girls in marriage when they are mere children, eleven to twelve years old, or else dress them up in boys' clothes, to preserve them undefiled. Nazo's husband was the son of the parish priest of Hertev. The Koords vowed vengeance upon me for saving the girl thus. Djundee beat my brother so seriously that he was ill in bed for nearly six months, and he and his men drove off my cattle, burned our grain, threshing-floor, and hay, and ruined us completely. When the girl came home on a visit, Djundee and his Koords attacked the house, and carried her off. We complained to all the authorities in the place and in Erzeroum too. By the time they agreed to examine the girl publicly, she had borne a child to the Koord, and shame prevented her return. She remained a Mohammedan. We then bought a gun for our protection, the law forbidding firearms not existing yet. In 1893 we sold the gun to a Koord named Hadji Daho, but in 1894 the police came and demanded it. We said we had sold it, and the Koord bore out our assertion. He even showed it to them. But they arrested my brother and myself, and compelled us to give our two buffaloes in exchange for two guns, which they took away as incriminating proof of our guilt; and then they sent us to Erzeroum prison. We were kept here, suffering great hardships, for a long time. When eight months had passed away, my brother died of ill-treatment. Then they promised me my liberty in consideration of large bribes, which reduced me to absolute beggary. I had no choice. I gave them all they asked, leaving myself and family of nineteen persons completely destitute. *And then they condemned me to five years' imprisonment.*"

Justice in all its aspects is rigorously denied to the Armenian. The mere fact that he dares to invoke it as plaintiff or prosecutor against a Koord or a Turk is always sufficient to metamorphose him into a defendant or a criminal, generally into both, whereupon he is invariably thrown into prison. In such cases the prison is intended to be no more than the halfway-house between relative comfort and absolute misery, the inmates being destined to be stripped of all they possess and then turned adrift. But what the prison really is cannot be made sufficiently clear in words. If the old English Star Chamber, the Spanish Inquisition, a Chinese opium den, the ward of a yellow fever hospital, and a nook in the lowest depths of Dante's Hell be conceived as blended and merged into one, the resulting picture will somewhat resemble a bad Turkish prison. Filth, stench, disease, deformity, pain in forms and degrees inconceivable in Europe, constitute the physical characteristics: the psychological include the bland despair that is final, fiendish, fierce malignity, hellish delight in human suffering, stoic self-sacrifice in the cultivation of loathsome vices, stark madness raging in the moral nature only—the whole incarnated in grotesque beings whose resemblance to man is a living blasphemy against the Deity. In these noisome dungeons, cries of exquisite suffering and shouts of unnatural delight continually commingle; ribald songs are sung to the accompaniment of heartrending groans; meanwhile the breath is passing away from bodies which had long before been soulless, and are unwept save by the clammy walls whereon the vapour of unimagined agonies and foul disease condenses into big drops and runs down in driblets to the reeking ground. Truly it is a horrid nightmare quickened into life.

Last March I despatched a friend of mine to visit the political prisoners in the Bitlis penitentiary, and to ask them to give me a succinct account of their condition. Four of them replied in a joint-letter, which is certainly the most gruesome piece of reading I have beheld ever since I first perused a description of the Black Hole. Only the least sensational passages can be stripped of the decent disguise of a foreign language and exposed to the light of day. It is dated "Bitlis Prison, Hell, March 28 (April 9th), 1895," and begins thus:

> "In Bitlis Prison there are seven cells, each one capable of containing from ten to twelve persons. The number they actually contain is from twenty to thirty. *There are no sanitary arrangements whatever*. Offal, vermin, and the filth that should find a special place elsewhere are heaped together in the same cell. . . . The water is undrinkable. Frequently the Armenian prisoners are forced to drink

'Khwlitsh' water—*i.e.* water from the tank in which the Mohammedans perform their ablutions. . . ."

Then follows a brief but suggestive account of the treatment endured by the writers' comrades, many of whom died from the effects. For example: "Malkhass Aghadjanian and Serop Malkhassian of Avzoot (Moush) were beaten till they lost consciousness. The former was branded in eight places, and the latter in twelve places, with a hot iron." The further outrage which was committed upon Serop must be nameless. "Hagop Seropian, of the village of Avzoot, was stripped and beaten till he lost consciousness; then a girdle was thrown round his neck, and having been dragged into the Zaptieh's room, he was branded in sixteen parts of his body with red-hot ramrods." Having described other sufferings to which he was subjected, such as the plucking out of his hair, standing motionless in one place without food or drink till nature could hold out no longer, the writer goes on to mention outrages for which the English tongue has no name, and civilized people no ears. Then he continues:

> "Sirko Minassian, Garabed Malkhassian, and Isro Ardvadzadoorian of the same village, having been violently beaten, were forced to remain in a standing position for a long time, and then had the contents of certain vessels poured upon their heads. Korki Mardoyan, of the village of Semol, was violently beaten; his hair was plucked out by the roots, and he was forced to stand motionless for twenty-four hours. Then Moolazim Hadji Ali and the gaoler, Abdoolkadir, forced him to perform the so-called *Sheitantopy*,[11] which resulted in his death. He was forty-five years of age. Mekhitar Saforian and Khatsho Baloyan of Kakarloo (Boolanyk) were subjected to the same treatment. Mekhitar was but fifteen and Khatsho only thirteen years old. Sogho Sharoyan, of Alvarindj (Moush), was conveyed from Moush to Bitlis prison handcuffed. Here he was cruelly beaten, and forced to maintain a standing position without food. Whenever he fainted they revived him with douches of cold water and stripes. They also plucked out his hair, and burned his body with red-hot irons. Then . . . (they subjected him to treatment which cannot be described.) . . . Hambartzoon Boyadjian, after his arrest, was exposed to the scorching heat of the sun for three days. Then he was taken to Semal, where he and his companions were beaten and shut up in a church. They were not only not allowed to leave the church to relieve the wants of nature, but were forced to defile the baptismal

fonts and the church altar. . . . Where are you, Christian Europe and America?"

The four signatures at the foot of this letter include that of a highly respected and God-fearing ecclesiastic.[12]

I am personally acquainted with scores of people who have passed through these prison mills. The stories they narrate of their experience there are gruesome, and would be hard to believe were they not amply confirmed by the still more eerie tales told by their broken spirits, their wasted bodies, and the deep scars and monstrous deformities that will abide with them till the grave or the vultures devour them. There is something so forbiddingly fantastic, and wildly grotesque in the tortures and outrages invented by their gaolers or their local governors that a simple unvarnished account of them sounds like the ravings of a diseased devil. But this is a subject upon which it is impossible to be explicit.

The manner in which men qualify for the Turkish prison in Armenia can be easily deduced from what has already been said. The possession of money, cattle, corn, land, a wife or daughter, or enemies, is enough. We are shocked to read of the cruelty of brutal Koords who ride to a village, attack the houses, drive off the sheep, seize all the portable property, dishonour the women, and return leisurely home, conscious of having done a good day's work. We call it a disgrace to civilisation, and perhaps the qualification is correct. But bad as it sounds, it is a mercy compared with the *Turkish* methods, which rely upon the machinery of the law and the horrors of the prison. A man whom poverty, nay, hunger, prevents from paying imaginary arrears of taxes, who declines to give up his cow or his buffalo as backsheesh to the Zaptiehs, who beseeches them to spare the honour of his wife or daughter, is thrown into one of these dungeons, which he never leaves until he has been branded with the indelible stigma of the place. But let us take one of the usual and by no means most revolting cases of arrest and imprisonment as an illustration.

A young man from the village of Avzood (Moush District) went to Russia in search of work, and found it. He also married, and lived there for several years. Towards the close of 1892 he came back to his native village, and the police, informed that "an Armenian who has lived in Russia is returned," despatched four of their number under the orders of Isaag Tshaush to Avzood. They arrived two hours after sundown, and while three of them guarded the house where the young man was staying, the leader entered. Shots were heard immediately after, and the young Armenian and Isaag lay dead. The authorities in Bitlis then sent a Colonel of the Zaptiehs to Avzood to see "justice" done. And it was done very speedily. The Colonel summoned the men of the village—none of whom were mixed up in the matter—and put them in prison. Then the officials deflowered all the girls, and dishonoured all the young women in Avzood, after which they liberated the men, except about twenty, whom they conveyed to the gaol of Bitlis. A few of these died there, and ten others were soon afterwards dismissed. Finally they decided to charge a young teacher, Markar, of the village of Vartenis with the murder of Isaag Tshaush, and as there was no evidence against him, the other prisoners were ordered to testify. Armenians have the reputation of being liars, but they certainly draw the line at swearing away an innocent man's life; and they refused in this case to commit the double crime of perjury and murder. Strenuous efforts were made to determine them; they were stripped naked, burned in various parts of the body with red-hot irons, till they yelled with pain. Then they were prevented from sleeping for several nights, and tortured acutely again, till, writhing and quivering, they promised to swear anything, everything if once relieved from their agony. A document declaring that Markar was in the village when Isaag Tshaush arrived there, and that he had shot Isaag in their presence, was drawn up in their names. To this they duly affixed their seals. Meanwhile Markar himself was being tortured in another part of the prison.

When the trial came on and the incriminating document was read, the signatories stripped themselves in court, exhibited the ugly marks left by the red-hot irons, and called God to witness that that evidence of theirs, wrung from them by maddening torture, was a lie. Markar, on the other hand, declared that he was not in Avzood village at all on the night in question. But these statements were unavailing; he was hanged last year, and the "witnesses" condemned to various terms in fortified towns. Some of the women dishonoured by the Zaptiehs died from the effects of the treatment to which they were subjected.

All accounts of the prisons in Armenia, Turkish, Koordish, and

Christian, agree in essential characteristics. I lately called on a very respectable Armenian—a man of good education and once a person of property—who has passed through several prisons, the object of his incarceration being the desire to deprive him of all he possessed. Him I questioned about the treatment of the prisoners, and what he said was this:

> "Armenian prisoners are very often tortured; but a good deal depends upon the place. Some prisons are very bad, being noted for the abominable things that go on inside their walls; others are not so horrible. The prison of Erzeroum, for example, is not nearly so bad as that of Bitlis, though there, too, torture is occasionally employed in a fiendish way. The reason is, I conjecture, that the foreign consuls in Erzeroum can nearly always get information about what goes on in the prison there, and the authorities are restrained by the knowledge of this."
>
> *Q*. "Then there is no torture in Erzeroum?"
>
> *A*. "There is sometimes, but not nearly so often as elsewhere. I have seen the 'Standing Box' there, and I know it was used some time ago, but I fancy it would not be often employed—certainly not nearly so often as in Bitlis."
>
> *Q*. "What is the Standing Box?"
>
> *A*. "It is a small cupboard hole, just large enough for one man to stand in, something like a sentry-box in shape. The prisoner put there could not sit, lean, or move."
>
> *Q*. "Surely he could lean, at least, against the wall?"
>
> *A*. "No; because it bristles all over with sharp iron points, and on the ground there is barely room enough for his two feet to stand. He is kept here for 24, 36, 48 hours, as the case may be; sometimes longer still. Two or more Zaptiehs always stand guard, and see that the thing is properly carried out. He receives nothing to eat or drink, and is not allowed to leave even to attend to the wants of nature. This is a horrible torture. It was applied to Markar, the teacher, and to numbers of my friends and acquaintances. Damadian's servant, Sogho Sharoyan, was subjected to it; so were Hagop Seropian of Avzood, Sirko Minassian, Garabed Molkhassian, Korki Mardoyan. Saghatiel Mirzoyan of Khosgheldi (Boolanyk), and scores of others. But this is by no means the worst. The torture of Sheitantopy, which is also an outrage that—"
>
> "Yes, I know about that."

The Armenians taken from Moush to the prison of Hassankaleh—many of whom were guilty only of giving evidence before the

Commission about what they had seen during the massacre—are used for perpetration of nameless crimes. The officials who thus abuse them are numerous and well known—I am in possession of their full names and addresses, and I could bring scores of witnesses to prove the charge. These scoundrels are generally Zaptiehs. I have seen and spoken with some of them, and they took very little pains to disguise the terrible facts.

The gaolers grow rich on the money they wring from the inmates of the cells. The prison-keeper of Bitlis Prison, Abdoolkader, a wretch who, God having presumably made him, may be called a man, earns enormous sums in this way. He lately spent £500 on his house, and two or three Turkish merchants are said to be doing business on his capital, although his salary is only about 50s. a month. These sums are received as bribes not for any positive return made to the prisoners, but for mere relief from torture employed solely for this purpose. The following case may give some idea of the nature of the relief thus highly paid for. Some five months ago three men of the village of Krtabaz were arrested and imprisoned.[13] The fact that they were released without trial ten weeks later is evidence enough of their innocence of crime. They were taken to the prison of Hassankaleh. The room in which they were confined was overcrowded. The term overcrowding does not connote the same thing in Armenia as in European prisons. *They had no room to lie down at all.* Some Koordish prisoners confined in the same dismal den, who enjoyed special privileges, had but two and a half feet space to sleep in. In one corner of the dungeon a hole in the wall represented the prison-equivalent of sanitation, and these three Armenians were told that they must stand up by this hole, and might lean against the wall to sleep. *This they did for fifteen consecutive nights.* The stench, the filth, the vermin exceed all conception. After the lapse of fifteen days, by dint of starving themselves, they were enabled to give part of their food to some of the Koords, one of whom allowed the Armenians to take his place in turn during the day. This was not much, for the Koords themselves had only sitting space, about 2½ feet long; still it did afford relief. But the Koord was severely punished for this benevolence or enterprise. His rations of bread were cut off, and he was put in irons for several days. The men he thus befriended, who now aver they owe their lives to him, were notables of their village, and innocent persons to boot, who were released some weeks later because "they had done no wrong."

And yet the Turk, we are told, is a true gentleman, while the Armenians are lying thieves. Seeing how much depends upon definitions, there may perhaps be a sense in which that is true. But even a gentleman is expected to kill his useless cats and dogs in a humane way, and should not an Oriental gentleman be asked to slaughter his Armenians without torture? Would it not be a humane act on the part of our late Liberal Government had it arranged at least for the painless destruction of Armenian men, women, and children? Chloroform, prussic acid, or electricity would surely be an improvement upon *Sheitantopy*, the Standing Box, and red-hot ramrods, and the Armenians or their friends would then have something to thank us for. The idea is not perhaps thoroughly Christian, but surely it is relatively humane. Whatever we may think of the suggestion in theory, few men would hesitate in practice to give their sisters, wives and sons the chance of putting an end to their sufferings, were they in the position of the Armenians.

"The Armenians could help themselves if they really wished," I lately heard an Englishman say, with a serious and convinced air; "they have only to turn Mohammedans. Surely God would not punish them for that." It is certainly true that the moment they embraced Islam their troubles would cease, and that now, though martyrs by suffering, deprived of the palm, they are but contemptible "criminals" in name. Many of those whose flesh was weak, however willingly may have been the spirit, did renounce their faith, and others are preparing to do likewise. Some of those with whom I conversed asked me whether I would advise them to save their families from dishonour and death by proclaiming that God is one and Mohammed is his prophet. I replied by expressing a hope, which I but partially entertained, that Christian Europe would come to their aid in good time and relieve them of the necessity of deciding between such painful alternatives. One thing is certain; if they embrace Islam, they must do it seriously and for good. There can be no recanting later on, as violent death in its most hideous forms would be the certain penalty. The following story is calculated to bring out in strong relief the temptation which the Armenians have to give up their faith. The narrative will be found interesting on other grounds besides.

Melik Agha was a notable and noble Armenian of the village of Abri (Boolanyk District), blessed with sons and grandsons, cattle, sheep, land, corn and hay in abundance—a sort of Armenian Job on a small scale. A noble Mohammedan of the same village, Kiamil Sheikh by name, envying his riches, desired to draw them to himself, and failing that, to destroy them and their owner. Last autumn for this purpose he had Melik's hay, corn, &c., burned to ashes. Then the Sheikh's men came and took away five of his horses and killed 150 of his sheep, leaving their carcases to rot where they fell. This was wanton waste in a country where people are continually poor and frequently hungry. Melik therefore went to Kop where the Kaimakam resides and invoked the strong arm of the law. While he was in Kop complaining, and his sons were away on business, the Sheikh's people, ever on the watch, dropped into his house, murdered the two children of Melik's eldest son and abducted their mother, who was very far gone with child. Melik Agha, hearing of this calamity, set out for Erzeroum to lay the matter before the chief authorities of the Vilayet. The upshot of his application was that Selim Pasha was deputed to inquire into the business and to get the woman back—the children, of course, could not be resuscitated nor could their murder be punished. The captor refused to deliver up the young woman, saying, "She will publicly declare that she embraces Islam." Then the Pasha, turning to Melik, asked: "What will you say or do if your daughter-in-law does publicly affirm that she becomes a Mohammedan?"

"I shall say that we too will become Mohammedans rather than allow our wives and daughters to pass into other hands." Then the woman was fetched, but seeing her surrounded by Sheikhs, and afraid of speaking the truth, Melik said to the Pasha: "She is ill. In a few days she will become a mother. Give her peace until then, and meanwhile send her to any Turkish house you like in Erzeroum. In a fortnight we shall hear what she has to say." To this all agreed, and the Pasha departed. Three days later the woman's husband (Melik's eldest son) was killed by Kiamil's people in broad daylight. Even the Turkish family in which the woman lived were horrified, and requested the Sheikhs to come and take her away, as they refused to have anything more to do with the business.

Soon after this, Melik's second son, Mgirdeetch, shot two of the Sheikhs in the field. It was a very wrong and un-Christian thing to do, and cases of the kind give correct people in Europe a pretext for complaining of the vindictiveness of the Armenians. What he should have done, we know, was to entertain the Sheikhs at dinner, or at least to let them pass on in peace; though there are certain highly civilised Europeans—nay, ministers of Christian Churches known to me, who virtually say:

> "God be praised for every instinct which rebels against a lot,
> Where the brute survives the human and man's upright form is not."

However this may be, Mgirdeetch and his younger brother, feeling that they and their relatives were doomed, ran into the house of Mussah Bey and proclaimed themselves Mohammedans. Then they sent a messenger to their father informing him of what they had done and exhorting him to go and do likewise. And he did. A Mullah was appointed to teach the newly converted family the doctrines and worship of Islam, and as fate would have it, the Mullah in question was a man who had been Melik's faithful servant for many long years, and was far more disposed to become a Christian than his former master was to recognise the teachings of the Koran. Melik having discussed his plans with his friendly Mullah,[14] sent his widowed daughter with a grown-up girl and three boys to Russia. When they drew near to the frontier, at Gara-Ghedook, the Koords attacked them and strove to obtain possession of the girl. But she held her mother's hand and refused to be delivered up to the lusts of these savages. Then the Koords shot her dead. Her mother took the body on her back, and carried it to the village Ghairavank, about three miles from Kaghziman, where it was buried by Father Raphael. After some time Melik himself and the other members of his family escaped to Russia, leaving behind his house, lands, hay, corn, cattle, &c., and taking only a little money, of which the Koords robbed him on the road. He was thankful to God for having allowed him to get across the frontier with his life.

And the feeling is fast growing among Armenians that this is the only favour, human or divine, for which they will ever be called upon to feel grateful. Not that they have not been told over and over again to hope, even by ourselves, who having first hindered Russia from coming to their assistance and undertaken to see them properly governed, gave a free hand to the Turks to inaugurate a

Dahomey in the five provinces. The darkest shadow, no doubt, is often no more than the proof and promise of a genial sun; but not for those creatures that live in the perpetual darkness of unexplored caverns. The Armenians are Christians, and they look up to God for protection, seeing that they have no one else to look to. But Baal on Mount Carmel was not more indifferent to the fate of his worshippers than He seems to be. Christianity is a good lode star, but not for those whose tears have made them blind.

It is no easy thing for an Armenian man to cross the frontier and enter Russia, if he possess a gold or silver coin or an article of clothing; nor for a woman to leave the country without first undergoing indignities the mere mention of which should make a man's blood boil with shame and indignation. "Oh, but these things are not felt so acutely by Armenians as they would be by Europeans," said an English lady to me a few days ago: "the wind is tempered to the shorn lamb, don't you know." It may be so; but I have seen and conversed with hundreds and hundreds of Armenian women lately, and I found no signs of the tempering process. Whatever vices or virtues may be predicated of Armenian women, chastity must be numbered among their essential characteristics. They carry it to an incredible extreme. In many places an Armenian woman never even speaks to any man but her husband, unless the latter is present. Even to her nearest and dearest male relatives and connections she has nothing to say; and her purity, in the slums of Erzeroum as in the valleys of Sassoun, is above suspicion. Yet these are the people who are being continually outraged by brutal Koords and beastly Turks, oftentimes until death releases them. But the difficulty of emigrating from Turkey, with money, clothing, or women, will be best understood in the light of a few concrete examples. Not that the Turks object to their leaving. On the contrary—and this is the most conclusive proof of the existence of the Plan of Extermination—they actually drive them over the frontier and then persistently refuse to allow them to return.

Sahag Garoyan, questioned as to the reasons why he and his family of ten persons emigrated from his village of Kheter (Sandjak of Bayazid), deposed as follows:

> "We could not remain because we were treated as beasts of burden by Rezekam Bey, son of Djaffar Agha, and his men, who

belong to his Majesty's Hamidieh corps, and can therefore neither be punished nor complained of. I emigrated towards the end of last year. Rezekam had come with his followers, as if it were war time, and taken possession of the houses of the Armenians, driving the occupants away. Only seven families were allowed to stay on. The others, having no place to go, took refuge in the church. We had to feed the Koords for three months, giving them our corn, sheep, & c., and keeping their cattle in fodder. We had to serve some of them as beasts of burden.[15] Rezekam himself paid a weekly visit to the village of Karakalisse, and levied a contribution of £10 Turkish on the inhabitants, besides hay, barley, &c., for his men. At last, unable to bear this burden any longer, we addressed a complaint to the authorities. They told us to be gone. Then a Koord, named Ghazaz Teamer, ordered us to sign a document setting forth that we were prosperous and happy. This was to be sent to Constantinople, as he wished to be appointed Yoozbashi of the Hamidiehs. No one signed the paper, whereat Teamer grew angry, and killed Avaki and his brother. Five months later he killed Minass, son of Kre, of the village of Mankassar. When the winter came on last year, Rezekam Bey imprisoned our neighbour Sarkiss, son of Sahag, had his head plunged in cold water and dried; after that it was steeped in petroleum and his hair burned off. Then he endeavoured to violate Sara, Sarkiss's sister, but she was smuggled away in time. Rezekam's servant, Kheto, dishonoured Moorad's wife; and a few days later entered the house of Abraham, an inhabitant of the same village, commanding him to go and work for Rezekam Bey. Abraham's wife, who was about to become a mother, begged that he might be allowed to stay at home; but Kheto kicked her in the stomach, and she was delivered of a dead child an hour or so after. Oh, we could not live there—not if we were beasts, instead of Christians."

Mgirdeetch Mekhoyan, aged thirty-five, of the village of Koopegheran (Sandjak of Bayazid), deposed: "I emigrated in 1894 because Aipa Pasha came with forty Koordish families, demolished our church, and took every thing we had." The same story, with variations, comes from every Sandjak, almost from every village, of the five Armenian provinces. Bedross Kozdyan, aged fifty-five, of the village of Arog (Sandjak of Van), testified:

"I left my village and my country with my family in August last year (1894), because we were driven away by the Koords under Tri, son of Tshalo, who was abetted by the Turkish authorities. He first came and violated three girls and three young married women, whom he took away in spite of their cries and prayers. Three Armenians tried to protect the wretched women, who implored them not to let them go. But the Koords killed the three on the spot. Their names were Sarkiss, Khatsho, and Keveark. Next day he and his men drove off the sheep of the villagers. We complained to the Governor of Van, but he said he could not move in the matter. Ten days later the Koords came again, and carried away our wheat, barley, and live stock, and burned the hay which they could not transport. Then they knocked down the altar of our church, hoping to find gold and silver hidden away there. We again besought the authorities to protect us, but they replied, 'We'll slaughter you like sheep if you dare to come again with your complaints against good Mohammedans.' Then we took what we could with us and set out for Russia. When we reached Sinak six armed Koords attacked us, robbed us of everything we had, and sent us over the frontier with nothing but our clothes."

Sarkiss Mardirossian, of the village of Utchkilisse (Sandjak of Alashkerd), said:

"I emigrated with my family of five persons because I could not live there. The Koords came and burnt all my hay, &c., and being very well off I had a large quantity. Then they drove off the 100 cows belonging to us villagers, fifty oxen and 300 sheep. We could no longer pay the taxes and, fearing tortures from the Zaptiehs and also hunger, we had to go. In Kiatoog we were stripped of everything we had by the Koords and sent over the frontier."

Ove Oviants of the village of Leez, Sandjak of Boolanyk deposed:

"I emigrated with my family of eight persons because we were driven off by the Koords under Terpoi Neato with the connivance of the Imperial authorities. He came to our village and took three yoke of oxen, seventy sheep, and two mules. A month later they drove off seventy more sheep and two mules, the latter and seventeen of the sheep my own property. We were 250 Armenian families, but against a handful of Koords we could do nothing, having no firearms. One night they broke open my door and took away the clothing and ornaments of the women of our family and two cows. Modego Tilo seeing that one of our neighbours had a handsome daughter, carried her off and forced her to become a Moslem. The girl's father appealed to the Vali of Bitlis, who ordered the Kaimakam of Kop to flog him soundly and then imprison him for seven

> days. This was done. He was warned on being released, that if he complained again he would be tortured to death. My family and four others then left for Russia. At Apazin the Koords attacked us and took everything we possessed."

Khatsho Garabedian, of the village of Kiavoormi (Sandjak of Khnouss), declared:

> "I am forty-five years of age. The reason I left with my family was because the Turkish authorities allowed the Koords under Heasso to strip me of nearly everything I possessed, and the Turkish Zaptiehs came and demanded the taxes, which I had no means of paying. The chief of these Zaptiehs then said: 'You have no money but have a pretty wife. Lend her to me and I will give you a receipt for the taxes.' I contrived to have my wife taken to another house, and when the Turkish official saw that he could not dishonour her, he punished me. First, cold water was poured over me, then dung and other filth was rubbed into my face, and a strap thrown round my neck. In this way I was dragged through the village. On my return they took my ox, the only possession that was still left me, and had it not been for that ox they would have taken my life. I then fled with my family, and we had only two Turkish pounds in money among us. The soldiers, however, stopped us and made us deliver up that, and we entered Russia as poor as the day we were born."

The Plan of Extermination is obviously working smoothly and well. The Christian population is decimated, villages are changing hands almost as quickly as the scenes shift in a comic opera, and the exodus to Russia and the processions to the churchyard are increasing. This is not the place to give a list of *islamised* villages, but a typical case may help to convey an idea of the process that is going on even now. In the province of Alashkerd, which borders upon Russia, there are five villages to the east of Karakilisse, named respectively, Khedr (or Kheter), Mangassar, Djoodjan, Ziro and Koopkheran. These villages Eyoob Pasha sent his sons to occupy. Koords of the Zilanlee tribe, they are all officers in the Hamidieh corps. General Eyoob has three sons, Rezgo Bey, Khalid Bey, and Yoossoof Bey, and these gallant officers with their followers set out last spring and took the villages for themselves. There were about 400 Armenian houses there at the time, or, say roughly, some 3000 Christian inhabitants. There is not one there to-day. Only one individual named Avedis Agha has remained, and even he lives not in one of the four villages, but in Yoondjaloo. He was a wealthy man when the Koords arrived; he is indigent now. The Armenians were completely driven out in the course of a few months by methods which may be termed somewhat drastic. For example: one day the Koords met Markar, son of Ghoogo, in the fields carrying home his corn. They demanded his *araba* (cart). He replied that it was engaged now, as they could see for themselves, but that he would give it later on. They killed him on the spot for disobedience and threw his body on the cart. Thirty villagers went with their children to complain to the Kaimakam in Karakilisse. The Kaimakam caused them to remain waiting in the open air for eleven days before he would hear them. And having heard them, he told them to go—to Russia.

In the Vilayet of Bitlis (Kaza of Boolanyk and Sandjak of Moush) there is a village named Kadjloo, which, being interpreted, means "Village of the Cross." It is a village of the Crescent now. The means by which the sudden change was effected are identical in character with those already described. Mohammed Emin led a number of Koords (outcasts from the Djibranlee and Hassnanlee tribes) against the village, took it, so to say, by storm, and, to use their own picturesque expression, "sat down in it." Happily it is situated only five miles distant from the seat of the Turkish Deputy-Governor, but, unhappily for the people, he refused to move a finger, and they were all driven off like sheep. Perhaps this is one of the cases in which the wind is tempered to the shorn sheep?

Then the conquerors set about raiding the neighbouring villages, and in particular Piran, which is about a mile further off. These would likewise have changed hands had it not been for a bright idea of one of the chief villagers, at whose suggestion a Koord named Assad Agha was invited to come and quarter his men in Piran, *accepting for himself twenty corn-fields, ten meadows,* and a spacious two-storey house, which was built expressly for him by an architect from Bitlis, in return for which he undertook to protect the Armenians from Mohammed Emin and his merry men.

Three hundred and six of the principal inhabitants of the District of Khnouss gave me a signed petition when I was leaving Armenia, and requested me to lay it before "the humane and noble people of England." In this document they truly say;

> "We now solemnly assure you that the butchery of Sassoun is but a drop in the ocean of Armenian blood shed gradually and silently all over the Empire since the late Turko-Russian war. Year by year, month by month, day by day, innocent men, women and children have been shot down, stabbed, or clubbed to death in their houses and their fields, tortured in strange fiendish ways in fetid prison cells, or left to rot in exile under the scorching sun of Arabia. During the progress of that long and horrible tragedy no voice was raised for mercy, no hand extended to help us. That process is still going on, but it has already entered upon its final phases, and the Armenian people are at the last gasp. Is European sympathy destined to take the form of a cross upon our graves?"

I have also received two touching appeals from the women of Armenia, sealed with their seals, and addressed to their sisters of England. What *they* ask is indeed little—that they be protected from dishonour. And, until the General Election gave us a strong Government, which knows its own mind, it seemed as if these women were asking for the moon.

English people have not even a remote notion of the extent to which young married women and girls are outraged all over Armenia by Turkish soldiers, imperial Zaptiehs, Koordish officers and brigands;—and outraged with such accompaniments of nameless brutality that their agonies often culminate in a horrible death. Girls of eleven and twelve—nay, of nine—are torn from their families and outraged in this way by a band of "men" whose names are known, and whose deeds are approved by the representatives of law and order. Indeed, these representatives are themselves the monsters, the bestial poison of whose loathsome passion is destroying "the subtle, pure, and innocent spirit of life."

Rape, violation, outrages that have no name, and whose authors should have no mercy, are become the commonplaces of daily life in Armenia. And the Turkish "gentleman" smiles approval. I have myself collected over 300 of these cases, and I have heard of countless others.

In 1893 the Hamidieh soldiers entered the house of Khoomar (village of Tortan), ordered couches to be prepared for them, and then had the young women of the house brought, and delivered up to their foul lusts.[16] In Baiboord, between Erzeroum and Trebizond, the Imperial soldiers ravished Fenedo, daughter of Heyerape, and then forced her to become a Mohammedan.[17] In Dooman (Sandjak of Khnooss) Khalo and his comrades seized the young daughter of the Armenian priest, raped her in turn, and forced her to profess the Mohammedan faith. In the same village Mootafee raped Varo, daughter of Shebo, and compelled her to become a Mohammedan. In Tortan a young girl, Dilbar, daughter of Asso, was raped by two Koords. Complaint was made to the Turkish authorities, but in vain. A few days later the Turks themselves, five in number, raped two other young girls, Toolerand and Yaghood. Mardiross Yengoyan, of the village of Badivegan,[18] was compelled to give up his twelve horses, then to entertain three Koords, and lastly, to deliver up his wife for them to dishonour.[19] Last year a young girl named Mariam, daughter of Solomon, of the village of Kortaz, was raped by Khalo, who carried her off, and forced her to embrace Islam. In 1893 six Koords came to the village of Tshekhi,[20] entered the house of Garabed Ghiragossian, and compelled the host to provide them with an abundant meal and their horses with fodder. Having eaten their fill, they went out into the garden and partook of green fruit and cucumbers till they sickened. Then they accused Garabed of having poisoned them, and set about punishing him condignly. They tied him tightly to a pillar in the apartment, then seized his wife and each of them dishonoured her in turn. After this they told the wretched man that they would set him free if he paid them a certain sum for his liberty.

On November 7 last a Turk of the city of Bayazid asked Avedis Krmoyan to pay a little debt. The Armenian, not having the money at the time, besought his creditor to wait a few weeks. The Turk refused, and insisted on taking Krmoyan's wife as a pledge that the money would be paid. Entreaties and tears were unavailing; the woman was carried off, and then forced to become a Moslem. She can never return to her husband again.

In the village of Khosso Veran (Bassen) a girl named Selvy was seized by a Turk as security for a debt contracted by her father. The creditor kept her three months and dishonoured her; nor would he consent to set her free until Giragoss Ohannissean went bail for her. As the debt, however, is unpaid, the Turk has a mortgage on her still. This sort of thing cannot be said to be uncommon, for although I knew but three cases of it from personal knowledge, I heard of more than a score in different parts of Armenia.

The day after last Christmas Serop Sarkassian, a peasant of the village of Osag (Moush), was suddenly reduced to misery by a Koord named Magson, who, like his colleagues, has no need to fear the law. Magson burned down Sarkassian's corn granaries, and then ravished and abducted his two daughters. It is perhaps worth noting, as an indication of the extent to which the wind is tempered to the shorn sheep, that of these two girls, one, Fidan, was exactly twelve years of age, while her sister, Alinasd, was a child of nine years. And Magson? Magson is highly respected by his co-religionists, who are always delighted when Christians, men or women, are converted, or abducted, from religious darkness to the light of the true faith. Moslems had nothing but praise, therefore, for the Koords who, on December 23, last year, raped and carried off the little daughter of Khatshig, of the village of Yondjaloo (Boolanyk), or for the two followers of the Koordish chieftain, Teadjeen, who, in the village of Shervansheig (Boolanyk), violated Vartoohi, niece of Serko Gooshdyan, and forced her to abjure her faith. For such deeds are meritorious.

It is not only absolutely useless, but often positively dangerous, to complain to the officials, who, from high to low, take an active part in this Oriental "sport" themselves. The Kiateeb of Alai entered the house of Ohannes Goolykian (village of Karatshoban in Khnouss) in the broad daylight, and raped the daughter of Ohannes, who was fifteen years old, and then sent her off to Trebizond. Her father complained, besought the authorities to restore her, and it is only fair to say that, so far as I know, he was not punished for his temerity.

The Deputy-Governor of Arabghir actually arrested and expelled a number of the men of the town whose wives were considered to be among the most handsome women in Armenia. He next approached the latter, but was received with the scorn he deserved. Then these women shut themselves up in their houses, refusing to allow him or his men to enter, whereupon he told them, publicly and shamelessly, that if they wished their husbands to return, they must yield to his desires.

The following case is one in which I took a very lively interest because I am well acquainted with the victim and her family. Her name is Lucine Mussegh, her native village Khnoossaberd. Born in 1878, Lucine was sent at an early age to the Armenian Missionary school at Erzeroum, where she was taught the doctrines of evangelical Christianity, her father, Aghadjan Kemalian, having always manifested a strong sympathy for Protestantism. Armenian girls are in chronic danger of being raped by Turks and Koords, and Armenian parents are continually scheming for the purpose of shielding them from this calamity which, as we have seen, occasionally results in death. The means usually employed are very early marriages or attempts to pass off the girls as boys.[21] I have known children to be taken from school, married, allowed to live a few months with their husbands or wives and then sent back to school again. This is what happened to Lucine, who, taken from school at the age of fourteen, was wedded to a boy of her own age, Milikean by name, and having lived some time with him under his father's roof, was sent to the Protestant school once more. One night, during her husband's absence from home, she was seized by some men, dragged by the hair, gagged, and taken to the house of Hussni Bey. *This man is the son of the Deputy Governor of the place.* He dishonoured the young woman and sent her home next day, but her husband refused to receive her any more, and she is now friendless and alone in the world.[22]

Lucine's father presented a complaint to the colonel of the Hamidiehs, and a petition to the parish priest. The Metropolitan Archbishop of Erzeroum likewise took the matter in hand, and appealed to the Governor-General of the Vilayet, and to the court of Khnouss. But all to no purpose. Lucine is now a pariah. In her Appeal to the Women of England, which is too long and too *naïve* to find a place here, Lucine says:

> "We suffered in patience when our corn, butter, and honey were seized, and we were left poor and hungry; we bowed our heads in sorrowful resignation when our kith and kin were cut down by the Koords and the Turks. Are we also to be silent and submissive now that our race is being poisoned at its source? Now that child-mothers and baby-daughters are being defiled and brutalised by savages? Say, Christian sisters, is there in truth no remedy? . . . We ask for no revenge, for no privileges; we ask only that . . . but need I be more explicit to English matrons, wives, and sisters? . . . Although we are Armenians we are Christians; I was brought up in a Protestant school, as you were; I drew my moral sustenance from the Bible, as you did; I was taught to feel and think, as you were. . . . For the love of the God, then, whom we worship in common, help us, Christian sisters,

> before it is too late, and take the thanks of the mothers, wives, sisters, and daughters of my people, and with them the gratitude of one for whom, in spite of her youth, death would come as a happy release.
>
> "(Signed) Lucine Mussegh"

I have also received a piteous appeal to the women of England from some hundreds of Armenian women of the District of Khnouss, begging as an inestimable favour to be shielded from the brutal treatment to which they are all subjected. It is needless to publish it here. Written appeals are seldom very forcible. If the reader had seen the wretched women themselves, as I saw them, and heard them tell their gruesome tales in the simplest of words, punctuated by sobs and groans, emphasised by misery and squalor, they would be in a condition to form some idea of the state of things in Armenia, which in the good old times of theocracy would have brought down consuming fire from heaven. In the village of Begli Akhmed, for example, I met a woman of about twenty-eight, clothed in ragged pieces of dirty carpets, with a pale emaciated boy of twelve, suffering from a terrible cough, who looked like a typhus patient aged only six or seven. I asked her to tell her story, and this is what she said:

> "My name is Atlass Manookian; I come from the village of Khrt (Khnouss District). We were very well off, but the Koords took away everything we had. Everything, Effendi; still my poor husband worked for me and the child here, though they told us to go. One day when I was bringing bread to my husband in the field, they struck me on the head and dishonoured me. That was in the daytime. . . ."

"It was at noon, mother, when father used to eat his bread, that they did that to you," broke in the ghost of a child. I never in my life witnessed anything more horrible than the sight of those two friendless, hopeless wretches, as they stood there trembling in the cold, the dying child thus simply bearing witness that his mother was dishonoured in the fields by a number of neighbouring Koords.[23] She then went on: "I complained to the head officer, Sheikh Moorad, but the Bimbashi beat me cruelly about the head and back, and knocked me down. Then, last spring, when my husband was sowing corn, Ali Mahmed came up and killed him." "With an axe, mother," said the boy. "We are now alone in the world, wandering and begging, and nobody knows us," said the woman. Having given her some coins, I hurried away, vainly striving to shake off the horrible impression which clung to me, like a hideous ghost, for weeks afterwards.

The massacre of Sassoun sends a shudder to the hearts of the most callous. But that butchery was a divine mercy compared with the hellish deeds that are being done every week and every day of the year. The piteous moans of famishing children; the groans of old men who have lived to see what can never be embodied in words; the piercing cries of violated maidenhood, nay, of tender childhood; the shrieks of mothers made childless by crimes compared with which murder would be a blessing; the screams, scarcely human, of women writhing under the lash; and all the vain voices of blood and agony that die away in that dreary desert without having found a responsive echo on earth or in heaven, combine to throw Sassoun and all its horrors into the shade.

Such are the things for which we are morally responsible; and in spite of the circumstance that the late Liberal Government was in possession of these and analogous facts, Lord Kimberley found it impossible to have them remedied and unadvisable to have them published. There is fortunately good reason to believe that Lord Salisbury, who alone among English statesmen seems accurately to gauge all the difficulties of this thorny question, will find efficacious means of putting a sudden and speedy end to the Armenian Pandemonium.

Mr. Gladstone on Armenia

Nothing could possibly have been better than the tone of Mr. Gladstone's speech on the Armenian question. Not a word was said by him which could rightly give the most timid Unionist an excuse for thinking that in supporting the agitation against Turkish misrule, and in favour of strong action by the Powers, he was injuring the present Government, or acting towards it an unfriendly part. Mr. Gladstone made it clear that the meeting was assembled not to protest against anything which the present Government have done or left undone, or are believed to intend, but simply and solely to strengthen their hands, and to give them that national and moral support without which no Government can have full power. Unionists, instead of embarrassing the Government, are helping it by insisting that the Porte should do its duty in Armenia. That they are smoothing the path of Lord Salisbury—not making it harder—will be seen by any one who takes the trouble to reflect upon the facts of the situation. The Powers are engaged in pressing upon the Sultan the carrying out of reforms in Armenia, and the giving of certain guarantees which shall prevent a renewal of the Armenian atrocities the moment that the attention of European public opinion is relaxed or diverted into new channels. At present the Sultan is fighting desperately against the proposals of the Powers, and trying by every diplomatic subterfuge—and the diplomatic subterfuges of the Turk are like the sands of the sea—to avoid the carrying out of reforms in Armenia. The Porte sincerely believes that the Armenian Christians are a band of dangerous revolutionaries, and that till they are harried out of existence, the Empire will have no peace. His hope is that by killing and imprisoning some, by driving others across the borders, and by converting the rest, the nest of disaffection around Lake Van will be destroyed. His position as ruler should not be mistaken. It is like that of Louis XIV., towards the Protestants of the Cevennes and elsewhere after the revocation of the Edict of Nantes. The French King was not a mere religious persecutor. He believed, however, that Protestants were necessarily bad subjects and a danger to the Empire, and he tried his best to get rid of them. The Sultan has a similar notion, and he will fight very hard to prevent the carrying out of a policy which appears to him as stereotyping the worst forms of disaffection in his great Asian province. How to force the Sultan to yield is the problem. Remember that here, all that is necessary is to solve the personal equation. If the Sultan can be forced to see that further resistance is useless, or more dangerous than yielding, the desired end is accomplished, for the Sultan's will is absolute. The Sultan is a real autocrat. The naked sword of his word cuts through obstacles even quicker than that of the Czar, for the Sultan has not, like the Czar, a great and well-organised bureaucracy standing between him and the execution of his orders. How can the Sultan be reached? By the fear of public opinion. Curiously enough, the Sultan is specially liable to be influenced by the pressure of organised public opinion. He watches carefully the news of what is done in England, and gauges the chances of resisting the demands of the English Ambassador by the support which the policy of that Ambassador is receiving at home. If the Sultan sees, or fancies he sees, that the English public is unmoved, he considers that it will be safe to do nothing. If, on the other hand, he finds not only the English Press unanimous against him, but great public meetings speaking in similar tones, he knows that resistance is hopeless. There is reason to think that the Sultan, first owing to the change of Ministry, and next owing to the Elections, hardened his heart in regard to the proposals of the Powers. A Conservative Government, he reckoned, would never go to extremities in putting pressure upon him. Under the new conditions, therefore, he might safely adopt a policy of procrastination. In a word, the very success of Lord Salisbury at the polls has injured his position at Constantinople. The Sultan has regarded the verdict of the country as one in his favour. It is the business of Unionists to show him that he is entirely mistaken, and to prove to him that when Lord Salisbury demands a prompt settlement of the Armenian question he is backed up by the whole force of English public opinion. The Sultan could not possibly make a greater mistake than to imagine that the country would not support Lord Salisbury in vigorous measures. The reverse is the case. We never remember an occasion when there was more unanimity of opinion in regard to a question of foreign policy. Depend upon it, there is little doubt as to unanimity when the *Times* and the *Daily Chronicle*, the *Standard* and the *Daily News* join hands with Mr. Gladstone in supporting and giving moral weight to the policy of Lord Salisbury. Indeed, this complete unanimity in the determination that Turkish misrule in Armenia must cease, and that the measures necessary to make it cease, however strong, must be taken, is almost to be regretted. It tends to prevent the indignation of England from fully manifesting itself. When people are all agreed, it is difficult for them to show, at any rate to an outsider, that they are in earnest. If we had a newspaper or two seriously defending the Turks, and a few public meetings in their defence, the Sultan would soon find out the depth and tenacity of the feeling which has been aroused by the stories from Armenia. But in all probability the Chester meeting will be enough to undeceive the Sultan. When he sees Mr. Gladstone denouncing Turkish misrule as he denounced it twenty years ago, the Sultan will look for comfort to the extracts which are supplied him from the *Times* and the *Standard*. But instead of comfort, he will find the declaration that he must yield to the demands of the Powers lest worse things befall him.

Our readers may perhaps have felt a certain sense of disappointment in finding that Mr. Gladstone's speech contained no specific suggestions for dealing with Armenia. That disappointment is most natural, but it is inevitable. Mr. Gladstone, speaking without first-hand knowledge of the negotiations, could not have made any practical suggestions without having done the very thing which he was of all others anxious to avoid doing,—without, that is, embarrassing Lord Salisbury. Under present circumstances, the only thing which can be done is, as it were, to give Lord Salisbury a blank cheque,—to tell him that he will be supported by public opinion in doing anything he may think necessary to force the Sultan to give way. The only thing which England will resent is his failure to make use of the power to fill up the cheque. Before we leave the subject of Armenia, there are two special points which we desire to deal with. The first is the question of publishing the reports as to the massacres which have recently been sent by our Consul in Asia

Minor. The late Government did not publish these, partly, we presume, for fear of unduly inflaming public opinion in England, and partly because of the horrible and disgusting nature of a great deal of the evidence contained in the reports. We would strongly urge the Government to reconsider this decision, and to give these reports to the public practically in their entirety. No one is going to be injured morally by records of devilish cruelty. Again, the dread of unduly inflaming public opinion is, we believe, unnecessary and over-scrupulous. It is right that people should know the whole facts of the case, even if they have to encounter much that shocks and pains them. The other point which we desire to dwell on is the mistake which is made by certain of the friends of Armenia in representing, or appearing to represent Mahommedanism as a creed which compels outrage and cruelty in its votaries. That is a mistake in fact and in policy. The enlightened and civilised, and yet deeply religious, Mahommedans of India feel no more compelled by their creed to slay, torture, and ravish those who differ from them in religion than do English Christians. It is an unjustice to attribute the wickedness of the Turks—a people at once demoralised and barbarous, a race that was rotten before it was ripe—entirely to the faith of Islam. The Turks are cruel. The Turks are Mahommedans. Therefore, all Mahommedans are cruel. That is very poor logic. When the Turks are denounced, they must be denounced as Turks, not as Mahommedans. If the friends of Armenia are not careful in this matter, they may lose much valuable sympathy for their cause. How, for example, can you expect Anglo Indians who have known and respected the Indian Mahommedans, to support a crusade against the Mahommedan? They will naturally say,—"We cannot join a movement which supposes what we know to be untrue,—the hopeless wickedness of all the followers of Islam." We are not concerned to defend Mahommedanism, and, indeed, regard it as in many ways a most injurious creed; but it is a great mistake, as well as most unfair, to attribute to it the vileness of the Turk. The Armenian movement must be kept free, not only from party feeling, but also from the *odium theologicum*.

Blackwood's Magazine,[1] Vol. 158 (October 1895): 483–92

An Unbiased View of the Armenian Question

Walter B. Harris

It may seem almost too late in the day to reopen the vexed question of Armenia and its massacres, and I would not venture to do so were it not that my travels have enabled me to see enough and procure sufficient evidence to make a clear statement as to the actual condition of affairs in Asia Minor at the present time, and to collect link by link the chain of events that led to the disturbances of last autumn. My route lay, if not in the actual districts in which the troubles took place, in parts where Kurd and Christian, Turk and Persian, find themselves living together in towns and villages of a country that presents almost the same features, moral and physical, as the mountains and plateaux of Van and Bitlis, Mush and Sassun.

The mixed Commission that was sent by the interested Powers, and the many correspondents who collected notes upon the question, have proved that without the least doubt the massacres which were reported in Europe toward the close of last year have taken place. They have proved also that every conceivable, and to us inconceivable, atrocity was committed by a lawless and ferocious soldiery upon Armenian men, women, and children; that soldiery were turned loose from the towns to ravish and kill to their heart's content, while their officers goaded them on to every manner of cruelty. Thus far the verdict is public news; but what I think has yet to be learned is, not only what absolutely led to these scenes of debauchery and horror, but also some idea as to the characters and lives of the persons engaged either as persecutors or persecuted, the actors in this terrible tragedy. The revolting facts that filled paper after paper in England at the commencement and during the early months of this year caused such a horror in England as is only possible amongst a philanthropic and generous nation; and these feelings of commiseration were stirred into a desire for revenge by the representatives of the Armenians in London, who were not slow to call attention to the pitiful state of their country.

This flood of pity, noble as it was in one way, was accompanied by at least one disadvantage, if not danger. It closed the eyes of the English people, and Europe in general, to any other side of the question that might exist, to any incentive the Turk may have had for bringing himself to such a pitch of exasperation that his cruelty knew no bounds. The innocent Armenians had been massacred, and not only massacred but horribly tortured, and women and children ravished and slain, and that was sufficient. It mattered not what had led to such a terrible state of affairs; no crime that the Armenians could have committed could merit such punishment. It was by the incessant appeal of the Armenian party in London, by their incessant calling of attention by every means of publicity to the last act in the drama, that they were able to obliterate all that had gone before, except to allude to a period of persecution; and in accomplishing this, no doubt they were highly satisfied with their success and with themselves. But before judgment can be passed upon the Turk, it is necessary to understand far more about Armenia and the Armenian question than the British public has had opportunity of learning. It is true articles and pamphlets were published, many of them absolutely unbiassed in their opinion, regarding the question; but while much stress was laid on the geographical, historical, and religious position of Armenia, there was a tendency to ignore more important elements of the case, the general character of the parties concerned. And it is, I think, upon this point that the greatest ignorance and even biassed opinion are found in England. To the ordinary British public the state of affairs is somewhat like this. Peaceful villages of Christians, much resembling our country population, are found surrounded on all sides by vast lawless hordes of semi-savages, who, when the innocent villagers are in church, steal their sheep and cattle, while troops of cruel soldiery are constantly engaged in exacting illegal taxes. Then every month or so the church, with its belfry and its timbered roof, is burnt, the priests flogged or dragged to prison, and the village destroyed, while the women and children are led captive. Such, so far as I can gather, is the idea of the general public upon the Armenian question. But how far is this from the truth! Instead of these homely villages with their churches and spires, surrounded with trees and gardens, the Armenians live in burrows in the earth, dirty and smoke-begrimed, passing their lives in agriculture or in petty trade, and, when rich enough, lending money at usurious rates to the very Kurds of whose depredations they so loudly complain. Some general estimate of the character of the Armenian must be conceived before any idea of the state of the country can be realised. Uneducated, a fanatical Christian who looks upon all other Churches than his own, the Gregorian, in much the same light as he does on Islam, immoral in his domestic life, practising vices which are supposed to be peculiarly those of Mohammedans, drinking more than is good for him, dishonest when he finds the opportunity in his business, the Armenian is a typical Oriental, lacking the thoroughness and manliness of the Turkish peasant, and much preferring to gain his ends by intrigue rather than by straightforward dealing.

Such is the Armenian of the country districts. In the towns, it is true, he is brought, if not under a moral, at least under a legal code, and here we find him diligent, an admirable linguist, an excellent man of commerce, so far as never letting a sou pass through his hands without making something by it, squeezing those under him, untrustworthy unless it be to his advantage to be the contrary, suave and plausible, without affection or regard for any one, and immoral where immorality does not cost him anything; an obedient and hard working clerk, a merciless and grasping master, and often marvellously clever withal. The Turk, on the contrary, is very different. Except those who fill official positions, where intrigue is part and parcel of their being, the Turk is straightforward, enjoying his life, as immoral as the Armenian, a lax Moslem, with no fanaticism but a firm conviction in predestination, ready to swindle when he finds the opportunity, which he is not usually sharp enough to do, affectionate in his nature, far too trusting in his disposition, and cruel to the backbone. He has never been able to rid himself of this great feature of the old tribes from which he is sprung, and when his blood is heated, his desires fired, there is no knowing to what pitch of devilish cruelty he will not proceed. Just as when the original hordes of his people, pouring out of Central Asia, flooded Persia,

Mesopotamia, and Asia Minor with every description of cruelty and bloodshed, so today, deep down in his heart, there lingers this inheritance. It requires, happily, much to exasperate him; but when a sufficient pitch is reached, his fury knows no bounds, and no constraint, moral or physical, can hold him back.

It has been said that the massacres in Armenia were due to religious persecution. This is not a fact, and there is no doubt in my mind whatever that this reason has been put forward by the agitators in Europe to obtain the more hearty co-operation of the Powers in redressing their wrongs. I think it will not be difficult to prove, on sufficient evidence, that until the actual massacres were taking place, when the cry of "Kill the Christian dogs!" was no doubt raised, no religious persecution of the Armenians had taken place. I have stated above, and I think all who know the oriental peoples well will agree with me, that the Turk is not a fanatic. It is true, occasional outbursts of fanaticism occur, but usually in the case of the *mollahs*, answering roughly to their priesthood. The Sunni doctrine, held by the Turks, is of the two great divisions of Islam by far the least narrow. It is the Sheiyas—such as the Persians from whom the Christian meets with a scowl and a curse—who often refuse him even a drop of water to drink; while the Turk receives one into his house, eats with one, and sometimes even drinks with one, allows Christians to enter his mosques—in fact, makes no practical difference between the followers of the two religions. It is for this laxity in his relations with Christians that the Sunni is so despised by the rigid and fanatical Sheiyas.

But so far as these words of mine go to prove that the late massacres were not of a religious character, it may be very justly said that they are only a general statement. Let us, then, look into the question more closely. Cast your eyes over that great country known as Asia Minor—in fact, I may say over Mesopotamia and the province of Baghdad as well—and look at the number of cities, and towns, and villages that exist. I believe I am absolutely correct in stating that with very few exceptions indeed—perhaps only those of the towns containing the tombs of the Imams, such as Kerbela and Nejef, or Meshed Ali—every city and town, and most of the villages, contain a mixed population of Christians and Moslems. Yet if, as has been stated, the Armenians of these districts were persecuted merely for upholding the Christian faith, how is it that we find in every other direction supporters of both religions living in peace one with the other, and mixing freely in commerce and social intercourse? How is it that the massacres of Bitlis and Sassun are not perpetrated every day in every quarter of the Turkish empire, until the hated and despised Christians are exterminated? In the towns of Turkey in Asia that I have visited I have found Moslems and Christians living in accord, enjoying the same prosperity, suffering the same disadvantages, the sole difference between their positions being that in the courts of law the judges are more prone to believe a Moslem than a Christian. In this the judges are wrong, for, generally speaking, neither ought to be believed. But we find a number of philanthropic and irrational men and women in England, who know nothing of the Turk or the Armenian, and nothing of the status in which they live, proclaiming from the platform and the pulpit that the Armenians were massacred because they refused to become converts, and because they upheld the religion of Christ. I never yet saw a Turk, and indeed few Moslems of any [region], who attempted either by persuasion or force to convert others to their belief. On the contrary, it is the Christians who are attempting to persuade the Moslems to change their religion, though in the case of the Turks their absolute failure has led to their abandoning them. Christian missionaries are allowed to reside, and do reside, in most of the larger towns of Asia Minor. The Armenians especially have opened schools and churches, and are doing good work amongst the native Christian children. Let one thing be clearly understood with regard to the Eastern Christians, and that is this—that their fanaticism and hatred toward the Turk are a hundred times greater than that of the Turk toward them. In talking to Moslems of Armenians during my travels, I heard not one curse or opprobrious epithet used; in talking to Armenians about the Moslems, no name was too bad, no insult too deep for them. In Erivan, an Armenian boasted to me of the exquisite tiles he had stolen from the lovely mosque in that city. On my rebuking him for sacrilege, he told me that he would, if he had the power, blow the place up with gunpowder, and that he rejoiced that every tile he took away—and he showed me the bare spot of his former thefts—disfigured the heathen temple. The following day he accompanied me to Echmiazin, the holy centre of the Gregorian Church, and there prayed for the destruction of all Moslems and heretics, and kissed, one after another, the relics in the church. Until my Arab servant entered Echmiazin with me, no Moslem, I was told, had ever been within the sacred walls, and I doubt not that he was allowed to enter only on account of the fact that it was the policy of those in authority to show every possible attention at that particular period to an Englishman. Yet the mosques in Erivan are visited by the Armenians, whose thefts of the exquisite tiles have disfigured beyond repair more than one beautiful spot. No; the Turk is not a fanatic, but the Armenian most assuredly is, and religious persecution will not blaze out in Asia Minor until the native Christian gains the upper hand.

To what cause, then, can the massacres be attributed?

Although, as I have pointed out, the Turk is by no means a bigot, his cruel nature naturally tends to render him a persecutor when he finds the opportunity, particularly if the persecution be a political one; for patriotism to his country, his people, and his Sultan, who, he believes, is the Khalifa of the Prophet, is deeply rooted in his heart. No one knows better than he that his system of government is rotten; but no one is more ready to defend it from outside attack. It was easy for him to see that the Christian population was an enemy to the State, and therefore he considered it an enemy to himself—and therein lies the key of the situation.

Here we must leave the discussion of generalities, to survey for a little what had been taking place in Armenia previous to the breaking out of hostilities. It is not necessary, in order to trace the course of these political events, to revert to any period previous to the Berlin Conference of 1878. When the representatives of the Powers then present were discussing the Eastern problem, the Armenians took advantage of the opportunity to state their case. They did so, however, with that disregard for correctness which characterises the statements of all Eastern people—owing more, perhaps, to their natural tendency to exaggeration than to the willful telling of untruth—with the result that the European delegates gave the question but little thought, merely calling the attention of the Sublime Porte to the matter by inserting a clause that "reforms should be instituted in the provinces inhabited by Armenians." This clause was as vague as it was impracticable, for every province of Asia Minor is inhabited by Armenians, and the members of the Conference could have little intended or expected that the Sultan should commence a series of practical reforms throughout his dominions in Asia. Had the Armenians understood, as they probably never will understand, that the practical minds of European politicians are influenced more by a few simple and unadulterated facts than by imaginary, or at least vague statements, there is no doubt that even as early as the Berlin Conference considerable attention would have been concentrated upon their position, and the matter treated as one of importance. But when, in the memorandum which they handed in—to Mr Goschen, I believe—they commenced by the assertion that in that vague district know as Armenia the Christian, or rather Armenian, population numbered three millions of souls, it was impossible that much credence could be put in the ensuing paragraphs of their statement of complaint against the Porte.

With regard to this question of population a few words must be said, for though in detail it is unimportant, except in proving the ratio of the Christians to the Moslems, it is interesting as showing to what extent the Armenians can be believed in the stories that they spread regarding their co-religionists in Asia Minor. Let us commence with 1878; we have there an official Armenian statement of their numbers—three millions. As soon as the clause was inserted, and what little public attention Armenia had attracted was withdrawn, and when there no longer remained any necessity to make out the Christian population as largely predominating, what do we find? This, that an Armenian in a position to be well informed puts down the population at between 300,000 and 400,000—that is to say, at *one-ninth* of the number officially stated to the delegates of the Berlin Conference. More recent and carefully prepared statistics, by far the most reliable that can be found, estimate the Armenians at about half a million, or *one-sixth* of the number given at Berlin. Then came the massacres of last autumn and the public feeling in Europe—and the population rises at a bound to two millions, a figure that was given me as correct not only in Echmiazin itself, but in many other places. As I said already, the details are of no importance; for it can safely be estimated that the Armenian population of the plateau of Asia Minor is about half, if as much, that of the Moslems—Turks and Kurds.

But I have drawn attention to the figures merely to show that in dealing with such oriental peoples as Turks and Armenians very little confidence can be placed in figures, or, unfortunately, for the matter of that, in statements, which are not proved by other evidence than that of report. I do not know whether the Turkish Government publishes a census of its Asiatic provinces; but I doubt not that if one has been drawn up during the last few months, or since the massacres, we should find it erring as largely, if not more so, in the other direction, and numbering the Moslems as the stars in the heavens and the Armenians as few and far between. In casting blame upon the Armenians for their perversion of details, it must not be thought that I am holding them up as below the level of the Turks. The Turkish point of view is one that is practically unimportant, as it has never been made public in England, whereas in the other case our papers have been filled with statements one and all of which are of Armenian origin. Rather I would point out to the Armenians how their case is weakened when few if any of its details will bear the least investigation—with the exception of the massacres themselves, which unhappily we know are only too true.

But to continue with the outline of the history of events that have been taking place since the clause was inserted in the Berlin Treaty, stating that reforms must be instituted in the provinces of Asia Minor inhabited by Armenians. This little clause, apparently so easy to attend to or to break, which seemed to mean neither trouble to Turkey nor betterment of their condition to the Armenians, grew quickly to such importance in the eyes of both, that it may be said to be the origin of all the trouble and sorrow. It gave hope to the Christians, and it opened the eyes of the Porte to a possible risk of disturbance and danger in the future. Little could the delegates have seen how so small a grain of mustard-seed could in the course of so few years grow into a political tree the branches of which have been filled with the discord and bloodshed of the birds who had built their nests therein.

For the Armenians there was a hope, while the Turk, silent and suspicious, watched for the dangers that he knew must come. Nor were they long in coming, though they took years to reach maturity. Secret political societies sprang into existence; leagues were formed; dreams of a free Armenia began to be spread about, and the fire of the souls of the people began to flicker. Old histories of the Armenian kings—half-fabulous records—were routed out and quoted from the pulpit, the voice of the priest preached freedom to the superstitious people, to whom their pastors are more than men, and the flickering flame began to blaze.

And what was the Turk doing meanwhile?

From the very first attempt of the Armenians to put forward their case the Sublime Porte had realised the danger. It was a danger that was a most difficult one to meet. Any attempt at force, at wholesale arrest, at crushing the secret societies of Armenia, would call once more the attention of Europe to the question, with what results it would be difficult to say—probably the same as had occurred in Bulgaria. At all costs this must be avoided. What, then, remained for the Turks to do? The sole policy which they found possible without the risk of measures of force was the following: to commence against the Armenians a system of petty persecution, which, without being sufficiently harsh or sufficiently tangible to call attention to the country, was ample to gain the ends desired—namely, the *voluntary* emigration of the Armenian population. But it was no easy matter to carry out such a system, for many of the districts where danger most threatened were wild mountain plateaux where the Turks themselves seldom if ever came into contact with the Armenian population. Here, however, there was a remedy, and in the wild tribes of Kurds, who share with the Christians these elevated plateaux, the Porte discovered a godsend. A few remarks must be here made about the Kurds. This race of hardy hillsmen are known to have inhabited the mountain ranges of Asia Minor from almost prehistoric times. They were known to the Assyrians; and mention is found of them and their doings on almost every page of the changeful history of Asia Minor. In appearance they are a fine hardy race of men, and in character possess some of the best features of Orientals. In their mountain districts, where the baneful influence of Turk and Persian has scarcely reached them, they are a most hospitable and kindly race, contented with their hard lot, living a life of morality unknown to the Armenian, but robbers withal. Nor can this last trait in their character be wondered at, when it is considered how much they have suffered in their time from the fact that their country has formed a continual battle-field from the earliest periods of history to the time of the Russo-Turkish war. How many armies have passed through and through their country, pillaging and robbing, it would be difficult to enumerate; but the fact that the old highroad to the great kingdoms of Babylonia, Mesopotamia, and Persia led through their territory is sufficient evidence of the checkered existence they have always led.

Living in mud hovels, much resembling those of the Armenians in winter, in summer they migrate with all their flocks and herds to the high mountain grazing-lands, where they inhabit for the most part brown tents of goat's hair. Sometimes these migratory journeys are of considerable length, some days in duration, and the passing Kurds have from time immemorial demanded and received a small tribute in kind from the Armenians whose villages they approach. In fact, in many cases a kind of feudal system has been in existence from time immemorial, a Kurdish tribe protecting an Armenian village from other robbers in return for a small annual tribute. It is a system that exists in many parts of the Mohammedan world, and seems to be identical with that in use to-day in the case of the Jews in trans-Atlas Morocco, who pay small sums to the Berbers for their protection.

It will be easily understood, then, that it wanted but a word on the part of the Turkish authorities to set the Kurds looting, and there is no doubt that a hint to this effect was given to them. That they had little to fear in return was very apparent, for had not the officials, as was undoubtedly the case, promised that no reparation would be made, the very fact that the Kurds inhabited wild mountain districts and are well armed would deter the Turks from the expensive, dangerous, and unremunerative course of attempting to punish them. But, in addition to this, there was a still more powerful reason why the Kurds ran no risk in giving vent to their pillaging propensities. Many of the wildest of these tribesmen have been enrolled in irregular troops known as the Hamidieh,—a sort of vagabond yeomanry founded upon, but little resembling, the Russian Cossacks. Armed by the Turkish Government, receiving a very irregular pay, and allowed to do as they please, there is little wonder that the Hamidieh took to looting their neighbours, tolerably safe from attack owing to the Sultan's uniform which they wore. In fact, it was no doubt an advantage in the eyes of the local officials that, instead of receiving their full pay, which found its way elsewhere, they should manage to satisfy themselves by robbing cattle and sheep. At the same time, these depredations of the Hamidieh were tending to carry out the policy of the Porte, and to drive the Armenians to emigrate.

But the very weapon which the Turks had raised to further their ends began at length to become a danger. Armed bodies of

Kurds, wearing the Turkish uniform, ravaged the country, and even the officials found that their tools had escaped their grasp, and that, had they desired to do so, they were powerless to hold the Kurds in check.

Meanwhile amongst the Armenians powerful influences had been at work. As complaint after complaint, based no doubt upon truth and embroidered upon by oriental imagination, reached their fellow-countrymen who were residing in England and in other European countries, these raised their voice in lamentation, and set their hands to work treason and revolution. And here an enormous blame rests upon the Armenian agitators, who may be said to have sacrificed their fellow-countrymen in order to gain their own political ends. I do not write these words without knowledge of what I am saying. The Armenians in Europe, safe from arrest and attack, wrote and sent emissaries to Asia Minor to agitate and stir up rebellion in those parts, and for several years this intrigue has been in progress. The district of Sassun refused to pay taxes, and ceased doing so, and in 1892, when the Turks attempted to bridge the river at Chenek, the only practical entrance to their wild mountain country, they fired upon the soldiers. From 1892 to 1894 the district was in a state of revolt, and their example of courage and bravery—or treason—stirred up their fellow-countrymen in other parts to imitation. Inflammatory literature, smuggled across the Russian and Persian frontiers, was poured over the country. Agitators stirred up the superstitious people by hopes of revenge and false promises of co-operation from England and elsewhere. Priests preached treason to the peasant from the pulpit, and the peasant, uneducated, understanding neither their political position nor the attitude of the foreign Powers, listened to their words as a divine message. The Armenians, like all Orientals, believed what their own people told them, and refused to hear the words of those who could give them, and did give them, better advice. They were told that many Armenians held high positions in British Government; they forgot that many did hold high positions at the Porte; and these idle and culpable words, written from London and Europe in general by men whose lives and persons were safe, and who were living in peace and plenty and had nothing to lose, egged the tribesmen on to actions which in other circumstances they would never have dreamed of. Had not the Armenians in England stirred up, directly or indirectly, their countrymen in Sassun, the pits would never have been dug in which to-day the bones of men, women, and children are rotting. Had affairs not reached so serious a turn as massacre, we should have long ago realised this fact in England; but the brutal barbarities perpetrated by the Turks have blinded the eyes of the public to all that has gone before, and for this, no doubt, the Armenian political agitators feel an immense gratitude and relief. So strong is the feeling in England that these words of unbiassed opinion may be scoffed at, for there is nothing so difficult as to change public opinion in the smallest and least important article of its belief; but personal knowledge and intercourse with the Armenians themselves have given me opportunities of seeing much of which the public have never heard. If my words be denied, as I quite expect they will be by interested persons, let inquiries be set on foot, Let one question alone be asked, Is it not true that as late as April of this year a caravan was stopped by the Turkish authorities at Kotur on the Persian frontier, and the pack-saddles of the mules found to be stuffed with inflammatory and revolutionary literature? And let reasoning men and women consider whether such a course as pouring treason into Armenia at such a moment was not an incentive to fresh massacre and equally appalling barbarities as those that had taken place the autumn before.

It may be asked, What is the ultimate aim of these political agitators? and they will tell you that it is merely the better government of their fellow-countrymen. But is this so? Let us look for a moment at the condition of the Armenians in Russia. There the Gregorian Church is still untouched, though that of the Georgians has long ago been swallowed up in the national religion of the country. Armenian schools flourish in every part; their worship is freely allowed; the dignitaries of their Church are chosen by the Armenians and appointed by the Emperor himself, who has never been known to object to the Catholicos elected by the people. In fact, they are allowed every religious and civil privilege, with the exception that children of mixed marriages shall be brought up in the Orthodox Church. Under the just rule of Russia the Armenian flourishes; all the petty offices, and many of the higher ones, in the Government of Transcaucasia are held by them; in trade they have ruined the less crafty Russian; and southern Russia to-day is an Armenian province. But ask the agitators whether they desire that the plateau of Asia Minor should fall under Russian rule, and what will they tell you? That they prefer Turkey to Russia. Astonishing as this reply is, it is heard throughout all the East wherever Armenians are found; and why is this? Because if Russia held Armenia, there would only be opportunities for the agitators and their friends to gain an honest livelihood by their labours or their efficiency, whereas what they are desirous of doing is to form a free and autonomous Armenia, in which their own personal enrichment and aggrandisement would take the place of patriotism and the welfare of their country. If you think that the Armenians are patriotic or sincere as a people, you are mistaken. At Echmiazin, the religious centre of the Armenians, one of the highest of the dignatories of the Gregorian Church spoke the following words to me. "We love England," he said. "After Armenia we love her best of all. We pray for her every day and many times a day. *She is so rich.*" In those ingenuous words you have the whole key-note of the Armenian policy, the whole character of her people—love of power and wealth. In an autonomous Armenia there would be every opportunity for the agitators to practise their powers of intrigue, a gentle art in which they excel. In a Russian Armenia intrigue means Siberia—at least such intrigue as the Armenians love to indulge in. No! the Armenian agitators and political aspirants with whom I came in contact in Southern Russia and in Persia, hovering about the frontiers, but careful never to run their necks into danger, one and all told me that they preferred Turkish to Russian rule, and that their war-cry was "Autonomy!" They pretend to be satisfied with such reforms as have been proposed by the Powers—and for a time they may rest tranquil—the calm before the coming storm; but as surely as the massacres have taken place, there will arise further and more serious troubles in the country—reforms or no reforms—troubles stirred up by men who are content to see their brethren suffer in the hopes of themselves some day gaining an end where power and fortune will be open to them. By all means let the European Powers insist upon the reforms proposed, and let them see that they are carried out; but once this is accomplished, once the Turk is morally and physically punished for the barbarities he has committed, barbarities almost unparalleled in the world's history, and when the solitary Sultan in the Yildiz Kiosk has eaten dirt in the presence of the world, then let it be clearly stated to the Armenians that no further support will be given to their political aims as long as Turkey holds to her promises and her practices of reform. If, however, the Porte becomes lax, and continues to allow the Kurds to rob and steal under the eyes of her provincial officials, it will be the duty of Europe once more to interfere. If, on the contrary, Turkey remains faithful to her promises she must be forced to give, then the time for interference is over, and the political atmosphere of the whole of Europe must not again be clouded in order to further the ends of unscrupulous adventurers.

The Spectator, Vol. 75 (October 12, 1895): 476–77

The Suspense in Constantinople

This business in Constantinople must gravely increase Lord Salisbury's already heavy anxieties. Sir John Tenniel in this week's *Punch* may depict "Ultimatum" as a bull-dog ready to be let loose, and irresistible by any worn-out dragon, but the Foreign Secretary has to remember that this offender is an old lion, and that other strong dogs will at once be in the arena on hearing the bull-dog's growl. The situation is bad enough anyhow, and so much may happen suddenly that is unexpected. Let us look at the facts, if that be possible, as we should be compelled to look at them if the responsibility of action were immediately upon our shoulders. We take it that the immigrant Armenians in Constantinople as distinguished from the resident Armenians, are half mad with rage at the recent atrocities, with fear for their relatives and families left behind in the province, and with hope deferred,—hope created by the representations of the Powers. They resolved therefore on a "demonstration"—which, remember, is the regular Oriental way as well as the Western way of expressing discontent—in the hope of hurrying on the dilatory Embassies, and perhaps of affecting the highly strung nerves of the Sultan himself. Some secret society, aware of the resolve, decided to turn it to account, and when the procession approached the Porte the officer in command of the police was shot by some one in the crowd, whose members, as is expedient in Turkey, all bore arms. The police, seeing their officer murdered, naturally charged the advancing crowd, and so far there is nothing for which to blame the Turks. The police no doubt cut down a great many men, more than was necessary; but no Asiatic will fight bravely without a sword, the police did not use rifles, and to call the deaths inflicted "a massacre" is to misuse words. The Italian or Austrian, or for that matter, the Irish gendarmerie, would have behaved just like the Turks. It was after the procession had been beaten that the inherent savagery of the Turks betrayed itself. There was no necessity for violence. The city is full of Ottoman troops, the few Christians armed, are armed only with revolvers, and Osman Ghazi could have coerced Constantinople into silent order without bloodshed in three hours. Instead of displaying irresistible force at once, the fanatic group in the Palace resolved to read the Christians a lesson; a hint was either sent out to the Softas, or, as is now believed, bodies of police in the disguise of Softas were set in motion, and the Armenians were in practice placed at their mercy. The Mussulman roughs, seeing mischief on foot, followed their co-religionists, and for twenty-four hours a reign of terror prevailed throughout Constantinople. All Armenians accessible were clubbed to death, the very gas-stokers killing twenty-one of their Armenian comrades, the bodies were rapidly conveyed to the shore in Government carts, and after some four hundred had been killed, such Armenians as were unable to barricade themselves, fled to the churches and the Patriarchate for protection. So completely were the police of opinion that they were released from law, that eight wounded and arrested Armenians, actually lying powerless in the Prefecture, were stabbed to death, that crime being witnessed by a dragoman of the Italian Embassy. So thoroughly was it understood that there was no protection for Armenians, that the unhappy race, whose crime is to be Christians and to be disaffected towards the Sovereign who allows his troops and police to slay and torture them at discretion, went wild with fear, while the lower Mussulmans, believing that a day of license, of which Constantinople has seen many, had arrived, showed all the symptoms of growing "fanatical,"—that is, of being ready to massacre Christians at sight. So menacing did affairs become that six Embassies, whose business it is to know the truth of what occurs in Constantinople, who are full of mad jealousies of one another, and who are divided by many profound and substantial causes of difference, united for the moment to represent to Yildiz Kiosk the facts as we have related them, and to demand of the strange little figure who sits there, so full at once of fears and power—a trembling prisoner in his gardens, yet Khalif throughout the Ottomans' vast dominion—that he should at once restore order and protect the Christians. It is probable that he complied, and that the only orders which would suffice were issued at last, for we see that immediately after, a few shots being heard in a local riot, the spot was instantly surrounded by troops, and order was restored, as it ought to have been at first, by the appearance of irresistible force. "Tranquillity" is therefore restored in Constantinople; but clearly the Embassies are not satisfied, and they have reason for their hesitation. The Sultan has not signed the order permanently protecting Armenians, the Armenians who fled to the churches have not returned to their homes, and the Mussulman ferment has not yet abated. The mob indeed probably believe that their ascendancy is threatened, and are ready to demand anything, the dethronement of the Sultan included, which they think the troops will permit. They may sink back into their angry quiet, as they have done many times before; they may content themselves with isolated murders, or they may explode in one wild burst of wrath against all Christians, and especially the English Ambassador, who is understood to be the special protector of those insolent slaves, the Armenians, who object to be massacred at the will of Colonels and Pashas. Therefore the Embassies keep their guardships close at hand, and therefore, we doubt not, the British Admiral at Lemnos has clear instructions how to act should the signal reach him that the English in Constantinople are in imminent danger of being clubbed to death. The great city waits, palpitating, for the next incident, which may be a grant of "reforms"—in other words, a fresh false promise from the Sultan to reign by European advice—or may be a catastrophe.

It is quite useless, almost impertinent, to suggest till that incident has occurred what next ought to be done. If, on the one hand, Constantinople sinks back into its normal condition of uneasy quiet, and the Sultan signs a paper placing all Armenians or all Christians under the guardianship of a Commission appointed by the Powers, nothing will be done until after a year or two's experience has proved that the paper is a nullity, the protection a farce, and Armenia as much misgoverned as before. If, on the other hand, the Mussulman masses, excited beyond bearing by what seems to them Christian defiance, should commence a massacre, or elect a fighting Sultan, or threaten the Ambassadors themselves, Europe, and especially England, must take steps so extreme that their results cannot be foreseen even by the most experienced. One shell falling in Constantinople would end the present condition of affairs throughout the Turkish Empire, calling at once every rebel to arms, all Macedonians, all Greeks, all Arabs, and also the Osmanli caste, which, we may rely on it, will follow its traditions and die fighting magnificently for Islam and its own ascendancy. They are not Hovas, the Turks. It is more useful to point out how completely Europe is acknowledging at last that the Ottoman Empire is a semi-barbarian Power, which must be controlled by force in the interests of humanity. If there is an acknowledged right in any Government, it is that of putting down disorder in its own capital, in its own way, and without attention to anything except its own judgment of what constitutes expedient severity. Not a remonstrance came up from Europe at the executions—which were, in fact, legal massacres—that followed the suppression of the Paris Commune. It is while he is exercising his undoubted rights, that Europe, for the moment coherent, informs the Sultan that his method is too uncivilised for endurance, that he must alter it at once, and that he must protect those whom he has condemned, and whom his policemen are destroying. Europe, in fact, assumes the ultimate right of regulating Turkey, not in her remoter provinces, not under any specific Treaty, but in her own capital, under her Sovereign eyes, and by virtue only of the right of civilisation to control barbarism. That is perfectly right, if "Europe" is to be the universal moderator in the world's affairs, which is now undoubtedly her pretension, whether or no it has been formulised; but then Europe must go a step farther and see that its will is obeyed. It is atrocious cruelty to interfere so far, and then retire, leaving the oppressors to wreak for years together their vengeance on the oppressed. The "reforms" and their operation must be steadily watched in the interior provinces, and that means the government of Turkey by six Powers, of whom no two have the same interests, the same views as to decent government, or the same method of applying pressure. We do not believe that effort can succeed, or that such a situation can endure; but that which must follow failure, the partition of Turkey, will tax the statecraft of Europe almost beyond endurance. The Eastern question is, in fact, upon us again, and though there may be, probably will be, one more postponement, the merest accident—a street riot, a fever-fit in the Sultan, a mutiny for pay—may compel a settlement at once with any means that happen to be at hand. Gunpowder is lying about all over Eastern Europe, and the Turk himself can fire it more readily and more effectually than anybody else. Of all the incidents of this *émeute*, no single one is so ominous or so significant as the execution of eight Armenians after they had been seized and laid safely by the heels. That is the spirit which will at last, and not long hence, bring Turkey and Europe into avowed and final collision. You may talk of reforms for ever, but if prisoners once arrested disappear, what is the use of your reforms?

The Spectator, Vol. 75 (October 19, 1895): 508–9

The Compromise at Constantinople

The Sultan, it is said, and we can readily believe, is much more disturbed by his great unpopularity among Mussulmans than by all the pressure which the Ambassadors of three Powers are just now applying to him. He can cheat the Powers, or divide the Powers by great concessions to Russia; but Mahommedan disaffection threatens his throne, and perhaps his life. With an intellect of wonderful keenness, though imperfectly supplied with information; with nerves perpetually quivering with vague apprehensions; and with a tenacity which has sometimes the effect of sullen obstinacy, and sometimes of genuine will-power, Abdul Hamid has in some ways been a successful Sultan. He has rebuilt the throne, which was, when he ascended it, crumbling under repeated shocks; and is at this moment as absolute as the strongest of his predecessors, who, with all their faults, have been marked among European dynasties for the number of strong rulers they have produced. The dread inspired in all Pashas by that trembling little figure is as deep as the dread inspired by Abdurrahman Khan, the boldest of soldiers and most severe of all civil administrators in Asia. The Sultan, however, has on other sides been most unsuccessful. He has ruined his fleet, which is essential to his sea-divided Empire; he has enfeebled discipline in his army by permitting irregularity of payment, and by raising hosts of irregulars—Kurds, Circassians, Albanians, and Arabs—none of whom have the Osmanli genius for military obedience; he has profoundly irritated and alarmed all Christians, and he has not conciliated even the Ottoman section of his Mussulman millions. He probably hates all Christians, partly because he has the Kalifate on his brain, partly because they furnish the lever for the detested pressure of Europe, and partly because he is aware that the fanatics in their malignity say that he himself looks just like an

Armenian. On the other hand, though he is a strict Mussulman, fulfils all the obligations of his faith, and trusts only his co-religionists with high office, Mussulmans do not love him. He is too far removed from their ideal Lord, the "Amurath" of tradition, the conquering, man-slaying, cruel, but efficient and visible ruler of their world. They do not mind his oppressions; he may kill a dozen Giaours an hour for all they care; but they hate his system of government by espionage, his endless precautions for his own safety, his seclusion, and his perpetual change of agents,—a practice wholly opposed to the Ottoman tradition. They are hungering, too, with their grand history, for a little success, for some policy which shall at least preserve them from endless bullying by Ambassadors; and we suspect, though we do not quite know, from endless hints from "protected" Christians as to their approaching downfall. That would be a disagreeable temper for any Government to meet, but in Constantinople it is a dangerous one. The loyalty of the Turks is of a special kind. They will die in heaps for the House of Othman which gave them their dominion, and which has in their tradition an indissoluble connection with Islam, but they do not quite forget that the Kalifate is not hereditary, and they vividly remember that within the House of Othman they have some right of choice. Soldiery and mob together have repeatedly altered the succession, and the old Sultans so feared this right that they used to kill out all Princes not in the direct line. It would be nothing unusual if the soldiers were to demand a stronger Sultan, or to approve a palace revolt which gave them another descendant of Othman as their Lord. Beyond this possibility they do not look, all the talk about new dynasties and Parliamentary institutions or "limitations upon absolutism" being café talk among men who repeat, like parrots, the ideas of the West, and who would be crushed as Midhat was, the only strong man they ever produced, by a wave of the Sultan's finger. This, however, is sufficient to give the Sultan agonies of apprehension, and it is between two fears—fear of a Mussulman rising and fear of seeing British ironclads in the Bosphorus—that he has been hesitating, begging for time, and trying in an adroit yet rather feeble way to set the Powers by the ears. He will probably fail, for there are only two Powers at Constantinople,—Russia and Great Britain; and sooner than retire absolutely defeated the British would have run the risk of seeing Armenia occupied by a Russian force. That is the only risk to be run in forcing the Dardanelles, and it is less than the risk of shocking opinion, as it would have been shocked if Lord Salisbury, by a visible retreat, had delivered up the Christians of the East to their oppressors. They would have been compelled to try insurrection; and though the Armenians are almost powerless for want of cartridges, and the Greeks not much better off, a real rising in Macedonia could not end without either a great war, or a partition of Turkey, which might not be confined to Europe.

It is the belief of some diplomatists of ability that the Mussulman rising in the near future is quite certain, though it may take the external form of a palace émeute; and if that occurs, anything may happen, for the chance of the Ottomans securing a competent Sultan is terribly remote. No doubt an efficient ruler has once or twice emerged from the harem, the race having the instinct of government in its blood; but that was in days when governing was a very different matter, when impudent Ambassadors were liable to arrest and confinement, and when the House dared delegate its absolutism to competent Viziers. A great Sultan is hardly to be looked for, and a little one would either irritate the Mussulmans by submission, or bring down Europe in wrath by continuing the persecution of the Christians. It is useless speculating on a contingency so vast, but if the rising does not occur, the Sultan will doubtless cease from persecuting, and there will be a momentary compromise between the warring influences. We entirely agree with those who argue that the compromise, which he has at last accepted, will be worthless, and that the Christians will not be protected. It is simply impossible to protect them unless they are territorially cut off from the Sultan's dominion. The evil is not that the Pashas will insist on cutting Armenian or Greek throats, but that the Mussulman mob will cut them, and that the police and soldiers will not coerce the Mussulman mob. Look at the last outbreak in Trebizond, right under foreigners' eyes, or the scene at Akhissar, in Anatolia, described in the *Daily News* of Tuesday, where the Mahommedan roughs of the market-place murdered forty-six Christians and wounded many more, no one resisting them except the Caimaican of a neighbouring station, who, "at the risk of his own life," induced the Mussulmans to abstain from completing their bloody work. That is the kind of scene which will go on over the whole Empire, until the

Sultan is changed, or the threat of partition has been carried into effect. The Imperial Hatt will be of no more use than any other piece of paper, and the only order which would be effective, one threatening death to the chief official if any Christian life were taken within his jurisdiction, will not be issued; indeed, from the point of view of justice, ought not to be. We cannot, however, blame Lord Salisbury as energetically as some of our contemporaries are inclined to do. It is excessively difficult to declare war single-handed—for that is the demand—when your enemy accepts your original terms; when your allies who have kept step with you, declare themselves contented; and when, if you act, it is nearly a certainty that all Europe will be in flames. We ourselves think, as we have persistently repeated, that the case is so extreme that we should be disposed to justify the risk; but we can understand that the British Premier, with the safety of an Empire to provide for, with a doubt in his heart as to the approval of his special party, and with his mind reluctant to face the terrible problems which a partition of Turkey would involve, may be reluctant to declare that hope is over. Probably he does hope that massacre, at all events, will stop. The Sultan in yielding implicitly pledges himself that it shall stop; and it is very difficult, either to assert boldly that the pledge is a fraud, or to devise a scheme which, without upsetting the Sultan altogether, shall be efficacious. The demand given up, if it has been given up, is the appointment of a Christian High Commissioner with power to communicate with the Embassies; but would the High Commissioner have been more than a post-office? What could he have actually *done* that the Ambassadors cannot do; or how could he have made any demand, not sanctioned by the policy of the three Christian Governments? It is natural to give up such a clause rather than run the risk of a great war. As we have said, we should have supported the running of the risk, and we think the majority of Englishmen would also, but then neither we nor the majority have the awful responsibility of giving the orders, or the knowledge of foreign designs which Lord Salisbury probably possesses. The situation does not content us; we should even have been relieved if Pharaoh had hardened his heart; but to shell Constantinople with the Sultan climbing down is a step upon which we had rather that the statesmen than the public gave the final decision. The one thing now left to be done, as the Sultan has "yielded," is to warn him emphatically that the slaughter of Christians must be stopped by his soldiers, or that his Empire will be thrown into the crucible of another Conference of Berlin, this time for the partition of the Ottoman dominions, and to carry out that warning inflexibly and at once.

The Spectator, Vol. 75 (November 30, 1895): 752

The Possible Extirpation of the Armenians

Englishmen have a great difficulty in believing that the dominant party in Yildiz Kiosk intend, or at least intended till Europe interfered, the total destruction of the Armenian people. It is impossible, they say, to kill out a nation, even if it only numbers a million; no one, they secretly think, would be wicked enough to make such an attempt, and they never give up the hope that the Armenians, driven to despair, would defend themselves as Montenegrins do. The first argument has, if by extirpation you mean wholesale slaughter, something to be said for it. It is nearly impossible to kill all the people of any race which has once become civilised enough to be aware of its danger, for the people either fight, and in defensible places win the battle, or they fly, and, after incredible hardships, some survive. It is not quite impossible, for Genseric and his Vandals probably did kill out the whole civilised populations of Northern Africa, and the Arabs must have killed more than one or even two millions of the older population of Egypt, but still extirpation in its literal sense is an extremely difficult work, and, except in the cases quoted, has probably never been carried out in the literal meaning of the word, the one apparent case, the total disappearance of the highly civilised Cambodians, having probably been due either to a long-continued drought, or to an outburst of malarial disease, such as emptied and desolated for ever the splendid city of Gour, the old capital of Bengal, whose sculptured ruins still occupy square miles of soil. If, however, by extirpation the speaker means destruction as a people, thus including dispersion as well as slaughter in his survey, the impossibility disappears. The Saxons probably "destroyed" the Britons in that fashion; and Titus, the "delight of the world," certainly in that fashion "extirpated" the Jews, who never again became a people, or attempted to cultivate the soil of their own land. The Spaniards, in that sense, "extirpated" the Moors, who had risen to a high civilisation, the few who remained in the Peninsula being absorbed in the white population, especially in Algarve, the southern province of Portugal, and disappearing finally from human ken. It would not only be possible, but easy, for the Ottomans to destroy the Armenian people in this way, for a third of them at least are scattered through the Empire, and can be massacred in detail, and the remaining two-thirds, if sufficiently persecuted and slaughtered, would fly, as the whole upper class is flying, into Russia. They were great soldiers once, but they are not fighters now; they are as visible among Mussulmans as goats among oxen; they have no arms and their efforts at self-defence are as futile against weapons of precision as those of the fighting Aztecs against Cortez's mail-clad cavalry. The operation would not take two spring seasons; after which the relics of the Armenian people would be wanderers, perhaps for ever, over earth, or perhaps, being Christians and full of industrial capacity, would be absorbed among the multitudes who now populate Southern Europe. It is, as we conceive, quite one of the chances of the present day that the ancient Armenian people, who are as Aryan as the ancient Persians or ourselves, may pass from the face of the earth, dying finally of Turkish violence and European betrayal.

The second reason for doubting the occurrence of such a calamity, the impossibility of believing that any one should form such a design as extirpation, has no foundation whatever. There is no reason for believing that Titus was a worse man than Abd-ul-Hamid; and he carried out to its logical conclusion towards the Jews precisely the policy which the Sultan is carrying out towards the Armenians. Ferdinand of Aragon was in no way worse than most Princes of his time, and he relentlessly carried out the expulsion of the Moors. Philip II. procured a decree from the Inquisition sentencing to death the whole Protestant population of the Netherlands. He was probably a specially bad man, but Louis XIV. was not, and he treated his Protestant subjects precisely as the Sultan is now treating the Armenians. Even in our own time a great Christian Sovereign has begun the expulsion of three millions of Jews, and only this week two orators in the Austrian Parliament demanded the deportation of the same race in tones which indicated that if the work were accomplished by mob violence—which would involve massacre—they at least would not be displeased. There is no reason why a Sultan should be more merciful than these men, and one strong reason why he should not. He probably shares to the full the impression of his Mahommedan subjects, that the Armenians are guilty of treason, and have become a danger to Islam. He knows, it is true, that they do not rise in insurrection, but he believes that they are appealing to the foreigner, and that it is in consequence of their hostility that European squadrons are gathering in menace on his coasts. Under those circumstances he, as Khalif, is not only entitled to "restore order," but is bound to do it, and may very easily, as Mahommedan and as Turk, believe as Titus believed, that the interest of the Faith or of the Empire requires a policy of extirpation. That those around him believe this is patent on the face of things, and it is probable that the ordinary Ottomans believe it too, for they have the instinct of a dominant caste, they see how Armenians hate them, and they know that whenever they are threatened, their Christian subjects appeal to Europe with more or less success. That the Armenians are comparatively rich and pleasant to plunder is true too, as a correspondent of the *Times* argued on Tuesday; but the grand motive of the massacres is not greed, but hatred, hatred like that of Ferdinand for Moors, Louis XIV. for Huguenots, or Dr. Lueger for Jews. There is no hope for Armenians in the second argument; and none in the final one that they can resist. They cannot resist effectually. Englishmen could not, if they were disarmed, undrilled, and surrounded at once by a regular and most formidable soldiery, and by a hostile and well-armed mob. You might as well expect the Jews to resist in Russia, or the gipsies in Roumania, or the Catholics in Great Britain. They have not the means to resist, and if they do, they are only crushed more completely and more quickly, for though the Regulars do not interfere at first, they will not stand by and see their co-religionists defeated by men whom they regard as "risen" and ungrateful slaves. The Americans would not assist blacks against whites in a local riot, and the hatred of the Turk for a Christian subject who disobeys is deeper than the hatred of an American for an "insolent" black, for he thinks he is justified by his creed, which the American does not, and he has a fear that his opponents may find foreign protection, from which the American is exempt. In plain English, the Armenian, having once aroused Ottoman jealousy as well as hate, must either be protected from the outside, or he will perish.

Our people will understand the whole situation if the Macedonians should rise in insurrection, and be put down as the Armenians are being "put down." The sympathy of Europeans and Asiatics is so imperfect, that even the modern passion of pity grows cold when the victims belong to the latter continent. The Japanese massacre of the Chinese in Port Arthur hardly stirred Europe more than a great railway disaster would have done. The great persecution of the Jews in Russia was no doubt condemned, especially by religious persons, but it woke none of the passionate feeling aroused two centuries before by the cruelties inflicted on the Huguenots of France. Not only were the flying Hebrews not welcomed here as the Huguenots, who were fed, comforted, and subsidised, but the mass of the population objected to their coming, sulkily declaring that Russian Jews were a dirty lot, and would bring down the general rate of wages. Even for these Armenians, though the existence of treaties and a general horror of Turks wakes in this country a certain energy of denunciation, the general sympathy is imperfect, the subscriptions for the ruined come in in driblets, and many of the journals are willing to believe not only that Armenians are disagreeable folk—which is true enough of classes among them, they often displaying the Asiatic tendency to insolence in prosperity—but they are capable of rising voluntarily upon Mussulmans, which is like saying that the Jews of our East-End are capable of organising a revolt. The Macedonians, on the other hand, are as European as we are. Every blow struck will be realised all through Europe; and if the Macedonian women are treated as Armenian women have been treated, nothing could save either the throne of the Sultan or the Osmanli caste. The mysterious comity of race will influence us as well as pity; and those who pity will not flush, but turn white round the lips as only Europeans do. Then, and we begin to fear not till then, we shall realise to the full extent what the Armenians have suffered and are suffering, and what the real danger is,—that they will be actually exterminated.

The Contemporary Review, Vol. 68 (November 1895): 744–60

The Constantinople Massacre and Its Lesson

Malcolm MacColl[1]

I have been challenged by a few English journals to reconcile my defence of the persecuted Armenians with the recent Armenian demonstration in Constantinople and its attendant horrors. "It can scarcely be denied, even by Canon MacColl," says the *Saturday Review* of October 5, "that the Armenians were responsible for the recent riots in Constantinople, and for the consequent loss of life." I do deny it most emphatically; nor do I consider myself refuted by the rejoinder which the Reviewer makes to the answer which he is good enough to put into my mouth. "The Canon," he proceeds, "will of course say that the Armenians rose against intolerable oppression; but as both their lives and property are secure, at least in Constantinople, we find in the recent disturbances another proof of Armenian cunning." If the writer were as well acquainted with Turkey as I am he would know that the life and property of a Christian subject of the Sultan are safe nowhere in the Ottoman Empire. For him there is no justice even in Constantinople. His life, property, honour are ever at the mercy of the meanest Mussulman who may choose to assail them. He can never prove that he has been wronged, for his evidence is inadmissible against a Mussulman. Nor, if he could prove it, would it make the smallest difference; for although the rayah[2] has some theoretical rights under Mussulman rule, these rights are of no sort of use to him, since he can never enforce them, and the violation of them is not punishable by law. The sacred law of Islâm forbids the murder of a rayah who has paid his yearly ransom for the right to live, and is otherwise innocent;

but it declares at the same time that if, nevertheless, a true believer should deliberately kill a rayah the murderer is not to be punished in any way. And he never is punished. Let the reader calmly reflect on the significance of the following extract from a report sent to the Foreign Office by one of the ablest and most experienced of our consuls in Turkey:

> "Within my experience of twenty-five years in Turkey I have not known a single instance in which a Mussulman has been condemned to death for the murder of a Christian upon purely Christian evidence."[3]

Purely Christian evidence is inadmissible, and a Muslim will not give evidence in favour of a Christian against a true believer; nor, as I have just explained, would it be of any use if he did. The plain truth is that Mussulman rule over non-Mussulman subjects is so abnormally iniquitous, so utterly repugnant to natural justice, that people are exceedingly slow to believe that such wickedness can exist under a Government which has its metropolis in Europe, and which the Christian Powers treat as if it were a civilised State. The very enormity of its offences against the primary conditions of civilised life is thus its strongest panoply against the indignant retribution of Christendom. If Christian Europe only realised that the government of Turkey is, in literal fact, an organised brigandage, under the cruel yoke of which the fairest and richest regions of the globe lie desolate, and human life has for centuries "groaned and travailed in pain together until now," it would soon put an end to the disgrace of allowing a horde of barbarians like the pashas and effendis of Stamboul to keep the civilised world in perpetual turmoil by the incorrigible infamy of their rule. And yet a slight exercise of the reasoning faculties ought to teach even the dullest of understandings that there is not a scintilla of exaggeration in my description of Turkish administration. Consider one illuminating fact. In spite of the Sultan's magniloquent prattle about his "independence," the Porte has been shorn for centuries of one of the most essential attributes of sovereign power. The States of Christendom, great and small, old and new, are so convinced of the incurable iniquity and corruption of Turkish rule and administration that they will not entrust the life, honour, or property of any of their subjects to Turkish justice or probity. They have in Turkey their own courts of justice, in which alone their subjects can be tried. They have also their own post-offices, because they have no faith in the honesty of Turkish officials. Christendom has thus for centuries put the stigma of incorrigible barbarism on the Sultan of Stamboul and his Government, and has wrested from their grasp the paramount exercise of sovereign independence. Now surely it requires no great penetration to understand that a Government which cannot be trusted to deal justly with the lives, property, and honour of the meanest subjects of Powers which are strong enough to protect their subjects even against the chicanery and brutality of Turkish officials, ought still less to be trusted to rule over populations which are absolutely at the Sultan's mercy; their normal condition being one of cruel and degrading slavery. Yet there are still among us, though they are a rapidly dwindling band, some who really believe that the Armenians and other non-Mussulman subjects of the Porte ought to be loyal to a ruler and a Government which deny them the elementary rights of humanity. These defenders of the Turk forget that in the mutual relations of human life duties are reciprocal. A Government which, so far from protecting its subjects in the secure enjoyment of their rights, is itself the *fons et origo malorum*, the prime transgressor against liberty and justice, and the corrupter of civic life, has no claim on the loyalty of those subjects, and ought not to receive it. Secret conspiracy, and insurrection when possible, are not only natural and inevitable in Turkey; they are the perennial right and the sacred duty of the rayahs. Length of tenure can never consecrate a brigand's rule, for time does not run against the primordial rights of humanity.

In Constantinople, therefore, as elsewhere in the Sultan's dominions, the Armenians are slaves, having no security for life, property, or honour, as the events of the last few weeks have shown to demonstration. But it is true that the Armenians of Constantinople enjoy more security than Christians in the interior, thanks to the presence of foreign ambassadors and the contiguity of fleets of ironclads. Still, the Armenians of Constantinople have grievances enough of their own to justify them in going by deputation to present a perfectly loyal petition to the Sultan. It is true, however, that it was not so much on their own behalf as on behalf of their kin in Armenia and other provinces that the Armenians of Constantinople organised their demonstration. Was that a crime? The Armenians would indeed deserve all the scorn which has been so wantonly and cruelly flung at them, if selfish regard for their own ease and comfort had made them obtuse to the sufferings of their brethren elsewhere. Surely any one with a spark of chivalry in his nature would admire them all the more for risking liberty and life in the forlorn hope of achieving some measure of deliverance for their brethren and sisters who are still enduring torture, dishonour, and death at the hands of the Sultan's soldiers and servants.

Let me glance briefly at the principal disabilities under which the Armenians, in common with all the non-Mussulman subjects of the Porte, lie without any hope of redress, unless the Powers which undertook to protect them in the Treaty of Berlin compel the Sultan to fulfil his Treaty obligations. Their evidence is inadmissible against a Muslim. They are forbidden to have arms of any kind. They are obliged by law to give three days' gratuitous hospitality to any Mussulman official or traveller who demands it; officials including soldiers, police, and tax-collectors; and travellers, anybody from a pasha to a beggar. These hateful guests demand the best rooms and food in the house and do as they please with the women. The men are helpless, for they have no arms, while their unwelcome guests are armed to the teeth; and if they presume to complain to any of the local authorities they are beaten or probably cast into prison. The peasantry pay their taxes in kind, which amounts in all to more than 60 per cent. of the produce. The tax-collectors are, as a rule, and in direct violation of the Sultan's engagement in the Hatti-humayoun of 1856, the police, who are among the most unmitigated ruffians on the face of the earth. The taxes are put up to auction, and so keen is the competition that the successful competitor not unfrequently pays more than the total value of the taxes. To recoup himself and make a profit in addition, he has recourse to the most grinding extortion. He quarters himself and his tribe of tax-collecting police on the unhappy villagers, and will not allow the harvest to be gathered till he has been bribed all round. The rayahs are, in addition, subject to forced labour at the bidding of the local authorities and landlords. They are obliged to wear a peculiar dress, to mark them off from the Muslims. They are forbidden to ride horses, but may ride donkeys, from which, however, they must dismount when they meet a Muslim, and bow low with downcast look while the true believer, who may be a beggar, passes, while the Christian may be a nobleman or an archbishop.

But we read and hear much about the extraordinary toleration of the Turkish authorities towards other creeds. Let us see what that toleration is. By the unchangeable law of Islâm, Jews are forbidden to build synagogues and Christians churches. They may repair old buildings, but on the same site and of the same dimensions. And even for this they must obtain a fireman from Constantinople, which means a series of bribes and a delay of months, perhaps of years. The churches must have no bells, for fear of offending the religious sensibilities of the Mussulman; and for the same reason there must be no loud singing inside churches or synagogues, or lamentation or singing at funerals. Apostasy from Islâm is death alike to converter and converted. On the other hand, it is a penal crime for a Jew or Christian to dissuade a relation or friend from becoming a Mohammedan. The most opprobrious language is applied in official documents and courts of justice to Christians and Jews. They are called "dogs" and "pigs," and in burial certificates and other legal documents they are said to be not "dead," but "damned." I could fill pages with evidence of all this out of the reports of British Consuls and the despatches of British Ambassadors. Here is a burial certificate, attested by a British Ambassador.

> "We certify to the priest of the Church of Mary (in Armenia) that the impure, putrid, stinking carcase of———, damned, (i.e. deceased) this day, may be concealed under ground."

No wonder Lord Clarendon, then Secretary for Foreign Affairs, denounced language of this sort as "a standing insult to Christendom," and sternly demanded that it should be discontinued. And it was discontinued in one of the numberless dishonoured promises of the Sultan and his Ministers, but not in fact. I saw one of those certificates quite lately. One of our Consuls reports as follows in 1867:

> "The grossest and most galling terms of abuse are habitually addressed to the Christian with absolute impunity, the very authorities being in this respect the worst offenders. In the councils and seats of justice there is no form of abuse of which the Turkish language, so pre-eminently rich therein, is capable, however gross, disgusting, and insulting to his faith, which is not hourly and openly

applied to the hated and despised 'Ghiaour' by the judges and authorities of the land."[4]

In a Blue Book on "Religious Persecution in Turkey," published in 1875, I find the following facts attested by her Majesty's Ambassador and Consuls in Turkey. The Porte "definitely refused" to permit the establishment of Christian schools; prohibited the publication of the Bible in the Turkish language; and, in direct violation of the Hatti-humayoun of 1856, the children, not only of Mussulmans, but of Pagan parents as well, can never be recognised as Christians, even if they have been baptized in infancy. "The law," said the Grand Vizier, "did not recognise such men as Christians at all, but as Mohammedans." The controversy arose out of the case of some young men, the sons of heathen converts to Christianity. These young men had been baptized in infancy, but when their parentage was found out they were imprisoned and put to the torture to force them to conform to Islâm. It was in vain that the British *chargé d'affaires* appealed to the promise to complete religious liberty solemnly given by the Sultan in the Hatti-humayoun. The Grand Vizier merely wondered at the obtuseness which could not see the invalidity of promises extorted from the Sultan's necessity, and blandly explained that any interpretation of the Hatti-humayoun which conflicted with the law of Islâm must be a wrong interpretation. By the law of Turkey the children of non-Christian parents can never become Christians.

But that was twenty years ago, and things may have improved since then? Things never improve in Turkey, except under coercion from one or more of the Great Powers. Left to itself, the progress is always from bad to worse. This could be proved in detail if space permitted; but it is not necessary. I will take official evidence, published this year in a document entitled: "Violations of the Hatti-humayoun, a Paper prepared at the request of Sir Philip Currie, British Ambassador to the Sublime Porte."

Although the building of places for public worship is by the sacred law of Islâm forbidden to Jews and Christians, the authorities, from 1856 to 1891, winked at meetings for worship in private houses. In the latter year the local authorities prohibited this scanty privilege; and in January 1892 an Imperial Edict was published, "decreeing the suppression of worship and schools not formally authorised and found to be without permits after, a stipulated delay."

This decree, however, was not at once strictly enforced. It was a feeler to test the forbearance of the Powers. There being no protest from any quarter against this outrageous violation of the solemn promise of toleration given by the Porte in the Hatti-humayoun, in 1894 the celebration of divine worship in private houses was peremptorily forbidden, on the ground that "every place where a Christian says his prayers is reckoned as a church, and a church cannot exist without an Imperial fireman." One of the results of this decree is thus described in the document prepared under the auspices of the British Ambassador:

> "At this moment congregations of from 150 to 300 Protestants are prohibited from worship in places which have been recognised as their meeting-houses during 10 to 20 years: at Fatza in the province of Trebizond, Inetzig and Aghn in the province of Harpoot, Kir Shehir in the province of Angora, and Osmaniye in the province of Adana, to say nothing of the case of congregations in Sidon and Gedik Pasha in Constantinople."

The opening of Christian schools after the Crimean War was also winked at till 1892, "when the Government suddenly commenced to suppress Christian schools." In the same year, 1892, another decree was issued closing all Government employment to all who are educated in other than Government schools—that is, virtually, to all but Muslims.

Having declared war against Christian schools, the next step was to destroy and exclude all but Islâmic literature, in accordance with the dictum of Khalif Omar, the destroyer of the liberties of Alexandria and Persia—that literature which agreed with the Koran was superfluous, while literature that differed from it was pernicious, and must be destroyed.

> "It has become a usual thing for travellers to be stripped of their books at any guard station in the interior of Turkey. The fact of authorisation printed on the title-page in Turkish makes no difference. The book must be sent to the headquarters of the province, perhaps a hundred miles away, for examination. The owner of the book is happy if he is not detained under arrest until the result of the examination is made known. Of course he surrenders his books rather than wait several days for the examination to be made. In fact, the suspicion exhibited against Christians who possess books . . . has

at last made the Christians of Asiatic Turkey almost as terrified at sight of a book as are the officials who are set over them. So complete is the destruction of Christian books in some districts through these causes, that the Christian children now growing up in those districts bid fair to be as ignorant as were their forefathers. The same causes operate to destroy the book trade.

"The censorship of foreign religious and literary works is so stringent as to deprive the Christians in Turkey of the ordinary means of keeping in touch with the advancement of knowledge among their co-religionists abroad. Such classics of English literature, for instance, as Shakespeare, Byron, Milton, Scott, are refused authorisation. So with the higher literature of any language. No standard history, no encyclopaedia, no treatise on metaphysics of any extended character, no full and extended theology or commentary on the Bible, can pass the censorship for introduction into the interior of Turkey. And if any minister or teacher, anxious to fill well his place, venture to smuggle such books through, or to possess the rudiments of a library, he is certain, sooner or later, to fall under the notice of the paid spy, and then must submit to condemnation for the crime which the authorities choose to consider to be 'incited' by the history or theological work concerned. The censorship of books published within the Empire is still more rigorous."

I can bear personal testimony to the rigour of this censorship. In the year 1892 I could not find a single copy of Dante, Shakespeare, or even Murray's handbook, in any bookseller's shop in Constantinople. They used to keep such books, but are now forbidden. In the same year Mr. Brooke Lambert, Vicar of Greenwich, had even his Bible confiscated on passing the frontier between Bulgaria and Turkey. I reached Constantinople in a yacht, and thus avoided such inconveniences and indignities. Nor has the Porte the wretched excuse of pretending that this forbidden literature might undermine the faith of Mussulmans, for it is written in languages of which the Mussulmans, with very few exceptions, do not understand a single word. It is, in fact, a crescentade against freedom of thought and intellectual progress. And this intolerance extends to details which would be incredible without authentic evidence. Christians must not publish articles in their own religious newspapers, in any language, "which contain the quotation of texts of Scripture," because anarchical doctrines might thus be furtively insinuated. "For instance, a text which alludes to rising from the dead may not be used, because the verb to 'rise' might suggest insurrection."

> "Any passage from the Bible is prohibited which contains any of the following words: persecution, courage, liberty, strength, rights, union, equality, star[5] (in astronomy one has to use the word 'luminary' instead), king, palace, arms, bloodshed, tyranny, hero, & c. &c. These words are prohibited in religious articles in any context whatever. A Christian religious newspaper may not place before its readers a hymn or other poetry; and from the hymn-books used in Christian worship many of the grand old hymns of the Church have been expunged, and the suppression sustained after appeal to the highest authority of the Porte."

Such expressions as the following are also forbidden:

> "'The guiding grace of God,' because Muslims do not admit that Christians can have this grace; 'good news or gospel,' because Muslims do not admit that the Gospel of Jesus Christ is 'good news'; 'apostle,' because the word implies that the Apostles of Jesus Christ were sent of God, which Muslims deny; references to our Saviour as 'the Saviour of the world,' or to His shedding His blood for the cleansing from sin."

Christian preachers are forbidden to recommend "the virtues of manliness, of moral courage, of resignation under affliction, of hope in God under adversity." Any transgression against these rules is severely punished.

> "Protestant pastors everywhere declare that they are compelled, in choosing texts from the Bible, and in framing their exhortations upon them, to hesitate, and paraphrase, and weigh words, through fear that if they speak of the consolations of Christianity, they will be charged with encouraging discontent; if they urge resistance to sin, they will be condemned for suggesting resistance to the Turkish Government; or if they speak of the demand of Christianity for pure and noble character, they will be charged with inciting to unlawful aspirations. On complaint being made of such restrictions upon the legitimate instruction of Christians, officials in high positions have answered that while provincial Governors are constantly sending extracts from the Bible to prove the necessity of their suppressing that book, Christians should be grateful for the privilege of being allowed to have the Bible, instead of complaining at being restricted in making or publishing comments upon it."

I have already given some instances of the insults which, to quote again the language of a British Consul, are "openly and hourly" flung at "the hated and despised Ghiaour" in official documents and by Turkish authorities, from pashas and judges to the ruffianly police. I have myself seen a Mussulman judge in a Mussulman court of so-called justice taking evidence against an accused Christian, and following the evidence with a running commentary of hard blows with his clenched fist on the face of the accused, who was then sentenced, without being allowed to a word in self-defence. The attempt to do so was treated as a fresh offence, and punished accordingly. The following extract from the document already quoted at some length casts a lurid light on the "humane" and "tolerant" temper of the cruel and unscrupulous despot whose mild manners and humanitarian "blarney" have so often imposed upon simple-minded British tourists.

> "In 1886 a book called the 'Mudafaa,' and in 1892 another called 'Resalei Hamidie,' were published in Constantinople. Both of these books were full of the most scurrilous attacks on Christianity and of the most contemptuous epithets applied to those who profess that religion. *The authors of those works were decorated by H.I.M. the Sultan, and many efforts were made to give the books the widest possible circulation.* Since that time, especially in 1892 and 1893, the Turkish newspapers of the capital have contained article after article which have thrown opprobrium upon the Christian religion. These articles have been published with the approval of a censorship that by law must decide beforehand whether an article may be published. But at the same time Christians have been rigorously prohibited from making in Turkish any answer to statements maliciously false concerning Christianity, by which these works have sought to excite the contempt and hatred of the Mohammden populace towards their Christian neighbours."

Let the reader carefully note the last sentence in this "Paper, prepared at the request of Sir Philip Currie, British Ambassador to the Sublime Porte," for the information of Lord Kimberley, in the spring of this year. It exhibits the Sultan at the head of a crescentade against Christianity, fomenting and disseminating "most scurrilous attacks on Christianity" and Christians, and decorating the authors of those attacks, which have for their object "to excite the contempt and hatred of the Mohammedan populace towards their Christian neighbours." I shall show presently that the recent massacres at Constantinople were part and parcel of this deliberate policy of organised fanaticism, which is at the beck and call of the craven tyrant of Yildiz Kiosk, and simply does his bidding. The exigencies of space will not permit me to do more than give a few typical examples of the hell upon earth in which the helpless Christians of Armenia are condemned to live. The British Consul at Erzeroum writes in 1891:

> "A band of thirty mounted police which were on the march were billeted for the night in a small Armenian village of ten houses, a few hours' distant from Bitlis. Four of them were quartered in the house of a young married Armenian. Overhearing them discussing plans against his wife's honour, he secretly sent her to the house of a neighbour. When the zaptiehs learnt this they ordered him to send for her, and, on his refusing to do so, beat him most cruelly. He fled to a neighbour's house, but, two days later, died from the effects of the ill treatment which he had received. Four doctors, three of them Turks, the other a Christian, examined the body, and the latter had the courage, in the face of the opinion given by the others, to certify to the real cause of death.
>
> "*In the houses where the other zaptiehs were quartered their designs against the female members of the family were carried out without resistance.*"[6]

Resistance was in truth impossible, for the police were armed, and the Armenians are not allowed to possess arms. That is one of the daily incidents of the hospitality tax. The women of the Christian subjects of the Sultan are at the mercy of the Mussulman police, soldiery, roving dervishes, and common tramps, who are all entitled to three days' gratuitous hospitality. Hardly any Christian woman escapes dishonour.

The British Vice-Consul at Van writes:

> "I learn that, on the 7th ultimo, a son of the Bitlis Ali Bey, accompanied by several zaptiehs, who were Circassians, and numbered forty, went to an Armenian hamlet, Hormuz, and passed the night at the house of a certain Kachik; this man was maltreated for taking measures to protect his honour, and died."[7]

The British Consul at Erzeroum reports as follows:

> "From the plain of Erzeroum, also, come many stories of ill-treatment of Christians. At Setaouk some Mussulmans forcibly entered the house of an Armenian, with the design of outraging his daughter. Failing in this, they violated his wife."[8]
>
> "Fifteen days ago Hussein, with his nephew, entered by night the house of an Armenian, named Caspar, in Patnoss, with the intention of carrying off Caspar's daughter-in-law, a very beautiful young woman. The inhabitants of the house cried out for help, on which Hussein drew his revolver and fired, killing the woman on the spot."[9]

This Hussein Agha was Mudir—i.e., Governor—of Patnoss in Armenia. The dry catalogue of his hideous atrocities and crimes fill a page and a half of a folio Blue Book. "He carried off over 2600 sheep, nine horses, many cattle, and property of all sorts. He set fire on nine villages, killed ten men, and cut off the right hands, noses, and ears of eleven more, some of which could, if necessary, be produced as witnesses." "A year ago Hussein carried off and ravished five Christian girls from Patnoss." In a dispatch to Lord Salisbury the British Ambassador denounces this man as "a monster," and Lord Salisbury laid the dispatch "before the Queen." This "monster," remember, filled the responsible post of Governor of a district where his word was law. Was any serious attempt made to punish him, or even stop his career of outrage? None. "Protected as he is supposed to be by the authorities," says the British Consul, "no one dares to raise a voice against him. Such is the terror that he now inspires that the Murakhass (Bishop) of Alashgird has fled to Bayazid."

The British Ambassador, by Lord Salisbury's instructions, denounced this notorious criminal to the Grand Vizier, and he was thereupon invited to visit the Sultan at Constantinople as a mark of special honour,[10] and promoted to the rank of a pasha and the command of a regiment of the Kurdish cavalry which the Sultan was then organising, and on which he bestowed the singular favour of bearing his own name, "the Hamidie"—"the King's Own," as we should say.

The reader will remember that it was in the year 1892 that the Imperial decrees were published against education and Christian worship even in private houses. In the previous year the Sultan began to form his force of 30,000 Kurdish cavalry, whom he officered with the most notorious brigands and criminals in Kurdistan—Hussein Agha among them. Representatives from the different regiments of the cut-throats were invited to visit the Sultan at Constantinople, where he had them fêted with every token of favour. On their return to Armenia they "openly state," says the British Consul at Erzeroum, "that they have been appointed to suppress the Armenians, and that they have received assurances that they will not be called to answer before the tribunals for any acts of oppression committed against Christians."[11] When everything was ready the Kurds were let loose on the helpless Christians, and the world was horrified by the massacre of Sassun, the rumour of which filtered through the cordon of troops and police with which the Sultan surrounded Armenia, and was revealed in all its horrors months afterwards by the enterprise of English journalists.

On discovering that his carefully prepared massacres came to light even in remote Armenia, the Sultan has adopted another method of "diminishing" the Armenians, and driving the survivors out of their ancestral home. The Kurds have been told to pasture their cattle in the meadows and cornfields of the Armenians. I state the following facts on the authority of Reuter's agent, whose impartiality has been generally acknowledged. He spent some months in Armenia this year, travelling about in disguise, and came to see me on his return last July. Wherever he went he saw Kurds' cattle, tended by their herds, browsing in the fields of the Armenians, and was told by the Armenians that they durst not remonstrate or complain. The crops having been thus destroyed, the next thing was to rob the Armenians of their cattle and household goods. A year's taxation was demanded in advance. The wretched Christians pleaded poverty through the ruin of their crops. The tax-gatherer answered: "You must pay at once." "Then give us a little time," implored the Christians, "till we can sell some of our cattle." The tax-gatherers, who are also the police, retorted by seizing all their cattle and household goods, and putting them up to auction: the neighbouring Kurds having been previously informed of the fact, while the Christians were forbidden to bid for their own property, which, after this sham sale, was divided between the Kurds and police. Thousands of Armenians have been thus reduced to feeding on roots and grasses for months, and crowds of them have perished from starvation and diseases bred by the garbage with which they have been endeavouring to keep soul and body together. Reuter's agent, a gentleman of independent means, and belonging to no political creed or party, showed me a sample of the cakes on which the starving Armenians had been feeding. It was a boiled concoction of roots, leaves, and grasses, and looked like a piece of concrete. "I went to Armenia," said this gentleman, "with my sympathies rather in favour of the Turks. I have come back with by blood boiling against their fiendish inhumanity. If the English people only realised the true state of the case they would not endure it for a week."

It was announced last summer that the Sultan had generously contributed £2000 for the relief of the surviving inhabitants of the villages destroyed by his own troops acting under his orders; the officer who presided over the massacre having afterwards been decorated by his humane Majesty. What the Sultan really did was to send orders to the Governor of the district to find the money. The Governor, knowing how to please his master, taxed the Armenian Christians for the amount of his Majesty's generous contribution, not a shilling of which went back to the Armenians. Truly a Turkish way of helping the needy and getting credit for benevolence!

The facts which I have thus placed before the reader point to the inevitable conclusion that the Sultan has been engaged for some years in laying his plans for the partial extermination and total degradation of the Armenians. He began by making war upon their schools and religious freedom. Education opens and enlarges the mind, and Christianity is a religion of hope, of progress, and of redemption. Intellectual development was therefore put under ban, and the preaching of the "Good News" of Christianity was sternly forbidden. But the Armenians had made considerable progress in education and in the aspirations for freedom which education inspires, before their oppression had realised the fact. They must, therefore, be taught a lesson. Hence the formation of 30,000 plundering and murdering Kurds into a cavalry force, bearing the Sultan's name, and officered by brigand chiefs, with a mission from the Sultan "to suppress the Armenians" without any fear of punishment "for any acts of oppression committed against the Christians." Hence the massacre of Sassun, and the recent massacres of Constantinople and Trebizond. Hence the persecution by torture, imprisonment, exile, and death of the intellectual leaders of the nation—schoolmasters and schoolmistresses, professors, physicians, ecclesiastics. Kill the aspirations of the Armenians by a reign of terror, by the death and expatriation of their leaders and educators and by confiscation of books, thus driving them back into the barbarism which comes of ignorance and helplessness under the dominion of armed force: there you have in a nutshell the explanation of the Sultan's dealings with the Armenians for the last few years. Their demonstration in Constantinople was quite legal and quite pacific. Even if the fatal shot which killed the officer of police was fired from an Armenian revolver,[12] was that an excuse for delivering the whole Armenian colony—men, women, and children—to three days' carnage? Was it any excuse for the murder by the police within their barrack-yard of thirty helpless prisoners? Armenians only were killed—a fact to which a Turk called the attention of the Correspondent of the *Standard* as a clear proof that it was not a case of fanaticism, but of a carefully planned massacre. The subsequent massacre of more than 400 Christians at Trebizond was marked by the same careful discrimination. "The mob did not touch any but orthodox Armenians, leaving even the shops of Catholic Armenians.[13] Only two persons outside the Armenians were killed." The orthodox Armenians are not in communion either with the Pope or with the Russian Church, and were therefore considered safe game. A heavy responsibility is laid on the Governments of France and Russia for having by their heartless diplomacy given currency to this impression. It is evident that very few of the Armenians in the Constantinople demonstration were armed. Armed men do not allow themselves to be bludgeoned and stabbed to death with impunity. The allegation that the Armenians were responsible for the massacres is disposed of by the damning fact that only three Turks were killed—by whom there is no evidence to show—while the number of the Armenians slain is known to have amounted to hundreds, including men, women, and children, who had nothing to do with the demonstration.

Now I ask the reader who has followed me thus far whether any scheme of reforms for Armenia is of the slightest value which is not placed under direct European control on the spot. I have shown how absolutely helpless the Christians are in the interior of Turkey. And now revenge will stimulate the ordinary brutality of the Muslims towards the Christians, whom they regard as their slaves. How are the Armenians to be protected unless there is to be some man at the top, as in the district of the Lebanon, who is practically independent of the Sultan? Some Christian subjects of the Sultan are to be appointed, forsooth! in subordinate positions. As if our experience of the Hatti-humayoun during the last fifty years did not *prove* not only the uselessness, but the mischief, of such an arrangement. These Christian assistants will have no power whatever, and their presence will only serve, as in the sham Councils created by the Hatti-humayoun, to give the semblance of Christian sanction to the unabated oppression of the Christian population. I should prefer, for my part, that Lord Salisbury had washed his hands of the whole business rather than sanction the scheme of his predecessors. But if he has felt bound to accept it, for reasons unknown to me, let us be just and lay the responsibility of the *fiasco* on the shoulders which ought to bear it.

Lord Rosebery's Government made four cardinal blunders in this matter. By suppressing the Consular reports from Armenia—Lord Beaconsfield's Government never did that even in the most Turkish mood—they not only concealed the truth from "their employers," to use the late Lord Derby's phrase; they encouraged the Sultan to believe either that they were not in earnest in the matter, or that they wished to screen his crimes for fear of raising that specter of timid diplomacy, the Eastern Question. Their next blunder was to sanction the appointment of a Turkish Commission of inquiry, which they knew must be an impudent imposture. Their third blunder was, after weeks of labour, to present a scheme of reforms so elaborate and complex as to delight the hearts of the Sultan and his pashas for the opportunity which it gave to endless discussion, and so entirely inadequate as to be perfectly futile. Their fourth blunder was not to accompany the presentation of their scheme with an ultimatum demanding acceptance or rejection within a given time; instead of which they sent their Ambassador, cap in hand, to ask the Sultan from time to time what he thought of the scheme, and why he objected to it. No wonder the Sultan allowed several weeks to pass before he deigned to give them any answer. There is only one effectual way of dealing with a Sultan of Turkey in a matter of this sort. Make up your mind what you want; put your demand into the clearest and shortest form possible; and then demand an answer, without discussion, within a given time, with an intimation of coercion in case of refusal; and if the Sultan sees that you mean it he will yield without more ado. And the late Government had all the less excuse for not taking a bolder line, for they had an instructive precedent to guide them, In the summer of 1880 Mr. Gladstone's Government assembled the fleets of the Great Powers at Dulcigno to compel the Sultan to surrender the lands which he had bound himself in the Treaty of Berlin to give up to Greece and Montenegro. The Sultan, doubting the determination of the Powers to enforce their demand, remained obdurate. Mr. Gladstone thereupon proposed that the combined fleet should appear before Smyrna and seize the customs—a *coup* which would soon have paralysed the administration of the Porte and starved it into submission. The other Powers refused, and then the English Government acted alone. It sent an ultimatum to the Sultan, barbed with a threat of seizing Smyrna, and the Sultan yielded with good grace at once. To talk of action like this involving us in war with Turkey is absurd. What could the Sultan do, without a single warship fit to go to sea, against the British fleet, which could with impunity cut his Empire in two and paralyse his whole machinery of government? Moreover, no one knows better than he how thoroughly his Empire is honeycombed with sedition even among his Mussulman subjects; and he is not quite such a fool as to imperil his throne by collision with England. He knows that he has no title whatever to the Khalifate; indeed, he had been far too prudent ever to have made a claim which the Mussulman world at large would regard as impious, and which would assuredly raise the standard of revolt throughout Arabia.

But what of France and Russia? France would have followed the lead of Russia, and if Russia were so selfish—which I shall not believe without proof—as to wish to thwart England in her righteous endeavour to secure effective reforms for Armenia, she would certainly not venture to proclaim such a feeling in action. To do so would be to abdicate her traditional *rôle* of protector of the Christians of Turkey. What happened at Dulcigno would have happened in this crisis if England had acted alone. No other Power, perhaps, would have joined her; but neither would any other Power have acted against her, and the Sultan would have yielded.

Instead of wasting weeks in drawing up an unworkable and useless scheme of reforms, the late Government should have called the Sultan's attention to the fact that the excellent reforms which the Porte had proclaimed, under the sanction of the Treaty of Paris, in the Hatti-humayoun of 1856, had never been carried out, and that he must consequently accept, for Armenia at least, a European Commissioner to see that these reforms were put in force; telling him, at the same time, that the alternative of refusal was coercion, if not on the part of other Powers, certainly on the part of England, which had a right to act alone, not only as one of the signatories of the Treaty of Paris, but still more imperatively by right of the Anglo-Turkish Convention. It does not much matter what the reforms are if there is a strong man to keep order and administer justice, who is not under the direct control of the Porte. On the other hand, the reforms may in themselves be admirable, but will remain entirely inoperative if they are left under the control of the Porte and its officials.

I recognise Lord Salisbury's difficulty in throwing overboard a scheme accepted by the previous Government as well as by France and Russia. But let there be no mistake as to the consequences if that scheme has been finally accepted without the necessary guarantee, of which Lord Salisbury recognised the necessity as soon as he came to examine it. It will not settle the Armenian question, even temporarily, for it will fail to make life tolerable for the Christians, who are now thoroughly roused. The Armenians are the most tenacious race in the Ottoman Empire, and they have no superiors in brain power. Those in Turkey will find powerful auxiliaries among their brethren across the Russian frontier, and also among Armenian colonies scattered over Europe and America. They are getting desperate—small blame to them—under their intolerable wrongs, and will do desperate things. Prudential arguments are thrown away on men whose lives, religion, and women are daily at the mercy of Turks and Kurds. To film an ulcerous sore is not to heal it; and Turkish reforms, without European control, are but a film which will not for long even conceal the open wound.

And, next to Armenia, England would be the principal sufferer from such a diplomatic defeat as a settlement which settles nothing. She has taken the lead in this matter, and, as she would have reaped the chief credit from a diplomatic triumph, she will proportionately suffer from a diplomatic failure. But it is among the Mussulmans of

India especially that defeat on the Armenian question will do mischief. The security of our rule over them rests mainly on their recognition of our determination and our strength. Let them once persuade themselves that we are a decaying nation which can be defied with impunity by the Sultan of Turkey, and, depend upon it, we shall have another mutiny. That of 1857 was due to their belief that a Power which it cost two years, in union with France, Sardinia and Turkey, to conquer Russia, could be broken in India. Why is it that the Mussulmans throughout the world stand in such awe of the Tzar? Because he has repeatedly invaded and conquered the Sultan of Turkey. It is the greatest possible error to imagine that we imperil our rule in India by compelling the Sultan to fulfil his treaty obligations. The real danger to our rule would be the belief on the part of the natives of India that the Sultan could defy our power with impunity.

Since these words were printed, a summary of the new reforms has been published. The Sultan is quite right in saying that, in so far as they deserve to be called reforms, they are all to be found in the Hatti-humayoun of 1856. But, like all Turkish reforms, they worsen the condition of the Christians. For example: the Christians "will be protected by gendarmes and troops . . . and will thus be able to conform to the laws regarding the carriage of weapons." That is to say, the Christians are to be dispossessed of the few arms which they have smuggled across the frontier.

"The nomadic tribes will be settled on lands granted by the Government"—i.e., taken from the Christians. This process has been going on ever since the Sassun massacres.

"A committee will be formed in order to examine and verify all titles to property." But Christians cannot obtain secure titles to property under Turkish law. This "reform" is therefore an ingenious device for depriving the Christians of their properties. Truly the last state of the Armenians is worse than the first.

The Spectator, Vol. 75 (December 7, 1895): 808

Lord Salisbury in Turkey

We have advised and still advise Unionists not to press Lord Salisbury too hardly in this Turkish affair. No one except the head of the Foreign Office can know precisely what chances there are of maintaining the European concert—which, considered by itself, is most desirable—what is the real risk of a general attack on Christians throughout the Turkish Empire, or what the combinations will be if the Powers ultimately part company. The Foreign Secretary, too, is responsible as even Members of Parliament are not, and may well dread his own best impulses if they lead him to give orders which may involve the whole future of the world. We fully acknowledge that the fall of Turkey, whenever it falls, means the commencement of a new era in European history. Lord Salisbury should be allowed a free hand; but we trust that while he claims, and should enjoy, national support, he will realise how completely his own future reputation as a great Minister depends upon his successful action. The whole people of both parties are watching him. They understand more or less the full difficulty of the situation, and will make allowances not only for delay, but for hesitation; but they nevertheless expect from Lord Salisbury success, which means in their eyes some permanent guarantee that the Turkish Pashas and their cruel master shall no longer misgovern the Christians of the Ottoman Empire. They think they have a right to expect this much. Lord Salisbury has the record of a great diplomatist; he has a special knowledge of the Turkish Court and its evil ways, he enjoys favour in Vienna, and he has in Italy a devoted ally, while he speaks on the Turkish subject [with] the voice of a united British people,—and he ought, therefore, to be successful. If he is not, the people, though they will not condemn him, but believe him to have been overmastered by his difficulties, will no longer consider him a great Foreign

Minister, but relegate him in their minds to a more ordinary category. So long as he goes forward step by step, they will not grudge the slowness of the steps; but if he stops, or throws up his hand, the revulsion of feeling will be very deep, and will, for one thing, greatly cool the present enthusiasm for the Unionist party. The greatness of men who are great is best tested under great difficulties, and the world expects from Lord Salisbury a plan which will succeed, or at least show some evidence of pre-eminent nerve. At present, it must not be forgotten, no real success has been attained, even if the extra six guardships are allowed to enter the Bosphorus. The Armenians, to whom we promised protection, have lost by murder some thirty thousand of their number, most of them heads of families, under circumstances of abominable tyranny. The Pashas who sanctioned or witnessed or condoned the massacres are still unpunished. The Sultan, who prompted the entire outbreak, is still absolute within his dominions, still dooms any subject who displeases him, still surrounds himself with advisers known to be hostile alike to Christians and to Western ideas of justice and wise government. The massacres have become fewer and smaller, but there is no security whatever against their recurrence, while; as regards individuals, no man in the Turkish Empire is safe if the Palace clique think it profitable to denounce him. Only this week a great Mussulman, an ex-Grand Vizier, has fled to the British Embassy after an interview with the Sultan, because he saw that he was suspected of Liberalism, and that means exile to Yemen or death. Lord Salisbury, in fact, with all his efforts, has accomplished nothing, although the efforts must have been great. He has kept the jealous Powers together, he has gathered a fleet such as has scarcely been seen in the harbour of Salonica,—a fleet to be joined, it is asserted, even by an American cruiser, so that not the six but the seven, greatest Powers will be represented; but still nothing of permanent value has been accomplished. There sits the Sultan safe in his park, unable, it is true, to resist any maritime movement, but on land master of all around him, able to baffle and confound the united Embassies, and to defy those who sent them instructions, with impunity. He promises reforms no doubt; but was it without his knowledge that his Foreign Office denied absolutely that any revolt had occurred in Yemen, the most detailed accounts of which have come to hand? The civilised world is hungering for something more real than such promises,—

for, if that were obtainable, a good Sultan, or if that is not obtainable, for a good and irremovable Vizier who shall at least grant security to the Christians of Turkey until the inevitable hour of partition shall arrive. No one of repute, unless we may count the *Spectator* among that number, objects to postpone sentence upon Turkey if her owner can be bound over for a time to good behaviour; but even that imperfect result has not yet been secured; and if it is not secured at last, Lord Salisbury's reputation as an adroit and successful manager will be materially diminished.

It will be said, we know, that we are testing the Premier by his ability to perform the impossible; but the retort is a mere begging of the question. Why is it impossible? The Turkish Empire, as Mr. Gladstone long since pointed out, of all Empires is the one most accessible to the sea Power. Its very substance is cloven in two by the sea; its chief revenues are derived from seaports; and it can be entered not only from the Mediterranean, but from the Red Sea and the Persian Gulf. Suppose for a moment—we beg pardon of the astute Monarch for the bare supposition—the Sultan executed Sir Philip Currie instead of a few thousand Armenians, how many days or hours or minutes would the impossibility continue? Yet we are pledged, if men can be pledged without formal contracts, not to let Armenians be murdered, or if they are murdered, to bring the murderers to justice. Does any one, in fact, doubt that Mr. Gladstone would have done it? That is a very serious reflection for the Foreign Minister who has defeated Mr. Gladstone—with our hearty concurrence—to ponder over while he waits the slow evolution of events at Constantinople. They will go right in the end, we do not doubt, as they went right in Naples, though King Ferdinand seemed so safe; but we want Lord Salisbury to be the agent in making them go right.

Our Failure in Turkey

The success of the Sultan in the affair of Said Pasha will be a great triumph for him in his own people's eyes, so great that his concession in the matter of the guardships will be at once forgotten. The subjects of a despotic Monarch are always interested first of all in personal questions; and to Mussulmans in Constantinople the Sultan must seem like "Ka," the mighty python of Rudyard Kipling's "Jungle Book," whose motionless gaze compels the monkeys to approach him. It is vain for a European to attempt to discuss the motives which govern the acts of an Oriental like Said Pasha. He fled to the British Embassy no doubt in an ordinary impulse of fear for his life; but why, having mortally affronted a master who never forgives those he fears, Said Pasha has once more placed himself in that master's power, it is impossible to guess. He may have dreaded poverty, for he had no fortune; he may have been tempted by the splendid bribe offered him, £4,000 a year for life, for Said is a Turk; he may have been afraid for his family, left at the mercy of his enemies; or he may have been dominated by the true Mussulman's shame at seeming to side with infidels against the faith; it is all a mystery, the two things certain being that he did not believe the promises made him, and that he will disappear, probably *not* into a grave, but into a remote lunatic asylum. Already among Turks the *mot d'ordre* is that Said is mad—an opinion which will shelter his life, even the Khalif sparing the afflicted of God, but will paralyse any "influence" he may have possessed. That influence, however, cannot be much, for in a Mussulman country there are but three sources of power,—the ruler, the preacher, and the army; and while he reigns, the first is strongest of all. Even in Afghanistan, where there are clan chiefs, and birth has a meaning unknown in most Mahommedan States, the frown of the Ameer means ruin; and, as

Dr. Gray relates in a remarkable book published to-day, the noble who in the morning rides out in cloth of gold, in the evening begs a little food in the street of the passer-by. A Grand Vizier is great while the Sultan speaks to him with a smile, then disappears like a man's shadow when night begins to descend.

The incident and the struggle about the guardships have broken the dreadful monotony of the news from Turkey, which, like a funeral too long protracted, has a benumbing as well as a moving effect upon the sympathies; but Englishmen should not lose sight of the main issue. A Christian people is being extirpated because in its misery it appealed for the help which English Ministers pledged themselves to give. Every week the evidence that the orders for massacre came from the Palace clique, that the regulars were instructed not to interfere, and that the irregulars were let loose to plunder and kill, grows stronger and more perfect. The process is always the same. If the Armenians reside in a village it is burned and the men killed; if they live in a town their quarter is fired, their men are slain, the Mahommedan priest utters the call to prayer from the ruined church, which can then never be entered by Christians again, the plunder, including often the women, is distributed, and the officials in Constantinople state that Armenians having attacked a mosque disturbances have occurred, but "tranquillity has been restored." In the single district of Van, a German writes, the irregular cavalry have destroyed two hundred villages. A Turkish merchant relates to his firm, not to the Press, how he saw in one ride in Anatolia two hundred Armenian women and children cut to pieces, under his horse's feet. A correspondent reports that in Trebizond a Bishop and five others who sought refuge in a church have been burned alive. These are but incidents, unimportant incidents in face of the fact that in six great counties—the six where the Sultan pledged his honour to Lord Salisbury to carry out his reforms—the Armenian population of the country-side is wandering homeless and starving, awaiting death from the winter on the mountains, or crowding into cities which have neither food nor shelter for so many. The Patriarch of Etchmiadzin declares that half a million of his people are homeless—remember, in Armenia snow falls as heavily as in our own Highlands—and though no Oriental, whether Christian or Mussulman, ever knows how to count heads, the number cannot be less than many tens of thousands. It is ruin which has fallen on these unhappy people, ruin such as followed the sack of Jerusalem, ruin such as the Western world, in its security and comfort as of a chestnut in its pod, has ceased even to be able to bring home to its own thoughts; and though the English are sinless, for they did not mean it, the ruin is due to them. But for the fear of an Armenian question, even this Asiatic Philip II. would not have dreamed of surrendering a million of taxpayers from whom he could have demanded a ransom that would have made Yildiz Kiosk all sunshine, to bands of irregulars who will never give up one piastre. It is in reliance on our promises, in hope of our assistance, that the wretched people have ventured on the murmurs, it may even be on the boastings, which have brought on them so horrible a doom. We are unable to believe that in failing to protect them, even to our own hurt, we are not shrinking from a responsibility which, whether we voluntarily assumed it or not, it has pleased Providence to fasten on us as a trial of conscience. It is not any opponents of this Government, but the *Spectator*, which knows as well as the Embassies how immense the difficulties are, which says that we are shrinking from a plain duty.

But what can Lord Salisbury do? This, for one thing,—it may very well be not the best thing. The source of all the mischief as acknowledged by all the serious and capable Turks is the Sultan himself. Let Lord Salisbury, therefore, inform the Powers that if England is not to act alone—as she can do without moving a man, by recognising the independence of Arabia and stopping the conveyance of Turkish soldiers thither by sea, and so shattering the Khalifate at a blow—the six Powers must announce that they consider Abd-ul-Hamid unfitted to reign, and that with him as Sovereign they will hold no further communication. There is precedent for that, for the same Powers in the same concert proclaimed the same decision about Napoleon. The Turks will comprehend that demand at once, will understand that the Christian Powers threaten neither the Turkish Empire nor Mahommedanism, but that if there is to be peace, the head of the Turkish Government must be changed. They are writhing under their oppressions as much as the Christians; they have the power of changing their ruler—such a change is in accord with every tradition of Constantinople—and they would, as we believe, exercise it at once, calling to the throne any Prince of the House of Othman in whom they have not had the opportunity of losing confidence. He might be no better than his predecessor, but he would have no quarrel with the Armenians; he would be compelled to rely on soldiers instead of favourites; and he would bring in a new group of men, among whom there might be one fairly competent to govern. Real power was trusted by the great Sultans to their Grand Viziers, who were often, like the Kiuprils, of foreign descent, and it is only this man who refuses to leave to Ministers an initiative. We cannot see that this course need irritate any of the Powers, for it would postpone the struggle which they all dread, and the partition which they all are willing to delay. It is folly to think, as some of our Liberal contemporaries think, that Russia will favour or tolerate a constitutional revolt in Turkey—even if such a movement is possible, which we disbelieve—but she has no attachment to one Sultan more than another, and her statesmen must be will aware, from M. de Nelidoff's reports, that the present misgovernment will end sooner or later—and by later we mean before next midsummer—in some grand catastrophe. The winds have been unchained in Turkey, and they will not go back to their caves till they have caused a wreck. It is not however our business to suggest. Lord Salisbury has probably a dozen plans before him, each of them more practicable than ours; the only contention on which we insist is that he, the author of the Treaty of Berlin, has no right, even for the sake of peace, to suffer the extinction of the Armenian people. That they will be saved at the eleventh hour we are unable to doubt; but if they are not saved by Britain she will be disgraced, and, scattered throughout Asia, there will be one more race which will bear, and bear justifiably, a permanent enmity to the British name.

The Nineteenth Century, Vol. 38 (December 1895): 991–1000

The Eastern Question: Turkish Reforms and Armenia

F. Heinrich Geffcken

The Turkish project of reform for six vilayets in Anatolia, in which the population is particularly composed of Mussulmans and Christians, is at last published, and Shakir Pasha is appointed high commissioner for superintending the application of the Sultan's Irade. It is, however, clear that this is only a diplomatic solution of the difficulty. The Ambassadors at Constantinople may be glad to have obtained this result after the weary negotiations of the last months; but in no country is there a wider margin between granting reforms and their real execution, as a short retrospect will amply show.

It is not the first time that equal rights for Christians and Mussulmans have been proclaimed by the Porte. Whilst it formerly staunchly refused to place both on the same footing, and preferred losing its Greek provinces rather than grant rights to the Rayah.[1] Reshid Pasha, who had observed the popularity won by Mehemed Ali by his energetic reforms, thought it necessary to show to the world by a solemn act that the Porte also was resolved upon entering the path of progress. He therefore, on the 3rd of November, 1839, in a gathering of the highest dignitaries, and in the presence of the young Sultan Abdul-Mejid, proclaimed the Hattisherif of Gulhane, which granted to all subjects, "to whatever religion or sects they might belong," equal guarantees for the security of life, honour, and property, and a just repartition of taxes. This act at that time was considered as a proof of great liberality; but it was overlooked that it contained a strange contradiction, ascribing in its entry the decay of the Empire to the neglect of the prescriptions of the Koran, which are in fundamental opposition, to granting equal rights to Mussulmans and infidels, and then coming to the illogical conclusion that *new* institutions were to secure the above said benefits to all subjects. Besides the Hat was not a law, but simply a proclamation of principles, which had to be converted into special laws by the Council of State. Very little came of it, and when in 1851 the Porte attempted to introduce certain reforms in Bosnia, the Begs revolted, and had to be put down in a bloody campaign by Omar Pasha. The pretension of Czar Nicholas to exercise a protectorate over the Christian subjects of the Sultan brought about the Crimean War; the Vienna Conferences admitted the Porte as a member of the European concert. But Lord Palmerston and Napoleon the Third discerned that for this purpose a regeneration of Turkey was necessary. Even in 1854 an Armenian renegade, who had [denied] Islam, was executed for apostasy at Adrianople. Lord Stratford therefore threw his whole energy into pressing the Porte to grant real reforms, particularly the equal evidence of Christians in the courts and the abolition of the capitation tax of the Rayah. After much difficulty the Porte yielded, and on the 26th February, 1856, the Hat-i-Humayun was issued, which embodied the gist of the reforms demanded by England, France, and Austria. It was communicated to the Congress of Paris, in the sitting of the 25th of March, 1856, and Baron Brunnow declared, perhaps not without a touch of irony, "he was happy to acknowledge that this act, testifying in every paragraph the well-meaning intentions of the illustrious monarch who had issued it, realized and even surpassed the expectations of the Russian plenipotentiaries." But Art. 9 of the Treaty of Paris (the 30th of March, 1856) expressly declared that the Hat had been a spontaneous action of the Sultan, which gave to no foreign Power the right of meddling with the internal affairs of the Porte.

In Turkey, however, the Hat-i-Humayun raised general discontent. The Christians were dissatisfied because, in return for the abolition of the capitation tax, it imposed upon them military service, which they abhorred. The Mussulmans were still more indignant that the Giaours should be allowed to wear arms, which hitherto had been their exclusive privilege. The Christians were much more numerous in the Balkan Peninsula than the Mahomedans: if they were militarily organized, they might rise or aid the enemies of the Porte; moreover, the right accorded to foreigners to acquire real property was opposed to the Mussulman law, according to which the whole soil belongs to the Caliph, who grants its usufruct only to Believers.

Thus both joined to prevent the execution of the Hat, and they succeeded so well that the Hat-i-Humayun remained a dead letter, in the same way as had been the case with that of Gulhane. In 1867, the French Ambassador, Marquis de Moustier, a man thoroughly well disposed to the Porte, was obliged to report to his Government that the execution of the Hat-i-Humayun "a depuis onze ans échoué devant l'inertie du gouvernement turc." It was, indeed, a strange illusion of Lord Stratford that the different creeds of the Ottoman Empire could be blended into one nation by decrees. True, its predecessors, the Byzantine emperors, also ruled over very different races, but these were at least united by the bond of a common religious faith—Bulgars, Serbs, Albanese, Valachs, had been converted to the Orthodox Church. But with the Turkish conquest the contest of the races had been embittered by that of the creeds; and there has never existed a Christian State which deserved that name in the sense as the Turkish dominion that of a Mussulman one: its one task is the realization of Allah's will as revealed by his Prophet. It is the essence of Islam that State and religious community are inseparably entwined: religion, politics, laws, and customs are only different manifestations of one idea: the Koran's prescriptions embrace the penal laws and the right of inheritance, as well as morals and prayers. The rigidity of this principle has been somewhat relaxed in civilized Mussulman dominions, such as those of the Caliphs of Bagdad or of Spain; but it was carried to the extreme by the Ottoman rulers and their followers. They adopted the Mussulman creed ready made, but they stuck to the letter of it. Accordingly, after having conquered Asia Minor and the Balkan Peninsula, they did not persecute the Christian faith in itself, nor try to convert the Christians to Islam:[2] they respected the different creeds, especially the Greek and the Armenian Churches, as they stood. But the Mussulmans were established as the dominant race; they alone had the right to wear arms and to hold offices. The Christians were the subject herd (Rayah) who had to submit, and as a token of their position had to pay the poll-tax. The Osmanlis are still the recognized chiefs of Islam; the Sultan is the Caliph of all the millions of Mussulmans; they are not opposed to reforms, for they suffer themselves from misgovernment, but they will accept only such as are compatible with their religion. When the French economist, M. Blanqui, endeavoured to persuade Kiamil-Pasha that all men were equal, and that all subjects of the Sultan ought to enjoy equal rights, the Turkish governor answered: "Yes, the chicken and the ducks are both birds, but not all birds can swim; the question is, which is the better government, that of the chicken or that of the ducks, and that is precisely what still in no country the chicken and the ducks have been able to decide." Equality of creeds can be enforced on Mussulmans in countries governed by a strong non-Mussulman Power, such as India and Egypt by England.[3] But a Mahomedan Power will never sincerely accept principles which are subversive of its *raison d'être*—namely, that Mussulmans should cease to be the dominant race. If pressed very hard by European diplomacy, the Porte will appear to yield, and promise much, then plead difficult circumstances which require time for the execution of what it has promised, and when events in other parts divert the attention of European cabinets from Turkey, it will try to evade the reforms altogether.[4] Besides, there is a stationary principle in Islam. Mussulmans do not accept the notions of the European State and of European progress; they may use the railways which we build in their country, but their conviction remains the same as that stated by the Chinese General Tscheng-ti-Kong: "Vos machines sont supérieures, mais notre philosophie vaut mieux." Travelling in Bosnia last year, I had frequent intercourse with the Mussulman Begs, and always met with the most dignified politeness; yet a high Austrian functionary, who had the management of the Vakuf, the property of the mosques, and knew Mussulmans well, assured me that these men, in their often ragged clothes, looked down upon every Christian as an inferior; because we believed in the Trinity, and had not the Prophet declared it blasphemy to say that God had a son?

Now it is quite true that, even admitting the principle of the dominant race, many useful reforms might be introduced; above all, maintaining order, preventing violence, establishing rational taxation, &c. That this is not done is due to the apparently irremediable Turkish misgovernment. It is, however, of comparatively recent date. Formerly the Ottoman Empire was a great feudal monarchy. The Dereg-Begs (princes of the valley), many of whom had governed their territories centuries before the Turkish conquest, corresponded to the great mediaeval barons; they enjoyed considerable independence, and the same was the case with their sub-vassals, the Timarlis (the landed gentry), which under Soliman the Magnificent numbered 53,352. They owed to the Sultan military service and the tithe, but had political authority in their domains, with which the central Government did not meddle. Together with this feudal system there existed a wide communal liberty; the Timarlis levied the tithe, the only direct tax, but could not interfere in local affairs, which were administered by self-elected functionaries of the commune. The same applied to the Christian communities. They had no political rights, and paid the capitation tax, but retained their autonomy under elected chiefs, Demogeronts, Nodjabachis, who collected the taxes and handed them over to the Government. With this system suppression of the Rayah was rare; it occurred principally there where renegades were the governing classes, such as the Begs in Bosnia, and it is remarkable that the Armenian troubles of which we hear much in the eighteenth century were mainly caused by the Jesuits, who endeavoured to convert the Gregorian Armenians to the Latin Creed, and were seconded by the Embassies of France and Austria.

The system of the old Turkish State fell into decay during the unfortunate wars which the Porte had to sustain during the eighteenth century. Some of the most powerful Dereg-Begs of Roumelia, Anatolia, and the Libanon took advantage of its defeats to aspire to complete independence, and refused to furnish their contingents. Mahmud the Second became the reformator. After having crushed the Janissaries, and created an army with the help of Moltke, he fell upon the refractory Dereg-Begs and reduced them to obedience. This was necessary, but unfortunately he went too far: he successively destroyed the Dereg-Begs, and by a stroke of the pen confiscated all the property of the Timarlis. Thus the whole provincial organization of the Empire was overthrown and replaced by the naked absolutism of the central Government—a step of fatal consequences. The administration of the Begs and Timarlis was, perhaps, not exemplary according to European ideas; but, on the whole, it corresponded to the local wants, and was limited by communal self-government; the taxes were moderate, and, with the exception of the fixed tribute to the Sultan, the money remained in the country. Mahmud introduced the infamous institution of the Iltizam, the farming-out of the provincial taxes to the highest bidder. Thus universal corruption became the rule; the pashas paid highly for their places, and endeavoured to suck out the double from the unfortunate provinces, as they were every moment in danger of being recalled; and in the same way every subordinate place was only to be had for money. "With us," a high dignitary naïvely said, "the Government exists for the governing class, not for the governed."[5]

Again and again the European Powers pressed the Porte to do away with this system, which must impoverish the country for the benefit of a few who amass riches. It subsists to this hour, and even the latest project of reform stipulates (ch. xv.) only that the farming-out in bulk of the taxes of a vilayet shall be replaced by a licitation of the tithes of each commune.

Finally, we have, at present, a dual Government at Constantinople; that of the so-called Sublime Porte, which actually decides very little, and that of the Palace, which is nominally that of the Sultan, but actually in the hands of a body of unscrupulous adventurers, astrologers, ulemahs, favourites, &c., who enrich themselves at the public expense.

The dual Government has been so well described by Professor Salmone in the May number of this Review, that I need not enlarge upon it, but will only mention that these men constantly repeat to the Sultan that his entire power rests upon his holding the high office of Caliph of the Islamitic world or the vicegerent of the Prophet on earth, and keep him in a constant terror of the possibility of his losing the position of Islam chieftain.

Now, given these leading facts, it is not astonishing that Art. 62 of the Treaty of Berlin (the 13th of July, 1878), by which the Sublime Porte promised anew equality of condition to all creeds, admission of evidence in the courts without any distinction, &c., should have remained a dead letter, just as the Hat-i-Humayun and the Hatti-sherif of Gulhane.

The only distinction of this treaty was that it contained a guarantee in favour of one special community. By Art. 61 the Sublime Porte engaged to realize without any delay the ameliorations and reforms required by the local exigencies in the provinces inhabited by Armenians, and to grant their security against the Circassians and Kurds.

This article was the consequence of the defensive alliance between Great Britain and Turkey of the 1st of July, 1878, by which, under certain conditions, the former engaged to defend the Sultan's possessions in Asia, as fixed by the definitive treaty of peace, and, "in return, the Sultan promised to England to introduce necessary reforms, *to be agreed upon later between the two Powers*, into the government, and for the protection of Christians and other subjects of the Porte in these territories."

The fatal weakness of this engagement lay in the clause "to be agreed upon later between the two Powers," for if the Porte did not consent to the proposals put forward by England, the whole reform came to a dead-lock. And so it turned out. England suggested the establishment of a gendarmerie commanded by European officers, the appointment of European inspectors of finance and justice in the provinces, and that of the Valis or governor-generals of each vilayet for five years.[6] But none of these reforms were executed, no inspectors were appointed, the Valis remained entirely dependent upon the Government at Constantinople, and as to the gendarmerie, the Porte declared it would be far too expensive. The mixed commissions sent into the provinces for inquiring into the state of things did more harm than good; for the Christians bringing forward their complaints, the Mahomedans took their revenge upon them as soon as the commissioners had left, and Sir H. Layard was soon obliged to report to his Government that the situation of the Armenians had become worse than it had been before the Treaty of Berlin. In vain did Mr. Gladstone send Mr. Goschen to Constantinople to impress upon the Porte the necessity of reforms, and to use even threatening language; in vain did the other Powers support the English envoy by a collective note—the Porte answered that it had already done everything in order to satisfy the wishes of the Powers, and presented a further project so nugatory that the Ambassadors protested in a second collective note. The Porte replied by extolling the difficulties "contre lesquelles elle a à lutter," and only made proposals, of which seven concerned the Armenians, but which widely differed from the demands of the Ambassadors. A renewed request of the English Government to the signatory Powers (the 12th of January, 1881) for a collective representation to the Porte came to nothing, as Prince Bismarck did not think it opportune to press the Sultan too much on this point, before the then acute frontier question of Greece and Turkey was settled. Other more pressing affairs cropped up in Afghanistan, Egypt, and Bulgaria, and matters remained in Anatolia *in status quo* until the massacres of last year forced anew the attention of Europe upon the Armenian Question.

Now justice requires us to avow that it is a most intricate one. The Armenians boast of very ancient descent, but already in the pre-Christian era were divided in two territories—Great Armenia, in the Caucasus, and Little Armenia, in the Anti-Taurus. The Turkish conquest swept away the national dynasties, and in 1515 Armenia was organised as a Turkish province. The Armenians belonging to the Gregorian Church were acknowledged, just as the orthodox Greeks, as a lawful Rayah-nation (Ermeni Milleti), and obtained as national authority three patriarchs. One, residing at Edshmiazin, had the supreme leadership in matters of faith, and was elected by the monks of that convent. So was the second, at Sis, in Little Armenia. The third, having jurisdiction in those secular affairs which Ottoman rule left to the autonomy of the recognised Rayah-nations, resided at Constantinople, and was appointed by the Porte, having twelve laymen assessors for the discharge of his office. The Armenians for the rest remained in their former condition; they had only to pay the capitation tax, and their relations with the Porte were for centuries so satisfactory that when, in 1724, the Persians made an inroad into Anatolia, the Armenians of Erivan sent an address of devotion into the camp of the Osman general.

The first to disturb this good understanding were, as above mentioned, the Jesuits, who, wanting to convert the Armenians to the Latin Church, erected a convent at Erzeroum. On the whole, their success was not very great, but their intrigues led to disturbances. They were several times banished, but always returned; and in 1831 the Catholic Armenians obtained by the support of France the same rights as the Gregorians (Katoluk Milleti), with a primate for the religious affairs and (1835) a patriarch for the secular jurisdiction, residing at Constantinople. A new religious scission arose when the Armenian Presbyterian ministers, supported by Lord Ponsonby's able secretary, Mr. Urquhart, began a Protestant propaganda among the Armenians; and, with the corrupt state of the Gregorian Church, met with great success. At the instigation of

Russia the converts were persecuted alike by the Patriarch of Edshmiazin and by the Porte; but the powerful influence of Sir Stratford Canning obtained for them the recognition as an independent community (Millet), with equal rights as the two others, by the Hatti-sherif of the 6th of June, 1853. Thus the Armenians were split into three groups, bitterly hostile to each other. Of those inhabiting Asiatic Turkey, it is reckoned that the number of Gregorians is about 75 per cent., that of the Protestants 15 per cent., and that of the Catholics 10 per cent.

Other important changes took place in the condition of the Armenians: parts of them came under Russian rule by conquest, and the Czar's Government were not slow to avail themselves of this fact as a pretext to intermeddle with Armenian questions in general, particularly with the elections of the patriarchs. Secondly, the Asiatic Armenians suffered greatly from the inroads of the Kurds, a race of indifferent Mussulmans, but of inveterate robbers. As long as the old provincial organization was in force, the Dereg-Begs and Timarlis kept them in check, but when greedy and lax pashas had taken their place it was different. As Mussulmans they did not think it their duty to protect the Giaours; they rather connived at the aggressions of the Kurds, if they did not share their plunder; and if blamed by the Porte under the pressure of foreign ambassadors, pretended that the guilt lay with the Armenians, who had provoked the Kurds. Finally the Porte committed the fatal blunder of forming from the Kurds a corps of irregular cavalry, which only made matters worse.

A third fact which requires special notice is the following. The Armenians, as an intelligent race, were welcome to the illiterate Turks as clerks, and in the course of time obtained even important places; we need only refer to Nubar Pasha, late Prime Minister of Egypt. But, above all, they ever were wily and successful merchants and bankers in all great commercial centers, so that now from Calcutta to London, Liverpool and Manchester, we find the prosperous members of this community. Influenced by the modern general movement of independent nationalities, and encouraged by the decay of Turkey, they founded the Armenian Committee in London, with branches at other capitals, the organ of which is the *Hasjadan*. The aim of this committee was at first not directed against Turkey. Perceiving how their co-religionists were treated by Russia, they feared nothing more than the absorption of further parts inhabited by Armenians into the Empire of the Czar. They only endeavoured to strengthen the national feeling of their Anatolian brethren by an agitation largely supported by money, newspapers, and agents, and tried to raise a "grido di dolore" for the Armenians by the petition to the Berlin Congress, forgetting that most of the tax-farmers were Armenians, and so were the bankers who advanced money to the Pashas for their places at usurious interest. This was already sufficient to embitter the good relations between Turks and Armenians, and to make the former renitent in executing Art. 61 of the Berlin Treaty, imposed upon them by the Powers. But it was the success of Bulgaria which turned the heads of the Armenian Committee: here was a State liberated by Russia, which, nevertheless, had shaken off the Russian yoke, had set aside the partition stipulated by the Berlin Treaty into Bulgaria proper and Eastern Roumelia, and, in spite of Turkey and Russia, had wellnigh achieved independence. Might not the Armenians do the same? These ardent patriots overlooked the slight circumstance that both cases were totally different. The Bulgarians were a homogeneous nationality, of one creed, with frontiers delimited by the Treaty of 1878, and with only a sprinkling of Mussulmans. But if there were about 600,000 Armenians in Asiatic Turkey, where was a compact Armenia similar to Bulgaria? Even in Great Armenia, which contains 50 per cent. of the above-mentioned number, the Armenians form only 33 per cent. of the entire population, the Kurds 35 per cent., Turks 17, non-Armenian Christians, Jews, &c. 15 per cent., and not one of these different races inhabits a fixed territory; they live intertwined with each other. In Little Armenia and Karamania there are only two larger and some smaller compact colonies; and 45 per cent. are dispersed in the cities of the vilayets of Brussa, Smyrna, and parts of Syria and Palestine. How is it possible to apply to a population so conditioned, which besides is divided into three creeds, the idea of autonomy?[7] But the committee did not stop at such considerations; they raised the cry of "Autonomous Armenia," and with the help of two patriarchs, Mighirditch at Edshmiazin and Ismirlian at Constantinople, they succeeded in rousing the masses, whom they instigated to refuse the taxes, and had the satisfaction, when the Turks promptly answered with the massacres of Sassoon, to see Lord Rosebery follow in the wake of Mr. Gladstone, take up cudgels for their persecuted brethren, and thus bring the Armenian question once more on to the diplomatic chessboard. Russia associated herself with the British complaints, and so did of course her obedient vassal France, while Germany, Austria-Hungary, and Italy kept back. But if England took the lead, she was not very fortunate. The Porte at once discerned that the league of the three was hollow. Russia, indeed, is always ready to take steps which may embarrass the Sultan, but it was never in earnest about the reforms; on the contrary, entrenched at Kars and Ardahan, she wishes the present confusion to go on in order to prepare future conquests. So whilst her Ambassador officially joined the representations of his British colleague, his dragoman gave at Yildiz-Kiosk very different advice, rather tending to resistance. Besides, the scheme of reform presented by Lord Rosebery was so intricate as to give the Porte opportunity for protracted negotiations, and of this the wily Turkish diplomatists amply availed themselves. Secure that Russia would not seriously embarrass them, they did not even yield to the strong language used by Lord Salisbury when he took up the work of his predecessor. At last the project of reform alluded to in the beginning of this article was agreed upon; but we greatly doubt whether the diplomatic solution will lead to an actual one. The first effect of its publication has been to plunge Anatolia into civil war. Mussulmans and Armenians stand against each other armed to the teeth, and blood is spilled like water. The Porte accuses the Armenians of having provoked the disorders, and it is certain that they have done all in their power to aggravate the situation; they caused the panic on the Exchange, the run on the Ottoman Bank and the "moratorium." On the other hand, it cannot be contested that Mussulman fanaticism has been roused, and that the Turkish troops frequently have made common cause with the Kurds. The Porte, pressed by the Ambassadors, has been obliged to call out the Redifs to restore order, which will heavily tell upon its dilapidated finances. The winter is at hand when, with its passes and bad roads, the country is rendered nearly inaccessible by snow. Lord Salisbury, in his speech at the Mansion House, has appealed to the existing concert of the European Powers; it is certainly very salutary as far as it goes, but will it hold when action becomes necessary? The Premier said: "How the Powers will act it is not for me to prophesy"; yet the whole question depends upon the point, what will the Powers do, if the Sultan does not succeed in re-establishing order? Until the primary question is solved, it cannot be attempted to put Armenian reforms into practice.

The Spectator, Vol. 75 (December 21, 1895): 885–86

The Death-Warrant of Armenia

Perhaps the greatest, decidedly the worst, result of President Cleveland's sensational Message will be its effect on the fate of the Armenians. It is for them almost a death-warrant. It will furnish a full excuse for all who are desirous of silently deserting that unhappy people. A nation, it will be said, cannot do more than it can, and it is impossible for Great Britain, with such a menace from the West hanging over her, to break loose from the concert of Europe, or to risk the outbreak of a European war in which, owing to American hostility, she might be powerless to interfere, or might even live to find a widespread coalition threatening her scattered dominion on many points at once. The English section of opinion represented by the *Pall Mall Gazette* will certainly argue thus, and a great majority of those who are careless what becomes of any people, if only they may trade with profit and live on the profit in podded luxury. Those statemen, too, and they are many, who, while pitying the Armenians, shrink from heavy responsibilities, will be all on the same side; and so will those who, esteeming themselves philanthropists, still look upon every war as an impediment to the realisation of a quasi-Socialistic ideal. There is another man, too, who is certain to take this view. The dreadful little being at Constantinople, who has decided to end the Armenian question within his dominion by extirpating the Armenians, will see in the Message the evidence that he is safe alike from England and from America. He knows that on this subject the enemy to be dreaded is Great Britain, and he has a vivid fear also of America, because she can act by sea, and is unencumbered by European jealousies. He has yielded three times to Mr. Terrell's energetic, not to say audacious, remonstrances on behalf of Americans, and at this moment his officers are guarding jealously the houses of American missionaries. If *they* are hurt, thinks his Majesty, shells may fall; and he has a horror of shells. If America and England quarrel, however, both restraints will be gone, and he will be able to carry out the second part of his policy to the bitter end. The first part has already been successful. He has cut down the tall poppies; has slain or banished or "arrested" the whole upper class of Armenians outside Constantinople, paying the irregular cavalry and the roughs with their plundered property; and he has now commenced the second. In all Armenian districts and in the villages scattered over Anatolia where Armenians exist, the same agents, the cavalry and the roughs, are now offering the wretched Armenians the alternatives of conversion or immediate death. Hundreds have rejected the alternative, but the mass of the people, cowed by the massacres, hopeless of aid from Europe, and in terror of the bayonets and sabres in sight, agree to be circumcised, recite the profession of faith, and rise from their knees members of the dominant caste. No Mussulman will touch them again, and they are free once more to do anything except to relapse back to Christianity. That the Mahommedans, like the old Inquisitors, will not bear in any country, regarding apostasy as a wilful blasphemy committed against the light. Mahommedanism, too, has a stronger grip than we Westerns think, the landholders of Bosnia, the Albanians, and the Armenian Kurds, who were Christians, and the peasants of the slopes of the Mysore plateau, who were Hindoos, being among the most bigoted of all Mahommedans. Take these instances from the correspondence of the *Daily News:*—

> "In Van, in Bitlis, in Kharput, Diarbekir, Erzeroum, Sivas, Trebizond, Adana, and Aleppo (that is to say, in the eight most important provinces of Turkey in Asia), there are countless villages, districts, quarters, whose entire remnant population has embraced Islam, in order to escape certain death. Last week, for instance, from Terchan (in the Baiburt district of the Erzeroum vilayet), where 1,225 Armenians were killed in the villages, 322 survivors were induced by threats to accept Islam, and were publicly circumcised, among them being the acting Bishop. In the Kharput vilayet, where 53 villages were burnt, their churches demolished, and 49 clergymen killed, the dead are to this day lying in the roads, there being none to bury them. Many of the surviving clergy have shaved their beards and become Moslems. In the village of Hussenik, close to Kharput,

> all the survivors of the massacre have accepted Islam. In the city of Kharput itself, a number of the Armenian notables have become Moslems, while the largest Christian quarter of the town has adopted Islam *en masse* in order to avoid slaughter. That slaughter was inevitable in the event of their refusal they had ample and terrible proof. For instance, a young Protestant pastor who had been educated in the American college fled during the massacre from the village of Hula Keni, where was his cure, to take refuge in Kharput. With his young wife he managed to reach his mother's house in the city in safety. Next day—the massacre being, be it noted, at an end—a troop of soldiers forced the door, and, hauling him and his wife out of the house, called on them to accept Islam. They refused, and at once, first his wife and then Mr. Atlasian himself, were ruthlessly murdered."

The broad statement as to forcible conversions is confirmed from other sources, and will, we doubt not, be found recorded in more general terms in the Consular reports. With England and America paralysed, the good work will go on more energetically still, and within a year the Sultan, triumphant over "united" Europe, will be able to record with exultation that there is now not only no disorder in Armenia, but no disaffection, all having accepted heartily the authority of the rightful Khalif. There is no hope of armed resistance, not even of such resistance as the Saxons offered to Charlemagne; and when there is no armed resistance history tells only one tale. Religious persecution always fails unless the penalty of recusancy is death; but then it usually succeeds.

Are we prepared, in fear of being attacked in Canada by Mr. Cleveland, to suffer this to go on? We say distinctly that the danger from America, be it great or small, ought to impel the British Government to more rapid and decisive action in the Near East, to a further and determined effort to make terms with Russia, and, failing that, to a withdrawal from the European "concert," and an attempt to obtain by force a full and honest protection for all Armenians. If Russia agrees to act, the protection could be obtained at once, for there is no force which could resist a Russian advance into Armenia, the province would be held as a material guarantee that the persecution should cease, and it would cease at once, Mussulmans, even when most excited, admitting the right of submission to *force majeure*. We are unable to believe that Russia would reject such an opportunity of posing as the protector of the Eastern Christians; or to see why, under circumstances so desperate, we should hesitate to allow her to increase her territorial dominion. It would not add to her strength; and if it did, it would be better to run the risks involved in that addition than to suffer a whole nation of clients to be extinguished for no other reason than that in reliance on our pledges they have ventured under intolerable tyranny to shriek aloud.

If this, which is at once the direct and the peaceful route, is really closed, if, that is, the men who govern Russia from cynical reasons of policy refuse our offer, we would have the British Government formally retreat from the European concert, and with such allies as it could find act decisively and at once against the Sultan, repeating the policy which in the case of Thessaly proved successful. That is, we would blockade Salonica, Smyrna, and Jeddah at the same time, and prepare from India for a descent upon the Euphrates. We believe that such a movement made in the interests of humanity would conciliate American opinion more than any amount of despatches; and if it did not, and if the Civil War arrived, we should be in no weaker position than at present, while we should have the relief of feeling that we had fully done our duty. It is as the fulfilment of a duty alone that we present this matter to our countrymen. We have nothing whatever to gain in Armenia or in the Turkish Empire, and we have much to lose in taxation, in expenditure of energy, and in the advance of the Power which, till it acquires Constantinople, will make a policy of embarrassing us in India. But there are great and heavy duties which fall to the lot of the nations that pretend to Empire; and if we are to continue to hold so immense a portion of the earth's surface we must rigidly perform them, even though we are already fatigued with our responsibilities. That Englishmen do not greatly love the Armenians, who are much too submissive to oppression, who are as saturated with the spirit of bargaining as Greeks or Jews, or London shopkeepers, and who cannot when they write keep from vague sentimentality, is but another reason for marching straight along the path we are bound to follow, and keeping our contract of eighteen years, that the Armenian people shall not be oppressed beyond what they can bear. No European outside Germany denies that this wide limit has been passed by the Sultan, and therefore, we repeat, our obligation of contract to interfere effectually has actually arisen. Action rests with Lord Salisbury, whom nobody is opposing; but that he should act, with Russia if possible, but if not, then alone, we feel no doubt whatever.

The Contemporary Review, Vol. 69 (January 1896): 1–19

Armenia: An Appeal

E. J. Dillon

The time has come for every reasoning inhabitant of these islands deliberately to accept or repudiate his share of the joint indirect responsibility of the British nation for a series of the hugest and foulest crimes that have ever stained the pages of human history. The Armenian people in Anatolia are being exterminated, root and branch, by Turks and Kurds—systematically and painfully exterminated by such abominable methods and with such fiendish accompaniments as may well cause the most sluggish blood to boil and seethe with shame and indignation.

For the Armenians are not lawless barbarians or brigands: nor are the Turks and Kurds the accredited torch-bearers of civilisation. That even if the *rôles* of the actors in this hideous drama were thus distributed, an excuse might at most be found for severity, but no pretext could be discovered for the slow torture and gradual vivisection employed by fanatic Mohammedans to end the lives of their Christian neighbours. If, for instance, it be expedient that Armenians should be exterminated, why chop them up piecemeal, and, in the intervals of this protracted process, banter the agonised victims who are wildly calling upon God and man to put them out of pain? Why must an honest, hard-working man be torn from his bed or his fireside, forced to witness the violation of his daughter by a band of all-pitiless demons, unable to rescue or help her, and then, his own turn come, have his hand cut off and stuffed into his mouth, while a short sermon is being preached to him on the text, "If your God be God, why does He not succour you?" at the peroration of which the other hand is hacked off, and, amid boisterous shouts of jubilation, his ears are torn from his head and his feet severed with a hatchet, while the piercing screams, the piteous prayers, the hideous contortions of the agonising victim intoxicate with physico-spiritual ecstasies the souls of the frantic fanatics around? And why, when the last and merciful stroke of death is being dealt, must obscene jokes and unutterable blasphemies sear the victim's soul and prolong his hell to the uttermost limits of time, to the very threshold of eternity? Surely, roasting alive, flaying, disembowelling, impaling, and all that elaborate and ingenious aggravation of savage pain on which the souls of these human fiends seem to feast and flourish, have nothing that can excuse them in the eyes of Christians, however deeply absorbed in politics.

But it is the Turks and Kurds who, at their best, are stagnant, sluggish, and utterly averse from progress; and at their worst are—the beings who conceive, perpetrate, and glory in the horrors just enumerated and in others that must be nameless. The Armenians, on the contrary, constitute the sole civilising—nay, with all their many faults, the sole humanising—element in Anatolia; peaceful to the degree of self-sacrifice, law-abiding to their own undoing, and industrious and hopeful under conditions which would appal the majority of mankind. At their best, they are the stuff of which heroes and martyrs are moulded. Christians, believing, as we believe, that God revealed Himself to the world in Jesus Christ, they have held fast to the teachings of our common Master in spite of disgrace and misery, in the face of fire and sword, in the agonies of torture and death. From the middle of the fifth century, when the hero Vartan and his dauntless companions died defending their faith against the Persian Mazdeans,[1] scarcely a year has elapsed in which Armenian men and women have not unhesitatingly and unostentatiously laid down their lives for their religious belief. The murdered of Sassoon, of Van, of Erzeroum were also Christian martyrs; and any or all of those whose eyes were lately gouged out, whose limbs were wrenched asunder, and whose quivering flesh was torn from their bodies, might have obtained life and comparative prosperity by merely pronouncing the formula of Islam and abjuring Christ. But, instead of this, they commended their souls to their Creator, delivered up their bodies to the tormentors, endured indescribable agonies, and died, like Christians martyrs, defying Heaven itself, so to say, by their boundless trust in God.

Identity of ideals, aspirations, and religious faith give this unfortunate but heroic people strong claims on the sympathy of the English people, whose ancestors, whatever their religious creed, never hesitated to die for it, and when the breath of God swept over them, breasted the hurricane of persecution.

But what special claims to our sympathy are needed by men and women whom we see treated by their masters as the damned were said to be dealt with by the devils in the deepest of hell's abysses? Our written laws condemn cruelty to a horse, a dog, a cat; our innate sense of justice moves us to punish the man who should wantonly torture a rat, say, by roasting it alive. And shall it be asserted that our instincts of justice, humanity, mercy need to be reinforced by extrinsic considerations before we consent to stretch out a helping hand, not to a brute or to a single individual, but to tens of thousands of honest, industrious Christian men, pure, virtuous women, and innocent little children to save them from protracted tortures, compared with some of which roasting alive is a swift and merciful death? Yet it is a melancholy fact that we have not alleviated the sufferings of these woe-stricken people by a single pang, and that the succour which no one of us, individually, would dream of withholding from a friend, a neighbour, nay, a bitter enemy were he in such straits, we all, as a nation, deny to our Christian brethren who are being bludgeoned, sawn in twain, burned or thrust fainting into a gory grave.

Why is it that our compassion for these, our fellow-men, has not yet assumed the form of effective help? For reasons of "higher politics"; because, forsooth, the Turks and Kurds, in whose soulless bodies the Gadarene legion of unclean spirits would seem to have taken up their abode, are indispensable to Christian civilisation—for the time being; and because the millions of soldiers, the deadly rifles and the destructive warships which are accounted the most costly possessions of contemporary Europe cannot be spared in such a cause—they are wanted by the Christian nations to mow each other down with. In a word, the civilisation built up on Christ's Gospel cannot stand, or at least cannot thrive, without the support of Kurdish cruelty and Turkish thuggery! It may be asked, on what grounds the people of Great Britain ought to show themselves more ready to pity, and more eager to succour, the Armenians than our Continental neighbours. The question differs little in spirit from that which the priest and the Levite asked themselves as they passed the helpless man mentioned by Jesus, who, on his way to Jericho, had fallen among thieves, and was left lying half-dead. But in the present case an answer is forthcoming, an answer which is calculated to satisfy the most callous among us, and transform us into Good Samaritans. Briefly, it is this: because we are primarily responsible for their sufferings; because they are the innocent victims of our selfish pursuit of political interests—which have none the less eluded our grasp, and left us empty-handed, and face to face with the calamitous results of our egotism.

In the first place, we refused to recognise the Treaty of San Stefano, and to allow the Christian subjects of the Sultan to owe the boon of humane treatment to Russia's policy or generosity. We insisted on delivering them back, bound hand and foot, to their rabid enemies, undertaking, however, to undo their fetters later on. But the "later on" never came. Oppression, persecution, incredible manifestations of savagery, characterised the dealings of the Turks with the Christians, but we closed our eyes and shut our ears until the Porte, encouraged by our connivance, organised the wholesale massacres of Sassoon. Then, for the first time, we interfered, striking out a line of action which we knew must prove disastrous if not completely successful, and without first assuring ourselves that we could and would work it out to a favourable issue. And the result was what was feared from the first. We acted as a surgeon might who, about to perform a dangerous operation, should lay the patient on the table, probe the wound, cut the flesh, and just when the last and decisive manipulation was needed to save the life of the sufferer, should turn away, and leave him to bleed to death.

These are reasons why we, and we more than any other people, are responsible for the misery of the Armenians.

The condition of Armenian Christians when we first interfered (1878) was, from a humane point of view, deplorable. Laws existed only on paper. Mohammedan crimes were punishable only in theory. Life and property depended for security solely on the neighbourly feeling which custom and community of interests had gradually fostered between Moslems and Christians, and which greed or fanaticism might at any moment suddenly uproot. Russia was willing to substitute law and order for crime and chaos, and to guarantee to Christians the treatment due to human beings. But we then denied her right to do this, as she refuses to admit our claim to undertake it single-handed. Our interference was inspired by purely political calculations, unredeemed by considerations of humanity. About this there is now no doubt, nor was there then any disguise. Our political interests needed, or our Government fancied they needed, the propping up of the Turkish Empire, when the Turkish Empire had already become the embodiment of the powers of darkness. And to these fancied interests were sacrificed the property, the honour, the lives of the Armenian people. But not to appear less generous or humane than our northern rival, we solemnly and emphatically promised to compel the Porte to deal fairly with its Christian subjects, and we undertook to see that such reforms were introduced as would enable Armenians to work without fear of legalised robbery or lawless brigandage, to marry without the certitude of having their wives dishonoured and their daughters violated, and to worship God after the manner of their fathers without being liable to imprisonment, torture, and death. We said in effect: "Though our political interests may clash with those of Russia, we will see to it that they are not subversive of the elementary principles of human justice and the immutable law of God. Therefore we declare that we are actuated by the will and possessed of the power to induce or compel the Porte to grant such political and administrative reforms as are essential to the well-being of its Armenian subjects."

This promise, and the events that rendered it necessary, constitute the main claim of the Armenian people in Turkey to English sympathy and assistance.

Yet we never took any efficacious step to fulfil that solemn promise. We never said or did anything the effect of which was to assuage the sufferings which owed their continued existence to our egotism. Nay, more; we allowed things to drift from bad to worse, mismanagement to develop into malignity, oppression to merge in extermination, and for the space of seventeen years we deliberately shut our eyes and closed our ears to the ghastly sights and lugubrious sounds that accompanied the horrors of Turkish misrule in Armenia. Our consuls forwarded exhaustive reports, the Press published heartrending details, Armenian ecclesiastics presented piteous appeals—all of them describing deeds more gruesome and nefarious than those which in patriarchal days brought down fire from heaven upon Sodom and Gomorrah. But we "pigeon-holed" the consular reports, pooh-poohed the particulars published by the Press, or characterised them as a tissue of gross exaggerations, and ignored the petition of the priests.

Let it not be supposed for a moment that this breach of faith was a mere "political peccadillo." It is often implicitly assumed, and sometimes flippantly affirmed, that politics postulate a code of morals different from that of private life. Even if this strange theory were true, it would furnish no justification, no excuse, no pretext for this indefensible conduct of a great nation towards a poor and downtrodden people. For the guiles and wiles, the subterfuges and stratagems which commonly characterise the diplomatic dealing of independent peoples and States are usually confined, even in their furthest consequences, by the narrow limits of the political sphere. They leave the real weal and woe of individuals practically untouched. National prestige, commercial advantages, or, at most, a strip of territory, is all that is at stake. But our unfortunate action and inaction made themselves immediately and fatally felt in the very homes and at the firesides of hundreds of thousands of Christian men and women, driving them into exile, shutting them up in noisome prisons, and subjecting them to every conceivable species of indignity, outrage, and death. We pressed a knob, as it were, in London, and thereby opened hell's portals in Asia Minor, letting loose legions of fiends in human shape, who set about torturing and exterminating the Christians there. And, lest it should be urged that our Government was ignorant of the wide-reaching effects of its ill-advised action, it is on record that for seventeen years it continued to watch the harrowing results of that action without once interfering to stop it, although at any moment during that long period of persecution it could have redeemed its promise, and rescued the Christians from their unbearable lot.

If a detailed description were possible of the horrors which our exclusive attention to our own mistaken interests let loose upon Turkish Armenians, there is not a man within the kingdom of Great Britain whose heartstrings would not be touched and thrilled by the gruesome stories of which it would be composed.

During all those seventeen years written law, traditional custom, the fundamental maxims of human and divine justice were suspended in favour of a Mohammedan saturnalia. The Christians by whose toil and thrift the empire was held together, were despoiled, beggared, chained, beaten and banished or butchered. First their movable wealth was seized, then their landed property was confiscated, next the absolute necessaries of life were wrested from them, and finally honour, liberty, and life were taken with as little ado as if these Christian men and women were wasps or mosquitoes. Thousands of Armenians were thrown into prison by governors like Tahsin Pasha and Bahri Pasha, and tortured and terrorized till they delivered up the savings of a lifetime, and the support of the helpless families, to ruffianly parasites. Whole villages were attacked in broad daylight by the Imperial Kurdish cavalry without pretext or warning, the male inhabitants turned adrift or killed, and their wives and daughters transformed into instruments to glut the foul lusts of these bestial murderers. In a few years the provinces were decimated, Aloghkerd, for instance, being almost entirely "purged" of Armenians. Over 20,000 woe-stricken wretches, once healthy and well-to-do, fled to Russia or to Persia in rags and misery, deformed, diseased, or dying; on the way they were seized over and over again by the soldiers of the Sultan, who deprived them of the little money they possessed, nay, of the clothes they were wearing, outraged the married women in presence of their sons and daughters, deflowered the tender girls before the eyes of their mothers and brothers, and then drove them over the frontier to hunger and die. Those who remained for a time behind were no better off. Kurdish brigands lifted the last cows and goats of the peasants, carried away their carpets and their valuables, raped their daughters, and dishonoured their wives. Turkish tax-gatherers followed these, gleaning what the brigands had left, and, lest anything should escape their avarice, bound the men, flogged them till their bodies were a bloody, mangled mass, cicatrized the wounds with red hot ramrods, plucked out their beards hair by hair, tore the flesh from their limbs with pincers, and often, even then, dissatisfied with the financial results of their exertions, hung the men whom they had thus beggared and maltreated from the rafters of the room and kept there to witness with burning shame, impotent rage, and incipient madness, the dishonouring of their wives and the deflowering of their daughters, some of whom died miserably during the hellish outrage.

Stories of this kind in connection with Turkish misrule in Armenia have grown familiar to English ears of late, and it is to be feared that people are now so much accustomed to them that they have lost the power of conveying corresponding definite impressions to the mind. The more is the pity. It is only meet that we should make some effort to realise the sufferings which we have brought down upon inoffensive men and women, and to understand somewhat of the shame, the terror, the despair that must take possession of the souls of Christians whose lives are a martyrdom of such unchronicled agonies, during which no ray of the life-giving light that plays about the throne of God ever pierces the mist of blood and tears that rises between the blue of heaven and the everlasting grey of the charnel-house called Armenia.

It should be remembered that these statements are neither rumours nor exaggerations concerning which we are justified in suspending our judgment. History has set its seal upon them; diplomacy has slowly verified and reluctantly recognised them as established facts, and religion and humanity are now called upon to place their emphatic protest against them on record. The Turks, in their confidential moods, have admitted these and worse acts of savagery; the Kurds glory in them at all times; trustworthy Europeans have witnessed and described them, and Armenians groaned over them in blank despair. Officers and nobles in the Sultan's own cavalry regiments, like Mostigo the Kurd, bruit abroad with unpardonable pride the story of the long series of rapes and murders which marked their official careers, and laugh to scorn the notion of being punished for robbing and killing the Armenians, whom the Sublime Porte desires them to exterminate. Nay, it was the Armenians themselves who were punished if they complained when their own relatives or friends were murdered. And they were punished, either on the charge of having cruelly done their own parents, sisters, children to death, or else on suspicion of having killed the murderers, who, however, were always found afterwards living and thriving *in the Sultan's employ*, and were never disturbed there. Three hundred and six of the principal inhabitants of the district of Khnouss, in a piteous appeal to the people of England, wrote:

> "Year by year, month by month, day by day, innocent men, women, and children have been shot down, stabbed, or clubbed to

> death, in their houses and their fields, tortured in strange fiendish ways in fetid prison cells, or left to rot in exile under the scorching sun of Arabia. During that long and horrible tragedy no voice was raised for mercy, no hand extended to help us. . . . Is European sympathy destined to take the form of a cross on our graves?"

Now the answer has been given. These ill-starred men might now know that European sympathy has taken a different form—that of a marine guard before the Sultan's palace to shield him and his from harm from without while they proceed with their orgies of blood and lust within. These simple men of Khnouss might now know and wonder at this—if they were still among the living; but most of them have been butchered since then, like the relatives and friends whose lot they lamented and yet envied.

In accordance with the plan of extermination, which has been carried out with such signal success during these long years of Turkish vigour and English sluggishness, all those Armenians who possessed money or money's worth were for a time allowed to purchase immunity from prison, and from all that prison life in Asia Minor implies. But, as soon as terror and summary confiscation took the place of slow and elaborate extortion, the gloomy dungeons of Erzeroum, Erzinghan, Marsovan, Hassankaleh, and Van were filled, till there was no place so sit down, *and scarcely sufficient standing room.* And this means more than English people can realise, or any person believe who has not actually witnessed it. It would have been a torture for Turkish troopers and Kurdish brigands, but it was worse than death to the educated schoolmasters, missionaries, priests, and physicians who were immured in these noisome hotbeds of infection, and forced to sleep night after night standing on their feet, leaning against the foul, reeking corner of the wall which all the prisoners were compelled to use as. . . . The very worst class of Tartar and Kurdish criminals were turned in here to make these hell-chambers more unbearable to the Christians. And the experiment was everywhere successful. Human hatred and diabolic spite, combined with the most disgusting sights and sounds and stenches, with their gnawing hunger and their putrid food, their parching thirst and the slimy water, fit only for sewers, rendered their agony maddening. Yet these were not criminals nor alleged criminals, but upright Christian men, who were never even accused of an infraction of the law. No man who has not seen these prisons with his own eyes, and heard these prisoners with his own ears, can be expected to conceive, much less realise, the sufferings inflicted and endured. The loathsome diseases, whose terrible ravages were freely displayed; the still more loathsome vices, which were continually and openly practised; the horrible blasphemies, revolting obscenities and ribald jests which alternated with cries of pain, songs of vice, and prayers to the unseen God, made these prisons, in some respects, nearly as bad as the Black Hole of Calcutta, and in others infinitely worse. In one corner of this foul fever-nest a man might be heard moaning and groaning with the pain of a shattered arm or leg; in another, a youth is convulsed with the death spasms of cholera or poison; in the centre, a knot of Turks, whose dull eyes are fired with bestial lust, surround a Christian boy, who pleads for mercy with heart-harrowing voice while the human fiends actually outrage him to death.

Into these prisons venerable old ministers of religion were dragged from their churches, teachers from their schools, missionaries from their meeting-houses, merchants, physicians, and peasants from their fire-sides. Those among them who refused to denounce their friends, or consent to some atrocious crime, were subjected to horrible agonies. Many a one, for instance, was put into a sentry-box bristling with sharp spikes, and forced to stand there motionless, without food or drink, for twenty-four and even thirty-six hours, was revived with stripes whenever he fell fainting to the prickly floor, and was carried out unconscious at the end. It was thus that hundreds of Armenian Christians, whose names and histories are on record, suffered for refusing to sign addresses to the Sultan accusing their neighbours and relatives of high treason. It was thus that Azo was treated by his judges, the Turkish officials, Talib Effendi, Captain Reshid, and Captain Hadji Fehim Agha, for declining to swear away the lives of the best men of his village. A whole night was spent in torturing him. He was first bastinadoed in a room close to which his female relatives and friends were shut up so that they could hear his cries. Then he was stripped naked, and two poles, extending from his armpits to his feet, were placed on each side of his body and tied tightly. His arms were next stretched out horizontally and poles arranged to support his hands. This living cross was then bound to a pillar, and the flogging began. The whips left livid traces behind. The wretched man was unable to make the slightest movement to ease his pain. His features alone, hideously distorted, revealed the anguish he endured. The louder he cried, the more heavily fell the whip. Over and over again he entreated his tormentors to put him out of pain, saying: "If you want my death, kill me with a bullet, but for God's sake don't torture me like this!" His head alone being free he, at last, maddened by excruciating pain, endeavoured to dash out his brains against the pillar, hoping in this way to end his agony. But this consummation was hindered by the police. They questioned him again; but in spite of his condition, Azo replied as before: "I cannot defile my soul with the blood of innocent people. I am a Christian." Enraged at this obstinacy, Talib Effendi, the Turkish official, ordered the application of other and more effective tortures. Pincers were fetched to pull out his teeth; but, Azo remaining firm, this method was not long persisted in. Then Talib commanded his servants to pluck out the prisoner's moustachios by the roots, one hair at a time. This order the gendarmes executed, with roars of infernal laughter. But this treatment proving equally ineffectual, Talib instructed his men to cauterise the unfortunate victim's body. A spit was heated in the fire. Azo's arms were freed from their supports, and two brawny policemen approached, one on each side, and seized him. Meanwhile another gendarme held to the middle of the wretched man's hands the glowing spit. While his flesh was thus burning, the victim shouted out in agony, "For the love of God kill me at once!"

Then the executioners, removing the red hot spit from his hands, applied it to his breast, then to his back, his face, his feet, and other parts. After this, they forced open his mouth, and burned his tongue with red hot pincers. During these inhuman operations, Azo fainted three several times, but on recovering consciousness maintained the same inflexibility of purpose. Meanwhile, in the adjoining apartment, a heartrending scene was being enacted. The women and the children, terrified by the groans and cries of the tortured man, fainted. When they revived, they endeavoured to rush out to call for help, but the gendarmes, stationed at the door, barred their passage, and brutally forced them back.[2]

Nights were passed in such hellish orgies and days in inventing new tortures or refining upon the old, with an ingenuity which reveals unimagined strata of malignity in the human heart. The results throw the most sickening horrors of the Middle Ages into the shade. Some of them cannot be described, nor even hinted at. The shock to people's sensibilities would be too terrible. And yet they were not merely described to, but endured by, men of education and refinement, whose sensibilities were as delicate as ours.

And when the prisons in which these and analogous doings were carried on had no more room for new comers, some of the least obnoxious of its actual inmates were released for a bribe, or, in case of poverty, were expeditiously poisoned off.

In the homes of these wretched people the fiendish fanatics were equally active and equally successful. Family life was poisoned at its very source. Rape and dishonour, with nameless accompaniments, menaced almost every girl and woman in the country. They could not stir out of their houses in the broad daylight to visit the bazaars, or to work in the fields, nor even lie down at night in their own homes without fearing the fall of that Damocles' sword ever suspended over their heads. Tender youth, childhood itself, was no guarantee. Children were often married at the age of eleven, even ten, in the vain hope of lessening this danger. But the protection of a husband proved unavailing; it merely meant one murder more, and one "Christian dog" less. A bride would be married in church yesterday and her body would be devoured by the beasts and birds of prey to-morrow—a band of ruffians, often officials, having within the intervening forty-eight hours seized her and outraged her to death. Others would be abducted, and, having for weeks been subjected to the loathsome lust of lawless Kurds, would end by abjuring their God and embracing Islam; not from any vulgar motive of gain, but to escape the burning shame of returning home as pariahs and lepers to be shunned by those near and dear to them for ever. Little girls of five and six were frequently forced to be present during these horrible scenes of lust, and they, too, were often sacrificed before the eyes of their mothers, who would have gladly, madly accepted death, ay, and damnation, to save their tender offspring from the corroding poison.

One of the abducted young women who, having been outraged by the son of the Deputy-Governor of Khnouss, Hussni Bey, returned, a pariah, and is now alone in the world, lately appealed to her English sisters for such aid as a heathen would give to a brute, and she besought it in the name of our common God. Lucine Mussegh—this is the name of that outraged young woman whose Protestant education gave her, as she thought, a special claim to act as the spokeswoman of Armenian mothers and daughters—Lucine Mussegh besought, last March, the women of England to obtain for the women of Armenia the *privilege* of living a pure and chaste life! This was the boon which she craved—but did not, could not, obtain. The interests of "higher politics," the civilising missions of the Christian Powers are, it seems, incompatible with it! "For the love of the God whom we worship in common," wrote this outraged, but still hopeful, Armenian lady, "help us, Christian sisters! Help us before it is too late, and take the thanks of the mothers, the wives, the sisters, and the daughters of my people, and with them the gratitude of one for whom, in spite of her youth, death would come as a happy release."

Neither the Christian sisters nor the Christian brethren in England have seen their way to comply with this strange request. But it may perhaps interest Lucine Mussegh to learn that the six Great Powers of Europe are quite unanimous, and are manfully resolved, come what will, to shield his Majesty the Sultan from harm, to support his rule, and to guarantee his kingdom from disintegration. These are objects worthy of the attention of the Great Powers; as for the privilege of leading pure and chaste lives—they cannot be importuned about such private matters.

What astonishes one throughout this long, sickening story of shame and crime is the religious faith of the sufferers. It envelops them like a Nessus' shirt, aggravating their agonies by the fear it inspires that they must have offended in some inexplicable way the omnipotent God who created them. What is not at all wonderful, but only symptomatic, is the mood of one of the women, who, having prayed to God in heaven, discovered no signs of His guiding hand upon earth, and whose husband was killed in presence of her daughter, after which each of the two terrified females was outraged by the band of ruffians in turn. When gazing, a few days later, on the lifeless corpse of that beloved child whom she had vainly endeavoured to save, that wretched, heart-broken mother, wrung to frenzy by her soul-searing anguish, accounted to her neighbours for the horrors that were spread over her people and her country by the startling theory that God Himself had gone mad, and that maniacs and demons incarnate were stalking about the world!

Such, in broad outline, has been the *normal* condition of Armenia ever since the Treaty of Berlin, owing at first to the disastrous action and subsequently to the equally disastrous inaction of the British Government. The above sketch contains but a few isolated instances of the daily commonplaces of the life of the Armenian Christians. When these have been multiplied by thousands and the colours duly heightened, a more or less adequate idea may be formed of the hideous reality. Now, during all those seventeen years, we took no serious step to put an end to the brigandage, rapes, tortures, and murders which all Christendom agreed with us in regarding as the *normal* state of things. No one deemed it his duty to insist on the punishment of the professional butchers and demoralisers, who founded their claims to preferment upon the maintenance of this inhuman system, and had their claims allowed, for the Sultan, whose intelligence and humanity it was the fashion to eulogise and admire, decorated and rewarded these faithful servants, making them participators in the joy of their lord. Indeed, the utter perversion of the ideas of justice and humanity which characterised the views of European Christendom during the long period of oppression and demoralisation has at last reached such a pitch that the Powers have agreed to give the Sultan a "reasonable" time to *re-establish once more the normal state of things.*

The Turks, encouraged by the seventeen years' connivance of the only Power which possessed any formal right to intervene in favour of the Armenians, and confident that the British nation was a consenting party to the policy of sheer extermination which was openly proclaimed again and again, organised a wholesale massacre of the Christians of Sassoon. The particular reason for this sweeping measure lay in the circumstance that the Armenian population in that part of the country consisted of the hardiest, bravest, and most resolute representatives of the race, and that their proportion to the Mohammedans there was more than twice greater than elsewhere. The systematic Turkeries which had impoverished and depopulated the other less favoured districts were consequently of little avail in Sassoon; therefore, a purgative measure on a grandiose scale was carefully prepared, for a whole year before, by Imperial officials, whose services the Sultan has since nobly requited.

The preparations were elaborate and open. The project was known to and canvassed by all. A long report was addressed by the Abbot of Moush, Kharakhanian, to the British representative at Erzeroum, informing him of this inhuman plan, proving its real existence, and appealing to the people of England to save their Christian brethren. But international comity forbade us to meddle with the "domestic affairs of a friendly Power," and the massacre took place as advertised. Momentary glimpses of the blood-curdling scenes, as described by Turkish, Kurdish, and Armenian eye-witnesses, have since been vouchsafed us; not by the Government, which "pigeon-holed" the reports of its consuls, but by the Press. And in these dissolving views we behold long processions of misery-stricken men and women, bearing witness to the light invisible to them, as they move onward to midnight martyrdom amid the howls of their frantic torturers. The rivulets were choked up with corpses; the streams ran red with human blood; the forest glades and rocky caves were peopled with the dead and the dying; among the black ruins of once prosperous villages lay roasted infants by their mangled mothers' corpses; pits were dug at night by the wretches destined to fill them, many of whom, flung in while but lightly wounded, awoke underneath a mountain of clammy corpses, and vainly wrestled with death and with the dead, who shut them out from light and life for ever.

It was then that our present Ambassador at Constantinople took action and displayed those remarkable gifts of energy and industry to which the Prime Minister lately alluded with pride. It was owing to his enlightened initiative and indefatigable perseverance that the unfortunate Armenians. . . . But what, ask the Armenians, have we to feel grateful for? What act of clemency, what deed of humanity, do we owe to British intervention?

The British Ambassador, however, did his best. He prosecuted inquiries, studied reports, made energetic representations to the Sultan, and at last carried the appointment of a Commission of investigation. An excellent result, apparently, and the beginning of much else. Yes, but on one condition—viz., that the British Government, before beginning this arduous work, saw its way to bring it to a successful issue, and, having irritated the Turks and Kurds to fury against the Armenians by this foreign intervention, were resolved not to abandon the Christians to the mercies of the Mohammedans without foreign protection. Otherwise it was only too clear that our tardy action would turn out to be a piece of inexcusable inhumanity. This view was expressed and maintained at the time by some of the leading organs of our Press. But the Government went its way unheeding. Yet while the Commission of Inquiry was still sitting at Moush the deeds of atrocious cruelty which it was assembled to investigate were outdone under the eyes of the delegates. Threats were openly uttered that on their withdrawal massacres would be organised all over the country—massacres, it was said, in comparison with which the Sassoon butchery would compare but as dust in the balance. And elaborate preparations were made—ay, openly made, in the presence of consuls and delegates—for the perpetration of these wholesale murders; and in spite of the warnings and appeals published in England nothing was done to prevent them.

In due time they began. Over 60,000 Armenians have been butchered, and the massacres are not quite ended yet. In Trebizond, Erzeroum, Erzinghan, Hassankaleh, and numberless other places the Christians were crushed like grapes during the vintage. The frantic mob, seething and surging in the streets of the cities, swept down upon the defenceless Armenians, plundered their shops, gutted their houses, then joked and jested with the terrified victims, as cats play with mice. As rapid whirling motion produces apparent rest, so the wild frenzy of those fierce fanatical crowds resulted in a condition of seeming calmness, composure, and gentleness which, taken in connection with the unutterable brutality of their acts, was of a nature to freeze men's blood with horror. In many cases they almost caressed their victims, and actually encouraged them to hope, while preparing the instruments of slaughter.

The French mob during the Terror were men—nay, angels of mercy—compared with these Turks. Those were not insensible to compassion; in these every instinct of humanity seemed atrophied or dead. In Trebizond, on the first day of the massacre, an Armenian was coming out of a baker's shop, where he had been purchasing bread for his sick wife and family, when he was surprised by the raging crowd. Fascinated with terror, he stood still, was seized, and dashed to the ground. He pleaded piteously for mercy and pardon, and they quietly promised it; and so grim and dry was the humour of this crowd that the trembling wretch took their promise seriously and offered them his heartfelt thanks. In truth they were only joking. When they were ready to be serious they tied the man's feet together, and taunted him, but at first with the assumed gentleness that might well be mistaken for the harbinger of mercy. Then they cut off one of his hands, slapped his face with the bloody wrist, and placed it between his quivering lips. Soon afterwards they chopped off the other hand, and inquired whether he would like pen and paper to write to his wife. Others requested him to make the sign of the cross with his stumps, or with his feet, while he still possessed them, while others desired him to shout louder that his God might hear his cries for help. One of the most active members of the crowd then stepped forward and tore the man's ears from his head, after which he put them between his lips, and then flung them in his face. "That Effendi's mouth deserves to be punished for refusing such a choice morsel," exclaimed a voice in the crowd, whereupon somebody stepped forward, knocked out some of his teeth, and proceeded to cut out his tongue. "He will never blaspheme again," a pious Moslem jocosely remarked. Thereupon a dagger was placed under one of his eyes, which was scooped clean out of its socket. The hideous contortions of the man's discoloured face, the quick convulsions of his quivering body, and the sight of the ebbing blood turning the dry dust to gory mud, literally intoxicated these furious fanatics, who, having gouged out his other eye and chopped off his feet, hit upon some other excruciating tortures before cutting his throat and sending his soul "to damnation," as they expressed it. These other ingenious pain-sharpening devices, however, were such as do not lend themselves to description.

In Erzeroum, where a large tract of country, from the lofty mountains of Devi Boyen to the Black Sea shore, has just been laid waste and completely purged of Armenians, similar scenes were enacted. The vilayet of Van, the town of Hassankaleh, and numerous other places have been deluged with blood, and polluted with unbridled lust. A man in Erzeroum, hearing the tumult, and fearing for his children, who were playing in the street, went out to seek and save them. He was borne down upon by the mob. He pleaded for his life, protesting that he had always lived in peace with his Moslem neighbours, and sincerely loved them. The statement may have represented a fact, or it may have been but a plea for pity. The ring-leader, however, told him that that was the proper spirit, and would be condignly rewarded. The man was then stripped, and a chunk of his flesh cut out of his body, and jestingly offered for sale: "Good fresh meat, and dirt cheap," exclaimed some of the crowd. "Who'll buy fine dogs' meat?" echoed the amused bystanders. The writhing wretch uttered piercing screams as some of the mob, who had just come from rifling the shops, opened a bottle, and poured vinegar or some acid into the gaping wound. He called on God and man to end his agonies. But they had only begun. Soon afterwards, two little boys came up, the elder crying, "*Hairik*, *Hairik*,[3] save me! See what they've done to me!" and pointed to his head, from which the blood was streaming over his handsome face, and down his neck. The younger brother—a child of about three—was playing with a wooden toy. The agonising man was silent for a second and then, glancing at these, his children, made a frantic but vain effort to snatch a dagger from a Turk by his side. This was the signal for the renewal of his torments. The bleeding boy was finally dashed with violence against the dying father, who began to lose strength and consciousness, and the two were then pounded to death where they lay. The younger child sat near, dabbling his wooden toy in the blood of his father and brother, and looking up, now through smiles at the prettily-dressed Kurds, and now through tears at the dust-begrimed thing that had lately been his father. A slash of a sabre wound up his short experience of God's world, and the crowd turned its attentions to others.

These are but isolated scenes revealed for a brief second by the light, as it were, of a momentary lightning flesh. The worst cannot be described. And, if it could be, no description, however vivid, would convey a true notion of the dread reality. At most of these manifestations of bestial passion and delirium the Sultan's troops, in uniform, stood by as delighted spectators when they did not actually take an active part as zealous executioners.

And these are the Turks, whom unanimous Europe has judged worthy of continuing to govern and guide the Christians of Asia Minor. True, the Powers have courteously signified their desire, and the Sultan has graciously pledged his "word of honour" that these massacres shall cease. His Majesty, in fact, undertakes, if a reasonable time be given him, to re-establish the *normal* state of things in Turkish Armenia; and we know that that *normal* condition implies the denial to Christians of the fundamental rights of human beings, the refusal of elementary justice, the prevalence of universal violence and brutality, the abolition of womanly purity, the disintegration of the family, the rape of tender children—in a word, a system of "government" for which the history of the world affords no parallel.

Yet unanimous Europe, we are told, entertains no doubt that the true interests of Christendom demand that Turkish rule, as thus understood, should be maintained. And, with the genuine interests of Christianity at heart, the Great Powers are agreed to maintain it, in God's name.

If the refusal of the Powers to compel the Mohammedans of Turkey to respect the manhood, the motherhood, and maidenhood of their Christian fellow-subjects could be, and had been, based upon their religious reluctance to employ force even against superlative evil, one might question the wisdom of such forbearance, but it would be impossible to withhold respect from the principle underlying it. But such is not the plea. Those same Governments who persistently proclaim Christianity on the one hand and unblushingly support the fiendish torturers of Christians in Turkey on the other, are eager to blow each other's Christian subjects in thousands off the face of the earth—ay, and to invoke God's blessing on the work over and above.

But indefensible as the conduct of Continental nations may appear to us, it is only fair to say that none of them was pledged specially and solemnly to see justice done to the Armenians; none of them broke any solemn promise by conniving for seventeen years at every species of human villainy in Asia Minor, nor could any of them reproach themselves with having roused the sleeping devils, lashed them to fury against the Armenians, and then left the latter to be trampled upon, burned, disembowelled, and pitchforked into eternity.

This unenviable *rôle* was reserved for Great Britain. Is it to be further persisted in? And if it is, are we, as Christians—nay, as men—to give the approval of silence to a line of conduct that would disgrace a tribe of heathens? Is there any political advantage so important and so seductive that the hope of ultimately securing it should harden our hearts to utter insensibility to the laws of God, the promptings of conscience, the inborn instincts of healthy human nature? To some, even among us, it may perhaps seem possible to imitate the Christian States of Continental Europe and keep the standard of true morality hidden away, to be applied only to bygone times and buried generations. But surely the bulk of normal

Englishmen are still capable of assuming a definite attitude towards contemporary crimes, even though they have a political aspect, without staggering and reeling from the centre of Christianity to the distant and dangerous circumference.

It cannot be too clearly stated nor too widely published that what is asked for is not the establishment of an Armenian kingdom or principality, not a "buffer State," not even Christian autonomy in any sense that might render it offensive or dangerous to any of the Powers of Europe; but only that by some *efficacious* means the human beings who profess the Christian religion in Anatolia and who professed and practised it there for centuries before the Turks or Kurds were heard of, shall be enabled to live and die as human beings, and that the unparalleled crimes of which for the past seventeen years they have been the silent victims, shall speedily and once for all be put a stop to.

What serious hope is there that the lot of the Armenians will be bettered in the future? The question of the promised reforms has already ceased to be actual. The Grand Vizier, explaining lately his reasons for not publishing the Sultan's recent undertaking to better the condition of the Christians, alleged, and very truly alleged, that the present Commander of the Faithful had brought no new factor into the question that needed to be published or made known. "His Imperial Majesty," he said, "made exactly the same kind of promise, respecting the same kind of reforms, as his illustrious predecessor seventeen years ago." Exactly; and it will have precisely the same kind of results. The Christian Powers of Europe will see to this, and England's duty is admittedly to follow the Powers. Continental jurisconsults have just given it as their conscientious opinion that any special reforms for the Armenians would necessarily involve a grave violation of the rights of man and of the law of God; and the jurisconsults ought to know. If this be so, the sensitive Sultan will naturally shrink from such lawlessness and godlessness and piously shelve the reforms. The reason given by these conscientious jurisconsults is intelligent enough: because to favour any one class of the population—say the Christians—to the exclusion of the others, would be to foster race hatred, to rouse religious fanaticism, and to unchain the most furious passions that now lie dormant (?) in the Mohammedan breast. They would strongly recommend—

would these learned spokesmen of the Christian Powers—the introduction of wide-reaching reforms for *all* Turkish subjects, were it not that insuperable objections render even such a course absolutely impossible; for, in the first place, the Powers have no right to interfere in favour of the Sultan's *Mohammedan* subjects, who in this case would be mainly concerned; in the second place, the Turks and Kurds themselves desire no such reforms, are, in fact, opposed to their introduction; in the third place, they are utterly unripe for them; and, in the fourth place, general reforms for all would necessarily prove as disastrous as special reforms for Armenian Christians, because the Armenians, as the most intelligent and only self-disciplined element of the population, would profit by the improvements to obtain political preponderance for themselves. Things had better, therefore, remain as they are, with the wholesale butcheries left out; that is to say, the *normal* condition of things must be re-established, which in a very few years will solve the Armenian Question by exterminating the Armenians.

And England—Christian, moral England—apparently endorses this view, and seeks to persuade herself that by combining with the Powers to carry it out, she will have discharged all her duties, general and special, to the Christians whom she solemnly promised to protect. Is it right and proper to acquiesce even by silence in such unqualifiable conduct as this? Have the tender humanities of the teachings of Jesus no longer any virtue that can pass into our souls and move us to condemn in emphatic terms the abominations which are even now turning the lives of our brothers and sisters in Armenia into tortures and their horrible deaths into the triumph of the most ferocious malignity that ever lurked in the abysses of the human heart?

If any Englishman in any walk of life, be he a Cabinet Minister or a Yorkshire boor, had been appealed to for help by the wretched woman whose little girl was outraged to death in her presence, after she had been dishonoured in the presence of her daughter, and her husband had been killed before the eyes of both, would he have taken much time to reflect before according it? Had he witnessed the living quivering Christian's flesh being offered for sale as "fresh dogs' meat," while the wretched man's children, whom he loved more than life, stood opposite him, the one with cloven skull asking for help, the other innocently plashing with his wooden toy in the red pool fed by his father's blood, would he have suspended his judgment until Continental Christians told him what opinion he should hold concerning these fiendish ferocities? Yet these are the deeds which, in thousands and tens of thousands, are being perpetrated, while we rejoice and thank God that at last all Europe is unanimous—unanimous in its resolve to shield the *Turks*, the doers of these deeds, from harm.

If there still be a spark of divinity in our souls, or a trace of healthy human sentiment in our hearts, we shall not hesitate to record our vehement protest against these hell-born crimes, that pollute one of the fairest portions of God's earth, and our strong condemnation of any and every line of policy that may tend directly or indirectly to perpetuate or condone them.

The Spectator, Vol. 76 (February 1, 1896): 156–57

Americans and Armenians

The gleam of hope for Armenia which some of our contemporaries find in the recent resolutions of Congress is, we fear, but a faint one. That the religious section of the American public is deeply stirred by the sudden effort to extirpate this unhappy people is no doubt true; indeed, there is full evidence of it in the religious journals. Pious Americans maintain more than two hundred missionaries in Turkey, besides a great college in Constantinople, and study their reports with greater zeal and more confidence in their accuracy than is always in England bestowed upon missionary statements. The missionaries, of course, have sent the truth home; they have no doubt that the extirpation of the Armenians is intended; and narratives as horrible as those in the *Daily News* are now circulating in all the villages of New England. There is, too, a vague perception among intelligent Americans that it was Mr. Cleveland's Message which arrested the last efforts made for the victims in England, and so terminated their last hope. The religious world in America is, therefore, boiling with a just and deep indignation, and Senators and Representatives know better than even to appear to neglect this division of the electors. They are not, however, so earnest as their supporters; and their vote, though passed by enthusiastic majorities, only calls upon the Governments of Europe to do their duty and protect Armenia. That does not pledge the people of America to anything, being, in truth, only a vote of censure upon the Sultan; and the political sense of the community is, we apprehend, opposed to going further. The tradition that their business is with their own hemisphere alone is almost immovable in American minds; and they are no more prepared to shell Constantinople for massacring Armenians than to shell Nagasaki because Japanese massacred the citizens of Port Arthur. They will only intervene if

American citizens are murdered, tortured, or fined over much; and rejoiced as the Pashas would be to slaughter out the missionaries as a hint to Christendom that Islam is not dead, the cunning despot who holds them in the hollow of his hand, would, if they gave way to their desire, execute them by dozens. He is not going to risk the despatch of an American squadron to the Sea of Marmora, and as he can protect any class he chooses, he does protect Americans. We wish there were more in the hope our contemporaries express, and yet we are ready to condemn ourselves even for wishing it. The business is ours, not that of our cousins across the Atlantic. We should welcome anything which brought American and English fleets into action side by side, and enabled us to repeat, with a variation, the scene on the Peiho; but to wait for an American initiative in protecting the Armenians is beneath our dignity, as well as a dereliction of duty. If in the judgment of the statesmen of both parties, to fire the European magazine on behalf of Armenia and trust to God to regulate the event, is too dangerous a risk to run, Englishmen can only submit, and wonder whether instinct is always an unsafe guide in foreign policy; but they cannot with decency transfer to the Americans a task which properly falls upon themselves. The Americans are not, like the Russians, on the spot; they are not pledged, like the Russians, to protect the Christians of the East; and they cannot, like the Russians, benefit them directly by bringing the cruelties to a final end. We do not believe, therefore, that they will interfere, and so relieve our own people of a responsibility which they are too weak or too nervous to take on their own shoulders. There is nothing to be done, we fear, in spite of Mr. Chamberlain's vague hopes, except to await the issue of negotiations, discussions, and intrigues which are obviously going on among the Powers, and which may end in a fresh lease of life for Turkey with new and exacting allies, or in a final partition of her remaining dominion. We have, we confess, but little hope of any good result, unless this country nerves herself to a supreme effort, and can only repeat, "The mills of God grind slowly," with what of faith we may. The retribution is certain, but the time seems long even to us who sit at home at ease, and what must it seem to those who, without houses, camped in the snow of the mountain districts of Armenia, are waiting without food for that break in their destiny which may enable them to return to their ruined homes, from which their wives and children have been dragged out to murder, and worse.

It is strictly of a piece with the whole miserable story, that just as the hope of retribution disappears, the Government should begin to publish Consular reports which prove the occurrence of the earlier massacres beyond dispute. We avoid, as we have avoided all along, the details of the horrors which always occur during these massacres by armed Asiatic savages, the torture of men, especially ecclesiastics who cannot fight, the dishonour of women, and the murder of children, and content ourselves with the grave words in which Mr. Shipley, the British delegate appointed on the Joint Commission of Inquiry into the massacres at Sassoon, records his deliberate opinion:—"Although, therefore, the Turkish soldiers cannot be convicted of the sensationally exaggerated stories of massacre attributed to them in certain of the English newspapers, I do not think, seeing, as I did, in company with my colleagues, the entire ruin of a whole district, not a house being left standing, the fields even having been wantonly devastated, as well as the abject misery and destitution to which these Armenians have been reduced, that the epithets applied to the conduct of the Turkish soldiers and Kurds by the same Press are in any way too strong. We have in our report given it as our conviction, arrived at by the evidence brought before us, that the Armenians were massacred without distinction of age or sex, and, indeed, for a period of some three weeks—viz., from August 12th to September 4th (O.S.)—it is not too much to say that the Armenians were absolutely hunted like wild beasts, being killed wherever they were met, and if the slaughter was not greater, it was, I believe, solely owing to the vastness of the mountain ranges of the district, which enabled the people to scatter and so facilitated their escape. In fact, and speaking with a full sense of responsibility, I am compelled to say that the conviction has forced itself on me that it was not so much the capture of the agitator Murad, or the suppression of a pseudo-revolt, which was desired by the Turkish authorities, as the extermination, pure and simple, of the Ghéliéguzan and Talori districts." There was no provocation given by the Armenians, and indeed the women and children could have given none, while even the men had at the utmost become only saucy in demeanour. Mr. Shipley says: "The case which it was sought to establish before the Commission against the Armenians—that the latter were in open revolt, and were committing outrages on the neighbouring Kurdish population—has been sufficiently dealt with in Chapter II of the annex to our report, and I do not therefore propose to discuss it in the present Memorandum. I would, however, remark that all the cases of outrage that the Commissioners could produce were some twenty-four in number, and of these the authenticated cases were finally reduced to some half-dozen,—a very slight cause on which to found such terrible reprisals. But, I venture to repeat again, the real cause of the sending of troops in 1894, and consequent destruction of the Talori and Ghéliéguzan regions, was not the pseudo-revolt of the Armenians or the pretended outrages against the surrounding Kurdish population, but lay in the fact that the Turkish authorities were unable to brook the feeling of independence which had survived among the Armenians of that district, especially among those of Talori, and had for some time past determined to make an example of them." These particular massacres which Mr. Shipley thinks, though with evident hesitation, may have included "only" nine hundred persons, were mere child's play compared to the subsequent ones committed after the Kurds and soldiery had fully understood that the intention was to extirpate the Armenians. The latter will be found described in coming reports with much more detail, for the Consuls can give their own testimony, instead of relying, as the delegates were forced to do, on the evidence of frightened witnesses, and will be published, we doubt not, just as Europe has begun to resign itself to the triumph of Abd-ul-Hamid, who now sits in smiling content, by his own callous astuteness and the aid of Germany and Russia victorious all along the line. It is a strange story, and one which will make most Englishmen doubt whether the savage old criticism on Christianity, that it is a feminine creed, had not in it something of melancholy truth. This much at least is certain, that there is not a Mussulman community in the world, Asiatic or negro, which thus assailed would not have caught up its scythes and hatchets and garden-poles, and so have died fighting to the last. We can find no evidence in any of the narratives which have reached London that the soldiers were ever beaten, or, except at Zeitun, that they were ever defied. And Europe, with two millions of soldiers under arms ready to be mobilised, looks on calmly, intent only on preventing any one nation from interfering, even to stop massacre, by itself.

The Spectator, Vol. 76 (February 8, 1896): 193–94

Lord Salisbury and Armenia

The powerful speech which Lord Salisbury, on Friday week, addressed to the Nonconformist Unionist Association, was full of brilliant passages and generally encouraging; but on one subject its effect is, to readers if not to the audience, most depressing. Lord Salisbury appears not only to give up the cause of the Armenians for the present, but to give it up for ever. He not only pleads that Great Britain cannot save that wretched people—which, of course, if true, is a final excuse for not doing it—but that it is under no special obligation to try. He says, and says truly, that the engagement implied in the Treaty of Berlin binds no one Power more than another, all the Powers only agreeing among themselves to superintend the application of future "reforms" which the Sultan undertook to carry out, and which he of course says he is carrying out as well as he is able. Great Britain is not bound under any agreement to do more than urge her co-signatories to make the reforms real by the necessary compulsion; and if Europe will not do it, then the obligation, so far as it is based upon that Treaty, may reasonably be held to be discharged. But the Foreign Secretary also says that there is no obligation under the Convention by virtue of which we hold the guardianship of Cyprus; and surely that is a very doubtful proposition. The words of the Convention upon the subject are:—"In return (for general protection against enemies) his Imperial Majesty the Sultan promises to England to introduce necessary reforms, to be agreed upon later between the two Powers, into the Government, and for the protection of the Christian and other subjects of the Porte in these territories; and in order to enable England to make necessary provision for executing her engagement, his Imperial Majesty the Sultan further consents to assign the Island of Cyprus to be occupied and administered by England." Surely, if words have any meaning, the Sultan agreed specially with England as a separate Power to introduce reforms "for the protection of the Christians and other subjects of the Porte," and Great Britain has therefore the right to urge, and if necessary compel, the Sultan to keep his promise. That is the meaning understood in every agreement with every Power, though in no agreement, out of international courtesy, is the use of force ever distinctly specified. Lord Salisbury says he drew the clause himself, and never intended to compel England to go to war with the Sultan; but surely the right to prevent a crime implies the obligation, if prevention be possible, to do it? If a policeman insists that a burglar shall get out of the area, and the burglar goes on burgling, the obligation on the policeman to use his muscles seems clearly to arise. Lord Salisbury will hardly contend that England is not in a position of policeman, for, if so, why did she demand better treatment for Christians from Turkey any more than from France or any other Power? Her existence depends, as Lord Salisbury himself recently pointed out, upon her obedience to laws laid down for her by those who keep her alive. Indeed, in all the negotiations of the past six months, Great Britain has either been guilty of rare impertinence, or she has been interfering as one of the police of the world, to prevent the continuance of a crime which Lord Salisbury himself acknowledges to be as bad as any crime committed by Tehengis Khan, or Tamerlane, or any other of the historic enemies of the human race. Moreover, had the work not been too dangerous, Lord Salisbury would never have dreamed of questioning what the obligation of England was, but would have appealed to the country to fulfil what he would have called its duty, by a direct application of naval and military force. We do not suppose he himself would question this for a moment, and we are therefore thrown back entirely upon his second excuse.

That, if it is well founded, is final, for it is the plea of inability put in its most absolute form. A paralytic is of course not to blame if he does not stop a murder, nor a healthy policeman if he cannot reach either the murderer or his victim. Lord Salisbury says the defence of the Armenians demands the military occupation of Armenia, and the British Army cannot get there. His words are:—"If the Sultan of Turkey came and met us in the open sea, I have no doubt we could cope with five or six Sultans; but if the Sultan of Turkey is in the Taurus, near Lake Van and the Armenian vilayets, in the impassable mountains inhabited by a population of the roughest and most fanatical character, it is really not worth arguing. England by herself could not have assumed the military occupation of those provinces." We doubt the fact, as a mere fact, if Turkey stood alone, for Persia would have been delighted to aid us at a price, and Lord Roberts is one of at least ten Generals who would be delighted to fight their way from Bagdad to Armenia against any force the Sultan could bring into the field. Lord Salisbury probably forgets, as every publicist who has written on the subject, we notice, forgets, the ease with which Turkey can be assailed from the Persian Gulf by an expedition, the mere landing of which would be the signal for a universal Arab insurrection. It would, however, be too unfair to press that argument. Lord Salisbury speaks as a great diplomatist must speak, and means that we could not reach Armenia, or coerce the Sultan, by open war, with the danger hanging over us that great Powers, perhaps many of them, would intervene. We could not, for example, hope to defeat Russia and Turkey acting together in Armenia, still less Russia, Germany, and France, all combined in defence of the Sultan. To that we have no reply of any kind to offer. The statement is undeniable and unanswerable. It is doubtful if England alone could perform such a task if she devoted her whole strength to the enterprise; certain that her people would not consent for any cause whatever to run a risk which they would consider positively immoral, the risk being one of destroying in fulfilment of a single good purpose, powers which may be devoted, indeed are devoted now, to the fulfilment of many. The *non possumus* is, the assumption being granted, therefore justified, and Lord Salisbury needs, and should rely upon, no other defence. But then, are the assumptions justified? It is round that question the battle of argument will rage, and until further information is before the public, we are bound to believe that Lord Salisbury, who alone knows the facts thoroughly, has full ground for his implications. He implies that Russia declined to act, and Mr. Balfour, who is so friendly to Russia that he would let her attain her great object of a safe port in the North Pacific, repeats the statement in a still more definite way. If that is true, and we see no valid reason to doubt it, then it is most probable that Russia would have resisted the coercion of the Sultan, and as that resistance carried the certain resistance of France, and the probable resistance of Germany—which has all along been fanatically anti-Armenian—the barrier may well have been one which could not be broken without an explosion, which would have caused calamities as great as the destruction of the Armenian people. Scores of people, many of them well-informed, are saying that Russia could not have refused; that the terms offered to her were not high enough; or that the opposition of Russia should have been risked in a cause so noble and so immediate; but little of that is consistent with political sense. It is mere foolishness for irresponsible persons like ourselves, or other journalists of the same opinions, or Mr. Gladstone, or Mr. Gore, to affirm that that could be done which the Foreign Office, which knows the facts, affirms to be physically impossible. Upon any other branch of the subject discussion may continue for ever; but as to the strength to be opposed to us the Foreign Office, and the Foreign Office alone, can know the truth. If it says, as it does say, that the strength is too great to be defeated without an effort it is impossible to make, there, till the facts are controverted, is an end of the discussion. We shall see when Parliament meets on what ground the Government has made up its mind, but till the grounds are published the big fact that the Foreign Office believes its facts sufficient to justify it in accepting a damaging diplomatic defeat is, and ought to be, reason for accepting with sorrowful resignation the apparently inevitable.

What motive has influenced Europe to such a decision we are at a loss even to conceive. It is utterly unlike Russia to refuse a great province to be obtained with the consent of mankind by doing work, the protection of the Christians of the East, which she has always declared to be her special mission in dealing with her secular foe. It is utterly unlike Germany to concern herself about objects in pursuit of which she could gain nothing, and which are not worth, as Prince Bismarck said, the "bones of one Pomeranian grenadier." And it is utterly unlike France to join Germany in enabling Russia, or compelling Russia, to abstain from a profitable seizure which would have brought her general honour. There must be some explanation; but what it can be is, for the present at all events, absolutely indiscernible. Of those put forward, only one is even intelligible; and this one, that Russia hopes to acquire all Turkey with the consent of the Sultan, is to us incredible or silly. That theory actually assumes that Abd-ul-Hamid, a timid Tiberius, is slaughtering his own Christian taxpayers in order that another Christian, whom his dynasty has fought for four hundred years, may reap all the profit of the transaction. Many things may be true, but that stretches credulity too far.

The Spectator, Vol. 76 (February 22, 1896): 262–63

The Policy of Russia in Turkey

The Russians remember Plevna, though the English do not. That brief sentence contains, as we believe, the most reasonable explanation of recent Russian policy in Turkey, which without the idea conveyed in those words is very nearly inexplicable. The permanent objects of Russia are not secret; they have been pursued steadily for a century at least, and they can never be abandoned until they are attained. So long as Russia remains an undivided whole, no Russian Government, even if it took the form of a constitutional Monarchy, or of a Republic, could rest content, or even quiet, until it had established itself in peace and for ever upon the shores of the North Pacific and of the Mediterranean. Without a safe and open port in the North Pacific, connected by railway with Moscow, the wonderful possession which we call "Russia in Asia" is comparatively valueless both to the Romanoffs and their people; with it, that region may become one of the greatest white colonies in the world,—far greater than Canada, equal perhaps to the United States as they were fifty years ago. European Russia is getting overcrowded, and there is room in Asia, and maintenance for fifty millions of peasants, if only they can have quick communication and an outlet to the main waters of the world. European Russia, again, needs entrance to the Mediterranean. Without it the great Russian people have no full control of their own export trade, most of which cannot pay for a long railway journey, or—what they value nearly as much—that great position and rank among the civilised and active Powers of the world, which they think their due. If follows that a Russian Government, whether despotic or liberal, ambitious or pacific, will always try to obtain Port Arthur, or a port like it, and the control of the Dardanelles as well as of the Bosphorus. They wish for Constantinople for traditional and, in a way, "religious" reasons, but for their permanent ends Constantinople is worthless without the Dardanelles. If another Power held Gallipoli the Russians would have the Sea of Marmora for a second dock, but they would be shut out from the open water just as they are now. They want, and in the end will have, a clear road, such as is enjoyed by every other independent nation in the world—even Persia and Siam—with the exceptions only of Switzerland and Ecuador. They cannot abandon these objects, nor should we in their place, and to study Russian policy without remembering them is only to arrive at a mental *impasse*.

Well, they have within the twelve months made immense strides towards both, and the question is why they do not go a little further and a little faster. They have their grip on the Far Eastern port, it may be Port Arthur, it may be all Corea with its natural dependency the Liau-tung Peninsula, and they are, if Bulgaria remains faithful, in a position to throttle Constantinople; but they were also offered Armenia, and the question arises why they did not take it. We know quite well that "it was not offered them" in any public way; but we believe it was offered them informally, but effectively, and whether it was or was not, does not signify a straw. Circumstances offered it to them. They must have known perfectly well that Lord Salisbury could no more declare war on them for occupying Armenia than he could cut the Armenian Patriarch's throat with his own hand; and except Lord Salisbury, who was there likely to interfere? Not France, which is for the moment a dependent ally; nor Germany, which has no means of reaching the Black Sea; nor Austria, which, if she ever fights Russia, will not do it to preserve an outlying province to the Sultan, for which she must fight, if at all, without allies. Except as owner of Constantinople, what is the Sultan to the Hapsburgs? The Russians had, in fact, free hands as far as Western Europe was concerned, and the question is why they did not choose to use that unexpected advantage of international position. The popular answer, which is also their own answer, that they were afraid of a European Conference which would end in the creation of a second Bulgaria upon their Armenian frontier, is no answer at all. Europe at large does not trouble itself about the destiny of Armenia, is not even pitiful when Armenians are massacred wholesale, and the English will be contented if the massacres are prevented for ever. They might fight to rescue a perishing Christian people from the Turk; they would not fight to secure to that people more or less independence of St. Petersburg. Really independent, Turkish Armenia cannot be; and the difference between government by a Russian Viceroy, or through an Armenian dependent Prince, is not sufficient, even in the eyes of fanatics of freedom, to justify a serious war. Russia could have kept Armenia had she rescued the Armenians; and we believe she had two reasons for shrinking back, neither of which do Russians choose to allege. One was that she desires no fresh quarrel with Turkey, until the hour arrives when she may seize Constantinople and either the European or the Asiatic gate to the open water, but rather desires to see Turkey still further weakened by anarchy, misgovernment, and that gradual waste of pecuniary resources which will very soon destroy Turkey as a fighting Power. For—and this is the true, second, and ultimate reason of refusal—the Russians do not, like the English, regard Turkey as a dead Power for battle. We instinctively reason like a people of maritime State, and recognise that Turkey cannot defend her coasts; but the Russians fight by land, remember Plevna, and think the contest might prove a very serious one. The Khalif could not evacuate Armenia, except under compulsion of defeat, without offending every Osmanli in his dominions, he can still summon three hundred thousand of the bravest soldiers in the world, he has still by his side the hard-fighting and hard-hearted General who defended Plevna, and he has still, to all appearance, enough of munitions in his arsenals for a long campaign. If a new Plevna were formed in Armenia the new Plevna must be carried, and with the Osmanlis fighting, as they would think, their battle of Armageddon, that might prove a very serious business. The struggle would be in a distant corner of the Russian Empire, the troops must be drawn from the huge garrisons now encamped in the West, and the Russian Generals, whenever far from their true base, lose men in a hardly explicable proportion. Many writers attribute this to corruption, the supply departments stealing the soldiers' food and clothing; but we fancy acute Anglo-Indian doctors, without rejecting or accepting that theory, would give a different additional explanation, and declare that with any troops but the English and German, a huge standing camp involves inevitably frightful sanitary dangers, such as, for instance, have repeatedly crippled unusually large armies of Sepoys. Lord Hastings was on one memorable occasion practically defeated by his own foul latrines. Be that as it may, the fact is certain that an Armenian Plevna might involve a greater exertion than Russia, with the Triple Alliance looking on, feels at all inclined to make. Her Generals probably exaggerate the meaning of the lesson of 1877, when the Roumanians were called in by a nearly exhausted Emperor; while her financial officers know that the disastrous effects of such a protracted struggle can hardly be exaggerated. Armenia is worth a good deal to Russia; but in the present circumstances of Europe, it might not be worth, or at all events might not be deemed worth, five or six years of financial exhaustion, and a large expenditure of her best-trained men.

We do not pretend to be in Russian secrets, least of all the secrets of her frequently puzzling military organisation; but this account seems to us more reasonable than most of those put forward. We cannot believe that Russia was insensible to the advantage of gaining a long step forward on the southern shore of the Black Sea, or indifferent to the loss of prestige which she must suffer through her desertion of the cause of the Asiatic Christians of Turkey. We quite admit that to Greek Christians the Armenians are heretics, and that the race as a race are not popular, their traders being a little too acute, and their pursuit of cash a little too vigorous and persistent. But still, the Russians do not massacre Christians themselves, and strongly object to their massacre by Mahommedans; they enjoy adventure, and they regard new provinces as new sources of wealth and strength for the Empire of which they are inordinately proud. We suspect strongly that had Armenia been obtainable by the decree of the Czar, as most Englishmen appear to think it would have been, the signal for mobilisation would have been given, and Russian agents would have declared all over Asia that while the English pitied the Eastern Christians, Russia, and Russia only, rescued them from the oppressor. There must have been some serious obstacle to the adoption of so very enticing and profitable a policy, and we think we have suggested accurately what it was. It is by a fleet, as Mr. Gladstone saw, not by an army, that Turkey is always and easily to he held in check.

The Contemporary Review, Vol. 69 (February 1896): 270–76

The Armenian Question: Europe or Russia?

H. F. B. Lynch

Africa, a Syracuse for Europe, may postpone or prevent the peaceful solution of the Armenian question; but it is at least probable that when Parliament assembles Armenian affairs will receive the anxious attention which they deserve. A statement of that question, with all its essential facts and features, has already appeared in the pages of this Review; I would refer the reader to the series of articles by the present writer in the June, July, and September numbers of 1894. Those articles embody the results on the political side of my long journey both in Russian and in Turkish Armenia during the years 1893 and 1894, which included a protracted stay in Erzeroum. They record the conclusions of a simple traveller and student, whose judgment was not affected by any preconceived sympathy with the Armenians or prejudice against their rulers, Russian or Turkish. It was my endeavour to approach the subject, not only from the standpoint of the governed, but also from that of the dominant peoples and of the authorities whose protection and hospitality I enjoyed. In what concerned the solution of the Armenian question in Turkey—and that is the question with which Europe is now called upon to deal—I indicated a policy and drew the outlines of an administrative scheme which, if the one had been adopted and the other placed into execution by the Turkish Government, would, I venture to think, have composed the growing fermentation in the Armenian provinces, while maintaining their power intact, and would have saved their empire from the series of catastrophes and political crises which during the past year have shaken it to the foundations, deprived the State of the services of its most capable advisers, and alienated the goodwill of many among it truest friends abroad.

Writing under a strong sense of the present sufferings of the Armenians, and realising to the full all the horrors and human misery of which Armenia has during the past year been the scene, I should find it difficult to withhold sympathy with the Christian population should they elect to cast in their lot with the Russian Empire and to petition Europe, which has failed to carry out her solemn obligations towards them, to invite Russia to come to their aid. It does not, however, appear that any such step has been taken by the Armenians themselves, although some among the most ardent of their supporters in England have paved the way for the adoption of this course. The Armenians may prefer to drink their cup to the dregs, rather than jeopardize still further their national individuality, already menaced by Russian rule. On this, as on so many other critical occasions in the painful annals of their national history, they may prefer to submit to all the consequences of a destiny which has placed them as an advance guard to Western civilisation on the bridge which leads through Asia to the West. "We are like a wheat-field reaped by bad husbandmen," writes an Armenian historian of the tenth century when bringing his work to a close; "it is surrounded on all sides by clouds and thick mist. I cannot foresee what will happen to us in the future. We shall bow to the decrees of Providence."

But Europe will be very foolish if she wraps herself up in the illusion that this question can be indefinitely postponed. Let us suppose that the Armenians, to whom she is bound by treaty, are extirpated: would the difficulties of the situation be lessened or disappear? What would happen under such a conceivable hypothesis? The Kurds, who inhabit the border ranges of Armenia, would swarm into the settled and cultivated area of the tableland itself. The Armenians gone, their depredations would be directed against that second line of resistance which has as yet been scarcely touched: the brunt of their incursions would fall upon the Mohammedan settled population; it would be the peaceful Mohammedans who would be required during the long Armenian winter to provide this pastoral people with fodder for their cattle and with grain. With the disappearance of the Armenians all the useful arts of life would vanish or fall into disuse. The country would lapse into complete barbarism, and we should be face to face with the situation of a province bordering upon the Russian frontier, over which the Kurdish tribes swarmed unchecked, and which formed the receptacle for all the worst elements in the population of the territory under Russian rule. Such a situation could not for a moment be tolerated by Russia, and even the bare requirements of frontier protection would compel her to intervene. Russian occupation, which is now a political alternative, would then be likely to become a political necessity.

No doubt there are many persons who would not view with disfavour the occupation by Russia of Turkish Armenia, and the deliverance of the Armenians at any price. The sentiments which inspire the advocates of such a policy are among the noblest that adorn human nature. It is not necessary in this place to dwell unduly upon the weak side of the modern humanitarian movement, or do more than allude to that element, I might almost say of oriental fatalism, which renders the humanitarian spirit infirm in action when confronted with a diplomatic check. Public opinion in England has spoken loudly and decisively in the Armenian question; two ministries have taken energetic action, yet, from some reason which has not yet been sufficiently explained, their intervention remains without result. Many minds are inclined, through a feeling of sheer weariness, to abandon the irksome task, and, although the proposal does not appear to have emanated from the Armenians, to adopt the solution which the attitude of the Russian Government tends to render imperative and to open the door to the forces of the Tsar.

Yet the humanitarian spirit is but the product of Western civilisation, and it is Western civilisation pressing eastward into Asia that has brought the Armenian question to an acute phase. Will it contribute to the true interests of our civilisation that Russia should occupy Armenia? In the first place, we shall be throwing into the arms of a people who are less capable of cultivation than they a race which not only belongs by long history and tradition to the family of cultivated nations, but has displayed the most surprising aptitude within the last few decades to assimilate Western ideas. The Armenian who turns his eyes towards Russia sees the more cultivated races either driven from the Russian Empire or made the object of a constant jealousy and antipathy rather than of increasing respect. If he turns for counsel in this crisis of his national history to the spiritual head of his religion and the former leader of his nation, the Catholikos at Etchmiadzin, he is confronted by the Russian power enthroned within his sanctuary, and inspiring or paralyzing, through the machinery of the Synod, the action of the supreme ruler of his Church. He feels that, once in possession of the Turkish half of Armenia, the mask, which has hitherto scarcely veiled the policy of Russia, will be completely cast aside, that there will be an end to his national individuality and to the language and religion which through so many long centuries of subservience he has upheld and preserved intact.

But, in the second place, the question raises wider and more momentous issues than the fate of the Armenian race. Once Russia has moved across her well-defined natural frontier, has occupied the provinces of Turkish Armenia and the passes which open west and south, she is in command of an imposing strategical position which is a menace alike to the Mediterranean Powers and to ourselves upon the Indian seas. Mere distance from the Mediterranean and from India is not an adequate—nay, it is a most fallacious—measure of the value of Armenia from a strategical point of view. We might avoid many grave political errors if our maps were constructed in relief. Never better than in Armenia was exemplified the saying that he who is master of the sources of a river is a master of the river itself. Vast alluvial plains, which were at one period an arm of the sea, extend uninterrupted from the mountain girdle of Armenia to the head of the Persian Gulf, and they are traversed by the mighty streams of the Euphrates and Tigris, which rise upon the Armenian tableland. From Balis which is only one hundred miles from the Mediterranean, from Mosul which is closer to Lake Van than is Tiflis, you have the navigable waterway of two magnificent rivers, which are so well adapted for transport on a large scale, and water countries so thinly populated that, in a military sense, they may almost be said to annihilate space. As a natural corollary Persia falls to Russia, and a Russian fleet rides in the Persian Gulf. Nor is the position less commanding if we turn our eyes towards the west. Erzeroum, the gate of Asia Minor, is situated at the head of that great natural passage which, branching off into numerous smaller bifurcations, leads westwards to the Mediterranean Sea.

Would Western civilisation be the gainer or the loser by such extension, amounting to predominance, of the Russian power? The many amiable qualities of the Russian character, which perhaps no person is better qualified to appreciate than the traveller who has enjoyed Russian hospitality, disarm those feelings of unreasoning antipathy which, when once they have arisen between nations, are the most difficult to allay. But the Russian Government has unhappily precluded itself from appealing to the higher instincts of the cultivated European peoples. Their ruthless treatment of the Jews, their crude panslavic policy, nay, the recent persecution of that handful of Russian colonists in Armenia who are religious exiles rather than colonists, debar them from such an appeal. Their commercial policy is not calculated to enlist the goodwill of the commercial classes in Europe: they have sealed up that natural avenue of western commerce with Asia by the Black Sea and the valley of the Kur. In this manner they have themselves afforded the strongest and most realistic arguments to those who still see in the Russian Empire a menace to all that Europe holds dear, and who quote the prophecy of the first Napoleon, that Europe would again be overrun, and her institutions overturned by the barbarians of the North.

Such are some of the larger issues raised by the Armenian question. I can do no more in this place than remind the reader of the true nature of that question itself, to the end that he may not be diverted by interested parties to the consideration of large schemes for the immediate regeneration of the Turkish Empire which they know cannot be carried out. As I have shown in the third of my previous articles, the Armenian question is by no means primarily a question of the better government of all the Asiatic provinces of the Sultan which contain an Armenian element in their population. Primarily it is a question of the better administration of the country inhabited by peaceable Armenians and Mohammedans, and overrun by the lawless Kurdish tribes. The same conditions, historical and social, which obtain in the country east of the Euphrates, I mean in Armenia proper, are not found, or are found only to a limited extent, in the provinces which lie upon the west. In those provinces there is no acute Kurdish-Armenian question, and it is that question which is the kernel of the Armenian question, and which is, in some respects, the most difficult to treat. To our failure to grapple with that administrative problem no less than to the squandering of the motive power at our disposal in the attempt to reform all Turkish abuses over the greater part of Asia Minor at once, may be attributed in a great measure the lamentable want of success which attended the efforts of our ambassador and his military consuls after the last Russo-Turkish war. If you journey over the whole extent of Armenia proper subject to the Sultan's rule, what are the grievances on the part of the Christian population which fill the eye and besiege the ear? Measures to redress the inequality of Christians and Mohammedans, reforms of the judicial system, an improved scheme of communal government—not a word will you hear of all these. Still less, in that dull atmosphere of poverty and misery, is the imagination roused by visions of an Armenian governor-general, and of an independent Armenian State. It is the absence of all security for life and property, it is the spectacle of an unarmed Christian population exposed to an organised system of outrage and exaction on the part of armed Kurdish tribes that arrest the traveller's interest, and divert it from those much less elementary questions which have been raised in connection with the Armenian cause.

The valuable "Memorandum" attached to the stillborn scheme of reforms which was the work of the Government of Lord Rosebery, and which is known as the "May scheme," lays particular emphasis upon the necessity of carefully selecting and strengthening the hands of the provincial governors, and contemplates an eventual reduction in the number of vilayets. Both this memorandum and these provisions appear to have been eliminated from the scheme accepted by the Government of Lord Salisbury, and sanctioned by the Sultan in October last. Had they been adopted it would at least have been possible, under the scheme, to lay the foundations of a strong and centralised provincial administration in the country east of the Euphrates, and to deal in a drastic manner with the Kurdish difficulty which lies at the root of the Armenian question itself. When once there has been established a sound system of social order in Armenia proper, in the provinces east of the Euphrates, the Turkish Empire well be relieved of the constant pressure upon its resources of military measures against the Kurds, and Europe will be freed from the standing menace to her highest interests which is offered by the condition of desolation and anarchy to which these provinces have gradually been reduced.

But there is a certain unreality in discussing at this hour the actual practical requirements of the case. Diplomacy has taken action, and our diplomacy has suffered a humiliating defeat. Who is the author and cause of that defeat and humiliation? I trust this question will be immediately cleared up. It is not the Sultan: he is unable to resist the will of the European Powers when once it has been decisively expressed. It is not the pressure of racial and anti-Christian feeling in Turkey, overriding the good intentions of the Porte: the Mohammedans themselves have joined in petitions for the redress of grievances which they share with their fellow-subjects of Christian faith. The leading Turkish statesmen, far from maintaining obstacles to the policy of reform, have themselves been overthrown from behind in their efforts to remove them and to effect an agreement with the Ambassadors. All that is best within the ranks of Turkish officialdom, all that is sturdiest in the national life, has been drawn, as might be expected, into the same vortex down which the sinking Armenians have disappeared. The Kurdish party, always strong at Constantinople, the party of destruction and disintegration, have seized upon the reins of State, and are involving Turks and Christians alike in the common ruin which no hand appears able to stay. That such a party should have been able, without assistance from outside, at once to defy the European Powers and to overrule the better elements in Turkey itself, it exceeds the bounds of possibility to suppose. It is a question, very plainly, of an undisclosed principal, and it is the question, inevitable in all such cases, *Cui bono*? Which of the Powers does it profit to see the Turkish Empire in tatters and its subjects beating at Europe's door?

That Europe is able to arrive at a satisfactory solution of the Armenian question without the extreme measure of a Russian occupation there can surely be little doubt. If it is indeed Russia who is thwarting all attempts at such a solution, Europe may well pause before she commits herself to the dangerous expedient of entrusting her with a mandate to occupy Armenia, and restore peace. Let Europe at least know the measure of her own pusillanimity and the Armenians know their true enemies. We are surely not so foolish as to be blinded by the diplomatic sophism that Russia is justified in resisting the forcible intervention of Europe in the affairs of the

Turkish Empire on the ground that she has on so many occasions been prevented by Europe from intervening in this manner herself. In the first place, the use of force becomes a most remote contingency if the voice of Russia and the voices of other European powers sound in concert upon this question. Secondly, the plain object of European intervention is not territorial aggrandisement, but the maintenance of the territorial *status quo*. Nor again, would it be necessary for any one Power to intervene singly, and by so doing perhaps to raise the suspicions of the rest. In Armenia itself, if the Turkish authorities are by themselves incompetent to deal with the present aggravated situation, the difficulty might be met by the enrolment of a police force recruited from all European nations alike.

European enterprise developing their resources, European commerce spreading over them her net of peace, the healthy rivalry of Germans and Belgians and Englishmen in a field which is open to all, America, foremost in the van of nations, sowing broadcast the seeds of her religion and culture which dare not cross the threshold of Russian soil—such are the better signs of the present times in the countries between India and the Mediterranean, and along this path let us hope that, in spite of many interruptions and much hard travelling, their people will continue to walk. No race is better fitted than is the Armenian to be the mediary between West and East, and it is not unreasonable to expect that he will some day reap the harvest which has been sown amongst such bitter tears.

For ourselves the special and extraordinary responsibilities under which we are placed in respect of the Armenians should incite us to make fresh efforts to fulfil our obligations, much as some may be inclined at the first sign of resistance to retire and abandon the field. The Government of Lord Rosebery, although supported by a slender and withering majority, and doomed to a precarious life, yet took a large view of our duties under our hereditary policy, and, gaining assistance from whatever quarter it chanced to offer, came near to enforcing measures of reform. Of the soundness of that hereditary policy, of the possibility of giving to it effect, I have myself never entertained any doubt; but I recognise that I speak without diplomatic experience, although I speak with some knowledge of the countries on the west of India, and with some practical acquaintance with their affairs. England is now placed under a Government entrusted with a long lease of power, and able to plan and to mature those combinations and calculations without which any policy, however straightforward, is liable to defeat. That Government will indeed have deserved well of the country if, far from squandering power over controversies more or less meritorious with the most civilised nations of the world, it proceeds with fixed concentration of purpose towards the fulfilment of that policy in respect of the population of the Turkish Empire to which we are so deeply pledged.

The Fortnightly Review, Vol. 65 (March 1, 1896): 341–58

The Fiasco in Armenia

E. J. Dillon

It is said that there is a special providence watching over children, tipplers, and other more or less helpless creatures who not unfrequently escape grave dangers without being aware of their proximity or understanding their nature. And a good deal might be urged in support of the assertion. But there would seem to be no doubt whatever that there is some analogous celestial machinery beneficently influencing the fate of favoured peoples at certain turning points in their history, when the national Palinurus is peacefully nodding at the helm. And few nations owe such a lasting debt of gratitude to their good genius as the British, whose heavenly patron, whether we call him St. Peter, St. George, or Good Luck, has extricated them from many an awkward difficulty into which they listlessly drifted of late years. Yet, strange to say, we, of all nations of the earth, should be least dependent upon the intervention of this *deus ex machina*—upon the presumptuous hope of "something turning up." For if our world-wide reputation be a safe guide, we alone adopt all conceivable measures for the attainment of our political aims, thoughtfully provide for the least probable contingencies, and leave practically nothing to chance; our diplomacy is a refinement upon Machiavelism; our foreign policy a maze of well-laid plans and audacious projects, which are being realised mainly by the folly of our neighbours; our intelligence office is the most perfectly organized in Christendom, and in the adjustment of means to ends we are firm believers in the purifying virtues of success.

In truth, we have as little reason to feel elated by the good, as depressed by the repulsive traits of this absurd description which is refuted by a series of alarming facts that no optimism can contrive to gloss over. Our information concerning the designs and the resources of other nations is seldom complete or trustworthy, and when it happens to be moment has irrevocably gone by. Our information concerning the designs and resources of other nations is seldom complete or trustworthy, and when it happens to be both, we never dream of drawing the practical consequences until the psychological moment has irrevocably gone by. Our professional politicians are hardly ever in touch, even indirectly, with the foreign people with whom they have to deal, and those upon whose reports they rely affect to despise the systematic calumnies of the Continental press and to ignore the misgivings with which foreign statesmen regard our most indifferent political moves and our most praiseworthy intentions. A lively Continental politician, unduly fond of exaggeration, once expressed his view of professional British politicians as follows: "Your representatives abroad move in well-worn grooves of old-world diplomacy which lead mainly to No-Thoroughfares. They stalk about in state carrying their heads erect *comme un saint sacrement*, proud in their consciousness of excellent intentions, and full of scorn for the opinions of the mere people in the street which often come to be the views of the people in the Ministries. They seem to take it for granted that good intentions leave an impress on the forehead of a halo round the head which all who run may see."

It is doubtless far better to hear accusations of this nature than to be confronted with complaints that our representatives have recourse to the doubtful methods of which foreign governments now and then avail themselves to acquire information and to silence press campaigns. But even here there are limits which cannot be outstepped with impunity, as we now know to our cost. No one who remembers the implicit reliance which we were ready to place upon China's inexhaustible resources, or, indeed, any of the numerous blunders which lack of information or of insight led us to commit during the past twenty years, will feel disposed to call for other instances of the danger we thus wantonly court.

If another instance were needeed, I should unhesitatingly point to our utter fiasco in Armenia, the avoidable causes of which constitute a superfluous proof of the fact that a good heart may become a curse instead of a blessing when divorced from a clear head.

Lord Salisbury has assured us, and it is impossible to doubt his assertion, that England is utterly powerless to alleviate the lot of the Armenians in Turkey, so that if the Commander of the true believers felt disposed to butcher all his unbelieving subjects tomorrow we should have to choose between the offer of our unavailing sympathy with the sufferers and a war with all Europe. It is natural to ask, and it would be interesting to learn, whether this unenviable situation is the result of very sudden and very recent events, or is identical with the position in which we found ourselves when our Government decided to place the Armenian question as the order of the day eighteen months ago. Who placed us in this awkward and cruel dilemma? Some say it was this Continental Power, others point to that; while it is admitted on all hands that the intentions of the English people were prompted by the spirit of true Christian charity, which their rulers failed to embody in efficacious acts. And these replies are substantially correct. The moral responsibility for the massacres that succeeded the butchery of Sassoon does undoubtedly lie at the door of foreign nations; but our blunder—in this case more fatal than a crime—consists in our culpable ignorance of the palpable fact that those nations were from the very first quite prepared to take upon themselves this responsibility. The situation to-day is exactly what it was eighteen months ago, and thousands of Armenian Christians have been murdered in cold blood, simply because we failed to read it aright. The ethical bearings of the Armenian massacres have been dwelt upon with such fulness of detail that nothing more remains to be done than apportion the blame—a task which may fitly be left to the historian; the diplomatic aspect of the question, however, the chain of causes which necessarily led to the fiasco of British policy in the East, is well deserving of a careful study.

Personally I am disposed to attribute our diplomatic defeat, which I ventured to predict as far back as December, 1894, to the unceremonious manner in which we baited the Sultan from the very first, without reflecting that we were driving him into the arms of Russia, and without taking means to prevent his cordial reception by that Power; to the reasonable distrust of our Eastern policy felt by the Tsar's Government, who are masters of the situation—a feeling which we took no pains whatever to dispel; to our ignorance of the fact that Germany was resolved to follow Russia through thick and thin, not merely against England, but even to the detriment of what heretofore were considered the interests of her Austrian ally; and to our taking it for granted that the co-operation promised and duly given to us by Russia, in a purely academic inquiry, would, as a matter of course, be continued to the extent of employing force against the Ottoman Empire. These causes, while they fully explain our diplomatic failure, in no wise lessen the moral responsibility of those who, by the facilities they unhesitatingly afforded for the shedding of innocent blood, have contributed to attach a new and odious meaning to the words Christianity and civilisation.

As soon as the rumours of a massacre of Christians in the Sassoon district were confirmed in essentials, the task which fell to our Foreign Secretary was of a most arduous and delicate nature. It was, of course, out of the question to treat the matter lightly without provoking an outburst of indignation against the Government of the day in England, although the crime was hardly more horrible than those which had been committed continuously for several years before. The difference was that the cruelties perpetrated previously were spread over a larger area, and the consular reports describing them could be conveniently withheld from the public, while the butchery of Sassoon was bound to leak out. Viewing the occurrence, therefore, in a tragic light, there were but two courses open: either to arrange the matter *à l'aimable* with the Sultan, skillfully working upon himself and his advisers, and endeavouring, by a judicious mixture of advice, persuasion, and veiled threats, to bring the responsible officials to punishment and obtain a guarantee that no such wholesale massacres would be permitted in future; or else to sound the international tocsin and call upon Europe to intervene. If there were reasonable grounds—and I hold that the grounds were conclusive—for believing that, under the actual circumstances, the latter course would be fraught with disastrous results and barren of good, then it was the primary duty of the Liberal Government to adopt the former of these alternatives, even at the risk of temporarily alienating the sympathies of the electors who were not acquainted with the essential factors of the problem, and were, therefore, incapable of forming an unbiased judgment.

And it cannot be doubted that this line of action would have proved fairly successful. Had we begun to deliver our strictures on the Sultan's conduct in a lower pitch, raising it very gradually to the point which we rashly took at the very beginning, we should have lost absolutely nothing and gained a triumph all the more substantial that it seemed hardly worth striving for. Several times during the course of the negotiations, the Sultan, trembling for his throne, yielded to our just demands: thus, he reluctantly instituted an inquiry into the massacre at Sassoon; he accepted the unpalatable conditions which our Government attached to the participation of our consular agent in that inquiry; he consented to make the investigation international by inviting the co-operation of France and Russia; he summarily dismissed Tahsin Pasha, the Vali of Bitlis, &c.; and his concessions might easily have been made to include the punishment of the principal murderers of Sassoon and a reasonable guarantee that wholesale massacres at least should not occur in future, had he had reason to suppose that our demands would, for the time being, stop here.

Unquestionably those results would have lacked the brilliancy of a triumph worthy of being paraded before the British electorate. But, modest as they must have appeared, any Government might well be proud of the foresight and diplomatic skill that enabled it to deliver thousands of Christians from the jaws of a horrible death. Moreover, when a man is playing a losing game, it may well be deemed a positive gain if he ceases play when he has lost but one-half of his substance. In like manner, it would have proved an enormous advantage to Armenia, to Great Britain, and to humanity at large, had we contented ourselves with saving the lives that had been spared, before the Sassoon massacre was followed and eclipsed by those of Trebizond, Erzeroum, Arabghir, &c.

As a matter of fact, however, neither of these two courses was adopted unreservedly; each was attempted in turn, and both begun at what the light of subsequent events reveals, even to the "man in the street," as the wrong end.

At first the Sultan was taken in hand, and was treated with a candid lack of consideration which, while exactly commensurate with his deserts, and admirably reflecting the just indignation of the British public, was diplomatically justifiable only on the condition that we were prepared to raise our tone *crescendo* until it became lost in the blast of bugles and the roar of heavy guns. And this is what we were not prepared to do. We began in the wrong key. Our feelings of horror and disgust were diplomatically expressed in remarkably emphatic language; threats, veiled and unveiled, were employed with a frequency which it might be expected would render their fulfillment superfluous, and every heroic expedient short of a diplomatic rupture was hopefully resorted to. But the Sultan refused to yield, because we had already appealed to Europe; and if he did not exactly apprehend that compliance with the demands of one Power might seriously embroil him with another, he might reasonably hope, what our Foreign Minister apparently never feared, that by playing off one Government against another, he might be allowed to go his way and sin as before. So he not only rejected but resented our "friendly advice," and sat still awaiting developments.

The Turk is a very peculiar person to deal with, and it must be allowed that our Liberal Government dealt with him in a very peculiar way. To manage him successfully is a task that requires uncommon skill. Practical psychology needs a special chapter to treat of his crotchets and idiosyncrasies. He takes nothing for granted. All propositions, including such as embody first principles, must be demonstrated before he accepts them as premises for argument, and something further has to be accomplished before he consents to regard them as a basis for action. In diplomacy he can give points to the "heathen Chinese." He never abandons a game of political chess till he is actually checkmated, and not even then unless the king is literally removed from the board. He sets greater store by form than by matter, and is more easily moved by an act of courtesy than persuaded by the most clinching of syllogisms.

On the other hand, the fact cannot be blinked that the Ottoman Government is practically inaccessible to mere argument, and can be influenced for good only by methods to which no diplomatist would dream of having recourse elsewhere. But then to be efficacious there must be brute force behind them. And if our Liberal Government had been prepared to enforce its demands at the mouth of the cannon or the point of the bayonet, we might now add up, with a sort of pious delight, the drops of gall and wormwood which it contrived to infuse into the unholy pleasures of the harem of Yeldiz Kiosk during the progress of negotiations. Certainly if emphasis, energy, and ardent zeal could have saved the lives or our *protégés*, many thousands of Armenians whom our well-meant efforts have hurled to destruction would now be living in hope, and possibly in peace, in Van, Arabghir, Trebizond, and Erzeroum. From the despatches recently published in the two bulky Blue Books we learn that athwart the seams in the courtly phraseology which it was difficult wholly to discard, frankness, indignation, and other homely qualities were continually struggling upwards to the light. Thus our Ambassador, whose manly, forcible, and menacing language is the exact reflex of the sentiments of the entire British people, telegraphs to Lord Kimberley:—"I am sending to the Palace a *strong* message in reply to this communication, and I am writing to Said Pasha *in still stronger* terms to point out the *danger* of delay."[1] "I spoke with *considerable warmth*, *and declined to remain and discuss the matter*."[2] "I impressed upon his Excellency (Said Pasha) *as forcibly as I could* that *the only safe* course for the Turkish Government was to authorize the Commission to make a fair and impartial inquiry; that failing this, they would be held responsible for the cruelties perpetrated on the Armenians by the local authorities, and *that the feeling aroused in Europe was such that if these cruelties were not punished, active interference from without must be looked for*. . . . Throughout our conversation I spoke in a *tone of friendly warning* and advice."[3]

And Lord Kimberley ably supported the Ambassador; thus he says of a conversation with Rustem Pasha, "who expressed this great concern at the aspect which the question had assumed":—"I told him that I deeply regretted the situation which had been created by the Sultan's action, and that I desired as earnestly as did his Excellency to avert, *if possible*, the consequences which might follow." The inference, of course, was clear: the evil had been done, and now no man could say where it would stop; if the Porte had only listened to the friendly warnings of England, the empire might hold together for an indefinite time to come, but now . . .

It is impossible for an Englishman to read these despatches, and to note the offhand, fearless, nay reckless, way in which the Turkish bull was taken by the horns, without feeling a thrill of pride at the thought, *civis Romanus sum*. It is only when we find the bull transformed into a cruel dilemma, on one of whose horns we must take our goring, that the angle of vision undergoes a change, and a very painful change. Every one will admit that the means chosen by the late Liberal Government to obtain surcease of sorrow for the Armenians were admirably adapted to the end in view, provided that they really meant all that they said and implied. And what they both said and implied by their words and their acts was, that a refusal on the part of the Porte to comply with the demands of Lord Kimberley and the requirements of civilisation would be punished with "active interference from without," and all that active interference might mean for the Ottoman Empire in general and for the Sultan in particular. Now this presupposed one of two things: either that England herself was prepared to interfere actively, and had made sure that the Continental Powers would stand by encouragingly, or at least be benevolently indifferent; or else that some other Government or Governments had promised to take the matter in hand, and, should the Porte prove obstinate, would proceed to extremities. In the certitude that one or other of these alternatives had been duly provided for lay the only justification, not merely for the very vigorous language employed in the course of the protracted negotiations, but likewise for the attitude assumed by our Government towards the Porte and towards Russia *from the very first.*

Let there be no mistake as to my meaning. If the Powers of Europe possessed Christianity as a grain of mustard-seed they would have swept away the Turkish Empire root and branch years ago; and if the Mohammedans who conceived and executed the massacre of Sassoon, and the tortures and murders that preceded it, had their deserts, it is not the diplomatist but the hangman who would have been called in, and with a *posse* of extra assistants. But the question which our Government was called on to tackle was not a point of ethics nor the bearings of a statute law, but a problem in practical diplomacy—viz., what attitude had best be adopted towards the Porte in order to obtain the punishment of the murderers of Sassoon and a guarantee that such crimes would be rendered impossible in future. Conciliation or coercion? The question cannot be said to have been sprung upon them by surprise. For a considerable time previous to the massacre they knew it was coming. They were in possession of numerous consular reports of an alarming character which, for reasons of their own, they persistently pigeon-holed, and the butchery itself was foretold clearly and definitely over a twelvemonth before in a memorandum drawn up by a high ecclesiastic in Armenia and addressed to a British consular agent.

But even if they had been in blameless ignorance of all this, Lord Kimberley and his colleagues might and should have known that to attempt to coerce the Turks without possessing or providing the means of doing so, without ascertaining whether force would be eventually employed, or at any rate permitted, by Russia and France; in a word, that reliance on a presumptuous hope that something would turn up and make things all right in the end was to jeopardise interests far more important than any which were apparently involved in the issue. Other people knew this, and the Government should have known it. As a matter of fact, they were either ignorant of all this, or at any rate they acted as if they were, and their extraordinary tactics utterly defeated the ends in view, irritated the morbid sensibilities of a fanatic people, cost the lives of twenty-six thousand Armenians, and brought shame and discredit upon our nation. The theory that a responsible government should stoop to the employment of mere bluff and bluster in the belief that the wily Turk could thus be bullied into compliance with its wishes, is one that Englishmen of all shades of political opinion will be very slow to accept as the explanation of the fiasco in Armenia. Yet it is the only theory that tallies with the known facts, and with these facts before us the utmost that charity moves us to assume is that our representatives, who, on receiving intelligence of the crime of Sassoon, dashed forward boldly and hopefully, as if executing a plan of campaign which had long since been carefully prepared, were inspired by the courage born of unblissful ignorance, and buoyed up by the confidence drawn from the harmlessness of past mistakes.

Few political blunders have proved more fruitful of disaster than the implicit trust with which our Government looked forward to the active co-operation of certain Continental Powers against the Turks. For that fatal mistake cost the lives of about thirty times the number of Christians slaughtered in Sassoon, and its far-reaching effects are not yet wholly exhausted. And, incredible though it may sound, there were no solid grounds for this hope, no reasonable excuse for this precipitate action. It was based neither upon a diplomatic promise nor upon the trend of European public opinion.

True, the despatches of the Blue Books that reproduce the conversations of our Foreign Secretary and Ambassador, allude to Continental co-operation with England as confidently as if it had been stipulated for in a formal treaty. But, on the other hand, it should be remembered that those allusions were made in conversations with the Turks to be coerced, and the only ground alleged for them in the despatches is one which it is impossible to read without a bitter smile. It occurs in the account of a conversation that passed between the British Ambassador in Constantinople and Said Pasha, Sir Ph. Currie assuring his Excellency that "the feeling aroused in Europe was such that if those cruelties were not punished, active interference from without must be looked for." [Blue Book No. 1, Despatch No. 66.]

Continental Europe is evidently meant here, because, without its active assistance or friendly permission, England could not resort to force against Turkey; and our statesmen were aware of this from the first. Now Continental Europe never felt the slightest thrill of indignation, probably not even of mild surprise, hardly knew indeed that it had any occasion to feel either. The German newspapers consistently ignored the stories of cruelty that were published in the English press, cordially supported the Turks and warmly eulogized the Sultan; when the truth at last came out, and could no longer conveniently be hushed up, it was summarized and euphemized as the severe but just repression of a wicked rebellion. Of indignation in Germany there never was a trace. The Austrian press simply sneered at the gullibility of the simple-minded English, and preached panegyrics of the Sultan, on the text, "Well done, thou good and faithful servant." The Italians remained indifferent down to last summer, when the publication of certain trustworthy details rendered them curious and interested. Their indignation resembled the light recently discovered by Professor Röntgen in that it was invisible to the human eye. The French mastered their feelings so successfully and preserved such an appearance of good humour that none but a Liberal politician could divine the rage that boiled beneath the surface. The Russian press alone was indignant, exceedingly indignant, that the Armenian question should be raised at such an inconvenient time, and, of all nations of the world, by England. "The feeling aroused in Europe!" How the wily Turk must have laughed in his sleeve when he was asked to believe in it and tremble! And if public opinion on the Continent was hardly of a nature to warrant the firm reliance upon energetic co-operation thus confidently expressed by British statesmen in their lively conversational encounters with their Mohammedan colleagues, the temper of Continental diplomacy was still less calculated to nourish this extraordinary delusion.

The Russian Government, which was most of all interested in the possible upshot of the Armenian Question, bitterly resented our methods, and profoundly distrusted our aims. And this on grounds which politicians cannot fail to appreciate, however sincerely moralists may deplore the consequences that ensued therefrom. Ever since the Treaty of Berlin the Oriental problem had been narrowed down to a vain but sharp competition for ascendancy over the Sultan among the foreign ambassadors at Constantinople; the German representative wisely hungering after commercial or financial concessions, and the others thirsting for purely political influence. As long as the prospect of actual hostilities was entirely shut out, this exciting game was played with varying results, which drew their importance from the optimism of the player; now the Sultan gives three-quarters-of-an-hour's audience to Sir William White, or Sir Philip Currie, and the momentous fact is telegraphed as a British victory to the four corners of the earth; now his Majesty chats with M. de Nelidoff for fully ninety minutes, and the existence of a Russo-Turkish Convention is inferred as probable; another day Abdul Hamid is peculiarly gracious to Baron Calice, and unusually amiable to Prince Radolin, or else invites General Brialmont to sail about the Bosphorus, and forthwith it is "credibly reported" that Turkey is negotiating for a place in the Triple Alliance. Ambassadors might come and ambassadors might go, but this time-killing game went on forever. All of a sudden, however, the rules of this interesting little whist party were rudely transgressed; the British ambassador, speaking figuratively, seized, instead of an ace of clubs from the regulation pack, a genuine gnarled oak bludgeon, and took to brandishing that as trumps. It practically came to that. For while the other ambassadors confined themselves in their dealings with the Sultan to reminiscences of past services, promises for the future, delicate flattery or covert criticism, Sir Philip Currie confronted him with a ready-made sphinx problem, which threatened to bring destruction, not merely upon the Ottoman Empire, but even upon the person of the Commander of the Faithful himself.

From a British point of view this seemed a most admirable move; for if the aim was political, it deserved our hearty approval as patriots; if the object was disinterested, it commanded our sympathy and support as Christians and as men, and bade fair to secure for us all desirable political advantages over and above. But there are other standpoints than the British, and it is worth while striving to realise how it looked from a more northerly angle of vision. Russia took greater umbrage at these tactics than even Turkey; for if successful they were capable of giving us the whip hand of the Sublime Porte, for which Muscovite diplomacy had been toiling and moiling for long years, and of rendering Great Britain the arbiter of the fate of the Ottoman Empire, a consummation which the Tsar's Foreign Secretary could not be expected to contemplate with equanimity.

And yet with this data before our eyes we were simple-minded enough to believe, and even to act upon the belief, that we should have no difficulty in obtaining the help of a Continental Power to carry out our plan; and that this Power was none other than Russia. What a golden age of innocence this nineteenth century of ours would be, were all diplomatists thus equipped with the simplicity of the dove, and untainted by the wisdom of the serpent!

But in sober truth this sudden raising of the Armenian Question by the Liberal Government was anything but a mere political manœuvre for selfish ends. Whatever considerations may have weighed with the British statesmen who, at the close of the Russo-Turkish war, insisted on handing back to Turkish misrule the Christian provinces that had just been ransomed from the Mohammedan yoke, our intervention after the massacre of Sassoon was inspired by unimpeachable motives of elementary humanity. We were fully prepared to forget, nay to sacrifice, what we had therefore regarded as our interests in the East, for the purpose of assuaging the sufferings of Armenian Christians. But when a sharp and protracted competition between two well-matched nations is complicated by present friction, and embittered by past memories, it is hardly natural that either should give its rival credit for a degree of unselfishness which beats the diplomatic record. And Russian statesmen were all the more distrustful that honesty was, in this case, the very best policy we could have pursued. What they practically said to our overtures on the subject was this: "Carry out your plan if you are equal to the task; if not, you have no business to arrogate to yourselves the right of taking the initiative and of garnering in all the political advantages which the leading *rôle*, if played successfully, is bound to confer." Outsiders who expected one of those noble outbursts of sympathy with human suffering which characterize the Slavonic race, are horrified at the thought that abandoned murderers who richly deserve the abhorrence of mankind should be thus shielded from human justice by the narrow-minded policy of a Christian power, which has eyes only for the petty triumphs of the diplomatic green table; but professional politicians who look upon selfish views as a matter of course, declare the arguments unanswerable and the attitude correct.

But it was not with our tactics only that the Russians found fault. They had no sympathy whatever with our avowed aim, and they received the theory of our unselfishness and Christian sympathy with a significant smile, hardly distinguishable from a sneer. A Saul, they admitted, might be found among the prophets, but a "nation of shopkeepers" could hardly stray into the regions of idealism without the operation of some marvellous miracle. For the sake of that very influence in Constantinople to which we now professed indifference, and which our tactics were none the less calculated to secure, we had for fifteen years connived at a state of things in Turkey which depopulated whole provinces and cost far more lives than were sacrificed at Sassoon. During that time the question was frequently asked, "Where is England's guarantee to Armenian and Macedonian Christians now?" That this awkward query, and still more unpalatable comments, were never couched in diplomatic forms is no excuse for ignoring them. The Russian press was not slow to give them prominence, and our deafness to the cries of the suffering Christian was a commonplace of journalistic politicians, who rightly ascribed it to a narrow-minded policy of which a great nation should be heartily ashamed.

Was it not natural that the moment we took a fresh departure the motives ascribed to our action should be equally selfish and egotistic? It is to be wondered at that when our Ambassador, with the reports from Consul Hallward in his possession, felt that he had a trump card in his hand, and played it with energy and confidence, he was informed by his partners in the game that it could not be allowed, as it was the result of a revoke? Why was the year 1894 chosen for opening up the Oriental Question instead of the year 1888 or 1892, seeing that the grounds were identical in all three? Was it not because the "psychological moment" had, in the opinion of the British Government, arrived? Why else were the damning reports of our consular agents withheld? Nay, why, even during these very negotiations, was the threat to publish them held over the Sultan's head and their suppression promised as a reward for submission? What other interpretation could be put upon such passages in the despatches as these: "I[4] intimated that if steps were not taken to satisfy her Majesty's Government that the Sultan's promise[5] would be fulfilled, they might find it necessary to inquire into the treatment of the Armenians, and *that they might also be forced to publish the consular reports from the Asiatic provinces which had been so long withheld*"?[6]

Was this play at fast and loose with a primary duty consistent with professions of Christianity, sympathy with human suffering, and all the rest of it, ask our Continental critics. If England was actuated solely by a sense of duty, how comes it that that duty is persistently ignored for years and remembered only at a time when its performance seems calculated to bring her in substantial political advantage? No doubt our responsible statesmen could furnish a plausible explanation of this curious procedure; but we can hardly affect surprise to learn that it was regarded by our Continental rivals as a political trick.

In politics the Russians are preternaturally suspicious of foreigners, and they affect to be particularly distrustful of Englishmen. Like Mrs. Snitchey when she gazed upon Craggs, they pretend that they can read a double purpose in our eye. And in this case they were enabled to impart a certain colour of probability to the assertion. For not only did they discern just reasons for our intervention in Armenia during the period of our indifference, but they denied that there were even plausible grounds for our interference in the occurrences at Sassoon, which, however cruel and unjustifiable in detail, were, they maintained, the result of a revolutionary agitation probably favoured and certainly connived at by England, whose money, moral sympathy, arms and printing-presses were all at the service of Armenian revolutionists. This view was very delicately embodied in Count Kapnist's remarks to Sir Frank Lascelles: "Count Kapnist said that there could be no doubt that there was a movement, which *was by no means confined to the Armenians living in Turkey*, for the purpose of establishing an independent Armenia. . . ."[7] I have stated, and, I think, proved, elsewhere, that this agitation played but a very insignificant part in the history of Turkish misrule in Armenia, and if the Armenians erred at all, it was on the side of unswerving loyalty and abject submission to their persecutors. But the Russians maintain, and they quote chapter and verse for the statement, that these Armenian "conspirators," whatever their number or their arms, were in constant communication with England, and were visited, encouraged and assisted by Englishmen, and that the fact is not unknown in London. These assertions might be reasonably discounted by the reluctance with which Russia in 1895 assumed the *rôle* which fell to England in 1878; but they now triumphantly point to the very categorical statement on the subject of the Armenian agitation, which has been very deliberately made by our own consular delegate at the Commission which sat in Moush to inquire into the causes of the massacre of Sassoon. Mr. Shipley, in his able memorandum on the joint report of the consular delegates, is the author of the following remarkable sentences: "I have no wish to be thought unduly partial to the Armenians, and I feel it *therefore* my duty to point to the *fact*[8] that an agitation subversive of the authority of the Ottoman Government has been carried on, not for one or two, but for several years past among the Armenians of the Moush and Talori regions by the Armenian Committees abroad, whose latest agent was Mourad, *and that it was the knowledge of their failure to successfully cope with this movement which ended by exasperating the Turkish authorities*."[9]

"What further proof is needed?" ask the opponents of intervention; "your own delegate, whose business it was to inquire into the causes of the massacre, has ascertained the fact that a revolutionary movement was carried on systematically and persistently among the Armenians; that it was supported and directed by *residents in foreign countries*, and that it was so cleverly organized and so well supplied with means that the Ottoman Government, with all their cunning machinery, their espionage, and tortures, not only failed to root it out but even to cope with it successfully, and that it was the *knowledge of their failure* which ended by exasperating the

Turkish authorities. "All this," they add, "was known to us long ago, and prevented us from interfering with the Turks. If it was unknown to the British Government, what an antiquated institution their Foreign Office must be. And, if known, what a flattering idea they must have of Russian simplicity!"

I may be allowed to repeat once more that I decline to be responsible for these views, which I put forward merely as included among the arguments which Continental publicists and statesmen advanced against foreign intervention in Turkey.

The Russians, it must be admitted, made their standpoint quite clear from the very beginning. They gave no countenance whatever to the supposition, no grounds for the hope that the Oriental Question in its Armenian guise would be raised by them or even discussed with a view to the introduction of serious practical changes in the administration of Turkey. *A priori* we had good grounds for believing that the topic was distasteful to them. But lest we should entertain the slightest doubt as to their intentious they gave clear and emphatic expression to their resolve on more than one occasion. Thus, when Sir Frank Lascelles, acting on instructions from Lord Kimberley, sounded the Russian Foreign Office, the reply he received was that the Russian Government wished their Consul at Erzeroum to participate in the inquiry, "*but they were most averse to raising any political question*, although ready to join in securing a full investigation of the case and the punishment of the guilty.[10] Lest this participation in an academic inquiry should be taken to mean solidarity with England in any but the theoretic question at issue, Count Kapnist, speaking in the name of M. de Giers, "*laid stress upon the fact that the Russian Government wished it to be understood that they had no arrière pensée politique*" on the subject, "*and were averse to raising any political question.*"

And in the face of these overwhelming facts, we went forward single-handed, threatening the Turks publicly and privately with armed intervention, well knowing that we could not, and that no other Power would, use force against them, however heinous their misdeeds. If we might reasonably have risked the employment of violent measures, there will be no two opinions in Great Britain or America that it was our duty to do so in God's name. But knowing this to be entirely out of the question, what was our duty? To awaken high hopes in the hearts of the down-trodden Christians, fan the flame of Moslem fanaticism to the very utmost, and then to leave the two peoples face to face in the hope that something would after all turn up to protect the weak against the strong, to supplement the agitation which had been going on for years in the districts of Moush and Talori, by a convulsive movement which swept over the entire Armenian people in Turkey, Russia, and Persia, and transformed every man and boy into an enthusiastic patriot? To add to the blood of the hundreds shed at Sassoon that of the thousands who were soon afterwards butchered at Trebizond, Erzeroum, Van, and Arabghir? This is precisely what we did, and it is difficult to characterize adequately without overstepping the bounds of desirable moderation, the puerile levity of a responsible government whose incredibly flighty experiments have embittered the Russians, inflicted a diplomatic defeat upon this country, and wantonly brought down terrible calamities upon a Christian people whose interest we were bound reasonably to consult and safeguard. If those disastrous effects had taken the Government by surprise, if it had been impossible or very difficult to foresee that they would follow from that policy of giddy adventure which scorns to adjust means to ends, there would be some excuse for Lord Kimberley and his colleagues, and the Armenians might be persuaded to ascribe their recent suffering to the curse which seems to have relentlessly pursued their race ever since the Sassanians ascended the throne of Cyrus and Darius. But no statesman worthy of the name, no observant journalist or well-informed outsider, was for a moment in doubt as to the inevitable consequences of Lord Kimberley's ill-judged action, which was at once a deadly insult to Russia, a serious danger to England, and a fatal snare to the Christian subjects of the Sultan.

The awful sufferings of the Armenian people are not a fitting subject for party controversy, and it would be in the worst possible taste to drag the painful topic into the wretched bickerings of the Tramecksan and Slamecksan of this country who, on the premises of the Foreign Office, at any rate, differ from each other hardly more than their prototypes of Lilliput. It is all the more to be regretted, therefore, that the Leaders of the Opposition in both Houses of Parliament have taken the inevitable failure of the flighty policy which they themselves inaugurated as the text for their attacks on the present Government, to whom they had left nought but the thankless task of choosing between a national humiliation and a sanguinary war. While it cannot be denied that the party now in power is primarily responsible for the baneful treaty of Berlin, no impartial observer can fail to see that the disastrous Armenian muddle is wholly the work of the late Liberal Government, who, if they possessed but a particle of the aptitude requisite for the conduct of the foreign policy of a great empire, must have foreseen what was clear to every politician in Europe, that a diplomatic reverse and a series of cold-blooded massacres would be among the least disastrous results of their misguided attempt to reopen the Eastern Question, without having first come to a clear, definite, and express understanding with Russia. That this is no exaggeration is evident from the confidence and almost historic detail with which these consequences were predicted from the very first by mere outsiders, who took the trouble to make themselves acquainted with the factors of the problem.

But the late Foreign Secretary, it has been urged, hoped that if the worst came to the worst, all difficulties could be readily smoothed away by conferring upon Russia a mandate to occupy Armenia, and restore order in the disturbed provinces. And it was universally believed that Russia would eagerly close with the flattering proposal.

This was but one of the many delusions under which the Foreign Office laboured from the beginning, and probably still continues to labour, and for which there was not the slightest foundation in fact. In the first place, Russia's intervention in Turkey, nay, even her co-operation in the raising of any question which was capable of assuming a political aspect, was expressly excluded by Count Kapnist, whose repeated and emphatic declarations have just been quoted. And, in the next place, all such hopes were nipped in the bud by the conditions of the Eastern Question, which a little calm reflection would have sufficed to make perfectly clear.

For the relative positions of Russia and Turkey have undergone a radical change since the war of 1877, the extent of which seems hardly to be realised even yet by our professional politicians, for whom the sun stands still in Westminster and the moon in the valley of the Thames. During the past eighteen years Turkey, from the position of a serious adversary has fallen to the level of a virtual vassal, in which respect she nowise differs from Persia. When farmers possess more beef than they can consume with impunity or dispose of with profit, they generally salt it until ready to digest and assimilate it. Turkey has thus been salted, and the Sultan, like the Shah, now occupies a position analogous to that of an evicted Irish tenant who has been temporarily reinstated in the capacity of caretaker.

How little this momentous change is realised in England was shown by the implicit belief accorded to the absurd rumour lately circulated, to the effect that Russia and Turkey had struck up an alliance, on the lines of that of Unkiar Skelessi. The notion is preposterous. Times have changed since 1833, and Turkey has changed with them. Russia's fleet in the Black Sea, and her troops in Transcaucasia, are the open sesame, the effect of which it will be no easy task to counteract. When they think fit, the Russians will occupy Erzeroum, Erzinghian, and the other Asiatic provinces of Turkey, with the same ease with which they will use Khorassan as a basis of military operations in another direction, when that seems opportune and advisable. Meanwhile, without any treaty, they will maintain the integrity of Turkey against all outsiders, with the same energy and determination as that of their own country. With the certitude that time is on her side, Russia has no temptation to violate that integrity until she can do so with such a minimum of political friction as accompanied her repudiation of the Black Sea Clause of the Treaty of Paris a quarter of [a] century ago. Now what motives could be held out powerful enough to induce her to imitate the precipitancy of our Liberal Government, and jeopardise the success of the policy of forty years by quarrelling with Turkey? To uphold British prestige, which British statesmen themselves made light of? To fulfill British promises which recorded Russia's humiliating defeat at the Berlin Conference? But perhaps Lord Kimberley relied upon the Christianity, the humane sympathy with suffering Armenians, and all the brilliant series of ideal virtues which statesmen are wont to descant upon with unction on the eve of every bloody war? To this implicit appeal the Russians replied in their press: "Where were all these glorious virtues of Englishmen when Lord Beaconsfield handed back the Christian subjects of the Sultan to the dismal fate which has only now begun to excite their pity when an improvement would suit their policy and further their designs? If England continued to be both Christian and humane, while suppressing those noble impulses eighteen years ago, it is hard to understand why we cannot remain both while holding them in control to-day." And the argument, though hardly creditable to a Christian, is somewhat embarrassing to a statesman.

But this is by no means all. Let us suppose that Russia was willing, in principle, to enter and maintain order in Armenia, but first wisely resolved to count up the cost of the transaction; what would have been the outcome of her calculations? Either the armed intervention would have been successful or unsuccessful. By failure I mean not a series of military reverses, which are out of the question, but the impossibility of accomplishing her mission satisfactorily without resorting to the employment of such measures as would certainly arouse the jealousy and perhaps provoke the opposition of her rivals in the East. Now there is no denying that this collision of interests, not directly emanating from the Armenian question, might easily culminate in a European war. And who vouched that in this case Great Britain would unmoor a single ship for the purpose of extricating her from the troubles incurred for our sake? Nay, who guaranteed that we would not take advantage of Russia's embarrassments and openly support her enemies? A Liberal Government could scarcely be suspected of such conduct, but who would answer for their successors and opponents? It is all very well to speak, in official conversations and despatches, of cordial friendship and neighbourly feelings; but in delicate cases like the present, express and formal engagements are the only safe basis for action. And the Liberal, no less than the Conservative Government, have sedulously avoided entering into any such engagements with Russia. They ought to be prepared, therefore, to take the consequences.

But the chances were that Russia's venture would be attended with success, the Turks would knuckle under, the Armenians breathe freely once more, and the reforms on paper would be embodied in permanent and beneficent changes in the administration of the provinces. What next? Then, argue the Russians, a tree would have rapidly grown up, from which a stick, nay many sticks, might have been cut for our own backs; and in lieu of the listless, lazy caretaker, who may at any moment be turned adrift, we should have found ourselves face to face with an able-bodied tenant surrounded by vigorous retainers, who instead of giving up the keys would bolt and bar the gates and throw scalding water on our bailiff.

It is certainly to the credit of the Armenian people that their intellectual, social, and commercial aptitudes qualify them to hold their own against the most ancient and experienced nations of the world, and if the shameful cause of the periodic decimation of the population ceased, they would increase and multiply at such a rate as to outnumber the Mohammedans in two generations. Many Armenian patriots desired, and some demanded, complete autonomy, to which of course the Russians would never assent. Nor was it needed. When Micky Free in the story was exhorted by the parish priest to pay for a mass to get his poor father's soul out of purgatory, on the ground that all previous prayers had barely liberated his head and shoulders, Micky replied, that no one who knew his late lamented father could doubt that if he once had his head and shoulders outside the bars of purgatory, all the devils in hell could not hold him back. In like manner, the Armenians, with security for life and property as a lever, would readily contrive to assume the political reins to a greater extent than the Hungarians in the Habsburg monarchy, and in a couple of generations they would have outnumbered the Turks, Armenized the Kurds, and attracted thousands of their compatriots from Russia. In this way new life-blood would have been transfused into the veins of the "sick man," and the "integrity of the Ottoman Empire," which Russia is so desirous of maintaining now that it is no more than a diplomatic phrase, would acquire a real and a most disagreeable meaning from her standpoint. Of course these eventualities might have been carefully discussed and prudently provided for, and Russia induced to prevent one of the most abominable crimes recorded in human history. But the Liberal Government were evidently not the people to do this. Everything which they did, and everything which they left undone from the moment that the report of the Sassoon massacre reached their ears, was eminently calculated to arouse the jealousy and provoke the anger of the one Power whose co-operation was absolutely indispensable to the satisfactory settlement of the Armenian question. The Sultan was threatened and bullied as if they were absolute masters of his fate; the Mohammedan population was incensed by the dispatch of a Commission which was a mockery and a snare. Russia's warnings were slighted, her interests ignored, and not a single attempt was made to overcome her objections or make provisions for the difficulties she might have to encounter by efficaciously intervening on behalf of the Armenians. The lack of statesmanship, of insight, and of ordinary tact that was manifested throughout the whole course of the negotiations down to the day on which the Liberal Government resigned, is probably without parallel in the records of British diplomacy.

And the Armenian fiasco is but one of an unbroken series of reverses which the musty traditions of our Foreign Office have inflicted upon this country during the past twenty years. It will probably be some time before we shall have seen the last of them. No branch of the State service is in greater need of a thorough reform, and it is sincerely to be hoped that, unlike so many others, it will come before it is too late. We have ample reason to thank our special providence that during the late crisis in South Africa, the Secretary of State for the Colonies was neither a diplomatist nor a statesman in the Foreign Office acceptation of the word, but a swallower of diplomatic formulas and a clear-headed man of business.

The Contemporary Review, Vol. 69 (April 1896): 513–28

Zeitun

Avetis Nazarbek[1]

I.

To the north of Armenian Cilicia, where the long, majestic chain of the Taurus throws out winding mountain arms away from the Cilician Mediterranean towards the north, the mountains group themselves, radiating into smaller ranges. Among the crests of these, which are covered with snow during part of the year, are upland valleys lying very high. In one of these valleys, all surrounded with rocks and forest, is hidden the town of Zeitun, clinging to the slopes of a mountain side—a great amphitheatre.

The country around is of rare beauty: on every hand you hear the roar of falling torrents and the gay music of waters pushing their way; everywhere you see fresh and icy springs, like mirrors, vast forests clothing the breast of the mountains, great plane trees, ilexes, tall pines, and verdure which lasts all the year round in spite of the devouring heat of the sun. South of Zeitun is the little district of Kapan, and by its side westward the community of Fernouz, renowned for its convent. The inhabitants of these two districts are as brave, open-hearted and open-eyed as those of Zeitun: their scenery has great cliffs and precipices, as well as the overflowing woodland charm common to all the land.

This name, Zeitun, is dear to all Armenians. Dear to us, because it belongs to Armenian Cilicia, where, up to 1393 was thriving the Armenian kingdom which fell at that date under the yoke of the Seld-joucides. The last House of Armenian kings, that of the Roubinian, reigned in Cilicia for four centuries, establishing there their throne after the devastation of Great Armenia by Tartars and

Persians, and while the greater part of Lesser Armenia was in the hands of the Greeks. Zeitun is dear to us because of its tradition of independence, which tradition it keeps sacredly to this day. Zeitun is dear to us because, until 1862, its people were able, as much by their courage as by favour of their mountain site, to keep themselves in a state of semi-independence. Having their native princes yet among them, the people of their own free will generally entrusted executive power to them, assisted by the elders of the city, men well known to the whole country: but the laws were always made and proclaimed by the people themselves in general assembly. Zeitun is dear to us because by its semi-independence it held aloft (and after all, it does so to this day) the national flag of the Armenians. All through the present century it has victoriously resisted the attempts of the Ottoman Government upon this semi-independence, surviving as by a miracle, an oasis in the desert of the empire which is rendered barren by barbarous and tyrannous laws, as Sahara by its sand. These attempts had no success up to 1872.

At this date the Zeitunlis were driven to insurrection, and after a month's successful defence, had the misfortune to believe the fair words of the foxes of the Turkish Government and fell into the snare cunningly set for them. And this time they were forced to recognise their own defeat, and to see for the first time Turkish officials set foot and remain in their beloved city. But this humiliation was not all. The Government of Turkey saddled the town of Zeitun, which has nearly eighteen thousand inhabitants entirely Armenian, with a great fortress on the European model. This fortress is set at the only entrance, just opposite the town, on which for eighteen years have been turned the black mouths of its cannon, gaping and fierce, ready at a moment's notice to destroy the city and all its inhabitants should they grow so bold as to think of a new rising or even so much as of resistance. The events of the last four months in and around Zeitun have shown conspicuously and startlingly how not even this fortress, with its Krupp guns ever loaded, can avail against a people which, drenched in its own blood, decides to do all to defend itself, even to the end.

Yes, Zeitun is dear to the Armenians, and to-day, holding high and scathless our national honour in this terrible crisis—this woeful, bloody, undreamt of crisis through which the Armenian people is passing—to-day Zeitun is dearer to us than ever.

I remember that when I was yet a child I often heard this name of Zeitun when the verses of our best poets were recited, or stories told of the deeds of the Zeitunlis. Such verses are sung by Armenians on every opportunity—at every festival, and above all in these fearful times as a supreme consolation—alas! only as a consolation.

Zeitun is the country in which our dream of liberty has been fostered and nursed, and the Zeitunlis are the heroes who bring the dream to life. Zeitun is the song of our hearts and in the Zeitunlis is our hope.

II.

What was the cause of this last rising or insurrection of Zeitun which began in the beginning of October 1895? Was it expected or not? Was it provoked by the action of the Turkish Government, or was it, as this same Government states, the result of ill-will on the part of the Armenians?

No one has yet forgotten the demonstration of last September the 18th, among the Armenians of Constantinople. It was organised both as a petition and a protest against the situation of the rural Armenians of Armenia, which situation was spoken of as one of "horror" by every one, from her Majesty the Queen and the Marquis of Salisbury down to the best of European journalists. For the organisers' own sakes the demonstration was bound to be of a pacific nature, and its object was to carry a petition to the Sublime Porte, requiring it to put a stop to the massacres, which, in spite of the intervention of some of the great Powers of Europe, still continued. In order to prove more fully that this demonstration had no warlike intent, it is enough to mention that the organising Committee of the Huntchak party thought it their duty to inform the Embassies of the six Powers at Constantinople, two or three days ahead, of the intended demonstration, and on the day immediately preceding it the Sultan's own Government was itself notified by the Committee of their intention. It has been made a matter of reproach since that those demonstrating carried arms, arms being assumed to indicate a hostile attitude. This reproach becomes too strange and ridiculous when one thinks a moment. Given a Government disposed to massacres and a Mahometan crowd with soldiers amongst them of the type of the murderers at Sassoun, the demonstrators could have done no otherwise than take this reasonable precaution.

It is known that by orders coming from the Palace itself, days followed in which the Mahometans slew the Armenians in the Sultan's very capital. Nevertheless, a very short time after the bloodshed, the Sultan was obliged to submit to pressure from some of the European Powers, and to grant (on paper, merely, it needs not to say) certain reforms. But, at the same time, something else took place, pointing only too plainly to all the later massacres, which began after this so-called concession on the part of Abdul Hamid. While signing with one hand, with the other he rubbed out; and by the mouth of his Ministers declared that he could not openly promise reforms to the Armenians and consent to carry them out, *without the risk*, by that very act, of provoking profound discontent among the Mussulmans, who, in order to escape reform, *might* go so far as to massacre all the Christians in Armenia. In this cynical declaration the mean and horrible tyrant preferred rather to appear helpless before his own subjects (he—Caliph of the Mussulmans!) than to repress his personal resentment, Asiatic vindictiveness, and ill-concealed ferocity against the defenceless Armenians, who lay at the mercy of their innumerable enemies. And what Abdul Hamid predicted was not only prophetic—rather it was a direct suggestion and marching order, meaning this: "To have done with the Armenian question, let us have done with the Armenians."

Another proof of criminal premeditation is the fact that the Central Government issued an order before the massacres had taken place, to make a thorough search in all Armenian houses, and to seize, not only arms, but *any common knife larger than a penknife*—thus elaborately to deprive the Armenians of any means of self-defence in case of need.

This snare (part of the policy of the Asiatic Reynard which is cherished and constantly practised in Turkey) was spread by the Sultan most sagaciously. He risked nothing for himself, being secure of the protection of Russia. This protection, so disastrous for the Armenians, Russia guaranteed him by the act of rolling the car of his Macchiavellian policy.

Such were the circumstances—the Armenians waking, morning after morning, to be murdered in thousands all over the Empire—such were the circumstances when, at the beginning of last

October, the local governor of Marash (in the province or vilayet of Aleppo) sent to Zeitun the official Hadji Aslan, a Circassian, with an escort of zaptiehs, under orders to make a "perquisition," or house to house search. The Zeitunlis, perfectly understanding what would be the end of such a visitation, and with the massacres over all Armenia before their eyes, definitely refused to submit to the rough requirements of the Circassian. The latter, disconcerted, retired next day to Bertous (a Mussulam district), and there got together over a hundred Bashi-Bazouks, and without loss of time attacked the Armenian village of Alabash, trying to burn it down. The Armenians had the courage to defend themselves. After this first attack, which failed, Hadji Aslan raised another hundred Bashi-Bazouks, and again, on October 6, attacked the village; but this time also the Armenians resolutely resisted and drove back the foe, dispersing them. On the 13th the Armenians of Alabash sent an express to the Zeitunlis asking them for help, as several thousand Bashi-Bazouks and regulars were about to fall upon them. The Zeitunlis, always brave, and ready to fight for their brethren, hastily organised a relief party, two hundred strong, which marched for Alabash. At Chakir Déré, where the historic river Jahan receives the stream from Bertous, the Zeitunlis met the Ottoman troops and the Bashi-Bazouks, who were all encamped on the top of a hill near the Mussulman village Maskhitli. The die was cast.

The next day at dawn firing began on both sides. The battle joined, lasting four hours without pause. Although their position was bad and the enemy eight times their number (there were two thousand Turks), yet the Zeitunlis both stood firm and gained new ground. There were more Turks than Armenians killed. Towards the end of the battle, while yet neither side prevailed, a messenger came into the Zeitunli camp to say that a large body of Turks and Bashi-Bazouks were preparing to attack the town of Zeitun.

Leaving one hundred of their comrades, the remainder of the Zeitunlis, night falling, hastened back; the other hundred that same night, attacked the Mussulman encampment and succeeded in putting the enemy to flight, after which first victory they also returned immediately to Zeitun.

Here the fight was already begun—bitter, bold, and decisive. Firing never ceased for a moment. Zeitun was beset by more than ten thousand men of the regular Ottoman troops and of Bashi-Bazouks. On this battle hung the fate of Zeitun. Our blood boiled. The thought of horrible martyrdoms of thousands of our innocents made every warrior tremble with rage. Before them and around them moved a mass of murderers—wild beasts, roused, savage, regardless of all but their thirst for blood, ready for any cruelty. In face of this terrible danger the Zeitunlis took the offensive, and detached bands to besiege on all sides the formidable fortress from which at intervals the cannon roared upon them. This struggle, as well as the incessant close fire of small arms on both sides, lasted more than fifty hours, after which, the Zeitunlis at last succeeded in driving back the besieging Mussulmans, and constraining the garrison in the fort, which numbered six hundred, to submit.

This took place on the 18th of October last.

The six hundred Turks became prisoners to the Zeitunlis, who took possession of the fortress with all its provisions of war and two Krupp guns. The same thing was done in regard to all the Turkish officials in Zeitun. The school building and bigger houses of the town were assigned to the prisoners. The national flag of the Armenians was floated on the top of the fortress; and the people for some days after this memorable victory held high festival. All the Turkish prisoners from the first day were treated by the Armenians as brothers.

To leave my story for a minute. In the report of the British Consul who wrote from Aleppo, it is stated that nearly two hundred prisoners had been massacred by the Zeitunlis. Upon this, all the anti-Armenian journals set up a moving chorus and redoubled their onslaught upon the Armenians. If it is true, this deed of massacre, certainly I will not defend this kind of practice! But the fact is beyond doubt, that in all their victories the Zeitun people have habitually behaved with chivalrous generosity, whether towards prisoners or towards the conquered populations of Turkish villages. This being so, it is difficult to believe that the Zeitunlis murdered 200 Turks who had already submitted. This massacring could only arise in case of a revolt among the prisoners. In any case, it is a bitter irony to accuse the Armenians of massacre after the human hecatombs, beyond all precedent and all parallel, achieved by the wish of the Sultan, and remaining not only unpunished but indirectly condoned by the attitude of European journalism towards the Armenians. A London evening paper speaks of these as "massacres," and terms Armenians "savages" who do not at all differ in point of fact from the Turks. This language is oratorical rather than truthful; but it should apply equally to certain European Powers who in their colonial wars often resort to slaughter, under quite different impulses from those of a handful of Armenians in the frenzy of their sorrow and their loss.

After their decisive and well earned victory the people elected a provisional government, composed of 16 members, four from each of the four quarters of the city; and a council of 40, to which each quarter contributes 10. They next organised a national guard to maintain order. Strange to say, perhaps, but up to the present time, ever since October 18, not a single case of theft, house breaking, brigandage, or crime of any kind has been committed in Zeitun. The food and necessary supplies have been distributed by the provisional government to the Armenian population and to the Turkish prisoners.

After these first victories of the Zeitunlis, the strength of the besieging troops (Ottoman regular army and Bashi-Bazouk) which were drawn up anew round the Zeitun district and that of Fernouz, has gone on increasing till now the number is thirty or forty thousand.

All this information I draw from letters which I have received from Zeitun itself almost regularly; consequently I can answer for their authenticity. Also from the same source come the facts and the events which I am about briefly to set forth, together with their dates.

III.

I have said already that at the beginning of the month of October last the Turkish officers and military, aided and followed by Bashi-Bazouks, made attacks upon Alabash. On the other hand, the Armenian villages of the following districts became the scene of horrible massacres—viz. Dash-Oloug, Kokisson, Boundouk, Keridje, Tavoud, Gueule-Pounar, Dejirmen-Déré, Jamaus-Heik. At the requisition of the local authorities the Armenian inhabitants of these districts gave up the few arms they possessed to the Government agents, and solemnly declared their fidelity to the Sultan, thinking in this way to escape the storm of massacre which Turkish agents were menacing. But, it need not be said, these poor Armenians deluded themselves. After having thus disarmed them, the regular troops of Eridjik and of Kokisson, and a considerable number of Bashi-Bazouks, Circassians, and Kurds, under the command of Mudir Mehemmed Bey, a Circassian, on the night of October 20, assaulted the Armenians of the districts above mentioned. The devastation, pillage, massacres, and cruelties they committed it is useless to describe: the European public, particularly the English, know it well enough and, alas! too well.

The same night the Turks of the districts Dejirmen-Déré, and Kokisson, whom I have already named once, gathered in the Mussulman village Choukour Hissar, and arranged to attack Fernouz. In pursuit of their ends they began to burn several Armenian dwellings near Fernouz, whose inhabitants, aware of the great preparations, tried first to come to friendly terms with them. But the Turks were encouraged by this proceeding on the part of the Armenians, and began a fusillade, counting on the strength of their position in Choukour Hissar, which is a fortified place. The Armenians, though few, replied to the fire, and after more than four hours, during which the Turks lost seventy men and the Armenians only four, this position was captured by the Armenians, who, during the struggle, were reinforced by friends from Fernouz who came out to their aid. The Turks were sent flying towards the Circassian village Tchamourlou.

Massacres, devastations, violation of women, &c., were committed by the regular troops, or by the Bashi-Bazouks, in the Armenian village Shivilki, belonging to the Kaimakamlik of Anderoun, as well as in the villages in the district of Yenidje Kale and Anapat. These horrors went on for six days under the command of a man named Yaij Ogli, a well-known brigand, though he was a public functionary. At this juncture Armenians of the village Thavoud, which is near Shivilki, and a small detachment from Fernouz, resolved to defend their brothers in Shivilki. They fought a battle with Yaij Ogli and his six hundred Bashi-Bazouks and succeeded in putting them to flight.

On October 29 the Turks of Nedir made a violent assault on

the Armenian village Thelemelik. The villagers, aided by a detachment from Zeitun, defended themselves valiantly, and drove off their enemies in the direction of Marash.

On November 1 a body of Zeitun men, several hundred strong, set off for Boundouk and Kapan to protect the Armenian inhabitants and their industry, which is very considerable—the keeping of silk-worms. In these two districts are a number of Turkish villages, the inhabitants of which, fearing to be punished for the crimes of the Bashi-Bazouks on their neighbours, the Armenians, offered submission and asked for pardon and protection; to which the Zeitun men, always generous, consented, and not a drop of blood was shed.

About this time news arrived that all the Armenian notables of the Kaimakamlik of Anderoun (or Andrine) had been shut up by the local authorities in infected places, that young girls were violated, houses and goods pillaged, &c. A detachment of 350 Zeitunlis straightway set off for Andrine, which is three days' journey from Zeitun. There, on November 3, began a fierce conflict between them and the Turkish combined forces, numbering 950. They were commanded by the Kaimakam (sub-governor) himself, by the Mudir and judge, Dourdou Bey, by Hadji Effendi and Youssouf Tchavoush. Although weaker in numbers, the Zeitunlis again won a brilliant victory, routed the foe, and arrived in the place exactly as the Turkish zaptiehs were about to fire the house in which the Armenian prisoners were confined. Setting them free (they were in a piteous condition, having had no food supplied for twelve days), the Zeitunlis collected together both these and all the Armenians—men, women, and children—of the country around, and sent them, and what property remained to them, in charge of a strong escort to Fernouz.

On November 5 some parties from Zeitun hurried towards the Yenidje Kale, Dounkalai, and Anapat districts, where the Armenian villages—four hundred houses altogether—were being stormed by the regular troops and by Bashi-Bazouks. But on the way they met the Turkish soldiers from Kertil and Nedir. Winning their way and continuing their march, just outside the Turkish village Keshirdje they met a fresh body of Ottomans, defeated them and arrived at Gaishli, which lies quite near the district which they were trying to reach, to deliver their brethren and three convents belonging to the Franciscan fathers. Father Salvator Lili of Cappadocia himself had written some days before to tell the Zeitunlis of the danger these convents were in, and had entreated them to go to their aid. (The Father was a Neapolitan of the province of Cappadocia, born in the village of Neutano.) However, the Zeitunlis were yet struggling with the Turkish troops on their route, when there came up from Marash more of the regular forces (500 soldiers and over 1000 Bashi-Bazouks), which laid waste, overthrew, burnt down all the Armenian dwellings, as well as two of the Franciscan convents, murdering Father Salvator and the greater part of the inhabitants. These things took place at Moudjik-Déré.

Meantime, a band of the Zeitunlis arrived at Keshirdje, whence they drove the enemy, passed on to Yenidje-Kale, where, raising a little help, with the two Franciscan fathers, a Spaniard, and part of the Armenian population, they directed their way to Fernouz. They had not long left Yenidje-Kale when the Turks fell upon the hamlet like a hailstorm and threw everything into chaos. Happily the massacre had hardly commenced when another body of Zeitunlis came upon the scene, having set out from Kapan to carry help to this quarter.

Then began a hard and terrible strife which lasted all day, from morning to nightfall, when the Turks began to yield, and at last, leaving their dead behind them, broke and fled.

The next day the Zeitunlis carried help to the three other villages of Armenians (containing more than one hundred and fifty houses) all belonging to the Yenidje-Kale district. However, the Armenians of Anapat and Dounkalai, with their two hundred and fifty houses, were literally wiped out and every single inhabitant murdered by the regular Ottoman troops and the Bashi-Bazouks.

All this happened at Zeitun and its neighbouring districts from the 1st of October up to the end of November 1895 (Old Style).

Since this date I have had more details of the other battles, which have never ceased up to the beginning of this January. They have ended always in speedier victory for the Zeitun champions, and more and more crushing defeats for the Turks and Bashi-Bazouks, who are now in a deplorable state.

The rising steadily spread, although the people of Zeitun and Fernouz have at one time had to keep and to feed near twenty-five thousand Armenians from different parts of Cilicia, these having escaped the massacre in a state of entire poverty, their homes and belongings being completely ruined.

IV.

In order to arrive at any conclusion on the subject of the rising of the Zeitunlis, upon its character and its bearing, it is necessary to set forth here, in its general features, the part played by the Armenian revolutionary party of the Huntchak in the said uprising, as well as generally in the national Armenian cause.

Our adversaries, and principally the agents of the Turkish Government, have so distorted the tendencies, principles, and character of the organisation of the Huntchak party, that English opinion is tempted to regard this party, which is patriotic in the best sense, as the enemy of its people. Our adversaries try to show that we, the Huntchakists, are Anarchists, that we are opposed to law, fomenters of trouble, disorder, and massacre—in short, that we are criminals. To prove this myth they dig in the dust of the archives of the Russian Embassy at Constantinople to find there "authentic documents." I know perfectly well that to find this sort of document, calling itself authentic, against the Huntchakists there is no place so good as the artificial archives of Hamid's Government, and again those of the Embassy named above. But as for me, who have not the privilege of visiting those archives, I would prefer to consult all the volumes of the *Huntchak*, the central organ of the Armenian revolutionary party, which has just passed into the ninth year of its publication, and ask to have pointed out to me one single line which is of an anarchist nature. I can, however, find for myself whole pages written *against* Anarchism.

In a pamphlet, published in English in London itself, nearly a year ago, I had an opportunity to expound the political programme considered most practical by the Huntchak party at the present day for the solution of the Armenian difficulty. This programme, far from being anarchist, certainly is very moderate in claiming for the Armenians only political rights of self-government, under a Christian governor, nominated and chosen for a fixed period by the great Powers. That is not, surely, an Anarchist's programme, but might in England be called a rather Conservative scheme; this no destructive policy.

We love our people. We want them to have a respite, a breathing space. When European diplomacy proffered mediation the Huntchak party risked its influence by setting its face against any insurrectionary movement. And we may claim for it the credit of being successful. The terrible year which followed the Sassoun massacre, that year of unknown anxiety, unheard-of sufferings and provocation, has been endured by the Armenian people in heroic calmness and self-control. We would have hailed any real concession as inaugurating a new era, a prospect of peaceful development for our people. But we have nothing to wait for any more. Since perish we must, let us perish like men, fighting our enemy face to face, not, like cowards, turning our backs on them.

The Huntchak party has existed and acted for more than eight years. From the first year of its existence it included young men from the universities—doctors, lawyers, professors, writers, and journalists. These almost all belonged to the well-to-do, some to the richest, Armenian families, noble and well known in their own country. Europe was their educator in science, both political and literary, and the great writers of the Armenian nation had made them know their national history. Their hearts beat with ardent love for the people who groaned degraded beneath a yoke of the most shameful kind—Asiatic tyranny undisguised—forced to beg for very existence under the yataghan of the Kurd. Thus as ardent patriots, the Huntchakists strive to do their utmost possible for the good of the Armenian people. They have displayed for years past and up to the present time a wonderful activity, inflexible energy, a capacity for the initiative, and inexhaustible resource. By their propaganda they have raised from the ground the nation's conscious dignity, probity, and natural courage, which were withering in the terror; they have spread large, generous, humanitarian ideas; in a word, they have regenerated Armenian intellect and *morale* in a few years. It is thanks to them and their work that the Huntchakist party has now for some years enjoyed the confidence of the Armenians and has a predominant influence over them. It is the representative of their political and social tendencies, and works for these.

The organisation of the Huntchak party is a secret organisation; it "conspires." It is needless to say why it is such, for it is more than clear that in Turkey it must be such to exist at all. At this moment its members are counted by thousands; it contains persons of every possible section of Armenian society, from the rich man to the peasant. It has ramifications in the whole of Turkish Armenia and in European Turkey, as well as in Europe and America. All these ramifications form a compact mass, acting under one direction and upon one line of general conduct, although all are not equally strong. Yet, during the years in which the party has grown to such proportions and such force, it has had much loss to bear. Hundreds of its members, whom the Ottoman Government's police have succeeded in arresting, have been—almost to a man—tortured, imprisoned, exiled, done to death; and fifteen have been formally condemned and executed.

The criminal tragedy which was to follow for some years in Armenia had these ill-omened beginnings.

But what was the *cause* of the appearance of "revolutionaries" on the Armenian soil? The cause was the conditions of the daily life of the people. Their life was one long suffering and pain; everything was degraded, commerce, industry, agriculture, education, thought, the entire life of the Armenian race. Here we have the natural causes of the revolutionary spirit. But this was not all.

Ever since 1878 there lay as a dead letter—dead to this day—the article of the Treaty of Berlin by which six great Powers of Europe recognised solemnly and internationally the pressing claims of the Armenians to a better existence; these Powers themselves took the responsibility for the introduction, "without further delay," of the reforms necessary to the Armenian Province. On the other hand, since 1878, instead of improving, the plight of the people has grown steadily more exasperating and intolerable. During this lapse of memory on the part of Europe the situation became as desperate for the Armenians as we see to-day. They began to murmur and to stir. The Huntchak party appeared, and took up the revolutionary movement. It has cried aloud from its birth in the heart of a ceaseless struggle with the Government and the police of Turkey, and kept on steadily organising for a rising, directing its propaganda and agitating to this end. It has spoken the word for self-defence, for falling back on our own forces, for insurrection. Logically it could do no otherwise. Since the Armenian nation was left defenceless by Europe, which had no regard for its own promise—since that was clear—the right of insurrection became the sacred right of this enslaved race, and henceforth it had to trust alone to its own inner forces and its own despair.

Thus all this revolutionary movement rests on a claim which cannot be gainsaid by persons whose life is led under political conditions which have absolutely nothing in common with those of Turkey; who cannot deny sympathy with, much less condemn, these efforts and these deeds of the Armenians, hard-driven by natural necessity, by the irresistible "force of circumstances." It is a great injustice to reproach the Armenian patriots for what they did under the cruel knowledge of the certain approaching death of their people. Their conduct is but the logical guarantee of all human rights—the Armenian people's too—and among them pre-eminently the *right to live.*

After the demonstration of September 18 at Constantinople, worked by the Huntchakists, when the Sultan made that too meagre concession which we know, the organ of the party advised waiting to the end of the "comedy" of the Sultan's concessions, in order not to precipitate events, although the massacres at Constantinople drew from the hearts of the Armenian community a cry for vengeance. The intention of the revolutionists then was very peaceable. But suddenly, instead of the execution of the "reforms," came the horrible series of massacres which began with Trebizond, Baibourt, Erzeroum.

Meanwhile the European Powers, after having given so much hope to the Armenians, now wavered with their fleets in the waters of the Mediterranean, and remained there as idle spectators of the bloody show in Armenia.

In such a case, in presence of such great horrors, which came on the nation like thunderbolts at the very moment when they were expecting just the contrary—that is to say, the realisation of reforms (however futile they might prove)—in such a case, I say, how could the Armenians feel, think, and act? What remained to the revolutionary patriots, in whose name I have a right to speak?

We reasoned thus: We are pressed to the wall, and we have very little to choose from. We may submit, with the apathy of dumb creatures, to our fate, waiting the day when the Turks shall have satisfied their revenge, and growing sick of murdering, shall allow the cowed remnants of our race to drag on the low life of hopeless slavery; or we may curse the day when we believed in the dream of freedom, and in the possibility of being men and citizens, and throw ourselves at the feet of the White Tsar, in the hope that he may deign to put upon us his yoke, instead of that of the Sultan. If we do not wish for either, then we have to take our fate in our own hands. The only desperate means left to us is open rebellion. We know full well what this means for us in Turkey. But we have so little to lose! And we know from history that people who have been bold enough to risk their all have often won their cause in spite of overwhelming odds.

This was our reasoning before the Zeitun insurrection began, and it remains in full force up till the present time, the situation in Armenian changing from bad to worse.

Our cry, uttered in such a case, such a desperate case, came back to us echoed from Zeitun. Huntchakist comrades who were there and had their Committee, by the means and under the direction of the Huntchak party, took the decisive resolution to defend themselves to the last. With this cry those comrades (heroes that they are!) coming to the head of the movement—they, the Huntchakists, took the fortress and town of Zeitun, and many other districts, which the Zeitunlis have held for four months past.

V.

"What fate awaits the Zeitunlis? What will be the end of this victory-lighted insurrection? What issue will the great Powers seek to give to it, by means of their Consuls, who are at this moment at Zeitun in negotiation with the Armenians?" Such were the disquieting questions put before us at the moment of the negotiations for the surrender of Zeitun.

There is nothing more difficult than to be the judge of others, and yet this is a *rôle* which is played on all hands—a part used and abused.

Here is a most unhappy nation, this of Armenia. Persecuted, martyred, massacred by the Government of the Sultan and his savage hordes; a prey to the extremest poverty and famine; drowned in its own blood; betrayed by the great Powers, and specially by England—it is moreover subject to every recrimination, every insult, every unjust condemnation on the part of a great number of European journalists. The last new ground for this is, that in the Report of the European Commission at Sassoun, it is said that the number of the Sassounlis massacred has been overstated. Yet no one has yet forgotten that the massacre at Sassoun bore such a character and was of such proportion that at first the number of slain might easily be misconceived in good faith, and in fact it was so misconceived, not only by the Armenians, but by the whole European press. What part did the Commission play? Its duty was first to establish the character of the massacres, next the true number of slain, and to throw light upon responsibilities. It has only established the number of one general massacre, and does not deny that it was unable to arrive at it exactly. Thus, it believes the number killed to have been near a thousand.

Thereupon on all sides the anti-Armenian journals have begun to cry out upon the exaggeration which went so far as six thousand, still more upon the figure repeated immediately after the massacre at Sassoun. It is heartrending that any civilised European journalist should stoop so low. Each human life is sacred, be it Armenian, German, or English, and when this human life is sacrificed unjustly, there should be no place for dispute over the corpse. If the lives so sacrificed count to twenty or a hundred, we dwell no longer on the number slain, at a time when there are none but victims. The capital point is that the massacres occurred. Because a thousand were killed at Sassoun, and not six thousand, the murder does not lose its significance and the responsibility of the Government for it is not diminished. This opinion is that also of the Commissioners. These thousand slain are victims of Turkish savagery. For this thousand also the great Powers must answer—they who actually eighteen years ago pledged themselves for the safety of Armenian lives.

But why go back to the massacres in Sassoun? In these few last months there have been tens and tens of thousands slain; and yet, on the eve of the twentieth century the Powers of Europe dare not, or will not, overcome the inhuman passions of a Government which they call a "sick man," or else "a putrefying corpse."

And now at this moment, from one day to another, we are in dread of massacres at and around the Zeitun district, such as have happened in other parts of Cilicia. The consuls of the European Powers have been there. What line did they take?

They urged the Zeitunlis, always in the name of an "honourable peace" to *give up their arms to the Turkish Government, whose troops they had beaten regularly up to the last moment.* This counsel could issue in nothing but the offering up, with hands tied, of all the people of Zeitun and all the 30,000 refugees who were sheltered at the time within its walls, to the ferocious vengeance of the Sultan, the Bashi-Bazouks, &c. Arms are the only guarantee against such a fate.

It was, therefore, a criminal error towards the Zeitunlis and their unfortunate *protégés* to think for a moment of disarming them the first. Further, the dangerous fortress, the cause of constant distrust and anxiety to the Zeitunlis, was to remain, together with a Turkish garrison and its cannon. Also the taxes were to remain—the crushing taxes, the payment of which is utterly out of the power of the ruined people, already a prey to the contagious maladies which are wasting the country. It is true that, side by side with this, in the conditions of the Porte, it is declared that the Sultan will disarm the Mahometans dwelling in the valleys that surround Zeitun; that he will appoint a Christian sub-Governor (a Kaimaikam); that he will introduce the famous administrative reforms promised (and signed by the Sultan) last September to all the Armenian provinces. Yes all these tales have been once more re-told by Abdul Hamid; but where are the guarantees for the performance of his promises? *When* and *by what means* will he have them carried out? Where is the European control which, alone, can be offered as a serious guarantee? Is he not laughing—this Sultan—under the very nose of European, and above all, of English diplomacy, and showing that the latter is for ever useless henceforward at Constantinople, thanks to the cordial understanding between the two despots of the East? It seems that the Consuls received from their Governments certain very strange instructions; they (one supposes) were to try and restore everything to the point it stood at *before the insurrection*, exactly the point at which things became intolerable and caused the rising.

What concerns England is that this supposition comes near the truth. Thus, in a discourse recently pronounced, Lord Salisbury thinks, with the other European Powers, that the Sultan may perhaps do something for the Armenians *if he is let alone*. And the great Powers wish to let the Sultan alone, at the same time sacrificing along with so many Armenians the people of Zeitun also. It is evident that the Powers at this moment desire to hush matters up.

This strange hope of Lord Salisbury's seems but a fugitive empty word, by which the First Minister of the Queen completes a solemn avowal of the absolute defeat of his Eastern policy, in which, as to the solution of the Armenian question, he has before him great difficulties, chiefly created by that same policy. This from the mouth of Lord Salisbury, along with his whole speech, means nothing but the retreat of Great Britain from the Armenian question. Still, it is impossible to admit of the idea of return to the state of things before the siege. Such a relapse might bring on the gravest complications; the people of Zeitun would be placed in the very same case again in which insurrection had become beyond all control. European intervention in the affairs of Zeitun should have had a character less cruel and less disastrous in its consequences, and juster, more impartial, more prudent. This intervention might have repaired the fault of European diplomacy through the whole terrible Armenian crisis. Europe cannot deny the right of self-defence to us, and particularly to the men of Zeitun, when this self-defence is recognised by every European nation and Government as a sacred law. Recognising this right, European diplomacy cannot exact submission pure and simple from the Zeitunlis. It should be admitted that these men are right when they claim for Armenian Cilicia a Christian governor named by the great European Powers and under their direct control; the political reorganisation of the country; non-intervention from the Ottoman Government in local affairs, and a general amnesty, &c. But, by their unfavourable attitude to the Zeitunlis during the negotiations, the representatives of the Powers have given a last blow to the hopes that the Armenians placed in the great Powers; and by this same attitude the Zeitunlis have been forced to submit to the conditions proposed by the Porte.

It was more than high time, and there was no occasion more favourable for Europe, and specially for Great Britain, to give this bare satisfaction to a part of the Armenians, who had shown by their conduct that they had decided to defend their lives, goods, and most human rights, and by that fact were capable and worthy of a life more human and politically less enslaved and more independent. The Armenians expected from diplomacy this act of justice and reparation, which was due to them.

In view of this, the Armenian patriots, and with them the whole nation, are obliged to adhere to their purpose of self-defence, their patriotic revolutionary programme, the consequences of which may have a much more serious bearing than at present appears upon European interests. But for us the prospect is no longer terrible. Bathed in our own blood which is shed without redress, having seen all our national property burnt, pillaged, wasted, ruined—after having lost either by massacre or by misery, by cold or famine, hundreds of thousands of our countrymen, we Armenians have nothing more to lose. But, on the other hand, what we gain will be for our good.

The Contemporary Review, Vol. 69 (April 1896): 628–43

Armenia and the Powers: From Behind the Scenes

On the 13th of last December the British Ambassador at Constantinople sent Lord Salisbury the following appalling telegram:

> "It may be roughly estimated that the recent disturbances have devastated, as far as the Armenians are concerned, the whole of the provinces to which the scheme of reforms was intended to apply; that over an extent of territory considerably larger than Great Britain all the large towns, with the exception of Van, Samsoun, and Mush, have been the scene of massacres of the Armenian population, while the Armenian villages have been almost entirely destroyed. A moderate estimate puts the loss of life at 30,000. The survivors are in a state of absolute destitution, and in many places they are forced to become Mussulman.
>
> "The charge against the Armenians of having been the first to offer provocation cannot be sustained. Non-Armenian Christians were spared, and the comparatively few Turks who fell were killed in self-defence.
>
> "The participation of the soldiers in the massacres is in many places established beyond a doubt."

Four days later the British Ambassador at Vienna handed a copy of this telegram to Count Goluchowski, Minister for Foreign Affairs, and begged him to peruse it carefully.

> "Count Goluchowski did so, and observed that the description is doubtless true enough, and very impressive; but that, as he had already stated, there is nothing to be done but to wait and see if the Sultan will be able to carry out his promises and restore order. Every kind of admonition had been given to him, and his Excellency did

not see what more could be said to him than has been already repeatedly urged. Intervention of any other kind must inevitably result in the further 'disaggregation' of the Ottoman Empire. But if Count Goluchowski rightly understands the situation, this is the last thing that the Powers desire. They know that unless the greatest precautions are taken Europe is threatened with the re-opening of the whole Eastern Question. Any further action will have the effect of raising it; will, in fact, 'apply the spark to the powder.' A catastrophe would ensue productive of results which would be infinitely grave. He must therefore maintain that, lamentable as the condition of affairs in Anatolia undoubtedly is, there is nothing whatever to be done but to give the Sultan the opportunity of doing what he has engaged to do. The prospect is not a hopeful one."

A fortnight later the Austrian Minister received new of more horrors:

"His Excellency went on to deplore that, beyond making representations [to the Sultan] the Powers can do nothing for the Armenians, of whom several thousands may now be computed to have perished by violence; while the rigours of winter, bringing famine, want of shelter and warmth—in fact, destitution in its most appalling shape—might be calculated to destroy many more before the return of spring."

This forecast has been too truly ratified by events. There is evidence that the number of Armenians massacred in cold blood to February was not less than 50,000,[1] while the addition of those who perished by famine and cold would raise the figure to little short of 200,000. Well might Count Goluchowski describe the prospect as appalling. But let us go on with his Excellency's most humiliating confession of the impotence of Christendom to stop, or even check, this carnival of horrors:

In presence of this heartrending prospect, it is intelligible that numbers of humane people are revolted at the idea that Europe is powerless; and, regardless of consequences, would wish that action should be taken by some, or even by one of the Powers, to put a stop to the extermination of the miserable Armenians. But practical statesmen are bound to consider the situation from another standpoint."

And again the bugbear of the Eastern Question is conjured up to frighten timorous statesmen. But the ghosts of the slaughtered Armenians and of the victims yet to follow still haunt his Excellency's imagination, and he goes on again in the course of a fortnight to disburden his troubled mind to the British Ambassador, and to bewail the impotence of Europe:

> "Count Goluchowski said that the prospect of the suffering through which the Armenians have passed, and which they have yet, in all probability, to undergo, is so terrible that pure humanitarians would naturally be prone to accuse those, in whose power they believe it to be to prevent such misery, of heartless cruelty, or, at any rate, of cynical indifference. . . . No one can more clearly than himself perceive the horrors of the situation, nor feel more acutely the bitterness of the incapacity of Europe to ameliorate it."

But there it is again! the spectre of the Eastern Question, which can only be laid by letting the Sultan go on with his bloody work, even to the "extermination of the miserable Armenians." Count Goluchowski's helpless lament that "there is nothing to be done but to wait and see if the Sultan will be able to carry out his promises and restore order," looks uncommonly like that "cynical indifference" which he pathetically disclaims. He knew perfectly well that it was want of will, not of power, that prevented the Sultan from carrying out his promises. For it was the Austrian Ambassador at Constantinople, as doyen of the Diplomatic Corps, who had, two months previously, accused the Sultan to his face of having ordered the massacres, and of not being sincere in his professed desire to stop them. Here is the stern message which Baron Calice, as the accredited organ of all the European Embassies, delivered in person to the Sultan on November 18, 1895:

> "The only means of restoring confidence is to put a stop to the massacres, *which we are convinced the Sultan can do if he is sincere in his professions.* It is not for us to indicate the measures to be taken, but we venture to make the following suggestions:
>
> "'That the functionaries responsible for the massacres should be dismissed.
>
> "'That an inquiry should be held as to the participation of soldiers in the outrages, and the guilty be punished.

> "'That the orders recently sent to the Valis and military commanders should be published, *and assurances given that previous orders have been cancelled.*
>
> "'That a Hatt should be issued by the Sultan ordering his subjects to obey his wishes.'"

Here we have the Sultan himself arraigned at the bar of the Great Powers of Europe as the author of the massacres, and accused in plain terms of being insincere "in his professions" of desire to stop them. Yet the Austrian Minister for Foreign Affairs, with these facts before him, says "there is nothing to be done but to wait and see if the Sultan will be able to carry out his promises." Surely one need not be a "pure humanitarian" to characterise diplomacy like this as "heartless cruelty, or, at any rate, cynical indifference." I believe that the annals of Christian Europe may be searched in vain for anything so abjectly humiliating, so entirely disgraceful, as this spectacle of the Great Powers of Christendom making so terrible an accusation against a barbarous despot who reigns by their sufferance, and then standing idly by while he goes calmly on with his work of extermination against a helpless and an innocent people. And the spectre which has smitten them with this ignoble paralysis—the raising of the Eastern Question—is it so certain that they have laid it by their cruel pusillanimity? The event will show whether it would not have been wiser to grasp the nettle firmly instead of stroking it with the open hand. A mandate from united Europe would have extorted obedience from the Sultan without the firing of a single shot. The apparition of the fleets of Europe, or even of a moiety of them, at the Dardanelles, with orders to pass in case of continued contumacy on the part of the Sultan, would have sufficed. At all events, the Austrian Government was itself at one time an advocate of that coercive policy which Count Goluchowski deprecated some months afterwards. The explanation of this *volte-face* may perhaps appear as we proceed. It happens that I have been a good deal behind the scenes in this matter, and I now propose to put the public in possession of the salient points of the diplomatic history of the Armenian Question during the last eighteen months. The two volumes of Blue Books, which have been so tardily published, are necessarily far from complete, and I am able, without committing any one, to supply some important omissions. I am entirely unconnected with party politics in England or elsewhere, and have no thesis to maintain. My sole motive is to place the public in possession of the leading facts, leaving them to distribute as they please the blame of one of the greatest tragedies to modern times, a tragedy which impartial history will characterise as the foulest stain as yet inflicted on the chivalry and manhood of civilised Europe.

The first thing to be noted is that the massacres which, in Lord Salisbury's phrase, have "made Europe pale," ought not to have taken the British Government unawares. They had been carefully prepared and organised for more than five years, and the British Government had been duly warned. Early in the year 1890 Colonel Chermside, then British Consul at Erzeroum, wrote that the cruelty and outrages inflicted on the defenceless Armenians were fostering a spirit of disaffection among the most docile and peaceable of the Sultan's subjects. In the same year Colonel Chermside's successor, Mr. Clifford Lloyd, of Land League fame, sounded a serious note of warning. "I am of opinion," he said, "that the question of protecting the Armenian peasantry from the attacks of the Kurds is of much greater importance than any other, and that if the Christians were shielded from the ever-existing apprehension of being pillaged and killed they would become a comparatively contented and prosperous people. All the Christians asked for was protection; but this was the one thing the Government failed to provide." And this failure was not due to ignorance or negligence or feebleness on the part of the Government at Constantinople; it was part of a deliberate policy, of which the object was to provoke the Armenians into some show of resistance that might furnish the Government with an excuse for massacring them. "The Kurds," says Mr. Clifford Lloyd, "here, as elsewhere, openly declare that their action meets with the approval of the Turkish Government." Small wonder if their intolerable wrongs made the Armenians "protest"—the only form which the discontent of an unarmed peasantry could take. "I believe that the idea of revolution is not entertained by any class of the Armenian people. An armed revolution is, besides, impossible," for the Armenians had no arms except some old flint-locks here and there to protect their crops and flocks from birds and beasts. "Discontent or any description of protest is, however, regarded by the Turkish local Government as seditious, and a policy such as I described in a previous despatch is pursued, depriving the Armenian subject of every liberty for his person, and for which no justification exists."

The pillage and murder of the Armenians proceeded on an increasing scale and with more open connivance on the part of the authorities, as Mr. Clifford Lloyd reported faithfully to his Government, although many of his reports—and they the most damaging to the Turkish Government—have not been published. He died at his post, and was succeeded at Erzeroum by Mr. Hampson, who reported in the beginning of 1891 a forward stride in the Sultan's policy of massacre. This was the enrolment of the Kurds into a cavalry force of 30,000, which the Sultan honoured by calling it after his own name, the "Hamidié," and over which he appointed as officers the most notorious criminals and brigand chiefs in Asia Minor, including Hussein Agha, whom the British Ambassador denounced as "a monster," and the dry inventory of whose crimes fills a page and a half of a folio Blue Book. This man, after being denounced to the Sultan by the British Ambassador, was invited to Constantinople, raised to the rank of a pasha by the Sultan, and given the command of one of the Hamidié regiments. Chosen representatives of this Kurdish cavalry were invited to Yildiz Kiosk by the Sultan, *fêted* right royally, and then sent back to Armenia "to suppress," as they openly declared, "the Armenians, with assurances that they will not be called to answer before the tribunals for any acts of oppression committed against Christians."

The Hamidié cavalry obeyed their master's instructions with great fidelity, and the lot of the wretched Armenians went from bad to worse. Still there was no attempt at rebellion, and the tyrant of Yildiz Kiosk began to wax impatient. Emissaries of sedition were therefore sent to provoke the Armenians to an abortive rising, and members of Armenian societies abroad were allowed to cross the frontier and agitate against the Sultan's Government. But all this had little effect on an unarmed and cowed peasantry. One Damadian, in particular, an Armenian Catholic from Constantinople, went, in 1892, about the villages of the Sasun district on a mission of agitation against the Government. He easily eluded the futile efforts which, for the sake of appearance, were made to arrest him. After nearly a year of this game of hide and seek, Damadian was arrested and sent to Constantinople, where, of course, he was immediately pardoned—a fact which speaks for itself.

What ought the British Government to have done in this state of things? The honour of England was more deeply concerned than that of any other Government in the protection of the Armenians. It was England which deprived them of the guarantees which Russia had provided for them in the Treaty of San Stefano. It was England, moreover, which had, in the Cyprus Convention, proclaimed to the world its intention to protect the Armenians. Yet the British Government, Liberal and Tory alike, did nothing to redeem the pledged honour of the nation.

What could the British Government have done? It might at least have followed the example of Lord John Russell's Government in 1850, and of the Russian Government in 1860. In the former case Lord Palmerston called the attention of the European Cabinets to the dangers to the general peace arising from the misgovernment of the kingdom of the Two Sicilies, as described in Mr. Gladstone's Letters to Lord Aberdeen. The publicity thus given to the tyranny of King Bomba had more to do with the overthrow of his son than the invasion of Garibaldi. Similarly, Prince Gortschakoff's circular despatch in 1860, warning the signatories of the Treaty of Paris of the intolerable oppression of its Christian subjects by the Porte, roused the slumbering conscience of Europe, so that there was no opposition to the prompt intervention of France and England on the outbreak of the Syrian massacres soon after Prince Gortschakoff's timely warning. Abdul Hamid II would not have dared to face the execration of civilised mankind, and his wholesale massacres would have not been. But instead of letting the light in upon the misdeeds and designs of the Sultan, the British Government did its best to screen them. It peremptorily refused to publish the reports of its own Consuls and the despatches of its Ambassador, and the nation was thus indebted to the enterprise of the press for the information which its own Government persistently concealed from it. And when the burst of indignation which the revelation of the facts occasioned forced the Government to act, it still took the course which of all others was best calculated to abet the Sultan in his fell designs. Two plans were open to the Government, either of which would probably have been successful. They might have appealed to a Congress of the signatories of the Berlin Treaty to join in compelling the Sultan to fulfil his treaty obligations towards the Armenians. Or they might have come to an understanding with Russia—which was then undoubtedly easy—for the pacification of Armenia. Instead of either of these obvious policies, they advised the Sultan to appoint a commission of inquiry into facts of which they had already ample knowledge in the reports of their own Consuls. The Sultan was only too delighted to fall in with so obliging a suggestion, provided, of course, that he was at liberty to conduct the inquiry in his own way. France and Russia then agreed, somewhat frigidly, to join England in sending Consuls to watch the proceedings of the Turkish Commission. As England had taken the lead, Prince Lobanoff naturally inquired what the Government proposed to do after the Commission had reported, for "it was evident that something must be done." On being told that "the Commission was not proceeding as satisfactorily as could be wished,"

> "His Excellency replied that he had never entertained much hope of a satisfactory result, and he doubted whether the perpetrators of the Sasun massacres would be brought to justice. In his opinion, however, the most important question to be considered was what was to be done when the Commission had finished its labours, and he sincerely hoped that some practical suggestion would be made."

But the British Government which originated this Commission had no suggestion to make, no policy to offer. Nay more, it meekly submitted to the indignity telegraphed by Sir Philip Currie in the following despatch:

> "The Ottoman Government have published Decrees conferring decorations on the Mufti of Moosh, who is said to have incited the troops against the Christians, and on Zeki Pasha, the Commandant of the 4th Army Corps. The Mutessarif of Moosh, who protested against the massacres, has been dismissed. The appointment of the Commission has been officially notified in the Press. The notice states that the Commission is sent to inquire into the criminal conduct of Armenian brigands, and denies absolutely the truth of massacres."

Lord Kimberley telegraphed back at once "his surprise and pain" at this exhibition of effrontery on the part of the Sultan; considered it "so grave in its nature that her Majesty's Government must give it their serious consideration without any delay"; and promised to send Sir P. Currie "instructions after I have consulted with my colleagues, as the matter cannot possibly be left in this position."

Nevertheless, the matter was "left in this position," and Russia and France, recognising the farce of the whole thing, but being apparently reluctant to separate from England, intimated that they would now send vice-consular delegates, not consuls, to accompany the Commission. The British Government followed suit, and sent a youthful vice-consul, who had no experience in that region, to accompany the Turkish Commission. At the same time it urged the Italian Government to sanction the sham inquiry by sending a delegate to accompany the Commission. But Italy, who had agreed, on England's invitation, and before the scope and purport of the Commission had been officially announced, to send a consul with the Commission, now refused to have anything to do with so palpable an imposture, and announced its intention to make an independent inquiry of its own.[2] The United States also, seeing that the undisguised object of the Commission was to screen the guilty and condemn the innocent, withdrew its previous sanction, and declined to have anything to do with it. The sanction of this monstrous Commission by Lord Rosebery's Government requires explanation, especially after Lord Kimberley's indignant despatch on learning that the intention of the Commission was to inquire into "the criminal conduct of Armenian brigands," the Sultan peremptorily declaring at the same time that there had been no massacre of Christians. Lord Kimberley took the decision of the Cabinet on the matter, with the result practically of sanctioning this outrage on the part of the Sultan. And when the foreign delegates, unable any longer to endure the gross travesty of justice with which the inquiry was conducted, washed their hands of the whole business and retired from the Commission, Lord Kimberley ordered the British delegate to resume his attendance.

Six months were wasted in this worse than bootless inquiry, and then a scheme of reform was offered to the Sultan for application in Armenia. Need we wonder that he doubted the sincerity of the reformers, and of England most of all, and refused contemptuously for three weeks to take any notice of the scheme? He might safely have sanctioned it, for without European control it was absolutely worthless. And he did sanction it after that period of tedious procrastination so dear to Turkish diplomacy.

Meanwhile the Liberal Government disappeared; and Lord Salisbury, seeing the worthlessness of the reforms as they stood, tried to make them effective by suggesting European control. But he was met by the reply that he was seeking to upset the policy of his predecessor, and his well-meant effort miscarried. In fact, the mistaken diplomacy of the Rosebery Cabinet began to show its fruits. Early in the negotiations an understanding with Russia in regard to Armenia was easy. The Government and people of Russia were still under the spell of that spontaneous outburst of British sympathy which the death of the Tsar, with its pathetic surroundings, had evoked, and which the genial diplomacy of the Prince of Wales—all the more effective from being unofficial—had intensified. Russia responded by promptly settling the question of the Pamirs in a sense satisfactory to England. After the flagitious conduct of the Sultan, Lord Rosebery might have cancelled the Cyprus Convention with the approbation of all parties, and thereby conciliated Russia by removing a standing menace against her, however little likely to be ever enforced. It was much easier for him to do this than for the author of the Convention. The opportunity was missed, but another chance of conciliating Russia presented itself later. Russia was seriously alarmed by the collapse of China and the terms of peace extorted from her by Japan, and the Tsar's Government proposed a friendly understanding with England on the subject. I state what I know when I say that England might then have practically made her own terms with Russia alike in the Far East and in the Near. No alliance was sought, only friendly cooperation; and the Russian Government would have met the British more than half-way both in China and Turkey. This would certainly have been greatly to the advantage of England, and would have been infinitely better for Japan. But so far were we from profiting by the friendly overture of Russia, it was promptly rejected, and the British squadron in the Far East was strengthened. This was probably a fortuitous coincidence, but Russia interpreted it as a menace, and at once invited France and Germany to the partnership which the British Government had spurned. From that moment Russia suspected the intentions of England and adopted an obstructive policy in regard to Armenia.

It was thus a fatal mistake on the part of Lord Rosebery to form a Russo-Franco-Anglican group unless he was prepared to give Russia some substantial guarantee of England's amity; for by forming a Triple Alliance on Oriental affairs he inevitably roused the suspicions and hostility of the other Triple Alliance, as the event soon proved.

After the scheme of reforms had been offered to the Sultan the members of the Triple Alliance complained that they had not been consulted, and Count Goluchowski intimated to Lord Salisbury (who had just returned to power) that it would be more comfortable to the Treaty of Berlin, and likely to be more effective, if the *six* Powers were to appoint a Commission of Surveillance for the application of reforms in Armenia. Lord Salisbury agreed, as, indeed, he could hardly help doing. But the result showed the fatal blunder made by his predecessor, either in not coming to terms with Russia in starting, or in not calling a conference of all the signatories of the Treaty of Berlin. Either plan would almost certainly have succeeded; but the policy which unfortunately prevailed was inevitably doomed to fall between the proverbial "two stools." Russia took alarm at the entrance of the Triple Alliance into any Commission of Surveillance in Armenia, and privately encouraged the passive resistance of the Sultan. Indeed, the scheme of reforms had already become an abortion. In the beginning of May 1895, an Ambassador at Constantinople wrote to the following effect to his Government: "The scheme of reforms presented by the three Powers," he said, "would be useless," an opinion for which he gives his reasons. Lord Rosebery's Government, said this authority, proposed that a Governor or High Commissioner should be appointed for a fixed term, subject to the approval of the Powers, to superintend the carrying out of the reforms, after the precedent established for the Lebanon—

> "a condition which the British Government had declared to be essential to the efficiency of the scheme. But this proposal was abandoned for the sake of keeping up the *entente* with France and Russia; which Governments, according to the information that reached the Porte, had expressed themselves rather sceptical as to

> the result of the reforms. And in truth it is plain that the scheme contains nothing which is not already the law of the country, but not applied, because not intended for home consumption, but for the purpose of silencing foreign Governments. Such laws, being opposed to the traditions of Islamic rule, will never be applied without foreign intervention. The Porte seems now to have obtained the support of Russia and France in rejecting the English proposal that the Governor should be appointed subject to the approval of the Powers."

Yet the British Government went on pressing on the Sultan a scheme of reforms which they had themselves thus reduced to nullity! An uncharitable critic might say that they were more intent on winning a majority at the impending General Election than on securing tolerable administration for the Armenians. I prefer to attribute their dogged perseverance in so inane a policy to that failure to grasp the situation which characterised their diplomacy from its inception to its close. And I regret that Lord Salisbury's loyalty to that fetich of diplomatists—continuity of foreign policy—restrained him from washing his hands of this *damnosa haereditas* and beginning *de novo.* A fresh start might have been difficult. But failure in overcoming the difficulty, and then an appeal to the conscience of Europe against the Powers, be they who they might, who were responsible for the continued anarchy in Asia Minor, would have been better that quiet acquiescence in so wretched a fiasco.

Lord Salisbury has been somewhat severely criticised for his menacing Guildhall speech, which has been characterised by some as mere *brutum fulmen*, signifying nothing. The fact, however, is that Lord Salisbury meant business. His solemn warning to the Sultan of the "ruin" that threatened his Empire, possibly resulting in dismemberment, was no empty menace. A great Power had proposed a naval demonstration in the neighbourhood of the Dardanelles, and it will probably be a surprise for England to learn that the Power which made that proposal was Austria. To conciliate Russia and France, it was suggested that the Powers taking part in the demonstration should pledge themselves not to annex any portion of Ottoman territory. France and Russia rejected the proposals. The other three Powers accepted them, constituting a group of four against two. It was then proposed that the four Powers should go on with the demonstration; that the fleets of England, Austria, and

Italy should pass the Dardanelles and dictate terms to the Sultan at Constantinople, deposing him in case of contumacy and appointing a successor. The German fleet was to be held in reserve, and join the other three in case of necessity. The English fleet went to Salonica, and the Italian fleet received orders to follow the lead of the British Admiral. So imminent at one time seemed the probability of action that Admiral Seymour sent a message to the Italian Admiral to hurry him up. These facts explain two brief despatches in the second volume of Blue Books (p. 73), which are obscure as they stand. The first is from the British Ambassador in Rome to Lord Salisbury:

> "I have the honour to inform your Lordship that I duly carried out your Lordship's instructions, as conveyed to me in your Lordship's telegram of the 23rd instant. Baron Blanc, Minister for Foreign Affairs, was absent from Rome at the time, but I have this day received a reply, a copy of which is herein enclosed, to the communication which I made him."

The gist of Baron Blanc's despatch is in the information that the Italian Ambassador at the Porte had received instructions "to support, in conjunction with the Embassies of Austria-Hungary and Germany, any steps which the British Embassy considers necessary or advisable to take." The meaning of this despatch is not a matter of inference, for on the 1st of last March, *àpropos* of a speech by Mr. Goschen on England's isolation, a semi-official article appeared in the organ of Crispi's Government, in which it is plainly stated that

> "the Anglo-Franco-Russian co-operation having failed, England addressed herself to Italy, Germany, and Austria-Hungary; and Italy replied that the three Powers were prepared to support any ulterior action that England might propose;"

and Baron Blanc's despatch in the Blue Book is referred to by way of confirmation. It was subsequently to this, I believe, that Austria made the definite proposal to which I have referred. Baron Blanc's despatch is dated October 26, and the article in the official organ says that "before receiving England's formal invitation, which was repeated at Vienna and Berlin," the Ambassadors of the Triple Alliance had received instructions to "support the action which the

British Ambassador was understood to be contemplating." The official article adds that

> "England having concentrated a powerful fleet near the Straits, Italy also sent a squadron, with open orders to co-operate with the English admiral when invited to do so, but not to provoke or anticipate the action of the British fleet."

The article is an explanation of Mr. Goschen's assertion that England's isolation was not compulsory, since, as a matter of fact, she had refused offers of support from other Powers. It is confessed that the retirement of the English fleet to Malta on the refusal of Russia and France to agree to the proposed naval demonstration was a great disappointment to the Italian Government, which evidently believed the demonstration would be successful, and would be more likely to prevent than to provoke a general war. Russia and France, the Italian Government thought, would hardly court collision with so powerful a combination of naval and military force, but would, on the contrary, probably end in joining the demonstration.

Lord Salisbury is, I believe, no great favourite with Russia, which has never forgiven him the Cyprus Convention and the speech, eight years ago, in which he indicated Austria as the destined heir of the throne of Constantine on the Bosphorus. Yet Lord Salisbury has twice at least done Russia a signal service. During the Russo-Turkish war in 1877, when the sword of England would probably have turned the scale against the Tsar, it was Lord Salisbury who prevented Lord Beaconsfield from fulfilling the threat of his "three campaigns" speech. And if he had accepted the proposal to dictate terms to the Sultan from the decks of the most powerful naval force that ever floated on the waters of the Bosphorus, Russia would certainly not be the Power which would now be predominant in Constantinople. Another result, however, would have been that England could then have hardly avoided becoming an integral member of the Triple Alliance.

These are facts on which both France and Russia may profitably ponder. For the moment their triumph in Turkey seems complete. Yet it may prove a Pyrrhic victory. It is well in such matters to look ahead beyond the exigencies of the hour. There are elements in the Russo-French Alliance which do not augur well for its permanence. The union of an Orthodox autocracy with a Catholic republic does not look promising, and some ominous symptoms of future antagonism are already appearing. The Russian nation hugs its religion not merely as a doctrine but as an essential element of its patriotism, and the reception of Prince Boris into the bosom of Orthodoxy was made a *sine qua non* of Russia's reconciliation to Bulgaria. The French nation, on the other hand, claims to be "the eldest son of the Church," and the head of that Church has lately consigned both Prince Boris and his father to perdition; the former for being received, the latter for letting him be received, into the Orthodox Church. And the Roman Catholic "Patriarch of Antioch" has lately sent the Pope, as the most acceptable offering for the anniversary of his Pontificate, the joyful tidings of 8000 Orthodox Christians frightened into the Papal fold in order to enjoy from Catholic France the protection for which they had till now looked to Russia. A diplomatist at Constantinople wrote to his Government last October that "his Beatitude the Catholic Armenian Patriarch, *in consequence of instructions received from the Vatican*, has always shown himself, down to those events (Constantinople massacres), exceedingly lukewarm in the cause of his countrymen, to whom he has refused any support. He has maintained the most cordial relations with the Sultan, and his attitude is severely criticised among the Armenians." And well it might be. The Armenians who have accepted Papal jurisdiction are, in Asia Minor at least, but a fraction of the Armenian population; and "the Catholic Patriarch," therefore, took no interest in them. He was quite satisfied when M. Cambon, the French Ambassador, assured him "that his flock had nothing to fear, since it was only the schismatic Armenians who were aimed at," because they had no protectors, not being in communion either with the Church of Russia or of Rome. Chivalrous M. Cambon! Apostolic Mgr. Azarian!

I must refer, as bearing on the same point, to a curious and most instructive document which was lately drawn up for the information of the Sultan. About a year ago the Pope addressed an encyclical letter to the Bishops of the Orthodox Church, exhorting them all to acknowledge his jurisdiction, and promising them in return to sanction all their present usages and customs, including marriage of the clergy, their native liturgy in the vernacular, their distinctive vestments and ritual, &c. The Sultan, who has a keen eye for any novel departure among his subjects, gave orders that a committee of experts should report to him on the advisability of encouraging or discountenancing the Pope's propaganda. The report of this Committee is a very able document, and its conclusion, after an able analysis of all the facts and contingencies, is that it will be wise to encourage the Papal propaganda in every way. The permanent enemy of Turkey being Russia, and Russia's influence depending so much on her protectorate of the Orthodox population, that influence would decrease with the decrease of Orthodoxy in Turkey. This decision was made known at the Vatican, and Mgr. Azarian, the Patriarch of the small minority of Armenian Roman Catholics, was ordered to hold no intercourse with the Gregorians, who form the great bulk of the Armenian nation, and to cultivate friendly relations with the Sultan. We have seen the result in the French Ambassador's assurance to Mgr. Azarian, that "not a single Armenian Catholic, who was known to be such, had been hurt, the Armenian schismatics alone being aimed at" in the massacres. In M. Cambon's phraseology the "schismatics" are those who cleave to the ancient Church of their fathers at the cost of life, while "the Catholic Armenians" are the minority of seceders who have in recent times accepted the jurisdiction of the Pope. It is hardly an edifying spectacle to see this *entente cordiale* solemnised between the Mussulman Sultan and "the Vicar of Christ" over the holocaust of martyred Armenians. Nor did the interchange of good offices end there. While Lord Salisbury's minatory language was still ringing in his ears and Russia had not yet covered him with her dangerous shield, the Sultan betook himself to the Pope for help.

> "The Sultan [wrote a Spanish statesman in the month of last December] has made a direct appeal to Leo XIII. imploring him to put pressure on England and Russia to induce them to withdraw their demands about Armenia. The Pope is highly flattered, this being the first time that an Ottoman Sultan has put himself formally *en rapport* with the Holy See instead of through some Catholic Power acting as intermediary."

The Vatican propaganda has made considerable progress among the Orthodox population of Bosnia and the Herzegovina, and has made no small inroads on the heretofore solid phalanx of the Bulgarian Church under the pressure of Prince Ferdinand and his zealous Catholic wife. Roumania, too, has recently yielded not a few conversions to the Papal fold. Russia's claim to a predominant protectorate over the Christian subjects of the Porte rests on her hitherto well-founded right to represent the creed of the large majority. Her abandonment of the Armenians, and her supineness in protecting even the Orthodox Christians of Turkey in the recent troubles, have seriously shaken her hold on her erstwhile *protégés*, as the conversion of 8000 Orthodox to Popery in the last six months, for the sake of French protection, shows. When these facts have filtered into the minds of the Russian people they may begin to think that the utility of the French alliance is somewhat onesided.

Considerations like these can hardly fail to make reflecting Russians doubt whether the French alliance is likely to be very stable. When the inevitable distribution of the Sick Man's inheritance takes place—and the catastrophe may happen suddenly and soon—the Franco-Russian Alliance will hardly bear the stress and strain of clashing interests and aspirations. France claims a dominant influence in Syria, and Syria holds Jerusalem and its holy places, which Holy Russia would never suffer to fall into alien and heterodox hands. And these coming events are likely to cast their shadows considerably before.

The English people, on the other hand, are pretty well cured of their Russophobia, and it is hardly too much to say that if Russia had taken the lead in securing tolerable government in Armenia, the public feeling of England would have given her a free hand in Turkey, and would even have left it to others, more directly interested, to bar her way to Constantinople. The evil legacy of the Crimean war would have vanished, and Russia and England might in future have devoted their energies to the peaceful rivalry of civilising the vast Asiatic empires over which they rule.

There was a moment when Russia and France might have broken up the Triple Alliance. The Transvaal incident, skilfully used, might easily have established cordial relations between England and Russia and France. Italy, which was getting weary of the burdens laid upon her by the Triple Alliance, would have gravitated towards England, and a combination would thus have been formed, without any formal alliance, which would have offered a better guarantee for peace than the present combination. But, just as Lord Rosebery's

Government missed its opportunity when Russia invited its partnership in the Far East, so Russia and France now missed a chance, which may not return, of dissolving the Triple Alliance. The disaster of Adowa shook the Italian monarchy to its foundation, and there was a week during which it was a question whether Italy would not abandon Abyssinia and come to terms with France. Austria was alarmed, and Berlin likewise. Another disaster in Abyssinia, such as the capture of Kassala, with the certain massacre of its garrison, might upset the throne of King Humbert. There was no time to be lost. England was urged to prevent a revolution in Italy by a diversion in Egypt, which would at the same time avert a Dervish invasion as the certain consequence of the fall of Kassala. Italy was advised from Berlin to cultivate friendly relations with England, and was assured that, while Germany might seek her own ends as regards Russia, she would energetically support any agreement that Italy might make with England. The expedition to Dongola was the result. By opposing that expedition France and Russia forced Germany and Austria into open co-operation with England and Italy; and perseverance in their anti-English policy may turn the Triple into a Quadruple Alliance. That can hardly be their aim, for it is the simple truth to say that England could practically make her own terms as a condition of joining the Triple Alliance; and the policy of France, backed by Russia, is remarkably well calculated to bring about that result.

It would be a pity to close this survey of the Armenian imbroglio without one more example of the Sultan's amazing effrontery. An official of rank, who was present when the Queen's letter was read to the Sultan last January, gives the following report of the scene:

> "The Queen appealed to the humane feelings of the Sultan, and said that it seemed incredible that such crimes could be verified as those which were reported to have been committed in Armenia, and she hoped that the Sultan would put an end to them in consideration of the friendly relations always existing between the two crowns. The Sultan received this communication with a puzzled look and more than ordinary surprise. His Majesty replied that he had proved his profound repugnance to any effusion of blood, and that his troops had always endeavoured to avoid it. As to the rest, order was now restored throughout his Empire, except at Zeitoun, as to

> which he was waiting the result of the mediation of the Consuls. That the Sultan should keep up the pretence of this apparent ignorance and indifference is not surprising, seeing that the system now in vogue in Ottoman official spheres is that of simply denying that any grave events have occurred in the Empire. That which the Embassies consider worthy of attention is the fact that England has now recourse to prayers and no longer to demands."

The last news from Constantinople, while I write, is that the Sultan has violated his solemn promise to the Powers to appoint a Christian Governor of Zeitoun, as one of the conditions of its surrender, and that he has again forbidden the distribution of relief to the destitute survivors of his massacres. His explanation that the appointment of a Mussulman Governor is only temporary is an expedient to gain time, in the hope and belief, hitherto only too well founded, that the Powers will get tired of remonstrating, and will acquiesce in accomplished facts. The next remonstrance will be met by the plea that the removal of the Governor would cause a disturbance. *Quousque tandem abutere patientia nostra?* Surely it is time that the Powers should address that question with an ultimatum to the miscreant whom they have already branded publicly as an arch-murderer and liar.

The Spectator, Vol. 77 (September 5, 1896): 292

The Massacres

Five thousand Armenians have been massacred in the streets of Constantinople. The Ambassadors of the Powers promptly showed their sense of the gravity of this fact. They expressed their regret to the Porte, and refused to put candles in their windows on the Sultan's Accession Day. Never was there so prompt and spirited a protest. It reminds one of Lady Catherine de Burgh:—"I take no leave of you, Miss Bennet. I send no compliments to your mother. I am seriously displeased." In truth, it is as if the neighbours in a suburban town, discovering that one of the householders in the square had been guilty of horrible cruelty to his wife and children, and held a meeting and determined that, in view of the fearful atrocity of Mr. S.'s conduct, they would only nod to him when they met at the station, and would on no account say it was a fine morning. The Powers are no doubt sincerely anxious to stop horrors like those of last week, when Galata was turned into a slaughter-house, and men, women, and children were killed under the eyes of the soldiers and police by a Turkish mob; but do they seriously imagine that the sort of action they are taking will have any result? The Sultan is not such a fool as to be frightened by their omission to illuminate in honour of his accession. The fact that he has been able to let the mob loose in the capital without any serious injury to his right to do what he will in Turkey, is ample compensation for a dull Fête-day. The knowledge that he can go as far as he likes in the way of suppressing anarchical tendencies among the Armenians, as he puts it, is worth any number of small snubs. The Sultan can now feel that the jealousies and fears of Europe make him master in his own house, and that he has nothing further to fear from outside pressure. He was no doubt rather nervous at testing his strength, but now that he has found how great it is, he must be exceedingly happy. If nothing is to happen to him, even when the Armenians get their deserts, not in a distant province, but in the streets of Constantinople, all fear of armed intervention is at an end.

The world is so saturated with Turkish horrors that it has lost all sense of proportion, and talks as if the recent doings in Constantinople were merely a regrettable street incident, reflecting little credit on the Sultan, no doubt, but still merely an ordinary piece of misgovernment of the kind that must be expected in Turkey. Yet in fact the massacre of last week was one of the greatest, if not the greatest, massacre in modern history. In the September massacres in Paris not a fourth of the number were killed, and the greatest slaughter during the Revolution, that which took place during the street fighting when the Swiss Guard were annihilated, only caused the death of five thousand people. But on that occasion there was something approaching a battle. At Constantinople it was pure butchery. The Armenians were hunted out and knocked on the head like rats in a barn. We are, then, face to face with this fact:—One of the bloodiest deeds in history has been committed in the face of Europe, and Europe can think of nothing better to do to punish the perpetrators than to keep its Embassies dark on the Sultan's Fête-day. Though England must to some extent share the disgrace with the rest of the Powers, we freely admit that Lord Salisbury would be most willing to take active measures to put an end to a Government which can create such a state of things. If the Powers would only agree, he would doubtless use the force of England to punish the perpetrator or tolerator of the massacres. But the Powers will not agree. What, then, ought to be England's attitude? It appears to us that the time has come when we must clearly define our position. Of course the ideally best of all courses to pursue would be to obtain an agreement among the Powers for the partition of the Turkish Empire. Russia should be asked to take Constantinople and Anatolia; France, Syria; Austria, Salonica; Greece, the islands; Italy, Tripoli; while we should remain in Egypt. Of course, this could be done, and done effectually, if only Russia would agree. Were she to consent, Austria, though angry, would be obliged to acquiesce. But, unfortunately, it seems impossible to get Russia to agree. She prefers that Turkey should advance yet a stage further towards complete putrefaction, and appears oblivious to the sufferings she thus inflicts upon the Christian subjects of the Sultan.

But even if the avenue of hope opened by a partition of Turkey is closed, is there not some other opening? There is, if the Powers will only take it. If they cannot agree as to the disposal of Turkey, and regard the maintenance of the *status quo* in Turkey as a necessary guarantee for European peace, why cannot they agree to depose the present Sultan, and to put in his place his brother or some other member of the house of Othman who may seem suitable. In this way the *status quo* would be preserved, and yet a lesson given to the Turks that Europe will not tolerate a regime of massacre and atrocity. The new Sultan, with his predecessor's fate before his eyes, would think twice before he let the Kurds loose in Armenia, or the mob in Constantinople.

But though we believe that the deposition of the Sultan might be accomplished, and yet the *status quo* be maintained, we feel very little real hope that the Powers will agree to such a course. They will, we fear, take the line that the deposition of the Sultan might mean armed intervention, and that armed intervention by six Powers might lead to jealousy and confusion, and so might imperil the peace of Europe. In fact, they would argue, "What is the massacre of five thousand Armenians compared with the interests of European peace?" If, then, England can neither obtain the partition of Turkey nor the deposition of the Sultan, what is she to do? Is she to sit down and let the spectacle of massacre and outrage go by without moving? It is a terrible alternative, but we fear she must. If she alone were to send her Fleet to Constantinople, she would probably secure nothing but the hatred of Europe. Suppose our Fleet to have forced the passage of the Dardanelles, to be anchored in the Bosphorus, and to have delivered an ultimatum to the Sultan. If we took this action in opposition to the Powers, they would probably advise the Sultan to resist. What could we do then? We might bombard the Seraglio and the city, but with little effect. After we had bombarded Alexandria, we found that we had an instant need for an army to occupy the streets and keep order. But Constantinople is a city of a million people, and to keep order would require an army of at least thirty thousand men. But the idea of landing thirty thousand men in the teeth of a united European opposition is absurd. Even if the Powers only offered a passive resistance, we should find ourselves in an intolerable position. Clearly it would be impossible for us to take action alone. Another alternative would be to retire altogether from the Concert of Europe, and to throw the blame entirely on the other Powers. But this would be not only dangerous, but a blow to the cause of the Armenians. As long as we keep in the Concert of Europe, we can do something to help the Christian subjects of the Porte. As the example of Crete shows, that something may often be really important.

It must be confessed that the whole prospect is gloomy and depressing. The only ray of hope, and that, we confess, is a faint one, is afforded by the Czar's visit to Balmoral. It is just possible that in the conversations in which he will doubtless engage with the statesmen who are to meet him there, he may become convinced that we have no sinister motives in urging Russia to take the lead in putting an end to Turkish misrule, and that we would loyally support Russia in any action she might take in the direction of freeing Armenia and possessing herself of Constantinople. If Russia could be persuaded to join with us in a settlement of the Turkish question, we might see an end put very shortly to the infamy of Mahommedans ruling Christians. As we have said, however, it is but a faint ray of hope. We fear that the Czar is more likely to listen to the views of those who call for the *status quo* at any price, than to listen to counsellors who may advise that if he comes to an agreement with England, his may be the glory of freeing Europe from the last remnant of Turkish rule.

The Contemporary Review, Vol. 70 (September 1896): 435–48

Two Massacres in Asia Minor

W. M. Ramsay

In the history of Asia Minor foreign invasion has often been accompanied by wholesale destruction of life. For example, to one who has the misfortune to read some pages of the old historians, unquoted and unquotable in modern books, the horrors of Tamerlane's inroad are a nightmare that haunts the mind at night and in solitude. But these and other terrible incidents have the excuse of war, of passion roused, when foreign conquerors were forcing their way into the country. There stand out above them in devilishness two great massacres, when a settled Government has essayed, with calculated policy, the extermination of a section of its own subjects, and has applied to the task all the resources of civilization, all the power that lies in organization, plan, co-operation, all the terrors of a standing army drilled and commanded to destroy a people. One of these massacres is hidden behind a double veil of the obscurity of ancient history—I mean Diocletian's persecution of the Christians. The other is in progress, its successive stages reported by telegraph, studied by experts, observed and recorded by consuls and ambassadors and special commissions, until we have grown sick to think of it, while we make an empty pretence of wishing that it should stop.

But, apart from the horror, the unspeakable cruelty and infamy of this last most gigantic crime in the history of the whole world, a crime in comparison with which everything that was hitherto most accursed in history sinks into insignificance, its effect in degrading the whole of Christendom and in retarding the progress of the civilized world is something that we cannot estimate, but which will surely be made manifest in the years that are to come. The comparison of the other great massacre in Asia Minor, and its effects on the civilized world in the centuries that followed, may give some conception of the loss that humanity sustains when it connives at the extermination of a race or of a party in the State. Leaving it to others to describe the miserable condition of the country, where the worst fate is to survive longest, I look back to past history. And if there be any resemblance in the results, as there is a marvelous resemblance in the antecedents and the facts of these two massacres, then we are as yet only at the beginning of events which will affect all Europe nearly, try as it may to "pass by on the other side."

Far more is recorded about the massacres inaugurated by the Emperor Diocletian in 303 A.D. than about any other of the "persecutions"; but it is hard to get from the records any clear idea of its meaning and its results. We shall better understand what that massacre meant to the world by looking at a Phrygian valley on the upper Maeander, at one of the two termini of the Ottoman Railway, beside the old city of Eumeneia, and observing how it acted there. We want to find out what was the effect on the mass of ordinary society: in what state did the massacre find, and in what state did it leave society? We hear, as a rule, about the prominent partisans and martyrs of Christianity: friends and enemies alike speak almost exclusively of them, neglecting entirely the great mass of undistinguished and obscure Christians. Those common persons (who, as a rule, had not the courage and heroism to stand forth prominently as martyrs, or the intellectual power to shine as leaders and teachers) are not represented to us in the Christian literature, except when their errors and backslidings have to be castigated; but they are shown to us in their epitaphs; and, if we want to see what Christianity practically was as a working influence in the Roman Empire, these common men are worth some share of the attention that is given usually only to the leaders.[1]

The questions before us, then, are: What was the condition of society in this Phrygian town during the third century (which is equivalent to asking what was the relation between pagans and Christians there), and what was the effect of Diocletian's action?

Christianity, when establishing itself amid an alien society, did not immediately re-make the whole life and manner of its converts.

They continued to live in many respects as before: they were characterized by most of the habits, and some, or many even, of the faults, of their old life and of the society in which they lived. That is clearly shown in St. Paul's letters to his early converts; it is the experience of missionaries in pagan countries; it is the lesson that we have to learn from the earliest Christian inscriptions of Phrygia. "It took centuries for Christianity to disengage itself from its surroundings and to re-make society and the rules of life."[2] Even Tertullian, who was disposed to go further than most in the direction of separating Christian from pagan society, speaks of the former as men living in company with the latter, similar in respect of food, dress, surroundings, and appliances, frequenting the same forum, market, baths, shops, fairs & etc.[3] We cannot doubt that the shopkeeper or trader who was converted did not as a rule alter the outward appearance of his life. People might converse with him in the street or the forum, and observe no reason to suspect him of Christianity. He did not break with "all his old thoughts and habits and feelings and friends when he was converted. He lived in externals much as before; he observed the same laws of politeness in society; his house, his surroundings continued much the same; he kept up the same family names, and when he died his grave, his tombstone, and his epitaph, were in the ordinary style."

The epitaphs prove that, under the imposed conditions of obedience to the existing Government, and laws and strict maintenance of order and peace within the city, there was established a *modus vivendi* between the two opposing religions; and the easiest way of showing its character is to invite the reader's attention to the evidence. The *modus vivendi* is exemplified in the epitaphs.

It is always difficult to eradicate ideas and superstitions connected with death and burial, and pagans and Christians in the early centuries tried in the same way to guarantee the sanctity of the grave, and to prevent unauthorised use being made of it; both alike enacted legal penalties, and invoked divine punishment, in case of intrusion. In legal penalties no religious scruple was violated; Christians and pagans met here on a common ground; and their epitaphs are undistinguishable so far as such penalties are concerned. But it was different in respect of divine protection. It was not possible for even the least instructed Christian to appeal to Helios, or Leto; and, as the desire to trust the safety of their graves to God was probably even stronger among the Christians than among the pagans, they sought after forms of adjuration which would conform to their religious views. Further, it was necessary that these forms should not be too openly Christian; they must be so general in expression as not to constitute an open declaration of their religion. Various expressions were devised to suit this need, to avoid at once offence against the common public feeling and outrage to private Christian feeling; but by far the most important was one, which seems to have originated in Eumeneia, and to have thence spread to some of the surrounding cities, "The violator shall account to the God." The pagans often used the term "the God" to indicate the great local deity; and it is also common in Christian books. In no respect could this formula jar on the most susceptible of pagans;[4] and yet it contains an idea, which was rarely expressed by them, while it has been at all times ready to the lips of every person trained in Christian society. The pagans often appealed to their God, but rarely to him as the judge; they often ask him to punish their enemy, but they rarely ask for fair treatment according to a reckoning of deserts.

It was probably during the first quarter of the third century that this formula was struck out; and it soon passed into very general use. There were twenty-six examples of it in Eumeneia alone (not to mention the cities round); and all belong to the period 220–300 A.D.[5] There is no demonstrably Christian epitaph of earlier time; for, although the church in Eumeneia dates back to the middle of the first century, the Christian character was still thoroughly suppressed in the epitaphs of the second century, and, though several are suspected of Christian origin, none can as yet be admitted in evidence.[6] In other neighbouring towns Christian epitaphs of earlier date have been detected by other indications. The most important of these was engraved on the tomb of a church leader of the second century, Avircius Marcellus, who, according to the native custom, prepared his own grave in his lifetime: he expressed in his epitaph the fundamental facts and mysteries of his faith; described their wide extension over the world from Rome to the regions beyond the Euphrates, and the universal agreement in regard to them, placing this as a monument and witness to the faith plan before the eyes of all. Yet, so skilfully veiled in his expression, that a German scholar has demonstrated, with true German learning and ingenuity, that there is no word or phrase in it which might not be used by a pagan; and he has inferred that the Christians of the valley, who admittedly regarded this monument as the gravestone of their great bishop, were mistaken, and that it is really the epitaph of a priest of Cybele. His argument has this great value, that it proves how pagans of the second century might fail to detect the religion of an epitaph, which has deceived even a German theologian.

But the twenty-six Eumeneian epitaphs are sufficient to give us some idea of the situation of thought and society in the city. We must bear in mind that what the Christians in Phrygia aimed at was the appearance of legality rather than absolute concealment. It is certain that they were numerous in Phrygia even in the second century; and it may be assumed that their strength was known in a vague way to the whole population. But their religion was forbidden, and any convicted Christian was put to death. Such was the theoretical principle; but in practice there was a great laxity in carrying it out. Trajan, Hadrian, and Antoninus Pius practically ordered provincial governors not to observe Christians, unless their attention was called to them by a prosecutor, who formally accused them. But prosecution in the Roman world could not be really effective, except where the government took the initiative, and sought out the Christians. In Rome there was no official prosecutor; regards were given to volunteers who prosecuted successfully; and the carrying out of the laws in general was left to private initiative. When Christianity was very strong, it would probably be rarely possible to find any private person ready both to brave the feeling generally entertained in ancient times against all volunteer prosecutors (*delatores)*, and to incur "the hatred of a united and energetic body like the Christians." The lack of martyrs in Phrygia between 180 and 303 A.D. conspires with all other signs to show that the Church in Phrygia developed in peace and prosperity during that period. There was a general indisposition among the officials and the pagans to begin any open action against the Christians; and the Church, on its side, studied to use all the outward forms that would give legality, and to avoid anything which would tend to draw attention to it or to provoke prosecution. A spirit of forbearance in practice was encouraged on both sides, and in the course of generations this became the rule of practical life.

In pursuance of this policy, the Christians put nothing in public documents, such as their epitaphs, which could be quoted as evidence of Christianity: if an official was mentioned, a title common to the pagans was used, as *episkopos* or *geraios*. Jewish festivals were legal; and their names could therefore be used. Benefit societies were allowed by law under certain restrictions; and the communities of Christians in the cities were therefore registered under suitable names, assimilated to those of trades or local guilds. Where anything clearly Christian was mentioned, it was hidden under a monogram, a symbol, or a strange name; and in all cases these resembled in appearance something that was pagan. For example, the Christian sign [*symbol*] was very like the pagan [*symbol*]; and the readiness with which the one might be taken for the other is shown by the fact that a skilful and learned epigraphist like the editor of the Berlin *Corpus* of Greek inscriptions actually made that mistake in one case, and conjecturally rewrote a correctly copied inscription in order to support his interpretation. That may be taken as an example of the errors which spring from the failure to recognise the true origin and character of the Christian epitaphs.

To judge from the proportion of epitaphs, the population of Eumeneia in the third century was in great part Christian. Of the seventy-one epitaphs which I have classed as pagan or doubtful, only eleven are clearly marked as later than 215 A.D., and several of these are suspected of Christianity. In the same period we posses twenty-six epitaphs that are certainly Christian. Three persons are mentioned as senators in the second century, and six in the third; the three are probably pagans, the six are all Christians.

These facts show that Eumeneia was to a large extent a Christian city during the third century. Naturally we should expect that the predominance of the Christian element would be more marked in the second half of the century; for the more vigorous and resolute character of the Christians would make them advance steadily in influence and the lighter elements would be drawn after them. The coinage of the city continued to bear the old types; but that does not prove the city to be pagan. The Fortune of the city is a very common type; but, in the spirit of concession which evidently ruled at Eumeneia, probably a Christian would not hesitate to authorise such types. The coinage ends about 260 A.D.; and it is not very varied. About 250–260, when persecution was being renewed, several Diana types occur, as if some acknowledgment of the established religion were necessitated at that crisis.

Further, the inscriptions convey the impression that there was no violent break between Greek and Christian culture in Eumeneia. There is no sign of bitterness on either side. One long inscription, which is distinctly anti-Christian, savours more of argument than of persecution: it seems to indicate deliberate choice of the better among two alternatives. The inscriptions bring before us a picture of rich and generous development, of concession, of liberality, in which people of diverse thoughts were practically reconciled in a single society. But they also show us Eumeneia as mainly a city of Christians. Nothing similar to this is known throughout the ancient world; Eumeneia stands before us as the earliest Christian city of which record remains; and, while the new religion was less strong in other cities, still Eumeneia may serve as the type of what went on in the whole region, exemplifying the practical conciliation of two hostile religions in a peaceful and ordinary city. Knowing that the first requirement of the Imperial Roman Government was order and quiet in the city, the citizens confined themselves in ordinary circumstances to verbal disagreement, while each avoided extremes in action. Further, the epigraphy of the city shows that attention was withdrawn from the empty kind of business that generally occupied the municipal senates, while energy was concentrated on the practical problem of working out, within the limits of "the Roman peace," a balance between the stronger Christian and the diminishing pagan party.

The resulting compromise cannot be described in detail. The forms of the State religion—*ie.*, the worship of Imperial Rome divine—had to be kept up, for it was "the keystone of the Imperial policy,"[7] and its maintenance was the test of loyalty; to the ancient mind "patriotism was another form of adherence to the national religion."[8] Thus it was a necessity for the city either to keep up extremes. How far the individual Christian might go in acceptance of the Roman forms we are denied all evidence, and need not speculate. Opinion and conduct varied widely, as is natural; some condemned as sinful a degree of compliance which others justified as merely the acceptance of outward forms of politeness. The courtesies of society and common life, as well as of municipal administration, had a non-Christian form; and wise toleration will admit great varieties of opinion as to how far politeness might honestly be carried in accepting the usual practices. During the following centuries the forms of courtesy became Christianised; but the process was only beginning in the third century. Probably the same policy which placed on the gravestone an appeal to "the god," leaving every one to understand in his own sense a term common to pagans and Christians, modified in similar delicate ways many of the forms of social and municipal life. But one thing is certain: if Christians entered the Imperial service or the municipal career, some sacrifice of strict principle was necessary, and, as magistrates, they had to comply with many non-Christian religious forms in a public way, for religion entered far more closely into the details of life in ancient times than it does in modern society and government. The mere fact that so many Christian senators of Eumeneia are known to us shows that the spirit of accommodation ruled there.

Even a casual glance over the Christian inscriptions in the Appendix to my chapter on the subject must suggest the question: Where are the later Christian inscriptions of Eumeneia? In the third century we have twenty-six certain, and several others probable; but only four can be classed to the fourth and following centuries. The contrast between the rich intellectual and political life of the Christians in the third century and the inarticulate monotony of the many centuries that follow is painful. We recognise in the dry pages of our catalogue the signs of some calamity to the race, the destruction of a vigorous and varied life. Two facts stand out prominently with regard to the change between the third and the fourth century. In the first place, it did not happen by a gradual process. The inscriptions are arrested suddenly about 300 A.D.; and there is no intermediate class between the earlier and the later styles. As M. Cumont first remarked, the reason lies in the great massacre by Diocletian and his coadjutors and successors, 303–313 A.D. In the second place, while it was a sudden calamity that arrested the development of the Christian city, the effects were permanent and irreparable: the life of the city was destroyed. Up to 300 A.D. we trace in its monuments the signs of active thought and work; after 300 there is a blank dotted with a few names of bishops at councils, with an archdeacon, a presbyter, and a single other individual. To a certain extent the stagnation is due to the causes described in other chapters[9]—the over-centralisation of government, the decay of municipal self-government, the indifference of the Imperial administration to the education of the people. But these causes were acting during the third century, and yet life was apparently more active then in the city than ever before; suddenly they became dominant and all-powerful. There seems no adequate explanation of the facts, except in the terrible calamity which destroyed the active and progressive section of the population, and gave free play to the forces in the Empire that were making for stagnation and ignorance.

These considerations point to the conclusion that the persecution of Diocletian took in Eumeneia the form of a thorough-going massacre; and a massacre could not be thorough unless it were deliberately planned. This is in perfect agreement with all that is recorded about the persecution. Private initiative in persecutions was no longer required; but the Christians were actively sought out by Government in pursuance of a carefully considered plan for annihilating their religion. To this end was directed all the power of a highly organised Government, moved by a single will, commanding almost unlimited resources for the space of ten years. The Government took advantage of a marked philosophical religious revival, characterised by strong anti-Christian feeling; and turned to its own uses the power of a strong emotion acting on men, many of whom were of lofty sentiments. In the first two centuries of its history, Christianity had to deal with a decaying and spiritless paganism; but now it met a reinvigorated and desperate religion, educated and spiritualised in the conflict against the Christians.

The "Acta" of Theodotus of Ancyra furnishes an example of the way in which the devoted fanaticism of such men made them convenient tools for Government at this crisis. The approach of a new governor, and the rumour of his intentions, struck terror into the hearts of Christians, as the "Acta" relates. The name of this governor was Theotecnus, "the child of God." Such a term might seem an impossible name for a Roman official; but the "Acta" is a document of the highest authenticity.[10] We recognize in the term one of those personal appellations assumed by some of the philosophic reactionaries, who vied with the Christian confidence in their divine mission and the Christian religious names assumed at baptism. In a Phrygian city not far from Eumeneia a long, dated inscription commemorates some of the leaders of the persecution; it imitates the language of St. John's Gospel, and speaks of the many who had been rescued from the evil torments (of Christianity).[11]

As an example of what happened in Phrygia, Eusebius mentions the fate of a city in which the people and the magistrates alike were all Christian. Combining his brief account with that of an even higher authority (at least on this point), Lactantius, we may state the facts as follows: the people collected at their church (which in itself was an act of defense). They were surrounded by a ring of soldiers, and the usual choice was offered, compliance or death. In ordinary circumstances we need not doubt that some, perhaps many, would have lacked the boldness to choose the latter alternative: but it lies in human nature that the general spirit of a crowd exercises a powerful influence on the individuals who compose it; and even those who, taken singly, might have shrunk from a terrible death, accepted it when inspired by the courage of the whole body. The entire people were burned with the church. And to those who by the patient toil of years have tracked out these Christians through their formula of appeal to "the god," it comes as one of those convincing details of real life and truth, that the one thing recorded about this destroyed people is that they died "calling upon the god over all." Unconsciously Eusebius writes as an epitaph over their ashes the words by which we have recognised the epitaphs of their own composition.

This was done by a governor, as Lactantius mentions; and no Roman governor could have ventured on such an act, unless he had a full commission to exterminate the Christians. A general massacre was evidently planned, and carried out by convenient agents. While this case has been selected for record as an extreme example of barbarity on the one side and of steadfastness on the other, it must be taken as indicative of the general policy. Hereafter it may be proved that Eumeneia was the city to which Eusebius and Lactantius allude.[12] At any rate, the punishment was everywhere proportionate to the guilt; and Eumeneia, as more deeply infected than any of the surrounding cities, would be treated with corresponding severity as an example to the rest. Historical and archaeological evidence conspire to prove that the active and courageous element in the Eumeneian people was annihilated with fire and sword about 303, and the development of the city was suddenly terminated.

While the Government used the anti-Christian revival for its own purpose, and while that revival was a contributory cause of the massacre, the main reason that induced Diocletian to give a reluctant consent to the policy was certainly not fanaticism. The measure was chosen after long consideration as politically expedient. The Christians were opposed to the government policy. They were the party of reform, and though they advocated their policy, as a rule, within the limits of strictest constitutional agitation, yet the Roman Government was never tolerant of political opinions among the people: it claimed to think politically for all. Now, the Christians, as a body, were necessarily desirous of change in the government policy, which proscribed them (even though this became under most Emperors more theoretical than practical). They were energetic as individuals and as a body; and therefore they were opposed, whether consciously or not, to the centralised and paternal Government policy, which more and more arrogated the right of ordering everything, managing everything, thinking for everybody. That policy, which ultimately ruined the Empire, was thwarted by the growth of freedom and individuality among the Christians; and the Government resolved to destroy the opposing elements in the State.

Freedom of spirit is a more delicate plant in the East than in Europe, in ancient than in modern times. Some, and especially those who have paid least heed to the new evidence that has been accumulating, may regard as fanciful the picture which we have drawn of the new Phrygian life of the third century as full of promise of a healthy and vigorous development for the Roman Empire. But none will deny that after Diocletian's time there are few signs of such a spirit, and that, if freedom of spirit had shown any signs of growth before, it was effectually destroyed then. Few can fail to be struck with the difference between the Church of the fourth century and the earlier Church, regarded simply as a force in society and in politics. From being the champion of education, it became more and more strongly its opponent, and regarded culture and literature and art with growing disfavour. Its bishops were worse educated, until in 448 we find a Phrygian bishop unable to write his own name, but still qualified to frame canons intended to bind the Christian world, at the Council of Constantinople. The Church became more and more identified with the policy of centralised despotism and the destruction of individual freedom. The massacre of Diocletian, by exterminating the most progressive party in the eastern cities, destroyed the last chance that the Empire had of regaining vitality and health. "Education had always been dependent on the vigour of municipal life, and now it sickened and died." When the pagan philosophical reaction had spent its short-lived force, there was no power left to withstand the barbarising anti-Grecian tendencies which the extremists and the bigots of the Christian party had always shown. The policy of massacre was proved to be, then as always, not merely a crime and a stupendous folly, but also a terrible blow to the world, to civilisation, and to humanity. The penalty of the Imperial crime was the enervation and consequent destruction of the Empire. The Roman Government, with many faults, had been the most effective civiliser of barbarians, probably, that history has revealed as yet. Diocletian betrayed its destiny, and barbarised its policy; and the Empire was delivered over to the barbarians. According to the stern law of nature, the whole of humanity must suffer for the sins of a part, and the children for the parents: in that way alone can the solidarity of human nature be forced on the unwilling minds of men. The Dark Ages, when civilization, peace, and knowledge seemed to have been overwhelmed by savagery and disorder, were the result of the massacre of Diocletian.

At the present time the same situation has recurred as in 303 A.D. The Government, or, rather, the despotic monarch acting against the advice of his responsible advisers under the interrogation of private favourites, resolved to exterminate what was probably the most energetic section of the population;[13] the policy was chosen for reasons of State (though religious bigotry was a contributory cause), and has employed and stimulated Mohammedan fanaticism for its own purposes. It has armed and trained the most barbarous elements in the country against the most peaceful and industrious, the Kurds against the Armenians; and by every means roused and exaggerated the barbarism which the Kurds are taught from infancy. I have no dislike for the Kurds; they are a race of considerable capacity and promise, and I have found them more pleasant in intercourse than the Armenians. Could anything be more charming than the welcome given to us by a young Kurdish Bey in a village on an affluent of the Euphrates, concluding with the words, "All our people are thieves; but, if you lose anything, come to me, and I'll get it back for you"? The force of hospitality could no further go.

Nor have I any prejudice against the Turks. On the contrary, I have a warm feeling of gratitude towards many of them, and the warmest sympathy for their position. For fifteen years I urged that poor Mohammedans suffered more than the Christians from their detestable Government, forced upon them and maintained in power by foreign ambassadors, long after the natural self-righting power of the East would have swept away an effete dynasty and replaced it by more vigorous rulers; and, until the recent development of palace policy, it was true that, so far as mere Government action was concerned, the Mohammedan villagers were, as a rule, the worst off. I know that many of the Turks feel now a similar emotion to that which made a Turkish soldier say to me about the last Russian war: "We deserved all we suffered for what we did to the Russian wounded." But fanaticism is a terrible emotion; and, when fanaticism and savagery are encouraged by rulers to exterminate a helpless "infidel" people, and seize their property, even a more educated and higher race than the Turkish peasantry would be capable of awful crimes.

Least of all have I any prejudice in favor of the Armenians. On that point I will not repeat what I said elsewhere as to the unlovable nature of the ordinary Armenian, nursed in the most debased form of religion to which Christianity has ever sunk, and bred for generations to slavery and insult, tempered only by cunning and bribery. Nor need what I have said as to their wonderful power of rapid development and improvement be here repeated. What I would urge is that it is not on account of their bad qualities that they are now being exterminated; it is because of their improvement. Had they continued in the same state of dull money-grabbing selfishness, hated and deserving hatred, they would have remained also in the same condition of strict repression, without the worse extremes of the last years. But the contemplation for the last thirty years of life on the higher level of the American missionaries produced a most profound and an entirely healthy effect on the Armenians; and at last it seemed as if the patient, quiet, generous life of the missionaries, guided by good sense and manly feeling, abstaining from all political connections, was about to reap its full reward. Already the missions had created an immense organization of schools and colleges; and the mere recognition of their higher standard of thought and living, apart from religious conversion, seemed about to make them a guiding power among the Armenian race. There lay the unpardonable crime: the inarticulate yearning of the Armenians for personal safety, for freedom from insult, for respect to the families and the women of their race, the vague desire for those elementary rights which the veriest worm is bound to claim as the first gift of God to all men; these feelings were beginning to stir and live, and struggle for articulate expression.

To lay down a constitution and system of rules that shall hold in balance these opposing religions in Asia Minor is beyond the power of man; and the attempts that have been made by commissions and congresses are mere empty verbiage, that can never exist except on paper. But fortunately they are as unnecessary as they are impossible. What is wanted is a Government that will strictly maintain order, and compel obedience to the simplest principles of peace. Wherever and whenever that experiment has been tried, whether on a great scale in the third century, or on a small scale under some official of average intelligence and honesty (as I have known it in various instances), the result has always been that the opposing religions establish an endurable *modus vivendi* among themselves, and intercourse goes on peacefully and easily.

What has been wanting in our own policy most of all has been decision of purpose. You can do anything with Orientals, if you know what you want, resolve to have it, and are honest and unselfish (as I believe we have been recently in Turkey, for the first time, perhaps, throughout our whole Turkish policy). Every one who has had any dealings with Orientals knows that the fatal error lies in wavering and in pretence. If the Oriental once begins to suspect that your word is stronger than your act all chance of moving him is lost. You must never threaten, unless you are ready to double your threat in action. You can never bluff the Oriental; he has an unerring instinct in detecting the empty threat, and a magnificent power of sitting quietly and letting the world rage and rave. The wobbling of our policy has been the reason why England, the ally and buttress of Turkey, has always been, so far back as my experience reaches, the Power which had least influence in Constantinople, the Power which the Turkish Government most frequently flouted and insulted. It makes one's cheek redden and one's blood boil to live in Turkey, and see the weakness and helplessness of our action. There have occurred in my time two great misfortunes in the carrying out of our Turkish policy, taking that policy as it was: the accession to power of Mr. Gladstone in 1880 and of Lord Salisbury in 1895. Those who had heard of the way in which the latter was deluded and played upon by Ignatieff, in Constantinople, before the outbreak of the last Russo-Turkish war, were in anxiety and tribulation last summer. Lord Salisbury began grandly; what a truly magnificent sound did he utter in his earlier speeches! You would have thought that the British Lion had opened his royal mouth and emitted his noblest roar. But, "God shield us, a lion is a most dreadful thing"; the Turks might have been afraid, and another prologue must tell that he was not a lion; and when you looked closer, half the face of old Snug the Joiner was seen through the lion's neck. 'Twas only a Midsummer Night's Dream. And every time he has opened his mouth we have heard more and more clearly the voice of the sucking dove. And yet people marvel at the audacity of the Sultan in disregarding the menaces of England and of Europe! Is there any child over the age of ten who would be dismayed at such empty brag?

Had that war to the death which Bismarck spoke about broken out between France and Germany, and had Germany succeeded in the first stages of the process which Bismarck sketched out, it would have been the duty of every civilised nation to interfere and tear the victor from the throat of the vanquished; and no nation can neglect its duty without suffering the full penalty of its crime. In the present case there is a great difference that the suffering nation has been neither lovable in its character nor great in its services to humanity, as France has been; but for its faults it has surely atoned by centuries of submission to stern and unmeasured repression, culminating in an exterminating process of such fiendish character. That it should be burned alive in thousands, slain in tortures in thousands more, killed by famine and nakedness and cold in tens of thousands,[14] should surely gain for it some mercy in the judgment of the Western nations; but that the scheme should be deliberately carried out to ensure by a system of outrage that no Armenian woman over a large tract of country shall become the mother of an Armenian child, is an enormity such as surely never before entered into the mind of man to devise. And yet the civilised peoples stand idly by and talk, and allow this poisoning of the fountains of life to proceed month after month unchecked; surely mere selfish apprehension of the punishments that must follow such callous indifference to crimes should have roused them to action.

Winter will soon be upon Armenia again, with snow lying deep for many months; the people will be almost naked, quite starving. Let us remember this time that the kindest way is to let them die quickly, and not dole out again enough bread to preserve them for longer misery. Let us kill them outright, rather than save them to suffer.

The Spectator, Vol. 77 (September 26, 1896): 389–90

The Czar's Visit

It is not good manners to criticise a guest, especially one whose presence is an honour, but this one is a public character as well as a guest, and there is something which appeals irresistibly to the imagination in the contrast between the figure of that slight young man with the weary face and the sad, anxious eyes, and the tremendous position to which Providence and events have raised the Czar. He is not only Autocrat of the Russian people, that is, of a hundred millions of white men who, if called upon, would elect him master and guide by a 90 per cent. majority, not only Commander-in-Chief of five million soldiers, not only the lord of the whole Northern world so completely that his telegraphed order would be a sufficient sentence of death on any man living between the Baltic and Japan, but he disposes of the armies and fleets of France, and throughout Europe he is for the moment the final referee. The German Emperor, to all other men so defiant, is to him all complaisance; and the head of the house of Hapsburg, who thinks of himself still as heir of the Cæsars, anxiously meditates whether the coldness of his recent visitor's speeches did or did not conceal a dangerous reserve. The King of Italy, a Sovereign with a descent of a thousand years, permits the marriage of his son with the daughter of a petty Prince in the Balkans, a Sheik rather than a King, because the alliance will conciliate the Czar; while the Sultan for the moment recognises the existence of no other Monarch, and if bidden in an autograph letter would abandon even the dear delight of slaughtering Christians who are unarmed. Even in Britain, which the Russian troops cannot reach, there is a disposition to defer to power so vast; and in a hall hung with Crimean trophies the aged Queen receives one who to her is a boy, with a feeling that on his fiat [depend] issues almost immeasurably great. Of the solidity of the power of

Russia we may judge from the fact that we, who won the struggle in the Crimea, are now pleading for aid to the heir and namesake of Nicholas I. It is said, of course, that the Czar is but travelling, as any other young noble might, to visit his wife's relatives, and enjoy, if that be possible, some approach to ordinary domestic life; but there are no relatives in France, and that heavy sceptre is not one which even for a fortnight can be lightly laid aside. Power dwells with an autocrat even if he is asleep, for till he wakes nothing can be resolved. It is not possible for those gathered at Balmoral to forget that peace or war in Europe [depends] on that young man's decision, that if he were offended he might change the whole future, that if he were pleased a few words from his lips would rescue one of the oldest of Christian peoples from the extinction by torture with which they are now threatened. To bid men forget how potent the Czar is, and regard him only as a welcome guest, is to bid them forget all facts, and occupy themselves with pleasant imaginings. The modern world is too conscious for such a bidding to be of the smallest effect. The situation is only the more strained if the Czar is, as reported, self-distrustful, reluctant to act, anxious for time and advice and guidance from the kind of events which move Sovereigns, for the passionate desire of all around him in the Queen's house is that he should decide, should take up his burden, should say the words which will terminate the European suspense, perhaps even the sick agony of Armenia. The reluctance of the jury to give a verdict does not terminate the consciousness of the accused that his fate is in their hands.

There is exaggeration in all that? We fear there is none, and that the failure of most men is to realise how true it all is, how terrible is the real power of the Queen's guest, how directly the responsibility for events rests on his personality. Be it through a certain weakness among her statesmen, be it because of a tremor which can be distinctly felt running through the nations, be it a mere result of complicated circumstances, nothing is strong in Europe at this moment except Russia, and the autocracy of the Czar in Russia is real, unhampered even by the existence of advisers whom he must not disregard. The power of decision rests with him exclusively, and his decision will practically be that of the entire Continent. It is folly to shut our eyes to that fact, or to the further one that on that decision rests, and for a long time to come will rest, the future disposition of the British people towards Russia. At present that disposition is singularly friendly, not only towards the Czar himself, but towards his State. They have neither been frightened nor annoyed by the great advance which Russia has made in the Far East, though that advance has made her the great influence at Pekin, and the formal Protector of Corea, which is rapidly becoming a Russian Principality almost as subordinate as Bokhara. They are willing, if the Czar will coerce Turkey into endurable order, to see the Russian flag advanced over Armenia, and would even as a people consent, on conditions, to see Constantinople pass into Russian hands. They wish, in fact, heartily wish, for a termination, or at least a suspension, of the antagonism between the two Empires. But if the decision goes the other way, if the counsellors at St. Petersburg persuade the Czar that Turkey must be suffered to go on rotting till the Ottoman Empire falls, if the Armenians are given up to massacre, and the Czar declares himself the benevolent ally of Abd-ul-Hamid, British feeling will undergo a strong revulsion. The whole nation will fall back into the attitude of cold suspicion out of which even now some British statesmen cannot be driven, and will mutter under its breath that one autocracy is as bad as another, and it does not become Great Britain to foster or even, if it can be avoided, permit any Russian advance, for there is no guarantee that such advance will be for the happiness of mankind. That was the temper of the British people a very few years ago, as witness the positively silly agitation about the Pamirs, and it would be their temper again, probably for a generation, to the immense embarrassment of Russia as well as of themselves. They need Russia in Asia as Russia, in Asia, needs them, but there will be no cordiality, no hearty co-operation, unless Russia will understand that neither in European nor Asiatic Turkey have we any selfish interests, and will make reasonable concessions to the outraged moral sense of the British people, who are burning with rage, justifiable rage, at what they consider a war on the human race, waged indeed by the Sultan, but sheltered by Powers far stronger and less blinded by ignorance than he. These are the facts of the hour, and as we ourselves urgently plead for an understanding with Russia, and would gratify her permanent aspirations in pursuit of it, we can see no failure of hospitality in describing them as they are.

The splendid position which the Czar, and therefore Russia,

occupies at this moment is a singular object lesson in the advantages and the drawbacks of autocratic government. It can hardly be denied, we think, by reasonable men that much of the prestige enjoyed by Nicholas II., a prestige almost bewildering in its grandeur, is due to the fact that he has really a free hand, that in the great decisions to be made every Russian will accept his guidance, and, if required, will follow him. His command, to employ a rather extravagant and yet true expression, will within his own dominions affect all wills as well as all acts. If he decides that the *status quo* must be maintained whatever its consequences, all Russians will rail at England as the peace-breaker of the world. If, on the other hand, he decides that Abd-ul-Hamid is too bad to bear, all Russians will recall their secular quarrel with Constantinople, and rejoice that Russia is making good her claim to be the protectress of all Christians in the East. That unity of the nation, which is the result, as it is also the source, of the autocracy, is an element in the power of Russia which it is impossible to exaggerate. The Czar can choose as ally whom he will, unfettered by anything save his own conscience, and therefore those who wish to be chosen—which just now is all Europe—wait humbly on his commands. There is solid strength as well as immense prestige in that freedom of action; but then look at the other side. Everything, the whole future of Russia, as well as of the Continent, hangs on the capacity of one man, who would be Czar whether he had the brain of Peter the Great or of Peter the Little, whether he possessed, like the first German Emperor, the power of choosing the exact instrument required, or whether, like Napoleon III., he never made a choice without making also a more or less grave blunder. The very liabilities of mortal life in an autocrat become to his nation enormous dangers, dangers which justify the apparently absurd precautions taken for the past month throughout the Western world. Moreover, Kings are conscious like other men, and it is impossible to doubt that the weight of this unshared power presses heavily upon autocrats, producing in some indecision, in some rashness, in some that ungovernable caprice which resembles the insanity which marked most of the Cæsars of the Julian line. To be uncontrolled, and to be human,—it is not a good combination. On the whole, we believe that Englishmen will prefer their own system even in external politics, though it is so nearly fatal to genius, produces such exhausting delays, and leaves so much to Cabinets which, like Councils of War, will do anything but act.

The Spectator, Vol. 77 (September 26, 1896): 390–91

The Fate of Constantinople

We do not like the way things are going. It is quite clear that a cue has been given to the Press, and that the cue is substantially this. Her Majesty's Government is deeply moved by the sufferings of the Armenian people, which still continue, and most indignant at the recent conduct of the Sultan; but it is not prepared without allies to apply coercion to him, nor is it prepared in order to secure allies to depart from the traditional policy of this country in respect to Eastern Europe. It is ready to make any appeal to the Czar's feelings or those of his people, but it is not ready to make any great concession to their interests or aspirations. In other words, her Majesty's Government will not promise to regard the occupation of Constantinople by a Russian force with approval or indifference. That seems to us equivalent to throwing up the sponge, and admitting that in the circumstances of the situation the Sultan must be allowed his own way, even though that way leads him to the final extirpation of the Armenian people. It is admitted, rightly or wrongly, that Great Britain, however furious with just indignation or however openly defied, cannot move against the Sultan without an ally, and it is clear on the face of the present position that the only ally worth having for the end in view is the Russian Government. We cannot obtain the hearty support of France without Russian consent; we cannot obtain the hearty support of Germany by anything we may do; and we cannot obtain the hearty support of Austria without accepting all the burdensome obligations which would be entailed on us by an entrance into the Triple Alliance. We must, in fact, either win Russia to an alliance, either active or passive, or sit quiet in bitter humiliation; and Russia will not be won without a guarantee that her permanent and unchangeable policy shall not be once again baffled by a new conference of Berlin, possibly by an armed defence of Constantinople. She was too bitterly disappointed in 1878 to run again a similar risk. That is the truth of the situation, and it seems to us that British policy, as described in inspired paragraphs, is based on two incorrect ideas. One is that we can go on declaring that we are still able to protect Constantinople from the Turks. We are not able. Wholly apart from all ideas of the possibility of a hostile coalition, in which, as we said last week, we are unable to believe, we cannot fight Russia, much less Russia *plus* France, without the hearty assent of the British people, and they would give no such assent. To wage a great war in order to maintain Turkish dominion would revolt their consciences too deeply. It would be like fighting a civilised Power in order that Barbary corsairs might have free range of the Mediterranean. The people would not do it, and any Government which proposed such a course would find itself either in a minority, or with a majority which had not the energy or the single-mindedness essential with Englishmen to success in a great war. The Opposition, however patriotic, would ask every day what we were fighting for, and the answer could only be the maintenance of the foulest and most destructive tyranny which now harasses mankind. Within a week of the declaration of war military considerations would force us into active and warm alliance with Abd-ul-Hamid,—that is, with a Prince regarded by nineteen out of every twenty Englishmen as outside the pale of humanity, a tyrant of the type which, according to optimist philosophers, has been extinguished by the progress of man. The situation would be unbearable, and would either produce a defeat or would be got rid of by some humiliating but "necessary" compromise. If, then, we cannot fight for Constantinople, what is the objection to say so frankly, and thereby convince all Russians that whether we are selfish or not—and we are selfish enough, except when we are moved, as in the present case, by loftier emotions—our selfishness will not stand in the way of their secular aspirations? They are free, we want to say to them, if they will help to do the world's work, to take the only pay which in their judgment will be sufficient compensation for the effort.

But we shall be told, indeed we practically are told by the action or inaction of British diplomacy, that there is another question to be considered. It is the traditional policy of Great Britain, acknowledged to be sound by all grave thinkers, to prevent the rise of any Power capable of founding a Universal Monarchy in the West, and Russia in possession of Constantinople could found such a monarchy. The "master of Constantinople," it is repeated every day, is master of the world. He would at all events be master of the Mediterranean. We are wholly unable to believe that statement, which, made in many quarters and in the broadest way, is based on inaccurate thought. It is utterly contrary to history, which shows us that the master of Constantinople, even when much the strongest military Power in the world, has never been able to master Europe; has usually, in fact, sunk gradually into a weaker Power, standing always on the defensive. In what way would the possession increase Russian ability to attack Germany, or Austria, or Great Britain? She might, it would be said, ally herself with France to drive us out of Egypt; but to whose advantage? and what prevents her from attempting that enterprise now? Is it, perchance, Turkish love for England which would induce the Sultan to close the Bosphorus and the Dardanelles against a Russian fleet? An alliance of Russia, Turkey, and France for our destruction could be arranged in a month even now, and would be at least as powerful as an alliance between Russia and France with the former in possession of Constantinople, a position, as Mr. Gladstone once pointed out, always singularly liable to attack from a maritime Power. The alliance, moreover, is, as a permanent policy, only an assumption. It is at least as probable that all States with interests in the Mediterranean would feel a new and keen dread of Russian ambition, a new and a strong disposition to seek the aid of the great maritime Power, which, allied with them, could keep the Mediterranean free and the road to Asia always open. This interest would always be vital to Italy; it would be enormously strengthened in Austria if she possessed Salonica; and it would be felt, we feel assured, even by France, though from her seat on the Atlantic she would remain as she is now, more independent. The subject is almost too large for a newspaper, but this belief, that Russia in a new position would be so much stronger than Russia as she is, seems to us to be part of the apprehensive view of politics which holds that there can be no freedom of the Mediterranean while France is seated at Biserta or England at Gibraltar. Positions are of a certain importance, but the mastery of positions is not the mastery of the world.

At all events, if this is the danger, the danger is incurred already. Turkey, with the Balkans in Bulgarian hands, with her Fleet rotting at anchor, with her Army unpaid, with her Christian population in despair, with a weak Sultan, and with Europe unanimously contemptuous of the Administration, lies, and it is believed is conscious of lying, at the mercy of Russia unless she is defended from outside; and who is there to defend her? Great Britain, as we have already said, and as almost all Englishmen admit, will not, lest she should share in the guilt of the recent massacres, or give their author a new lease of the power he has so fearfully misused. France will not, because she hopes some day to recover her provinces through Russian assistance. Germany will not, because she has no direct interest in the matter sufficient to justify the Emperor in risking a war upon two frontiers, or calling on his whole people to sacrifice themselves for a diplomatic idea. And Austria will not, because, as we have so repeatedly argued, Austria, when it comes to the point, will prefer Salonica and the chance or certainty of a great Asiatic trade to the infinite risks of a war, with half her soldiers Slavs, against the head of the Slavic world. Russia can take Constantinople if she pleases, and the choice before us is that of suffering her to acquire it apparently in our despite, and possibly through a Protectorate, which would make of the Ottoman Army Russian soldiers, or permitting her to acquire it upon terms, the first of which would be that Ottoman oppression of Christians should cease for ever. Those are the true alternatives before us, and we cannot honestly say that the Government, if they are accurately represented in inspired accounts, are choosing either the wiser or the better one. Most certainly, if their decision is based upon the idea that Lord Salisbury's "free hand" will include permission to defend Turkey by force, they are lamentably deceived.

The Situation of To-day

There never was a question upon which verbal controversy was so futile as this of the Armenians. There is nothing, in fact, to be controversial about. No person entitled to express an opinion on the facts doubts that the policy of the Sultan includes conduct which is an outrage on civilisation and humanity, and which would justify Europe in dethroning him by force as unworthy to reign over a State which is, and is admitted to be, a European dependency. Controversy as to the right of anybody to commit piracy is in our age imbecile, and the action of the Sultan is more distinctly an offence against the common interest of mankind, and especially of Christian mankind, than any of the historical instances of piracy. Nor, we conceive, does anybody doubt that, as Mr. Gladstone says, Great Britain did pledge herself when she took Cyprus to secure protection for the Armenians, if not for all the Christians of the East, and has therefore the right, if Europe will not move, to move by herself. And we doubt if there are many of us who do not feel that in not moving we are shrinking from an obvious duty because we are afraid of the consequences of doing it. Those facts are not subjects of controversy, but are admitted, the difficulty that worries us all being not a disagreement as to facts, but a perception that recognition of the facts does not help us a step farther forward. Grant that Abd-ul-Hamid is, as Mr. Gladstone so perpetually calls him, an "Assassin," grant that Europe ought to arrest the career of an assassin, grant that England specially pledged herself to prevent the special assassinations which are occurring, grant that England is humiliated almost to dishonour by not fulfilling her pledge—all of which things we fully grant, though we should use other words to describe them—the grand question remains unsolved. What are we to do? Are we to blow up the house to get to the assassin? Are we to hurl policemen on soldiers in order to clear a way for the arrest? Or is there any way in which the end, which is not only expedient but obligatory to seek, can be attained without serious risk of a struggle in which the assassin might ultimately win the game, and triumphantly proclaiming that there is no law for him, extend indefinitely the area and the horror of the assassinations?

That is the precise truth of the situation, though it is expressed for once, for obvious reasons, in terms which we dislike as inconsistent with the ways of Englishmen when really at white-heat, and in some ways the situation has not this week been improved. Austria, with its massive though slow-moving armies and its geographical position, is of all the Powers except Russia the one that can do most to defend or to coerce the Sultan; and Austria has been expressing in the most public way her reluctance to see the *status quo* disturbed. All that grand display on the Danube means that if Constantinople is threatened Austria will resist, lest Russia should demand a right-of-way across the Danube to Constantinople, and it is so accepted by all the minor States, which, frightened for their independence, turn to the great Power which, as they think, can defend them. Germany could not allow Austria to be crushed, and it looks therefore as if the Triple Alliance were guaranteeing the *status quo* in Turkey, and therefore permitting Abd-ul-Hamid to work his will. That is bad news for Lord Salisbury, and for those who, like ourselves, have believed that if the crisis arrived the house of Hapsburg would assent to a compromise, and accept a road to the Ægean as compensation. That house may take that course still, but undoubtedly pledges given to Roumania and Servia—and there can be no reasonable doubt of pledges having been given to the former State—would be serious difficulties in its way. "By going to Salonica," the Emperor Francis Joseph may say, "I sanction the partition of the Balkans, and that means for Roumania and Servia servitude or extinction. I am pledged to prohibit either."

The one gleam of light comes from the other European combination. There is no proof as yet, and can be none till the Czar's visit to Paris is over, that the Russian Emperor and Lord Salisbury have arrived at any efficacious understanding. All that is certainly known is that they have "conferred" for some hours, and that the chasm between Great Britain and Russia has not in that conference been widened. An impression prevails, however, of that kind which is rarely without foundation, that the Czar has been convinced at Balmoral of the danger to European order involved in the Sultan's bloodthirsty policy, that he is willing to sanction new efforts to arrest it, and that in consequence the French Government, which has all along watched the massacres with repugnance, as events which strengthen the hands of both the Clericals and the Radicals in France, has felt itself more free to act at Constantinople. M. Cambon, too, the French Ambassador there, has been visiting Paris, and has doubtless brought home to M. Hanotaux the true situation in the Turkish capital, which has made a much deeper impression upon Ambassadors whose wives' throats may be cut by Kurds and Lazes, than upon Foreign Secretaries who are only looking on. He has accordingly returned to his post charged with warnings, has communicated those warnings to the Sultan, and has received from the potentate the usual number of promises of reform. Not one of them will be acted on for any length of time, but it is possible that Abd-ul-Hamid, upon whom all warnings produce for the moment a bewildering impression, may pause in his career, may hesitate for a month to sanction further outbreaks, may even order his lieutenants, if outbreaks occur, to use military force for their repression. The pause may be worthless as far as Armenians are concerned, for the Sultan's hatred of that unfortunate people is quenchless, but it will give Europe time to reflect, to study the situation, and to recognise the precipice upon which it stands. Its peace, by its own confession, is at the mercy of a man whose mind is subject to impulses which no European statesman understands, who dare run the most desperate political risks in pursuit of that supreme gratification of an Asiatic, the making his own will executive, and who must either be a fanatic or penetrated through and through with the belief that the fanaticism of his Mussulman subjects is the rock below his throne. It is exceedingly difficult to believe that cool statesmen, anxious for their own interests and honestly desirous that a cataclysm should be averted, can be blind to the danger involved in such a position, or can fail to see that the only way to avert it is to deprive the man who produces it of his power for evil. Abd-ul-Hamid can at any moment fire the magazine, he is known to like playing with matches, and to have his pockets full of them; is it probable or possible that decent policemen, all of them experienced sergeants, will hesitate to take his explosives away from him? It seems to us nearly, if not quite, incredible. The change in the European attitude is all the more probable because France, as we ventured to recommend a fortnight ago, has been pushed into the first place. She will not arouse the jealousies of the Continent as Great Britain would do, and she does not want Constantinople as Russia does, yet behind her if she moves is the whole strength of those two Powers. We think it more than likely that M. Cambon, who is said to be a determined man, and who earned during the crisis great credit from all correspondents for his energy and humanity, may be the agent authorised by all Europe to make the last attempt to preserve the *status quo*, that his representations may increase in urgency, and that he may at last be the Ambassador instructed with the pleasing task of informing Yildiz Kiosk that the alternatives are the deposition of the Sultan or the dismemberment of Turkey.

It will come to that in the end. We do not believe in reformed Pharaohs. The system which allows such a scene as has been presented for the last eighteen months in Turkey is a system which must be swept away, and it will not be swept away until shells have exploded in Constantinople. We agree with Mr. Gladstone that the "Eastern question," the final redistribution of Turkey, is upon us again, and leaves before the Powers of Europe but two alternatives. They can agree upon a peaceful partition to be carried out, if the Ottomans obtain their just share, by a moderate exertion of force steadily but resistlessly applied from all sides at once, or they can agree to a partition after an exhausting and entirely needless war among themselves, in which a million of men and the surplus revenues of a generation will have been consumed together. The diplomatists all say that the second alternative is the one which will certainly be adopted, and they may, being trained experts, prove to have been in the right. Only if they are so proved, let us hear no more for the future of the value of diplomacy, or of Europe being governed by men of great sense and some philanthropy. Asia could not make a worse muddle of its affairs than Europe will have made, or have shed more needlessly more innocent blood.

The Spectator, Vol. 77 (October 17, 1896): 504–5

Lord Rosebery's Deliverance

Lord Rosebery has, indeed, as he promised, cleared the air,—of most of the Armenian people. We do not see how any one can read his Edinburg speech without perceiving clearly that he is opposed to isolated action on the part of Great Britain in the Armenian quarrel, disinclined to offer Russia heavy terms for her assistance, resolute against the denunciation of the Cyprus Convention, full of scorn at the proposal to withdraw our Ambassador, and convinced that the Armenian question is not for this country one of those which would justify any large risk. He does, indeed, welcome the agitation, because he thinks it will help to prove the disinterestedness of the country, and he expresses, being a kindly man and a Scotchman, his horror of the brutalities perpetrated on Armenians, brutalities of which he knows, as he admits, far more than his audience, because he has read the suppressed Consular reports; but all the same "the policy of this country consists, if you like it, of a thousand portions or a thousand interests, and we cannot allow nine hundred and ninety-nine of these portions or interests to be sacrificed to the remaining one, however important that one may be." The destruction of the Armenian people is only, he implies, a thousandth part of the concern to Great Britain that her general policy is, or, in other words, that destruction is, when contemplated from a proper height of statesmanship, rather an insignificant affair. What other meaning can those words—and remember Lord Rosebery is a master of words as well as an experienced diplomatist—be made to bear? Suppose he had said them to Russia or to Turkey, and he has said them to both, and to all the world beside. The real evil to be dealt with—for he admits the existence of the evil, though he minimizes the political importance of the one now oppressing the national conscience—is that Turks govern Turkey, and that evil, he says, covers such an area, and involves issues arousing so much jealousy, that Great Britain is powerless to deal with it. There must be a concert of all Europe, which Lord Rosebery knows quite well we shall never obtain. "I advocate concerted action as the only solid, safe, and effectual method of dealing with this question. I deprecate any other method as both futile and dangerous. Against any other which may imply the solitary intervention of England, I will raise my voice and my strength as long as I have voice and strength to exert. I am not less haunted than you are by the horrors of Armenia, by the horrors that have transformed an earthly paradise into an organised hell. For all that, I would not attempt to do away with those horrors by adding to them a horror a hundredfold greater. We are a great nation and a just nation; but, to employ the fine phrase of Mr. Gladstone, 'we do not wield the sword of the Almighty.' It is not ours to dispense in this world universally the punishment of wrong and the reward of right. We have to balance, as it were, between two evils, and of the two I cannot balance between the evil of Armenian massacre alone and the evil of Armenian massacre *plus* European war. There is no doubt a certain concord that reigns over the aspect of Europe at this moment. *But that concord is chiefly directed, not in your favour, but against you.*"

What do those measured and eloquent words mean if they do not mean this,—that unless the whole of Europe moves in concert against Turkey, it will probably move against Great Britain? As for making an agreement with Russia, Lord Rosebery asks why the popular feeling has so changed, why we have forgotten the administrative methods of Russia, methods which he illustrates by the cases of the Poles, the Jews, and the Stundist Dissenters, the obvious intention being to imply that the Russian despotism is hardly to be preferred to the Turkish. As to any less drastic method of interference, except indeed by advice, Lord Rosebery pours scorn on all suggestions. He will not denounce the Cyprus Convention because it is dead, so dead that there is no dishonour in not acting on its provisions,—a statement so opposed to the facts that at this moment every Russian quotes that Convention as the grand reason against Russian interference, alleging that even if they interfere the Convention binds us to prevent their obtaining their reward. The withdrawal of the Ambassador he deprecates as being only an "affront" to the Sultan, leading possibly to war, and rendering the action of the Concert nearly impossible; while in speaking of the proposal, no doubt a silly proposal, to stop the tribute of Cyprus, he grows actually sarcastic. That tribute is pledged to the bondholders, and he asks if the Sultan will care for injuries inflicted upon them. You might as well, he says—borrowing an epigram from Sydney Smith—tickle a tortoise's back to make it laugh. Every plan, in fact, as yet suggested is rejected, and Lord Rosebery has no other to propose. England is to make the Triple Alliance and the Dual Alliance pull together if she can, and to set them on the task of partitioning the Turkish Empire; or, if that is not possible, is to remain quiescent, and watch the extirpation of the Armenian people, as the Americans are doing, and as Lord Rosebery believes the free Colonies would all rather that we did. This counsel is for the future as well as for the present, would hold good even if the Sultan cleaned Broussa of Armenians, as his advisers are believed to be meditating, or even, so far as appears, if he slaughtered out all Europeans in Constantinople, as his spokesmen all threaten he will do, should active interference be so much as imminent. For, and on this point Lord Rosebery rose to genuine and even lofty eloquence, of all calamities a European war is the most dreadful, especially for this country, which, in Lord Rosebery's judgment, so far from being stronger for the recent expansion of its Empire, is far weaker. Here are the speaker's own words, taken from the *Times*' report, which was evidently intended to be verbatim:—

> "For the last twenty years, still more during the last twelve, you have been laying your hands, with almost frantic eagerness, on every tract of territory adjacent to your own or desirable from any point of view which you thought it desirable to take. That has had two results. I daresay it has been quite right; but it has had two results. The first result is this,—that you have excited to an almost intolerable degree the envy of other colonising nations, and that, in the case of many countries, or several countries rather, which were formerly friendly to you, you can reckon, in consequence of your Colonial policy, whether right or wrong—and I myself am supposed to be rather a sinner in that respect—you can reckon not on their active benevolence, but on their active malevolence. And, secondly, you have acquired so enormous a mass of territory that it will be years before you can settle it or control it, or make it capable of defence, or make it amenable to the arts of your administration. Have you any notion what it is that you have added to the Empire

> in the last few years? I have taken the trouble to make a computation which I believe to be correct. In twelve years you have added to the Empire, whether in the shape of actual annexation or of dominion, or what is called a sphere of influence, 2,600,000 square miles of territory. I observe you sigh. Whether it is with a sense of repletion or relief at hearing you have so much undigested empire about you I will not stop to inquire; but just compare these figures. It will show you more clearly what you have done. While the area of the United Kingdom—England, Scotland, Wales, and Ireland, the Channel Islands, and so forth—has 120,000 square miles, therefore to the 120,000 square miles of the United Kingdom, which is part of your Empire, you have added during the past twelve years twenty-two areas as large as that United Kingdom itself. I say this, that that marks out for many years a policy from which you cannot depart if you would. You may be compelled to draw the sword—I hope you may not be—but the foreign policy of Great Britain until its territory is consolidated, filled up, settled, civilised, must inevitably be a policy of peace."

England, in short, ought not to fight for the Armenians because war in Europe would be a worse misfortune than the extirpation of a Christian people, and because also she has become too weak to fight successfully, having scattered her strength so greatly that unless directly attacked her only possible policy is peace. And the man who says this has been Foreign Secretary, and knows that his statement will be read with exultation in all the Cabinets of Europe, and especially in that of Constantinople.

We should ask our readers gravely and soberly whether they would now trust the destinies of the Empire to Lord Rosebery's hands. We ask without the smallest *arrière pensée*, for we supported Lord Rosebery's accession to the Premiership; we not only recognise but fully enjoy his gifts as an orator, and we would rather but for this speech have seen the Liberal party led by him than by Sir William Harcourt, in whom we are able to recognise only a gladiator statesman. But we see in every sentence of this speech the traces of the defect which we have recently denounced in Lord Rosebery's civil policy, an inherent and incurable want of moral nerve and capacity of final decision. We had expected those qualities from him, as all Whigs, we believe, also expected them, and they are not there. With much that Lord Rosebery said as a man of reflection we heartily agree. Like him we believe that to fight all Europe is a course which could be risked only if our existence as a Great Power was at stake. Like him we believe, but unlike him we have for twelve years preached, the doctrine that it was madness to let the Empire grow so fast unless our military force was allowed to grow *pari passu* with it. Like him we object to little cures for the Armenian trouble, little threats addressed to the Sultan, and little warnings like the withdrawal of our Ambassador. But we utterly repudiate the policy to which these reflections lead Lord Rosebery, and would prefer any alliances, or any sacrifices for the increase of our own military strength and security, to sitting down groaning but inert, with a confession that Britain has grown too fat ever again to make an exertion at the call either of civilisation or of her own honour. Is that attitude, an attitude as of an overgorged lion powerless because of his very feasts, the fitting one for the close of the Victorian Era? We do not believe that the British people, when once it has realised what the attitude is, will think so for an hour.

The Nineteenth Century, Vol. 40 (October 1896): 654–80

The Massacres in Turkey

I.

The Rev. Dr. J. Guinness Rogers

Whatever doubt may have existed in any mind as to the feeling of the nation in regard to the successive outbursts of insane fury at Constantinople has been set at rest by the extraordinary demonstrations of the opening weeks of September. On the 5th of that month the *Speaker* expressed the keen disappointment which was being felt by numbers who were concerned alike for the safety of the persecuted Armenians, and the good faith of the British people, which was virtually pledged on their behalf, at the seeming apathy with which the Constantinople Terror was viewed. The challenge was distinct, the reply was immediate, and in its volume and intensity leaves nothing to be desired. The passionate feeling of the hour is sweeping everything before it, and the fire blazes all the more fiercely because of the persistent efforts which have been made to keep it under. My own conviction is that it would have been possible at any time within the last few months to kindle a feeling in the country as strong and resolute as that which put an end to the Bulgarian atrocities of twenty years ago. But so far from any movement in that direction, the contrary course has been adopted. Popular agitation has been discouraged, and then it was confidently said that the country had reached a state of callous indifference, like that of Prince Bismarck when he said the Eastern question was not worth the sacrifice of a single Pomeranian soldier.

For days after the present movement began it was the fashion of the London correspondent of country journals to assure his readers that any appearance of excitement was delusive, and as I happened to be the first who took up the *Speaker's* challenge, I was treated as the victim of a midsummer madness. These correspondents were quite right as to their own field of observation. But that field was not the world, was not even the country. These gentlemen may be very useful, if their readers remember that they are only repeating the gossip picked up in lobbies and smoking rooms, and that outside these there is a wide circle of opinion—opinion which is intelligent and influential—of which they know nothing. It has proved so in the present instance. Clubland was all but unanimous, and they reflected its views. It was extremely inconvenient for various reasons that the country should be stirred, and it was therefore dogmatically asserted that it cared nothing for the whole matter. Was not Lord Salisbury, strongest and bravest of Foreign Ministers, at the helm? Was not the European concert in active operation? What more could be done, or indeed desired, in the best of all possible worlds? Meanwhile if the people did not speak they observed and they reflected; while they were musing the fire burned (and now, to use the old Psalmist's words) they speak with their tongue.

Whether, even now, there is a clear perception of the extent to which the character and influence of Great Britain are involved in the matter, is open to very serious doubt. Passion is at white heat, but mere sentiment, whether of indignation at the tyrant or of sympathy with his victims, however natural and laudable, is not statesmanship. It is affected, rightly affected, by the outrage done to our common humanity, but it does not take the trouble to appraise the exact measure of our natural responsibility, nor does it care to inquire how far our national status is likely to be affected by the decision that is reached. Sober-minded politicians will be more affected by considerations of this nature, and they are certainly those which must be pressed home upon every statesman. This is not one of the occasions on which a nation can stand by with the cynical and scoffing question, "Am I my brother's keeper?" Our own honour is at stake, and what some seem to value more than our honour, our influence and position in the world.

It is not necessary here to repeat the long and melancholy story of that Berlin treaty which at the time was said to have brought us peace with honour, but which it is now seen scattered seeds of disaster and trouble, whose harvest we are reaping. The connection between it and the present Armenian persecution is too direct and obvious to admit of doubt or require demonstration. Had the treaty of San Stefano been confirmed, the crimes which have shocked all Europe could never have been perpetrated; and as on Great Britain rests the responsibility for tearing up that treaty, on her must come also a large measure of responsibility for the crimes resulting from this fatal indulgence to the Turkish tyrant. Alas! the memory of that ill-advised act has haunted our diplomacy ever since, and it paralyses its efforts still. There is one of the facts that must be borne in mind in shaping the policy which is to deal with this emergency. In some way or other its evil effect has to be counteracted. But however this is done, it is, at all events, clear that the whole transaction has fixed on us obligations which we cannot evade.

But if there are any who are inaccessible to an appeal of this kind, there is another of an entirely different character which it is impossible to ignore. The Sultan hardly conceals the fact that his action is a distinct defiance of Great Britain. It is Great Britain which has sought to check him in the exercise of his murderous proclivities, and it is her policy which he has been endeavouring to circumvent, unfortunately with only too much success. He will humiliate himself before Russia, he will intrigue with Germany, he will send his ribbons to French statesmen, he will even try to conciliate Austria in order that he may be able successfully to defy Great Britain. Unfortunately these Continental Powers have shown themselves only too ready to fall into line and to support him in his resistance. We have been assured over and over again that Great Britain is without a friend on the Continent, and, it must sorrowfully be said, if she has any they are very slow to act in her support. It is in vain that the sympathy and aid of the Great Powers have been sought; in vain that we have waited upon their convenience, until that waiting has come very near to a humiliation to ourselves; in vain that such excessive stress has been laid upon the European concert that it might almost seem as though we were afraid to call murder murder until the European concert had first given us permission to speak the truth; in vain that this European concert has, in fact, been exalted into a very demigod, on whose fiats the statesmen and people of this free nation must wait in humble submission. The more our statesmen have sought thus to clear themselves of any suspicion of selfish aim or sinister purpose by consultation at every point, the more cold and chilling has been the response which they have received. If this were to be the end, and the Sultan, resting upon the indirect help which he receives from other Powers, were able to laugh to scorn the remonstrances of Great Britain, it is hardly possible to exaggerate the blow which would be given to our national influence. The present insulting attitude of the Sultan may seem ridiculous enough looked at from one side. But there is another side of a very different character. Here is a monarch who sits on his throne solely in virtue of the tolerance of other Powers, assuming the airs of a mighty prince who can afford to meet sober and rational remonstrance with lies and insults, can pose as the victim of misrepresentation and calumny at the very time when his deeds are crying to heaven for vengeance, and secure in the immunity which he enjoys through the mutual jealousies of those who ought to suppress him and his crimes, can still persevere in his career of cruelty and blood. The spectacle is too ludicrous, but, alas! this miserable caricature of a monarch is able to work his own will. Our Government may enter its protests, and this may be soothing to our consciences, but it is humiliating to the last degree. What it really means is that England has parted with the power which she wielded when Milton sang, and Cromwell, "before whose genius" (to use Macaulay's words) "the young pride of Louis and the veteran craft of Mazarin stood rebuked," and "whose imperial voice arrested the sails of the Libyan pirates and the persecuting fires of Rome," interposed on behalf of the persecuted Piedmontese, and that on the suggestion of our modern Imperialists. For her own sake as well as for the sake of those who are looking up for her protection, England is bound to see that her remonstrances have another and a different issue.

The first and most essential condition of this is, that we get rid both of the party and international intrigues which in reality make the capital on which the Sultan trades. So far as our internal affairs are concerned, our first business is to lift the whole question out of the region of party strife. Our one concern should be to put an end once and for ever to the possibilities of Turkish despotism. How that may best be secured is a problem which statesmen have to solve. It is ours to make it clear to them that it must be done, and that no apology will be accepted for failure, or at all events until every possible method has been exhausted. It is simply pitiable to find men trying to turn incidents of a crisis like this to the advantage or disadvantage of any particular statesman. Policies must be judged, but it should be on their own merits, and not on their bearing on the interests of a particular leader or party. It is for this reason that I personally welcome the letter which Lord Rosebery addressed to myself. That does not mean that I agree in every word or in every opinion, but simply that I approve of his attitude as worthy of a statesman occupying his distinctive position as leader of the Opposition. When Mr. Gladstone raised his trumpet voice in 1876 he was not hampered by his relation to a party, and yet his work had hardly commenced before the Prime Minister of that day took fright and treated the whole as an attack upon the Government. Much more certainly would this have occurred had Lord Rosebery put himself forward as the leader of any opposing policy.

Never indeed was there a subject in relation to which a party strife would be more utterly discreditable. Unfortunately there are those who seem unable to contemplate any subject except through party spectacles. They are so intent upon the battles of factions, and even of individuals, that they seem to forget that there are numbers of earnest politicians in the country, who care little or nothing about the personnel of a ministry, but who are intensely anxious as to the success of principles. They have no axe of their own to grind, are far removed from the temptations of place, have not even the faintest desire for a title. Naturally they are disgusted by the intrigues of the lobbies and the log-rolling of journalists. It is these unselfish politicians who are the strength of the present movement, and they are determined that it shall not have a party character. It is bad enough that the Armenians should suffer from the jealousies of contending potentates. It would be worse still if they were sacrificed to the ambitions of English parties. But it would be worst of all if their cause were to be prejudiced by intestine dissensions in the English party which specially prides itself upon undertaking the defence of its interests. In saying this, I do not for a moment mean to suggest that any Foreign Secretary ought to be sustained in power regardless altogether of the character and success of his policy. Speaking as a Liberal I must express my strong opinion that any attempt to promote the interests of Liberalism by an Armenian agitation would be impolitic in the highest degree. If we are to help these unfortunate people, we must have a singleness of eye. The law holds good here: we cannot serve God and Mammon.

But the second point which I wish to emphasise is not less important than the first. Personally, I do not share the anxiety which so many express as to the possible results of our taking an independent position in defence of Armenia. Every one outside diplomatic circles ought to speak with extreme reserve on such a point, since his knowledge of the situation must necessarily be very restricted. But it would require a good deal to convince me that the European Powers could ever be brought to unite to save the Sultan from the righteous penalty of his own misdeeds. Their bond of union is distrust of England rather than sympathy with Turkey, and it is hard to understand how, with views so divergent that they must necessarily become antagonistic as soon as any positive action was attempted, they could agree on measures of hostility to this country. It is, to say the least, extremely doubtful whether any resistance would have been offered if Great Britain, having invited the other Powers to unite in repressive measures and been refused, had taken independent action.

Be this as it may, it is eminently desirable that a work of humanity in which all the Powers are interested, should be undertaken by them conjointly. It is idle to deny that the chief difficulty in our way is distrust and jealousy of Great Britain which evidently prevails on the Continent and perhaps especially in Russia. Russia has certainly been the most powerful obstacle to the success of our policy. Her representatives have hitherto thwarted us at every point, and there is no reason to hope for anything different until some better understanding is established between us. I venture to think that it should be the aim of our statesmen to secure this. Diplomacy has not yet exhausted all its resources. But if it is to succeed it must be prepared to exercise trust in order that it may inspire it in return. Russia is in no sense our natural enemy. It is not even an ancient foe. The policy which began with the Crimean War set aside the best traditions of our Foreign Office, and our action at the Berlin Conference fostered the antagonism which had thus been engendered between two hitherto friendly peoples. That alienation and rivalry must cease, or there is little hope for the Armenians. The Berlin Convention blocks the way. The obstacle ought to be removed. If our Government are unprepared for this, what is the alternative? We are told that everything possible has been done, and now that we have simply to wait until the European Powers come to a different mind. Advice more cowardly and pusillanimous could hardly be tendered, and it is safe to say that the English people are not in the mood to brook such a confession of impotence. We can at least withdraw our Ambassador, and so cease to play our part in consultations which have too much the character of a farce, and at the same time save ourselves from giving any sanction to so detestable a rule. What further action we take must be determined by events. No sane man counsels war, but to say that we will do nothing that would lead up to it is to make war a certainty. Even were we compelled to act alone, Great Britain is not so impotent as some would fain represent her. But for myself I have no love even for splendid isolation; I long to see the end of the insane jealousies which have separated Russia and this country, and I believe that the establishment of better relations between these two great peoples would inaugurate a new era in the history of the world.

II.

The Right Hon. the Earl of Meath

"Constantinople Riots. Further details of massacres. Six thousand defenceless people murdered." So run the headlines of a sober, unsensational, leading newspaper, appearing this 9th day of September, in the year of our Lord 1896.

Six thousand defenceless people murdered! One's breath is taken away if one thinks of the meaning of these words. If 6,000 people had passed away within a few days by the visitation of God; if they had died of, say, the cholera, or of any similar deadly disease; if they had suddenly been swallowed up by an earthquake, or had been overwhelmed, as sometimes has occurred in China, by a gigantic flood, we should all have been horrified; but to be murdered, and murdered in cold blood by their fellow-subjects and fellow-citizens, suddenly and without warning, not in China or in some far-off, semi-civilised or uncivilized land in Asia or Africa, but in Europe, and in a capital largely inhabited by Europeans, under the very walls of the palace of their sovereign, to whose ears their dying shrieks may quite possibly have reached, within sight of the Embassies representing the most powerful and most civilized countries of the world, and under the very eyes of the police and soldiery paid by them for their protection and defence, but who, under the spell of some mysterious influence, stood passive spectators of these horrible scenes of carnage! What more sickening and ghastly story of wholesale murder is it in the power of the imagination of man to conceive?

One has to return in thought to the awful massacres of St. Bartholomew, when a sovereign hounded on his soldiery to the destruction of his own people, for a parallel to the fearful situation which now reigns in Constantinople. But this dreadful crime occurred more than three centuries ago, and it might have been hoped that the world had made some progress since those days.

Let it not be said that the 6,000 men suffered for the crime committed by some twenty-five of their co-religionists in seizing by violence the Ottoman Bank and in hurling bombs at the Turkish soldiers.

These few misguided men were responsible for their own crimes and assuredly deserved punishment, but what had the innocent 6,000 done that they should be massacred in cold blood? As well say that because some Protestant Englishmen have been wounded by the bombs of Roman Catholic Irish dynamiters, that therefore it would be legitimate for the British to massacre 6,000 Irish Roman Catholics in the streets of London.

The Sultan is directly responsible for these murders, and should not be allowed to escape from the just punishment of such an awful crime. When massacres occurred in Armenia it was possible for him to plead inability to restrain the passions of his Mohammedan subjects in distant portions of the Empire. He could urge that inefficient police and undisciplined soldiery far from the restraining hand of his centralized power had broken loose from his control, and, excited by their Mussulman fanaticism, had committed crimes in the heart of Asia which he greatly regretted and which should never be repeated. He might, I say, plead this in extenuation of the horrible massacres in Asia Minor which have justly excited the wrath and indignation of Europe, though every indication has gone to show that, far from restraining his soldiery and officials in these distant regions, he directly encouraged them in their bloody work of massacre; but no such excuse can be made in the present case.

The Sultan of Turkey, whatever may be his power in the distant portions of his Empire, is certainly supreme and all-powerful in his own capital. He surrounds himself with the most trustworthy and best disciplined men both in the army and in the police. It is notorious that nothing can take place in his capital without his being instantly acquainted with it. His spies are in all parts of the city, and report direct to him the conversation and movements of all suspected persons. A revolutionary movement in which so many persons were engaged as in the attack on the Ottoman Bank could hardly have been organized without some intimation of the intention of the conspirators having reached the ears of the Sultan through his numerous detectives, and in the excited state of the populace it would only have been natural to anticipate that some reprisals would be made by the Mussulmans on the Christians, if precautions were not taken to prevent them.

Had the Sultan desired the massacre of the Armenian Christians in his capital he could not have planned a better course of action than to allow these twenty-five mad revolutionaries to carry out their foolish and wicked designs, knowing that the Mussulmans would certainly revenge the outrage, and that if the police and soldiers were held aloof from the disturbances for forty-eight hours, the discontented and, from his point of view, dangerous Christian Armenians, the source of so much trouble and annoyance, would be wiped out of existence, and that he and his advisers would be freed for ever from their hateful presence in the capital of his Empire. It is impossible to say what actually occurred in the palace, but knowing the power of the Sultan, and the means at his disposal for becoming acquainted with all that was going on in the capital, and for suppressing at once any riot or disturbance, and considering that murder was permitted to go on practically unchecked for some forty-eight hours, and that 6,000 men lost their lives during that time, almost within sight of the palace of the all-powerful autocrat, the men who can acquit him of some share in these atrocious crimes must indeed be gifted with a charitable spirit.

"The Assassin who sits on the throne of Turkey. . . . Him whom I wish always to call the Great Assassin."

Such are the terms applied in recently published letters by Mr. Gladstone to the Sultan. To most men the name will not appear exaggerated or undeserved.

Righteous as is the indignation which we may feel towards the Assassin on the throne, we cannot, in justice, forget that there are exalted and distinguished personages in other countries who cannot be exonerated from all blame in regard to these massacres. We know from the dispatches published in the official Blue-books that the Prime Minister of England was prepared after the first massacres of Armenians in Asia Minor to have put a stop, if necessary by force, to any recurrence of these horrors, had he received the smallest encouragement from the great European Powers, and that he reluctantly desisted from interference on hearing that Russia would not only not assist England in her efforts to stop further massacres, but would resent any independent action on her part. It has been stated, with what truth I know not, that private approaches were made by the Government of Great Britain to that of the United States (whose people had shown marked sympathy with the victims of persecution, and whose missionaries had been eye-witnesses of many atrocities, and had personally suffered from the disturbed state of the country), and that Lord Salisbury declared his readiness to risk the dangers of foreign hostility could he be assured of the support of the Republic of the West, but that such an assurance could not be given, as American traditional policy did not permit the Republic to entangle herself in European alliances, or to take any part in the political affairs of the Old World.

Whatever others may have done, the Prime Minister of Great Britain has, at all events, performed his duty. Short of plunging his country and Europe into a general war for the sake of the Armenians—an act of quixotic madness, which even such a righteous cause would have failed to justify—he could not have done more. If he has failed to bring about a concert of Europe for the purpose of compelling the Turk to cease his murders and brutalities and to conduct himself like a civilised being, the fault lies not with Great Britain, but with those Powers whose selfish jealousy forbids them to combine with their neighbours in enforcing peace and respect for law and order on the bloodthirsty tyrant of the Bosphorus.

As I write, a telegram from Paris states that while at breakfast together on the journey from Breslau to Goerlitz, the German Emperor spoke with the Czar upon his approaching visit to France. His Majesty is said to have alluded to his projected stay in the French capital as a fresh pledge of peace, and then, referring to his late visit to Vienna, he announced that a complete understanding had been arrived at between Russia and Austria, with the object of effecting a pacific solution of the Eastern Question. In any case, the telegram continues, the Czar stated that Russia and Austria would only actively intervene in the event of any third Power endeavouring to act alone.

Of course, this statement may be perfectly untrue, and may have its sole foundation in the brain of a Parisian reporter; but if it be true, it means that whilst Russia and Austria decline to interfere in the internal affairs of Turkey, they will not permit any other Power to do so.

In the meantime the blood of 6,000 men, murdered in Europe, in addition to that of the thousands who have already met their deaths during the last six months in the Sultan's dominions on the other side of the Bosphorus, cries aloud to Heaven for vengeance.

How long will the populations of Christian Europe permit these atrocities to be committed with impunity by the crowned assassin of the Yildiz Kiosk?

His object is evidently to sweep from his dominions the hated Giaour—either by death or banishment. Having murdered 6,000 Armenians, he is now deporting the rest to the inhospitable shores of Anatolia and to other distant portions of his Empire, where death awaits them either by starvation or at the hands of mobs of fanatical Mussulmans, who assuredly await their arrival.

Encouraged by the jealousies between the Powers, which in the past have ensured him impunity, the Sultan seems to have become reckless. If he be permitted to destroy the Armenians, who can guarantee that in his madness he will not attempt similar violence against Christian foreigners residing within his dominions? Are we to wait for justice to be executed until he commits such a final act of murderous folly? In such a case, the one remaining satisfaction would be that this scene would be the last in the horrible drama, as the Assassin, his throne, and his dynasty would once for all be swept from the soil of Europe amidst the universal execrations of an outraged world.

Let us hope that the Powers of Europe will awake to their responsibilities and anticipate such a fell catastrophe by deposing the reckless Imperial madman before he can shed further blood, or finally exterminate the last remnants of an ancient Christian race.

III.

John Burns, M.P.[1]

There is a time in the history of a nation like Great Britain, whose general interests are best served by permanent peace, when it should face dauntlessly, and with a heart of steel accept, the alternative even of war for a just, inevitable, and humanitarian act towards a suffering people.

Such a time and crisis have arrived for our common country over the Armenian atrocities.

By doing the right thing boldly, through the inspiring influence and contagious example of a speedy intervention, England can palliate the awful reproach that Europe has incurred, stop the flagrant injustice in Armenia, and avert the continued stain on our common humanity. Unless some step is taken by England somehow, a further policy of drift will be disastrous, and our masterly inactivity in the East will cause us to regret, perhaps in India, the day when our statesmen construed indifference as neutrality and desertion as diplomacy. Further delay on the Armenian Question will be dangerous for England's prestige. The waiting upon others is inimical to her power and that strength amongst nations which have almost solely been sustained by the spontaneity and independence of her "splendid isolation."

The gravity of the last phase of the Eastern Question, serious thought it be, is fortunately not accentuated by political partisanship. Our Ministry, without fear of men or favour for any particular method of intercession, can, if they have a prompt remedy, have a unanimous country at their back. Certain it is that other Powers are expectant of England's lead. In them that attitude is instinctive; because, as has been often proved, England is alone "the one free voice in Europe." The civilised world hopes and believes England will lead the way in telling the Sultan, and if necessary compel him, to cease the ruthless slaughter of an unarmed people. For less provocation England has often risked life and treasure. In her highest moral interests which have been assailed she should exercise her traditional responsibility and carry out the international obligation due to a weaker people from such a first-class Power. That the time for active intervention by some Power has arrived is beyond question.

Whether through joint or by isolated action England does her bounden duty is immaterial. As the country to which oppressed people have always turned, and, I hope, will ever appeal, England is by virtue of her geographical situation and her political isolation the only Power that can take the initiative. I want that dutiful honour to be England's, and in so being and doing save the Armenians from that effacement evidently now intended. Any objection that may have been urged for delay has been removed. Every corroboration of past massacre has been produced, and the horrors of the recent holocaust established. The universal denunciation of the character and extent of Constantinople murders compels England, failing co-operation from others, which is improbable, to chivalrously suppress, single-handed if necessary, the satanic lust for blood that the Sultan has displayed.

A year ago, perhaps, active isolated intervention by England would have been premature and inexpedient, and might have led to international complications. But since then in other crises activity in well doing led to arbitration over Venezuela. A flying squadron to deliver a firm message taught an Emperor the art of polite letter-writing whilst England was daring to curb her own rebellious Praetorians in South Africa. These and other acts show that "grasping the nettle" within and without our Empire pays. But is this alarm as to the possibility of war through our intervention justified? I think not. The undue apprehension of war over the right issue has often, by the excessive fear of it, made war inevitable, and enabled the daring despotisms to exploit the nervous scruples of their more civilised neighbours and opponents. Less consideration for the material and commercial interests at stake, and a greater regard for the moral obligation, has by its transcendent influence averted what under less noble impulses and ideals, would have been forcible action.

But why speculate upon results of intervention and hypothetical combinations of Powers and other complications when all the signs of the times point to practical unanimity? The co-operation of the Powers through their ambassadors by the collective notes to the Porte on the 27th and 31st of August would of itself justify any action England may take, and cause the chief Powers, if diplomacy is not duplicity, to support her demands upon the Porte. The refusal of France to hand over the bank raiders, our past waste of blood and treasure for Turkey, her indebtedness to England, all prove our *bona fides*. Whether or no, England, not for the first time, must do her duty, even though it be alone, in demanding reforms. What those reforms may be can best be determined as recent past action and present negotiation determine.

If England for the moment specifically confines her action to the prevention of further outrages, and the concession of such reforms or autonomy to Armenia as will secure its people there, and through the Turkish dominion, life and liberty, that temporarily will suffice.

And it is only because British aggrandisement is feared that some Powers do not join England. That fear dispelled by pledges, they will allow England to be the Garrison Police of Europe to keep the Turks in order.

If doing this, however, should open up, as it may, the deposition of the Sultan, the repartition of Turkey, and the allocation of its dominions to other states in Europe, that must be faced.

But I believe the cost of Europe's armed peace, in the main due to the untenable position of Turkey, will very soon lead all the Powers to settle without war, perhaps by arbitration, as soon they must, the distribution of the Turkish Empire to better hands than those who now palter with its possibilities, plunder its people, and prey upon its resources. Pending that decision, which is inevitable, England would be supported in her attempt to secure an armistice from assassination for the Armenians.

It does not need enthusiasm for the social and political aims of the Armenians as a people to justify their prompt rescue from their present condition on the part of England.

I cannot enthuse over the Armenian. He is not an ideal subject for help or sympathy, but he is, with all his faults, human, and should not be hunted like a beast. That the Armenians are the least favoured of the polyglot peoples that submit to, but do not accept, Turkish rule is true.

I have no love for the Armenian, his Christianity is in many instances a cloak for crafty commercialism, his huckstering and usurious pursuits are incapable of defence. That he is the Jew of the East we know, and, like the Jew of the other hemisphere, he may look upon the Mussulman as his commercial Mecca and to prey upon him his religion. A dash of the vigour the Cretans recently displayed would have been to his credit. The undue cultivation of the worst form of commercial spirit has evolved in the Armenian faculties that do not endear him to the Turk. We have the same thing under another name nearer home. The Jewification of the Armenian is in no small degree the cause of the recent troubles; but that is no excuse for persecution as a preliminary to extinction. All this given and admitted, the senseless slaughter of otherwise innocent, if undesirable, people must be stopped.

On the other hand, I do not share even now the wholesale denunciation of the Turks as a people. Not even the number of Armenians killed by them decides my opinion for intervention. I venture to believe that the ordinary Turks, if left to themselves, are incapable of the organized brutality that, under the inspiration from their rulers, the dregs of its population have assisted in.

The broad fact that tells with me is that, without sufficient cause or provocation, an Eastern oligarchy is plundering and murdering a section of its people under the corrupt domination of its pashas. Worse than this, they were secretly, then openly, now defiantly stirring up the fanaticism of its otherwise decent people, and for their own ends importing the most savage of their auxiliaries to carry out what the real Turkish people at Constantinople do not approve.

The fact is, and the past and present history of the Ottoman Empire proves, that there are two Turks to be reckoned with: the governing element, which is nearly always criminal and corrupt, and the governed, who, considering their race, religion, and Oriental customs, are not the unmoral replicas of their infamous rulers. In a word, the autocracy of degeneracy which stands for government in Turkey has to be destroyed, and in its destruction the overtaxed, blackmailed, Turkish people would rejoice, and good administration for Armenia would begin.

Turkey has for generations been in the hands of a brutal bureaucracy. This official despotism that combines Oriental craft with Western hypocrisy, and both with Eastern vice, must go. Its puppet and embodiment, the Sultan, must be deposed. In the permanent interests of Turkey itself the Sultan and all his *entourage* must be sacrificed, or, for lack of this, the Turks will provoke universal hostility and, as a nation, must disappear.

As a Turkish proverb pertinently says, "Their fish now stinks at the head." That ghoulish head must be severed to save the whole

Eastern peoples from moral putrefaction, administrative decay, and social dissolution.

How best and quickest can relief to the Armenians be given and the better Turkey saved from its wicked parts? For any one, not of the Government, it is difficult to say, and through the curse of our secret diplomacy it is difficult to suggest what to do. That is the business of our governors and parliamentary pashas, the Cabinet. The details of it is their work, its necessity is their mandate, and their political responsibility as an administration makes it their duty.

When they will apply the vital spark of kindling action I cannot say. Europe is indignant, England is agreed, and it commands the only voice that can order the Porte to desist. Such an order given by our fleet in forcing the Dardanelles would suffice. This decisive act, once before taken for less justification than has recently occurred, would have created a situation the outcome of which would not be war, but the agreed dismemberment of Turkey.

Risks must always be run. England was made and lives by them at home and abroad.

A bold venture would have exposed the bluff of the reptile Press of Europe, and disclosed not a unity of Powers against England, but a rupture amongst them over the division of an empire that England alone can and must tumble to its doom.

But what has come over our statesmen that they should hesitate even at strenuous mediation, when a real *casus belli*, as the condition of Armenia is, exists? Is their hesitancy and apprehension due to a knowledge of factors in the Eastern Question that the public do not possess? If so, it is time the English people were informed, so that if the dread arbitrament of war alone will suffice, they should know it, and on that knowledge decide, or if a bargain with Russia is needed, discuss the terms, accepting or rejecting as humanity, not territory, decides. There have been few European troubles that possessed the justification for English initiative and collective action of the Powers which these massacres have furnished. Had some crisis been wanted for reasons of *la haute politique*, it would have arisen and been created over the matrimonial alliance of some petty prince with another member of a royal house, and war would have been declared ere this. Had some irritable ambassador had a violent dislike to another, means would have been found for the "suspension of friendly relations."

Had the Sultan been at Coomassie instead of Constantinople, at Zanzibar or Khartoum, or anywhere else than in his lair at Yildiz Kiosk, the long fingers of our commercial interests would have found some sordid trade reason for pulling him up, as our sailors say, with a round turn. If the sanctified political exigencies of palm oil, cotton, and trade gin have driven us to the splendid and heroic audacity that has marked some of our expeditions, and often illumined the pages of our history, we have yet, I am certain, conscience and courage enough for the rescue of millions of human beings from a cruel and obsolete despotism.

Surely in the heyday of our naval supremacy and military preparedness, our statesmen have the firmness to indicate what our sailors and soldiers would cheerfully do and dare?

Over the Armenian atrocities there has been greater incentive for interference than evoked the courage of the Crusaders. In some form, in varying degrees, the subject peoples of Turkey have been oppressed by a continuity of crime in their rulers. What in more barbarous times we could have tolerated, we now must take active steps to suppress.

I decline to accept the view which recent events have seemed to justify, namely, that women and children, the aged, and the deliberately unarmed, must continue to be killed in Turkey because the armed giants of Europe are jealous as to who shall be the first or last to stay the murderer's hand.

Have the "Big Battalions" taken the other side and now become the bodyguard of his Satanic Majesty the Sultan? Is it safer for the Great Assassin to ply his murderous mission with an armed host surrounding him, while he, in proportion to their strength, craftily exploits their rival plans, their hidden antagonisms, and their secret policies? If this be so, England, exempt from territorial aggrandisement in that part of Europe, is driven to plainly telling the other Powers that, in their desire to divide the Turkish dominions in the future, they must help to stay the annihilation of its people in the present.

If war is out of the question, singlehanded and collective deposition impossible, these do not exhaust the versatility and resources of the potential Pitts and embryonic Cromwells who aspire to direct our policies and govern our Empire. I at least await their action with some degree of doubt. But if they can prove that their hand is stayed because intervention will mean the intensification of Armenian massacres and universal persecution, we perhaps will have to wait. But how long? Judging by recent references to the impotency of England, Armenia is always to be theatre of atrocity because some statesmen and journalists regard England as weak and as nervous as themselves.

But at least the convening of a conference of the Powers is possible. Let the world know which nation shields the Sultan, and what for. Let England at that conference or now boldly exploit for humanity the real divisions amongst the Powers, with a full knowledge that some of them dare not attempt war abroad for fear of revolution at home, whilst at the same time subordinating those "British interests" that a false pride and a mistaken policy have maintained too long in Turkey, and caused the present difficulty.

The pity of it all is, that the impression created on Europe and the Porte by the spirited action of our Consul at Constantinople was allowed to pass away. It was the plucky preliminary of further action by his superiors at home; at least it foreshadowed what their policy should have been.

The withdrawal then or even now of our Ambassador, and the substitution of an admiral with an hour's notice for all four-footed beasts to vacate Yildiz Kiosk and a bombardment if reforms were not granted within an hour. Audacious well-doing would have solved the situation.

The Concert of Europe, however, is to be waited upon, and the chief element in it, as I regard England to be, must await, I suppose, another tragedy to invoke its aid. If that should come—and vacillation is its chief stimulus—then even with the Powers against us, but America and our colonies helping England, the Sultan must be thrown from that pivotal position he now occupies, and from which he has dexterously lured, or drawn to his side, or kept neutral, the very forces and powers that, in preserving their diplomatic balance, sent the Armenians to their fate and made a murderer master of the Eastern Question.

IV.

Professor H. Anthony Salmoné[2]

The darkest record in the pages of modern history is unquestionably that of the reign of Abdul Hamid. What is still more lamentable is the fact that an indelible stain blemishes the fair repute of

European chivalry and honour. With all the boasted claim of Western nations to civilisation, culture, love of justice and humanity, and the protection of the oppressed, they have of late remained inert witnesses of the most barbaric treatment that a subjugated people ever received from its rulers. All this notwithstanding that the six Great Powers stand pledged by treaties to afford protection to the persecuted subjects of the Sultan. But they have continued passive, lest by active intervention some spoke may thereby be put in the wheel of their political machinery.

It is true that the Powers, following the lead of Great Britain and Russia (I do not mention France, for her latter-day statesmen have made her the puppet of the Tzar), made strong representation last year to the Sultan. This was followed by several others. Every one is now acquainted with the result. His Sultanic Majesty, after months of tedious exchange of polite remonstrances, granted some modified reforms—on paper. This, be it understood, he took the precaution to make publicly known to the world, and especially for the edification of his wretched subjects, as voluntarily "emanating from the fountain of his limitless mercy and boundless love for his people!" Despite the apparent absurdity of the whole affair, the representatives of the Powers were constrained to make a virtue of necessity and accept this magnanimous concession. Months elapsed and not a sign was made as to putting this into force. On the contrary, the officers and officials at whose instigation and by whose aid the atrocities in Armenia took place were decorated and promoted.

The tone of the press on the Continent has been, throughout the period of the sad occurrences, modified and extremely cautious. But, on the other hand, I venture to ask what real good has accrued from the voluminous writings in this country and the tirades made against the Sultan and his Government. Worse than nothing. Abdul Hamid retaliated by a repetition of his former dark deeds of blood! Numerous indignation meetings were held, eloquent platform speeches were delivered, and every feasible step was taken to prove that the feelings of Christian England were outraged at the merciless slaughter of so many thousand Armenians. Surely, no greater or more influential and representative meeting was ever held than that which took place at the St. James's Hall last year in May! Yet, after the lapse of fifteen months, over five thousand Christians are butchered by orders of the Sultan within a stone's-throw of his fastness, Yildiz, and actually within sight of some representatives of the European Powers. Can history furnish a greater outrage upon the honour of the civilised human community?

With regard to the St. James's Hall meeting, I venture here to state briefly that it is my firm conviction that (1) had the speakers refrained from attacking the Muhammadan faith; (2) had they expressed the desire for the introduction of general reform in Turkey (both to Christians and non-Christians alike); (3) had a formal resolution been passed appealing to the other Powers to support Great Britain in taking immediate measures to compel the Sultan to carry out those reforms—long ere now the desired end would have been attained. This would have contributed, in a great measure, to lubricate much of that friction which has since existed between Great Britain and the Powers over the Turkish Question. It would have helped to allay the discontent of the Muhammadans and brought about peace and contentment throughout Turkish dominion. That meeting, with all its subsequent appendages, had a baneful effect! It increased the madness and fury of the bloodthirsty Sultan, roused the suspicion of foreign politicians, and augmented the hostility of Russian statesmen to this country.

The question of imminent importance at present is to consider the manner in which this complex problem can be solved. Affairs have now reached so acute a stage that unless some speedy solution be found a disastrous European war is inevitable. It must be evident to all that the persecuted suffering subjects of the Sultan are determined to maintain their present attitude, and will not rest until they get the much-needed reforms. The voice of the leaders of the reform movement has had a telling effect. Committees have sprung up in every part of the Turkish Empire. Some of these are absolutely revolutionary, as has been proved; but their action was independent of the leaders of the Central Committee at Paris. The power of the latter has grown to enormous dimensions, and I have the best authority for stating that these have the support of the bulk of the Turkish Army officers. Indeed, with the exception of a small minority (who surround the Sultan), every inhabitant of the Empire secretly supports the league of reform.

The only solution of the difficulty—the only means of checking the flow of bloodshed in perturbed Turkey—*is the immediate deposition of Abdul Hamid!* In this idea the Press and public of this country are unanimous. On the other hand, no practical suggestion has been offered as to the manner of procedure. It is true some have advocated that England should, single-handed if needs be, effect the dethronement. Such a step without some understanding with Russia would be fraught with danger. I do not mean that this country in reality need fear any active opposition on the part of Russia or of the other European Powers. The Government of the Tzar knows right well that, by supporting Abdul Hamid actively against the will of the whole nation, Russia would defeat her own ends and jeopardise her policy in appearing as the champion of Turkey. The danger would really emanate from the people of the country themselves—I refer to the Muhammadan population. These—although they have been equally the victims of misrule, and are in reality anxious to terminate the existing *régime*—would resent the active intervention of England, which they would regard as made on behalf of the Armenians and Christians alone. Unless these doubts be dissipated they would resort to arms, and—though powerless to withstand the power of Great Britain—they would avenge themselves upon the hapless Christians. I repeat what I have often said before, that it is much to be regretted that the country should have so strenuously striven to obtain redress for the Armenian sufferers, with such total disregard of the condition of the non-Christians of Turkey. But this may yet be amended. I rejoice at the fact that Mr. Gladstone has latterly in one of his letters stated that it is not the Muhammadans who are to blame, but the Sultan. It would be beneficial if his lead were to be followed by others who have waged an incessant war against the creed of Islam.

The time has arrived when the Young Turkey party should be fully recognised by the European Powers. Without their support, direct or indirect, nothing can be effectually or peaceably done. They, on the other hand, should have some countenance from one or more of the European Powers, so that when the hour arrives for them (especially those at Constantinople) to openly proclaim themselves opponents of the present *régime*, they may do so securely and effectively. They would, moreover, take the necessary means to ensure the fulfilment of reforms by Abdul Hamid's successor.

The deposition of Abdul Hamid could be effected in a single

night without the shedding of one drop of blood; for should it be felt that Europe would even only stand neutral the whole nation would openly rise, and the *Sheikh-ul-Islam*, the chief Turkish Muhammadan dignitary, himself would be at their head and readily grant the necessary *fetwah* for his deposition. In this connection I may add that, according to Muhammadan law, the edict of a few priests of Islam is all that is needed to dethrone the Kaliph and appoint a successor. Such was the case with the four former Sovereigns of Turkey who have been deposed during this century.

It is somewhat strange that in all that has been said regarding the deposition of the Sultan no mention has been made of his possible successor, and no reference made to the possible condition of the country after the event. Does this not show a heedless disregard of the future—with all its possible complications? Does it not show the irresponsible ignorance of those who would at any cost have their country plunged in a hazardous situation?

It is both amusing and painful to reflect upon the conduct of a person who, while labouring under mortal fear and in imminent danger, seeks to dispel from his mind the inevitable evil by thinking of some fantastic good. Such has been the case with some of the leading men in this country over "the Eastern Question." At the time of the appearance in this Review of my article in May 1895, the editors of two leading London morning papers expostulated with me for having so strongly shown the real condition of Turkey, intimating "that such exposures may lead to the re-opening of the Eastern Question, which is most undesirable at present." This wilful blindness is almost incomprehensible, and I even venture to say that its consequences are as disastrous as those of the conduct of people who imagine they see what does not exist. The conduct alike of those who ignore a fact and of those who exaggerate it is reprehensible.

I trust that I may be pardoned for referring to my past writings in this Review, but it may somewhat serve to emphasise what I feel it my duty now to say. As far back as May 1895 I declared that the persecuted suffering subjects of Turkey have at last realised that they must no longer hope for succour from Europe, and that they are determined to endure their sufferings no longer; that they were resolved by themselves, unaided to fight for liberty or die in the struggle. And this statement has since been fully realized. Macedonia, Crete, Mount Lebanon, and again the Armenians, have risen in arms, and many thousands in truth have died in the struggle.

The British nation and its Government have repeatedly been accused of seeking self-benefit at whatever sacrifice it may entail to others, and that self-considerations alone for the purposes of national aggrandisement sway the mind of public men in this country. There may be some amount of truth in the indictment. On the other hand, can the other Christian nations of Europe plead guiltless of the crime of aiding and abetting the shedding of the blood of thousands upon thousands of innocent lives in Turkey at the close of the nineteenth century? Should not France, once the mighty champion of Christendom, with all its historic chivalry, bow its head in shame for helping to support a cold-blooded tyrant upon his throne? And how can Russia—the avowed enemy, until within a year or so ago, of Turkey and of all oppressors of Christians—reconcile her former attitude with her present conduct in giving encouragement to that worthless craven who has during his reign caused more suffering to his subjects than all his predecessors put together.

In conclusion I will briefly summarise the opinions of one of the most influential leaders of the Young Turkey Party and the chief editor of *La Jeune Turquie*, of Paris, as expressed to me in a conversation a few days ago. He said:

> "Present affairs in Turkey are replete with danger—not only as regards that Empire, but as threatening the peace of the world. The danger does not arise so much from the disturbances in the country as from the attitude of the Powers in connection therewith. Their apathy and contentment with diplomatic remonstrances (instead of taking decisive steps) have made affairs much worse than they would have been. It was thought that the matter would blow over. Mere protests and threats had no effect upon the Sultan, who has become well acquainted with 'European representations.' But things now have gone beyond all the arts of diplomacy. Further disturbance and massacres are inevitable! These sparks in Turkey will cause a European conflagration, the result of which God alone knows. The Muhammadans are wrongly accused of fanaticism. The idea is erroneous. They likewise cry out for reforms and are sick of the present Sultan. Moreover Muhammadans are always ready to

submit to superior power, as is the case in India, Algeria, Egypt, and other places.

"As to the Sultan, he is possessed of intelligence, but he is in reality insane—and who would not be so after twenty years' imprisonment at his palace, surrounded by adventurers and liars, knowing only what he is told? There is only one way to save Turkey, and save Europe thereby from a fruitless war; and that is by the deposition of Abdul Hamid. Why should not Queen Victoria, for instance, ask the Tzar, as a humane act, to agree to the deposition, for the sake of saving the heartless massacre of thousand of innocent helpless people? Such a step would be hailed with acclamation throughout the civilised world, no less than by the people throughout Turkey."

The above is, with some reserve, what was said. I can only add, from my intimate knowledge of the forces at the disposal of and employed by "awakened Turkey," that nothing but the speedy deposition of Abdul Hamid can possibly remove the danger which now threatens all the subjects of Turkey with destruction and Europe with a disastrous war.

V.

The Right Hon. W. E. Gladstone

The foregoing articles, with which I have become acquainted through the kindness of the Editor, appear to me likely to attract the public attention, not only by ability and integrity, but by the remarkable diversity in the points of view from which the several authors approach the discussion, and the not less remarkable decision with which they arrive at a common conclusion: that conclusion being, that the "situation" in the East is intolerable, and that action with a view to a remedy has become indispensable, and ought not to be delayed.

It may be worth while to remark that that situation, besides being intolerable, is unexampled. It is not without example that the Great Assassin, now Sultan of Turkey, should have defied all Europe: but on two occasions when he made the attempt, in 1876–7, and in 1880, it cost him the severance of fourteen millions of people from his Empire, whereas his daring has now effected this defiance, up to the present point, with absolute impunity, and with triumphant success. In a witty and pungent sarcasm Dean Swift set forth that, when ten men well armed enter into conflict with one man in his shirt, the man in the shirt is nearly sure to be beaten. In the present case, not indeed ten but six men well armed have fought with one man in his shirt, and that a very ragged one, but the man in the shirt has thus far been victorious, and has exhibited his consciousness of victory by the periodical repetition of his crimes now blazoned throughout the world.

Nor (to do the six men justice) has this been because they were insensible to the enormity of the offences. On the contrary, though we do not know all, yet it has become known even to us on the outside of all charmed circles, through channels which if accidental are authentic, that a remedy the strongest and most direct of all has been deliberately proposed and variously advanced in their deliberations, and has only failed to take effect through certain reciprocal jealousies, independent of the merits of this particular controversy before us. Now it may be laid down as a general rule that the failure of strong remedial propositions is not a mere return to the *status ante*, but worsens the general position. They are sure to have become known to the criminal who is unhappily also a sovereign: their collapse is like an assurance of impunity: and that assurance of impunity becomes for the time absolute, when the Six Powers cast aside their weapons of offence, and descend to the prosecution of an illimitable diplomatic war, which has been based upon the method of stillborn remonstrance, and which, not from fault of execution, but from the law of its nature, was doomed from the first to be, and to become with the lapse of time more and more, a thing pitiable and contemptible.

The last feature of strangeness, in this successful contumacy by the single hand, remains to be stated. When a particular sovereign defies the world, it is sometimes with the love and veneration, always at least with the assent and support, of his subjects. There is no evidence that the Sultan has any one of these props to sustain him. His people are not indeed permitted to express their sentiments; but all the evidence before us is to the effect that as a body they, the Mahommedans as well as the Christians, are thoroughly disaffected. The motive power, which has directed these atrocities, and is only watching the movement of the hand on the clock to direct more, consists in the Sultan himself, sitting in the Yildiz Kiosk, with his dishes tasted lest his cook should poison him, and surrounded by ten or, as some believe, twenty thousand troops in his capital, whom, contrary to his general practice, he regularly pays, feeds, and clothes, and on whom, rightly or wrongly, he thinks he can rely.

Such is the unexampled character of the Eastern controversy in its present phase. The interrogation, however, of the hour, to which the British nation is from day to day heaping mountain high the materials of an affirmative reply, is whether, besides being unexampled, it is also intolerable. I venture to add that we have already passed the point at which a doubt could be raised whether the Eastern Question had been really opened or not. Quite apart from the present national movement, or its immediate consequences, opened that question is by the weight of facts, and so effectually opened that unless by the application of effective remedies it never can again be closed.

Upon the humiliation, which Europe has been suffering for the last eighteen months through its diplomacy, the people of this country appear to be well agreed. They seem also to be of one mind in the belief that action is absolutely demanded by the intolerable character of the situation. Further they have no doubt as to the title of the Powers collectively, or it may be individually, to undertake such action; the ground or reason of it being found in the hideous character, and the vast extent, of the Armenian massacres, together with the certainty that nothing but fear on the part of the Assassin will prevent their indefinite repetition. For, though the wonder be scarcely less than the crime, it really seems as if he had marked out for himself as an infernal mission, even the extirpation of the race whose blood, as we understand, he shares; and as if he would not consider his business was at an end until the last Armenian was at his last gasp.

Now, the action which is contemplated is humane; and it is also of the class which is called humanitarian. But, as between nations, the fact that a given course is agreeable to humanity does not of itself amount to a sufficient justification for entering upon it. Neither is it enough to say that we have made a careful examination of means and ends, and are well convinced that the undertaking is within our power. But there is still something more that we lack: for we have not had the sword of the Almighty entrusted to our keeping, and while we are bound to follow and require humanity in our own house, we may not have a title to enforce it in the house of our neighbour. We ought therefore to examine whether our case is complete, and whether we have the specific rights and obligations, which suffice, in the case that may be before us, to invest us with a jurisdiction that, apart from these specific rights, would not properly belong to us.

The specific right, then, which the Powers of Europe possess, and which entails a corresponding obligation, to prevent the recurrence of atrocious and wholesale crime in the Turkish Empire, is the right conferred, and the obligation imposed, by Treaty; let us say *nominatim* by the Treaty of Berlin. This right, and this obligation, attach to all the Powers. It is the shameless violation of it by Turkey which entails her liability as towards them all. There are two of them, however, from whom sound moral judgment would entitle us to expect a special forwardness. One of them is Russia, who by the Treaty of San Stefano had promised so much to the Christians. And the other is England, to whom unhappily were owing in a principal degree such shortcomings as attach to the Treaty of Berlin in comparison with the Treaty of San Stefano.

But while the argument for action as opposed to mere expostulation is under the Treaty of Berlin complete and even imperative for all the Powers, it cannot be too pointedly borne in mind that over and above everything which belongs to the five sister States, England is invested with an altogether separate right, and bound by an equally separate obligation, in which they have no share whatever. Were the Treaty of Berlin swept to the bottom of the sea, the Five Powers would have no rights in the matter save those of generalised humanity. But, in that same contingency, the rights and obligations of England would remain absolutely unaffected, as she draws them, distinctly but cumulatively, from another source.

It pleased us, in the year 1878, to conclude, without the intervention of the Powers, a separate Treaty with Turkey, which however became known to them before the transactions at Berlin were completed. It was thus tacitly accepted or allowed by them; but, whatever their attitudes in regard to it may now have been, it is absolutely binding as between the contracting parties. This Treaty differs from most others in two important particulars, of which the joint effect is, if I mistake not, to give a great amount of additional point and force to the obligations we have spontaneously incurred.

The name of honour is one, which has often been abused in

political discussion. It has been made a cover for miscarriage, for mistake, for crime. It has been profaned for evil purposes quite as much as the name of Liberty, even (perhaps) almost as much as the name of Order. But it is a great and a sacred name: and, where it can be invoked under a valid plea, the man who hesitates to make whatever sacrifices it may require, degrades both himself and the nature which he bears.

Under the Treaty or Convention of 1878, a great advantage was obtained by Turkey; for England became engaged to defend not Armenia only, but the whole Turkish Empire in Asia against Russian attack. On the other hand, the Sultan undertook to reform his government in concert with England. So that we actually made ourselves in honour partakers of the government of those widely extended countries, and such we should have been in act, had the Sultan fulfilled his promise. He not only did not fulfil it. In Armenia, he read Reform to mean "Massacre." The peculiarity of the Treaty was that his promise of reform was stipulated as being "in return" for the truly valuable engagement he had already obtained. Not only was the pledge broken, but it was broken after he had received actual and weighty value in return.

The Armenians were no parties to the Convention. They have no treaty rights, no international existence. They are only men: for, though they happen to be also Christians, this does not affect the substance of the case. But who can deny with "honour" that, when we made this Treaty over their heads, we undertook not only heavy juridical obligations as towards Turkey, but also real and profound moral obligations as towards them?

But there is another enhancing consideration, which has not I think as yet been sufficiently borne in mind. We too in this Treaty took "value received"; and we have it, so to speak, at this moment in our pockets. The Sultan made over to us, without limit of time, the occupation and administration, that is the virtual dominion, of the island of Cyprus.

Perhaps it may be said, and I might concur in the opinion, that Cyprus is of no value to us. But that reply is wholly foreign to the purpose. If it did not add to our strength or resources, it added, as we were told, to our *prestige*. It was boasted of in Parliament at the time as a territorial acquisition, and was highly popular. We cannot now turn round upon it and declare it valueless. We took it as value, and as value we have now to abide by it in the present argument.

The case then stands briefly thus.

We are entitled to demand of the Sultan the immediate fulfilment, under his treaty with us, of his engagements, and to treat his non-compliance as, under the law of nations, other breaches of treaty are, or may be, dealt with.

We have in the face of the world bound ourselves to secure good government for Armenia and for Asiatic Turkey.

And for thus binding ourselves we have received what we have declared to be valuable consideration in a virtual addition to the territory of the Empire.

And all this we have done, not in concert with Europe, but by our own sole action, on our own sole responsibility.

However we may desire and strive to obtain the co-operation of others, is it possible for us to lay down this doctrine: *England may give for herself the most solemn pledges in the most binding shape, but she now claims the right of referring it to some other person or persons, State or States, not consulted or concerned in her act, to determine whether she shall endeavour to the utmost of her ability to fulfil them?*

If this doctrine is really to be adopted, I would respectfully propose that the old word "honour" should be effaced from our dictionaries, and dropped from our language.

The Contemporary Review, Vol. 70 (October 1896): 457–65

The Constantinople Massacre

[The following article, though for obvious reasons it cannot be signed, may be taken as thoroughly well-informed.—Ed. Contemporary Review]

It is about two years since the massacre in Sassoon which led England, France, and Russia to intervene in a feeble way for the protection of the Armenians in Turkey. It is just a year since several hundred Armenians were beaten to death by Softas and Zabtieh in the streets of Constantinople. This brought the fleets to the vicinity of the Dardanelles, and after much negotiation brought five small gunboats to Constantinople. Beginning in October in Trebizond, there were massacres and looting in all the principal cities of seven provinces, and a general destruction of villages and rural population in the same provinces. According to the latest estimates, about 100,000 were killed, and about half a million reduced to want. The Great Powers did nothing, and, England and Italy excepted, looked on with indifference. Russia entered into a new alliance with the Sultan to guarantee the integrity of his Empire.

On the continent the people generally were in sympathy with the policy of the Governments and took no interest in the fate of the Christian subjects of the Sultan—which naturally confirmed him in his belief that he could treat them as he pleased without fear of Europe. In the spring the Cretans revolted, and in August, through the intervention of the Powers, secured all that they asked for in the way of autonomy.

The Armenian revolutionists, encouraged by the outbreaks in Crete, Syria, and Macedonia, appealed anew to the Embassies and to the Turkish Government to secure some reasonable reforms for the Armenians, and accompanied this demand with the threat that they would create disturbances if their demands were not heeded.

They planned outbreaks at Adana, Angora and Van. Only the last came to a head, and it resulted in the death of most of the revolutionists and the massacre of several thousand innocent persons. This outbreak at Van was utterly foolish in its conception, without any possible hope of success, and very badly managed. Then early in August came the threat of an outbreak at Constantinople, which was treated, as all such threats have been by the Ambassadors, with contempt. But those who knew the city have known for many months that some such outbreak was sure to occur if the persecution of the Armenians continued unchecked, and have foreseen the consequences. If the Armenians were not the most peaceable and submissive people in the world, this city would have been in ashes before this time, for they have had everything to drive them to desperation. They have bowed their heads and submitted to this also; but it was certain that the revolutionists would try to rouse them and to startle Europe in some way. The Turks also seem to have desired this outbreak. They were fully informed as to the plan of seizing the Ottoman Bank on August 26. This is stated in the proclamation of the Sultan, published in the Turkish papers the next day, and has been affirmed by many of the officers since. They did nothing to prevent it; but spent all their energy in preparing for the massacre which was to follow.

The theory of the Russian Armenian revolutionists who seized the Ottoman Bank was, that if they could hold it with the threat of blowing it up if their demands were not listened to, the Ambassadors would force the Sultan to grant the reasonable reforms which they demanded for the Armenians, rather than permit the destruction of the Bank and its staff. It was a scheme borrowed from the theatre, absurd in itself, and made ridiculous by the way in which they failed to carry it out. They went in bravely, and nothing hindered their destroying the Bank, but they allowed themselves to be talked out of it by Mr. Maximoff, the Russian dragoman, and would have been the laughing stock of the world if its attention had not been absorbed by the massacre which followed. The real heroism of that day was displayed in another quarter of the city, by another small party of Russian Armenians, men and women, who took possession of two stone houses and fought the Turkish troops to the death, the survivors killing themselves when they could fight no longer. There was no serious fighting anywhere else, although dynamite bombs were thrown from the windows of houses and khans upon the troops in a number of places, showing that some preparation had been made for a more extended outbreak. There is nothing to be said in justification of this attempt of the revolutionists. They had provocation enough to justify anything in reason, but there was nothing reasonable in this plan, nothing in it to attract the sympathy of the Powers or to conciliate public opinion; and if the statements are true which have been made by Armenians as to certain unexecuted parts of the plan, it was diabolical. This only can be said on behalf of these revolutionary committees. They are the natural outcome of the treatment of the Armenians by the Turkish Government during the last twenty years. When oppression passes a certain limit and men become desperate, such revolutionary organisations always appear. They are the fruit and not the cause of the existing state of things in Turkey, and if we can judge by the experience of other countries, the worse things become here, the more violent will be the action of the committees, whether Europe enjoys it or not.

Revolutionists are the same all the world over, but the Turkish Government is unique, and it is not the attack on the Bank which interests us but the action of the Government which followed. As we have said, the authorities had full information of what was to be attempted and did nothing to prevent it, but they made every preparation for carrying out their own plan. Bands of ruffians were gathered in Stamboul, Galata, and Pera, made up of Kurds, Lazes, and the lower class of Turks, armed with clubs, knives, and firearms; and care was taken that no one should kill or plunder in the quarter to which he belonged, lest he should be recognised and complaint made afterwards by the Embassies, with a demand for punishment. A large number of carts were in readiness to carry off the dead. The troops and police were in great force to prevent any resistance, and assist the mob if necessary. It was a beautiful day, the streets were crowded, and few had any idea of what had happened at the Bank, when suddenly, without any warning, the work of slaughter and plunder began, everywhere at once. European ladies on the way to the Bosphorus steamers suddenly found themselves surrounded by assassins, and saw men beaten to death at their feet. Foreign merchants saw their own employés cut to pieces at their doors. Every man who was recognised as an Armenian was killed without mercy. In general the soldiers took no part in the slaughter and behaved well, and they somewhat reassured those in the streets who were not Armenians, but in a few moments the shops were closed and a wild panic spread through the city. The one idea of every one was to get home; and as the foreigners and better classes live out of the city in summer they had to go to the Galata bridge to take the steamers, which ran as usual all through the three days of massacre. This took them through the streets where the slaughter was going on, and consequently we have the testimony of hundreds of eye-witnesses as to what took place. The work of death and plunder continued unchecked for two days. On Friday there were isolated outbreaks, and occasional assassinations occurred up to Tuesday. The number killed will never be known. The Ambassadors put it at 5000 or 6000; the official report to the palace at 8750, besides those thrown into the sea. Thousands of houses, shops and offices were plundered, including a number belonging to Greeks and foreigners. Everything was done in the most systematic way, and there was not a moment of anarchy, not a moment when the army and police had not perfect control of the city during all these days. Certain Armenian quarters—Scutari, Koom Kapou and others—were for some reason protected, and were as quiet and undisturbed as usual. The outbreaks of violence at Bebec and Candilli on the Bosphorus were probably spontaneous and contrary to orders, as was everything done after Friday morning in town.

The quarters where slaughter and pillage were most terrible were along the Golden Horn—from the Dolma Baghtchè Palace to Hasskuei and from Seraglio Point to Aivan Serai; also at Samatia, near the Seven Towers, and at the Adrianople gate. Large numbers were killed in Pera. The majority of those massacred belonged to the working class—especially the *hamals* (porters)—but a large number of gentlemen, merchants and other wealthy men, were killed, together with about fifty women and children. The savage brutality of the Moslem mob was something beyond all imagination, and in many cases the police joined in beating men to death and hacking others to death with knives, in the very face of Europeans. A friend of mine saw eighteen men dragged by the police, one after another, out of a building in Galata, and cut to pieces at the door. A lady friend saw a procession of Catholic school girls in Pera

Street. An Armenian, flying from the mob, took refuge in the midst of them, and was cut to pieces there—his blood spattered over the children's dresses. Some twenty employés at the railway station were seized by the police and beaten to death on the premises. Mr. Maximoff, the Russian dragoman, saw two men beating an Armenian to death in the street. With the help of his cavass he captured one of them, took him to the nearest police station, and demanded his imprisonment. This was refused, and he took him to Yildiz—he turned out to be a well-known official there. Mr. Herbert, H.M. Chargé d'Affaires, to whom the highest honour is due for his action during the massacres, saw many terrible sights with his own eyes—among others a Moslem crowd jeering at a man on the top of a cartload of dead, who was still in the agonies of death. A man whom I knew very well was beaten to death, stripped, and a big cross cut on his breast with a sword. A living child was found in the pile of 700 mutilated bodies in the Chichli Cemetery. A friend of mine saw a mob of Turkish women looting the little shop of an Armenian just killed—shouting and laughing, and treading under foot what they did not care to take away. When there were no more Armenians in the streets they were sought out in the khans, shops, and houses, and here in many cases the military officers took an active part in the plunder—if not in the killing. At Hasskuei—where there is a large Jewish population—after the Turks had murdered the inmates of a house, officers sold the right to plunder it to the Jews. I know one case where an officer received nine pounds for the plunder of a house. The Jews also assisted the Turks in hunting the Armenians out of their hiding-places, and in some cases killed them themselves. At Hasskuei, Samatia, and Kassim Pacha the women and children left alive are without any means of living. The brutality of the mob in these attacks upon the houses was even more horrible than in the streets, for the women pleaded and sometimes fought for the lives of their husbands and sons, who were mercilessly cut to pieces before their faces. I know of one case where a widow prayed for the life of her only son—an innocent boy. Even the murderers were touched but the mob of Turkish women behind cried out, "Don't listen; kill him!" and they killed him in his mother's arms.

At Bebec the mob was made up of the Turkish *hamals* of the village, and at a signal from the *Imam* of the mosque they attacked the bakery, where they bought their daily bread, generally on credit, murdered every man they could find, and plundered everything—a Turkish woman in a neighbouring house pointing out the hiding place of one poor boy.

In many cases European officials appealed to the officers in command of the troops, who were looking on at the slaughter of helpless unarmed men, to interfere and put a stop to it. The reply was "We have our orders." It was an officer who killed the clerk of the British Post-office on the steps. And some of the most cold-blooded and horrible murders took place in front of the guard house, at the Galata end of the bridge, in the presence of officers of the Sultan's household of the highest rank. They also had their orders.

Happily for the honour of the Turkish people, there is another side to the story. It was the Government and not the people that conducted this massacre. And although the vile instruments employed were told that they were acting in the name of the Prophet, and freely used his name, and are boasting to-day of what they did for Islam, the Sheik-ul-Islam forbad the Softas taking any part in the slaughter and many a pious Turk did what he could to protect his neighbours. Some of them sheltered scores in their own houses, and there are *Ulema* who condemn the whole thing as directly contrary to the teaching of the Koran. The common people accept it as the work of the Caliph, which is not to be criticised. One poor woman who had an Armenian family in her house said: "I will protect you against the mob, but if they demand you in the name of the Prophet I must give you up to be killed." I think that many of the common Turks are as much afraid of the Armenians as the Armenians are of them. It is not the people, not even the mob, who are responsible for this great crime. It was deliberately committed by the Government. The Ambassadors of the six Powers have declared this to be an unquestionable fact in the Joint Note addressed to the Porte.

Since the massacre this same Government has been carrying on a warfare against the Armenians which is hardly less inhuman than beating out their brains with clubs. There were from 150,000 to 200,000 Armenians in Constantinople. They were merchants, shop-keepers, confidential clerks, employés in banks and offices of every kind—the chief business men of the city. They were the bakers of the city, they had charge of the khans and bazaars and the wealth of the city; they were the porters, house-servants, and navvies. Many thousands of them were from the interior—from the provinces which have been devastated during the past two years—earning money in Constantinople to pay their taxes and support their families. It is this money which has kept alive tens of thousands of families since the massacres. Now the Government has undertaken to ruin this whole population. They are hunted about the city and over the hills, like wild beasts. Every day we see gangs of them brought in, hungry, ragged, with utter despair in their faces. The banks, the Debt Commission, the Régie, and all public companies have been required to dismiss their Armenian employés, they have taken them from the Custom House, the coal wharves, the khans, shops, and offices, and even from private houses. Thousands have been sent off at once to the Black Sea ports, to find their way as best they can without money or food to their desolated villages in the interior. Other thousands, on paying blackmail to the officers, have been allowed a few days to close up their business. Thousands have fled to foreign countries, leaving everything behind them, taking advantage of the intervention of the foreign consuls, who have put them on the steamers in the harbour without passports. The wealthy families are getting away by paying enormous bribes for passports. The terror, the distress, the hopeless anguish of these people, which we see constantly, cannot be described, but, as we can do nothing for them, it makes Constantinople seem like a hell. It is not only the ruin of the Armenians, but the ruin of the city. Many kinds of business have become impossible. The wild Kurds who have taken the place of the Armenians at the Custom House cannot do the work. It takes about five times as long to coal a steamer as formerly.

There is no one in the city to fill the place of the Armenians in the offices and houses, or to run the bakeries. But these statements convey no true impression of the real state of things. It is not simply that men are wanting, or that shops are closed. The foundations of society have been overthrown and all confidence has disappeared. There is no longer any trusted power in the city to represent the principles of law and order. Any Government, however severe, which represents these is tolerable. Every man knows what to expect. But when a so-called Government uses its power for the destruction rather than the preservation of the lives and property of its subjects; when it organises mobs to massacre quiet and unoffending men in the streets, and to plunder the town; when it destroys the means of doing business, and exiles by the thousand its most industrious subjects without a pretence of law, then we have a condition of society which is worse than anarchy. It is a reign of terror. It is the Armenians to-day. It may be the Greeks or foreigners to-morrow, and there is no power in Constantinople to resist the forces at the disposal of the palace. There is no security anywhere; and no hope of relief from the present terror. Every one feels that we are on the eve of events even more terrible than what we have seen. It is this which has brought about the financial ruin of the city, which is in itself a source of danger. We have the remnant of the Armenians starving and without the means of earning a living, and the Armenian revolutionists driven to desperation by the action of the Government, and we have the whole Turkish population and the army—dependent directly or indirectly upon the Government, which has no money and is rapidly destroying all its own resources. The Turkish population is not only in distress for money, but it has been demoralised by the action of the Government. Its natural respect for law has been shaken, and we see evidence every day of disorder and disorganisation among the common people. Lawlessness in all the relations of life is an inevitable result of such events, and it is surprising to see how rapidly this spirit is developed in Constantinople. How far it has extended to the army will appear at the next massacre.

The action of the Embassies during the massacre is worthy of special attention. The Austrian, Russian, Italian and German Ambassadors were here, England and France were well represented by very able Chargés d'Affaires. So far as I can learn, all were left for ten days without any instructions from their Governments and acted on their own responsibility. They acted together in perfect harmony, and so far as words could go they acted with energy, but the experience of the past two years has not been such as to give much weight to Ambassadorial threats. It was no doubt known at the Palace that they were not acting under instructions, and it was not until they had sent an open telegram to the Sultan such as he had never seen before that, after two days of slaughter, orders were given to stop the massacre. Such use as was possible was made of the small gunboats, and men were landed to protect the embassies and other official buildings. The Ambassadors or their secretaries and dragomans went about the city and saw for themselves what was going on. They remonstrated at the Palace again and again, and finally, as we have said, threatened the overthrow of the Sultan. They sent a formal note to the Porte, declaring that the massacre was the deliberate work of the Government, and that it would be held responsible for it by the Great Powers. They still hold to this position. With the small force at their disposal I do not see what more they could have done; but the result was a very humiliating one, one which would have been deemed impossible a few years ago. The Sultan laughed at their threats and the massacre went on unchecked for two days. He was startled by their telegram into giving orders to stop it, but he has gone on with the work of destroying the Armenians in another way as unconcernedly as though the Ambassadors did not exist. So far as we can see, he feels as sure of his absolute security from all interference as he did last January—after he had come to an understanding with Russia. And he seems to have no idea that he is himself ruining his empire. On the contrary, he believes, as he told his Ministers two years ago, that he is the wisest and most powerful sovereign in the world. There is no possibility of any change here for the better so long as the Great Powers maintain their present attitude, and abstain from armed intervention. The work of destruction will go on. Lawlessness will increase and extend to the army. New massacres will take place, involving other nationalities, until the ruin of the city is complete. I believe that there is not an Ambassador in Constantinople who is not of this opinion. No one familiar with the principles of political science can doubt it. Constantinople is a doomed city. It will not be the first time that Europe has looked on with indifference at its destruction. In 1453 it was the last bulwark in the way of the progress of Mohammedan conquest. Europe turned a deaf ear to its cry for help, and suffered the penalty in centuries of conflict with the Turks. We look back with contempt upon the petty jealousies of that day which led to such a lamentable result. We belong to a higher civilisation, the fruit of all these centuries of development, and have broader views of the mutual interdependence of nations. It would have been a hard struggle for the Europe of that day to save Constantinople, but we have armies and fleets enough to work our will almost without an effort. Yet once more the cry has gone up from this devoted city to enlightened, Christian Europe to save it from destruction, and again a deaf ear has been turned to this cry. The city is once more left to its fate—a far more base and ignoble fate than that which befell it when it became the proud capital of the great conqueror.

To me the indifference of Europe is inexplicable. It is not true that there could be no interference here without endangering the peace of Europe. It is not true that nothing could be done without a full settlement of the Eastern question. The Sultan might be deposed within a week and a responsible Government established here to the great joy of Turks and Christians, and this without disturbing the limits of the empire, if England, France, and Russia could agree between themselves to do it—or better, if all the six Powers would consent. In my opinion, the anxiety not to disturb the peace of Europe at the present time is so great that war would not result if a single Power, either Russia, France or England, should intervene by force to put an end to this *régime* and save Constantinople. This is a matter of opinion—but it is certain that the simple reason why there has been no intervention thus far in the name of civilisation and humanity, is that no one of the Powers has been sufficiently moved by events here to be willing to make sacrifices and incur risks, or endanger prospective advantages to rescue this empire from its present ruler. That they have not been so moved is what is to me inexplicable. Is there no God in Europe but mammon? Is our boasted civilisation a degeneration rather than a development? Has Russia forgotten all her sympathy for the Christians of the East, to care only for dominion in Europe? Has England no longer any care for the oppressed? Has France abandoned her place among the nations, and her time-honoured policy in Turkey? Whatever the explanation of this incredible indifference may be, the consequences of it will not be confined to Constantinople any more than they were in 1453. The retribution will not come again in the form of Moslem conquest, but probably in that very European war which has been made the excuse for leaving the Christians of Turkey to their fate.

The Nineteenth Century, Vol. 40 (November 1896): 838–48

Turkish Misgovernment

I.

Wilfrid Scawen Blunt[1]

The retirement of Lord Rosebery from the Liberal leadership relieves the Radical Opposition of its chief difficulty in regard to Eastern politics, or at least makes it possible to propose a true line of conduct to the party which shall not be met by a jingo *non possumus*. Mr. Gladstone, Sir William Harcourt, Mr. John Morley, are always open to friendly argument where this is based on a true sympathy for liberty; and it is not, perhaps, altogether vain to remind them at times of their own past lapses where a wider interpretation of their admitted principles is pleaded for. I make bold, therefore, to put my view before them of their present Armenian agitation, to point out where I think they are in error, and to suggest what seems to me a more practical plan than any they have yet suggested for gaining the end they have in view. This I take to be the speedy relief of the Armenians from their present persecution, and an early, humane, and perhaps final, settlement of the whole Eastern Question. I believe all to be within their reach; but it can only be through their initial acknowledgment of great errors in the past, and the conversion of England, through their own conversion, to as great a work of reparation in the present.

First, then, as to their past lapses. The Liberal leaders in their pronouncements are astonished and indignant at the crimes they see perpetrated at Constantinople and in Asia Minor, at the Sultan Abdul Hamid's duplicity in the matter of reforms, at his arbitrary misgovernment, and at the Armenian blood that he has shed in torrents. I think, nevertheless, that if they would examine their own consciences a little closely, they would find that the present outrageous condition of things at Constantinople is one very largely, indeed principally, of their own contriving.

To begin at the very beginning—the Cyprus Convention and the Treaty of Berlin. It is true that out of office Mr. Gladstone and his colleagues denounced these arrangements strongly, but in office afterwards they persistently upheld and made use of them, and, indeed, on some points intensified their ill consequences. The full story of the Cyprus double-dealing has never, I think, been told in print, and its results have been so far-reaching, and are still so vitally affecting the situation, that I will make no apology for relating its chief episode here. The story, as I remember it well at the time—and it cannot in its main facts be gainsaid—is this. When the Congress met at Berlin in the early summer of 1878, one of the first of its acts was to take from each of the Ambassadors present a declaration that he came to it with clean hands—that is to say, free of all secret engagement between his Government and any other Government represented at the Congress. This declaration Lord Beaconsfield and Lord Salisbury gave with the rest. A few days after, however, the text of the Cyprus Convention was published in London by the *Globe* newspaper, which had obtained it from Mr. Marvin, a man employed as a translator at the Foreign Office, and who had for money betrayed it to the press. The incident was within a little of breaking up the Congress. The French and Russian Ambassadors declared themselves outraged at the English ill-faith, and M. Waddington went so far as to order his trunks to be packed for leaving Berlin. The situation was only saved by Prince Bismarck's intervention and the great personal ascendancy Lord Beaconsfield had acquired at the Congress. It was compromised on the following terms of English surrender. Lord Beaconsfield agreed with M. Waddington:

1. That France, as a set-off for Cyprus, should be allowed on the first convenient pretext and without opposition from England to occupy Tunis;

2. That, in the appointments then making in Egypt by the Finance Commission, France should march *pari passu* with England; and

3. That the old French claim of protecting the Latin Church in Syria should be acknowledged.

On these conditions M. Waddington was for the time detached from the Russian influence, and Lord Beaconsfield was able to return to London in triumph, having secured, according to his well-known boast, a "Peace with Honour." Nevertheless, the germ of the whole of our subsequent troubles in the East, including the French and Russian alliance, may be distinctly traced to the incident above related, and it is necessary to remember it now if we are to understand the full difficulty in which we are involved. Its first embarrassing result was the establishment in 1879 of the Anglo-French financial control in Egypt; its second, the violation of the Ottoman territory in Tunis, with our connivance, in 1881; the third, the failure of our moral influence with Turkey and all the Powers, leaving us charged with the fate of Asia Minor, and, at the same time, impotent to control it for good. Now, of course the initial blame in this scandalous affair was not the Liberal Party's. Mr. Gladstone denounced it as strongly as the rules of official etiquette, which always screen the worst Foreign Office delinquencies, would allow. But what I would beg Liberals to consider is, that neither in 1880, when Mr. Gladstone returned to office, nor at any subsequent period of Liberal ascendancy, has the smallest serious attempt been made to undo or repair the wrong. Mr. Gladstone in office became indistinguishable in his treatment of the Eastern Question from Lord Beaconsfield. He neither withdrew from the responsibility in Egypt, nor refused his connivance with France when the time came for redeeming Lord Beaconsfield's bond in Tunis, nor did he abrogate the Cyprus engagement. All that he did to modify his predecessor's policy was to relax the vigilance of English supervision in Asia Minor by withdrawing the perambulating Consuls Lord Salisbury had appointed, and so to leave the Armenians and other Ottoman subjects more completely than ever at the Sultan's mercy. He retained unaltered the obligations of the Convention, while neutralizing its purpose—what little there was in it—for good; and, above all, and to the disappointment of everyone who had followed his noble declarations of disinterestedness out of office, he retained Cyprus, England's unholy "backshish" in the affair. To the present day it is inexplicable to me how the great Liberal statesman of 1880 should thus have stultified his declarations and swerved from his principles.

A still stronger case for Liberal repentance is that of Mr. Gladstone's action two years later in Egypt, and one that more vitally affects the present unhappy situation among the Sultan's subjects. In 1881 and 1882 there was everywhere in the Ottoman Empire a strong movement in favour of reform. All the intelligence, all the education, all the humanity of the empire was on the side of a liberal interpretation of the Sheria, or Moslem law, of religious tolerance, and, above all, of constitutional government. Rightly or wrongly, all that was best in the empire had turned to this European panacea for a remedy. On the other side stood the reactionist fanaticism of the uneducated, the rabble of the towns, and this same Sultan Abdul Hamid. The moment was a critical one. The constitutional party, weakened by the issue of the Russian war, was being hard pressed by Abdul Hamid at Constantinople; the liberal Grand Sherif of Mecca had just been assassinated and replaced by a reactionist; the Sultan was beginning to assert his leadership of the Panislamic movement. Still the issue of the struggle was far from decided against liberty, and in Egypt, at any rate, the constitutional party were carrying all before them. They had wrung a Constitution from the Khedive, and were determined on reform. All the enlightened Moslem world, and in large measure the Christian world, too, of the Ottoman provinces were looking on, their hopes centred on the Egyptian success. It was at this critical juncture that Mr. Gladstone allowed himself to be persuaded—we all remember in what financial interests—to intervene and crush the movement. He pleaded in excuse that he was paying a debt of honour, that he was bound by international engagements and I know not what else. What he seems, however, to have forgotten, but it is very necessary Liberals should remember it, is that in order to effect his purpose he called in the aid of the very forces of inhumanity he is now denouncing, with an effect altogether disastrous to Eastern liberty. It is on historical record that in the month of June 1882, after threatening the Egyptian nationalists in vain, Her Majesty's Government appealed to this very Sultan, Abdul Hamid, for help to crush their movement and dispose of their leader, *by Oriental methods.* The English Liberal press of the day even went so far as to explain that Dervish Pasha, the Sultan's right-hand man, borrowed for the occasion, was specially fitted for his work, inasmuch as he was "notoriously unscrupulous." It is also historical that within a few days only of Dervish's arrival in Egypt the Alexandrian riots and massacres occurred. Our ships then bombarded Alexandria; but meeting still with a national resistance, we obtained from Abdul Hamid a decree of rebellion against Arabi, armed with which our English army finally occupied

Cairo. It is not too much to say that the overthrow of the Egyptian nationalists at Tel-el-Kebir, *under warrant of the Sultan*, and the non-fulfilment of Mr. Gladstone's promise, made through Lord Dufferin, of restoring some kind of constitutional government at Cairo, sealed the fate of liberty throughout the Ottoman Empire, and with it of all chance of internal reform.

Nor is this quite all. Abdul Hamid, supreme now over the constitutional party in Turkey, was resolved to take vengeance on the defeated Liberal leaders. In 1883, encouraged by the complicity of the Powers, including England, he had Midhat, the constitutional ex-Prime Minister, arrested and tried on a false charge of murder, brought before a packed tribunal at Constantinople, condemned, and sentenced to death. It is within my personal knowledge that English evidence of the highest official kind could have been adduced at the trial, clearing Midhat of the charge. Yet, for reasons of English state, that evidence was withheld. Midhat's sentence, momentarily commuted to perpetual imprisonment, was carried out as soon as the public had ceased to busy itself about him. By the Sultan's order he was beheaded privately in prison at Taïf, in Arabia, and his head was forwarded to Constantinople.

Things having been so in the past, however completely now forgotten (to me they are poignant and ever-living memories), I confess to a little scepticism as to the fundamental right of the Liberal leaders of the present agitation to act as justiciaries on Abdul Hamid, or to "wield the sword of the Almighty" in a new crusade. I will, however, assume that in their inner consciences they acknowledge they were wrong, and are anxious seriously now to repair the ruin of the Eastern world. It is terribly late to begin. They are no longer in office. Their full opportunity is past. They are discredited in Europe, doubly discredited in the Turkish Empire. But still they can do something, if only they have the courage to come forward and say fairly to their followers: "We have misled you all these sixteen years. We have been blind, leaders of the blind. Our eyes are now open; we will go back to our principles of 1880."

Assuming this, let us see how the Armenian question really stands. Down to the year 1893 our responsibility for reforms in Asia Minor was studiously forgotten and left alone by our diplomacy. The Armenian question was considered impossible of solution at the Foreign Office, and all that was done with it was from time to time to trot it out as a possible counter-question to the troublesome one of Egypt. It was a common saying with our diplomatists that there were two "clichés," or stock answers, with which Abdul Hamid could always be met and frightened if he showed any inclination to join France on the Egyptian question. The Arabian Caliphate was one of them; Armenia was the other. It was in this spirit, and no other, that Lord Rosebery, who held a brief for the occupation of Egypt, approached the question in 1893. I was at Constantinople in that year, and I know well that there was nothing more serious in his earlier moves than this: a special inquiry had just been made, in conjunction with the American Embassy, into the condition of affairs in Armenia, but its result had been to show that there was no sufficient element there of resident Armenian population to justify an attempt at encouraging the creation of an autonomous State. The whole Christian population of the provinces was less than one in five compared with the Mohammedan, and in only one small villayet did it stand in a majority. It was therefore admitted by both Embassies that the autonomous movement could not be supported with any chance of success. The Armenians were suffering great oppression, morally justifying them in their resort to a trial of strength with their master; but it was without chance of success, nor had it become as yet even a "desperate necessity," caused by any fixed purpose of their destruction. The Armenian movement was already a political one, having its base in England, and it enjoyed the sympathy and assistance of the Armenians in Russia. Such was the report of 1893, which has not, I think, been published. Nevertheless, Lord Rosebery, little in earnest except diplomatically, encouraged the movement from time to time, toying with it for the sake of Egypt, and to please Armenian sympathisers in the Liberal camp at home. Later, it is quite certain that the stronger action taken by our Embassy at Constantinople was due to his direct orders. The misfortune of the affair is this—that the encouragement of England, official and unofficial, is beyond all doubt the cause of the present Armenian disasters. These poor people, not understanding the needs of our diplomacy, and believing that their hour of political deliverance, under English protection, was at hand, resolved in 1895 upon a great venture, and organised their movement on the active revolutionary lines which in other countries have proved successful. This hardened the Sultan's heart, and it is clear that he then resolved on their destruction. I was again in Constantinople in September and October 1895, when the first riots there occurred, and I was never in the smallest doubt of the Sultan's personal responsibility. Abdul Hamid is far too powerful a despot for a single blow to have been struck against a single Armenian in his capital without his orders. His motive, however, must not be mistaken. Abdul Hamid, though the head of the reactionary party, is not himself a fanatic. His action has been dictated solely in the interest of a political or, perhaps, to speak more accurately still, a dynastic and personal end. He stood, indeed, according to the phrase, between the devil and the deep sea; and he knew that he must crush the Armenians—or himself be crushed. This is his one excuse. I do not give it as a sufficient one, but still as a fact to be noted. His mode of repression is only the old-fashioned Turkish one of massacre, which we ourselves made it possible for him to use in this year of grace, 1896, when we helped him, fourteen years ago, to put down the constitutional party and become the absolute lord he is.

Another matter which it much behoves our Liberal leaders to consider, and which they do not seem as yet to realise, is that in Abdul Hamid's terrible work of repression he has throughout had the countenance and approval of Russia. Of this my visit to Constantinople last year gave me a complete assurance; and its reason is not difficult to seize. Half the Armenian provinces have for the last twenty years been incorporated in the Russian Empire, and from the moment the Armenian movement became one for autonomy it was doomed in Russian opinion. The Russians have a jingoism of their own, which tolerates no other national sentiment within the empire but the Russian; and the Armenians, with their undying tradition of an independent kingdom, one of the most ancient in the world, are, in their eyes, an obstacle and a rock of offence to be removed. As Christians even they do not command full sympathy in Russia, for they belong to a branch of the Orthodox Church which is out of communion with the Russian, and which especially repudiates the religious headship of the Czar. Lastly, their alliance with Russian Nihilists, and their Anarchist methods, have closed the door against official sympathy. As long as M. de Giers was alive something of the old tradition of Russian policy, which championed the Christians in Turkey, survived; but with the advent of Prince

Lobanof this finally disappeared, and has given place to a new policy of alliance with the Sultan, as representative there of order. English sympathy has only made matters worse for the Armenians in Russian eyes, and the Russian attitude towards them now is: "We leave you to England to help you if she can." Even in the matter of the Sultan's methods I could not help being reminded at Constantinople of their close similarity to those used by Russia towards the Ruthenian Poles. These have been ground under the harrow of the Czar's penal laws, and occasionally of popular violences, now systematically for thirty years, man, woman, and child, till they have abandoned their Catholic faith and are to-day fanatic members of the Russian orthodoxy. The Polish question has thereby been solved for ever; and, coming as I did from Russian Poland, I seemed to see in the forced conversion of the Armenians of Asia Minor only a page of violence a little overdone, but taken from the Russian book. It is the extreme, therefore, of rashness on the part of the Liberal leaders of the present agitation to rest their hopes of dethroning Abdul Hamid on Russian intervention. Abdul Hamid has, I fear, too faithfully been doing Russian work to be seriously dealt with by Russia as a criminal.

What, then, is it possible for England to do? There are here, as usual, the traditional three courses. The first is to go blindly into a war with the Sultan. With regard to this I am bound to say that every law of honour—unless, as Mr. Gladstone puts it, the word "honour" is to be expunged from our dictionaries—prescribes and necessitates such a war. We have taken the Armenians solemnly by treaty under our protection, receiving substantial payment from their master, for the protective right, in the island of Cyprus. We have encouraged them for our own purposes to organise themselves and rebel, and the Sultan now has got them by the throat, and, backed by Europe, is defying us to come on and deliver them. If we do not go to war we shall be sitting down under the greatest affront we ever suffered as a nation. We bombarded Alexandria because a couple of hundred of the Alexandrian rabble, with Sir Beauchamp Seymour's valet, had lost their lives. Here some scores of thousands of peaceful citizens have perished through our fault, and we have done nothing but talk. Nevertheless, I do not suppose we shall fight. We never do except against the half-armed foe; and here we should find all Europe fully armed at the Sultan's back. The second course therefore—to do nothing—will be open to us, and I am inclined to think we shall choose it. Lord Rosebery recommends it, and Lord Rosebery represents trade and finance, our great English gods. A third course, however, I will recommend to the consideration of Liberal England, which I believe to be perfectly sound and feasible, and, if we have the moral courage to confess our wrong, perfectly within our reach. This is to advocate and insist on our Government arranging without delay with the Powers most interested for a new European Congress. I do not see anywhere that this has been suggested in England, yet it is the only true and worthy solution of the problem for us, the only practical escape we have from our dishonour.

The conditions on which Lord Salisbury could, if he would, move the great European Powers to meet in a new Congress on the Eastern question are these. First, England must go into the matter absolutely clean handed; not as at Berlin, but with a firm and avowed determination to take nothing whatever of advantage for herself in the arrangements to be made. The clearing of her own honour, now dragged vilely in the mire, must be her sole and all-sufficient reward. Secondly, she must come as a suppliant for her Armenian *protégés*, not as one with rights, for she is not ready to fight for them. Thirdly, she must not expect the question of the Armenians to be settled alone. Europe would not fash herself only for these. England must be ready to see the whole Ottoman case treated without any reserve whatever, her one condition being the rescue of her Christian friends. Fourthly, it follows from this that the Egyptian question must be discussed with the rest of the Ottoman questions. It is mere folly to imagine that France and Russia, having got complete control of the Armenian case, will solve it to our liking, except as part and parcel of a general bargain. It is equally folly to suppose that they would be content with Cyprus. Neither Power cares a straw for Cyprus, nor, I imagine, would take it [as] a gift. The only proof we can show of our disinterested zeal for the Armenians is to put Egypt with them on the table in the Congress. Fifthly, there must be no subterfuge or mental reservation about the Soudan. I hear people talk about ending the occupation of Egypt some day by an annexation of the Upper Nile. But such talk is useless now. The powers would not consent to it in any arrangements being made, short, perhaps, of a final partition of the

Ottoman Empire. Sixthly, we must not expect such a partition to be agreed to. None of the Powers are quite ready for it. It would be too dangerous a scramble. All that could this and next year be reasonably expected would be an intervention at Constantinople to re-establish the authority of the Porte as opposed to the Palace, to disband the Sultan's guard, and to establish some sort of financial control on the Bosphorus, with a throwing open of the Dardanelles. In the Armenian provinces, Russia might at the same time consent to give protection to the Christians, and secure them from further massacre. I believe this to be the extreme outside of what it would be reasonable to expect. But we should have gained our object—the highest one of all. Our honour would have been saved, and we should have regained the right to speak with authority as an honest Government in regard to the final settlement.

Let those, therefore, who really care about honour and duty and humanity, not for the sake of self-laudation on platforms, or for the amusement of denouncing the sins of others, but because they are sincerely ashamed of England's shame, rally to this idea. It is a far more practical one than any of the little half-measures as yet propounded, and, as I have said before, is one easily within our reach. All we have to do is persuade our fellow-countrymen to keep their promises about Egypt, and face the truth that we cannot remain there for ever, and arrange the terms of our going. The rest will come easily and pleasantly. Lord Rosebery, with his brief for the occupation, is fortunately gone from the supreme Liberal councils. Let the Liberal Party rise to the full height of the occasion, and it will convert England again, as it did in 1880; while if, on the contrary, we harden our hearts in the face of a pretty well united world, which laughs angrily at our fine moral talk, and points contemptuously at Cyprus and Egypt hanging out of our coat-tail pockets, it may well happen that we shall lose not only these and our honour before many years are out, but the whole of our overgrown Empire besides—God forbid that I should be justified in adding our national independence at home as well as Empire.

II.

E. F. Du Cane

The time seems to have come when discussion of the measures that should be taken to settle the Turkish question should be carried beyond the limit to which it has hitherto been confined.

Various proposals have been made, some very drastic. We have been invited to force the Dardanelles—to depose the Sultan—to write a joint Note demanding reforms—to give Russia a free hand to adopt certain unrevealed, indirect methods of exciting pressure, and so on; but these are only the first steps, and give no clue to what the succeeding steps should be, still less to the ultimate aim which should be kept in view in order to permanently dispose of this dangerous question.

The accompanying letter, which was written by General Charles Gordon in 1881, is remarkably *à propos* to the present situation. This keen observer and experienced administrator rejects at once two methods which may be suggested, either that the country should be governed and administered by a foreign power, or that the existing government ("The Pachas") should be trusted to reform the administration under foreign pressure. He falls back on the idea that the Turkish peoples themselves should be given the power to control and check those whose misgovernment has turned countries once rich and flourishing into poor and depopulated deserts whose only idea of administration is by robbery, and whose only method of preserving order is by terror and massacre.

This object he would effect, broadly speaking, by extending to the provinces which are still under the Turkish Government constitutions such as have been taken away from it, viz. Roumania, Bulgaria, Eastern Roumelia, &c., countries which apparently only require to be let alone in order that they may develop their strength and regain their prosperity.

Difficulties in carrying out this proposal may no doubt be suggested, but it may be that still greater difficulties would attend any other solution of the question; and it has at least the merit that it evades many of the thorny obstacles which arise from the mutual jealousy of the Powers.

"8 Victoria Grove, Gloucester Road, Kensington
"January 16, 1881
"My dear Du Cane,

"I send you the Blue Book, Condition of Asia Minor &c., but I think you will, on looking over it, see that it merely contains for the most part a description of the deplorable state of the Turkish provinces, and does not in any way—or at any rate only indirectly—show how the misgovernment is to be remedied.

"In fact the perusal is wearisome, as there is no decided remedy proposed, though amelioration is suggested by insisting on this and that being forced on the Porte.

"I consider that any promise or statement of the Turkish Pachas to improve or remedy any evil are to be deemed utterly insincere, will be carried out with a pure intuition to evade the spirit, and only to comply with the letter while under pressure.

"I consider that enforced reform can be only exotic and ephemeral, that it will fall to the ground when it is no longer enforced.

"I consider it is quite hopeless for foreigners to attempt to dictate how the administration, collection of taxes, &c, (of which this Blue Book is full) are to be performed.

"I consider that unless the people of Turkey will [now] take up the remedy of the abuses of their government, it is hopeless thinking of any progress against the Turkish Pachas by foreigners which will be permanent.

"I therefore say that the unique way to deal with misgovernment in Turkey is to call on the Turkish peoples to execute them.

"1. The Turkish peoples know exactly the full extent of the corruption and rottenness of their government; they know how and in what way any remedy they may enact will act on the country. They are in every way interested, for themselves and their children, in obtaining a good government; whereas to the Turkish Pachas, so long as they can fill their purses it is all they care.

"2. To put the power in the hands of the Turkish peoples is a fair, perfectly just effort on the part of foreign governments; it is merely the supporting of the Sultan's own design when he gave his constitution. Foreign governments who support this liberation of the Turkish people cannot be accused of intrigue or selfishness; they will gain the sympathy of the peoples, whereas now what have they got? Have they the sympathy of either the Sultan or Pachas or peoples? And, judging from the Blue Book, they, or at least our government, are overloading their heads with details of administration, when the whole foundation on which the success of these details rests is thoroughly rotten.

"A foreign government is no match for the Sultan and the Pachas: it has not the knowledge necessary to cope with them: it is the Turkish peoples who alone have the power to hold their own, besides which no foreign government has any right to interfere. It may be said that the foreign government interferes in virtue of promises, but these promises were *extorted* and are not valid.

"By the way foreign governments are now working they are

inevitably drifting, day by day, into still increasing interference with the internal affairs of Turkey, and are helping to band Sultan, Pachas, and peoples against any improvement. Such interference must end in serious complications, and can in no way further the professed object—improved government.

"No individual Pacha, let him be one of the exceptions to the usual rule, can now stand against the influence of the Sultan and the parasite Pachas; the fact of his being backed by this or that foreign government will be (whenever the time comes when that foreign government becomes urgent in its demands for reform) the cause of his downfall, and will be explained at large that he is dismissed because he is a tool of this or that government; but if this *rara avis*, an upright Pacha, was found, and if he was backed by the peoples of Turkey, it would go hard with the Sultan and his ring ere they flew in the face of their peoples in dismissing him.

"It is urged that the Turkish peoples are not fit for representative government. Well, look at Roumania and Bulgaria, and, in some degree, to Roumelia; they succeed very fairly. If the peoples never have a chance, they will never be able to show what they can do. Had we waited till our monarchs or our lords had given us representative assemblies, we would be without them to this day.

"What I maintain, therefore, is that our government should unceasingly try, with other governments, *to get the Midhat constitution reconstituted;* that they should leave that very dubiously just (in fact it may be called iniquitous) policy of forcing unwilling peoples under the yoke of other peoples, which is not only unfair to the coerced and ceded peoples, but is a grave mistake, for by it are laid the seeds of future troubles.

"To collect all these reports may be useful enough for those who have the time and patience to read them, but what do all these reports tend to elucidate? Simply that the government of Turkey is utterly rotten, that the peoples are miserable and discontented, that the sole object of the Sultan and his Pachas is to drag the entrails of the provinces into their palaces at Constantinople. There may be petty schemes here and there for improvements, but it is like painting up the bulwarks of a vessel which is rotten at the bottom.

"I say, too, that at any moment, in the event of the death of the Sultan, most serious events may take place: who is to take his place? who is to nominate his successor? The reconstituted chamber of the Midhat Constitution would at any rate prevent any great catastrophe, and I have no doubt would so coerce the new Sultan as to obtain full promise to benefit the country.

"Believe me, my dear Du Cane,

"Yours sincerely,

"C. E. Gordon"

The Spectator, Vol. 77 (November 7, 1896): 633–34

The Armenian Policy of France

The long speech on Armenia which M. Hanotaux read to the French Chamber on Tuesday is very depressing to all who care either for humanity or for the future of Eastern Europe; but it does, in however unsatisfactory a way, to a certain extent clear up the situation. M. Hanotaux is most reticent as to details, but he does admit that somewhat precise arrangements were made with the Czar while he was in Paris, and as the Czar had already conferred with Lord Salisbury, it is reasonable to suppose that the arrangements have the provisional sanction of the three great Powers. It is implied also throughout the speech, though it is nowhere explicitly asserted, that the other three Powers either approve or will not oppose, and that the executive machinery will be the a "Concert of Europe," acting through a conclave of Ambassadors in Constantinople itself. That conclave will not, it is settled, either seek or permit any partition of Turkey, which is to be maintained as an unbroken dominion "from Persia to the valley of the Nile." Nor will it allow any substantial alteration in the treaties already existing, such, for instance, as those which forbid the free navigation of the Dardanelles and the Bosphorus to men-of-war. There is, moreover, to be no direct control exercised over Turkish administration, and no kind of *condominium*, which, indeed, M. Hanotaux, possibly with certain plans for Egypt in the back of his mind, characterises as "the most precarious and dangerous of expedients." The instrument of government is still to be the Sultan, who, if he chooses to modify his methods, may still reign the absolute master and tax-gatherer of his subjects, of one half of whom he is recognised, even in M. Hanotaux's speech, as the merciless enemy. The conclave is, however, to point out to him that the source of all troubles is the bad management of his affairs, "political, financial, and administrative." It will *indicate to him certain means of putting that management into order*—probably the restoration of power to decent Ministers, or a competent Grand Vizier—and it will insist that he shall carry out certain reforms, pointing out to him that in those reforms, which will not be local, but universal, lies "the only path of safety." This plan, as thus explained, was attacked only by M. Jaurés, the Socialist orator, who denounced it as "making France an accomplice in the massacres." It was endorsed by the Deputies by a vote of 402 to 90, and it may therefore be considered the accepted policy of France.

We need not say that to us it seems a most unsatisfactory policy. In the first place, to speak plainly, it leaves the Sultan himself unpunished for the most grievous offence against humanity and civilisation which has been committed in modern times. That offence was nothing less than the slaughter, under circumstances of the most atrocious cruelty, of at least a hundred thousand Christians, men, women, and children, who had never rebelled, who had been guilty of no crime, who at the worst were only suspected of detesting in their hearts a régime which is proved by the very massacres to be worthy of their detestation. That immense crime is by this arrangement condoned, the Sultan remaining not only master within his Empire, but the object of all diplomatic respect, and a necessary factor in every future effort to improve the condition of his territories. Moreover, he is allowed to an enormous extent a free hand for the future, for the very plan itself will tell him how safe he is, how reluctant, if only he will give plausible promises, Europe is to interfere. He must not, it is true, verbally set the Powers at defiance, because if he does one of them may be irritated into action; but if he quietly hints to the mob at Broussa that there really are too many Armenians about, and the race is consequently extirpated there, he will only be in the position in which he is now, that of a man who has misused his powers to gratify a thirst for blood, but who is so rich that until the succession to his heritage is settled, the Magistrates cannot bear to interfere. In the second place, no guarantee is given to the Christians that they shall not endure all the suffering a malignant and absolute Sovereign can inflict short of being executed in batches, shall not, for example, be arrested in crowds, tortured in prison, deprived of all property, and forced to see their women violated or insulted by every irregular soldier who may happen to desire them. If these things deserve no vengeance now, why should they deserve it hereafter? If it is too inconvenient to punish them in 1896, why will it be convenient in 1900? The plan assumes, even as regards the future, that the Sultan can himself be reformed; but where is the evidence of that, or even the probability that a man who is to be rewarded by impunity for the misdoing he loves, will abjure such misdoing because he is assured that it will if repeated bring on him a torrent of good advice? Why should he mind the advice if his position is still to be left to him intact? Do the Powers hope that the Abd-ul-Hamid whom they have known in Bulgaria as well as Armenia will be shocked into humanity by finding that a parcel of infidels regard him as a monster, but fearing the result of the division of his property, will remain satisfied with that pious opinion?

But, it is said, behind the advice will come a distinct threat of deposition. Very good, if it is so, the deposition of the Sultan being the next best expedient to the partition of Turkey; but where is the evidence that such an "extreme resolution," as it is called on the Continent, has been taken, or if it has been taken, will be acted on? The Sultan cannot be dethroned until the Fleets have entered the Bosphorus, and if that entrance would to-day be so terrible an event, why will it not be terrible when a few more Armenians are dead? People talk as if the Ambassadors could blow away the Sultan with the wind of their mouths, but he would fight for his throne in his way, that is, by massacres, just as energetically as he would fight for Turkey. We may be perfectly sure that two at least of the Sovereigns will be reluctant to hold a legitimate ruler personally responsible for his acts, and if they are reluctant how is the threat, which no official person utters, to be invested with such controlling power? The Sultan, no doubt, will for a moment be alarmed and make promises by the score; but he recovers himself from those spasms of humanity in a few hours, and in a few days he will believe that the jealousies of the Powers which prevent them from making an end of Turkey will also prevent their making an end of him. Suppose he applies his policy of removing inconvenient races to his own family, and remains, as so many of his ancestors did, except for his own children, the last of the race of Othman. Are the Powers to depose the dynasty as well as the individual, and yet not excite the international jealousies of which they stand in such dread?

So far as we can see, if M. Hanotaux describes the situation correctly, Europe is to look on at Constantinople as a schoolmaster looks on at a barring out, with the deepest of frowns on his brow, but with a clear impression that the punishment of a whole school is difficult, and that he has his own future income to remember. All that has been positively gained by recent negotiations is that the Powers are not quarrelling—which, of course, is something—that they will remonstrate in threatening terms if more massacres occur, but not if the method adopted is that of wholesale arrests, and that they may if a revolution occurs within Turkey itself, which is probable if money to pay the troops cannot speedily be obtained, look on without interference. If that revolution, however, produces civil war, they must interfere, and the total result of their plan, therefore, is continued expectancy, without retribution for the past or security for the future. Even M. Hanotaux admits that the ultimate causes of the evil will not have been affected. The gangrene, as Lord Salisbury described it, will still exist in the body corporate of Europe, waiting either for the surgeon who will cut it out—an impossibility without bloodshedding—or for the death which sooner or later all such gangrenes must produce. Diplomacy has perhaps postponed a war; it has obviously not even thought of a plan by which that war, which so far from being inevitable is absolutely needless, might be permanently prevented.

The Contemporary Review, Vol. 70 (November 1896): 695–709

Travels amongst the Armenians

J. Theodore Bent[1]

The Armenians, perhaps one of the oldest nationalities of the world, have now known bondage for many centuries.

Mount Ararat is the cradle of the race, the Araxis is their river, and their lake is Urumia, or, as the Persians call it, Darya Armeni, the lake of the Armenians. Their country is now divided between three States, Russia, Turkey, and Persia, and, inasmuch as it has been our good fortune to see the Armenians under each of the three sways, I think I cannot do better than divide this account of them into three distinct parts. When the Byzantine emperors crushed the power of the Armenians, they initiated the policy of scattering them. This is why we find so many Armenian villages dotted over Asia Minor where we least expect them; the Turks continued this policy, and so did the Persians, with the result that in the East the Armenians are almost as ubiquitous as the Jews, and equally crafty in getting a livelihood.

Orthodox Armenians are divided into two, the northern Armenians owing allegiance to the Patriarch of Etchmiazin in Russian territory; the southern are under the Patriarch of Sis in Cilicia; hence jealousies naturally exist. Again, there are Roman Catholic Armenians, and many Armenian converts to Islam; and the American missionaries in Asia Minor have been much more successful with the Armenians than the Greeks; the result of changing religious belief so easily being that this race has never been as united as the Greeks, and never showed that bold religious front against the Mussulmans which preserved the unity of Hellenism through the centuries of Moslem rule. Take, for instance, the Armenians of a town like Tarsus in Cilicia, where we first came into direct contact with them. They are here divided into three sects, Armenians proper, Roman Catholics, and Protestants; each community has its church, and each cordially detests the others.

It is, however, with the Armenians proper that we have most to do, and we will first visit them in the Patriarchate of Sis. During a few days we spent at Tarsus we visited all the points of interest connected with the Armenians there. Their legends and traditions are everywhere of the most extravagant order; consequently at Tarsus the Armenians had much to tell us regarding St. Paul. Their church they believe to be built on the site of an older edifice originally founded by the great Apostle on one of his visits to Cilicia, and they tell you that a tree in the churchyard was actually planted by him; around it are gathered the Armenian graves, each with the symbol of the departed thereon. The defunct merchant is known by his weights and measures, the blacksmith by his anvil and hammer, the scribe by his inkstand and pen, the woman by her distaff and spindle. They show, too, St. Paul's well, spots to which the pious still repair in pilgrimages.

The Armenians of Cilicia were the last to succumb to Islamism, for during the Crusades the Armenian kingdom was supported by the soldiers of the Cross, and the Roupenian dynasty maintained its independence in its strongholds of Anazarba and Sis until the Crusades were over.

A visit to the town of Sis was impossible a few years ago, owing to the Turkoman robbers who dwelt in the Taurus, but we got there easily enough seven years ago, with only the necessary discomforts attending travel in Asia Minor. Dotted over the plain behind Adana and Tarsus are the old castles of the Armenian kings, built on solitary rocks during the three centuries that the Roupenian dynasty ruled over Cilicia until the last of the line died in Paris in 1393, and was buried at St. Denis, where to this day the Armenian residents in Paris pay an annual visit to his tomb. It is easy to see why the Roupenian kings chose Sis for their capital. Tarsus was too exposed in troublous times. Anazarba, though almost impregnable, is isolated and could be surrounded, whereas Sis is built on a rocky hill separated from the Taurus mountains only by a narrow valley, and those mountains behind it are still full of ruined castles and places of refuge in time of danger.

Wet and weary we reached Sis, and found a hospitable roof placed over our heads by a Protestant Armenian named Kasarian, to whom we had a letter. Sis is but a poor town now, nestling under the great fortress-crowned rock where 550 years ago the kings had their palace; flat-roofed houses, with open fronts like dolls' houses, climb one over the other to the enclosure of the great monastery, where the patriarchs still keep up the faint shadow of a royal inheritance. There is one long street or bazaar, busy on the weekly market day with camels, mules, and wild, quaint-dressed nomads from the mountains, but dead-alive on any other day. Every Armenian man is called a baron, the title being used by every man not of sufficient position to be styled "Effendi"; it is quaint to hear your muleteer addressed as Baron So-and-so, and Armenian names are very high sounding. A gunsmith in the bazaar rejoiced in the name of Baron Sennacherib Toufenkian, literally meaning "son of a gun," having, of course, reference to his trade. In this part of the world Armenian is only spoken in secret, and many only speak Turkish, so that the services in the cathedral conducted in the old tongue are quite unintelligible to the majority of the worshippers.

The patriarch of Sis claims, and probably with justice, to be the direct descendant of the patriarchs who ruled the Armenian Church during the days of the Roupenian kings, consequently he hurls anathemas at the head of the patriarch of Etchmiazin and calls him a usurper. This latter place certainly did not possess a katholicos or patriarch until the 15th century, when a schism arose amongst the faithful, and the northern Armenians set up a patriarch for themselves at the monastery which Gregory the Illuminator, the apostle of the Armenians, had founded. Probably Sis is therefore the original patriarchate; but sunk in squalor as it is, and terrified for its very existence in the land of its enemies, it offers to-day a sorry contrast to the flourishing patriarchate under the protection of Russia.

The present occupant of the patriarchal throne of Sis is called Katholicos Mogaditch or Baptism; he is well-off himself and somewhat unscrupulous in the way he raises money. He visited Constantinople some years ago, and by the outlay of a sum of money he obtained from the Sultan a recognition of his right to call himself the head of all the Armenians. In his own country, however, he is no prophet, so much so that he dare not reside at Sis but spends his time up in the mountains at Marash, only coming down to Sis for the ceremony of blessing the holy oil. He often travels about, too, amongst the scattered Armenian population, and generally takes with him his treasure, by which he finds it easy to raise money, namely, the much venerated arm of Gregory the Illuminator, and to the title of Katholicos is added that of "Keeper of the Holy Arm." At Adana, at Kaisarea, at Kharput, at Aintab, at the time of famine or pestilence Patriarch Mogaditch and his holy arm are sure to turn up and make a goodly sum of money amongst the credulous.

We were sorry to find both of them away when we visited Sis, but Bishop Kyragos did the honours well and showed us everything. The morning after our arrival we climbed up to the monastery, passing on our way the two towers, which are all that is left of the palace of the kings, about which a German prelate, Wildebrand of Oldenburg, wrote so glowing an account in 1211. To build the present monastery Patriarch Kyragos used most of the masonry of this palace early in this century. We were received in the council chamber by the bishop, who wore a tall black hat with fluted top, and the elders in purple sat around. The palace which the patriarchs inhabit is in a sad state of repair, but it must have been handsome at one time, and was decorated by artists brought from Persia on purpose. The church is rich in blue tiles and quaint pictures of Armenian hagiology, and contains the marble throne on which the Armenian kings are said to have sat. In a side chapel, at the top of a flight of steps, is the gilded throne on which the patriarch sits when he consecrates bishops. To the side of this is a cupboard in which resides the gorgeous silver gilt bowl in which the holy oil or *meiron* is produced every four years.

The ceremony of blessing the oil is one of the most strikingly characteristic in all Armenia, and pilgrims come from afar to be present at it. The bowl, with its manifold decorations, its turrets, and its pinnacles, is placed outside the church. It holds about a gallon of oil, into which flowers are put, and then amidst prayers and chants it is stirred by the arm of St. Gregory, and let us suppose by some chemical process it is made to assume the appearance of boiling. The privilege of lifting off the lid of the bowl is on this occasion put up to auction, and once a wealthy Armenian bid no less than 100 Turkish pounds for this distinction. The oil is then sold in small quantities to the pilgrims, and as much as £1000 is sometimes realised on this occasion. Armenians lay great store by their oil, and generally have a phial of it in their houses; it figures in baptisms, marriages, and funerals, and has wonderful medical properties. We wanted to photograph the silver bowl, but Bishop Kyragos, with the talent inherent in his race, said the charge for so doing would be one pound, and considering that he would get decidedly the best of the bargain we declined his offer.

The treasury and reliquary of the Cathedral of Sis is a most curious spot. The bishop, before showing it to us, dismissed all idle spectators, and led us alone to a room where he showed us their vestments and their books; then with hushed voice and stealthy step he lifted a cupboard from before a false door into an inner and perfectly dark room, where by the light of a taper we feasted our eyes on silver croziers, silver-backed gospels, richly-jewelled mitres, and the whole paraphernalia of the sacerdotal treasury. In a silver chalice we were shown some red stains; "blood," said the bishop, "into which the wine was changed when the new cathedral was consecrated," and which had never been touched since. The treasure chamber contains also many relics, and it is guarded with great care for fear the Turks or the wandering nomads should learn how much it contains.

Before leaving the monastic precincts we visited a school, which the present patriarch has established and maintains at his own expense. The pupils are taught French, Turkish, algebra, astronomy, and physical science, and are then sent out themselves as teachers in the mountain villages. They sang us a song in Armenian, which we were told was a lament over the departed glory of their country, and inspiring courage for the future, and we felt a keen interest in these poor scholars, whose battle with ignorance and oppression for the years to come would be so severe.

We spent several days pleasantly at Sis. One day a stiff climb took me to the fortress of the old kings, the highest summit of the rock on which it is built being 2000 feet above the level of the plain. Three rugged peaks divide it into three distinct parts, and the whole is surrounded by a wall in excellent preservation, and the space enclosed is scattered with the débris of churches, palaces with dungeons, and buildings of great strategical importance. In one corner at the summit is a stream of water which never runs dry, and during the summer months the inhabitants come and fetch it from here; that is to say those who are obliged to stay there, for in summer Sis is one of the most unhealthy and fever-stricken spots, and all who can go up to the mountain farms or *yaelas* during the hot season.

The view from the fortress of Sis is enchanting over the far-stretching Cilician plain on the one hand, with its net-work of rivers and the snow-clad Taurus range on the other. Here and there a few inscriptions tell of the old kings and the buildings they erected, but for the most part the views of the town are hidden by brushwood, which forms an admirable pasturage for flocks.

Descending to the town, we were shown the house of one Emin Effendi just outside the monastery wall. This individual had once been Bishop of Sis and next in succession to the Patriarchate, but he fell in love with the wife of a neighbouring Armenian, and the only way to get married was for them both to turn Mussulmans, which they accordingly did.

Undoubtedly the condition of the Armenian Church in Sis is exceedingly degraded, and the better class amongst them are most anxious for reform, and this fact has contributed not a little to the success of the American missionaries in Asia Minor, whose establishments at Marash, Zeitoun, and other Armenian centers have produced a large number of converts. The dogmas of the Armenian Church are even more stringent than the Greek; their fasts are more severe, neither shellfish nor olives being eaten in Lent. Before ordination a total abstinence of forty days is inculcated, and during that period a residence in the church, perpetually praying and chanting; but then these things are never observed. The ignorance amongst the clergy is most lamentable; even the bishops and monks, who are supposed to be educated, know absolutely nothing, and the lower clergy generally ply some humble trade in conjunction with their holy office. They have no stipends attached to their cures, but make money by blessing houses, exorcising demons and cursing rats; then they get marriage fees and prayers for the dead. All endowments are kept in the hands of the upper clergy, and if it was not for the gross superstition of the multitude the lower clergy could not possibly gain a livelihood.

The Armenians of Sis seem to live perpetually in the open fronts of their homes, even when the weather is cold and wet, only retiring to sleep in winter in the dark, vermin-filled recesses at the back. In the summer they sleep on wooden platforms erected on poles and approached by ladders, where they can obtain the largest amount of fresh air, and the smallest amount of vermin. All day long the Armenian women are busy in the open front of the house bread making, sorting grain, spinning and talking, the baby hangs from the rafters, and the water-jars are picturesquely placed around. Below this balcony we find the stables for the mules and the flocks redolent with pestilential smells.

The women of Sis wear a fez on their heads, and if they are rich it is bound round with a frontlet of gold coins; they are not such gad-abouts as the Greeks, and rarely take part in those festive pilgrimages so beloved by the young folks of modern Hellas. Sometimes they will go to a little open air shrine in the mountains, about two hours from Sis, dedicated to St. George of Cappadocia; it is a delicious spot surrounded by rocks, trees, and lovely flowers, and adjoining it is an old Armenian fort. They are fond of Passion plays and wax figures representing various scenes in the life of Christ.

The men are active in their own amusements, playing leap-frog, and wrestling on Sunday afternoon on a green sward by the cemetery, gaily dressed in their long coloured cotton gowns. Also they play various horseback games, probably learnt from their unpleasant neighbors the Kourds in the mountains at Hadgin, Zeitoun, and Marash. The Armenians are strong, hardy fellows, very different from the cringeing courtiers of their race in Constantinople and the Armenian merchant class of Smyrna. When brought into contact with commerce the Armenian develops a subtlety and sharpness which put into the shade both Jew and Greek. Stories of such Armenians as Barbeck of Zeitoun, who defied a Turkish army in his mountain fastness, and only gave himself up when it was represented to him that if he and his band did not surrender his native town would be shelled by the Turkish cannon, show that there is most excellent material in them if they ever had a chance; but centuries of slavery and oppression have made the wits of some of them too sharp, and the disregard of cruelty and bloodshed too marked in others.

Another Armenian centre in which we passed some time is at Julfa, near Ispahan, and, in considering them, we pass on to the Armenian race under the rule of the Shah of Persia. Perhaps, of all the Armenians scattered about in the East, those of Julfa and the mountainous villages around retain the old customs of the race in the most unadulterated form. The women here go about the streets with the old national red costume, and the girdle, a broad belt, ornamented with knobs, two buttons, and clasped in front by an oval piece of silver heavily embossed. At a mountain village, Kurd-i-Bala, some 50 miles from Ispahan, they still wear the tall, nodding head-dress, which makes the Armenian ladies not unlike pictures of Aaron when officiating at the altar; the women do all the tilling in the fields at this village, and they wear the veil over their mouths, looking upon it as very indecent to show the mouth to a member of the opposite sex, the veil often being attached to the nose by a dab of wax for fear of any indecent exposure of the lips. At Ispahan they say husbands exist who have been married for years and yet never seen their wives' mouths, and the doctors who wish to look at their female patients' tongues are nearly driven to the point of distraction. Not only are the lips hidden, but, what is still more marvellous, the tongue of the women is also tied. A bride does not speak before men before her first child is born or a year has elapsed, and after that she only is allowed to converse freely with her husband until six years of married life have gone by.

We spent a night at Kurd-i-Bala in an Armenian house, and marvelled at the women, who hovered inquisitively around us, their tall head-dresses, with silver chains, nodding the while as they discussed us in a whisper; these head-dresses, called *kotlas*, have a flat crown and stand as high as a tall hat; beneath their red dresses appear drawers with embroidered edges, presenting a truly quaint picture of primitive humanity. These Armenians have lived a life of curious isolation in and around Julfa since the Shah Abbas persuaded them 300 years ago to leave their home of Julfa on the Araxis and settle at Ispahan. He gave them extensive tracts of land across the river, where they built a second Julfa, and they flourished like the Children of Israel in Egypt for a considerable period; they had religious toleration and handsome mercantile privileges, so that during the Suffean dynasty they grew to be the richest body of men in the whole of Persia, and tradition says Julfa then contained 10,000 souls. But a century later a Shah ruled who knew not Joseph, his dominions were threatened by Afghan hordes, and he could not resist the temptation of falling upon the peaceful Armenians and betraying them to the Afghan conqueror as the price of peace. Since then every ruler of Persia, in his turn, has robbed, pillaged and massacred the wretched inhabitants of Julfa when occasion required, and Julfa to-day is a half-ruined, miserable place.

Even in its ruins Julfa has traces of bygone wealth—its churches are very fine, and the walls of the cathedral are adorned with frescoes representing the tortures of St. Gregory the Illuminator. The church of St. George is also a fine one, and contains a large stone which tradition says came all the way in the air from Etchmiazin, and on which sick Armenians lie to heal themselves of diseases. Julfa is under the patriarchate of Etchmiazin, and every four years the Bishop of Julfa travels to that place to bring a sufficiency of the holy oil to last until the next blessing takes place. In the cemetery the tombs are handsome, and, as elsewhere in Armenia, the symbol of the trade of the defunct is carved on his tombstone. But the glory has departed from Julfa, and a century and a half of oppression has knocked all the spirit out of one of the most interesting Armenian revivals of modern times. But, at the same time, the revival under the Suffean dynasty is interesting, as showing what Armenians can do when liberally governed and protected from rapine.

The Armenians are not modest when they talk of their pedigree and their ancestors. Theirs was the first country populated after the universal deluge, for did not the ark rest on Mount Ararat? They claim as the more immediate founder of their race one, Haik, grandson of Japhet, and they sometimes still use the name Haistan for their country.

Legends, too, are rife amongst them that they received Christianity during the lifetime of Christ, and, furthermore, they tell you about the letter which King Abkar wrote to Christ, and to which he received an autograph reply; also, that he wrote to Pilate concerning our Lord, and that SS. Thaddeus, Bartholomew, and Judas (not Iscariot) came to Armenia and preached in their land.

On the walls of the church at Julfa one may see their conception of their great apostle, St. Gregory the Illuminator. We see there depicted with hideous realism the various tortures to which he was put by his cousin Tiridates; and then we see how the story of Nebuchadnezzar again repeats itself, for Tiridates and his courtiers were turned by divine wrath into wild boars for casting lustful eyes on the fair Christian girl Ripsima and her nurse Gaiana. They were eventually restored to their former existence by the prayers of St. Gregory, who thereupon instituted a five days' fast, called *Aradchavok*, which is still rigidly observed. Finally, the illustrations show us Tiridates and his courtiers laying the foundations of a church in A.D. 302 on the spot where St. Gregory affirmed that he saw the holy light descend, and they called it Etchmiazin, which, in the Armenian tongue, means "the descent of the light," thereby carrying on into Christianity the old legend of the Zoroastrians, whose sacred places were always built on spots supposed to have been illuminated by fire from on high, and whose religion was the accepted one at the time when St. Gregory lived. All over ancient Armenia such temples are still visible, and it is another instance of how the earlier Christian divines made use of pagan customs and planted Christianity as it were upon them.

One day at Julfa interested us much in the condition of the Persian Armenians, and we quite looked forward to coming across them again on the shores of their own lake, the salt lake of Urumia. At Mianduwab, a considerable town at the southern extremity of this lake, we met them once more, and here we felt that they were the indigenous race—a race who claimed to trace their pedigree from Noah, and still dwelling under the shadow of the mountain on which tradition tells us the ark alighted.

The lake of Urumia is a very somber-looking one—a vast sea of salt, heavier in consistency than the Dead Sea, so that no storms ever raise its waters to a dangerous height. No fish live in it, and its shores are decked with no verdure. Legends, similar to those of Sodom and Gomorrah, are also told about it, and at certain seasons of the year the walls of submerged cities are supposed to be visible in it. The rivers which flow into it from the north are all salt, and its coasts are rugged, mountainous and barren; it is closed in by the great mountain chains on the west which spring from Mount Ararat, and on the east by those which spring from Seehend. Of a truth Lake Urumia is an uncanny spot to look upon, and in the towns around it Armenians are the predominant race. Here, too, we find Nestorians, Syrians, and fragments of races who once were under the Armenian kings, but now owe allegiance to the Shah. About 35 years ago an energetic Persian governor tried to develop the resources of Lake Urumia; he got a few boats on it, and started a colony on one of its islands, and actually talked of a steamer; but his efforts, like many things Persian, died with the man, and the lake of the Armenians returned to its wonted solitude.

Nevertheless, the plains around Urumia are amongst the most fertile in Persia, and the Armenian towns on it are infinitely better than those under Turkish sway. We stayed a night at Binab, and passed through miles of vineyards, the fruit of which the Mussulmans turn into raisins and the Armenians into wine. With its running streams passing through the center of its bazaars, with its houses buried in vines and fig-trees, Binab will equal in fertility most places in the world. Behind it rise the stupendous mountains of Seehend, which send down countless streams towards the lake and earn for Binab its name of "amongst the waters." Armenian tombs in the cemeteries here are rich in quaint devices, and bits of Armenian architecture, with its wealth of tracery, almost Byzantine in character, are constantly to be seen.

Each step we took northwards increased the number of Armenian inhabitants who occupy the towns and villages. Tabriz is full of them, and, as we approached the great mountain and the River Araxis, we felt that we were approaching what once was the heart of the Armenian kingdom. Around Ararat the three kingdoms of Persia, Turkey and Russia meet, and here the three kingdoms have sliced up Armenia amongst themselves much as Poland has been sliced up in Europe.

Turkish Armenia, as we have seen, is in the last stage of squalor and decay. Persian Armenia is better, but, as we have seen at Julfa, things are not all that could be desired. The towns on Lake Urumia have been, from time to time, drained by exorbitant governors and subject to Kourdish raids, but they have survived the attack better than their unfortunate countrymen across the frontier, and may, by comparison, be said to be in a flourishing condition.

When once we reach the Araxis all is changed as if by magic. Under the beneficent rule of Russia the Armenian towns flourish exceedingly. Erivan is a thoroughly western town, with its shops, its boulevards, its opera and its bands—a town which 30 years ago, when governed by Persia, was no better than Julfa, near Ispahan. The old Persian palace, with its Tarpeian rock, from which the governor used to hurl those who offended him into the abyss below, is now kept only as a museum of the past. The question at once forces itself upon one, Is it right to check the advance of a Power which has done so much to civilise the East? Should we not rather permit Russia tacitly to assume the care of the whole Armenian nation, that she may replace the rotten governments which massacre and destroy the remnants of what once was and could be again a flourishing community of civilised Christians?

As Ararat is approached Deluge stories come upon one with increased vigour. We stopped for a few hours' halt at the village of Maranda, on the Persian side, and were shown a tomb of mean size and aspect which they said contained the bones of Noah's wife, whose name had been Miriam, and from which the name of their own town was derived; but, if they had looked into history a little more closely, I think they would have been convinced that the name of their place came from Maranda, a Roman colony established here, and not from the mythical lady who sailed in the ark. Maranda is watered by a delicious stream, and is shaded by large trees. Here, and in every village around Ararat, grows the jujube, or singate tree, with a dull green foliage, so like the olive that we thought we had got into the region of olives once more; but the climate is not suited to the olive, and it is not found here. The question occurred to us, Did Noah mistake, like us, the jujube branch for an olive? A dove with a jujube branch in its mouth would sound far less romantic.

Soon after leaving Maranda we descended by a romantic gorge, with the whole range of the Karabagh mountains before us, into the Araxis valley, the river of the Armenians, and under a broiling sun we rode into all that is left of the once thriving town of Julfa, from whence Shah Abbas brought his Armenian colony to Ispahan. It is a poor spot now, with but three Government houses on the Persian side of the Araxis, and little more on the Russian, and is principally remarkable now for a perfect army of millstones, cut in the neighbouring mountains, and waiting to be dragged by bullocks into the heart of Persia, probably just like those Xenophon mentions as being brought into Babylon.

Our first halt in Russian Armenia was Nachitevan, or the "town of Noah," as the Armenians call it, rich in fertility and streams. Good roads, handsome houses, and an air of prosperity made it hard to believe that we were still in Armenia. What a contrast to the squalor of Sis, the decay of Julfa, and the backwardness of those unfortunate Armenian towns which have the misfortune to remain under the yoke of Islam. If the statesmen of western Europe could all be made to take a journey through Turkish and Persian Armenia, and then find themselves comfortably housed in a good hotel in Russian Armenia, I think there would be no further talk of bolstering up Mohammedan countries.

Here dwelt Noah, the Armenians have it, both before and after the Deluge, and close to this place they show the vineyard from the fruit of which the patriarch made that wine of which he partook too freely. We went to the church, and visited Noah's tomb, an octagonal vaulted place supported by a single pillar, before which stands a shrine for the burning of incense whilst the Armenian pilgrims, who visit the spot in large numbers, say their prayers. Then we went to the cemetery, and saw the large, ugly building where the mourners have a repast at funerals, and make merry after the fashion of an Irish wake. We admired the exquisite view over the plain and Karabagh mountains, but what struck us most in this town was the condition of the inhabitants themselves.

An Armenian at Nachitevan dares to be rich, and builds himself a handsome house without fear of a visit from an extortionate pasha. He dresses in European costume, and his wife has abandoned the primitive and picturesque for the silks and satins of Europe, the bonnet and the parasol.

As for those underground houses, of which there are many in these towns, they are now handed over to the remnant of the Persians who still remain here. An Armenian would consider it derogatory now to inhabit them.

Twelve miles after leaving Nachitevan we got our first view of the Mount Ararats, great and small. Two sugar loaves of unequal height, placed on a billiard table, would give some idea of how these mountains rise out of the plain of the Araxis. At their foot lie scattered the ruins of the towns, where in former ages lived, as around a great center, thousands of rich and prosperous Armenians. Ani is there, with its 300 churches, the former capital of the race. Here now one finds only a few priests, for Russia does not care for the Armenian race to congregate too much in one given spot. Of all these once flourishing towns there is nothing now to be seen save a few columns with rich tracery and a few churches, which have escaped the ravages of the many enemies who have swept over Armenia.

Erivan, our next halting-place, claims also to have been

founded by Noah, and also has a vineyard which claims the honour of having caused the intoxication of the Patriarch. It is a large and thriving place with very emerald green Russian domes and a very emerald green Armenian church, which fight horribly with the more subdued green of the surrounding trees. Erivan was in holiday attire as we approached, and the Armenian population was on its way to worship at an old church outside the town. We hated those gaudy dresses and vile imitations of *modes de Paris* after our quaint Armenian costumes of Persia, and we sighed to think that civilisation so agreeable to the individual is so destructive to the individuality. Erivan is a curious mixture of West and East. The Persians are there with their mosques and Oriental bazaars, and they jostle up against smart Russian soldiers, in this, one of their most important frontier towns. Here one realizes how the great flood of Western civilisation is swamping, as in a second Deluge, all that is primitive in mankind, all that is quaint and picturesque, all that is cruel and horrible; a deluge which cannot be checked, and which one could not wish to check. Only sixty-five years have passed by since Russia set foot in Erivan; they have in this time quite metamorphosed the town; the streets are good; there are shops, squares, promenades, all the necessities of civilised life. An Armenian lady of Erivan would pass unnoticed in Hyde Park, whereas her compatriots of Julfa or Sis could be shown at the Aquarium for a considerable profit.

From Erivan we made a pilgrimage to Etchmiazin, the See of the northern patriarchate of the Armenians, so that we might compare it with Sis.

We drove thither in a carriage along a good road with lovely views of the Ararats all the way, and before reaching the chief monastic building we alighted to see the old church of St. Ripsima, dedicated to the chaste maiden already alluded to. This church is a very good specimen of early Armenian architecture; it is round, with small apses appended, and a pretty bell tower over the porch. In it we found a curious collection of young men preparing to be priests, and going through the forty days' fast and instruction within the church. At the end of the time they have a *viva voce* examination in what they have learnt, and those who fail to pass return to mundane occupations.

St. Ripsima's church is surrounded by a mud fort, after the

fashion of those one sees all over Persia, telling of troublous times, now happily gone by. Within the sacred precincts dwells a farmer, who acts as guardian of the church, and at the same time makes butter in one of those quaint terra-cotta churns found commonly in this district.

We passed another church of inferior merit, and then reached the flourishing village of Valarsapat, which has grown up around the convent of "the descent of the sacred light."

Etchmiazin may be said to represent all the national vitality that the Armenians now possess. Here, under the wing of Russia, they have ventured to assert themselves as a nation once more. Here they keep a museum of their national curiosities; here they have an academy for the instruction of 300 young Armenians, a fine building with a council hall, containing the picture of the Patriarch George, who founded it about twenty years ago. Class rooms for various grades occupy two long corridors; a library of choice books of all nations is attached, the latest addition to which we found to be a beautifully illustrated edition of Farrar's "Life of Christ." There are dormitories for the young men, which in cleanliness would not disgrace a first-class English school, and a playground where the swarthy Armenian boys were enjoying themselves like boys in England. What a striking contrast to the miserable school at Sis, where the scholars dare scarcely speak their own language and terror reigned supreme.

We entered the large quadrangle of the convent and visited the church of St. Mary in the midst, erected, as they say, on the spot where St. Gregory the Illuminator saw the sacred light descend. Parts of this church are said to date from the seventh century; its porch is very finely decorated with intricate patterns closely akin to Byzantine; and the central dome is twelve-sided, and on each side is a medallion representing an apostle, but the bright colour with which the church is painted spoils the effect, the bright red of the belfry and the reddish stone of the porch give to the whole a rather more startling than pleasing effect.

Let us enter now with the venerable Patriarch Makar, for he alone keeps the key of the precious relics for which Etchmiazin is so renowned—the very core, so to speak, of Armenia. Inside, the church is exceedingly rich in paintings; there are five thrones in mother of pearl, and the holy of holies is the replica of an old Greek stage with the proscenium of alabaster richly illuminated with pictures of the apostles. On either side of this are two rooms, rich in vestments and relics and curiosities of the Armenian nation, more suited, we thought, to the secular museum; amongst them are rich copes and embroidered stoles, mitres and very old tiaras, all of which had been brought from Ani, the ancient capital, and have been stored here. There are croziers with emeralds and rubies and diamonds in them, and orders and jewels dating from the days of the old kings of Armenia, not the upstart Roupenians, but the old kings who fought and conquered the Romans.

But the relics are even more wonderful still. We were shown a portion of the ark which, tradition says, an angel gave to St. James of Nisibis as a reward for trying in vain to ascend Mount Ararat for three years. No one has ever been permitted to ascend Mount Ararat, the Armenian patriarch told us, since Noah came down, quite ignoring Mr. Bryce and members of the Alpine Club who have found the summit of Ararat far easier to reach than Mount Blanc or the Matterhorn.

Here are to be seen both hands of St. Thaddeus, but poor St. Gregory the Illuminator's body has been as much torn asunder in death as it was in life. We have met one arm already in Cilicia, Etchmiazin boasts of his right arm, whilst his head is in Italy, and his trunk is somewhere else where he died. Many other equally astounding relics we were shown.

We attended vespers in due course, and were pointed out the richest man of Etchmiazin saying his prayers. He is reputed to have a million roubles, another instance of the prosperity of Russian rule; in Persia or Turkey so rich a man would soon find his way into prison, and his money into the coffers of a governor

The monkish refectory is a quite old-world building, consisting of two long, narrow rooms, with stone tables and stone seats; at dinner time they put cushions on these seats and a cloth on the table. On Saturdays and Sundays the monks are given wine, on the other days only water. There is a canopied seat for the patriarch, where he eats in regal solitude, and there is a balcony from which a novice used to read a book aloud during meals; but this custom has been abandoned now.

In the library we were shown not only all the beautiful old

MSS. which had been brought from Ani, containing much interesting Armenian lore, but also the great diploma which Patriarch Makar received from the Czar of Russia on his elevation to the seat of Katholicos. The Czar has also decorated Makar with all kinds of orders, and the Armenian clergy have the same status as those of the Orthodox Church. Armenia has always been a petted child of Russia's and prospered accordingly.

We were given a very comfortable apartment in the monastery, and dinner and breakfast of a highly satisfactory nature, and on the following morning, before our return to Erivan, we visited the church erected to the memory of Gaiana, St. Ripsima's pious nurse, and the lake and garden constructed by the late patriarch, and then we bid the monks of Etchmiazin and their comfortable quarters farewell.

Our last look over the valley of Armenia and the Ararat was a glorious one, with Erivan and the plain as a rich foreground.

Our last look at Armenians was on Lake Savanga, where a convent is built on a tiny islet; thither all naughty monks from Etchmiazin are banished, that they may have a strip of water between them and their temptations to iniquity; their sublime solitude on this islet can be only relieved by fishing for those very excellent fish for which Lake Savanga is celebrated through all the country round.

Another steep ascent, another mountain pass, and we had left the Armenians behind us and entered Georgia.

The Spectator, Vol. 77 (December 12, 1896): 846–47

The Rumours about Turkey

It seems to be possible that Justice, leaden-footed though she has seemed, is at last approaching the Sultan. The Foreign Offices are naturally and wisely silent, but the rumour comes from too many quarters, and is too well defined, to be entirely without foundation. According to an account which is getting believed in St. Petersburg, Paris, and London, the Czar has at last been satisfied, by evidence laid before him at Balmoral and confirmed by M. Nelidoff on his visit to St. Petersburg, that to wait in passive expectancy the fall of the Turkish Empire is to risk a sudden explosion which may shatter the very foundations upon which peace is built. A fresh massacre, a rising in Macedonia, a military revolt in the camp at Yildiz Kiosk, may on any day raise the Eastern question in such a form that it must be settled by action, which action may—or, according to very great diplomatists, must—involve the risk of a European war. The three Powers, therefore, Russia, Great Britain, and France, with the approval of Austria, and with assurances of the neutrality of Germany, have agreed to demand of the Sultan certain reforms which, as they consider, will render the continued existence of Turkey endurable to the civilised world, and to inform him that if he refuses to accept their proposals they will be compelled to resort to measures of coercion. It is calculated that the Sultan, thus deprived of his usual source of confidence—namely, his reliance on the latent jealousies of the Powers—will submit, will make the changes in his Administration which are essential to any reforms whatever, and will, for the time at all events, give up his exclusive control of public affairs. He is not brave, he is well acquainted with the maritime strength of the Powers, and he is devoted to himself, not to the counsellors around him, who will be ruined by his submission. If he submits, all is well for the time, for the mere fact of his submission will break the evil spell of terror which renders all decent Turks powerless before him, and the new men who will be appointed "to carry out reforms" will know how to hold their own. In the conceivable though unlikely event, however, of the Sultan continuing to resist, or unduly protracting the negotiations, or in the quite possible contingency of a general massacre of Europeans by an infuriated mob, the fleets of the three Powers will force their way to Constantinople, and under the menace of dethronement, compel order and submissive obedience to their "counsels." It is not believed that the Sultan will fly, and mobs do not rise in cities commanded by fleets which they know to be irresistible, and which they can actually see.

This is the story, and reading an account which we conceive to be "inspired," we believe it to be true, with the reserve that, unless there is danger to Europeans in the capital, some telegrams will remain to be exchanged before the fleets which are hovering near the Dardanelles and the Bosphorus would, in the event of refusal, be actually in motion. Certainly we hope it is true, for even from the Continental point of view the course to be adopted is a wise one. It is evident from the hideous massacre at Eghin in September, a massacre of nine hundred Armenians, in which the soldiers took part, that the Sultan has in no way changed his policy of killing out the Armenian nation, and every such massacre renders it more difficult for the civilised Governments to refuse to act. Moreover, it has for some time been evident to the well informed that, apart from the question of the Armenians, an explosion within Constantinople itself, whether from the bankruptcy of the State, or a mutiny among the guards, or an outbreak of civil war in the streets, is ultimately inevitable. Such an explosion, which in an Oriental State is always sudden and usually sanguinary, might, and probably would, be followed by a period of anarchy which would compel the Powers to occupy Constantinople,—that is, would set in motion all the ambitions which diplomatists believe would lead to war. It is far wiser, if Turkey is to be maintained, to remove the causes of disorder, which, it seems to be agreed among those who have to act, are to be most conveniently sought not in the fevered brain of the Sultan, but in the evil counsellors by whom he is surrounded. The experiment of governing through better men may, of course, fail; will fail, if the Sultan retains his belief in his own position as chief of the Mahommedan world; but it is an easier experiment than the dethronement of the Monarch himself or the partition of his dominions, and it is, therefore, quite legitimate to try it. It may even succeed beyond expectation provided that two conditions can be observed. One is that the Sultan can be convinced, be it by an autograph letter from the Czar, or by the appearance of a fleet, or in any other way, that Europe has made up its mind, and that the alternatives before him are armed resistance to its decrees, submission, or abdication. The other is that the representatives of the Powers should act with peremptory decision, that submission or refusal should be required at once, that no facilities should be given for the flight of the Sultan, who might carry with him the heir to the throne, that no time should be allowed for rumours to circulate in Constantinople, or to be forwarded to the provinces; that, in fact, before the Ambassadors leave the Sultan's Cabinet, power within Constantinople should be transferred to strong and trustworthy hands, say those of the released Commander-in-Chief, Osman Ghazi. If there is any of the usual procrastination, if the Sultan is allowed to offer compromises, above all, if the Mussulman mob is granted time to arm itself and descend into the streets, there will be a catastrophe yet which may bring all the skill of all the diplomatists at once to naught. The Ambassadors must speak like officers in command of an irresistible army, not like men intent on respectfully insinuating wise counsels to a Sovereign misled by his information. It is not true that Asiatics understand only visible force. They are not such fools. But it is true that they understand with singular shrewdness when the end has come, when they must use force themselves, or submit, as they all know how, to the inexplicable will of Allah.

We need not say that we have no atom of confidence in the "reforms" themselves, whatever they may be, which are to be submitted to the Sultan. The Czar could not, for very fear of ridicule, require him to call a Parliament, or revive Midhat's constitution, and petty rules about the police, or the right of the Armenians to fair trail, or even the dismissal of civil officers in whose districts massacres occur, will do no good whatever. Reams of paper "reforms" will leave the three forces which rule Turkey—viz., the Sultan, the soldiers, and the Mussulman mob—equally unaffected, and equally on the watch for an opportunity of venting their fanaticism or their spite. If the Indian Criminal Code were in force in Turkey to-morrow it would not prevent such a scene as that at Eghin, or such a "riot" as that which recently occurred in Constantinople. The sole hope is in a change in the depositaries of power, who can if they please protect the unarmed, raise revenue without pillage, and bring all who murder in the name of a creed before summary Courts-martial. A strong Grand Vizier to whom the good soldiers of the Empire and the more decent among the Ottomans can rally, may keep the edifice standing for a few more years, and as its fall will involve such calamities, it is well the experiment should be tried. It is not, however, a hopeful one. A riding Sultan who visited every corner of his dominions, reinvigorated the Army, and executed half the civil Pashas for peculation might keep things going for another generation; but the house of Othman is worn out, no other has any hold upon the people, and those people themselves are about as capable of self-government as the animals in the Zoological Gardens are of electing their own keepers. There are plenty of educated Turks, and good Turks, and Turks who are Western in sympathy; but the Turkish Empire rests on the Ottomans, and the Ottomans are a tribe of the Far East, encamped in Europe for purposes of destruction, out of sympathy with their time, their surroundings, and their own leaders. They are utterly pessimist, they are boiling with rage at their position, they will find some day a soldier to lead them, and then they will fight their last fight, die like the brave men they are round their standards, and pass from the scene, leaving this repute, that they were Mongols who left their deserts to plunder, that they conquered half the Roman world, and that in four hundred years of sovereignty they never founded a city, or built an edifice, or made a discovery, or composed a book. They were, in fact, to the Arabs what the Vandals were to the Lombards or the Teutons, not merely barbarians for all the conquering tribes were that, but barbarians having in them no vivifying quality or rule of action. The Arab brought his subtle brain, the Teuton brought the seed of all progress, but the Ottoman brought nothing except a readiness to die. That readiness gave him everything that he could take, but he made nothing for himself, and when his hour arrives at last every man he ever governed will draw a deep breath of thankfulness to the God who has waited, as all good men think, so inexplicably long.

The Contemporary Review, Vol. 71 (January 1897): 21–29

Armenia and the Forward Movement

George W. E. Russell[1]

I gladly comply with the request of the Editor that I would supply some account of the "Forward Movement" in reference to Armenia. I do so the more willingly because the movement has been widely misunderstood; and in many quarters, as I believe, knowingly and wilfully misinterpreted.

I.

And, first, of the name. We did not christen the movement; the name came to us of its own accord. People began to talk of "The Forward Movement," and we welcomed the phrase because, in these great causes where public morality is involved, *non progredi est regredi.* Now, as of old, the word of command in every enterprise for the right is: "Speak into the children of Israel, *that they go forward.*"

II.

The Forward Movement in relation to Armenia is an attempt to do by the moral force of the Liberal party that which the "Non-party" movement, so grandly auspicated a year and a half ago, has signally failed to do. In August 1895 Lord Rosebery said: "I am convinced of this, that the noble Marquis, in proceeding *even alone* to deal with this question vigorously and efficiently, will find that he has behind him not a party, however overwhelming, but the entire nation." Let me hasten to admit that this was a magnificent ideal. We had a Prime Minister to whom the country had just given a plenary commission, supported by an unprecedented majority in both Houses of Parliament, and wielding single-handed all the moral and material forces of England; and we were bidden to see him, in the eye of faith, confronting the crowned Assassin with the demand that his butcheries should cease at once and for ever, and backing his brave words by resolute acts. Truly said Lord Rosebery that, in such an enterprise, Lord Salisbury, even though acting alone, would have behind him the entire nation; and what Lord Rosebery said was echoed and re-echoed with unanimous assent at all the "Non-party" meetings which were held throughout the country between September 1895 and September 1896.

III.

In those meetings I took no part. No nobler ideal was ever held up before the mind of a civilised nation; but, when one came to consider it in relation to realities, a fatal insincerity became apparent. Every "Non-party" meeting proceeded on the hypothesis, always understood and generally formulated in a definite resolution, that we could trust Lord Salisbury to deal with the Armenian question.

Now this was an effort of faith to which I found myself quite unequal. No one questions Lord Salisbury's abilities, his patriotism, or his humanity. He is generally believed to be quite free from any Turkish sympathies. But a public man must be judged by his public record; and, amid these loud protestations of confidence in our Prime Minister, the still, small voice of memory kept asking, "Is not this the man who, as a party to the Treaty of Berlin, handed back more than a million of liberated Christians to Turkish slavery?" Of course his admirers have always tried to excuse that most miserable episode of Lord Salisbury's career by saying that his own intentions were everything that is human, but that he was overcrowed by Lord Beaconsfield's imperious will. When, on the day of the ambassadors' return from Berlin in July 1878, Lord Salisbury was drawn through the streets of London on the back seat of Lord Beaconsfield's carriage, his position aptly symbolised the realities of the situation. He was chained as a captive to the triumphal car of his victorious chief.

But the old excuse will no longer serve. Lord Salisbury, who in 1878 occupied the back seat and played the second fiddle, was made by the Election of 1895 absolute master of the British Empire. If it could harden his heart to coerce the Sultan, he would, as

Lord Rosebury said, have the whole nation behind him. But the history of twenty years ago repeats itself in every detail. Now as then, we see on the one hand the great anti-Christian and anti-social Power, standing where it ought not, in the fairest provinces of desecrated Christendom; founded on slavery and polygamy; operating by massacre and rape. And on the other hand we see, as the representative of England, the weak man with the strong style, meaning everything that is honourable and chivalrous, but evermore "letting *I dare not* wait upon I would"; screwing up his courage to the sticking-point, and finding it fail him just when the moment arrives.

Certainly in this case, if ever, wisdom was justified of her children; and those who declined to declare their confidence in Lord Salisbury, found their scepticism daily and hourly confirmed. As at Berlin, so at Constantinople, our heaven-sent Minister was still the lath painted to look like iron—the lath which crumbles into matchwood when a strong grasp grips it, and pierces the confiding hand which leaned upon it for support.

IV.

These sentiments, I imagine, or something very like them, restrained certain Liberals in each constituency from taking part in the "Non-party" agitation which proceeded, flickeringly and spasmodically, during the spring, summer, and early autumn of 1896.

A few of those who had felt themselves so restrained, being profoundly moved by the repeated and ever-increasing horrors in Turkey, and by our apparent impotence to cope with them, arranged a small private conference in London at the beginning of last October. To this conference I was invited. Just before we assembled came Lord Rosebery's resignation, and then his speech at Edinburgh. The effect of that speech on the "Non-party" agitation may be illustrated by the prayer with which an American preacher concluded his Sunday's services—"And, if any spark has been kindled by the exercises of this day, oh, *water that spark.*" The "Non-party" agitation was most effectually watered by Lord Rosebery's speech, and not merely watered, but drenched and drowned. As far as I am concerned, it perished unwept. Vitiated from its birth by a fundamental unreality, it has passed away into the ignominious limbo of lost causes and forgotten ideals.

But even then my friends would not move. The inconsiderate haste, the hot eagerness in mischief-making, which have been freely attributed to them, were wholly absent from their counsels. "We must wait," they said, "till the 9th of November, and see what Lord Salisbury has to tell us. Perhaps he will be able to announce some notable victory as the result of twelve months' diplomacy, and our work will be done."

The 9th of November came, and with it the long expected speech. In order properly to appraise that speech, we must look back to the corresponding performance of the previous year—to the 9th of November, 1895. Then Lord Salisbury, in language more menacing than any Minister had ever before addressed to a foreign Sovereign with whom he still maintained diplomatic relations, warned the Sultan that, unless his barbarities ceased, the wrath of God would descend upon him. And this, translated into language of common life, was taken to mean that some human agency was about to execute the just purposes of heaven. Twelve months passed. The massacres continued, increased, and spread from outlying provinces to Constantinople itself. The Christian Powers looked on. No hand was stirred to save Armenia. Diplomacy pursued the provokingly even tenor of its way. The "Non-party" movement went on voting blind confidence in Lord Salisbury, and backed his diplomacy, and deplored the massacres, and hoped that "something would be done." The 9th of November—that fatal day of compulsory confession—returned in due course, and what had Lord Salisbury to report? What were the fruits of his diplomacy? What were the consolations reserved for the patriots of no-party?

In order that I may not overstate my case by a hair's breadth, I forbear to characterise Lord Salisbury's speech in words of my own. I prefer to borrow those of a friend, never to be named by me without affection and respect, Henry Scott Holland, Canon of St. Paul's—a man who has persistently refused to lend any countenance to party-dealing with this question; who has trusted Lord Salisbury to the uttermost; and has clung with desperate tenacity to the hope of some good issue from the concert of Europe. What says Mr. Holland of the speech at the Guildhall?

> "It is not that we are so starched with seriousness that we cannot tolerate a touch of levity, though, to us, the total incapacity of

England to save a nation which it is pledged to defend from murder and starvation is a poor subject for laughter at a city dinner. But apart from this, our complaint is that the humour is so cheap and so thin.

"The joke about the incapacity of the British fleet to scale the Taurus mountains might just have done a year and a half ago for an after-dinner retort, when not everybody had yet been convinced that the sole source of these inland massacres lay, not in Armenia, but at Constantinople. But the one gain of the ghastly butchery that occurred in Constantinople itself has been that it has, at last, opened everybody's eyes to the fact which we had continually asserted, and 'every schoolboy' now is aware that the scene of all action lies in the Yildiz kiosk. The whole question for European diplomacy is, not how to get to Armenia, but how to get *at* the Sultan. The pressure, the compulsion that is demanded, can only be exercised at one spot—Constantinople. And whatever other obstacles may hinder our fleets from arriving there, it is not the lack of water. Constantinople is, at least, on the sea. Jokes about the Taurus are absolutely meaningless.

"And then, Egypt! Is Lord Salisbury really going to try to persuade us that the idea of coming to terms with Europe about Egypt is only due to the idyllic imaginations of Mr. Morley and Mr. Courtney? Does he suppose that we never read the European Press, or the speeches of foreign Ministers? Or that we are totally ignorant of the inside of foreign Chancelleries? For all these, Egypt is the determinant issue. For France, for Russia—the only two powers that seriously matter—it is the pivot of their diplomatic attitude towards England. To ignore this in a speech of this importance is only to make evident our Premier's supreme contempt for our intelligence.

"And then, in the face of this acute European suspicion, to flaunt our expedition to Dongola, in rousing language that deliberately suggests the advance of the British Empire, which is the very thing that we have pledged ourselves to Europe *not* to do in Egypt! Could indiscretion go further?

"And all the time, the real defence of the expedition was so ready to hand, so strong, and so conciliatory! For, of course, the expedition hastens the possibility of discussing our retirement. We could never have retired while Dongola remained in the hands of the Dervishes. Egypt would never settle down to peace until her southern frontier was assured, and the black cloud of savagery that hung over her ancient province and its rich commerce had been dispersed. We can sincerely claim that we are fulfilling our European mandate by this brilliant success. Why not, then, say so? Why turn aside to glorify it in terms the most provoking and aggressive that it was possible to use?

"Worse than this! To fling our Egyptian success in Europe's face was to deny the need of reparation, of humility, of sacrifice, if we are to get this terrible Eastern business straight.

"Yet Lord Salisbury at the very moment was speaking of 'burying an antiquated policy.' What was the antiquated policy? His own—England's own. He had been one of its chief authors. Over it England has steadily gloried. How can we throw it over, and not be prepared for the sacrificial reparations which all great blunders involve? Blunders are not undone by mere confession. The confession has to be justified by acts. If Lord Salisbury, if England, are to own to the tremendous blunder committed in this discarded policy, Europe will expect something more than this light and airy dismissal of it in an after dinner speech.

"We are to bury it, are we? Good! But what shall we bury with it? Fifty thousand dead Armenians. They have been killed through that antiquated policy of ours. Four hundred thousand of them—men, women, children—are now starving, in rags, houseless and homeless, under the pitiless Armenian winter, because of our antiquated policy.

"How many of them will go down into the deep grave in which we are to bury it?

"And shall we dig the grave, then, with a phrase? Will this burial involve no penance? Lord Salisbury denied Mr. Morley's reference to England's 'bitter humiliation.' Is it not humiliating, then, to have led Europe to undertake the defence of suffering populations, and then to find ourselves totally unable to reach the people whom we undertook to defend? Surely it was the authors of the Berlin Treaty who should have been the first to consider how the British fleet could scale the heights of Taurus, and secure there the justice to which England had pledged her good name.

"We shall never get out of the present trouble so long as we stubbornly refuse to realise the shame involved in it. Only under its sting shall we find force to escape from an intolerable ignominy."

It is true that Mr. Holland winds up this scathing criticism with some desperate attempts to extract comfort out of occasional phrases in Lord Salisbury's speech. But we were not all endowed with this miraculous faculty of hoping against hope, and deriving nourishment from the stones and serpents of cynical rhetoric. After the Guildhall speech, it seemed to us that the time had come to "go forward." So we formulated our views in the following resolutions:

"1. This meeting is of opinion that the policy of Non-party agitation in relation to the Armenian question has been a failure, and that the question should be taken up by the Liberal party, on party lines.

"2. This meeting recognizes that the present Eastern situation is mainly the result of the Conservative policy in the past; that Lord Salisbury, as a member of the Berlin Congress, is especially responsible for the existing state of affairs in Armenia; and therefore that the present Ministry cannot be trusted to deal with the Armenian question."

These resolutions we sent to probable sympathisers, to leading Liberals in different parts of the country, and to the Press. Their reception was exactly what we expected. Good men sympathised; brave men were glad; timid men were frightened; and the smug philistinism of the comfortable classes found it incredible that sensible men should take an unpopular side for the sake of a moral cause.

V.

So the Forward Movement began, and before I say precisely what it aims at, let me rebut the two main charges which have been brought against it. First, it is not a sectarian movement. If the Sultan's victims were Mohammedans or Parsees, the butchery would be an equally horrid crime, and it would be equally the duty of the Christian Powers to punish it and end it. At the same time it is true that the religious element enters into the case, not as making the crimes more heinous, but as causing them. It is my firm belief now, as in 1876, that the Christian subjects of the Porte are tortured and killed because they are Christians. Civil and political pretexts are invented to cover a religious persecution; and the governing impulse of the Turk in his fiendish handiwork is hatred of the religion of the Cross. And certainly our fellow-Christians should not be shut out from the sympathy and the championship which we should be eager to extend to Mohammedans or Parsees if they were the victims of similar cruelty.

Then, we are not seeking the advancement of the Liberal party. We know that no change of Government is possible for five years at least. If by a miracle Lord Salisbury were dethroned in the meantime, we do not know who would take his place. We are not contending for office, or emolument, or honours; we are fighting for humanity, for the salvation of Armenia, and for the fair fame of England; and we seek to employ the moral force of the Liberal party as the most effective implement known to us for the attainment of our ends.

Having rebutted these two principal charges against us, let me say briefly what the Forward Movement has in view.

1. *Freedom of Criticism.*—We claim the right to remove Lord Salisbury's Armenian policy out of the sacred enclosure in which for eighteen months it has been screened from all hostile comment, and to place it in the category of topics to which criticism may be freely applied. We say that we are entitled to apply to that policy exactly the same process of examination and of censure which every opposition is entitled to apply to all the acts of every government. The right to criticise carries with it a corresponding duty; and the Liberal party is false to its trust if, in a matter vitally affecting national honour, it continues a policy of indolent acquiescence.

2. *Light.*—We want information. Diplomacy has been working in the dark for a year and a half, and has nothing to show for its trouble. After such ignominious failure, no reasonable people would trust our diplomatists blindfold in matters affecting our own interests. Why should we trust them about Armenia? And it is not only Armenia that is involved. England is involved also. We are the guardian of our honour, and we have a right to know that Lord Salisbury is not bartering away, behind our backs, the hereditary glory of England as the champion of the oppressed throughout the world.

3. *Russia.*—My own view is that Russia is the Power to whom naturally belongs the duty of coercing the Turk. She is pre-eminently fitted for it by her Oriental character; by her religious sympathy with the Christian subjects of the Porte; by her geographical position; by her military strength. But she has no reason to trust us. She has not forgotten the Crimean War or the Congress of Berlin. It is for us to make the first move. We must ask oblivion of the past. We must give to Russia public and binding assurances that we are not seeking our own aggrandisement. We must pledge ourselves that, even if it became necessary for her to seize Constantinople, we, at any rate, should not oppose her. Have these things been

done? Has Russia received these assurances? Has she refused the task assigned to her by humanity? We have a right to know.

4. *Single-handed Action.*—This, as we have seen, was contemplated as a possibility by Lord Rosebery in 1895. No one in the Forward Movement puts it higher. It would be the terrible *ultima ratio* of an empire which had failed to secure the aid of other nations, but could not shuffle off her own responsibilities on to those of cowardly or selfish rivals. No one desires it. Every one must shrink from it. But we must not forswear it. If we enter the concert of Europe proclaiming to all the world that in no possible event will we act alone, we tie our hands behind our back, and make our remonstrances as impotent as those of Portugal or Belgium.

VI.

It is said by our critics that the leaders of the Liberal party discourage the Forward Movement. This statement would be more impressive if we knew precisely who our leaders are, and to what they are leading us. "The leaders of the people," said Lord Beaconsfield, "are those whom the people trust," and the leaders of a party are those whom the party follows. Whom does the Liberal party follow just now? It follows no one absolutely; the leadership is in commission, and the party picks and chooses, and follows one man on one subject and another on another. Lord Rosebery gives us the right lead on Home Rule, Sir William Harcourt on finance, Mr. Asquith on social reform. But as no one seems inclined to give the faintest indication of a lead on the moral aspects of the Armenian question we must perforce lead ourselves.

Will not the clergy of the Established Church help us? Or will the authorised and endowed teachers of national religion be content yet once more to pass by on the other side, while the work of guiding the national conscience in a great issue between right and wrong is performed by the ministers of the Nonconformist communions?

Is it possible that the priests of the Church of England know the facts? I can hardly conceive that they do. If they did, the shame and guilt of silence would press on their souls with insupportable weight. May I pray any clergyman of my own communion, into whose hands this paper may fall, to ponder one extract from Vice-Consul Fitzmaurice's report on the massacre at Ourfa?

"On Saturday, December 28th [1895], . . . Towards noon, a muezzin gave out the midday prayer from one minaret, . . . while a mollah waved a green banner. . . . A trumpet sounded the attack. . . . The Armenian men . . . had given up all their armes; and, in abject terror, . . . pleaded for mercy for the sake of their women and children, and the Prophet Jesus. With insulting language they were dragged out, one by one, . . . and brutally butchered. . . . About 100 stalwart young Armenians were thrown on their backs, held down by their hands and feet, while the Sheikh . . . proceeded, while reciting verses of the Koran, to cut their throats after the Mecca rite of sacrificing sheep.

"Many Armenian men secreted themselves at the bottom of wells, . . . but their destroyers hurled down jars and stones, and then fired down revolver shots, or flung down matting saturated with petroleum, which they then set on fire.

"On the following day . . . the massacre was resumed, the trumpet having been sounded at early dawn.

"The savage butchery of the previous day was continued till noon, when took place the burning of the Ourfa Armenian cathedral, an act which for fiendish barbarity has been unsurpassed by any of the horrors of recent massacres of Armenians, and for which the annals of history can furnish few, if any, parallels.

"On Saturday night crowds of Armenian men, women, and children took refuge in their fine cathedral, capable of holding some 8000 persons, and the priest administered the Sacrament, the last Sacrament as it proved to be, to 1800 souls, recording the figure on one of the pillars of the church. These remained in the cathedral overnight, and were joined on Sunday by several hundreds more who sought the protection of a building which they considered safe from the mob-violence of the Mussulman even in his fanaticism. It is computed that at least 3000 individuals were congregated in the edifice when the mob attacked it.

"They at first fired in through the windows, then smashed in the iron door, and proceeded to massacre all those, mostly men, who were on the ground floor.

"Having thus disposed of the men, and having removed some of the younger women, they rifled the church treasure, shrines, and ornaments to the extent of some £4000, destroying the pictures and relics, mockingly calling on Christ now to prove Himself a greater prophet than Mohammed.

"A huge, partly stone, partly wooden, gallery running round the upper portion of the cathedral was packed with a shrieking and terrified mass of women, children, and some men.

"Some of the mob, jumping on the raised altar-platform, began picking off the latter with revolver shots, but, as this process seemed too tedious, they bethought themselves of the more expeditious method employed against those who had hidden in the wells. Having collected a quantity of bedding and the church matting, they poured some thirty cans of kerosene on it, as also on the dead bodies lying about, and then *set fire to the whole.* The gallery beams and wooden framework soon caught fire, whereupon, blocking up the staircases leading to the gallery with similar inflammable materials, *they left the mass of struggling human beings to become the prey of the flames.*

"During several hours the sickening odour of roasting flesh pervaded the town, and even to-day, two months and a half after the massacre, the smell of putrescent and charred remains in the church is unbearable."—From Vice-Consul Fitz-Maurice's Report (Blue Book. Turkey, No. 5, 1896. C. 8100, pp. 11 and 12).

Last month some of us, kneeling in an Anglican church, almost under the shadow of our august Abbey, saw with wet eyes the infinite pathos of the Armenian Liturgy. As those poor refugees from Moslem persecution bowed before the Sacramental Presence and the Cross of Christ, singing with mournful cadence the Lord's song in a strange land, there seemed to mingle with their wailing supplication the voices of the martyrs beneath the apocalyptic altar—"How long, O Lord, Holy and True, dost Thou not judge and avenge our blood?" Then, if never before, we realised that the offence of the Cross has not ceased; we felt the binding pressure of a common Christianity; we longed to do something which should prove, in very fact and deed, that each of us was a "brother and companion in tribulation, and in the kingdom and patience of Jesus Christ."

As long as memory retains its office, that service will live in our hearts, and will add its own sad emphasis to the inexorable command of conscience which bids us GO FORWARD.

NOTES

Note: For author's own notes, his initials "A.K." are included in boldface at the ends of the appropriate notes.

Introduction

1. This introduction draws heavily from my book *British Diplomacy and the Armenian Question, from the 1830s to 1914* (Princeton and London: Gomidas Institute Books, 2003).
2. D. Beales, *From Castlereagh to Gladstone 1815–85* (London, 1971), p. 159.
3. J. H. Gleason, *The Genesis of Russophobia in Great Britain* (London, 1950), p. 12.
4. Henry John Temple, Third Viscount of Palmerston, British politician and diplomat, notable for his efforts to maintain the balance of power in Europe. He served as war secretary (1809–28), foreign secretary (1830–34, 1835–41, and 1846–51) and prime minister (1855–58 and 1859–65).
5. A. Palmer, *The Decline and Fall of the Ottoman Empire* (New York, 1992), pp. 106–7.
6. Kirakossian, *British Diplomacy*, pp. 13–18.
7. *Eastern Papers*, Part XVII, Firman and Hatti-Sherif by the Sultan, relative to Privileges and Reforms in Turkey (London, 1856), pp. 4–7.
8. *Papers Relating to Administrative and Financial Reforms in Turkey 1858–1861* (London, 1861), pp. 2–13, 15, 16.
9. Ibid., p. 21.
10. William Ewart Gladstone (1809–98), British statesman. He served as president of the Board of Trade (1843–45), colonial secretary (1845–47), chancellor of the exchequer (1852–55, 1859–66), and, after becoming leader of the Liberal Party, prime minister (1868–74, 1880–85, 1886, 1892–94).
11. S. M. Ivanov, *Vneshneekonomicheskie sviazi Osmanskoi imperii v novoe vremia (konets XVIII—nachalo XX v.)* (Moscow, 1989), pp. 94–96.
12. Benjamin Disraeli, First Earl of Beaconsfield (1804–81), British statesman and leader of the Conservative Party (1848–81). He was a member of the House of Commons from 1837 to 1876 and of the House of Lords from 1876 until his death. He served as chancellor of the exchequer (1852, 1858–59, 1866–68) and prime minister (1868, 1874–80).
13. Robert Arthur Talbot Gascoyne, Third Marquis of Salisbury (1830–1903), British statesman and Conservative politician. He served as

secretary of state for India (1866–67, 1874–78), foreign secretary (1878–80). A member of the House of Lords, he assumed the leadership of the Conservative Party in 1881 and served as prime minister in 1885–86, 1886–92, 1895–1902 and, concurrently until 1900, as foreign secretary.

14. *Turkey*, no. 15 (1877), pp. 194–95.
15. Ibid., pp. 297–98.
16. Ibid., p. 286.
17. Robert F. Zeidner, "Britain and the Launching of the Armenian Question," *International Journal of Middle East Studies* 4, no. 7 (1976), p. 468.
18. FO 424/63/124, pp. 86–89.
19. *Turkey*, no. 22 (1878), p. 262.
20. Christopher J. Walker, *Armenia: The Survival of a Nation* (New York, 1980), p. 112.
21. G. Cecil, *Life of Robert Marquis of Salisbury* (London, 1921), p. 242.
22. R. W. Seton-Watson, *Disraeli, Gladstone and the Eastern Question: A Study in Diplomacy and Party Politics* (New York, 1962), p. 410.
23. Kirakossian, *British Diplomacy*, pp. 73–74.
24. *Hansard's Parliamentary Debates, 1878*, Vol. 240, pp. 1242–46.
25. *Turkey*, no. 39, *Correspondence relating to the Congress of Berlin with the Protocol of the Congress* (London, 1878), p. 1.
26. Ibid., p. 186.
27. Ibid., p. 225.
28. *Turkey*, no. 38 (1878), p. 384.
29. J. H. Park, *British Prime Ministers of the Nineteenth Century: Policies and Speeches* (New York and London, 1950), p. 286.
30. *Turkey*, no. 7, *Correspondence Respecting the Affairs of Turkey* (London, 1880), pp. 1–2.
31. FO 424/99, No. 449/2, pp. 231–32.
32. *Turkey*, no. 23, *Further Correspondence Respecting the Condition of the Populations in Asia Minor and Syria* (London, 1880), pp. 279–80.
33. Ibid., pp. 280–82.
34. FO 424/122, no. 5, p. 7.
35. FO 424/122, no. 23, p. 46.
36. FO 424/122, nos. 27, 28, p. 52.
37. FO 424/122, no. 33, p. 56.
38. FO 424/123, no. 126, p. 176.
39. M. MacColl, "The Constantinople Massacre and Its Lesson," *The Contemporary Review* 68 (1895), pp. 750–52.
40. John Wodehouse, First Earl of Kimberley (1826–1902), British politician. He served as undersecretary of state for foreign affairs (1852–56, 1858–61), ambassador to Russia (1856–58), colonial secretary (1870–74, 1880–82), secretary of state for India (1882–86, 1892–94), and foreign secretary (1894–95).
41. E. J. Dillon, "The Fiasco in Armenia," *The Fortnightly Review* 65 (March 1, 1896), p. 348.

42. *Turkey*, no. 1, *Correspondence Relative to the Armenian Question and Reports from Her Majesty's Consular Officers in Asiatic Turkey* (London, 1895), part 1, p. 10; S. Shahid Bey, *Islam, Turkey and Armenia and How They Happened* (St. Louis, 1898), pp. 198–99; E. M. Bliss, *Turkey and Armenian Atrocities* (Philadelphia, 1896), pp. 368–73.
43. *Turkey*, no. 1 (1895), p. 8.
44. Ibid., p. 7.
45. Ibid., pp. 7–8.
46. Ibid., pp. 19–20.
47. Ibid., p. 21.
48. MacColl, "The Constantinople Massacre," p. 257.
49. "Lord Rosebery's Deliverance," *The Spectator* 77 (October 17, 1896), p. 504.
50. *Turkey*, no. 1, 1895, part 1, pp. 40–41.
51. R. Douglas, "Britain and the Armenian Question," *Historical Journal* 19, no. 1 (1976), p. 117.
52. *Turkey*, no. 1 (1895), part 1, pp. 39–40.
53. Ibid., p. 42.
54. Ibid., p. 79.
55. Ibid., pp. 74–75, 82.
56. Ibid., pp. 76–78.
57. *Turkey*, No. 1, *Correspondence Relative to the Armenian Question and Reports from Her Majesty's Consular Officers in Asiatic Turkey* (London, 1896), pp. 9–10.
58. Kirakossian, *British Diplomacy*, pp. 209–10.
59. *Turkey*, no. 1 (1895), part 2, p. 66.
60. Douglas, "Britain and the Armenian Question," pp. 121–22.
61. G. W. E. Russell, "Armenia and the Forward Movement," *The Contemporary Review* 71 (1897), p. 21.
62. *Turkey*, no. 1 (1895), part 1, pp. 134–46; "Americans and Armenians," *The Spectator* 76 (February 1, 1896), pp. 156–57.
63. *Turkey*, no. 1 (1895), part 1, pp. 198, 200–203; *Turkey*, no. 1 (1896), pp. 118–19; *Turkey*, no. 2, *Correspondence Relative to the Armenian Question and Reports from Her Majesty's Consular Officers in Asiatic Provinces* (London, 1896), pp. 2–4, 9–10, 14, 16–17, 21; FO 424/183, no. 208/2, p. 240; no. 219/2, pp. 255–56; no. 251/2, pp. 398–99; no. 280/1, p. 413.
64. H. Hepworth, *Through Armenia on Horseback* (London, 1898), p. 282; E. Pears, *Turkey and Its People* (London, 1911); G. H. Paelian, *Landmarks in Armenian History* (New York, 1942), p. 62.
65. FO 424/183, no. 371, p. 476.
66. *Turkey*, no. 2 (1896), p. 22.
67. Shahid Bey, *Islam, Turkey and Armenia*, p. 201.
68. *Turkey*, no. 2 (1896), pp. 22, 36.
69. FO 424/184, no. 6, p. 3.
70. Douglas, "Britain and the Armenian Question," pp. 124–25.
71. *Turkey*, no. 2 (1896), p. 25.

72. Ibid., pp. 41–42.
73. *Turkey*, no. 1 (1896), p. 158.
74. *Turkey*, no. 1 (1896), p. 158; *Turkey*, no. 2 (1896), p. 57.
75. FO 424/184, no. 118, p. 68; no. 140, p. 95; no. 121, p. 68; no. 124, p. 69; no. 126, p. 69.
76. *Turkey*, no. 2 (1896), pp. 107–8.
77. Ibid., p. 124.
78. Ibid., pp. 137–38.
79. Ibid., p. 176.
80. Ibid., p. 141.
81. L. M. Penson, "The Principles and Methods of Lord Salisbury's Foreign Policy," *Cambridge Historical Journal*, Vols. 87–106, 1935, p. 101; G. S. Papadopoulos, *England and the Near East 1896–98* (Thessalonika, 1969), pp. 45–47.
82. C. D. Clayton, *Britain and the Eastern Question: Missolonghi to Gallipoli* (London, 1971), pp. 185–86; R. Taylor, *Salisbury* (London, 1975), p. 169.
83. J. A. S. Grenville, *Lord Salisbury and Foreign Policy* (London, 1964), p. 47.
84. FO 424/184, no. 701, p. 385.
85. *Turkey*, no. 2, 1896, pp. 208, 211, 224.
86. FO 424/184, no. 703, p. 386; no. 750, pp. 424–25; *Turkey*, no. 2 (1896), p. 210.
87. *Turkey*, no. 2, pp. 254–55.
88. FO 424/184, no. 821, p. 487.
89. FO 424/184, no. 828, p. 490.
90. FO 424/184, no. 830, p. 491.
91. FO 424/184, no. 831, p. 491.
92. FO 424/184, no. 834, p. 492.
93. *Turkey*, no. 2 (1896), p. 285.
94. Ibid., p. 281.
95. Ibid., pp. 289, 291.
96. *Turkey*, no. 8, *Further Correspondence Relating to the Asiatic Provinces of Turkey (In Continuation of Turkey No. 2 [1896]* (London, 1896), pp. 51–54.
97. Levon Mkrtch'yan, *Zeyt'uni apstambut'yune, 1895–1896 t't'* (Zeytoun Uprising of 1895–96) (Erevan, 1995), pp. 180, 182, 190–91.
98. See R. Melson, "A Theoretical Inquiry into the Armenian Massacres of 1894–96," *Comparative Studies in Society and History* 24, no. 3 (July 1982), pp. 481–505.
99. *Turkey*, no. 2 (1896), pp. 318–22.
100. Bliss, *Turkey and Armenian Atrocities*, p. 463.
101. *Turkey*, no. 2 (1896), p. 325; Bliss, *Turkey and Armenian Atrocities*, pp. 428–34, 475–76.
102. Bliss, *Turkey and Armenian Atrocities*, p. 477.

103. *Turkey*, no. 2 (1896), pp. 320–22; Bliss, *Turkey and Armenian Atrocities*, pp. 425, 451–66, 478.
104. *Turkey*, no. 2 (1896), pp. 323–30.
105. Central Historical Archive of the Republic of Armenia, *Collection of Excerpts from Documents*, List 1, Chapter 51, Part 2, p. 10.
106. "The Constantinople Massacre," *The Contemporary Review* 70 (1896), p. 458; "The Massacres," *The Spectator* 77 (September 5, 1896), pp. 292, 296.
107. Central Historical Archive, *Collection of Excerpts*, p. 11.
108. A. Wittlin, *Abdul Hamid: The Shadow of God* (London, 1949), pp. 177–78.
109. Central Historical Archive, *Collection of Excerpts*, p. 14.
110. L. Abbott, "Armenian Question," *The Outlook* 54 (1896), p. 1036; "The Constantinople Massacre," pp. 459–60; J. Bryce, *Transcaucasia and Ararat* (London, 1896), p. 516.
111. C. Roberts, "A Mother of Martyrs," *The Atlantic Monthly* 83, p. 90.
112. E. Antoine, *Les Massacres d'Armenie* (Brussels, 1897), p. 90.
113. *Turkey*, no. 1 (London, 1897), pp. 21, 29, 52.
114. M. H. Gulesian, "Armenian Refugees," *The Arena* 17 (1897), p. 652.
115. Antoine, *Les Massacres*, p. 79.
116. M. MacColl, *The Sultan and the Powers* (London, 1896), p. 53.
117. M. S. Gabrielian, *Armenia. A Martyr Nation* (New York, 1918), pp. 257–58.
118. W. L. Langer, *Diplomacy of Imperialism 1890–1902*, vol. 1 (New York, 1935), pp. 333–34.
119. Grenville, *Lord Salisbury*, p. 85.
120. Papadopoulos, *England and the Near East*, p. 103.
121. Ibid., p. 107.
122. Ibid., p. 103.
123. Ibid., p. 111.
124. Ibid., p. 103.
125. Ibid., p. 111.
126. Ibid., p. 112.
127. Clayton, *Britain and the Eastern Question*, p. 187.
128. R. Adalian, "Young Turks and the Armenian Genocide," in *Encyclopedia of Genocide* (Santa Barbara, CA, 1999), vol. 2, p. 631
129. A. Kirakossian, *The Armenian Question and the Armenian Genocide* (Erevan, 2007), pp. 80–81.
130. A. Nassibian, *Britain and the Armenian Question 1915–1923* (London and New York, 1984), pp. 45–46.
131. Ibid., p. 59.
132. Ibid., p. 44.
133. "Armenia's Desolation and Woe," *The Review of Reviews* 15 (1897), p. 626; J. R. Harris and H. B. Harris, *Letters from the Scenes of the Recent Massacres in Armenia* (London, 1897).

134. *Nor Kyank* (in Armenian), no. 98 (November 1, 1898), pp. 333–34.
135. Nassibian, *Britain and the Armenian Question*, p. 45.

A Vanishing Treaty

1. Weekly magazine of news and opinion, published in London and widely noted for its critical reviews and essays on political, literary, and economic issues. *The Spectator* has been a serious journal of intellectual discussion since it was founded in 1828, Its editorial stance is moderately conservative and much more conservative than the larger journals with which it shares its eminence, *The Economist* and *New Statesman & Society*. For many years, it was noted for its witty essays, but in modern times, it has turned to more straightforward treatment of political and cultural affairs.—**A.K.**
2. James Bryce, First Viscount (1838–1922), British statesman, lawyer, and historian. He was a member of Parliament since 1874 and became a Liberal Party leader in 1880. He served as undersecretary of state for foreign affairs (1886), president of the Board of Trade (1894–95), chief secretary for Ireland (1905–06), ambassador to the United States (1907–13). He founded the Anglo-Armenian Society in 1876 and the Armenian Association of England in 1893. He traveled in Armenia, Caucasus, Smyrna, and Constantinople and published *Transcaucasia and Ararat* in 1877. Bryce was one of the first Western politicians to respond to the 1915 Armenian genocide and was active in forming the British-Armenian Red Cross Society and Fund for Relief. In 1916, he published a collection of documents entitled *The Condition of the Armenians in the Ottoman Empire, 1915–1916*.—**A.K.**
3. James Fergusson, undersecretary of state for foreign affairs.—**A.K.**

Armenia and the Armenian People

1. Monthly magazine founded in 1865 in London by Escott Trollope, Frederic Chapman, George Eliot, and first editor George Henry Lewes. The object of the magazine was to become an organ for unbiased expression on topics of general interest in politics, literature, philosophy, science, and art. Although *The Fortnightly Review* was considered a liberal periodical, its liberalism, however, should not be equated with the political party of that name. It later was incorporated by *The Contemporary Review*.—**A.K.**
2. *Novoye Vremya*, 9th December, 1889. Also *Kavkaz*, 26th November, 1889.
3. Cf. *Novoye Vremya*, 9th October, 1889.
4. The correspondent of the *Odessa Messenger* was an eye-witness of this scene, which he describes in the above terms in the *Odessa Messenger* of August, 1885. Cf. also *Yuschny Krai*, 7th September, 1885.
5. It is interesting to read in the light of these facts the statements, as rash as they are circumstantial, made by publicists, magazine writers and

others who for some reason or other desire to see an Anglo-Russian alliance. Take, for instance, the following passage which appeared in *The Fortnightly Review*, for October 1889:—"People are too prone to conclude that the Pomaks migrated from Bulgaria after the war in order to escape living under a Christian flag. As a matter of fact, religion was only the indirect cause of their flight. They left because they feared that the new government would not be able to protect them against an excited peasantry. . . . *In the districts annexed to Russia no exodus of importance occurred.* The Mohamedans of those parts had not been cutting Christian throats in the garb of Bashi-Bazouks and *knew that the conqueror would place them on a footing of perfect equality with his other subjects.* Their confidence was amply repaid and in consequence they are *not loyal and happy*." P. 541.

6. I am giving this account of the election from memory. If I inadvertently fall into an error it will be found to be very slight and quite immaterial to the main issue.
7. Although country ceded by Turkey to Russia has been ten years in the hands of the latter country, the question has not yet been decided whether private ownership in land exist there or not. In Batoum, for instance, that question is being hotly debated just now, the Government maintaining that it does not. To prove this thesis, it is taking measures to evict present private owners. Cf. *Novoye Vremya*, 15th October, 1889.
8. The editor of this Review possesses copies of two of these primers.

The Armenian Question I

1. Founded in 1866 by Alexander Strahan, *The Contemporary Review* was designed to be *The Fortnightly Review* of the established church. The first editor was the dean of Canterbury, poet, musician, painter, and traveler Henry Alford. The *Contemporary* was the first British journal of its day to devote extensive space to art and music. With the accession of Percy William Bunting to the editorship in 1882, the *Contemporary* became a practical promoter of social reform and political liberalism, establishing a tie between the magazine and the Liberal Party. Currently, *The Contemporary Review* is a forum for discussion of a broad spectrum of topics, including international affairs, politics, literature, and the arts.—**A.K.**
2. Harry Finnis Blosse Lynch (1862–1913), British traveler. He traveled extensively in the countries between India and the Mediterranean for purposes of scientific, political, and commercial research. First journey 1889, Alexandretta, Aleppo, Diarbekir, and down the Tigris on a raft to Baghdad; inaugurated a new river service under the British flag on the Karun River. Second journey 1893–94, the Caucasus and Armenia; climbed Mount Ararat. Third journey 1893, Armenia; surveyed the great crater of Nimrud and mapped the country. Publications: *Armenia:*

Travels and Studies, 2 vols., 1901; various articles in the reviews and proceedings of learned societies; map of Armenia, 1901.—**A.K.**

3. See Sir H. Layard's despatch dated May 30, 1877.
4. The Armenian delegates to the Berlin Congress presented a memoir to the European plenipotentiaries in which they set forth their cause. It is published by De la Jonquière in his "Histoire de l'Empire Ottoman," Paris, 1881. They also drew out a project for an Organic Regulation to be applied to the new province. It was to be administered by an Armenian Governor-General appointed by the Porte with the consent of the Powers. The Organic Regulation defines the area of the province as comprising all the country between the Russian and Persian frontiers, the Black Sea, a line of demarcation starting from Tireboli on the coast to the confluence of the Kizil-Tchibuk Tchai with the Euphrates on the south in about 38° latitude, and thence extending eastwards across the Upper Tigris to the Bitlis river, the mountains of Mukus south of Lake Van and the Persian frontier. I believe, however, that changes were made in the extent of the area which it was considered that the new province ought to embrace. How unsound was the foundation upon which, as it seems, the Armenian delegates were building is shown by the statistics of population which, according to Major Trotter, were unofficially supplied to the plenipotentiaries at Berlin. In the table, which he furnishes, of different statistical estimates of population for the vilayets of Erzerum, Van, and Bitlis (excluding Sert) the Berlin Project gives the number of non-Moslems within that area as 1,172,000 and of Moslems as 528,000, a proportion between the two which a slender acquaintance with the country would be sufficient to disprove. *See* Blue Book, Turkey, No. 6, 1881, p. 127.
5. Article 61. "La sublime Porte s'engage à réaliser san plus de retard les améliorations et les réformes qu'exigent les besoins locaux dans les provinces habitées par les Arméniens et à garantir leur sécurité contre les Circassiens et les Kurdes. Elle donnera connaissance périodiquement des mesures prises à cet effet aux puissances qui en surveilleront l'application." The Powers collectively appear not to have taken the smallest interest in the question since the Berlin Congress. Inasmuch as the Armenians are scattered in considerable numbers over the whole extent of Asia Minor reforms introduced in *the provinces inhabited by the Armenians* would have a very wide application indeed and would be almost impossible to supervise unless Europe took the whole of Turkey in tutelage.
6. The statistics of population were supplied by the Patriarch Nerses to Mr. Goschen. They may be found in Blue Book, Turkey, No. 23, 1880, p. 274. Mr. Goschen, writing to Lord Granville on July 15, 1880, says: "My strong feeling is that the Powers cannot commit themselves to any plan until they know the real facts about the population. It would not do to build on a mistaken basis, and I feel convinced that no one has sure ground. The Patriarch's figures are as exaggerated as those of the

Porte on the other side. Again, how to deal with the nomad Kurds? All must depend on the physical force of the two different races and religions. If the Armenians should be in a minority it will be dangerous to give them the same institutions which we should give if they were in a majority, dangerous to themselves." Blue Book, Turkey, No. 6, 1881, p. 16. And, again, in another despatch of July 23: "With regard to the actual project of reforms, the letter of the Patriarch is conceived in such vague phrases that but little advantage is to be derived from it in elucidating the problem to be solved." *Ibid.* p. 20.

7. See Lord Granville's despatch of February 10, 1881: "In consequence of the objections raised by the German Government Mr. Goschen will not be instructed to put forward the Armenian question immediately on his return to Constantinople."
8. I have already pointed out that the Armenian plateau is a part of that continuous system of high land which includes Asia Minor and Persia, and that therefore there are no definite natural limits on the west and east. I take the Persian frontier as a convenient political limit of Armenia on the east. According to General Schindler, quoted by Curzon (*Persia,* ii., 493), the number of Armenians in Persia may be placed at 43,000. The Armenian population of Azerbaijan—that is, of the northern province of Persia, which adjoins the Russian and the Turkish territory—is placed by Curzon at 4815 families, or 20,890 souls (*Ibid* i. 548). I am informed that of the inhabitants of this border-province the Armenians to the number of 40,000 followed the army of Lazareff into Russia after the treaty of Turkomantchai in 1828.

The Armenian Question II

1. Sophocles, "Oedipus Tyrannus," I. 58.

The Armenian Question III

1. It is interesting to compare these results, which were obtained quite independently and before I had seen his estimate, with the figures given by the late Mr. Taylor, for many years British Consul for Erzerum and the surrounding country. Mr. Taylor knew the country intimately, and had travelled extensively in it. On his figures are based those which have been given by his successors in office, and which appear in the Blue Books. After making the necessary deductions for districts annexed to Russia since the date of Mr. Taylor's reports, his estimate of the population, as adapted to the area with which we are dealing, is as follows: Turks, 348,350, Kurds, 466,982, Christians, 352,657—total, 1,167,989. This estimate corresponds in a satisfactory manner with mine, after we have made allowance for information, either new or more complete, which has appeared with reference to certain districts since Taylor's time. The census shows that Taylor under-estimated the Turks who inhabit the northern Cazas of Erzerum Vilaet. Taylor also

placed the Kizzilbash Kurds of the Deyrsim at 110,000. Relying on more recent reports, I place them at 50,000.

2. This tax is known in the country under the name of *Kishlak*, or winter quarter.
3. The emigration of the Armenians into Russia is conducted under considerable difficulties; it is no easy matter for the Russian Government to find a provision for the more needy refugees, and, unless they are provided with passports, they are always liable to be turned back at the frontier. It is only a very desperate situation at home that drives the Armenian peasantry into Russian territory. During 1893 upwards of 3500 of such passports were registered by the Russian Consulate in Erzerum, and, in addition to these emigrants who were able to comply with the proper formalities, a large number, chiefly from the district of Khinis, contrived to find a refuge upon Russian soil. The country was suffering from the effects of the disastrous harvest of 1892, and, owing to the scarcity of all grain and to the raids of the Kurds, who were carrying off what yet remained, the Armenian peasantry of some districts were face to face with starvation.
4. Vahan Vartabed, in an Armenian newspaper published at Constantinople, the *Djeridei Sharkié*, under date the 3/15 December, 1886.
5. See the *Nineteenth Century Magazine* for September, 1878.

Turkey and Armenia

1. These irregular troops are so called after the Sultan.

Armenia

1. British MP, chairman of the Anglo-Armenian Association.—**A.K.**

The Mussalmans of India and the Armenian Question

1. British monthly periodical founded in 1877 by editor James T. Knowles as an organ of the Metaphysical Society. *The Nineteenth Century* was a forum for discussion of topics related to practical science, social justice, and politics. In the 1880s and '90s, it adopted a Liberal position. In 1901, the periodical became *The Nineteenth Century and After*, and in 1951 *The Twentieth Century*.—**A.K.**

The Condition of Armenia

1. Emil J. Dillon (1854–1933), Irish linguist and reporter, a specialist in Oriental languages and comparative linguistics. He worked in the St. Petersburg and Kharkov Universities and the Mekhitarian Order in Venice in the 1880s and studied Armenian language and literature. Author of several monographs on the Armenian language and translations. He traveled in the Ottoman Empire in 1895, working as a correspondent for the *Daily Telegraph*, and made a trip to Western Armenia. —**A.K.**

2. A Turkish coin. Forty paras are equivalent to twopence.
3. Bairam is the festival which follows the long fast of Ramazan.
4. I have published elsewhere a comparison between the prosperity of Armenians who lived in the epoch of misgovernment and the indigence of those who languish in the present era of extermination; but this interesting subject has never been exhaustively treated.
5. Khorzo, a well-to-do inhabitant of Prkhooss near Lake Nazig (District of Akhlat) was a lucky exception. True, he did not exactly possess a gun, but he was suspected of having one. His house was searched, the floor dug up, the roof examined, in vain. Then he was imprisoned for a month and allowed to purchase his liberty by paying £70 in gold and signing a paper to the effect that he never had firearms of any kind.
6. Cows, horses, &c., are frequently lodged in the apartment in which the inmates live and sleep. I have passed many a restless night in a spacious room along with horses, buffaloes, oxen, sheep and goats.
7. This narrative has been abridged by me.
8. The Koords call all Europeans hat-wearers, and generally regard them with respect and awe.
9. I.e., to the whole universe.
10. The Koords are divided into *Torens* or nobles, who lead in war time, and possess and enjoy in peace; and *Rayahs*, who sacrifice their lives for their lords in all raids and feuds, and are wholly dependent on them at all times. A *rayah's* life may be taken by a *toren* with almost the same impunity as a Christian's.
11. Literally "Devil's ring." The hands are tightly bound together, and the feet, tied together by the great toes, are forced up over the hands. The remainder of the *Sheitantopy* consists of a severe torture and a beastly crime.
12. As three of the writers are still in prison, prudence forbids me to publish their names, which are in the possession of our Foreign Office.
13. Their names are Vehret, Mardiross Der Kasparian, and Goolbeg.
14. The Mullah also went to the famous Armenian monastery Etchmiadyin, where, it is said, he embraced Christianity.
15. This is no uncommon thing in Armenia.
16. Deposition of Hagop Der Mardirossian and others.
17. Deposition of Haroothioon Haroothioonian.
18. Sandjak of Hassankaleh.
19. Deposition of the man himself.
20. Sandjak of Hassankaleh.
21. In the village of Ishkhoo, for instance, the daughter of Tepan Agha was brought up as a boy. She was arrested and imprisoned some time ago in Erzeroum, for this, too, is a crime.
22. She gave me an appeal to the women of England signed by herself, together with her photograph.
23. I possess the photograph of the wretched woman.

An Unbiased View of the Armenian Question

1. Conservative monthly periodical founded in 1817 in Edinburgh by William Blackwood.—**A.K.**

The Constantinople Massacre and Its Lesson

1. Rev. Malcolm MacColl, British clergyman and publicist; curate of St. Mary's, Soho; of St. Barnabas's, Pimlico; of St. Paul's, Knightsbridge; chaplain to the British ambassador, St. Petersburg; rector of St. George's, City; canon of Ripon from 1884; member of pro-Armenian group Grosvenor House Association. Publications: *The Reformation in England; Science and Prayer; The Eastern Question: Its Facts and Fallacies; Three Years of the Eastern Question; Reasons for Home Rule; Responsibility of England towards Armenia; The Sultan and the Powers; The Education Question and Liberal Party.*—**A.K.**
2. Rayah is the common designation of Christians, Jews, and Parsees, in Turkey. It means a flock—very appropriately, since the non-Mussulman subjects of the Sultan are regarded and treated by their rulers as a flock of defenceless sheep, whose *raison d'être* is to be fleeced or slaughtered at the discretion of their masters.
3. Consular Reports of 1867, p. 67.
4. Consular Reports of 1867, p. 28.
5. Because the Magi were led by a star to worship the Messiah, and this might encourage Jews and Christians to look for a Deliverer.
6. "Turkey," No. I. (1892), p. 9.
7. *Ibid.*, p. 24.
8. *Ibid.* p. 60.
9. *Ibid.* p. 25.
10. To achieve special notoriety by outrages on Christians, and then to be denounced by the British Government, is the surest passport to the Sultan's favour. It was just after he had been denounced to the Sultan by Lord Beaconsfield's Government "in the name of the Queen," that Chefket Pasha, the butcher of Batak, was promoted to a high post in the palace and decorated.
11. "Turkey," No. I. (1892) p. 23.
12. There is no proof that the shot was fired by an Armenian. An eye-witness has stated in a Roman paper that the shot was fired by one of the Grand Vizier's escort, shooting the officer by mistake, or purposely by way of excuse for the massacre.
13. *Daily News* Correspondent, October 18.

The Eastern Question: Turkish Reforms and Armenia

1. The Hat of 1831 promised protection to all Rayahs "who come into the shade of Islam, and of our Imperial justice," but gave them no rights.
2. The Koran strictly distinguishes idolaters and the possessors of a divine

revelation. The first are to be destroyed unless they adopt Islam; the latter only to be subjected and to pay a tribute to the ruler of the believers (Sura ix., "The repentance").

3. Algeria and Tunis by France, Bosnia and Herzegovina by Austria.
4. "You think us weak," said Fuad Pasha. "It is an error; our solidity is not factitious, because it reposes upon your divisions."
5. Achmed Vefic Effendi (Senior: 1 *Journal kept in Turkey and Greece*, 1853, p. 17). The Finance Minister of Tripoli frankly avowed that he collected annually about 250,000*l.*, of which sum he transmitted half to Constantinople, and divided the other half between himself and his subordinates (ibid. p. 21).
6. Despatch of Sir H. Layard to the Foreign Office, the 27th of April, 1880.
7. In citing the example of the "règlement" of 1862 for the Libanon, it is overlooked that Druses and Maronites mostly live in separate territories.

Armenia: An Appeal

1. Yezdiged II., King of Persia, insisted on the apostacy of the Armenian people, whom he commanded to embrace the garbled doctrines of Zoroaster. Vartan, the chieftain of the race, gathered 287 members of the royal family around him, and with a following of 749 others, manfully died on the field of battle after a bloody combat with the Persian troops, on June 2, 450.
2. The above description is taken literally from a report of the Bitlis Vice-Consul of Erzeroum. Copies are in possession of the diplomatic representatives of the Powers at Constantinople. The scene occurred in the village of Semal *before* the massacres, during the *normal* condition of things.
3. Father, father.

The Fiasco in Armenia

1. No. 40. The italics are mine throughout.
2. Despatch No. 31.
3. No. 66.
4. *I.e.* , the British Ambassador at Constantinople.
5. Respecting the Commission.
6. Blue Book, Turkey, Part I., No. 66.
7. Despatch No. 119, p. 59.
8. The italics throughout are mine.
9. Blue Book, p. 207.
10. Despatch No. 91.

Zeitun

1. Avetis Nazarbekian (1866–1936), founder of the Armenian social-democratic Hunchakian Party with six fellow students in Geneva in 1887.

Edited newspaper *Hunchak* ("The Bell"). Traveled to London 1892–1893 as organizer of the party branch; traveled extensively to Paris, Athens, and Geneva. Returned to London for the first general congress of the party, 1896. The party congress of 1905 in Paris sided against Nazarbekian, who had sought virtually to dissolve the party's identity. The same congress emerged at the eighth party congress, in Athens, 1924; he was elected vice chairman of the party committee, but his views were criticized.—**A.K.**

Armenia and the Powers: From Behind the Scenes

1. This is the calculation of Signor Monaco, who conducted an independent inquiry on behalf of the Italian Government. He calls attention not only to the fact, noted in the estimate of 30,000 testified by the great Powers, that that estimate embraces a limited area, but to the important consideration that the estimate stops at December, whereas there have been massacres on a large scale in many other places since then. Sir Philip Currie's suggestion that the object of the massacres was to destroy the majority of Christians in the districts to which the reforms were to apply is proved by a recent report of the Grand Vizir to the Sultan, which assures his Majesty that his mind may now be at ease, "since a majority is everywhere assured to the Mussulman element."
2. The British Foreign Office made repeated applications to the Italian Government to send a delegate to accompany the Turkish Commission. But Baron Blanc emphatically refused, and gave as his reason that it would not only be futile, but mischievous in addition, to accompany a Commission whose action was officially directed to the justification of the Turkish functionaries and officers who committed the massacres, and to the fixing of the sole responsibility on "the Armenian brigands." The persistence of the British Government in an inquiry which was avowedly instituted by the Sultan to suppress the truth and propagate falsehood is inexplicable. This manly protest of the Italian Government does not appear in the Blue Books.

Two Massacres in Asia Minor

1. The following remarks are not, as might seem to be the case, written to bring out the similarity with the Armenian massacres. They are extracted from the printed pages of ch. XII of my "Cities and Bishoprics of Phrygia," vol. II; the evidence will soon be accessible in the "Appendices" containing the text and analysis of the documents on which the chapter is based. The epitaph of a Christian butcher at Apameia, twenty-five miles from Eumeneia, is quite an interesting monument.
2. "St. Paul the Traveller," p. 208.
3. "Apolog.," 42.
4. "St. Paul the Traveller," p. 208*f.*
5. As M. Cumont has pointed out, it is modified from a very rare pagan

form, "The violator shall account to the departed" (who were now identified with "the god").

6. Seven are dated: the rest are assured by less direct evidence. There is a number of others, of the third and second centuries, which are suspected of Christian origin, but at present they cannot be used in evidence.
7. I admit nothing that does not satisfy the canons laid down by M. Cumont in his careful and critical study of "Les Inscr. Chrét. de l'Asie Min." ("Mélanges d'Arch. et de l'Histoire," 1895). Without knowing the articles on this subject that appeared in the *Expositor* 1888 and 1889, he has in many respects come to the same views.
8. "Church in Rom. Emp.," p. 324, quoted with approval by Prof. Mommsen in *Expositor*, 1893, viii, p. 2.
9. *Ibid*, p. 190.
10. *I.e.* of my "Cities and Bishoprics of Phrygia."
11. It is admitted in Ruinart's "Acta Sincera," and bears all the signs of firsthand knowledge and truth.
12. Lactantius mentions it was a special subject of pride to any governor if he had been able to induce any Christian to recant.—"Div. Inst.," v. II.
13. There were some other places in the neighbourhood of Iconium where Christianity was also very strong; these may compete with Eumeneia for the honour of being an entirely Christian city in 303 A.D.
14. I do not except even the Greeks (though I like them better).
15. I might say "hundreds of thousands," without the slightest fear of exaggerating. But I purposely understate, because there are many who, if they could find any excuse for believing that only 199,000 had perished in this way, would imagine that the counter-charge of exaggeration was a sufficient answer.

The Massacres in Turkey

1. John Burns (1858–1943), British labor leader, sentenced to six weeks' imprisonment for his part in the Trafalgar Square demonstration on "Bloody Sunday," November 13, 1887, and leader of the dockers strike in 1889. An independent Labor MP, 1892–1918, he was the first working-class person to be a member of the cabinet, as president of the Local Government Board, 1906–14.—**A.K.**
2. H. Anthony Salmoné (1860–1904), professor of Arabic, King's College, London University; author and writer. For many years, he labored to draw public attention to the necessity of encouraging Oriental studies in England; his main endeavor was to bring the East nearer to the West and to forward imperial affairs. Publications: *An Arabic-English and English-Arabic Lexicon; The Fall and Resurrection of Turkey; The Imperial Souvenir.*—**A.K.**

Turkish Misgovernment

1. Wilfrid Scawen Blunt (1840–1922), English poet. He married Lady Anne Noel, Byron's granddaughter, and traveled with her in the Middle

East, becoming a supporter of Arab nationalism. He also supported Irish Home Rule (he was imprisoned 1887–88) and wrote anti-imperialist books, poetry, and diaries.—**A.K.**

Travels amongst the Armenians

1. James Theodore Bent (1852–1897), British traveler, archaeologist, and author. Traveled in Greece, Asia Minor, Persia, Mashonaland, Abyssinia, Arabia. Publications: *The Cyclades, or Life amongst the Insular Greeks; The Ruined Cities of Mashonaland; The Sacred City of the Ethiopians.*—**A.K.**

Armenia and the Forward Movement

1. George William Russell (1853–1919), British Liberal politician. Elected to the House of Commons in 1880 and served as undersecretary of state for India (1892–94), undersecretary at the Home Office (1894–95), and a member of the London City Council (1889–95) and the Privy Council (from 1907).—**A.K.**

INDEX